W9-DAQ-071

THE SOUTH

The
SOUTH

ITS
ECONOMIC-GEOGRAPHIC
DEVELOPMENT

by A. E. Parkins

GREENWOOD PRESS, PUBLISHERS
WESTPORT, CONNECTICUT

TO A COMPANION OF MANY YEARS

ELEANOR GRACE PARKINS

MY WIFE

THIS BOOK IS DEDICATED

CONTENTS

PREFACE

This volume is an attempt to describe the civilization of the South, mainly in its economic-geographic aspects, and to interpret this civilization in terms of its regional setting and its historical antecedents. In brief, it is a study of the evolution of Southern civilization.

To develop the theme thus outlined the author considers his task to be:

First, to describe the Southern environment, i.e., natural and man-modified—the surface features, the climate, the biota, the soils, the mineral and power resources, and the natural transportational facilities.

Second, to describe, interpret, and explain, in so far as possible, the cultural features and patterns and institutions that Europeans and their descendants have evolved, in their occupancy of this region, the South. Cultural features and patterns as here used embrace means of transportation and communication, cities, rural and industrial landscapes, types of agriculture, mines, factories and workshops, and what not. Some of the cultural characteristics are to be read from the cultural landscapes; others do not exist or have not existed in material forms, perhaps merely in the mind of man as an idea, ideal, tendency, or pattern of thinking. The author has made no conscious effort to keep the material presented in this volume within the recognized boundaries of any one or two academic subject-matter fields.

Archeology and history show that cultures in the course of time undergo changes, which as a rule may be correlated with advances made in man's economic development, i.e., the improvements he makes in his attempt to wrest a living from his environment. Economic goods with which he satisfies his needs are produced in increasing amounts and with a relative decrease in the expenditure of human and physical energy. Stages, steps, eras, periods, or epochs are recognized and so recorded in the advancing order. The writer (along with many other geographers) recognizes a normal order of economic development and a corresponding normal order of cultural development. Such an order is considered normal because the majority of regions in their economic evolution seem to have followed this order. Departures from this normal order there are, but these are attributed to abnormalities. Accidents, diseases, lessened water supply, worn-out soils, and other unfavorable conditions result in abnormalities in the economic-geographic evolution of a region. The author tries to show that the South has tended to follow a normal order of development but has met with accidents and its normal order of evolution, for a time, was misdirected and delayed.

The writer assumes that the South is a region, not apart from but different from other sections of our country. It requires no array of figures and a long dissertation to prove this assumption. The press, literature, history, and people in general recognize differentiations in our country. Notions about the major differences natural to the North, South, and West are as much a part of our thinking as are those related to day and night. Exactly what differentiates the South from the other sections of our country, however, and the existence of well-differentiated subregions or areas within the major region are not so well recognized. Facts and concepts relative to these items form the larger part of this volume.

This volume is written for the well-read layman, the thoughtful student of Southern institutions. It does not essay to prove the superiority of this section, the South, over others or to emphasize its inferiority, but to present its past and present-day status, scientifically and without bias. It is not written in a controversial mood. The author has no set hypotheses to support or theories to prove, no planned economic order to propagandize. He has endeavored to follow the advice of the Jewish historian, Josephus, who wrote, "The principal scope that authors ought to aim at, above all the rest, is to speak accurately and to speak truly for the satisfaction of those that are otherwise unacquainted with such transactions, and obliged to believe what those writers inform them of."*

---

* Flavius Josephus, *Antiquities of the Jews,* translations by Wm. Whiston, A. M., 1845, 278.

ACKNOWLEDGMENTS

Said George Peabody, "Education [is] a debt from present to future generations." This was the philosophy underlying his establishment of the Peabody Educational Board and his magnificent gift for education in the South. Equally well might one say that education is a legacy from past to present and future generations and that the teacher is the custodian and the executor, the bearer of "the light." So quietly and subtly does he work at the task of fitting us the better to live and meet our obligations, that we often fail to appreciate the importance of his contributions. To his many great teachers the author wishes to acknowledge his indebtedness: to Mark Jefferson, the late W. H. Sherzer, the late R. D. Salisbury, Henry Cowles, the late Ellen C. Semple, H. H. Barrows, the late J. Paul Goode, and many others.

Federal Government reports, descriptive and statistical, the work of hundreds of experts, have been used freely, for which due credit is given throughout this book. But especially among those experts does the author wish to mention the late Curtis F. Marbut, H. H. Bennett, and O. E. Baker.

In addition he wishes to acknowledge direct assistance of the following in the critical reading of certain portions of this book: Professor W. H. Haas, Northwestern University; Mr. Roscoe Nunn, United States Weather Bureau, St. Louis; Professor Robert Brown, Rhode Island College of Education; Professor L. C. Glenn, Vanderbilt University; the late ·Professor K. C. Davis, Peabody College; Professor Jesse Shaver, Peabody College; Mr. Carl Peterson, Tennessee State Forestry Department; Mr. L. G. Waldrop, Superintendent of the Nashville Railroad Terminals; Dr. Louis Wolfanger, Columbia University; Professor Fremont P. Wirth, Peabody College; and the several county agricultural agents and others who have read the sections on agriculture.

THE SOUTH

CHAPTER I

INTRODUCTION

THE ADVANCING SOUTH

Man's greatest task is to provide himself with the necessities of life. What he works at and how he works in a given region depend largely upon

1. The physical conditions of that region—the soils, the minerals, and mechanical power; the climate, the climatic stimulus and likewise healthfulness.

2. The experience he has had in utilizing the resources of his environment.

3. The urge he has, the necessity, to exploit these resources.

The urge to work is largely a matter of (a) climate, which greatly affects and conditions his needs; and (b) the density of population, which determines the demand society in general makes upon him.

In thinly settled regions, where opportunities for getting a living are numerous, man makes but superficial use of the resources of his environment. The structure of his economic, social, and political institutions is likewise simple. As population increases in density, the demands upon him and upon the natural environment in which he happens to be operating increase and multiply. Accordingly, he intensifies his economic endeavors; and under the strong interactive life of a dense population, his institutions become complex, and science and inventions are developed to enable him the better to meet the demands upon his time and energy.

An increasing population is thus a dynamic force that pushes man on from the exploitive stage of his occupancy of a region; on through the pastoral stage and hoe culture; later, exploitive tillage characteristic of pioneer agriculture; then extensive agriculture on to intensive agriculture; and finally, into manufacturing, mining, and highly organized trade and commerce. The writer is not insisting that all these stages are to be found in the development of all peoples. He

1

wishes you to think of this generalization as expressing or indicating a trend in the normal history of a people.

The stage to which such economic-geographic development may be carried, the institutions and devices man establishes to aid him in making these adjustments, and the number of people a given region may support, provided the occupants behave normally, are determined (the writer uses this word advisedly) by the variety and extent of the resources of the region, its suitability for human living, and the standards of living of the occupants.

For every stage in the economic-geographic development there tends to be a concomitant stage or pattern in cultural development. A region does not take on an advanced cultural pattern until it has developed the concomitant economic stage or pattern. Culture and resource utilization advance together.

And what of the South? Does this section of the United States, generally recognized (and here assumed) as a region, possess the requisite natural conditions for an advanced economic development and an advanced cultural pattern? Has it had a normal development as compared with other regions in the United States or western Europe? To answer these questions is the task of this volume.

This chapter is but an introduction to a more detailed development of this theme in later chapters. There will first be presented in this chapter an epitome of how the South came to be. This will be followed by a statement of its present-day status as one of the sections or regions of the American nation, and the advance being made.

AN EPITOME OF THE DEVELOPMENT OF THE SOUTH

The past always casts its spell to a greater or lesser degree upon the present, and in no other section of the United States is this quite so true as in that group of states we have long since come to call the South.*

Land, land, land, because of its low relief, its admirable natural transportation facilities, its mild humid climate eminently suitable to supply man's needs, has ever been quite the most important natural environmental condition to which man has given consideration in his economic operations in the South. The major, possibly dominating, social-economic condition has been the low density of population.

In the early seventeenth century, European colonists, migrating,

---

* The South as used in this book is the South of the Census. It includes Delaware, Maryland, Virginia, West Virginia, North Carolina, South Carolina, Georgia, Florida, Alabama, Mississippi, Tennessee, Kentucky, Arkansas, Louisiana, Oklahoma, and Texas.

partly because of civil strife but largely because of the crowded condition of agrarian Britain, sought agricultural lands on the shores of
the Chesapeake. For nearly a century they were busy clearing the
forests of the Coastal Plain, always within easy reach of navigable,
tidal waters over which were transported their greatest export staple,
tobacco, along with hewn timber, naval stores, and a few other products. Over these waters also returning ships bore the essential fabricated goods, as well as fineries for the wealthier planters. Every colony,
to be successful, must have export products that command profitable
returns. In Virginia these came from the fields and the forests—in
short, they were products of the soil. Land here was the basis of
subsistence.

In the seventeenth century and the first half of the eighteenth began
also the conquest of the seaboard lands of the Lower South* by English colonists from the dispersal centers about and at Charleston
(dating from about 1670 to 1672) and Savannah (dating from 1733).
With the exception of a few Spanish and French near the Gulf Coast
in Florida and along the Lower Mississippi, the whole South of that
day was therefore the domain of British-American farmer settlers.

By the close of the eighteenth century white men had spread over
most of the Piedmont, pierced the many passes of the Southern Appalachian Highlands, settled many of the mountain valleys and coves,
and even planted a few active settlements within the Mississippi
Basin, ready for the conquest of the vast Mississippi plains (Fig. 44).

During these two hundred years (nearly) that the people of the
Upper South were slowly taking possession of the lands, checked for
a time in their westward migration by ridges, escarpments, and forests, only a beginning had been made in manufacturing. Iron and
iron goods—bulky and thus difficult to transport—were produced in
many parts of the Piedmont and in a score or more plants in the
Great Valley. The fabrication of clothing, harness, boots, and implements was to be found in nearly every home. All such industries were
in the handicraft stage, for nowhere in America, or in fact in the
world, except in northwestern Europe, was there even the beginning
of factory manufacture. Only in old England had factory machinery
been devised and put to use; and though waterfalls had been harnessed
for factory use, steam power was still in the experimental stage. The

---

* The terms Upper and Lower South have long been in use. The Upper South
now includes Delaware, Maryland, the Virginias (once one), North Carolina,
Kentucky, Tennessee, and a part of Arkansas and Oklahoma. The Lower South
is largely the states of the Cotton Belt and Florida.

first machine-equipped, power-driven textile factory in New England dates from about 1790. Although textile machinery was introduced into the South about this time, it was several decades before power-driven machines were found there in large numbers.

By 1810, largely because of a general lack of transportation, and thus isolation from the markets where manufactured goods could be secured at reasonable prices, the South was manufacturing about 28 to 30 per cent of the value of manufactured products of the United States. (See discussion, Chapter X.) At that time it had 46 per cent of the country's population—an excellent showing in manufacturing, but far below the developments of the North. The Southerners found on the land full scope for the utilization of their capital, enterprise, and energy. They turned to manufactures through necessity, not from choice. Land was the magnet that attracted the attention of the vast bulk of the population, and particularly was this true in the forty or more years that followed.

From 1800 to 1840 the frontier in the Upper South was carried from the Appalachian escarpments and the frontier outliers in the Nashville and Blue Grass basins (see Figs. 40, 43, 45, and 46) on to the edge of the Indian country, which the Federal Government had set aside for those native primitive Americans, victims of greedy, white land seekers. Land was dominant in the thoughts of most people. The abundance of cheap, fertile land and its acquisition were talked about in every city, hamlet, and country home in the Upper South. Moving lines of settlers were daily sights on all the trails, which soon became well-traveled roads, that led westward through mountain passes and across the fertile plains of the Mississippi Basin. Rivers too bore their quota of flatboats and barges; and beginning with the 1820's steamboats became the chief means of conveyance for that part of the journey in which such a luxury could be utilized.

The Lower South, the Cotton Belt, saw even more activity in the acquisition of land. The desire for cotton lands was the major motive. Families with little wealth mingled with the large planters who had sold out in the Carolinas or Georgia, and who with their slaves were seeking lands to the west, preferably lands near rivers down which flatboats and steamboats would carry to the Gulf ports the valuable bales of cotton that brought large returns. Cheap, virgin, cotton land, therefore, was the main cause of the westward movement in the Lower South. By 1840 all the Indian tribes had been removed to the Indian country (to which reference has just been made) beyond Arkansas and their lands quickly taken.

Texas, even before Mexican independence was won from Spain, was being settled by Americans seeking cotton lands, and after 1836, when Mexican control was removed, the movement was rapid and Texas was annexed to the Cotton Kingdom (in 1845) as the largest of its states.

Thus in the fifty years after the westward-moving frontier had barely passed the Appalachian Highlands (Figs. 40 and 43), its location in 1800, American settlers, largely Southerners, had laid claim to more than 400,000,000 acres of agricultural land, nearly a fifth of the entire area of the United States. Is it any wonder that man's chief attention should be directed to the land? The prospect of wealth has ever been a magnet that attracts men wherever this will-o-the-wisp may rest. The Transappalachian country in the South and the Gulf States had about 4,800,000 more inhabitants in 1850 than in 1800. A large portion of this increase represented westward-moving pioneers interested in the acquisition of land. Is it surprising then that manufacturing, mining, trade, and commerce received less attention than agriculture? Transportation was not neglected, for this activity was associated with the westward movement, the marketing of agricultural products, and the transportation of personal and household necessities and foods.

In 1850 the factories of the South were turning out less than 14 per cent of the manufactured products of the United States. Its population was 39 per cent of that of the country.

Although the rapid expansion of the agricultural lands in any section greatly retards the growth of manufactures, the frontier period of any region's history is stimulating. It is a period of vigor and enterprise, a mad rush for the acquisition of easily won wealth. For a time there is economic retrogression in the frontier zone due to the people's moving from a more advanced to a more primitive environment, but this is followed, within a short while, by a rapid advance in economic development and in experience as well as in intellectual growth. New and diverse economic and social elements are being introduced and new ideas brought by the newcomers who hail from as many points of the compass as there are natural lines of communication from the "mother regions." The increasing population and the new physical environment call for rapid economic-geographic adjustments. A hardy type of citizen is developed, partly the result of natural selection, and partly because frontier conditions demand boldness, bravery, resourcefulness, aggressiveness, and optimism. These were the sterling qualities that characterized the folk of each successive new section of the South as generation after generation moved westward with the advancing frontier.

Gradually, in all the frontier regions, one after another, life—eco-

nomic and social—settles down to the routine characteristic of a
regime in which man has met most of the problems of life and has
learned to settle them largely through force of habit. Nothing is quite
so conservative, unchanging, as life in an old, long-settled agricultural
area, with a static population and established lines of traffic and communication. When perfection is once reached in man's adjustments,
that is the end of development, until new forces come in. The writer
is not implying that man is bound down to a blind determinism from
which there is no escape. Man always finds it to his advantage to
adapt his living, as far as possible, to the changing order and to the
condition of the times in which he lives. Life is easier if it conforms
to the social-economic pattern of each order.

A westward-moving frontier of conservatism followed in the wake
of the earlier westward-moving frontier of progress. The eastern
South, most of the land east of the Southern Appalachian Mountains
and Blue Ridge, had, in the early periods of the nineteenth century,
settled down to a regime characteristic of old, long-settled regions.
Tobacco, rice, indigo, timber, and naval stores had, since early in
the eighteenth century, and even before, been the money crops; and
for decade after decade there had been no great increase in the volume of production, certainly not after the early tobacco boom in
Virginia, sufficient to disturb the equilibrium of the Southern agricultural world. The son lived in much the same economic and social
environment that his father had.

Beginning in the early part of the nineteenth century, cotton culture, however, which drew capital and enterprise from all parts of
the older sections of the South, energized nearly every phase of
Southern life. A rapidly expanding market, increasing prices for many
decades, and corresponding rich financial returns attracted thousands
to the Cotton Kingdom. Southern philosophy of life, social and political, responded admirably to the changing economic conditions.
Judge Winston writes, "The notion that Southern civilization was the
best in the world and that slavery was of God held the South in a
grip that seemed unbreakable."*

All went well until the production of cotton came to equal or surpass the demand. Prices fell, money returns dropped below expenditures, and distress was felt on every hand. Valorization as a national
or regional scheme of marketing crops was unknown at that time.
Farm blocs, those administration nightmares of our day, had not yet

---

* Robt. W. Winston, "Rebirth of the Southern States," Current History, XXII,
1925, 538.

evolved. No assistance was rendered by legislative action. There were no FFCA's to make loans nor AAA's to regulate production. Manufacturing was suggested as a cure for the ills of the South, a tonic for the rejuvenation of its economic life. Such certainly was needed to lead it out of the old age of agrarianism into which it had again drifted.

But before new ventures, for which the South was undoubtedly ripe, could be launched, the whole country drifted into a sectional war which resulted in almost utter ruin to the South. In many sections buildings were burned, and livestock and supplies useful to invading armies were confiscated to the extent of hundreds of millions of dollars. Everywhere land was abandoned and allowed to wash and gully. A precious heritage was being lost. The few industries that had arisen during the earlier years of the War either were destroyed or ceased operation. The transportation systems were demoralized, and the capital invested in 4,000,000 slaves, certainly $2,000,000,000 and more, was shifted from assets to liabilities and labor so demoralized as to be wholly unfit as free workers for the task of rehabilitating the war-rent South.

In 1860 the true value of real and personal property in the United States was $16,200,000,000; and that of the South, $6,300,000,000, i.e., 39 per cent of the country's total. In 1870 that of the entire country was $30,068,000,000, whereas the value of Southern property had shrunk to $4,200,000,000, or 14 per cent of that for the nation. South Carolina, which in 1860 held eleventh rank among the states in the Union in "true value" of property, dropped to twenty-seventh place in 1870; Georgia dropped from eighth place to twenty-first; and Mississippi from ninth to twenty-sixth.*

While the Civil War exhausted the South, Reconstruction, during which the impoverished, yet proud, whites fought to maintain white supremacy in a third of our domain, brought the whole section to the verge of despair. It was not until the late 1870's and early 1880's (see Figs. 1-3) that the "beaten and insulted" whites of the South regained control of local affairs and took up the task of developing the resources with which nature through eons of time has endowed it. Says one writer, "She [the South] was not saved by a Dawes' plan as was Germany, but what she did [and has done] she did in weakness but her faith was great" (Thomas Preston).

Agriculture, the basis of material wealth for two and a half centuries, continued to be the main support for the New South that

---

* Ninth Census of the United States, *Industry and Wealth*, 1870, 10.

arose out of the ruins of the Civil War and Reconstruction. It was
a New South in one sense; a new regime of labor had been substituted for one largely founded, in most sections and for some products, on the chattel slave. But it was an old economic order. Cotton

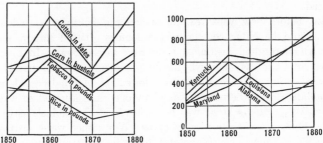

FIG. 1.—Graphs of Leading Agricultural Products of the South, 1850, 1860,
1870, 1880.

Scales adjusted to fit the four items in one rectangle. Data from Census Reports for 1850, 1860,
1870, and 1880.

FIG. 2.—Real Estate and Personal Property in the South, 1850, 1860, 1870, and 1880.
Data from *Report of Tenth Census*, 1880, Vol. VII, 3, 4, 6, 12.

and tobacco remained the dominant money crops. Rice culture was
practically destroyed and when revived, two or more decades later,
shifted westward to the Coastal Prairies of Louisiana. Elsewhere the
farmers carried on under greater burdens of debt, under the same

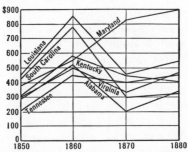

FIG. 3.—Per Capita Wealth of Selected States in South in 1850, 1860, 1870,
and 1880.
Data from *Report of Tenth Census*, 1880, Vol. VII, 3, 4, 6.

isolated conditions, and therefore under the same old practices. Conservatism was even more evident than before the War. It is only within
the last three or four decades that the New South has experienced in
some parts a rejuvenation in agriculture. The opening of new and
rapid lines of transportation to the great Northern industrial centers

has been of material benefit in the attempts at agricultural intensification to be found in many parts of the Southern States. The rise of Southern industries has also served as a stimulus, not entirely because of the creation of large Southern markets, except for a few raw materials, such as cotton, but because of the new outlook in the economic life. The South is still in an agricultural regime and will long remain so; on such a basis its economic life and cultural development, if judged properly and fairly, should be evaluated.

THE PRESENT-DAY SOUTH: ITS ADVANCEMENT

AGRICULTURAL ADVANCEMENT

Agriculture, on the basis of percentage of total population classed as rural and of the relative number of people gainfully employed, is still the major activity of the South. In three major divisions of the Southern States the percentage of rural population of the total in 1930 was, for the South Atlantic States, 63.9; for the East South Central States, 71.9; and for the West South Central, 63.6.* In 1930, out of the 14,300,000 "persons ten years of age and over engaged in gainful occupations" in the South, 5,600,000 were in "agriculture."†

The total value of agricultural products of the South in 1929 (based on calculations for 67 crops) was 37 per cent of the total for the United States and these returns came from 31 per cent of the land in crops. Obviously agriculture in the South in 1929 brought much larger returns to the acre than in the country at large. Not only returns to the acre but also returns on the investment in farm property were larger. The value of farm buildings in the South was 23 per cent of that of the country at large; of implements and machinery used, 21 per cent of the total; and of all farm property, 25 per cent. In other words, the Southern farmers were producing 37 per cent (in value) of the crops of the country on 31 per cent of the land in crops and with 25 per cent of total capital investment.‡

Many Southern farmers in most communities are thoroughly alive to the changing order in agriculture. The boll weevil has brought diversification in many parts of the Cotton Belt. More and more

---

* *Statistical Abstract,* 1932, 46, based on *Report* of *Fifteenth Census.*

† Calculated from data in *Statistical Abstract,* 1932, 62, 64.

‡ Calculated from data, *Statistical Abstract,* 1930, 681; 1935, 559, 561. No statistics are available for a comparison of labor expenditures. As of January 1, 1935, the value of the farms of the South was 26.6 per cent of the total for the country (*U. S. Census of Agriculture,* 1935, I, p. xx).

cattle are being raised. Much blooded stock is being introduced.
Dairying is increasing in many parts. Special crops as truck, strawberries, and orchard fruits are increasingly grown. More machinery
is being used. Cooperative societies are becoming active and effective,
as are other farmers' organizations, such as pig, calf, poultry, and
corn clubs for boys and girls, and county and state fairs. Farm demonstration and home demonstration work is to be found in most parts
of the South. Pupil enrollment in Federal-aided vocational agricultural schools is increasing rapidly. In 1900 the Southern States had
only about 10 per cent of the total enrollment of the country, but
in 1929, nearly 20 per cent.* North Carolina was the first state in
the Union to establish a regular state office to supervise the marketing
of farm products and the first to organize rural credit unions similar
to those of European countries.

There has been in some parts of the South, particularly in the older
parts, a decrease in number of farms, crop acreage, value of and number of farm animals, and other items. This decline is not peculiar to the
South alone. From 1930 to 1935 the crop acreage in the United States
declined 8 per cent and production 10 per cent.† The decline was greater
in the older and rougher parts of the South because there were and still
are more "marginal farmers" who are cultivating land simply because there is little else for them to do; cultivating land that would return far greater revenues if in forest. We in the South have many thousands of farmers yet who should seek other forms of labor. They are
wasting the major part of their time and energy in a pursuit that gives
them at most a bare existence. For them, as Sidney Lanier well expressed it, "Most of living consists simply in not dying." They make
little or no contribution to the economic life of either the South or
the nation, and certainly their farms are no ornament to any agricultural landscape. The factory in both South and North at present
offers them, and will continue to offer them, about the only means
by which they may make a living and educate their children. For
them industrialization is a godsend. It means material, physical, and
intellectual betterment. The advancing South demands farmers with
that intelligence which enables them to adjust themselves to new situations. Conservatism means death sooner or later. In the face of constantly changing economic conditions Southern farmers *must* develop
new adjustments.

---

* *Statistical Abstract*, 1930, 126.

† *Agriculture*, II, Part 2, *Southern States*, Fifteenth Census, 1930, 12, 13. Data
also from Bureau of Farm Economics, Graphs.

Advance in Education

That the New South is laying firm foundations for the future is seen in every state in the tremendous advance made in public education in the last two or three decades. The increase in public expenditures for public (elementary and secondary) school education between 1900 and 1930 was phenomenal. (See Graph I, Fig. 8.)

The amounts spent in 1930, in comparison with the expenditures for 1900, were as follows:

Oklahoma	48 times
North Carolina	38 times
Florida	24 times
Alabama	23 times
Louisiana	19 times
Texas	17 times
West Virginia	14 times
Tennessee	13 times

For the whole South in 1900 the sum was $28,000,000, and for 1930, $415,600,000. This latter sum is almost 15 times that for 1900. For comparison, Wisconsin has increased its expenditures nearly 10 times; Nebraska, about 6 times; Iowa, by less than 6 times; and Missouri, by about 7 times.* *There was, however, a greater need for improvement in the South.* In 1900 North Carolina and Alabama were each spending only 50 cents per capita of total population on public school education. *No other section in late years has made a greater advance in education than the South.* Said the late Wallace Butterick of the General Educational Board, in 1927, "I have travelled extensively throughout the country and am prepared to say that, for fine and modern school houses the South leads the North. . . . This zeal for education anticipated the material progress of the South and has conditioned it. It is an educated people that make real and enduring progress . . . The South is not spoiled by its economic development because education and culture go along with economic progress." (See Fig. 4.)

There is yet much opportunity for improvement. The median expenditure for the South for 1930 was about $10.80 per capita of total population. This includes expenditures for both negroes and whites of course. For New England it was $19.55; the Middle Atlantic States,

---

* Data from *Statistical Abstract* for 1924, 89; 1935, 114.

$25.20; the Rocky Mountain States, $23.51; and the Pacific States, $24.40.* But further advance will come in the South with increasing population and increasing wealth. The South is doing well for a region in which agriculture dominates the economic life and in which economic recovery from the turmoil of a war three-quarters of a

A. E. P.

FIG. 4.—One of the Scores of Central High Schools of North Carolina. This is at Currituck.

Less than a decade ago North Carolina plunged into school house and road building. The state is now deeply in debt, but these improvements are certain to bring rich returns in future years.

century ago is not yet entirely attained. The biracial school system adds materiall_ to the burden of providing adequate educational facilities.

ADVANCE IN MINING

The South today is making substantial contributions to the nation's output of minerals. For the first time in three hundred years of its history, its stores of underground wealth are being actively exploited. (See Graph IV, Fig. 5.) In 1932 it produced 65 per cent of the petroleum of the country, which means that it was pumping about 40 per cent of the output of the entire world. (See Graph V, Fig. 5.) It also produced about two-thirds of the natural gas. It mined 45 per cent of the total bituminous coal of the country. West Virginia was the leading Southern mineral-producing state, and some years it is the leading state of the Union in the production of soft coal. (See

* Data from *Statistical Abstract*, 1935, 114.

Graph III, Fig. 5.) The total value of minerals mined in the South in 1930 was $1,529,000,000, or more than 36 per cent of the total, by value, for the country; and only a beginning has been made. In the decade between 1919 and 1929 the growth in mineral production in the South was 59 per cent in comparison with 16 per cent for the rest of the country.*

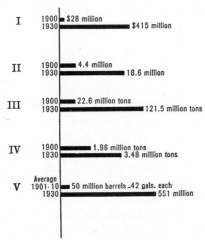

FIG. 5.—Some Selected Indices of Advancement.

I—Increase in Expenditures for Public Education in the South, 1900 to 1930. Data from *Statistical Abstract*, 1924, 89; 1935, 114.

II—Growth in Number of Active Spindles in South. Data from *Statistical Abstract*, 1934, 746.

III—Growth in Coal Production in West Virginia in Thirty Years. *Statistical Abstract*, 1926, 725; 1935, 698.

IV—Increase in Production of Pig Iron. *Statistical Abstract*, 1926, 711; 1935, 682.

V—Increase in Production of Petroleum. *Statistical Abstract*, 1935, 706.

ITS PLACE IN LUMBER PRODUCTION

For many decades the Southern States have supplied a large part of the lumber requirements of eastern United States. The total value of forest products from Southern forests was probably a billion dollars in 1928. Like other sections of our country the South is cutting each year far more than it grows, yet, if all the land not suited for agriculture were reforested and the forests protected, the demands in the South could readily be met and a surplus remain for export. With

* Data from *Statistical Abstract*, 1925, 707; 1935, 678, 706.

a long growing season, high temperatures, and abundant rains, forests grow more rapidly in the Southern States than in any other section of our country. A tree (longleaf pine) reaches commercial lumber size in about thirty years.

Recent developments (now far beyond the experimental stage) in the making of newsprint and rayon from Southern pine point to the South's becoming an important pulp and paper section and thus in time breaking the monopoly Canada now holds on our newsprint paper market. A Dr. Herty is the chemical wizard.

Advance in Manufacturing

In manufacturing the South is making only a beginning. In 1929 the output of Southern factories (based on value added by manufacture) was only 13.9 per cent of the value added by all the manufactures of the United States, and only about 87 per cent of the value added by the plants of the single state of New York. On the basis of value of product the output of Southern factories is 14.2 per cent of the total for the country. In manufacturing, then, the Southern States fall far below the quota that their area (30 per cent) and their population (31 per cent) would call for. This section is advancing more rapidly in the growth of manufactures, however, than the older well-established sections and even the United States as a whole. From 1919 to 1929 the value of manufactures in the Southern States had increased exactly 20 per cent while the increase for the country at large was only 11.9 per cent.*

The most rapid industrial advance is in the textile industry, cotton and rayon. Today the South (most of the factories are centered in the South Atlantic States) is the leading cotton-manufacturing section of our country. Whereas this section is advancing in the number of spindles from year to year, New England is declining rapidly. For example, the consumption of cotton in the mills of the Northern States fell off 55 per cent in the decade between 1919 and 1934, and the consumption in Southern mills increased 37.7 per cent.† So far the output of the mills of the South is the staple sort and not subject to the vagaries of changing styles as are high-class luxury goods. The southward movement of cotton manufacturing is no more active than the development of the rayon industry.

* *Fifteenth Census*, 1929, "Manufactures," II, 16.
† Calculated, data from *Statistical Abstract*, 1935, 766.

ACTIVITY AT SOUTHERN PORTS

From the head of Chesapeake Bay to the Rio Grande there is much activity at the numerous Southern ports through which passed about 30 per cent (in 1933) of the export foreign, water-borne, cargo tonnage of the nation. The foreign water-borne export tonnage of the ports of the Gulf Coast in 1935 was more than twice that of New York and nearly twice that of the ports of the North Atlantic, north

A. E. P.

FIG. 6.—A Small Portion of the New Harbor at Mobile.

On the left is a great British freighter loading Birmingham steel from flatboats; in the middle ground, a Warrior River steamer and flatboats or barges; on the extreme right, a warehouse and an American freighter loading with lumber; and projecting above the roof of the warehouse may be seen the spars of a schooner also loading, in another slip.

of the Chesapeake. The greatest activity in the South is centered at the Chesapeake Bay ports, New Orleans, and Houston-Port Arthur. The exports of the Lower Chesapeake Bay ports nearly equaled that of Philadelphia; New Orleans had nearly five times the tonnage of exports of Boston, and the ports of Texas (combined) more than New York. In tonnage of imports and in value of imports the Southern ports fall far below those of the North Atlantic. The ports of the South had about 33 per cent of the import tonnage of the North Atlantic District in 1935 and in value of imports about 20 per cent. Its value of exports was about 88 per cent.* The explanation of all this is that the South is still a large exporter of raw products which find short and easy

* *Statistical Abstract,* 1936, 417, 455 (calculated).

routes by rail and river (limited chiefly to the Mississippi) to the widely spaced ports on the ocean's margin. Cotton and cotton products formed about 17 per cent of all Southern exports by value.

To handle still larger volume of freight, many Southern ports are arranging more active and direct rail contacts with the interior and providing larger and deeper harbors, more docking space, larger warehouses, and better dock machinery. Louisiana and Alabama, recognizing the benefits that accrue to the state in general in ocean commerce, have made liberal contributions to their Gulf Coast cities for port improvement. (Fig. 6.) These have been supplemented by Federal appropriations.

As has been pointed out frequently by various writers, America's future trade region lies for the most part to the south—both the cis- and trans-equatorial regions. No other section lies so advantageously as the South to participate in this trade, which must increase year by year.

THE CONTRIBUTIONS OF THE RAILROADS TO SOUTHERN ADVANCEMENT

Of railroads, the Southern States have their share, about 33 per cent of the mileage of the country. The mileage increase in the last twenty-eight years is one-half the increased mileage of the whole country for the same period.

In no other section are the legislatures and people in general so friendly to railroads, and in no other sections are the railroads striving more to supply the farmer, mine operator, lumberman, manufacturer, and business man with reliable and speedy transportation facilities. No more capable developers are to be found anywhere than the industrial and agricultural bureaus of the railroads of the South.

THE CHANGING SOUTH

The Solid (Democratic) South, in which "one can take a census of all the Republicans by counting the postmasters and the cotton pickers"; the land of one-crop agriculture, where the chief implements of tillage are "a nigger, a mule, and a one-horse plow"; the land of "glorious agrarianism and the easy life," "where the niggers put the crops in and the sheriff takes them off"; the land of illiteracy and class education; the land of "Judge Lynch" and "special privilege"—that land, though we cannot say that it no longer exists, is disappearing. Such apothegms, wrongly or rightly descriptive of the Southern States, belong for the most part to another day and may well serve as epitaphs in the graveyard of a past and passing order. A new day, a new spirit, a new economic order, a new vision of the relation of man to nature, is sweeping the South. The sway of a regime in which agriculture dominated to the almost complete exclusion of other economic activities, in which the South served only as a producer of raw products and a consumer of the fabricated goods of the Northeast and of Europe, is being disputed by a higher type of agriculture and manufacturing.

If the South, to the critical observer, seems slow in swinging into the new order and hesitant to move with the force that characterized the older manufacturing sections of our country, it should be remembered that it is still young in its industrialization and is still under the spell of agrarianism. Its earliest settlers on the shores of the Atlantic tidewater were lovers of the land; and, in the expansion of the frontier from the Atlantic to the foothills of the Rockies and the arid lands of the Southwest, land, land, cheap land, productive and easily cultivated land has, as we have previously described, absorbed the energy and capital and enterprise of the ever-increasing population. Abundance of land, war, the abandonment of an outworn labor regime, financial losses, political suppression in the days of Reconstruction, a constant emigration, and a weak immigration have been factors retarding the normal economic-geographic development.

It is undoubtedly true that the South is conservative. Conservatism is born in an atmosphere of unchanging economic conditions characteristic of an old agricultural regime. Certainly the South has more ties that tend to bind it to the past than has either the North or the West. The fundamental economic order has not been greatly disturbed so far by innovations. There has never been an influx of hordes of discordant nationalities to break up the continuity of family ties, or to introduce new ideas and ideals in politics, theology, and society. The stamp set upon society in the South in the early eighteenth century has come on down to our day but slightly changed. But it is changing.

The lack of respect, developed largely during slavery days, for manual labor and the lowly born (whites) and for the middle-class artisan out of whose group must come leaders in the new economic order, has had a retarding influence. But these conditions, too, are being modified. In many parts of the South, until of late, the "lowly" born who have risen to power, prosperity, and prominence have not found it to their advantage to discuss their beginnings and struggles in polite society. The ideals of what constitutes success are changing. Once, only law, medicine, theology, education, and agriculture commanded respect. In addition to these high callings, we now pay our homage to engineering, business, and manufacturing, in fact, to all the occupations in which man, in a highly complex civilization, is engaged.

An atmosphere of conservatism is never a nursery for the rearing of advanced thinkers and rapid social and economic movements. Few contributions to science, art, and literature have come in modern times from an agrarian regime, for such is not the environment for intellectual flowering and fruition. Progress is born where man meets man in intellectual competition, where man is stimulated to supreme effort by example and desire to surpass, where life is complex and subject to frequent changes such as exist in an industrial atmosphere. The new order means much to the South.

The South is in a state of becoming. Silent forces are at work. Traditions are toppling. It has made great progress, but it is still new, filled with a desire for greater progress. It sees visions of new opportunities, which call for new developments that will bring rich returns for spiritual progress as well, let us hope, as for material wealth and advancement.

A REGIONAL PLANNING EXPERIMENT IN THE SOUTH

In May, 1933, Congress, at the suggestion of the President, provided for an experiment in regional planning in the valley of the Tennessee River, an experiment which if successful will be repeated in many sections of our country, it is predicted. The development work is under the supervision of a non-partisan board, known as the Tennessee Valley Authority. An area as large as an average American state, rich in a wide variety of natural resources and occupied by some 2,000,000 people, is its field of activity (Fig. 7). The tentative plans as outlined by the President, Congress, and the Authority call for:

First, the development of a part, at least, of the large waterpower resources (3,000,000 horsepower in the Tennessee River and its tributaries, as estimated by army engineers) that there may be an efficient measuring stick to judge of the fairness of the rates now being charged the public by public utility companies.

Second, industrial development, the abundance of cheap steam-electric and hydroelectric power, cheap, contented labor, and a wide variety of raw product being the major factors in deciding upon the location.

Third, the agricultural rehabilitation of the Valley—the checking of soil erosion, the removal of marginal and submarginal crop lands from production, and soil improvement.

Fourth, the conservation of the forest resources, reforestation, and the conservation of wild life and forest recreational resources.

Fifth, social betterment. This is the "end product" of the whole scheme of regional planning, i.e., the creation of prosperous agricultural and industrial communities, peopled by contented, educated, healthy, law-abiding, forward-looking citizens. The regional planners have visions of cultural landscapes dominated by small industrial centers each with well-kept factories, neat, clean stores, schoolhouses, churches, and community houses, all surrounded by gardens; and

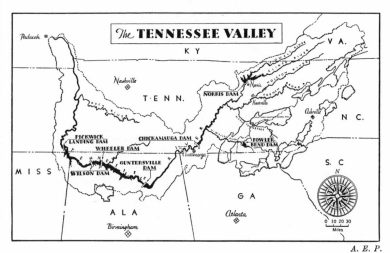

Fig. 7.

From booklet by Tennessee Valley Authority.
By 1937 Wilson, Wheeler, and Norris dams were completed. Work was well along on Pickwick Landing dam and just started on the Chickamauga and Hiwassee dams.

poultry, fruit, and dairy farms, on which the majority of the factory workers will live. Large-scale industry will not be barred, but efforts will be made to prevent, if possible, the development of large urban centers. Regional planning in the Tennessee Valley is an undertaking whose consummation will take decades of time. It is not for our day alone.

The Authority is wise in not attempting to formulate complete, detailed, idealistic plans. In 1936 it had before it only a few major objectives, such as those stated in the previous paragraphs in this section. It leaves the way clear for readjustments in the general plans, as such readjustments are found necessary. It does not overlook the difficulties to be encountered. It is dealing with both nature and man;

and Mother Nature perhaps will prove more amenable to leadership,
certainly to discipline, than man. Full authority to do as it sees best
with the Muscle Shoals power and the associated fertilizer plants and
the erection of other power dams, reservoirs, transmission lines, and
distributing stations has been conferred on the Authority, as well as
the right to condemn property in the name of the Federal Government for public use. The man to be dealt with, however, has well-
established, inherited rights of ownership that cannot be violated, and
his cooperation must be secured in most undertakings. Property rights,
majority rule, individual freedom, and initiative will need be respected
if the regional planning schemes of the Authority are to bear fruit.

Regional planning or a "planned economy" rather than the hap-
hazard, uncoordinated, individualistic economic development that has
prevailed under the competitive, capitalistic system since the beginning of white civilization on this continent is a new venture in America, largely the child of the 1929 to 1936 depression. Whether the new
economic and cultural order will be superior to the old is the question
that the Tennessee Valley experiment is supposed to answer.

The effectiveness of any economic system is measured by the quality of citizens that evolves in or under it. We must leave to future
generations (and taxpayers in particular) the decision as to whether
the new order will offer greater opportunities for individual development and will produce a manhood and womanhood healthier, happier,
more tolerant of the rights of others, and possessed of a higher sense
of moral and social obligations than the present.

PART I

THE SOUTHERN ENVIRONMENT

CHAPTER II

NATURE'S LEGACY

INTRODUCTION

The natural environment is the stage on which man plays the drama of life. The type of drama which can be played is closely related to the natural environment, as asserted in Chapter I. Simple economic dramas, like grazing and pioneer agriculture, are played in a simple setting in which few resources are exploited; complex dramas, like commercial agriculture, manufacturing, and the active exchange of goods, involve the use of many resources. In a region of diverse resources man adapts the stage setting, the kinds of resources utilized, to harmonize to a greater or less degree to the play being enacted. More and more resources come to be needed as the complexities of economic life are multiplied. Our interest in this chapter is the degree of suitability of the Southern environment for civilized man and his institutions. We will deal in this chapter with the natural environment, that is, the environment as nature prepared it. The chapter that follows will discuss the modifications that civilized man has made of this environment in the three hundred or more years of his occupancy.

Man's discovery of the economic possibilities of the Southern environment, as known today, is a matter of several centuries of hard work on the part of hundreds of "explorers." History records the explorations of Ponce de Leon on the Florida coast, of de Narváez, De Soto, and La Salle in the Gulf region, the sad experiences of Raleigh's colonists in Albemarle Sound, John Smith's exploration of Chesapeake Bay, Governor Spotswood's *de luxe* expedition to the crest of the Blue Ridge; but the annals of only a few of the hundreds of trappers and traders who traversed valleys, passes, and plains of the vast interior have ever been told. They brought back information that stimulated the cupidity of thousands and sent westward wave after wave of land seekers that continued for two centuries or more until the agricultural lands of every section of the South were taken up. These pioneer trappers and farmers picked up practical information concerning the lands, the vegetation, and the climate of the Southern environment. But the definite scientific information regarding the to-

pography, the geology, mineralogy, soils, and climate that we now possess is largely the work of scientists of the last half century.

In an area with as much plains land as the South has, and therefore
mantled by deep soil and dense vegetation, prospecting for minerals
proceeds slowly. In such an environment borings and careful geologic
exploration are necessary. It is in mountainous and desert lands that
the casual discoveries of mineral deposits are made. Mineral discoveries and particularly mining have made only a beginning in the
South. Our agrarian civilization tends to utilize only the resources
that are basic to crop production. Coal, oil, gas, bauxite, Portland
cement materials, barite, fuller's earth, and clays, now produced in
large quantities in the South, were in little or no demand in Southern
economy until well into the nineteenth century. Little attention, therefore, was given to mineral exploration and discoveries. As industrial
technology advances still further, many mineral products now considered worthless will come to have great value.

Though we have been several centuries in discovering the resources
which we are now utilizing, we are far from having reached the limits
of discovery. In our analysis of what has been discovered about our
Southern environment we will consider:

1. The lands and the minerals beneath the surface.
2. The weather and climate.
3. The biota.
4. The soils.

THE LANDS

Two mountain and plateau areas—the Southern Appalachian Highlands and the Ozark-Ouachita area—break the monotony of plains
land that spreads from the Potomac to the Rio Grande. Fully three-
fourths of the area of the South has elevations less than 1,000 feet
above sea level (Fig. 8).

The only formidable topographic barrier to the free movement of
man and goods is the Cumberland-Allegheny Front, the eastern scarp
of the Cumberland-Allegheny plateaus. From the Potomac southward
to northeastern Alabama this 800- to 1,000-foot wall (above the Great
Valley at its eastern base) has only a few breaks that open westward
to the lowlands of the Mississippi basin. The westward-moving pioneers
in the South used, for the most part, only one break, the Cumberland
Gap, and through this, between 1790 and 1830, streamed more than
100,000 people in search of the rich farming lands of the Transappalachian region.

The Mississippi, though serving in the past as the South's greatest

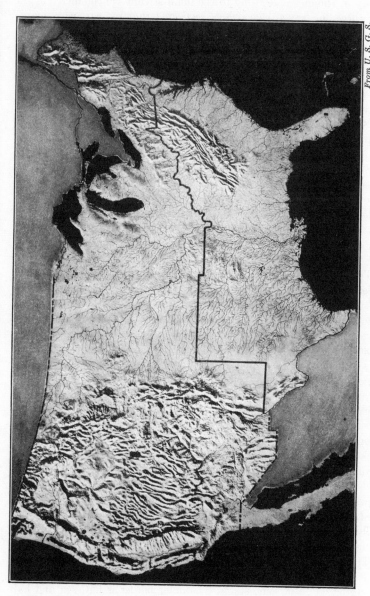

Fig. 8.—The United States in Relief, with boundary of the South indicated.

From U. S. G. S.

artery of commerce, drawing to the main stream the commerce of the widespreading areas, has always restricted the free east-west movement of commerce and people by land. Wide, marshy, pestilential flood plains, a broad strip of water, and valleys filled with unconsolidated mud and sand so deep and soft that finding a substantial footing for heavy bridge piers is difficult have greatly retarded the number of crossing places. In the days of westward movement there were only two important crossing places: one near St. Louis, the other at Natchez. The presence of Indians in western Tennessee and Mississippi was also a deterrent factor. Until the last few years the only bridges across this mighty river between the mouth of the Ohio and the Gulf were at Memphis. Here a high bluff on the east side of the river was a contributing factor in the localization of these causeways. More recently bridges have been constructed at Vicksburg and New Orleans. Ferries have long been in operation and fairly numerous, but slow, inconvenient, and costly.

Figure 9 shows the physiographic provinces, or land regions, of the South.

The largest of the physiographic regions is the Coastal Plain, divided into the Atlantic and the Gulf plains. Its area is about 255,000 square miles, larger than France, Belgium, and the Netherlands combined, and nearly a third of the total area of the South. It includes parts of Maryland, Virginia, Kentucky, Arkansas, Oklahoma, and Texas, and the whole of Florida, Mississippi, and Louisiana. It is physiographically the youngest province, so young that in only a few areas are the deposits consolidated. In fact, its outer border is now advancing on the sea in the same way that the whole plain, much as it exists today, was formed. The oldest part of the plain is along the inner border. A few million years ago the waves of the ocean beat upon the old land at this inner border. Rivers brought sediment and rock in solution from the old lands to the sea. The sediment was deposited and worked over by waves and alongshore currents. The minerals carried in solution were extracted from the sea water by various types of sea animals whose remains were deposited when the animals died, sometimes in large quantities in a short while. And thus gradually the land advanced upon the sea, assisted now and then by elevations of the land or subsidences of the sea.

The Coastal Plain is the flattest of the plains lands of the South. It is highest along the inner border, and here rather conspicuous hills are to be found in some states. The outer border is half sea and half land. Shelving sandy barrier beaches topped by sand dunes behind which are lagoons, marshes, and wet flatwoods are the features, in

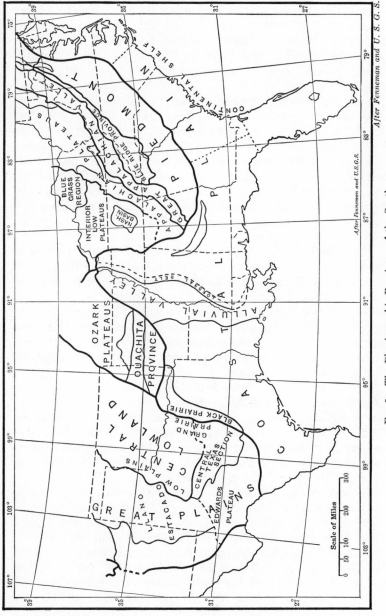

FIG. 9.—The Physiographic Provinces of the South.

After Fenneman and U. S. G. S.

order described, along most of the coasts of the South from the ocean's edge inland. The width of this low outer tidal border varies greatly. It is widest in eastern North Carolina, the brackish water of Albemarle and Pamlico sounds extending 50 to 70 miles inland from the ocean. Tidewater lagoons and bays along the Atlantic farther south and likewise along the Gulf extend 20 to 30 or more miles inland. Marshes and flatwoods occur still farther to the interior. The greatest of all tidewater indentations of the Coastal Plain is Chesapeake Bay and its numerous tidal estuaries, caused by the drowning of a larger river system.

Between the low outer marshy, tidal portion of the Coastal Plain and the inner dissected section is the broad flat Middle Coastal Plain, well drained yet flat enough to reduce surface erosion to the minimum. Before the coming of white men this portion of the Coastal Plain bore the best of the longleaf pine forests. It was, and still is, the section most used for agriculture.

The outer belt of the Coastal Plain, except here and there where truck gardens and seaports dominate the landscape, remains much the domain of nature. Several generations of lumbermen in the seventeenth, eighteenth, and nineteenth centuries battled with nature, at times almost obliterating the forest trees with axe, saw, and fire, but each time the trees have come back, though the last generation shows terrible scars of battle. Today much of the cut-over land of the Coastal Plain is in this outer belt. It may become the most active pulpwood-producing area of our country.

Most of the harbors of the South are the drowned mouths of the Coastal Plain rivers, and though they are shallow and subject to silting man finds it easy to deepen them and excavate new channels. Baltimore and Richmond are at the inner edge of the Plain at its meeting with the Piedmont, but most of their harbor improvements have been made in the Coastal Plain. All the other large ports are at or near the outer border of the Plain.

The inner border of the Coastal Plain from central Alabama northeastward is the Fall Line, an "imaginary" line connecting the row of rapids of the rivers that flow across both Piedmont and Coastal Plain. From central Alabama to the Rio Grande a fall line is scarcely discernible. The lower rapids of the Tennessee near Muscle Shoals and the hard rock in the Arkansas River at Little Rock are comparable to the Fall Line rapids, but elsewhere the inner boundary of the Coastal Plain is not sharp. The physiographer must call upon the geologist to assist him in its location.

West of the Atlantic Coastal Plain is the Piedmont Plateau, extending from central Alabama northeastward beyond the northern border of the South, on into Pennsylvania. Though called a plateau it is really a plain, a plain of denudation, with only a few hills (monadnocks) rising above the otherwise gently rolling surface. King's Mountain and Stone Mountain are the best known of these monadnocks. They are composed of granite more resistant to erosion than the gneisses, schists, and other old crystalline rocks that dominate in the Piedmont. The Piedmont is higher, drier, and healthier than the Coastal Plain. Its flat surface like that of the Coastal Plain in no way erects barriers to man's movements. Except where erosion has been active its mantle rock is deep. The pioneers found the outer border of the Piedmont clothed with coniferous forests, but a mixed forest of hardwood and conifers dominates most of its area.

The western edge of the Piedmont is irregular, for the numerous flats along the streams that extend back into the Southern Appalachian Mountains in North Carolina and Georgia and into the Blue Ridge in Virginia are really extensions of the Piedmont surface. Between the valley flats are ridges and outlying hills.

The Blue Ridge forming the western border of the Piedmont in Virginia is continuous, though cut here and there by water gaps. Southward from Virginia the name Blue Ridge covers all the easternmost ridges of the Southern Appalachians, some low, some lofty. This ridge in Georgia, South Carolina, and for the most part in North Carolina is the divide between the Atlantic and Mississippi rivers that rise in these states. Though formidable in appearance when seen from a distance, shrouded in a blue haze, the Blue Ridge is not a barrier, for it has many wind gaps and water gaps that permit a fairly free movement of commerce and people. The more important water gaps have been cut by the Potomac, the James, and the Roanoke. Farther south Swannanoah, Hickory Nut, and Salida are the best known of the gaps.

The Southern Appalachian Mountains that lie mostly in western North Carolina and northern Georgia are a jumble of short ridges and isolated peaks separated by large open valleys and basins. Although most of the short ridges have a northeast-southwest trend there are many transverse ranges. Near some of the large rivers the original lofty surface has been so reduced by denuding agencies that the intermontane basins have the appearance of dissected plateaus. The relief in these is low; mountains are discernible only on distant horizons. On or near the Blue Ridge and the Great Smoky Mountains are found the loftiest peaks. Mount Mitchell, 6,711 feet; Grandfather

Mountain, 5,964 feet; Cattail Peak, 6,609 feet; Roan Mountain, 6,287 feet; Pisgah, 5,749 feet; Mount Guyot, 6,620 feet; Mount LeConte, 6,593 feet; and Clingman's Dome, 6,640 feet, are the better known.

How many hundreds of millions of years old the rocks of the eastern part of the Southern Appalachian Mountains and the Piedmont are no geologist can tell. Perhaps they are as old as the so-called crust of the earth. There is no geologic evidence that these rocks as a whole were ever beneath the sea. The large size of the crystals that form some of the granites indicates that at one time lofty mountains once existed where now there are plains. These two old physiographic

A. E. P.

Fig. 10.—The Level Floor of the Great Appalachian Valley near Lexington, Virginia.

From Lexington northward to the Potomac, the eastern side of the Great Valley is a broad plain, the Shenandoah Valley. The western side of the Valley is a ridge and valley section.

provinces and the Blue Ridge are known as Older Appalachia. At one time Older Appalachia extended farther to the east than it now does, far beyond the outer border of the Coastal Plain.

West of the Southern Appalachians and west of the Blue Ridge of Virginia and Maryland is a long narrow depression of valleys and ridges that extends from central Alabama northeastward all across the South and on into Pennsylvania and New York to the plains that lie south of Montreal, Canada This physiographic province is known as the Great Appalachian Valley, the Great Valley, or the Valley and the Ridge Province. Though varying in width throughout its entire length nevertheless it presents many features that are similar. In Alabama, largely in the Coosa Valley, it is about 25 miles wide; in Tennes-

see and southwestern Virginia in the Tennessee Basin, 35 to 50 miles.
For most of its length in the South the eastern portion of the Appalachian Valley is a plain (Fig. 10); in the western half, ridges and
valleys dominate (Fig. 11). The best agricultural lands and the densest
and more prosperous populations are on the flat lands. The ridges are
largely used for the growing of forests, although apples and peach
orchards cover many of the low ridges in the Shenandoah Valley and
a few of the ridges in the Valley of East Tennessee.

The cap rock of the Cumberland and Allegheny plateaus, that lie
as Fig. 11 shows to the west of the Great Appalachian Valley, is

A. E. P.

FIG. 11.—A Rough Section of the Great Appalachian Valley, near Monterey,
Virginia.

This is the ridge and valley region. Flat-floored valleys some three or four miles wide alternate
with prominent ridges. The landscape is about twenty-five miles west of Staunton. The highest
ridge in the background is Bull Pasture Mountain.

sandstone and conglomerate made by the consolidation of sea sands
and gravels. Beneath the sandstone conglomerate strata are shale beds.
In these are bituminous coal seams; beneath the shale is limestone.
And thereon hangs a geologic tale which briefly and simply is as follows: For many scores of millions of years, during the middle periods
of geologic history, there lay a long, broad seaway to the west of
Older Appalachia. Into this seaway poured many great rivers from
the east, from Older Appalachia with its lofty mountains and plateaus.
They carried great quantities of sediment and likewise minerals in solution. Period after period this deposition went on, and the deposits sank
deeper and deeper into the "crust" of the earth, owing to their great

weight, until some 50,000 feet of sand, mud, the remains of sea animals, and ooze (these later became sandstone, shale, and limestone)
were laid down. The last to be deposited were the sand and gravel
which later were indurated into the sandstone and conglomerate that
now occur on the top of the Cumberland Plateau. Following this long
period of deposition came great earth movements; the rocks in the
eastern part of the region were folded and faulted and lofty mountains
formed. The region of folding and faulting was nearest the eastern
shores of the old seaway, that is, on what is now the Great Appalachian
Valley and the western part of the Southern Appalachian Mountains.

Since this period of upheaval most of the mountains have been removed by the usual process of weathering and river transportation.
The ridges now to be found in the Great Valley and the mountains
to the east are but the lower flanks of the folds of the ancient mountains. This is the geologic history of the Great Valley, in brief. The
immense amount of erosion that is implied in the above brief story and
the immensity of time necessary for the changes are almost beyond
the layman's comprehension. Yet there is abundant evidence for all
the facts just presented.

The Cumberland and Allegheny plateaus have a history somewhat
comparable to that of the Valley except that they were not folded.
The old sea bottom and shore were elevated into a plateau. If you
should ever pass an exposure of sandstone or conglomerate on the
Cumberland Plateau, stop and examine some of the rounded quartz
pebbles that have weathered out of the hard rock. You are holding
in your hands indubitable evidence that the surface of the Cumberland
Plateau was at sea level when these sands and gravels were deposited.
The geologic "antiques" you are holding are many thousand times
as old as any human artifact taken from the mounds of a Cretan,
Babylonian, or Hittite civilization.

The almost interminable winding valleys of the Allegheny Plateau
and the steep escarpments and the infertile surface of the Cumberland
Plateau, neither of which has attracted landseekers in numbers, have
served to divide the Upper South into a Cisappalachian region and a
Transappalachian region. Kentucky, West Virginia, and Tennessee have
never had the close commercial relations with the Atlantic Coast cities
in the South that the Lake States have with the ports of the Northern
States. Even today the railroad and road engineers are forced to use
all the devices known to their profession to provide feasible traffic
ways across these plateaus (Fig. 12).

Beneath the cap rocks of sandstone, conglomerate, and shale of the
plateau are several hundred feet of limestone as previously stated.

Where the dissection of the cap rock is deep enough to reach the lime-stone and the valleys are wide enough to have flats, as in many parts of the Allegheny Plateau in the South, there is excellent agricultural land. The great distances to market are the farmers' chief problem, for conditions do not favor the development of large urban centers within the valleys. The coal-mining towns that occur scattered here

Courtesy Harper's Magazine.

FIG. 12.—The Narrows of Wills Creek, western Maryland, along the Baltimore and Ohio Railroad. Wills Creek Gap is one of the few passes across the Appalachian Barrier. From Harper's Magazine, IV, 1856, 600.

and there in the Allegheny Plateau offer the best markets, but these are small.

The eastern border of the Cumberland and Allegheny plateaus is a distinct topographic feature, as stated above, so conspicuous as to be called an escarpment or front (Fig. 13). It is the Cumberland Plateau that has the most distinct escarpment. The dissection of the western front of the Allegheny Plateau produces only high hills that rise above the low hills of the physiographic province to the west; the western side of the Cumberland Plateau is a distinct escarpment.

Westward from the west-facing escarpment and "foothills" of the plateaus stretch the Interior Low Plateaus on to the Coastal Plain of the Mississippi Basin. These plateaus are plains, for the most part, but with hilly land near the major streams. The Pennyroyal is the name given to the flat land of the Interior Low Plateaus in Kentucky. In Tennessee the Low Plateaus region is called the Highland Rim Plain. Below the general surface of the Low Plateaus in north central Kentucky and middle Tennessee are two basins, famous in Southern agriculture for their productive lands, the Blue Grass and the Nashville Basin. The bedrock of both plateaus and basins is limestone yet

A. E. P.

FIG. 13.—The Western Escarpment of the Cumberland Plateau, near Sparta, Tennessee, on the Nashville to Knoxville Highway.

The plateau level (top of bluff) is shown on the left, the ridges in the background are outliers of the Plateau, somewhat reduced in elevation, rising above the Highland Rim Plain.

of different geologic age and composition. That of the plateau surface has much chert. The basin limestone is comparatively pure, suitable for the manufacture of lime and cement, and is also much used for buildings and for rock walls. It also has phosphate rock as one of its "impurities," concentrated by weathering agencies in middle Tennessee to rock phosphate.

The Ozark Plateau and Ouachita Mountains form a highland with the Coastal Plain to the east and south and the great Central Plains to the west. The Ozark Plateau physiographically resembles the Cumberland plateau; and the Ouachita Mountains and the Arkansas Valley, the Great Appalachian Valley. The Boston Mountains on the southern border of the Ozarks resemble the Cumberland escarpment, particularly that part near Cumberland Gap, known as the Cumberland Mountains. The Ozark region has fertile limestone valleys separated by forested ridges and slopes. The whole is thoroughly dissected (Fig. 14).

The Central Lowlands or Plains, broad and flat and extensive, cover most of Oklahoma and extend southward into Texas. Only a small part of this vast physiographic province is in the South. There are some interruptions in the continuity of the plains—low mountains or rocky ridges. The most conspicuous are the Arbuckle and Wichita mountains in southern Oklahoma.

A. E. P.

FIG. 14.—A Landscape in the Ozarks, North of Fayetteville, Arkansas.
The relief is far more subdued here than at Eureka Springs.

West of the Central Lowlands is the Great Plains Province; only a small part of this likewise is in the South. In western Texas the High Plains region, a subdivision of the Great Plains, is known as the Llano Estacado or Staked Plains. In reality it is a low plateau with escarpments on both the eastern and western borders, that on the eastern border being the most conspicuous. This eastern escarpment is known as the "Break of the Plains." Over most of the Llano Estacado is a deep, brown colored loam that under dry-farming techniques yields abundantly when consideration is given to the fact that the annual rainfall is little more than 20 inches. South of the Llano Estacado is the stony Edwards Plateau, used almost exclusively for grazing. The plateau and mountain area west of the Pecos River is likewise too arid for farming (Fig. 15).

The general location, limits, and some of the major features of the physiographic provinces just outlined, are familiar to many people of

the South; but few realize that a large part of the geographic, economic, and social phenomena of these Southern States are directly
associated with these provinces or regions. The physical characteristics
and chemical composition of the soils, the drainage conditions, mineral
deposits, natural conditions affecting land and riverway transportation, the utilization of water resources, the health conditions, and
even to a marked degree the climatic conditions are best understood
and will be given a more orderly place in man's thinking, if their

A. E. P.

FIG. 15.—A Large Salina near the Guadalupe Mountains, Texas.

This lake, or salt flats, is ninety-three miles east of El Paso, in the arid section of Texas. A pipe
line across the flats is carried on piling above the salt.

proper association with these major physiographic regions is made.
Many of these relationships will be brought out throughout the remainder of the book. We wish now to direct, briefly, the reader's attention to the distribution of the useful minerals of the South by
physiographic regions.

THE USEFUL MINERALS OF THE SOUTH

In the minds of most people the occurrence and distribution of
minerals is all a mystery. Yet there are natural laws regarding their
occurrence. It is comparatively easy to tell whether a certain mineral
may occur in a certain class of rock, but no one can tell whether or
not the mineral is present in that rock before a thorough investigation
is made. It is this uncertainty that mystifies the uninitiated. The
mineralogist knows that beds of coal cannot be found in a region
of igneous or meta-igneous rock like that of the Piedmont Plateau. He

knows that veins of metallic minerals are normally associated with igneous rock and therefore are generally not to be found in sandstone, shale, or limestone unless these rocks have igneous intrusions (Figs. 16 and 17).

The Coastal Plain, as previously stated, is young, geologically. The mineral materials forming it are of marine origin derived from animals or are land material that has been deposited in the borders of the sea and worked over on the shores by waves and currents. No metallic minerals occur except bog iron ore that accumulated or was

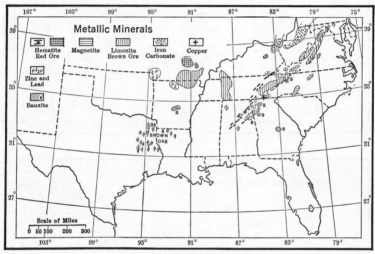

FIG. 16

This map shows the distribution of metallic minerals. Not all deposits here shown are worked and there is no relation of amount of production to area of exposure.

assembled in boggy areas after the Coastal Plain was formed. Sands, gravel, and shell marl are widely distributed. Clay is less abundant. Fuller's earth and diatomaceous earth are fairly common. Limestone is confined mostly to Florida and near-by portions of Georgia and Alabama (Fig. 18). A form of limestone known as Selma chalk is the bedrock of the Black Belt of Alabama. Two similar limestone areas occur in Texas, the best known being the Black Prairie of Texas. The Coastal Plain limestone is soft. On the Florida Keys it is shaped for building purposes by axes and saws. The general abundance of shells and casts and molds of seashells in the limestone is evidence enough that this rock was formed from the less perishable parts of shelled sea animals of various sizes. Some limestones have come from

coral and were formed just as the living coral reefs are now being
built off the Florida Keys. Phosphate rock occurs in South Carolina

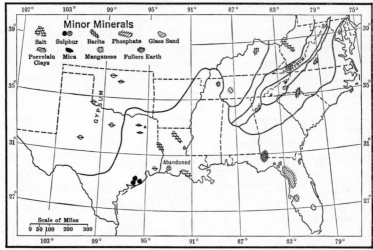

FIG. 17*

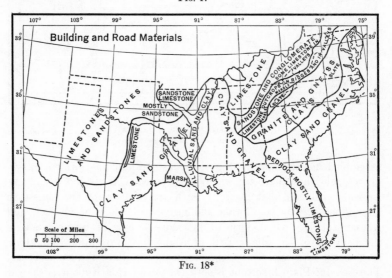

FIG. 18*

and western Florida. Florida has the more important and richer deposits; in fact, those of South Carolina are now too exhausted for
economic production.

---

* The heavy lines in Figs. 17 and 18 are the boundaries of the Physiographic
regions.

For some unexplainable cause the petroleum and gas deposits of the Coastal Plain, so far discovered, with one exception, are in the West Gulf Coastal Plain. Salt and sulphur are likewise confined to the West Gulf Plain. The Coastal Plain also has peat and lignite deposits. Peat is now being formed in most of the marshes like the Dismal Swamp, and lignite, derived from peat, occurs beneath many hundreds of square miles in Texas and Mississippi. As long as bituminous coal is available at low prices the lignite deposits will remain mostly unworked.

In the Piedmont, the Blue Ridge, and the eastern part of the Southern Appalachian Mountains igneous and meta-igneous rock predominate. Old granites have been subjected to pressure and distortion and recrystallization. These old rocks have been intruded by younger igneous rock. The minerals of Older Appalachia are therefore quite unlike those of the Coastal Plain. Most metallic minerals are associated with molten magmas and with magmatic waters, that is, waters that have come from great depths and are likely to be saturated with mineral compounds. Gold and silver have been found in the Southern Appalachians but for the most part not in paying quantities sufficient to develop a mining industry. Copper is mined in several localities in North Carolina and southwestern Virginia. Copper mining at Ducktown, Tennessee, was begun about the 1850's. At one time the Ducktown region was among the leading sources for copper in our country. Mozanite was once mined profitably—until the cheaper imports from Brazil supplanted the American product in American markets. Other mineral deposits worked in Old Appalachia are mica, feldspar, kaolin (weathered feldspar), soapstone, talc, and magnetite. Granite of excellent quality is taken from many quarries in the mountains and hills of the Piedmont.

The quicksilver of Texas and diamonds of Arkansas are to be associated with igneous rock. These are, however, of little importance among minerals when judged by value of production.

In the remainder of the South, the Great Valley, the Cumberland and Allegheny plateaus, the Interior Low Plateaus, the Ozark and Ouachita regions, the Great Central Lowlands, and the Highlands areas in western Texas and Oklahoma the bedrock is of marine origin, as we have learned, but vastly older than the unconsolidated materials that make up the Coastal Plain. Although tens, even hundreds, of millions of years have elapsed since the rocks of some of these regions were formed under the sea and many changes have occurred, such as induration, recrystallization, and vein-forming, there is a great similarity in the useful mineral deposits of these regions and those of the Coastal Plain. One finds sand and gravel and muds of much the same sort as those of the Coastal Plain. But in the hard-rock regions these unconsolidated materials are weathered products of the hard rock. The older regions have limestone as does the Coastal Plain, but in the former the limestone is hard and highly crystalline, in some sections even to the point of being marble.

All the old limestone areas, the Great Appalachian Valley, the deep valleys of the plateaus, the Interior Low Plateaus with the Nashville and Blue Grass basins, and the valleys of the Ozarks, have suffered profound denudation. In the Great Valley, as we have seen, there once were lofty mountain ranges and the two limestone basins were domes. The limestone areas in the South were leveled and denuded largely by solution. In such a process there is a tendency for the insoluble materials of the limestone, widely scattered and distributed in the bedrock, to be left as residuum and concentrate into beds. This is the origin of the phosphate rock beds in the Nashville Basin, of the zinc ore, bauxite, and brown iron ore in the Great Valley. The concentration of many of these deposits is not sufficient to make them economically workable. Sulphur springs and wells and salt licks are common in the limestone areas. The mineral waters of limestone areas may contain, besides three or four forms of sulphur, compounds of sodium, magnesium, calcium, lithium, potassium, and iron. These are dissolved from the limestone as the underground waters circulate through cracks of the rock. The hot springs of Hot Springs, Arkansas, are probably due to the presence of hot rock from igneous intrusions some distance below the surface.

The Cumberland and Allegheny plateaus, as previously stated, have excellent beds of coal, some bearing the best coal in America. The coal originated from vegetable accumulations in the great marshes that existed in the plateau areas when these areas were at or near sea level, that is, before the great uplift and folding previously described.

Gypsum occurs in both the Coastal Plain and the older rocks of marine origin. The most active workings in the South are in central Oklahoma and northern Texas.

The bauxite of Arkansas, the chief American source of aluminum ore, and of Alabama and eastern Tennessee is in the hard marine rock and was derived from the chemical action on a grand scale in nature's laboratory. In Georgia aluminum ore occurs in the older formations of the Coastal Plain.

The iron ores of the South are of several sorts and ages and therefore in several kinds of rock (Fig. 16). The magnetite of North Carolina and Georgia Piedmont is of great geologic age. Very low-grade brown or bog ore of the Coastal Plain was worked in Colonial days. The brown ore of the Great Valley and the western edge of the Blue Ridge and the Southern Appalachian Mountains is partly a residual deposit from the weathering of limestone and partly the result of concentration in pockets of the harder rock by ground water. Brown ore of low grade also occurs in the Highland Rim west of the Nashville Basin. The hematite (red ore) of the South, known as Clinton ore, outcrops here and there from central Alabama northeastward beyond the borders of the South into New York. The name Clinton is applied to this type of ore because the ore was first studied near Clinton, New York. The Clinton ore is thought by geologists to be of sedimentary origin. Soluble iron compounds were carried by water to bogs. By the aid of iron bacteria the soluble compounds were changed to insoluble compounds. Through a long period of time large quantities of ore may thus be accumulated. The brown bog ore may have been changed to red or hematite by metamorphosis incident to mountain forming. The chief outcrop of Clinton ore in the Birmingham district is Red Mountain in the Great Valley. Red ore outcrops here and there in the Great Valley from central Alabama far on into Pennsylvania.

THE CLIMATE AND WEATHER OF THE SOUTH

The location of the South, (1) between 25° N and 39° N latitude, (2) in the southern edge of the belt of Westerlies, and (3) in the southeastern portion of the continent with the sea on the east and the south, and the low relief of the land determine the characteristics of its climate and weather.

Owing to its comparatively low latitude, the South has a high sun during the year as compared to the North. The length of the growing season is longer than in the North, and the length of the day in winter and in summer does not vary so markedly. The median growing season for the Lower South is 240 days and for the Upper South 180 to 210 days, except in the plateau and mountain sections. The growing season for more than half of the South is long enough for two harvests of some crops; and in the Lower South for three.* This also means that the hot season is longer. If we assume that a monthly average of 68° and above is *hot* and below 32° is *cold*, the length of the hot season and of the cold season at selected places is as follows:

	Hot	Cold
St Paul, Minnesota	2 months	4 or 5 months
St. Louis	4	1
Nashville	5	0
Montgomery	5	0
New Orleans	7	0
Miami	12	0

* Rarely is the land worked as intensively, however, except in some trucking areas where interplanting is often practiced.

A high sun is a hot sun. The evaporation of water from the ground and the transpiration from plants are high in most of the South. Much more water is needed for crops in general than in the North, and droughts are more frequent and disastrous. But, surprisingly, the maximum temperatures in the summer is, as a rule, little above that of more northerly localities. A comparison of the absolute maximum (the highest temperature ever recorded), up to December 31, 1929, at a few cities is interesting: Atlanta 102°, Montgomery 107°, Louisville 107°, Little Rock 108°, Nashville 106°, Omaha 110°, St. Paul 104°, Bismarck 108°, St. Louis 107°. The summers of the South differ from those in the North in the greater length of the hot spells and their more frequent occurrence. The reverse is of course true of the winter in the two sections. Cold spells are short and infrequent in the South.

The location of the South in the southern border of the Westerlies means that it lies south of the main paths of the highs and lows (the atmospheric formations with which our weather is associated), yet does have variable weather. When a well-developed low is passing eastward to the north of the South warm moist Gulf and Atlantic winds, southerly winds, dominate; when a high is passing eastward, north of the South, cold dry northerly winds prevail. In terms of air mass analysis, it is an equatorial air mass that dominates the weather of the South in the former situation and a Polar Pacific or Polar Continental in the second. Gulf and Atlantic winds bring warm weather and generally rain; and north winds, if they are strong and persist for several days, give cool, dry, bracing weather. In the winter the north winds may carry freezing weather to the Gulf Coast and far down into Florida. The flatness of the Mississippi Basin permits the free movement of the winds whether from the south or from the north. South winds tend to cool off as they move northward, and north winds warm up as they move southward. The Gulf and Atlantic winds tend to give coastal lands for one hundred or more miles inland cooler temperatures than those at localities farther north. The hottest section of the South in the summer is the northern half of the Gulf Coast States.

The Appalachian Highlands are barriers to the movement of winds to only a slight degree, but the ridges do affect the distribution of rainfall. The regions of heaviest rainfall are near the coast and on the east-facing slopes of the ridges of the Southern Appalachian Highlands, as Fig. 20 shows.

Figure 19 is a map of the temperature regions of the South. This map makes use of the widely used terms hot, mild, cool, and cold as descriptive of temperatures. But here these names are assigned definite numerical values. A hot month has an average temperature of 68° or

higher. A month having an average between 50° and 68° is a mild
month. One with an average temperature between 32° and 50° is a
cool month, and a cold month has an average of 32° or lower. The
temperatures of the hottest and coldest months give the name to the
region. The South is largely in the Hot Summer and Cool Winter
Region. Only a small part of the Appalachian Highlands has Hot Summer and Cold Winter temperatures, and only the Gulf Coastal lands
and Florida have Hot Summer and Mild Winter temperatures. This

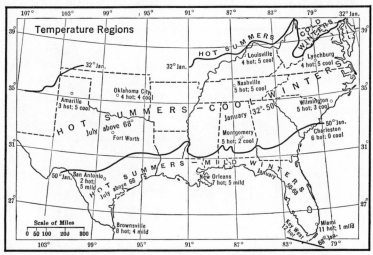

Fig. 19

A temperature region is an area having temperature conditions somewhat similar, within certain
limits. The temperatures of the warmest and the coldest months are used to determine the
boundaries of the regions. A month with an average of 68° or above is a hot month; one with an
average between 68° and 50° is a mild month; between 50° and 32°, a cool month; with an
average below 32° is a cold month.

latter temperature region is often known as the Subtropical. The one
to the north may be called Warm Temperate.

The distribution of the rainfall is shown in Fig. 20, from which it is
readily seen that about three-fourths of the South has more than 30
inches of rainfall on the average during the year. This we may call
the humid portion. Most of the remainder of the South may well be
called subhumid, grading into semiarid. The east-facing slope of the
Blue Ridge has the heaviest rainfall in the Southern States, one station recording more than 80 inches.

The sufficiency of the precipitation for crops depends largely upon
the seasonal distribution of the rainfall, the relative sink-in and

run-off as affected by the porosity of the sod, the slope, the plant cover, and the rate of downpour; and lastly to the rate of evaporation. These conditions vary so greatly over the South and the data regarding them if not entirely lacking are so meager that the presenting of even a general picture of each of these is impossible.

Rain water may be stored in the ground for weeks and months and in the deep porous soils of the High Plains of Texas for a year or two, yet in most parts of the Southern States, with much of the surface in slope and a high summer sun, it is but a matter of a few rainless days before the vegetation with superficial root systems be-

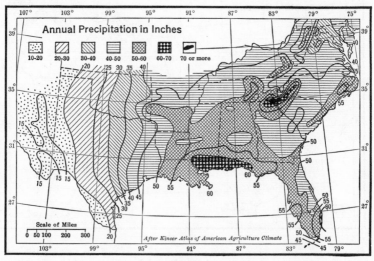

FIG. 20

gins to hang out a distress sign. Figure 21 is a map of the distribution of and number of droughts in a 10-year period. A drought as defined by the weather bureau is a 30-day period (consecutive) in which the precipitation during any day is below one-tenth of an inch. Such a criterion may suffice for the weather bureau, for the bureau has to consider large areas with diverse drainage and soil conditions, but it is of little practical value to the farmer. Low flat lands suffer less from droughts than hilly lands. A drought of 60 days or more results in a leaf fall in deciduous trees, such as happened in 1925, particularly on slopes. From 15 to 20 per cent (or more) of the forest trees in the drought area were killed. The writer is firmly convinced that *dry spells* (mostly less than 30 days' duration) *are the most widespread and destructive*

of all weather phenomena to agricultural operators in the South. The
ratio of evaporation to precipitation is a factor of interest in the study
of droughts. Precipitation data are collected at every weather station,
but there have been few studies of the rate of evaporation of water
from a free surface. One measurement obtained at Birmingham showed
a total evaporation from a free surface of water of 38.3 inches between
April 1 and September 30. The normal precipitation during that period
was less than 25 inches. At Amarillo, Texas, the normal evaporation

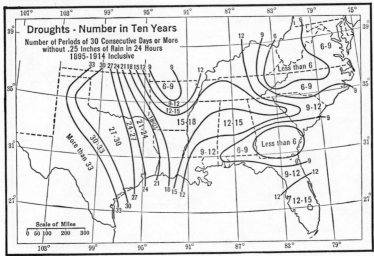

After Kincer, Atlas of American Agriculture, Precipitation and Humidity.
FIG. 21

(based on an 11-year record) from an open pan was 52.7 inches,
whereas the normal precipitation is about 25 inches. The total evaporation varies from year to year. At Spur, Texas, in 1922 it was 71.8
inches but only 52 in 1926.*

Figure 22 is a map of the climatic regions of the South.

"Cold spells" or "cold waves" form a second weather phenomenon
that affects agricultural operators adversely. The greatest damage is
felt in the Lower South where such weather is considered abnormal.
In the northern part of the South freezing temperatures are normal
experiences from early December to early March though at any time
during this period there may be several days in succession of spring-
like weather. The severest "cold spells" in the winter come in the rear
of well-developed elliptical lows that pass slowly eastward across

* Charles E. Linney, *Monthly Weather Review*, July, 1927, 320, 325.

4

46 NATURE'S LEGACY

the Gulf States, provided there is to the northwest of this low a well-developed, slowly moving high. Under such conditions great volumes of cold, clear, dry, biting blasts move southward down the flat Mississippi Basin plains to the Gulf Coast and Florida.

Official records show that the severest cold waves in Florida occurred in January, 1886; December, 1894; February, 1895, 1899, and 1915. There are no records before 1886. There are unofficial records

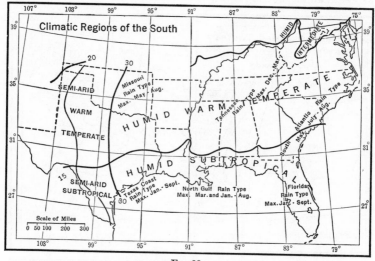

Fig. 22

Five climatic regions are delimited. The western boundary of the humid South is the 30-inch isohyet (equal rainfall); the semiarid area is to the west. Lands between the 20-inch and 30-inch isohyets may be called subhumid, but for simplicity not so named here. The east-west boundaries of the climatic regions are the isotherms used to delimit the temperature regions. The dominant rainfall types of the South are also shown. Rain types after Ward.

of a very severe freeze in 1766 during which fruit trees were killed in St. Augustine. In 1774 a snow storm extended over the whole of Florida. On April 6, 1799, vegetation was killed over more than half of the state. Probably the coldest weather ever recorded in Florida was in February, 1835, when the temperature at Jacksonville was 7°. The St. Johns River was frozen several rods from the banks, and fruit trees were killed over a large part of the state.*

The cold waves of Texas are known as Northers. Between 1871 and 1927, twenty-seven cold waves with temperatures of 27° or lower reached the coast. At one time the thermometer dropped to 8°. On

* Bull. Q, U. S. Weather Bureau, 346 (First Edition).

the open High Plains where shelter is not to be had and where man even today makes little provision for housing cattle the loss of livestock is great. During some cold spells cattle by the thousands are frozen to death even in the Rio Grande Valley. In Minnesota stock men would consider temperatures that kill cattle in the Rio Grande as balmy weather. It is the unusualness of the weather that plays havoc.

A third type of destructive weather phenomenon in the South is the tropical hurricane. Its fury is felt mostly along the Atlantic and Gulf coasts, especially in lower Florida. The newspapers in recent years have so fully described the paths and the destruction wrought that further comments are not necessary here. Some data on the frequency and period of occurrence may be of value. In the 38 years between 1887 and 1925, records show that a total of 240 hurricanes struck or came near our southeastern coasts. Of these 62 came in October, 60 in September, 32 in August, 11 in July, 13 in June, 1 in May, 13 in November, and 2 in December. Only a few of these 240 were destructive. Wireless on Caribbean vessels has been of great service in locating the paths of these hurricanes and keeping the public informed of their progress day by day. The most destructive hurricanes to date are the Galveston of September 8, 1900, that caused the loss of 6,000 lives and $30,000,000 worth of property; and the Florida hurricane of September 18, 1926 (at Miami). The property damage at Miami alone was $76,000,000, and the known loss of lives in the district 114.

Tornadoes, similar in some respect to tropical hurricanes except that they develop on land and cover a much narrower and shorter path, are characteristic of the interior of the Mississippi Basin from the Gulf States to Wisconsin and Michigan. They may be thought of as concentrated hurricanes. The velocity of the wind in the hurricane rarely reaches more than 100 to 125 miles an hour, but in the tornado it may be 300 to 500. Tornadoes are associated with thunderstorms but are distinguished from thunderstorms by their funnel shape. The area of the base of the funnel covers much less than a mile, some not more than a quarter mile. A single tornado may travel a hundred or hundreds of miles before working itself out. Rarely is a path of destruction continuous for this distance, but the tornado may come down to the surface of the earth and leave a record of its presence at only a half dozen places. Tornadoes are highly destructive of life and property—several hundred lives may be lost in the path of a single tornado and the property damage may amount to a score or more millions of dollars—yet there is little reason for one in the Mississippi Basin to worry about tornadoes. Professor Ward has estimated that the chances are 1 in 625,000 that a given square mile within the tornado region of the United States may be visited by a destructive tornado. The insurance companies handling windstorm and lightning coverage demand higher rates in the tornado belts based on previous tornadoes. There is little evidence, however, for supposing that an area once visited will ever have a second visitation. The writer does know of a farm in northern Alabama being visited by three destructive tornadoes in the course of a few years. On two occasions most of the buildings were destroyed. But even this must be considered as unusual and not the rule.

Has the expression the "Sunny South" any scientific evidence? The following data for a few selected cities (selected at random) will answer the question:

PERCENTAGE OF POSSIBLE SUNSHINE FOR YEAR

Cities in the South		Cities in the North	
New Orleans	58	Buffalo	49
Louisville	58	Concord	53
Nashville	59	Indianapolis	56
Montgomery	62	St. Paul	56
Little Rock	62	Chicago	58
Vicksburg	64	St. Louis	59
Galveston	64	Des Moines	61
Charleston	65	Huron	63
Miami	67		
Ft. Worth	71		

For some non-Southern readers it may not be amiss to be reminded that one does not step into Florida and Gulf climate as soon as one crosses Mason and Dixon's line or the Ohio River. Under normal weather conditions it gets warmer in both summer and winter the farther south one goes, yet every year Nashville, for example, may have colder weather than Illinois in winter and cooler temperatures in the summer, for several days in succession. The summers are not so enjoyable in the middle South as in the middle North; but the winters in the middle North are not as enjoyable as those in the middle South. Both sections have good features, both have bad features, of weather and climate.

THE ORIGINAL BIOTA OF THE SOUTH

Humboldt, the greatest scientific traveler of his time (1769-1859), recognized the zonal arrangement of plants and animals. In the romantic style of his day he writes, "Unlike in design and weave, is the carpet which the plant world in the abundance of its flower has spread over the naked crust of the earth, more densely woven where the sun ascends higher on the cloudless sky, looser toward the sluggish poles, where the early returning frost nips the undeveloped bud and snatches the barely matured fruit. Every zone is endowed with peculiar charms—the tropical in the variety and grand development of its production, the northern in its fresh meadows and in periodical revival of nature and the influences of the first breezes of the spring. Besides having its own special advantages, every zone is marked by a peculiar character."* Humboldt stressed only temperatures as an element of the environment.

Present-day ecologists have come to see that temperature is by no means the only factor in the environment to which plant life adapts itself. Indeed the environment is exceedingly complex. The maximum and minimum temperatures, length of growing season, length of periods of extremes of heat or cold, amount of sunlight, length of periods of droughts or deluges, amount of rain, seasonal distribution of rain, as well as winds, and humidity are some of the conditions of the atmosphere to which plants are or tend to be adapted. Soil with its complex environmental condition, to be sketched in the following section of this chapter, is also a factor. In ecological plant geography it is climate that is considered the dominant factor in fixing the limits of the various major plant regions. Some of the variations within this plant region may be due to differences in soils, drainage, and sun-slope. For example, the deciduous forest belt covers a large region (many states) that has climatic conditions similar, in their major aspects, throughout. Within this large area it is not difficult to trace a close correlation of certain tree species to soil conditions (known in ecology as edaphic conditions). Beech, maple, and hickory grow on deep rich soils; some of the oaks, on drier ridges with light soil; the hackberry, on thin soil; the red cedar, on almost no soil; the water maple, willow, slippery elm, and others on alluvial lands—all within the major climatic plant region.

The map used in this chapter (Fig. 23) shows the distribution of certain classes, orders, families, genera, or species of plants, particularly trees, that *seem* naturally to group themselves. An ecological interpretation of these groups will not be attempted; only the correlation of plant groups to climatic and soil conditions will be undertaken. The emphasis will be largely on such plants as have an economic value or that condition man's utilization of the land. Although for the most part most of the original vegetation is gone, enough of the

---

* Quoted by Charles Mohr, *Plant Life of Alabama*, Geologic Survey of Alabama, 28.

original is left here and there for us to know the species that composed it perfectly. We will discuss these original types as if they still existed, and hence we use the present tense.

It will be noted from the map that east of, approximately, the ninety-fifth to ninety-eighth meridian the plant regions have a linear

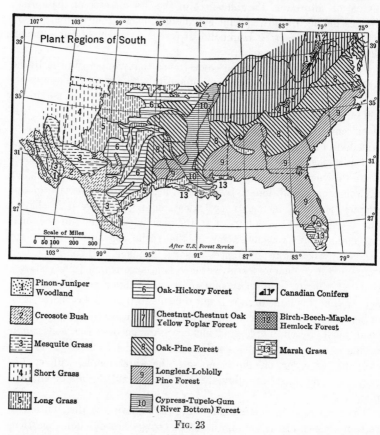

FIG. 23

east and west distribution. Since the isotherms of the Southern States extend roughly east and west and deviate poleward near the Atlantic Coast, these plant regions undoubtedly may be correlated with temperature conditions. So also do the soil regions extend east and west (Fig. 27). This should be expected, for it will be shown in the succeeding section that the major soil groups hold a causal relationship to climate conditions, both temperature and rainfall. We have also seen that within the major climatic regions soil is a factor in the localization of plant life. In Texas there seems to be a closer correlation of plant life with rainfall than with temperature.

Savannahs, everglades, and flatwoods dominate in the low, wet outer portion of the Coastal Plains (Atlantic and Gulf) and the estuarian sections of the rivers that cross the plains. The soil is waterlogged most of the year, and even in the dry seasons the water is near the surface. Because of the heavy rainfall and the flat surface, natural

Courtesy Harper's Magazine

Fig. 24.—A Typical Natural Landscape in the Louisiana Prairie, about 1850.

The trees are live oaks. This was the Attakapas Country, famous as a grazing region. Cane and corn fields dominate the cultural landscape today. From *Harper's Magazine*, VII, 1853, 751.

drainage is poor and artificial drainage expensive. In most of this vast area nature reigns almost as supreme as in pre-Columbian days. This low, hydrophytic section varies greatly in width from a few rods to a score or more miles. Most of the southern third of Florida is a great marsh, the Everglades. Marsh land is extensive in eastern North Carolina, and far inland from the head of Mobile Bay. In Louisiana and Texas coastal prairies border the Gulf. There are marsh lands also between the distributaries and bayous in Louisiana (Figs. 24 and 25).

From eastern Texas eastward, the natural plant life on the drier portions of the outer and on the middle Coastal Plain sections is pine— longleaf, loblolly, and slash. In this belt the rainfall varies from 30 to 60 inches or more, everywhere sufficient, except in years of drought, for a luxuriant growth of trees. This belt lies almost wholly on the Coastal Plain. The loose, porous soil permits rapid drainage except on the flat lands near the streams. A difference in species is recognized in the different portions of the Coastal Plain. This forest region lies mainly in the Hot Summer and Cool Winter belt of temperatures with the southern edge in the Hot and Mild belt. Conifers the world over, as a rule, dominate in regions of cold winters and moderate summers. The presence of coniferous vegetation in such temperatures as here prevail is probably to be attributed to the dominance of soil (edaphic)

A. E. P.

Fig. 25.—A Bit of the Coastal Prairie of Southern Texas, between Houston and Corpus Christi.

Traveling over this flat monotonous plain hour after hour, even in a speedy automobile of today, one readily senses its endlessness. Wild and tame grass pastures, fields of rice and cotton (the latter on the dryer lands) are the types of land utilization. Some farmers have herds of tick-immune cattle developed by crossbreeding with imported humped, creamy gray Brahman bulls. The Brahman cattle exude a sticky wax that repels insects. Immunity extends to cattle with as little as one-eighth Brahman blood.

conditions over climatic. The pine, racially, is a primitive type of plant. The soil student considers the soils of the Coastal Plain young or primitive. Primitive life dominates in a primitive soil environment. It is because the pine is a primitive type that it finds little difficulty in getting a foothold in land badly eroded or denuded of its humus by burning—a factor of great moment in the reforestation of cut-over lands.

Bordering this pine belt on the north is a transition belt in which deciduous trees, largely oak, and pines compete; yet the competition is not strong. The pines occupy the sandier and better-drained lands; the oak the more fertile tracts on the gentle slopes and flats. In the long run, were the natural forces and tendencies not disturbed, much of the pine would likely be replaced by the oak or other deciduous trees owing to changes in the humus and life conditions of the soil. This change in plant life proceeds in successive steps and stages and is known as plant succession. Oak-pine vegetation dominates on the Piedmont but it also appears on the Coastal Plain of the Chesapeake Bay region, on the Cumberland Plateau in Alabama, the dry sandy and loessal lands in Mississippi, and the dry, hilly, sandy lands (primitive or young soil) in Louisiana and Arkansas.

The deciduous or hardwood belt covers the Upper South and extends far to the southwest into Texas. East of the Mississippi the variety of species is largely chestnut, chestnut oak, and Carolina poplar. On the higher mountain slopes species of more northern climes are numerous, even those of Canada. West of the Alluvial Valley of the Mississippi, the oak takes precedence among the trees, an adaptation, no doubt, if one may judge from many observations as to the habits of certain oaks, to the drier conditions.

Proceeding from east to west across Texas from the oak-pine forest, there come the oak-hickory formation, then the prairie region with grass five feet or more high, followed by the short grass vegetation of the High Plains. These types of plant life, in order, are undoubtedly correlated with lower and lower amounts of rainfall to the west. In southwestern Texas the rainfall is so low that semiarid conditions of life are approached. Mesquite grass, mesquite, and piñon-juniper vegetation merge into the semi-desert creosote bush near the Rio Grande. These plants are perennials. Ephemeral types that spring up after each warm season rain, blossom, and die down as drought conditions come, give an unexpected charm to a landscape that ordinarily is unattractive to one accustomed to verdure.

An east to west plant profile in North Carolina would begin with the formations of dune and barrier beach, followed by those of the coastal marsh and flatwoods, the drier belts of the Coastal Plain, the Piedmont, and the mountains. The major conditioning factors in this vegetational profile are undoubtedly temperature, type of soil, and soil water, since the rainfall is much the same over the area covered. The differences in temperature, and to some extent in soil, are largely due to differences in altitude.*

A north-south profile from the Gulf to the Ohio through Alabama and across Tennessee and Kentucky would show types very similar to those in the Caroline profile, except that the high-altitude, and there-

---

* *Naturalist's Guide to the Americas,* 413-417.

fore high-latitude, types are absent. There is nothing comparable to
the Black Belt of Alabama in North Carolina.

The Black Belt of Alabama is generally referred to as a prairie
region. Mohr who studied it in the nineties of the last century writes
regarding the original vegetation, "The term 'prairie region' refers less
to the timberless tracts, which originally formed a small fraction of
its area, than to the black, calcareous, highly fertile soil of these
uplands, which being rich in humus as a result of the reaction of its

A. E. P.

FIG. 26.—Mangroves Bordering a Channel of Key Largo, Florida Keys.
The mangrove covers immense areas of mud flats in southern and western Florida.

calcareous constituents upon vegetable matter, closely resembles the
equally productive soil of the western treeless prairies."*

The vegetation of Florida is transitional between the tropics and
the temperate regions and likewise varies with the drainage conditions. On the keys tropical palms are reflected from the clear, lime-
impregnated waters of the Florida Strait and the lagoons behind the
keys, but where the waters are stagnant and mud has collected, the
tropical mangrove (Fig. 26) forms vast thickets that are persistently
advancing seaward. Mangrove dominates on the Gulf shores of southern Florida and along the quiet lagoons. The tall grass and sedge
of the Everglades cover most of the southern third of Florida. Here
and there the continuity of marsh vegetation is interrupted by hammocks (or hummocks) of tropical forms, which, like the palms and

* Mohr, *op. cit.*, 99-100.

mangrove, were probably brought from the West Indies by winds, ocean currents, and birds. Rubber trees, banyans, the coral bean, one of the coffee beans, and two members of *Euphorbia* are common. Beneath the trees and entwining or resting on the branches are lianas and orchids. These tropical plants are confined to those portions of Florida not visited by frosts. They are evergreens.*

North of the Everglades and along both the east and west dry land borders that lie between the marshes and the seashores, pine forests dominate. The sand palmetto is conspicuous everywhere, as undergrowth. Within the pine region are small scattered hammocks with plant formations of two types. The high hammocks with deep, rich, well-drained soil, containing some clay or underlain by limestone, have broadleaved evergreens, like the magnolia, bay, and holly. These are climax types of a wet subtropical region. Ecologists believe that but for the intervention of man—removal of the forests and annual burning of undergrowth—the larger part of the longleaf pine lands would eventually have come to have a wet subtropical flora. In the northern part of Florida the broadleaved evergreens, the subtropical climax type, are fewer in number than farther south, the hammocks being covered with black, red, white, and bur oaks, black walnut, wild cherry, hickory, and others that are characteristic of the forests north of 40° N. Simpson thinks they are relics of species that pushed southward into Florida in the Glacial Period when all the South was much colder. With the change in climate in Post Glacial times some species died out but other species, those listed above, adjusted their structures or were hardy enough (generalized in type) to fit into the new environment.†

Spanish moss is restricted mostly to the northern two-thirds of Florida, that is, north of about 27°. Its northern limit in the South is approximately 32°-33°, mostly in the river valleys in these latitudes. It is an epiphyte, not a parasite. In the moister parts of the South it grows even on telegraph wires and poles.

THE ORIGINAL ANIMAL LIFE OF THE SOUTH

Animal ecologists have generally accepted the life regions worked out by plant ecologists and plant geographers. They recognize a coastal marsh fauna, a sand dune fauna, a coniferous forest fauna, a

---

* D. H. Campbell, *An Outline of Plant Geography*, 110-113; *Naturalist's Guide to the Americas*, 427.

† Charles T. Simpson, "The Plant Life of Florida," in a publication of the *Florida State Department of Agriculture*, 1926, 19, 20.

savanna fauna, a deciduous forest fauna, and so on. That certain birds show a preference for low bushes, others for marshes, coniferous trees, open prairie, or the margins of lakes, is recognized by every bird student. Certain animals like the buffalo show preference for grasslands yet do live in forested areas. Others like the prairie dog are rarely seen apart from the open plains. Their habits of life are adjusted to a prairie environment.

It is not intended to give in detail a list of the animal characteristics of each of the many plant regions of the South but rather to discuss the range of a few of the larger forms as elements of Southern environment that have had some effect in the development of civilization. To most of the pioneers (and even the farmer and hunter of today), the only animals of importance were those which furnished food, furs, and sport in hunting and fishing; and those classed as predatory on both man and domestic animals.

The bison and elk roamed the forest tracts of the Upper South until the middle of the eighteenth century in Virginia, and the early part of the nineteenth in the transmontane sections of the Mississippi Basin. It is only during the last six or seven decades that the bison has become extinct as a free animal in western Texas. Beaver in small numbers in the sluggish streams of the Appalachian Highlands are within the recollection of our older mountaineers. Bears, wild cats, pumas, wolves, and the lynx have been seen in the sections remote from civilized man's habitations within the present generation. Foxes are common, so also are the general varieties of deer. Among the game birds are the turkey, mallard duck, wild goose, partridge, and quail and the prairie chicken in the west. These are fairly common. The opossum, rabbit,, and squirrel have furnished a limited amount of food since the earliest occupancy of the lands.

A beginning is now being made in the restocking of some of the national forests and parks in the South with selected types which civilization either drove westward or destroyed. Most of the states have or are providing state parks, state forests, or game preserves. The National Government maintains several forests in the South.

In the last century or more coastal, commercial fisheries in the South have been active. The inland waters have trout, bass, perch, catfish, crappie, pike, drum, buffalo, carp, and suckers and eels; the salt-water shad, alewives (herring), drum, weakfish (sea trout), blue fish, Spanish mackerel, crab, shrimp, oyster, and terrapin. The tarpon, kingfish, cavalla, the pompanos, and red snapper are confined largely to the Gulf Coastal waters. The inedible menhaden is taken off the Atlantic Coast.*

THE SOILS OF THE SOUTH

Soil has come to be considered an evolving thing. It is more than just dirt, mineral matter with a little humus. The soil body is, in its maturity (when completely developed), the result of a long series of complex changes, the particular type of development and quality of soil being affected by the natural environment. A soil in its evolution starts as a mass of disintegrated rock. This parent soil material is further weathered. Water moving through it shifts soluble mineral matter and colloidal bodies, even the finer mineral particles. Chemical changes of many sorts take place. Leaching goes on where the rainfall is sufficient to give a downward movement of the water. Capillary water brings materials from the lower to the upper horizons. Microscopic and ultramicroscopic organisms come to make the evolving soil their home and become an integral part of it. They multiply rapidly under certain conditions and are destroyed under adverse ones. A cubic inch of soil may contain many tens of millions. Beside these microscopic forms of life there are many sorts of beetles and worms. The earthworm contributes much to the soil-making process. It opens up channels in the ground from a few inches to five feet long, and Darwin found that its excreta—castings—annually formed a layer a fifth of an inch thick. In the course of thirty years, he discovered, earthworms has converted a stony field in England into a meadow. The remains of all forms of ground burrowers produce organic matter and gases in the soil. The plant cover makes its contribution. The roots shift soluble minerals from the soil to the leaves and stems which later are added to the topsoil. Some roots harbor nitrogen-making bacteria. Thus the solum is a busy place, a workshop, in which are produced, directly or indirectly, the essentials for all land life, the soil. The raw material is the parent soil material. The processes that the raw material undergoes depend upon the temperature, rainfall, topography, and many other conditions. It takes hundreds of years, no doubt, to make a mature or completely developed soil. The best topographic environment is gently sloping land with the soil porous enough to permit freedom of movement of air and moisture. Poorly drained lands, lands subject to sheet wash and gullying or too frequent deposition as in river valleys, do not develop a mature soil.

Formerly soil science classified soils on the bases of the parent soil

---

* Data on fish checked with David Starr Jordan and Bartin R. Everman, *American Food and Game Fishes.*

material and the bedrock from which it was derived. Thus they
recognized limestone soils, sandy soils, clay soils, silty soils, loams, etc.
Although it is now recognized that the parent soil material is not the
sole criterion for classifying mature or fully developed soils, it is
conceded that the physical and chemical composition determine the
workability, porosity, rate of movement of air and water, and the
availability of the essential mineral plant foods. Until the soil has
reached maturity in its evolution the parent soil material serves to
some degree to give it its character. Theoretically all mature soils, no
matter what their parent rocks were, have similar characteristics in a
given region.

The parent soil material of the Coastal Plain is marine sand and
silt. The soils of the Middle Coastal Plain on flat lands have probably
reached maturity; those of the wet outer border are considered immature; in the hilly inner border region erosion has greatly if not completely destroyed the A horizon, the topsoil. The Coastal Plain in
general is easily worked, drains readily, leaches rapidly, warms up
rapidly, aerates well, yet has very little soluble mineral matter for
the plants. Heavy and frequent fertilizing is necessary to secure
economic returns. Similar conditions prevail on the top of the Cumberland Plateau.

The Piedmont parent soil material is heavy, being composed largely
of clay derived from the chemical weathering of the feldspar of granite
and meta-igneous rocks. Much of the quartz and mica of the granites
has been carried away to the ocean to make up the Coastal Plain.
Piedmont soils even though the parent material has undergone much
change in their evolution are stiff and hard to work, aerate poorly, and
are "cold." Leaching is less active than on the Coastal Plain.

The parent soil material of much of the Great Valley, the valleys
of the Plateaus and the Ozarks, the Highland Rim, and the Nashville
and Blue Grass basins is derived from limestone, and the developed
soils of these regions are among the most productive of the South. They
are not all of equal fertility, for the limestones from which the parent
soil material was derived varied greatly in purity. The drainage, erosion, and plant cover during the period of their development have
been unlike in the various physiographic regions.

Figure 27 is a map of the soils regions of the South, after the most
recent maps prepared by the Bureau of Chemistry and Soils. To the
late C. F. Marbut should be given the credit for the development
of this new conception of soils in the United States. The map as presented is based on the work of Dr. Marbut and associates at Washington. There are many hundreds of soil types (a few shown in Fig. 27

as Hagerstown, Houston, Norfolk, etc.), but these types may be organized into soil groups and subgroups.

There are two major soil groups in the South, the pedalfers and the pedocals. Each of these is divided into subgroups. The pedalfers are leached soils. In the leaching, the carbonates and other soluble minerals are carried from the topsoil (known as the A horizon) down into the subsoil (known as the B horizon) and some on out of the soil into springs and finally rivers. The A horizon comes to have an increased

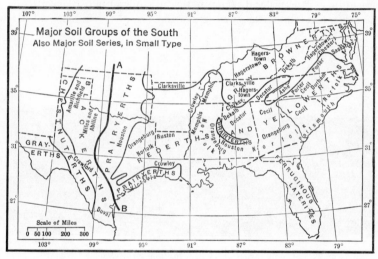

Fig. 27

amount of aluminum and iron compounds, hence the name *ped* (from soil), *al* (aluminum), and *fer* (iron). The pedalfers tend to be acid. The B horizon is more compact than the A horizon. All the pedalfers, except the prairie soils, developed under a forest cover. The annual leaf fall returned to the surface of the soil much humus and mineral matter, and upon the decay of the leaf much of this was carried downward into the soil. This process is still going on where there is a forest cover. But when the land is denuded of the forests, natural fertilizing is stopped and, unless man systematically returns humus and mineral fertilizers in some form to the land, it deteriorates. The heavier the rainfall and the more denuded the land, the more rapid the deterioration.

The pedocals are soils that contain more carbonates than the parent soil beneath. There tends to be developed a calcium carbonate layer a few inches beneath the surface. The depth depends upon the rainfall, the more the rainfall the deeper the layer. These soils have developed under semiarid to arid conditions and hence are little leached. The term pedocal comes from *pedo* (soil) and *cal* (calcium). They are porous soils, and thus absorb moisture and retain it well and tend to be fairly stable in composition under natural conditions. Fertilizers are not needed on these soils though they should be handled so as to retain a fair amount of humus. The greatest obstacle to productive agriculture in the pedocal region is the lack of rainfall. Blackerths or chernozem, chestnuterths, and grayerths are the subgroups of the

A. E. P.

FIG. 28.—Sheep Grazing on Cotton Stubble, near Coleman, Texas.

This is in the dark brown or chestnut pedocal soil region. The topography is favorable for the development of a mature profile in this soil. There is very little soil erosion.

major pedocal group. Their plant cover, where moisture permits, is grass—longleaf, shortleaf, and bunch grass. The color of the soil is readily correlated with type of grass and thus with the amount of rainfall. The Blackerth or Chernozem Region, where the rainfall is 25 to 30 inches, grows tall grass. Under lower moisture conditions the chestnuterths (Fig. 28) to the west grow short grass, and under still lower rainfall a short grass in bunches. Farther west as in western Texas the grayerths, rich in soluble minerals but poor in humus, yield abundantly when irrigated. The natural plant cover, as previously stated, is creosote bush and piñon-cedar.

Three subgroups of pedalfers are recognized in the South, namely, the graybrownerths, the rederths and yellowerths, and the prairyerths.

The graybrownerths dominate in the Upper South. These, as the name indicates, are prevailingly gray-brown in color when dry, brown when moist. In their virgin condition the A horizon of the fully developed soils has a layer of humus derived from forest leaves and other organic matter about 3 inches thick. Beneath this is a pale yellowish or light brown layer. The B horizon is heavier in texture than the A, owing to the presence of colloidal material as well as iron oxide and alumina, and, in some sections, calcium, potash, magnesium, and phosphates. Phosphates and calcium compounds are generally present in the Nashville Basin and the Blue Grass of Kentucky.

Certainly there is no unity in the topography of the Graybrownerth Region, nor is the bedrock the same throughout, though limestone underlies most of the belt. The unifying genetic and evolutionary factors are climate and vegetation. These soils lie in the northern portion of the Hot Summer and Cool Winter temperature belt. The ground is frozen for only a few weeks during a year sufficiently to check the movement of soil moisture. The rainfall is moderate, 45 to 50 inches, and with rather moderate summers the evaporation is far less than in the soil belt to the south. Conditions favor a persistent ground cover and therefore a constant supply of humus. The soils though acid are only mildly so and therefore are suitable for a wide variety of crops—wheat, corn, tobacco, grass, orchards. The limestone areas, especially, in the Shenandoah Valley, the Blue Grass, and the Nashville Basin, when cleared of forests, are well adapted to the growing of blue grass.

The rederths and yellowerths have the greatest areal extent in the South of any of the subregions. (See Figure 29, a profile of a red and yellow soil.) The A horizon of the soils of this region is light yellow or gray (on flat moist lands a light brown), but the B horizon is either red or yellow, depending upon the character of the parent soil material. On the Piedmont red dominates, but yellow on the Costal Plain. In the Appalachian Valley in Alabama and a part of Tennessee red dominates. In hilly regions and on slopes, even moderate slopes, erosion has been so active as to remove much or all of the A horizon. These soils for the most part developed originally in a pine forest. The rainfall is moderate to heavy, 40 to 60 inches, the summer temperature high, the evaporation rate high, and over most of the region the ground is rarely frozen. Because of these conditions the soil in its virgin state is low in organic matter and soluble minerals. These soils are not so productive as the graybrownerths to the north but with care and patience can be built up to be fairly productive. Heavy and frequent applications of fertilizers are necessary to maintain the moderate fertility. The sandy soils of the Costal Plain if well drained warm up rapidly in the spring and are thus well adapted to truck gardening.

The prairyerths, the westernmost of the pedalfers, are the most productive in the South. Figure 78 is an agricultural landscape in the Prairyerth Region. Leaching is slight for two reasons. The rainfall is

A. E. P.

FIG. 29.—Sample of One of the Soils of the Norfolk Series-Middle Coastal Plain, Georgia, near Tifton.

A Horizon.—Light texture sandy loam, light brown in color, about 3 inches; lighter in color beneath. 8-10 inches. B. Horizon.—Yellow to brown yellow. Compact owing to some clay. Yet crumples when either wet or dry. Thickness about 3 feet. C Horizon.—Iron-stained nodules, and coarse gravel and angular stone, probably water laid. But little changed.

low, yet high enough for humid crops, and the lands flat. The natural vegetation is tall grass. It has a deep root system which carries soluble minerals from the calcareous clay of the subsoil to the leaves and stems. These upon dying supply humus, calcium, and other minerals to the topsoil. The calcium in the upper part of the soil tends to prevent the downward movement of the colloidal material of the clay. Thus the A horizon is about as heavy as the B. These soils are dark in color on account of the large quantity of humus. They are lasting soils under natural conditions for they tend ever to renew themselves. Soil students consider the discovery of the Prairyerth Region one of the greatest events in the history of agriculture in America in the last century. The prairyerths are found in many counties in central Texas (the Black Prairie Region) and Oklahoma and cover smaller areas in southeastern Texas, southwestern Louisiana, and parts of Alabama and Mississippi (the Black Belt).

CHAPTER III

MAN'S MODIFICATION OF THE NATURAL ENVIRONMENT

INTRODUCTION

On the mountain is freedom! The breath of decay
Never sullies the fresh flowing air.
Oh, Nature is perfect wherever we stray;
'Tis man that deforms it with care.

SCHILLER

"The despoiler" is the term that has been applied to man in his relations with nature in his attempt to procure a living; and the term is particularly applicable to white man in most parts of America. Much of this seeming despolation, however, was necessary, and not all the changes he has made in his physical environment have been destructive. Civilized man, as distinguished from culturally and economically undeveloped man, is a producer of economic goods, not merely a "plucker" or collector. He must get to the soil wherever it is productive, exploit the mineral resources, and tap the power resources. Three centuries of civilization in the United States of America have transformed a land that was supporting but a million or more Indians, living a "hand-to-mouth" existence, into a civilized country of 130 million people who stand at the top among the national groups of the world in wealth, prosperity, and personal comfort. In the midst of such abundance of nature's resources it is natural to be wasteful. It is only within the last two decades or more (since about 1908) that we have come to a realization of the great need of conservation, to the need of husbanding the resources of which we as settlers and descendants of settlers have come into possession. There is no sin in condoning one's conduct in the utilization that has been made in a realm of plenty, but not to mend one's ways when one's obligations to present and future generations are known is the greatest of sins.

In this section the attempt primarily is to trace man's modification of the natural environment in the South; but also to indicate wherein man has been wasteful and suggest methods for improvement, and also point out the improvements over nature he has made.

64

THE DESTRUCTION OF THE FORESTS

White man found the South for the most part a land of untouched resources. The few hundred thousand Indians had a few small widely scattered clearings here and there in the immense forests that stretched eastward from eastern Texas and Oklahoma to the Atlantic. The corn, pumpkin, and bean patches here and there in the forest were tilled in a superficial way for a few years and then abandoned. Nature soon obliterated the scars with a plant cover, and in a few score years abandoned clearings could not be told from virgin lands. As for the animal life, the Indians, until the coming of the fur trader, hunted largely to secure food and hides and fur for clothing.* Being few in number these primitive men made only slight inroads on the game. Thus during the few thousand years that the Indians held dominion over the land no appreciable change had taken place in either plant or animal life.

When white man came to what we call the South and entered upon the task of clearing the forest for his agricultural activities, he began the destruction of life forms that in their racial development were hoary with geologic age. He disturbed an order of development, which if it were to start all over again, as it must on badly eroded lands, and continue on to the climax stage, would take a period several times as long as our written history.

Land had to be cleared for agricultural production, forests had to be cut to provide for the multitude of demands for timber and wood; but often man destroyed when there was little call. And, what is more, he has neglected to reforest lands that are not at all suited for agriculture, under present standards of cultivation. It will be many decades, possibly a century, if our population should continue to increase, before we will need to bring into agricultural production such lands as those in many parts of the Baltic plain that the Germans are now cultivating. If legislators knew what ecologists know about plant succession and the evil effect of the total destruction of forest tracts, which is generally followed by excessive soil erosion, laws would be enacted to regulate the cutting of trees in a private forest as cutting is now regulated on our great national forests.†

MODIFICATION OF THE FAUNA

Along with the destruction of the forests and the dominance of civilization there has been a tremendous loss of animal life. Not every forest tree had a bird's nest, housed a squirrel, opossum, or coon, or

* Some Indians used hides for shelter.
† For extent of removal of the forests see Chapter XIV.

protected a deer, bear, or fox. No records of a scientific census of animals are available. We have no data, therefore, on which to base conclusions. The fur-bearing animals had not been greatly reduced in numbers by the Indian hunters, until the coming of white fur traders. Before the white fur traders entered into the life of the Indians, animals were killed to supply clothing and food for the scanty population that occupied the forests. The fur trader led the Indians away from the tillage of their patches of corn, beans, and pumpkins and their desultory hunting excursions into the life of hunters for furs. Very often the flesh of animals killed for furs was not used for food.

Then came the white farmer. At first he cleared only small pieces of forests here and there for patches of corn. This disturbed the animal life but little. But as each white man's clearing expanded and continued to expand most forms of wild life retreated to the untouched forests. We still find in the primeval forests of the Southern Appalachians a few representatives of the original fauna; and the original fauna may be found in the larger forests and less-frequented marshes of the outer Coastal Plain quite undisturbed, except the larger animals. Florida, with only about 14.3 per cent of its area in farms, and Louisiana, with only 32.2 per cent, must have much of its original wild life; but in all the other states where farms take up from 48 per cent of the total area (as in Arkansas) to about 77.5 per cent* (as in Kentucky) much of the wild life is gone, particularly since much of the area not in farms is cut-over land. Taking the South as a whole, the black bear, the Virginia deer, the bobcat, the red fox, gray fox, otter, and wolf, as we have seen, have disappeared from most parts. The bison and beaver have long since become extinct.

Bird life suffered least by white man's invasion. Few bird censuses have been made even in our day and none in the past. At most the number of birds to the square mile can be mere guesses for most of the country. We do not know whether bird life is increasing or declining in numbers in the South. Some species we know are fewer in number than formerly, and a few species, like the wild pigeon, are to most people in the South matters of history. The establishment of bird and wild animal reservations, like those of Southern Louisiana, the bird sanctuary at Lake Wales, Florida, by Edward Bok, and the few national parks and forests in the South, is to be commended. The value of such reservations cannot be measured in terms of dollars. They stimulate an interest in nature which leads to one of the most intellectual, profitable, interesting, and healthful forms of recreation.

---

* *Statistical Abstract*, 1934, 543.

In the modification man makes in the biota of a region, he shows, as he can in no other way, his dominance in the world of living things. He bows to the great forces of the physical world—earthquakes, tidal waves, tropical hurricanes, tornadoes, and other adverse climatic conditions as cold waves and hot waves—but he feels himself master in the animate world when he enters a new region for the purpose of making it his home. He destroys what he wishes and protects those life elements of his environment that will contribute to his economic well-being and happiness. Against the unwelcome he wages an unremitting war, the warfare becoming more intensive as human population increases and the demand for sustenance becomes an ever-increasing problem.

MAN'S GREATEST ENEMIES

Against insects, bacteria, and other blights, man has had to wage unrelenting warfare. Indeed some entomologists assert that the present age is not a human, a psychic age, the Age of Man, but an insect age. Just as in the past we have had the age of fishes, the age of reptiles, the age of mammals, we are now in the age of insects. But our superior mental powers have always made us victorious in the struggle with insects, although at times they have held almost undisputed sway in some parts of our country. The Bureau of Entomology for the fiscal year ending June 30, 1934, spent nearly $6,000,000 (nearly $1,600,000 was classed as "emergency") in its work in the United States,* a large part of which was in the study of insects and the means for their extermination. This is small as compared with the money spent for insecticides and germicides by the public. The destruction to our crops for some single insect pest like the boll weevil or the Mediterranean fruit fly amounts in some years to many tens, even hundreds, of millions of dollars. The best we can do in most of our warfare with those enemies is to reduce their ravages to the minimum. Few of them have been entirely destroyed. By destroying the original native vegetation and introducing old-world economic plants we have prepared a way for the introduction of many sorts of troublesome foreign pests. Indeed, not all the insects that now tax our energies and pocketbooks are indigenous to our environment.

Space will permit only a brief discussion of a few of the pests known in the South.

The boll weevil is a Mexican pest that first entered southern Texas in 1892. By 1922 it had spread over the entire Cotton Belt. In 1921

* *Statistical Abstract*, 1935, 170.

it was estimated that this one pest reduced the prospective total yield of cotton for the United States 31 to 34 per cent. The loss for Georgia was estimated at 45 per cent, and that for Oklahoma at 41 per cent.* The boll weevil, however, has little affected the total crop of cotton. Since it is known that the yield per acre will be less, to maintain the normal cotton crop, the acreage must necessarily be increased and the cost of production is increased.

The cattle tick which carries the germ of the Texas cattle fever has been known in North America since Colonial days, probably having been introduced along with Spanish cattle into Mexico, Texas, and Florida. It was first discovered as a *possible* cause of cattle fever near the close of the eighteenth century by a Mr. Pease of Pennsylvania. Cattle from North Carolina, it was believed, carried it into Pennsylvania. Frequently, when Southern cattle were driven through regions otherwise free from the tick, many of the cattle near the roads of the section crossed contracted fevers. That the fever was due to a protozoan carried by the tick was proved by Theobald Smith in 1889. It is only in recent decades that a thorough study of the disease has been made and a method for the eradication of the tick devised, namely, dipping the animals in a vat of insecticide. In 1906 there were 985 quarantined counties in the South in the infested area. By 1934 the number that had been released was 914.†

A careful estimate made in 1906 placed the annual loss to Southern farmers at $40,000,000, and to this should be added $30,000,000 more (an estimate) of "lowered assets of the South." Where the tick has been eliminated a surprising improvement and development in the cattle industry have usually resulted. Packing plants have been introduced in many sections, so also have creameries, condenseries, and ice-cream plants.‡

The Mediterranean fruit fly has been the South's most recent insect scare. Early in 1929 this pest was found well established in central Florida in the citrus-fruit sections. The center was near Orlando. Upon a careful survey it was found to be in 980 localities scattered over 20 counties, or about 8,000,000 acres in all. This area produced 67 per cent of the citrus fruit of Florida in 1928, and 76 per cent of the three years' average. Utter ruin to the citrus-fruit industry of Florida was the prospect unless the fly could be exterminated. The impending loss to the state and the nation may be judged from the fact that the

---

* *Yearbook of Agriculture,* 1922, 714.

† *Yearbook of Agriculture,* 1935, 566.

‡ *Farmers' Bulletin* 1625, 1930.

annual yield was from 10,000,000 to 19,000,000 boxes of oranges a year worth $2.00 to $3.00 a box; and 10,000,000 to 16,000,000 boxes of grapefruit at a normal price of $3.00 to $6.00 a box.*

Both state and nation began the work of eradication. Many millions of dollars were appropriated. The active measures used won the day for man. This is the first instance in America of an insect pest being entirely destroyed over a large area within a few months.†

Owing to the hot moist weather that prevails over a large area, the South is open to ravages by subtropical, tropical, and warm-weather diseases such as yellow fever, cholera, and malaria. But this susceptibility of the region to such ravages has stimulated Southern medical

NORTH CAROLINA
GIVING LOCATIONS OF DEATHS BY MALARIA

DEATHS BY COUNTIES
1921-1927

Trend by Years

Years	1921	1922	1923	1924	1925	1926	1927
Deaths	172	177	151	123	123	85	55

Courtesy Southern Medical Journal (Vol. XXII, April 1929).

FIG. 30.—Distribution of Deaths by Malaria.

There is much marsh land bordering the sounds in eastern counties. The cool well-drained mountain area has no deaths from malaria and the Piedmont also has a low death rate because no marshes are present.

men and sanitary engineers to energetic efforts. Only one disease, malaria, will be discussed here.

Malaria, known to our early settlers as ague, is the most persistent and widespread of the warm-weather and warm-climate diseases. It is more prevalent in the marshy sections, and since marshes are widespread and cover large sections of the South, the malaria districts total an immense area. The map of North Carolina (Fig. 30) shows conclusively the relation of the relative prevalence of malaria cases to surface features. In all swampy districts malaria constitutes a serious problem. But every Southern state has taken active measures against this disease, and in spite of the poverty and ignorance with which health authorities have had to contend—malaria, ignorance,

* Data for production and price from *Yearbook of Agriculture,* 1935, 480.

† Report of Secretary of Agriculture in the *Yearbook of Agriculture,* 1930, 50-52.

and poverty are concomitant phenomena—surprising results have been attained. The International Health Board of the Rockefeller Foundation has offered financial aid to many states. The success attained during a ten-year campaign in western Tennessee, in the improvement of health impaired by malaria, has been phenomenal.

SOIL EROSION

Studies conducted throughout some twenty years have shown that the Savannah River, which drains the adjacent parts of Georgia and South Carolina, is carrying 135 carloads (50 tons each) of soil (mantle rock) daily to the Atlantic Ocean—more than 2,500,000 tons of suspended material annually. Similar investigations of the Mississippi give the stupendous figure of 340,500,000 tons of suspended rock material being deposited in the Gulf each year. In terms of train loads (of 40 cars, each carrying 50 tons), 466 trains would need leave the mouth of the Mississippi daily to return this immense amount of rock debris to its original home. According to a report of the United States Bureau of Chemistry and Soils several years ago, Fairfield County, South Carolina, in the Piedmont, had lost 90,000 acres of productive land by gullying. In Stewart County, Georgia, the inner part of the Coastal Plain, 70,000 acres have been made practically useless for agriculture by excessive erosion.* In western Tennessee 300,000 acres are reported as having been destroyed (Fig. 31). These instances are typical of a process that is going on over a large part of the South.

Erosion, even the sheet wash that is scarcely noticeable, is responsible for much soil depletion, unprofitable farming, tax delinquency, and farm abandonment. The total loss for the country at large, it is estimated by competent Federal Government experts, amounts to $400,000,000 a year. Fully 100,000 acres of productive land are destroyed each year, and in addition a much larger area is being hopelessly impaired. About 50,000,000 acres have been essentially destroyed in the United States, an area equivalent to nearly 625,000 farms of 80 acres each; another 50,000,000 acres are in almost as bad condition.† The total loss already is at least $10,000,000,000. More than a third of this—the area of the South is about one-third of the total of the country—should be assigned to the South, for nowhere else in United

---

* Quoted by H. H. Bennett, *Geographical Review*, XVIII, 1928, 590-605.

† H. H. Bennett, "Combating the Menace of Soil Erosion," *Literary Digest*, April 14, 1934, 15; L. C. Gray and O. E. Baker, *Land Utilization and the Farm Problem*, November, 1930, U. S. Department of Agriculture, Pub. 97; A. E. Parkins and J. R. Whitaker, Editors, *Our Natural Resources and Their Conservation*, Ch. IV (by Bennett), 75.

States are the conditions quite so favorable for loss by soil erosion. Man, if he intends to build a permanent civilization in the South, must awaken to a realization of the ultimate effects of the slow but relentless destruction of his most valuable of all resources. The vast stores of iron ore, coal, oil, gas, sulphur, and salt, and the power of the thousand streams that roll onward down the slopes to the ocean, can amount to little if the productive power of the soil is impaired. *Soil is a resource that belongs to the public, present and future. Permitting its destruction should be considered a crime!*

Surface water erosion there has always been, since the earth had an atmosphere and rains fell. During the geologic ages many tower-

A. E. P.

FIG. 31.—A Great Gully in the Red Hill Section of Western Tennessee.
Erosion is very active in the hilly area to the west of the Tennessee River.

ing mountain ranges in the South have been (some more than once) reduced to low plains. Running water was the chief transporting agency. Soil erosion is a normal natural phenomenon. But man, the despoiler—the term as applied to man in relation to soil has its greatest significance—by the removal of the plant cover has permitted the destructive erosive forces to work as they have never worked before. It is probably, if not certainly, no exaggeration to declare that in the South in the course of one or two centuries the land surface has been reduced more rapidly as a result of soil erosion than in 20, yes perhaps 200, centuries before man came and removed the forest cover, opened furrows and ditches, and left the land "naked" for most of the year. Not only has man permitted this destruction, but he has aided and abetted "innocent nature."

How long does it take nature to make soil? Measured in years no one can tell. We are certain it requires many thousands of years for the change from solid rock to mother (or parent) soil material.

To make soil from solid rock there must be a disintegrating of the rock by mechanical and/or chemical processes, into fine rock debris, as gravel, sand, silt, and clay. Chemical processes produce both rock debris and soluble minerals. While these processes are going on, under suitable topographic conditions such as on hills, the transporting agencies, chiefly running water in the South, are carrying away some of the material toward the sea, to be deposited in alluvial fans, bars, flood plains, natural levees, and deltas. Thus, over a weathering rock mass, mantle rock accumulates but slowly. As the rock debris accumulates and buries the parent ledge the rate of weathering is greatly reduced. This is the process by which mantle rock is being produced on the uplands of all the topographic provinces of the South that have cores of bedrock.

Rock debris or mantle rock is not soil as previously described (Chapter II). Few plants there are that will grow in crushed rock even though rich in soluble mineral matter. The productive soils of today have required a long time to reach the climax stages of their development. Thus when we permit the erosive forces to attack our soils, unchecked, we destroy a priceless resource that has taken the forces of nature ages and ages to produce.

There are two phases of soil erosion: surface or sheet wash and gullying. There is hardly an area in the South, outside the flat lands near the coast and in the river flood plains, that is not suffering from excessive loss of topsoil, and many parts have had hitherto productive lands rendered worthless by gullying. Gullying is most active in the loessal districts of Kentucky, Tennessee, and Mississippi, on many of the slopes of the plateaus, the Great Valley, and the Piedmont, and in the inner hilly sections of the Coastal Plain. In Georgia the writer has seen scores of gullies in the Coastal Plain 50 or more feet deep that are the product of 50 years or less of unchecked erosion.

Sir Charles Lyell, the great British geologist, in his *A Second Visit to the United States*, gives a graphic description of a large gully near Milledgeville, Georgia, which he visited in January, 1846. "The surprising depth of some of the modern ravines," he writes, "in the neighborhood of Milledgeville, suggests matters of curious speculation. At a distance of three and a half miles west of the town, on the direct road to Macon, on the farm of Pomona, is the ravine represented in the annexed wood cut. (See Fig. 32.) Twenty years ago it had no existence; in the course of twenty years, a chasm, measuring no less than 55 feet deep and 300 yards in length, and varying in width from 20 to 180 feet was the result. The high road has been several times turned to avoid the cavity, the enlargement of which is still proceeding, and the old line of the road may be seen [in 1846] to have held its course directly over what is now the widest part of the ravine. . . ." *

Over the South there are hundreds of ravines of dimensions as great as these cited by Lyell, and gullies of lesser dimensions destined to be as great as the Milledgeville ravine are numbered by the thousands.

From Sir Charles Lyell, loc. cit., Vol. II, 29 and 49.

FIG. 32.—Gully near Milledgeville, Georgia, 1846.

In lands deeply gullied nothing can be done toward reclamation, for reclamation should have been undertaken when the small rivulet first creased the slope. With gullies 20 to 60 feet deep one can but wait until the intermittent streams that flow through them complete their work of land reduction. It may take fifty years to make a gully. Several hundred will be required to bring to grade the land in the vicinity of the original gully. It will take a vastly longer time, a matter of many, many scores of generations of human beings, for the soil to attain the productiveness that the former upland soil possessed when covered with the primeval forests—and tens of thousands if the soil is removed to the bedrock.

Soil erosion—wash and gullying—is active in the South because
1. During only a few weeks each year, even in the Upper South,

* Sir Charles Lyell, *A Second Visit to the United States,* II, 29-30.

is the ground frozen. In middle Tennessee it is a rare winter that the ground is frozen for more than a week or so at a time. Southward the winters are even more open. Erosion, therefore, goes on almost unimpeded twelve months in a year. In the Lake States, by contrast, the ground remains frozen most winters to depths of two or three feet from November to early, even late, March.

2. The staple crops, as cotton and corn, leave the surface of the soil uncovered during the off season, unless the farmer grows winter oats, rye, or wheat, and even these leave much opportunity for erosion. More grass is needed in the rotation schemes in the South. At present the millions of acres of weeds, though a despoiler of the appearance of the cultural landscape, serve to check erosion and therefore are not an unmitigated evil.

3. Most of the land is in slope, that is, it has a mature topography and much of the topsoil is of a sort that washes and gullies readily— a light porous upper soil on a denser subsoil.

4. Lastly, because of the cheapness of the land and the prevalence of tenancy (on a large number of the farms it is shiftlessness and ignorance), little is done to prevent surface wash and check gullying in its incipient stages.

But little labor is required to check soil erosion if preventive measures are started early. The writer interviewed one farmer in the Piedmont of Virginia who prevents the formation of "poverty spots"— surface wash—by covering the slope that has the first appearance of soil wash with cured hay or straw to the depth of one or two feet, and turning out his cattle and horses to feed on the scattered hay and straw. These preventive measures are generally undertaken in the winter. Hay is used on the pastures, straw on other lands. The livestock scatter the seed and tramp much of the uneaten hay and the straw into the ground. Furrows in areas subject to wash or gullying should always be thrown up along the contours of the slope (Figs. 33 and 78). Rivulets frequently start in harrow depressions or streaks if the harrow is run up and down or oblique to the slope. Care should be taken to scatter the water, to prevent its collecting. Deep plowing, leaving the upturned or overturned sod or soil in the plowed or harrowed rows until it is necessary to prepare the land for crops, is advisable. On some slopes it is advisable to throw up terraces with the plow. The terraces may be tilled (the mangum terrace) or planted to grass in strips three to four feet wide. The writer has seen many thousands of acres thus protected in central Georgia and parts of Alabama. If gullies have been started, further erosion may be checked by dumping straw, brush, or stones in the gullies at frequent intervals and at numerous places. Lastly, all lands that are likely to get beyond the control of man should be kept as forests, or if deforested should be reforested before washing or erosion starts actively.

Another point of attack is on the soil itself and is directly associated with the maintenance of soil fertility—that is by maintaining (or increasing) the humus content of the soil. When forests are cut down the wood's earth—the humus—is soon removed in most parts of the South. Much of it dries up and is blown away. One might say that the hot sun "burns" it out. Surface erosion, of course, also

A. E. P.

Fig. 33.—Contour Plowing, near Forsyth, Georgia.

In many counties in Georgia soil erosion is reduced to a minimum by contour plowing. This photograph was obtained just after the plowman had completed his work. Where the slope is steeper terracing is usually necessary.

removes it. Humus in the soil tends to make it porous so that more water is absorbed and retained and thus there is less leaching. Soil solutions are more readily formed. Less water runs off the surface. There should be a constant return of humus-making material to the soil. Since the South is not a natural perennial grass region, and little barnyard manure is available (except in dairy regions and dairying is not active) for most of the cattle range during a large part of the year, the source of the humus must, therefore, be green cover crops. Even though winter cover crops do not, for the present, pay, as some agriculturists claim, such crops certainly will pay in the course of years.

Soil wash and gullying *can be prevented.* Such waste of land is practically unheard-of in Europe. For forty centuries lands have been cultivated in China and Japan and are better today than 4,000 years ago, partly because soil erosion is not permitted. If the South is more susceptible to such processes of land deterioration, *and it is*, the farmers of the South should adjust themselves more than they have hitherto done to the adverse natural conditions and redouble their effort to prevent such losses. Many thousands of acres of slopes now tilled should be reforested. The prevention of soil wash and gullying is an economic burden; but unless the problem is faced squarely, nature in the end will dominate and man will lose out.

Every bit of rock or soil on the surface of the earth above the base level of the streams that flow into the oceans is destined in time* to find a resting place, unless earth movements interfere, in the oceans. This has been the regime of the surface of the land since the earth came to have an atmosphere and a hydrosphere and streams have wended their tortuous courses to the seas. The best that man can do is to utilize the mantle rock as it is delayed here and there on flat lands and the gentler slopes in its journey to its inevitable destination. On steeper slopes subject to erosion he must, with all the ingenuity at his command, throw up barriers to its movement. On many of these, i.e., on lands that are likely to be harmed within a few years by soil wash or gullying, he would better call nature's forests to his aid.

Soil wash and gullying affect man in many ways other than through the harm done to agriculture. Much of the material eroded from farms in surface wash and gullying goes directly into the streams, and tends to fill up the channels or to be deposited in excessive quantities on the fertile flood plains. The streams become muddy, thus destroying certain forms of fresh-water life accustomed only to clear water. Mud and silt in the streams render the water unsuited for domestic use unless expensive settling basins are provided. Industries using large quantities of clear water are not attracted to sites on such rivers, or are put to a great expense to provide evaporators or settling basins. Abundant supplies of clear water are often decisive factors in establishing such industries as pulp and paper making and the dyeing and bleaching of cloth.

The sediment carried in suspension or rolled along the bottom tends to fill the basins above dams constructed for power and navigation, and the sand and silt bars in the channels of the streams greatly reduce the value of the streams for navigation. On some streams slackwater dams and winged dams have to be built, and an increas-

---

* Geologic time is here considered.

ing amount of dredging is necessary to maintain an unobstructed navigable channel.

In the previous sections of this chapter, dealing with man's modification of the natural environment, forest removal and its effects on the biota and on the soils have been considered. It reveals man as a despoiler. In the following section we are to look upon man, in a happier mood, as a rectifier of nature's shortcomings.

THE DRAINAGE OF WET AND OVERFLOW LANDS

The total area of wet and overflow lands in the South is about 65,000,000 acres (Fig. 34). The area of wet lands varies from season to season and from year to year. About 50,000,000 acres of this is potential crop land,* but not necessarily economically possible of reclamation at present.

The Atlantic and Gulf Coastal Plain and the Alluvial Valley of the Mississippi (see Fig. 35) have almost the entire acreage of wet lands in the South. In the South Atlantic and Gulf States all estuaries, bays, and sounds, and most of the alluvial lands of the rivers below the Fall Line, are bordered by salt-water and fresh-water marshes. The strips of marshes along the rivers are five to ten or more miles in width. Some of the streams draining the flat alluvial lands bear the title swamps, not rivers. The South Carolina synclinorium has marshes even beyond the inner edge of the Coastal Plain. The many pocosins on the uplands between the Coastal Plain rivers also need drainage. So also do the Flatwood sections of the South Atlantic and East Gulf states. The more elevated portions of Georgia and Florida, the anticlinorium sections of these states, have better natural drainage than most parts of the Coastal Plain. Georgia has the Okefenokee Swamp, similar to the Dismal Swamp of Virginia and North Carolina, and most of the southern third of Florida must be drained to fit the land for truck gardens. Smaller swamps in partially filled sinkholes are to be found widely scattered over most of Florida. They are least numerous near the northern border of the state. Alabama has a large area of wet lands, mainly along its rivers in the Coastal Plain. One of the largest wet areas in the South is the Mississippi Alluvial Valley from Cairo to the Gulf. (See Figure 35.)

---

* *Technical Bulletin,* October, 1930, U.S.D.A., 194. Some data are presented in the *Yearbook of Agriculture,* 1921. The report on drainage in the Fifteenth Census gives data on areas of enterprises not on land needing drainage to fit them for cultivation. The first drainage census was in 1920. "Drainage of Agricultural Lands," *Fifteenth Census,* 1930, various pages.

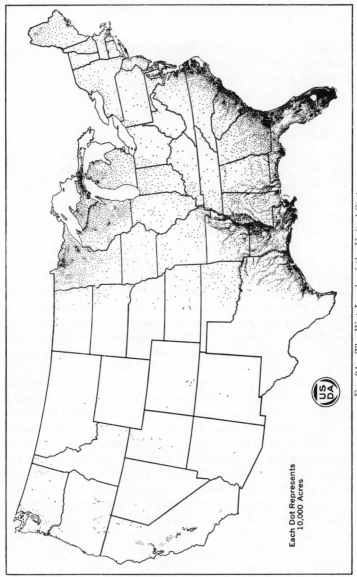

Fig. 34.—The Wet Lands of the United States.
The map shows that the South has the bulk of the wet lands of our country.

Almost the entire areas of the St. Francis Basin, the Yazoo delta, the Tensas and Atchafalaya basins, all highly productive sections of the Southern States, will need millions of dollars spent on levees, drainage ditches, and pumping plants to fit them for agriculture.

Of the total area of wet land in "operating enterprises" (large areas only considered) in the United States in 1930 only 27 per cent was in the South. The North had 68 per cent of the reclaimed wet land and the West only 5.6 per cent.*

The legal machinery for wet-land reclamation has already been provided in all the Southern States, but the demand at present for agricultural land is not sufficient to induce the owners of wet lands to attempt further reclamation. North Carolina, as far back as 1795, passed a law which enabled a farmer who wished to drain his land to "secure easement to construct and maintain a private drain across his neighbor's land" by payment of damages. Florida passed a similar law in 1834, Tennessee in 1846, and Virginia in 1848.

It is probable that an acre of reclaimed wet land, if devoted to intensive cultivation, is capable of supporting a person. This means that the South by the reclamation of the total area of its potential agricultural wet lands will provide sustenance for 50,000,000 or more people in addition to the number that may be supported on naturally well-drained lands. If we assume, because of the high standards of living in America, that it will require two acres to a person, 25,000,-000 people may be supported on the South's reclaimed lands. These figures may seem chimerical, yet it means only 320 people to the square mile. Belgium has an average population density of 670 to the square mile; many parts of the Po Valley have a density of 600; in the lower Nile Valley there are about 14,000,000 people on less than 12,000 square miles, including the area of the canals, marshes, lakes, roads, and date plantations; and Java in the Dutch East Indies, with large areas of mountain and forest land, has an average density of 717 to the square mile.†

MODIFICATION OF STREAMS AND HARBORS

Few harbors and rivers in their natural condition satisfy the requirements for rapid, safe, and cheap transportation. The policy of putting river and harbor improvement under Federal control and paying for the same out of Federal moneys had its inception in 1824. Work to the end of making the harbors accessible to the ever-increas-

---

* *Ibid.*

† *Statistical Abstract,* 1930, 193, 504-505, 508-512, 550-552, 556-560; *Statesman's Yearbook,* 1935, 695, 834, 1039, 1146.

ing size of ocean carriers and of giving all-year transportation (excluding closures by ice) on the larger rivers has been carried on continuously ever since, although not continuously on any one harbor or stream. During the fiscal year closing June, 1934, work was being done on some 200 harbors, about 290 rivers, and 47 canals and other waterways in the United States—969 projects in all, exclusive of flood control. The total amount expended on improvement and maintenance for the fiscal year 1934 was nearly $99,000,000. This did not include the expenditures on flood-control work which amounted to more than $48,000,000. The estimated amount needed to complete the river and harbor projects adopted by Congress was $383,600,000. Up to the close of the fiscal year June 30, 1934, there had been expended on our waterways, coastal and inland, for navigation and flood control about $2,128,000,000, of which about $566,000,000 was for maintenance.*

This is the price man pays to improve nature's waterways in the United States to hold them in bound and fit them for use.

It is a common opinion of American economic geographers, economists, and conservationists that an appreciable fraction of these huge sums of money spent on our waterways is unwisely spent. Each river and harbor appropriation is a "pork barrel" out of which many senators and representatives extract money on the plea of rendering more serviceable the water-transportation facilities of their respective districts, but in reality indirectly to buy votes. These sums therefore do not measure man's need of modifying the rivers and harbors of our country to meet modern transportation demands. Some improvements are economically possible, others not. The sums spent for river-and-harbor-improvements a half century or more ago were small indeed in comparison with those of recent years. The South has not always had the proportion of the total that it now has, particularly during the Civil War and the Period of Reconstruction. The rapid industrial development of the last few decades, the development of more active traffic routes to Latin America, the opening of the Panama Canal, the allocation of government-owned boats to Southern ports after the World War, and the increase of export crops (particularly cotton), export minerals, such as phosphate, oil, and sulphur as well as export lumber, and many other commercial commodities that seek markets or factories in the Northeastern States or across the seas, have called for harbor improvements. The long coastline, the wide distribution of harbors and the shallow

---

* Data from *Report of Chief of Engineers*, U. S. Army, 1934, Part I, 1, 13.

waters, characteristic of drowned, sandy coasts, have all contributed in making it necessary for man to expend huge sums in modifying his natural environment to satisfy the demands of modern transportation. See Chapter VI for discussion of improvement of waterways.

FLOODS AND FLOOD CONTROL OF THE MISSISSIPPI

Floods are perfectly normal phenomena, for most rivers. Southern rivers certainly are no exception. The Southern river that has received the most attention in this country because of its destructive floods is the Mississippi. Nearly every year it has a period or periods of high water, but it is only occasionally that the height of its flood waters becomes excessive. During such times a large area of the flood plain, with its agricultural lands and buildings, cities, and traffic lines, is covered by water, and the usual trend of business affairs is interrupted. Yet these unusual floods are normal, for small floods and large floods must have been the regular order in the life history of the Mississippi for hundreds of thousands of years. We have physiographic evidences for this.

One of De Soto's men wrote an account of a Mississippi River flood that occurred in 1543. "Then God Our Lord," his report runs, "hindered the work with a mighty flood of the great river, which at that time [about eighth or tenth of March, 1543] began to come down with an enormous increase of water, which in the beginning overflowed the wide level ground between the river and the cliffs. Soon it began to flow over the fields in an immense flood, and as the land was level, without hills, there was nothing to stop the inundation." There are thus early historic records of floods.

Gayarré, a chronicler of early French Louisiana, reported that during the great flood of 1735 New Orleans was inundated and much damage was done. High water lasted from late December until late June.* Other great floods are reported to have occurred in 1776, 1782, 1799, 1809, 1815, 1818, 1823, 1828, and every few years since. The destructiveness of the flood waters is ever increasing, not necessarily because the floods are higher, although they probably are; but because the number of people that take chances in areas subject to inundation is increasing, and more and more property is being accumulated. No statistical data are available for determining whether the floods of late decades are higher than those of the earlier decades of the historic period. It seems very clear, however, that though floods are natural happenings man has in various ways (see later discus-

---

* Charles Gayarré, *History of Louisiana*, I, 469.

sion) in his modification of the natural environment, particularly in
the removal of the forests, added a few inches, if not feet, to the
"peak" height of the flood waters.

Experiments at Spur, Texas, and at an experimental station on the
Piedmont, show that grass cover reduces the run-off materially, as
stated previously in this chapter. Forest cover is equally if not more
effective. We know that dense mesophytic woods, like the broad-
leaved hardwood forests of central United States, are damp and cool,
that many forest springs dry up when forests are removed, and that
small streams from cleared lands do not have the uniformity of flow
that is characteristic of streams from forested tracts. All this would
lead us to believe that forests do regulate stream flow to a material
degree. That the reforestation of the watersheds of the streams would
prevent all floods is not to be thought of, but that such an operation
would somewhat reduce the height of the water in the streams during
flood seasons seems reasonable. Although no comparative data are
available to which one may turn for evidence, it is quite certain that
the floods of the lower Mississippi have been much higher since the
creation of the levees than before, when the flood plains took care of
the heavy overflow.

The levee system of the Mississippi was devised in the beginning to
protect the lowlands from flood; later it was constructed chiefly
to improve navigation of the Mississippi. The first levees, thrown
up in 1717 by Le Blond de la Tour, were to protect New Orleans.
By 1828 the levees were continuous almost to the Red River, 190 miles,
except where bluffs bordered the channel, and for 65 miles below
New Orleans. Congressional action in 1849-1850, which turned over
to the several states unsold swamp lands within their borders to be
sold and the funds devoted to flood protection, was a great stimulus
to levee building. The people of Louisiana about the middle of the last
century, becoming alarmed lest the building of levees along the
Mississippi above the northern boundary should greatly endanger life
and property on the vast area of alluvial lands within the state, com-
plained to the Federal Government through their representatives in
Congress. A careful survey of the whole scheme of flood control and
improvements to navigation along the Mississippi was decided on by
Congress, the work to be done by army engineers. Andrew A. Humphreys was put in charge, and after ten years of field observations he
rendered his report.* This report, published by the War Department

---

* A. A. Humphreys and H. L. Abbot, *The Physics and Hydraulics of the
Mississippi River*.

in 1874, has been the chief guide for much of the work done on the river since. Humphreys and his co-workers contended that the bottom lands about the Red River, before levees were constructed, did not function as reservoirs during high flood stages; that reservoirs in the headwaters of the tributaries would have little effect on restraining floods; that straightening the course of the river by making cutoffs artificially would be dangerous; that there were no suitable sites for distributaries to be developed artificially; and, finally, that a levee system properly constructed would, when completed, protect the alluvial lands adequately, against all floods. And so the work of extending the levee system went on.

The flood of 1874, which resulted in tremendous losses, gave further impetus to levee building. Congress that year provided for a commission to study the problem of reclamation of the whole alluvial valley. Their report accepted the findings of the Humphreys commission and again fixed on levee construction as the only means of flood control. It also recommended supplementary levees where caving and undercutting along the river were imminent. Up to this time, protection to the inhabited alluvial lands had been the primary consideration. However, the navigation interests had long been asking for help. The railroads had by now begun to displace the steamboat to an alarming degree, and shipping interests turned to the Federal Government for assistance.* Congress in 1879 made provisions for the Mississippi River Commission to study navigation and flood-control problems along the Ohio and Mississippi rivers. It, too, decided in favor of the levees.

It seems certain, on *a posteriori* grounds, that the removal of forests (as discussed above), the drainage of swamps, the opening of ditches in tilled lands, the partial filling of the pools of streams by bars, and the deepening of the water at shallows in navigable streams have all increased the run-off and thus also increased the velocity of water in the tributaries of the Mississippi. The tributaries, therefore, pour their waters into the main stream much more rapidly than they did before man came to modify the natural environment. This increased delivery of water would have little effect in increasing the height of the floods in the lower Alluvial Valley of the Mississippi were the waters of the master stream permitted to spread over the alluvial plains and were the waters that reach the extreme lower section of the Alluvial Valley (say below the Red or Baton Rouge)

---

* A. DeW. Frank, *The Development of the Federal Program of Flood Control on the Mississippi River,* 1930, 16.

permitted to enter the many bayous and thus be carried on to the Gulf. The most important of these bayous west of the Mississippi are the bayous Lafourche, Grand, and Atchafalaya. But levees prevent this water from getting to the heads of these bayous and have confined it to a comparatively narrow channel. Along the Mississippi from Cairo southward the distance between the levees (the *batture*) is not more than eight or ten times the width of the normal channel. The water, therefore, that enters the upper end of the Alluvial Valley is constrained to work its meandering way toward the Gulf between walls of dirt, as previously explained, and owing to decreasing slope (concave profile) tends to pile up and become higher and higher the farther downstream it moves. Levees, therefore, tend to increase the height of flood waters.

A river is certainly a marvel of the physical world. Fundamentally it is only a liquid pulled down a slope by gravity. Simple, but yet how difficult thoroughly to understand! One has but to stand on the banks of the mighty Mississippi in flood to appreciate the magnitude of the forces involved as its waters silently move to the sea. How insignificant is man in the face of "ole man ribber." Science has yet to discover many of its mysteries that concern the relationship of load, volume, slope, and velocity. But an attempt is being made. Since about 1930 there has been in operation near Vicksburg, Mississippi, a hydrographic experimental laboratory, called the United States Waterways Experiment Station, manned by a group of highly trained men who are attacking some of the many problems of river improvement and river control. With miniature models, twenty-five, fifty, one hundred, or more, feet long, they are able within a few weeks to determine the effect of engineering works on the channel of a stream that would require years of careful study and observation "in nature." Already the laboratory has saved the taxpayers of our country many millions of dollars by supplying the field men workable data and principles to guide them in their work. This is one phase of the attempt to control the Mississippi.

Apparently the most logical procedure in flood control is to approximate nature's disposal of floods, in so far as possible. Such a generalization requires no great amount of knowledge of the problem, but it is in harmony with what we have learned regarding man's experiences in dealing with nature. It generally takes less energy and time to work with nature than against her. The building of levees and the closing of distributaries are certainly unnatural and dangerous; yet one would not suggest the destruction of these works that have cost the Federal Government, state, levee district, and individuals such huge sums,* for they do handle the average high flood. The levee system is certain to remain as a basic engineering work.

Spillways should be (and are being) provided in the Lower Mississippi to function as distributaries, through which or by which flood waters can reach natural distributaries and be carried away to the Gulf as the water was carried before man interfered, are a second feature worked out for flood control. The Jadwin Plan includes these features. The army engineers have provided two efficient spillways in the lower Mississippi, namely, the Bayou Atchafalaya, leading southward from near the mouth of the Red, and the Bonnet Carré that directs overflow water into Lake Pontchartrain. Lesser spillways are provided below New Orleans. Of lesser importance is the New Madrid floodway, which, however, probably saved Cairo in the flood of 1937. See Fig. 35 for the location of the New Madrid floodway and spillways on the lower Mississippi, shown in black on the map. In portions of the Alluvial Valley the original condition is approached, and yet the work of man is preserved, to some degree at least, by providing a series of overflow basins enclosed by levees. The overflow basins are the cross-lined areas on the map, Fig. 35. There are several of these overflow basins. Such of the basins as are subject to frequent overflow will be devoted to the growing of forests or to such crops as may mature quickly. The building of homes in the basins most subject to overflow should not be permitted. The construction of reservoirs at the headwaters of the tributaries, though of benefit in many floods, cannot be relied upon to function at all times, for often the heavy rains that cause floods do not fall at the headwaters as previously stated.

However efficacious reforestation may be in retarding run-off, it is a matter of three or four decades to get a dense stand of trees and underbrush and humus; yet it should be undertaken. Each farm should be required, *as far as possible,* to handle the rain that falls on it, through dams in drainage ditches and the terracing of slopes.

The Jadwin Plan, with its systems of levees, spillways, and overflow basins just described, presented to the Secretary of War December 1, 1927 (the works called for nearly completed before the winter flood of 1937), may not be the last word in flood control, but it is an improvement over previous plans. The engineers, profiting by the experiences of the 1927 flood, constructed works designed to handle a

---

* Bernard F. Walker, "Curbing the Mississippi," *Scientific American,* CXXXVIII, 1928, 145.

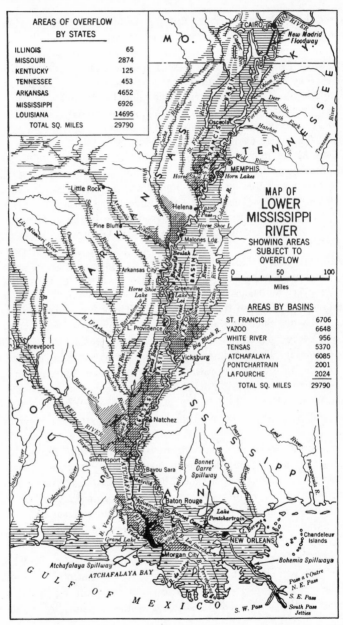

AREAS OF OVERFLOW BY STATES	
ILLINOIS	65
MISSOURI	2874
KENTUCKY	125
TENNESSEE	453
ARKANSAS	4652
MISSISSIPPI	6926
LOUISIANA	14695
TOTAL SQ. MILES	29790

MAP OF
LOWER MISSISSIPPI RIVER
SHOWING AREAS SUBJECT TO OVERFLOW

0   50   100
Miles

AREAS BY BASINS	
ST. FRANCIS	6706
YAZOO	6648
WHITE RIVER	956
TENSAS	5370
ATCHAFALAYA	6085
PONTCHARTRAIN	2001
LAFOURCHE	2024
TOTAL SQ. MILES	29790

Fig. 35

This map shows not only the natural overflow lands before levees were built but also the new Madrid floodway and the spillways in the lower part of the valley. The Ferguson cut-offs are not shown. The crosslined areas are the overflow basins provided in the flood-control plans.

super flood 25 per cent greater than that in 1927. About $325,000,000 was expended.*

A new type of engineering, the making of cut-offs, has been introduced, General Ferguson being the originator. Since a successful try-out at the waterways laboratory at Vicksburg, eleven have been completed (by summer of 1937) between Arkansas City and Natchez (Fig. 36). They have shortened the river by about a hundred miles and thus speeded up the movement toward the Gulf spillways. The

A. E. P.

FIG. 36.—The Giles Cut-off, one of the Ferguson cut-offs, across a westward swinging meander of the Mississippi above Natchez, Mississippi (1937). This is entirely man-made, completed in May, 1933.

1937 flood waters were carried at a gauge much lower than the waters of the 1929 flood, that is, before the cut-offs were made. Much work remains to be done on this river below Natchez.

That the present works will handle *all* future floods no one, of course, can assert, for every now and then nature does the unexpected. The flood of 1937, that brought such appalling disaster to the Ohio Valley, was handled with ease by the Mississippi works after the flood waters had passed the Tiptonville meander some fifty miles downstream from

* The report of the army engineers was submitted to the Secretary of War December 1, 1927, and may be found in full in *House Document* 90, 70th Congress, 1st Session, 1927, 83-85; *Report of the Chief of Engineers*, U. S. Army 1927, 1924; *Report of the Mississippi Valley Committee of the Public Works Commission*, 1934, 209-212.

Cairo. But would the task have been so easy if the "unprecedented" rains had continued to fall instead of ceasing as they did shortly after the crest of the flood had passed Louisville and Paducah?

The Ohio flood of 1937 with its damages mounting to scores of millions of dollars (more than $75,000,000 on the Kentucky side, reported in the press) and its 1,000,000 refugees clearly demonstrated that the skill and experience of the army engineers must now be applied to the control of the angry waters of the Ohio Valley. Flood-control works on the Ohio must be coordinated with the works already constructed on the Mississippi. The Ohio is one of the main if not the main contributor of the water that floods the lower Mississippi. When its discharge at Cairo reaches much above 1,000,000 cubic feet a second, the levee system of the major stream below is taxed to its capacity.

PART II

THE PEOPLING OF THE SOUTH

WHITE MAN TAKES POSSESSION

CHAPTER IV

WHITE MAN TAKES POSSESSION

INTRODUCTION

The little party of Europeans, scarcely more than a hundred men, that landed on the shores of the James River estuary in 1607 was the vanguard of a mighty host, nearly forty million in number, that has crossed the Atlantic to seek homes in America during the three hundred or more years between then and now. This was the mightiest migration to a single country the world has ever seen, or probably ever will see again; but it was no new venture for the human race. Every country today has within its borders racial strains from other lands.

When European met Indian on the shores of the James estuary it was the meeting of brothers whose ancestors parted company hundreds or thousands of generations ago, one group going westward, the other eastward. They had thus encircled the world. The one had tarried long enough in the tight little continent of Europe, where an invigorating and healthful climate and crowding had encouraged the abandonment of the ways of primitive man for those of the civilized; the other through endless wandering over the vast stretches of little-used continents had remained fishers and hunters. Wandering develops a hardy race, but a people needs to be anchored in a rich environment for centuries to make cultural and economic progress.

In the South, civilized man experienced in the ways and the tools of the farmer, the trader, the miner, and the organized conquerer, was matched against the primitive tribesman whose hold upon the land was but superficial and whose tools were of the crudest sort. The outcome was as it always has been and ever will be, the world over.

Although in possession of English America for many hundreds or thousands of years, the Indian had made little or no modification of his environment. He girdled groups of trees here and there and removed underbrush to prepare small patches of ground for his potatoes, corn, beans, and pumpkins. He tilled these forest gardens two or three years and then abandoned them to nature. In a generation or so such "scars" became so reclothed with verdure that all traces of man's having once lived there were wholly obliterated. He removed no forests, he dug no minerals, he drained no swamps, and he deepened no rivers or harbors. The animals that he killed to supply the needed meat and clothing and shelter were few in number. Nature ruled as nearly undisputed during the Indian's period of occupancy as it had for hundreds of millions of years previous to his coming. White man, then, when he came to establish his home found a region of "pristine richness." He came from a continent where civilized man in fairly close settlements (the term settlement as used in this chapter refers merely to groups of people, small and large, and not to organized villages and towns) had held sway for centuries. The vast forests that once covered western Europe had been reduced to mere patches of woods. Most of the agricultural lands in some of the countries of western Europe had passed into the hands of large landowners. There were few or no mineral deposits suitable for small-scale exploitation; others lacked the richness that leads to early exploitation. America with its untouched resources, America where a new civilization might be conceived along new lines and on a new basis, became the haven for the landless, the poor, the aggressive, the progressive, the persecuted. Europeans fairly swarmed to our eastern seaboard, planting settlements here and there, which eventually became dispersal centers, in preparation for the conquest of the American continent.

THE ATLANTIC SETTLEMENTS AND DISPERSAL CENTERS

Jamestown on the James River in Virginia was the first dispersal center to be established in the South in white man's conquest of this vast territory (Figs. 37, 38 and 39). Though the original site was abandoned, the James River area has shown continuous growth from the first and was the major dispersal center on the Atlantic Coast of the South. The long coastline of this portion of the continent and the numerous natural harbors, however, gave abundant opportunity for the establishment of many more bases of operation. In 1634 a settlement was made at the head of navigation, at the Fall Line of the Patapsco River. This later developed into the active city of Baltimore. The Charleston center had its start on the west bank of the Ashley River in 1670, but, finding this shallow and the lands marshy, the settlers moved to the present site in 1680. The Georgia center, the youngest of the group, was established in 1733 when Oglethorpe founded Savannah on the lower Savannah River. This latter was an outpost in English North America established chiefly to serve as a buffer to the Carolina province against the Spanish and French to the South. Cape Fear River was selected for a settlement by land-lookers from New England in 1661 but was soon abandoned. In 1664

FIG. 37.—The Island of Jamestown, as seen from the James River.
Here began Southern civilization.

FIG. 38.—A Corn Field on the Mainland, near Jamestown, Virginia.

Tobacco and corn, both Indian crops, were the money crops and the food crops that sustained the people of Jamestown in their early attempts to establish homes in Virginia and, down to our day, they have been among the more important crops of the Old Dominion State.

a colony of Englishmen came from the Barbadoes, but three years later they in turn abandoned the venture. A settlement called Brunswick was made in 1712, some fifteen miles below the site of Wilmington. This date marks the beginning of permanent occupation of the Cape Fear region; but in 1739 the governmental and commercial center was shifted to Wilmington, which, "by reason of depth of water capable of receiving vessels of considerable burthen, safety of its roads beyond any other part of the river, and the secure and easy access from all parts of the different branches,"* was likely, it was predicted, to develop into a great commercial center.

From these five centers of British civilization on the Atlantic Coast land seekers spread, in the main, westward. The Jamestown settle-

A. E. P.

Fig. 39.—A Tobacco Patch on the Island of Jamestown, Virginia.

This crop is on ground that grew tobacco three centuries ago. The land may have grown several "crops" of trees since then.

ment was the most active in expansion, because it was the oldest and had the closest political, economic, and social contact with the Mother Country. Land was first taken up along the shores of the numerous estuaries of the West Shore of the bay. Later the East Shore was invaded, and by 1700 settlers were spreading out upon the Piedmont to the west of the Fall Line.

During the eighteenth century the population growth was rapid, the number in 1800 being nearly ten times that in 1700. The population was largely rural. A chronicle, written about 1760, records that there were no "towns of any considerable note. This last circumstance," the chronicle comments, "is owing to the vast commodiousness of water carriage, which every where presents itself to the plantations

---

* Quoted from the Act of Incorporation, 1739, in James Sprunt, *Chronicles of the Cape Fear River,* 46.

of private planters, and the scarcity of handicrafts. James Town is now scarcely to be mentioned, and Williamsburg is considered only as being the seat of provincial government and of learning."*

PEOPLING THE PIEDMONT

The Piedmont of Virginia offered no barriers to expansion from the lower Chesapeake population centers, and there were few natural features to give direction to the movement. The James, the York, the Rappahannock, and the Potomac, no doubt, directed the movement of many migrating groups, although the numerous shallows and rapids produced by ledges of resistant rock in the stream bed rendered them unfit for continuous navigation. But these rivers led westward and northwestward. The movement of population was for the most part westward and northwestward, but also southward and southwestward, i.e., as a whole, roughly radial. The movement westward carried people through the numerous passes of the Blue Ridge into the Great Appalachian Valley. The frontier moving northwestward eventually reached the Ohio Country.

In the Albemarle Sound country of North Carolina was planted the first permanent settlement in that colony, the colonists having come from the lower James River center. Later people from the Albemarle country spread westward and southwestward over the Piedmont and there were joined by migrants from Virginia.

The Maryland colony with its nuclear settlement at Baltimore, on the Upper Chesapeake, underwent, in many respects, the same evolution as the lower Chesapeake. The earliest settlements were made largely on or at the edge of the Coastal Plain. The Eastern Shore in Maryland is much larger than in Virginia, hence a larger population could be accommodated. The Western Shore is smaller and the Piedmont nearer the Chesapeake. Expansion of settlements to the Piedmont was relatively earlier than in Virginia.

The Wilmington settlement on Cape Fear River in the Old North State was more closely associated with the Mother Country in its commercial relations than was the Albemarle colony. Lumber, naval stores, and tobacco shipped across the Atlantic brought wealth to the numerous plantation owners along Cape Fear. The fame of the region attracted a goodly number of land seekers. As in Virginia and Maryland the Coastal Plain lands on or near the navigable waterways were the first settled; the overflow took up lands on the Piedmont, and

* From *Universal History*, XLI, 556, quoted in Abiel Holmes, the *Annals of America*, II, 117.

eventually supplied migrants to the westward-moving stream of land seekers.

The Piedmont of South Carolina and Georgia was taken up mostly by people from the northeast, and for several decades the land between the coastal settlements and the Piedmont was a thinly peopled, hilly area (the sand hill and clay hill section), called the "Middle Country,"* ill-suited to the needs of agriculturists.

The supply of settlers for the white occupancy of the Piedmont thus came largely from the older settled sections to the northeast, from the shore of Chesapeake Bay and Albemarle Sound, one, two, or three generations removed from the earliest settlers, and from the Cape Fear settlements. Scotch Irish came southward from Pennsylvania; some Scotch, French, Swiss, Welsh, and Germans migrated directly, from their European homes. With some of these groups there was a tendency toward national and linguistic segregation, a phenomenon characteristic of plains wherever wide dispersal of the migrants is possible. By 1750 most of the Piedmont was occupied by the whites.

TAKING POSSESSION OF THE GREAT VALLEY

The Great Valley was, in striking contrast to the Piedmont, a "mixing bowl," where families from Virginia, Maryland, Pennsylvania, and colonies farther northeast—English, Scotch-Irish, Germans and French; Non-conformists, Anglicans, English Catholics, French Protestants, and Quakers—mingled, forgot fealty to king or prince and state, and became as one under the stress of similar undertakings, similar dangers, and similar successes. There were settlers at the site of Winchester in the lower Shenandoah Valley in 1733. The southwestward-moving frontier reached Staunton shortly after 1740, and a few cabins were constructed on the banks of the Watauga and Holston rivers in northeastern Tennessee by 1769.

The settlements in northeastern Tennessee developed into a minor dispersal center, migrants coming from all the older settlements to the northeast and east. Here many tarried for a time then moved on westward. And here developed the beginnings of a state, the Watauga Association, which later evolved into the short-lived Independent State of Franklin. Both were called into being through the necessity of having some form of government for an aggregate of people that was slowly advancing toward a commonwealth. Most community phenomena have physical environmental bases. The Independent State of Franklin had natural boundaries. To the east and west were topographic boundaries; southward was the boundary of Indian lands. It

---

* This does not mean the middle Coastal Plain belt.

was isolated from the older settlements in the Valley and east of the
Blue Ridge and Southern Appalachians. Population was becoming
dense enough and diverse enough to have many conflicting interests.
As it was far from the seats of government of North Carolina and
Virginia, many fugitives from justice sought here an asylum and a
place in which they could continue the practice of their unsocial professions. Some form of government was necessary to hold them in
check. The pioneers from Virginia did not feel any loyalty to North
Carolina. The control of North Carolina was weak. Debts had been
contracted in Indian Wars, and North Carolina refused to assume
these debts.*

THE FRONTIER OF WHITE OCCUPANCY IN 1790 AND ITS OUTLIERS

By 1790 the vanguard of the migrating population, the frontier (see
Fig. 40), had advanced in Maryland and Virginia to the eastern edge

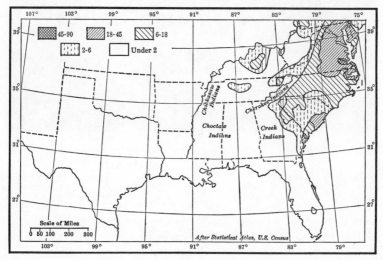

FIG. 40.—The Distribution and Density of Population in 1790. Boundaries as
of 1930.

The land east of the Mississippi and south of 31°N. was Spanish territory: that west of the
Mississippi, French.

of the escarpments of the Appalachian Plateaus; and in the Carolinas,
to the eastern edge of the Southern Appalachians. In Georgia the
whites found their advance bitterly disputed by the strong, half-
civilized Indian tribes, the Cherokees and Creeks, who were finally
suppressed only after a struggle that lasted nearly half a century.

To the west of this frontier line, the map shows, there were three

*J. G. M. Ramsey, *The Annals of Tennessee*, 107, 109.

outliers, one centering about the Forks of the Ohio, a second in northern Kentucky (the Blue Grass Region), and the third in the Middle Basin of Tennessee. These three outliers were in areas possessing abundant attractions for migrating people and natural advantages for the development of prosperous population groups. The Forks of the Ohio region had large areas of deep alluvial lands in the terraces and flood plains of the rivers. The Kentucky and Tennessee centers were in limestone basins with soils rich in phosphate. Though isolated

A. E. P.

FIG. 41.—The Road through Cumberland Gap—the white streak, partly obscured by the vegetation—about 1935.

This gap for several decades was the most-used pass in the South. Through it poured hundreds of thousands of people into Kentucky and Tennessee. It is the most feasible pass across the Cumberland and Allegheny fronts from Will's Gap (Fig. 12) in Maryland to northern Alabama.

from the Atlantic Slope settlements by escarpments, ridges, and gorges of the Southern Appalachian Highlands, they were not cut off from world market contacts. Their commercial channels merely assumed a new, though circuitous, orientation. New Orleans was their ocean port.

Their location opposite, or nearly so, to the most easily traversed passes across the Appalachian Barrier was still another environmental condition that contributed to their growth. Forbes' Road and Braddock's Road converged toward the Upper Ohio; and just beyond Cumberland Gap (Fig. 41), the route from the eastern Tennessee dispersal center forked, one leading northward to the Blue Grass and the other westward to Middle Tennessee. These Transappalachian settlements grew rapidly. In 1780 there were about 45,000 people west of the mountains in American territory. By 1790 more than 74,000 whites had established themselves in Kentucky and 30,000 or more in middle Tennessee. Beyond the boundaries of American territory, however, there were, in 1790, thousands of Europeans, mainly of French and Spanish nationality, who later were absorbed by the westward-moving Anglo Saxon frontier.

ACTIVITY IN THE SPANISH AND FRENCH TERRITORIES

The Spanish settlements in Florida, St. Augustine, and Pensacola, the former 225 years old in 1790, the latter nearly a century, had remained static in population growth, and neither can be considered a center of dispersal. The French were the active colonizers in the middle Gulf-Mississippi Valley area. Their first attempts were the building of forts on Mississippi Sound (1702); but their main effort at establishing European civilization in the South was expended on the Lower Mississippi River, under the leadership of Bienville who founded New Orleans in 1718. New Orleans became the active commercial center of Louisiana and the center of dispersal of the French population along the rivers of the lower Mississippi Basin.

By 1762, at which time by a secret treaty it was ceded to Spain,* the population of greater Louisiana was estimated at 8,000 to 12,000, nearly half of whom were negro slaves. Scattered settlements lay along the lower Missouri and lower Red, but most of the people lived on the Mississippi between New Orleans and Pointe Coupee. A few French herders had homes on the Attakapas and Opelousas prairies of Louisiana (see Fig. 24). Natchitoches, which when built was at the foot of the great Red River raft, was nearly a hundred years old in 1790; Natchez was a town of a hundred homes. The colony was prosperous. Cotton growing was begun in 1740, and the Jesuits introduced sugar cane from Santo Domingo in 1751. Tafia rum and cane syrup were exported. By about 1790, after much experimenting, a method of crystallizing sugar from concentrated cane juice was worked out. The population was greatly augmented about 1766-1768 by the arrival of Acadians from Nova Scotia. Most of them settled in the Attakapas country where their descendants are found today. Indian traders in their canoes or with pack animals traversed most of the territory shown to be vacant on the map; and hundreds of flatboats had been carrying the products of the Ohio, Cumberland,

---

* It was not transferred to Spain, formally, until 1769, owing to a delay due to opposition of the French Louisianians to Spanish rule.

and Tennessee valleys' farms and forests—salt beef and pork, grain, whiskey, medicine, herbs and roots, hides, and furs—for a decade or more. Thus this area west of the frontier line of 1790 and outside the settlements in Kentucky and Tennessee was not an uninhabited, unknown wilderness.*

Active though the French were for more than a half century in the lower Mississippi Basin, these efforts were at an end when in 1762 they delivered to the Spanish, just noted, one of the largest tracts of land ever exchanged on the American continent; but the Spanish were hardly more successful in the Mississippi Basin than in Florida. French and Spanish creoles under American rule, after 1803,† were no more active. For more than forty years the frontier of French settlements (thirty years and more after the Louisiana Purchase) remained practically stationary. New Orleans ceased to be an active dispersal center of population until engulfed by the Anglo-Saxon frontier that moved westward over Georgia, Alabama, and Mississippi.

The active centers of dispersal to the west of the Appalachians between 1790 and 1810 were in Kentucky and Tennessee. From these two centers came the most aggressive of the pioneers in the movement that pushed the frontier to the western boundary of the South.

THE TRANSAPPALACHIAN REGION AND ITS PEOPLE IN 1790

These early Transappalachian pioneers (Fig. 42), the vanguard of the thousands that were to follow, knew little of the vastness of the land and of its potential wealth of grazing lands, forests, farm lands, mineral resources, water power, and the natural opportunities for transportation and trade offered by the 26,000 miles of waterways that lay to the west of them. Even by 1790 four nations had contended for the control of the Mississippi Valley, but mainly for the control of the fur trade and the major waterways that made the fur trade possible. Real possession, development, and exploitation were to await the coming of the young nation from over the mountains on the eastern border of the continent, whose lands stretched from Maine to Georgia, and which in the next sixty years was to push the American political frontier from the escarpments of the Appalachian Plateaus, where it lay in 1790, across the fertile tracts of the Mississippi Basin, across semiarid plains, the Rockies, the arid intermontane plateaus, across the Sierra Nevada-Cascade ramparts, and on to the waters of the

---

* H. E. Bolton, *The Spanish Borderlands*, 235-236; John Pope, *A Tour through the Southern and Western Territories of the United States*, 28-35.

† Louisiana at Napoleon's dictation was transferred from Spanish to French rule in 1800. It became American territory late in 1803—the Louisiana Purchase.

Pacific. Two thousand and more miles the population frontier was to be pushed in one-third the time it required the Virginians and New Englanders to reach the escarpments of the Appalachian Plateaus, one-fourth the distance. But it is of Southerners we are writing, with all due respect and admiration for the enterprise, daring, and energy of the Northerners. On every frontier to the West were to be found "men from Tennessee, and men from Kentucky." It was the New Englander who took the initiative in starting out America's claim to the Oregon Country, but it required the hardy frontiersmen of the

FIG. 42.—A Pageant Commemorating the Arrival of the Founders of Nashville.

The original good ship "Adventure," which carried many of the first settlers, was floated down the Tennessee River from the Watauga settlement in northeastern Tennessee and poled or cordoned up the Ohio and the Cumberland. Many of the actors in the celebration pictured above are descendants of the original settlers. Recently (1930) there has been erected at the top of the bluff a replica of the original palisaded Fort Nashboro.

Mississippi Valley in the 1840's to make good the claim by actual settlement.

THE AMERICAN PIONEER IN GENERAL

The American pioneer was probably a distinct type, a variant. When frontiers were to be manned he withdrew himself (natural selection) from regions grown mature or old, or stagnant in economic development, forsook the easy conditions of well-organized society, and sought young regions that offered richer economic returns for the energy and time expended in the pursuit of a living, a surplus for old age, a dowry for his children, and social and political preferment. New situations in his new environment quickened his wits, exercised his intellectual powers, developed independence of thought and action. The constant meeting with new situations led to versatility and adaptability. He thought in big units, of land, of distances, and of future wealth. "He was the child of progress. He looked forward not backward. His star of empire moved westward and thither he followed it." The adjectives which most truly describe the frontiersmen of the Mississippi Valley in the early part of the nineteenth century, and the farther west even in our day—aggressive, optimistic, assertive, independent, adaptable, realistic, broad-minded, open-minded, trustful, and others—all seem to grow out of the adaptations that the pioneers and frontiersmen had to make to the environment that was peculiarly American. This type of American was the product of both nature and nurture. Variation, natural selection, adaptation in his living to environmental conditions were the biological processes in his development.

The frontiersman, however, had his "seamy" side, and many of his characteristics have come down to our day, so integrated with our social, political, and economic being as to be difficult to eradicate. Much crudeness, ignorance of civilized living, aggressiveness, loudness, conceit, and self-adoration were mingled with the many sturdy characteristics, sketched above, of the manhood and womanhood of that day. These "seamy" characteristics were normal to a wild, crude environment in which the non-essentials of living were sloughed off in the struggle to live. Our lack of respect for authority seems a natural outcome of the freedom and independence of the frontier and of democratic institutions in general. Our adulation for loud-mouthed mediocrity and ignorance, for the practical tinkerer rather than the scientific expert, for him who has arisen from the ranks rather than for the well-born; the deprecation of what the majority of our citizens consider good art, good music, good literature; the crudeness of architecture of many of our homes, churches, public buildings, factories, and even schools, and the unkept condition of many of our villages and most parts of our larger towns and cities may all be traced back to frontier conditions. In a realm of plenty the problem of making a living does not require the prolonged effort it does in a land of meager resources or dense population. The fruits of labor come easy. Skill, training, and long service are not required to procure them. "Good enough" is a cardinal conception of our philosophy rather than "the best." Yet one is not to get the impression that work, hard work, is not a characteristic of Americans—a characteristic that has come down to us from pioneer days. It is doubtful that any people has the genuine respect for labor that we have in America.

It is to be hoped that the sturdy, honest, genuine characteristics of our frontier forbears may be preserved; they are much to be desired above the senseless, sentimental, sophisticated manners and practices found in some of the social strata of our times; but we must learn to judge between the false and the genuine, between brass and true gold, between the crude and the beautiful. A civilization and a people are remembered by the enduring things they leave to posterity. Tradition has clearly established what is enduring. Democracy cannot afford to break entirely with tradition.

THE EXPANSION OF POPULATION FROM 1790 TO 1810

Space will not permit the discussion of the spread of population by decades. Instead the reader is asked to consider the distribution

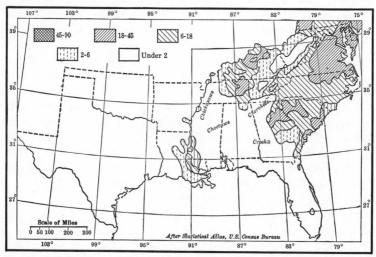

Fig. 43.—Distribution and Density of Population in 1810. (Boundaries as of 1930.)

Spain still held the Gulf Coast east of the Pearl River.

of population in the years 1810, 1830, and 1850, as stages in the great sixty-year movement that resulted in pushing the frontier from the eastern edge of the Appalachian Plateaus well on to the westernmost edge of the section we call the South.

To the east of the Appalachian, on most of the Central Plain and the Piedmont, there was little change in the distribution of people between 1790 and 1810 (Figs. 40 and 43). The "18-45" (persons-to-the-square-mile) area in Virginia and Maryland had expanded so as to cover most of the Piedmont. The west shore of Chesapeake Bay experienced little change. The east shore—the Peninsula—had increased in density in the Maryland section. There had been an increase of densities in all parts of Maryland, Virginia, and North Carolina, the result both of immigration and of natural growth.

The greatest changes in the east had taken place in South Carolina and Georgia, both of which were in 1790, as has been seen, little more than frontier settlements.

The Piedmont in Georgia and South Carolina about 1800 to 1810 was receiving additions to its population from both the northeast and the southeast. The old movement continued, but a new cross movement was now starting. The increasing demand for cotton land was just beginning to be a factor in westward migration in the Lower South; and this demand continued to be the prime urge for many decades to follow until cotton culture and negro slavery had been pushed to the semiarid plains of central Texas. The increasing demand for land by the large planter was pushing out the smaller landowners, and these sought land in the Piedmont, or forsook the South entirely, emigrating even to the distant Pacific after the late 1830's. It was mainly in the 1820's and 1830's that cotton culture reached its first importance on the Piedmont.

In Georgia the frontier had advanced slightly to the westward along the whole western front, but was being retarded in its advance by the Creeks. The pressure behind was great; there were no thinly settled fringes and enclaves in the lower Piedmont at this time; the "18-45" area extended to the very border of the Indian lands. The struggle between whites and Indians became more intense along this frontier during the two decades following 1810.

The Appalachian Valley was still being settled. The eastern and more easily reached portion was as densely peopled as many portions of the North Carolina Piedmont. Settlers all along the Valley were pushing westward into the eastern edge of the dissected Allegheny Plateau. There had been a further advance down the Valley of East Tennessee at the sacrifice of Indian claims, and a "45-90" area was developing in and about Knoxville. The Cumberland and Allegheny plateaus remained for the most part unsettled.

THE PLATEAUS, RETARDED FRONTIERS

The unattractiveness of the Cumberland Plateau, because of its infertile soil and poor natural transportation facilities, led to the rejection of this large area for settlement by the earliest pioneers into Kentucky and Tennessee. It remained almost a wilderness for two or more decades after 1790; but when the productive lands to the east and west became less available it was gradually taken up by farmers. Its infertility is to be read (a hundred and twenty-five years and more after 1810) in the low population density, the low productivity, the wide extent of the forest lands (mostly second growth), the poor quality of the roads, houses, and schools, the high percentage of illiteracy, the primitive home life and living, and the small number of great leaders in the professions, politics, or business. As a stream which in its headwaters carries detritus of many kinds and distributes its load in its lower stretches, depositing here boulders, there gravel, here sand, there silt, so a great stream of migrating peoples, peoples of many kinds—wise and foolish, farsighted and thoughtless, enterprising and shiftless, energetic and lazy, and what not—sorts out, or rather has sorted out of it (natural selection), certain groups which are satisfied to take "lean" areas where they and their posterity must remain in, or degenerate into, ignorance, squalor, and penury. Others are content only with the best and are willing to travel far and work hard to attain the object of their desires. The dominance of the Blue Grass and the Nashville Basin in the affairs of Kentucky and Tennessee and the high rank they hold, past and present, in the affairs of our nation are fundamentally geographic phenomena. The superiority of their economic-geographic advantages led to their selection as homes by a superior people, and in the exploitation of their resources the returns were so abundant that here a surplus of wealth developed to enable the people to build beautiful homes, provide their children with excellent schools and colleges, and thus continue to develop a superior people.

To the bulk of a population success in life is largely a matter of opportunity. In retarded frontier regions the list of opportunities is exceedingly limited. This is as true of the North and West as of the South. The coal mine, the lumber camp, the sawmill, and the store in the small plateau towns, along with pioneer farming, constitute the list of opportunities open to the young boy or girl or the father. None of these offers returns that can lift the worker above the mere-existence level. The ambitious are forced to seek more favorable opportunities elsewhere.

EXPANSION FROM THE KENTUCKY-TENNESSEE CENTERS BETWEEN 1790 AND 1810

The settled areas in Kentucky and Tennessee during the twenty years between 1790 and 1810 had greatly expanded, people spreading out in nearly every direction within the basins and out upon the sur-

rounding Highland Rim plain (Figs. 40 and 43). The western frontier
in Kentucky and Tennessee was pressing on the Chickasaw lands west
of the Tennessee River. These two centers were growing much more
rapidly than the older center of dispersal of eastern Tennessee, where
the farmers had much greater difficulty in getting their products to
and supplies from large markets, and the more fertile land was limited in area. The eastern section thus had less attractive power. Phila-

From Edward King, The Great South, 1874, 291.

FIG. 44.—Natchez-under-the-Hill, about 1870.

Fort Rosalie was built by the French on the bluff to the left in 1716. Both the English and
the Spanish controlled this site before it was taken by the Americans in 1798. As the town grew,
it expanded out upon the flat lands back from the river bluff. Here were and still are the residences
of the large plantation owners. The lands they tilled, with slaves before emancipation, lay across
the river in Louisiana. The flood plain lands were inundated at every high flood. A levee now
protects them.

delphia, Baltimore, and Richmond, even Charleston, were the trading
centers for eastern Tennessee. Kentucky and Tennessee in 1790 had a
population of 110,000. By 1810 it was 668,000.* Jay's treaty in 1795
and the purchase of Louisiana in 1803 removed forever the possibility
that the Mississippi River, the natural outlet for the products of the
Transappalachian settlements, would be the western boundary of
America and that the free movement of the products of this region to
world markets would be checked.

---

* *Statistical Abstract,* 1935, 4.

THE MOVEMENT OF THE FRONTIER IN THE EAST GULF REGION BETWEEN 1790 AND 1810

Much of the eastern Gulf area from the Mississippi to central Georgia was Indian lands, and thus was not open to occupancy, legally, until treaties could be arranged between the Federal Government and the various tribes. Here and there were isolated settlements. James Wilkerson reported to the Secretary of War in 1801 that there were "many unlicensed settlements . . . thinly scattered along the western banks of the Mobile and Tombigbee for more than seventy miles and extended nearly twenty-five miles up the Mobile and Alabama." There were about 500 whites and 250 negro slaves of all ages and of both sexes. The Indians viewed with jealousy the advance of the whites because the "destruction of game had diminished the resorts of their ancestors, and the chase [had] become a precarious resource for the support of life."*

Natchez in 1810 (see Fig. 44) was a center of a thinly populated area that stretched along the eastern bank of the Mississippi, and on the western border of the Indian territory. The Natchez settlement (area not stated) had a population of about 5,000 whites and 3,000 negro slaves. For many decades it was a minor dispersal center. It drew to its wharf and its business houses men of every rank and nationality that passed that way. It was the eastern terminus of a route that led westward across Louisiana through Natchitoches to Nacogdoches in the Spanish territory, now Texas. It was the southern terminus of the Natchez Trace (to be discussed later) that traversed the Indian country of Mississippi in a fairly direct line to the Nashville settlement in middle Tennessee.

THE DISTRIBUTION OF PEOPLE IN LOUISIANA AND ARKANSAS IN 1810

That the Transappalachian pioneers considered a navigable river an essential for a successful settlement is shown by the numerous settlements on rivers. In a new country, before people are numerous enough to cooperate successfully in the building of roads, the rivers are the highways of travel and transportation. They are often the routes taken by the pioneers in seeking new homes, and it is upon them that the earliest products are floated to market.

There are many reasons why man in the alluvial environment of Louisiana associated himself with rivers. It is only on natural levees

---

* *American State Papers*, "Indian Affairs," I, 659.

that land sufficiently dry for cultivation is to be found (see Fig. 35).
New Orleans and Natchez were the two centers of departure of settlers bound for the riverine sections of Louisiana: Natchez, for northern Louisiana settlers who took up lands along the Mississippi; New
Orleans, for those bound for the Red River, the Black, Tensas, and
Ouachita, the natural levees of the bayous Atchafalaya, Teche, Lafourche, and Vermilion, and the Attakapas and Opelousas countries. All
these bayous head in the western and southern slopes of the broad
natural levees of the Mississippi and Red Rivers. Each bayou with
its two strips of dry farming land (natural levees) was (and still is
except for a few cross roads) separated from its neighbors by a broad
almost impassable marsh. To get to these bayou lands it was necessary
to go up the Mississippi or the Red to or near the headwaters and
then follow the bayous southward. Well on into the nineteenth century one could see the great majority of the plantation homes in lower
eastern Louisiana from a boat navigating the rivers and bayous. Such
certainly was the distribution of the population in 1810. Brackenridge,
a most careful observer and interesting writer, who visited Louisiana
in 1810, says that from New Orleans upstream to Lafourche, one
hundred miles distant, there was an unbroken succession of plantations
"laid off with great regularity and taste." The plantation homes were
embowered in groves of ornamental and useful (fruit and nut) trees.
From Lafourche to Pointe Coupee (near St. Francisville) about two-
thirds of the lands were cleared and cultivated. Strangely, this section of Louisiana was known as "the Coast." He considered this the
most beautiful part of Louisiana. It shows, he writes, "what may be
done by the art and industry of man even in those parts which Nature
left rude and unsightly." The Lafourche region (southwest and west
of New Orleans) was settled by a "poor, lazy, careless, miserable lot
of people, mostly Spaniards, mostly small planters, who were known
to the French as *petits habitants*."* The principal settlements on the
Red were Natchitoches, Bayou Rapide, Bayou Robert, Bayou Boeuf,
and Bayou Atchafalaya.

Natchitoches, a town of about forty families, was described as a
"small, irregular, meanly built village, half a dozen houses excepted."
It had been much larger thirty or forty years previous. The first
homes were built on a hill where it was dry; but this was inconvenient, for the river was the life of the settlement. Hence many
families moved to the banks of the river where it would be "more
convenient for loading and unloading of boats" and where the garden-

---

* H. M. Brackenridge, *Views of Louisiana*, 157-173.

ers found superior soil.* For forty or fifty miles up and down the Red from Natchitoches there were continuous stretches of cultivated lands. The bayous (streams) to the south of the Red were likewise settled; so also were the low flat plains of the Attakapas country and open plains or meadows of the Opelousas.†

Far in the interior of Louisiana, beyond Natchitoches, and beyond the settlements on the Black and its tributaries, always along some stream navigable by a canoe, there were scattered hamlets and small settlements of typical trappers, traders, and cattle herders.‡

It was the abundance of pasturage that led the American pioneers into the prairie sections of Louisiana. Many of these settlers had probably followed the life of the pastoralist, or half hunter-half pastoralist, on the frontiers to the east. Here where conditions did not permit of close settlement they were able to "come still nearer the pastoral state." Yet here one found many of the institutions of the more advanced cultural stages. Reports one traveler, "The most trifling settlement will contrive to have a school master who can teach reading, writing, and some arithmetic. Very different from the good natured creole, who does not know a letter of the alphabet."§ Cultural evolution moved swiftly on the Louisiana frontier as in other states and territories after American influence began to be felt. In the first few years of a frontier's history the people suffer retrogression in their economic and social life, but with the incoming of new settlers the advance becomes rapid and in the course of a few decades an air of maturity permeates the settlement.

Arkansas in 1810 had but one small settlement, Arkansas Post, near the mouth of the Arkansas River. It was established as a fur-collecting settlement in 1686. Because of the location at the junction of the Arkansas and Mississippi, it included in its trade territory a large area in the middle Mississippi Valley.¶

MIGRATION BETWEEN 1810 AND 1830

Between 1810 and 1830 the western frontier made many significant advances. Figure 45 shows the distribution of people and the location of the western frontier, as well as the retarded frontiers, in 1830. Compare with Figure 43. The Kentucky settlement had already, by

---

* John Sibley, in *American State Papers*, "Indian Affairs," I, 727.

† H. M. Brackenridge, *op. cit.*, 166-171.

‡ John Sibley, in *American State Papers*, "Indian Affairs," I, 732.

§ H. M. Brackenridge, *Views of Louisiana*, 117; Humphrey Marshall, *The History of Kentucky*, 356.

¶ Sibley, *loc. cit.*; also Brackenridge, *op. cit.*, 113-117.

1810, expanded to the Ohio River. The Chickasaw Purchase in 1818 opened a fertile tract of land in western Kentucky and Tennessee and Mississippi for settlement, and it took less than twelve years to transform this from a wilderness to settled communities. Settlers here avoided the rivers and river bottoms, for they were too marshy to be cleared. It is only now that drainage reclamation is being undertaken. The flat-lying, brown silt area, midway between the Tennessee and the Mississippi, had, by 1830, a population density approaching

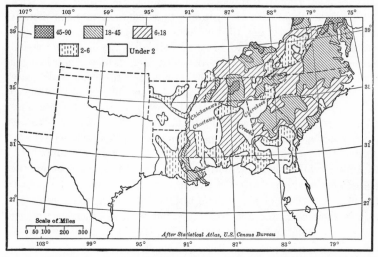

FIG. 45.—Distribution and Density of Population of the South in 1830. (Boundaries of States as in 1930.)

that of the old-settled portion of the Piedmont and Coastal Plain. Tennessee, during the twenty-year period between 1810 and 1830, was the most rapidly growing state in the entire South. Its population increased 420,000.

In Louisiana, expansion was along the lines laid out in 1810. By 1818 some eight hundred families had taken up lands above the Red River raft,* and there were numerous plantations along the Mississippi. The total gain in population during these two decades was 139,000. The population in 1830 was nearly three times that in 1810. The Mississippi continued to be the major route to the interior.

The distribution-of-population map for 1830 shows a thin line of

---

* John Bach McMasters, *A History of the People of the United States,* IV, 395.

settlements in Arkansas spread along both the Red and the Mississippi. The upland settlements numbered three. The southernmost was in the Ouachita Mountain section on a tableland between the Ouachita (or Washita) River and its tributary, the Little Missouri.* In this same area were the celebrated hot springs, later the site of the city of Hot Springs. There were a few huts of split boards for summer encampment of health seekers near the springs in 1804 when Doctor Hunter and William Dunbar visited the area.† Far up the Arkansas was the Mulberry settlement, and near the eastern border of the Ozarks on the White River was the third. About 1821 settlers began to come to these areas from Kentucky, Tennessee, and Carolina. Although all these settlements were on or near waterways navigated by small boats, the people practiced, for the most part, a local economy.

THE ADVANCE IN THE EAST GULF STATES BETWEEN 1810 AND 1830

The Eastern Gulf States likewise showed much advance of the frontier. The strength and the spirit of the Creek Indians had been broken in 1813 and 1814 by Jackson who administered to them a telling defeat, and they were too weak to withstand the advance of the white frontier. By 1830 the whole Georgia Piedmont had been taken up by settlers from the states to the east and northeast. Cotton was now becoming the dominant crop. The Cherokees still held the Great Valley in Georgia and eastern Alabama, and the Choctaws and Chickasaws the northern half of Mississippi. The central Alabama enclave of white man's territory, shown on the 1810 map, was rapidly enlarging, because of the active demand for virgin cotton land. In the next ten years, by 1840, the entire East Gulf area was made available for white occupancy. The frontier in Mississippi in the two decades after 1810 moved eastward from the borders of the Mississippi River and northward from the Gulf. The swampy Yazoo Delta was the last to be opened up to cotton culture. Florida was still largely unsettled, for civil government by the United States had been established only in 1822. By 1830, 35,000 settlers had pushed into the northern portions, mainly from Georgia, South Carolina, and Alabama.

THE DISTRIBUTION OF POPULATION IN 1850

By 1850 all enclaves, or retarded frontiers, east of the Mississippi, except one small area of marsh in the Yazoo Delta, had been occupied, though some were but thinly settled (Fig. 46). Florida alone had a

---

* Ellen Semple, *American History and Its Geographic Conditions,* 166.
† *American State Papers,* "Indian Affairs," I, 737.

frontier, advancing slowly southward, as settlers from Georgia, Alabama, the Carolinas, and other Southern States pushed into its forests in search of new lands. Cotton land was wanted, and little of such was to be found in Florida. Already the lands of South Carolina and Georgia were showing a decreasing yield and cotton growers were actively pushing westward into Alabama, Mississippi, Louisiana, Arkansas, and Texas. One observer who visited Alabama about 1835 writes that a negro hand in South Carolina and Georgia could produce on the average about 310 pounds of cotton; but in Alabama,

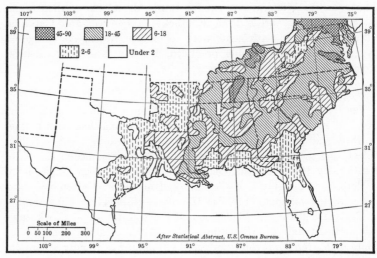

Fig. 46.—Distribution and Density of Population of the South in 1850. (Boundaries of States as in 1930.)

owing to the virgin soils, the average was 430 pounds to the hand and on some plantations even 1,000 pounds. He reports that 10,000 families left South Carolina and Georgia in one season. On a journey across Georgia, via Augusta, Milledgeville, and Macon, he passed many camps in the woods along the road. The numbers on the move were to him almost incredible. During the day he passed caravans of "tilt wagons . . . long and low roofed . . . each laden with provisions and household goods." Both the poor and the comfortably well-off were on the move. The former suffered great hardships from cold, lack of food, and "breakdowns"; the latter traveled more comfortably, for their equipment was better and they carried their slaves to perform the difficult tasks. Each caravan of the wealthier migrants was "preceded or surrounded by field slaves, a half dozen to fifty or sixty."

"Thus they crawl onward," he writes, "from day to day for weeks and months. . . ." But most of them were certain of a rich reward at the journey's end. "The rich alluvial lands of Alabama, recently belonging to the Indian reserves and now [about 1835] on sale by the government or through land speculators," were attractive enough for the thousands "from the worked-out and impoverished soil of the older Southern States."*

Occasionallly he met a returning party, broken in spirit at the loss of a father or mother, or the failure to secure land to their taste. The homes of their dreams, to the west, were dreams after all.

From Edward King, The Great South, 1874, 314.

FIG. 47.—Emigrant Wagons in a Town in Mississippi, about 1870, but applicable to a period from 1825 to 1870.

"At the proper season, one sees in the long main street of town lines of emigrant wagons." For more than a half century the Cotton Belt seemed on the move; the older portion in the east moved westward to virgin cotton lands.

In the early forties Lyell reports a similar movement from parts of Alabama to Texas and Arkansas. He was told that Monroe County, Alabama, alone, had lost 1,500 inhabitants (about 1841). Much capital was leaving the state, for the wealthier planters were "reduced to the alternative of high taxes to pay the interest of money so improvidently borrowed from England or suffer the disgrace of repudiation. . . ."†

MIGRATION INTO THE TRANSMISSISSIPPI AREAS

Arkansas and Louisiana ceased to be frontier states long before 1850, though they continued to receive settlers. With the "re-annexa-

---

* Tyrone Power, *Impressions of America*, II, 80, 135.

† Sir Charles Lyell, *A Second Visit to the United States of North America*, II, 56. Figure 47 depicts a movement in Mississippi in the 1870's.

tion" of Texas in 1845, the American frontier had pushed rapidly westward to the western edge of the Grand Prairie and nearly to the Balcones Escarpment in south central Texas (see Figure 48).

Texas won its independence from Mexico in 1836, and next year asked for annexation to the United States. No action was taken by Congress until 1844. The South favored annexation, for it would open up a large territory under the American flag suitable for the growing of cotton and the use of slaves. The non-slaveholding North, and

From Edward King, The Great South, 1874, 161.

FIG. 48.—Military Plaza, San Antonio, about 1870.

For a century or more San Antonio was an outpost in an Indian Country.

particularly the Northeast, opposed annexation, but lost. The "Lone Star State" added one more star to the American flag in 1845. Mexico claimed that the international boundary should be the Nueces River; this led to the Mexican War. For a strip of semiarid land the United States fought a war that cost it the respect of the whole of Latin America. Present generations have been reaping the calumny of the victory today, in the distrust and fear in which this country has so long been held in the Western Hemisphere. Only in the closing weeks of 1936 did there come to be a return of the confidence that existed more than a century ago (before the annexation of Texas and the Mexican War) between the republics of the Americas.

THE ANNEXATION OF TEXAS JUSTIFIED ON GEOGRAPHICAL GROUNDS

Disgraceful as the Mexican War seems to us, three-quarters of a century removed from the spirit of those times when territorial aggrandizement was the factor that dominated our national policy, we must confess that American expansion to the Rio Grande and the Pacific was in full accordance with the laws of geographic adjustment that a virile nation makes when its potential economic energy is devoted solely to land-using occupations. Somewhere near or at the location of the present international boundary on the south, is the logical (geographic) line of demarcation between English America and Latin America. A glance at a rainfall map, a plant map, a crop map, and a population map of North America shows clearly that Texas is in every respect a continuation of the South that lies east of the Sabine. Geographically, Texas is peripheral to Mexico and continuous with America.

The decennial population maps from 1850 to the present are a confirmation of the "destiny" that carried the American flag to the Rio Grande. Coastlines that give ready access to the world ocean, mountain ranges, and desert tracts are the logical geographic locations for national boundaries. Thus though we may blush at the spectacle of America fighting small Mexico, weakened by almost incessant revolutions, the expansion of our political frontier was logical. This much must be said in justice to America's action: our country made many attempts at purchasing Texas even before Texas independence. The President of the United States, about 1829, when American settlers first began their rapid migration, realized that eventually the American frontier must go to the Rio Grande.

In 1850 the western frontier in the South ran, roughly, from Corpus Christi on the Gulf, through San Antonio, Austin, and Fort Worth (Fig. 46). At the Red River it bore eastward to the western boundary of Arkansas around Indian Territory.

FRONTIER ADAPTATIONS TO ARIDITY

After 1850 the westward movement of the frontier in Texas was slow. This was not because there was a loss of vitality of the Southern people or a decline in population increase. Although the South had passed through a great war and the nightmare of a long period of reconstruction, population had increased from 9,000,000 in 1850 to more than 24,000,000 in 1900, and 35,000,000 in 1920. The frontier after 1850 had reached its greatest and most effective barrier since it started on its westward journey from the borders of the Atlantic in the early seventeenth century. Mountains, Indians, and marshes were nothing to overcome compared with aridity. Entirely new adaptations had to be made in land utilization. White man did make a slight advance over the Indian in this semiarid area in substituting pastoral pursuits for hunting; yet, as carried on in western Texas, cattle raising was little in advance of buffalo hunting. Man for a time did little more than substitute a domesticated animal for a wild grazer. The farmer, to utilize western Texas, had to devise new methods of cultivation—land-moisture conservation methods—and find crops that could withstand droughts and give economic yields with the minimum of soil water available.* The great discovery of the last few decades that has changed much of western Texas from a land of cattle ranches to productive farms is dry land farming. The High Plains have been occupied by agriculturists largely in the last twenty years.

THE LAST FRONTIER IN THE SOUTH

The last of the states of the South to experience the passing of the frontier was Oklahoma. There was much excitement and a "rush" for lands, that showed little of the character of the orderly, quiet, unannounced movement that characterized the migrations of the eighteenth and nineteenth centuries in America. Much the same desire motivated the people—land for farming; but there was added another attraction, the possible existence of mineral wealth beneath the surface. This possibility was rarely if ever considered by the pioneers of Arkansas, Louisiana, and the other states to the east. The possibility of discovering gold or silver no doubt was ever in the minds of the migrants; but coal, oil, gas, zinc, glass sand, clays, gypsum, and building stones had little or no place as economic goods in their world. The twentieth-century pioneers in Oklahoma might have given a real pioneer atmosphere to their movement had they traveled on foot with most of their worldly goods on their backs, by pack animals, or ox cart; but instead they utilized the railroad (for part of the way), horses and carriages, and even automobiles in the later "rushes."

The great interest in the frontier in Oklahoma is the rapidity of its movement. The first legal opening (only a small part of the total territory) was in 1883. The state with its present boundaries was admitted to statehood in 1907. In 1910 its population was nearly 1,700,-000, Indians making up only 4.5 per cent of the total population. Oklahoma City had grown from a cow pasture in 1883 to a busy modern city of 64,000 people.†

The movement of the frontier into Oklahoma was rapid because under the protection of the Federal Government a primitive culture

---

* The active wind erosion, and resulting dust storms, of the late 1930's showed that he has not yet applied all the essential techniques for this environment. He must learn to conserve soil humus.

† Data from *Statistical Abstract*, 1935, 4 and 5.

was permitted to exist on land capable of supporting a high civilization, and bordered on all sides, except on the west, by densely populated, highly developed areas, with redundant populations; and beyond these bordering states were others even more highly developed and densely populated. Here were resources in lands and minerals which if once possessed would, overnight, give their possessors sustenance and possibly the comforts and affluence that otherwise, even for the few, would require years of effort.

The population of Oklahoma in 1910 (first census after statehood) was composed largely of people "who had come from somewhere." Only about one-third of the total 1,657,000 people had been born in Oklahoma. The distribution of the birthplaces, by states, is illuminating. Of the total number:

205,000 people had come from				Texas
162,000	"	"	"	"	Missouri
133,000	"	"	"	"	Arkansas
101,000	"	"	"	"	Kansas
71,000	"	"	"	"	Illinois
62,000	"	"	"	"	Tennessee
43,000	"	"	"	"	Kentucky
41,000	"	"	"	"	Iowa
41,000	"	"	"	"	Indiana
33,000	"	"	"	"	Ohio
33,000	"	"	"	"	Alabama
28,000	"	"	"	"	Mississippi

The remainder were from more distant states. Thus the movement into Oklahoma drew in its wake people from a large area but most of them from the nearest states.* By 1920 Indians formed only 2.8 per cent of the population of the state.†

The admission of Oklahoma to statehood in 1907 and the assumption of its control by white man closed the struggle between Indian and white, between uncultured and civilized man, for mastery in the South. It required three hundred years for white man to take full possession.

A BASIS OF SOUTHERN UNITY

The frontier in the South, as in the North and West, has always been "a zone of assimilation and amalgamation," a melting pot, in which people from many regions, differing in ideals, aspirations, equipments, and philosophies of life, with different methods of economic adaptations to environmental conditions, mingle, exchange ideas, and,

---

* Data from *Report of Thirteenth Census*, 1910, I, 730-734.
† *Report of Fourteenth Census*, 1920, III, 812.

consciously or unconsciously, break down provincialism and realign
themselves into unified groups under the spell of common conditions
and common problems.

Lyell writes charmingly of his observations of Southern society in
the forties—"The different stages of civilization to which families
have attained, who live here on terms of the strictest equality is often
amazing to a stranger. . . . Sometimes, in the morning, my host would
be of the humblest class of 'crackers' or some low illiterate German
or Irish emigrant, the wife sitting with a pipe in her mouth doing no
work and reading no books. In the evening I came to a neighbor,
whose library was well-stored with the works of French and English
authors and whose first question to me was, 'Pray tell me who do
you really think is the author of the Vestiges of Creation?' "*

In the tremendous mixing of peoples that has characterized the
westward movement during the three hundred years of Southern history there have been for the most part the dispersal and reassembling
of the same families. The individuals participating on each successive
frontier were removed by one, two, or more generations. One will find
the family names of Colonial Virginia all over the South even to the
western border of Texas. There are few communities, even, that do
not have one or more members bearing the name Calhoun, Payne,
Wilson, King, and Marshall, and scores of others, not to mention
Smith and Brown. These are a few of the families whose ancestors
may be traced back to immigrants who entered the eastern South in
the seventeenth and eighteenth centuries.

In Georgia in 1850, out of a total white and free colored population
of 524,500, about 404,000 had been born in Georgia, 52,000 in South
Carolina, 38,000 in North Carolina, 8,200 in Tennessee, 7,300 in Virginia, 3,000 in Alabama, 642 in Pennsylvania, 1,203 in New York,
594 in Massachusetts, and 712 in Connecticut. In Alabama, of the
total population of 429,000, about 238,000 had been born in Alabama,
59,000 in Georgia, 48,700 in South Carolina, 28,500 in North Carolina,
22,500 in Tennessee, but only 876 in Pennsylvania, 1,443 in New
York, and 654 in Massachusetts. In 1850 Georgia had 4,261 who had
been born in Great Britain and Ireland, 972 in Germany, 13 in Aus-
tria, and 11 in Holland. For Alabama the data were similar.†

Although there has been a slow infiltration of Northern and foreign peoples, most of the families on every frontier have been Southerners. There were thus two broad streams of migrating people passing

* Sir Charles Lyell, *A Second Visit to the United States of North America*,
II, 64.
† *Compendium of Seventh Census*, 1850, p. xxxvi.

over the North American continent in the part called the United States, one starting at Plymouth Rock, the other at Jamestown. Each had notable accessions from other ocean landing places—New York and Philadelphia, Charleston, Savannah, and New Orleans. People from New England and Pennsylvania in the early days, when the coast lands and the lands east of the mountains were being settled, established homes in the South and became Southerners in a few generations. People from the South moved into Indiana, Illinois, and Missouri, and many into Oregon. In the last fifty years some Northern farmers have taken up lands in Louisiana, Texas, and Oklahoma. But these, all, have been minor movements. Even within the South there has been a general tendency for migrants to follow isotherms largely because isotherms in humid states form the northern and southern borders of the major crop areas. Old agricultural practices could be followed in the new regions. Man is prone to avoid new adaptations unless forced by necessity.

Unity in the South, then, to some degree, possibly to a large degree, is based on the widespread dispersal of the descendants of the original families as the respective successive frontiers of this vast area were being peopled. And this in spite of natural conditions which, we know, had a tendency to separate the people of the various sections. The "grain" of the country in the Upper South runs northeast and southwest. Commerce even today tends to follow the slope of the lands. Kentucky and Virginia have few reciprocal commercial or political relations. In the Lower South until the coming of the railroads commerce moved by river, and therefore roughly at right angles to the coast. In the Civil War the Southern Appalachian region was a wedge that tended to split the Confederacy. Clearly the *anthropo* factors were, and are, more contributory to unity than the *geo*. Taking the South as a whole, the unifying environmental factors are the great areal extent of the Coastal Plain with its unified climatic conditions and unified agriculture and the transverse location of the Mississippi River. Coastwise traffic has never been a factor in bringing about a comity of feeling in the Seaboard and Gulf States. Florida has always served as a barrier between these two groups. Capes Hatteras and Fear, the former "the graveyard of the Atlantic," made the coastwise movement of small vessels dangerous.

FRONTIERS OF TODAY AND TOMORROW

The grazing-agricultural frontier in the South disappeared with the conquest of the High Plains of Texas and Oklahoma by the dry land farmers. But a new frontier (or must we say frontiers?) is arising, an industrial one. It is not, like the slow-moving, grazing-agricultural frontier, advancing along a broad front and taking possession of all lands in its path. It is more intelligently directed. Its sponsors select with care the sites where it begins its development. It is being established near coal fields, and waterfalls and rapids, near or in oil, gas, and iron ore regions, in sections where there is a supply of cheap labor or where traffic lines can assemble raw products from wide distances and carry factory products to extensive markets. Some industries are being located in cities that are conspicuous because of their extensive commercial activities. No industrial area as large and as active as those in many parts of the Northeastern States has yet developed; but a beginning has been made along the Ohio, in the Piedmont in North and South Carolina, in eastern Tennessee, in central Alabama, and about or in most of the major cities of the South.

Industrialization has already started a new movement of population similar to that which has been going on in the industrial countries of Western Europe and Northeastern and North Central United States for a century or more, a movement toward the city. So far the industrial sections have been manned largely by "home folks," as were the successive grazing-agricultural frontiers. Eventually if opportunities multiply and become more attractive there may set in a movement from sections outside the South, even from Europe, Latin America, and perhaps Asia. The South may cease to be the last great stronghold of the Anglo-Saxons in America, the nationality that found the vast area that we call the South a wilderness and made it a land of farms and factories.

In this new industrial frontier the pioneer is the local millman who makes his factory both a neighborhood and a family institution. He works with his employees, plays with them, and prays with them, and his factory is free from strife. He will be (and is even now being) superseded by "foreign" capitalists and corporations whose factories are run by managers and whose interests are largely in factory dividends and such factory betterment work as will keep the employees contented. In this change the frontier region passes from industrial democracy to industrial autocracy; and turmoil, if not open warfare, is on. Will the South in the more advanced stages of its industrial evolution experience the growing pains of the manufacturing Northeast? That remains to be seen. May the spirit of the old frontier of democracy and independence, a respect for the individual and a love for the free life, remain!

PART III

PROVIDING TRANSPORTATION FACILITIES

CHAPTER V

THE HIGHWAYS OF THE SOUTH

THE ROADS OF THE PIONEER

The earliest pioneers in advancing into a new region in the forested sections of the South rarely cleared a way for wagons. Their household goods, bare necessities, were transported on their own or their animals' backs. They used the waterways where possible for conveyance, or if they traversed settled sections, before striking lands beyond the frontier, they followed beaten paths or roads. Their transportation problems were not difficult if the frontier left no gaps (unsettled areas) in its advance, for roads by necessity were provided, or developed without much thought, as the frontier moved onward. But if they sought fertile lands beyond mountains, or infertile plateaus, or deserts, their civilized methods of travel and transportation had to be forsaken and they traveled as did their Indian predecessors and contemporaries.

The first settlements in the South, as previously stated, were on tidal waters. As long as the expansion from the initial centers was along rivers, roads were little needed; but when the frontier moved inland, roads became an essential in the economic life of the people. There were a few roads on each of the peninsulas of Tidewater Virginia and Maryland, but since most of the plantations faced the waterways and the plantation homes were widely distributed, road building was not active. It was when the frontier advanced upon the Piedmont that the call came for roads to markets or shipping points on the rivers. By 1700 most of the colonies of the South had passed laws much like those of England, governing the construction and upkeep of roads. The farther the frontier moved from tidewater, the more essential roads became. State aid was invoked, and even Federal aid when roads were demanded to connect the transmontane regions with the seaboard. Maryland and Virginia, the oldest of the Southern colonies and the first to send pioneers into the "back country" and across the Appalachians, took the lead in lending state assistance. Assistance was given for the construction of a road from the Potomac to Fort Pitt at the head of the Ohio, along the route of the old Brad-

123

dock Road. This first American transmontane road was later followed, in general, by the National Pike.

It was the pioneers of the advanced settlements of western Pennsylvania and of Kentucky and Tennessee, isolated from their former markets by hundreds of miles of forest-covered mountains and plateaus, who needed assistance in the construction of Transappalachian highways. The need for such contacts was usually felt many years before they were provided.

About 1790, when the Transappalachian population in Kentucky and Tennessee alone numbered more than 110,000, there were but two wagon roads crossing the mountains. One led westward from Maryland and Virginia and southern Pennsylvania, up the "Potowmac" to Cumberland Fort and thence to Redstone Old Fort on the Monongahela. The road was described as being rough but nowhere in the least difficult for wagons. At Redstone boats could be purchased, or travel could be continued on horseback. Another route lay to the south "through the wilderness through which it was hardly possible for a carriage to pass, a great part of the way being over high steep hills, up the banks of rivers and along defiles which in some places seem to threaten you at every step with danger."* This was the route through the Cumberland Gap. (See Figures 41 and 49.)

Boone had blazed this latter route, the Wilderness Road (to Cumberland Gap), about 1775. The Wilderness Road was for a time but a mere trail that could be traversed only by pack animals and people on foot.

In the Great Valley in eastern Tennessee and southwestern Virginia, the settlers had certain though distant contacts with the seaboard from the beginning of the occupancy. The road to Philadelphia was about 650 miles long, and to Richmond, across southern Virginia, some 490 miles (Fig. 49). These were fair wagon roads, the cost of transportation being about $4.00 per hundredweight to Richmond or return.† Eastern Tennessee also had a road eastward to Morganton east of the Southern Appalachian Mountains and from there to Charleston. Michaux writes of his trip along this road, "On the 21st of September 1802, I set out from Jonesborough to cross the Alleghanies [old name for mountains of North Carolina] for North Carolina. About nine miles from Jonesborough the road divides into two branches which unite again fifty-six miles beyond the mountains. The left which is principally for carriages cuts through Yellow Moun-

---

* Gilbert Imlay, *A Topographical Description of the Western Territory of North America,* 170.

† F. A. Michaux, *Travels to the West of the Alleghany Mountains,* 255.

tain and the other through Iron Mountain.* I took the latter as I
had been informed it was much the shortest. I only made nineteen
miles that day and put up at Cayerd's at the Limestone Cow. . . . I
had the day following twenty-three miles to make without meeting
with the least kind of a plantation. After having made the most minute inquiry with regard to the path I had to take I set out about
eight o'clock . . . and after a journey of three hours reached the
summit of the mountain, which I recognized by several trees with

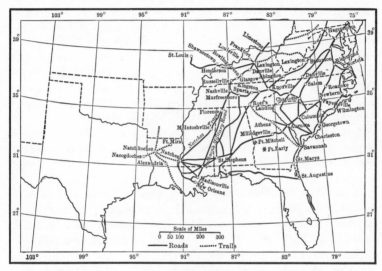

FIG. 49.—The Major Early Roads of the South, up to about 1830.
Compiled from maps by Jno. Melish, M. Lovoisene, Gilbert Imly, Finley, and others.

'the road' marked on each, and on the same directions [signboards] to
indicate the line of demarcation that separates the state of Tennessee
from that of North Carolina." On the third day out from Jones-
borough he traveled twenty-two miles to the house of one Davenport.
Morganton, which he eventually reached, contained "about fifty
houses of wood and almost all inhabited by tradesmen. One warehouse only, supported by a commercial house at Charleston, is established in this town," he writes, "where the inhabitants for twenty
miles round come and purchase mercury and jewellery goods from
England, or give in exchange their products which consist chiefly of
dried hams, butter, tallow, bear and stag skins, and ginseng which

* These ridges are the westernmost of the ridges of the Southern Appalachian
Mountains.

they bring from the mountains." He states that between Morganton and Charleston, a distance of 285 miles, there were several roads, "which do [did] not vary in point of distance above twenty miles."* There were regular lines of wagons engaged in commerce between Charleston and the back country.

Returning now to a further consideration of the Cumberland Gap Road, "This," says a contemporary traveler, "is the only route the people coming from the upper [western] part of Virginia and North Carolina can take at present to get into the country [Transappalachian Region]; the gap of Cumberland Mountains, being the only place where it can be passed without the greatest difficulty."† A road for wagons was laid out through Cumberland Gap in the summer of 1795 and some "30 or 40 wagons passed over it in the fall of that year." That such a road was needed is shown by the report that several thousand settlers in detached families passed through the Gap in September, October, and November of the year previous.‡

It is written that in Kentucky, beginning with 1782, the people "began to open roads for carriages in the interior of the country; prior to this there were only paths practicable for persons on foot or horseback."§

Before 1790 the Blue Grass settlers were in touch with those of the Nashville Basin by a "beautiful [for the time] road through the barrens," about 190 miles long. This road extended from Maysville, on the south bank of the Ohio, on through Lexington, southwestward to Nashville. Except for the necessity of using wagons for the transportation of goods and products, people apparently preferred horseback to the vehicles (springless and necessarily slow) of the day; and even to the keelboats when and where they could be had. Birkbeck wrote, regarding horseback riding, "Women, of advanced age, often, take long journeys in this manner without inconvenience. Yesterday, I heard of a lady, mentioned familiarly, with no mark of admiration, who is coming from Tennessee 1,200 miles to Pittsburg with an infant, preferring horseback to boating up the river."¶ The usual rate of travel of moderately heavy-wheeled vehicles and by horseback was about 25-45 miles per day.‖

---

* F. A. Michaux, *Travels to the West of the Alleghany Mountains*, etc., 251-266.

† Gilbert Imlay, *A Topographical Description of the Western Territory of North America*, 170.

‡ *Ibid.*, 516.

§ F. A. Michaux, *op. cit.*, 159.

¶ Morris Birkbeck, *Notes on a Journey in America*, 44, 45.

‖ *Ibid.*

HIGHWAYS IN OLDER SETTLED AREAS

Road building east of the mountains where there were continuous settlements and low grades presented little financial or topographic difficulties. Such sections were fairly well supplied with highways by 1800, as the quotation from Michaux indicates. In the Report of the United States Secretary of the Treasury, Albert Gallatin, in 1807, it is stated that there were several roads leading out from Baltimore, some under construction. Most of the larger towns south of the Potomac were connected by dirt roads especially in those sections wherever there was a "more compact population." The cost of these highways ranged from $1,000 a mile to $14,000, the average being about $7,000.*

TRANSAPPALACHIAN HIGHWAYS

The Secretary in this report of 1807 recommended Federal aid to four roads across the Appalachian to connect four sets of rivers on either side of the mountain barrier. The Susquehanna, Potomac, James, and Santee on the east should be connected, he recommended, with the Allegheny, Monongahela, Kanawha, and Tennessee on the west. These roads, together with the necessary improvements to navigation in the rivers so as to give commodities freedom of movement from the Atlantic to the Mississippi, would cost, it was estimated, some $4,800,-000.† The only road, however, that received Federal aid about this time was the National Pike from Cumberland, Maryland, westward to Wheeling and on into Ohio. Many, if not most, travelers from the Transappalachian Region used this route, so far as it extended, in their journeys to and from Washington and the East.

THE NATCHEZ TRACE

The most historic road in the South, east of the Mississippi River, was the Natchez Trace. This ran in almost a beeline from Nashville to Natchez on the Mississippi (Fig. 49). It was also the oldest land route in the Transappalachian section in the South, and from 1785 on to 1820 or 1825 was the most traveled of any trace, trail, or road. It (part at least) was first an Indian trail used by the Chickasaws and Choctaws in going from village to village or making hunting trips into the Cumberland River country. Later, traders with their pack horses, laden with such articles as would attract the fancy

---

* *Historical Register, III,* State Papers, 13th Congress, 2nd Session, Part I, 1814, 274.

† *Ibid.,* 283.

of the savage mind, sought the Indian villages on the Natchez trail. During the flatboat era of navigation on the Mississippi (discussed in the next chapter) and before the coming of the steamboats, the boatmen—those "wild men of the western waters," who floated the products of the forests, the mines, and the farms of the Ohio, the Cumberland, and the Tennessee rivers down the Mississippi to Natchez, and New Orleans—quite generally used the Trace on the return journey to Nashville, Lexington, Louisville, or other up-river shipping points. "On foot" was the most common mode of travel, even though not so desirable as horseback, for Spanish horses in New Orleans or Natchez ranged from $40 to $60 each, the equivalent of a month's pay of a riverman.

The "opening of the Mississippi" (1795), and particularly the purchase of Louisiana (1803), opened the floodgates for down-river flatboats, manned by thousands of rough, boisterous, daring rivermen. As a result the number of boatmen moving northward over the Trace became greater. The number using the trail may be judged by the fact that in the year 1817 (ending in October) 1,500 flatboats and 500 barges reached the lower Mississippi from the "up country."

It was a veritable wilderness that these travelers traversed between Nashville and Natchez. The traveler Baily who passed over it in 1796 or 1797 characterized this territory as "the desert," not because it was devoid of vegetation but because it was destitute of provisions. Travelers for many years had to carry provisions for the entire journey of some 500 (Michaux states 600) miles which, even on horseback, took from fifteen to twenty days.*

After 1801 the Federal Government improved the Natchez Trace, that year having made a treaty with the Chickasaws who thereby were bound not to molest travelers and to maintain ferries at the large rivers, charging not more than the price fixed by the Government. It became a mail route. The valuable mails which sometimes passed to and from New Orleans and Tennessee, Kentucky, the Great Valley of East Tennessee, and Virginia, and even Washington, and the large sums of money carried by returning rivermen made

---

* Francis Baily, *Journal of a Tour in the Unsettled Parts of America,* 348, 357; F. A. Michaux, *op. cit.,* 202; *American State Papers,* Class VII, Post Office Department, 1789-1833, 28.

Baily was twenty-six days on this trip, traveling on foot. He provided himself with 15 lbs. of biscuits, 6 lbs. of flour, 12 lbs. of bacon, 3 lbs. of rice, 1½ lbs. of coffee, 4 lbs. of sugar, besides crushed corn. He experienced a delay of one day at the Tennessee River, occasioned by the necessity of making a raft. *Op. cit.,* 348, 357.

robbing a profitable occupation along the Trace. Federal troops were dispatched at times to make the way safe.

It bore diverse names at different times, such as the Government Road, Robinson Road, and the Nashville-Natchez Road; but the name most popularly applied to it was and is the Natchez Trace.

The returning river boatmen were not the only whites that traversed this route. It was the main land throughfare for two decades or more between the Ohio and the Cumberland and Tennessee valleys on the north, and Natchez and New Orleans to the south. Settlers moved along it from the Kentucky and Tennessee dispersal centers to southern Mississippi and on into Louisiana.

The coming of the steamboat on the Mississippi (about 1820), which marks the beginning of the era of successful upstream navigation, reduced the traffic over the Trace, and within a few years it ceased to exist as a road except in history or in exciting stories of the exploits of travelers. These exploits have long since become traditional.* Work has already started (1937) on a (Federal built) modern hard-surfaced road along the route of the Natchez Trace.

A WASHINGTON TO NEW ORLEANS HIGHWAY

The increasing population in the Transappalachian Region (after 1790), the opening of the Mississippi (1795), and the Purchase of Louisiana (1803), all advanced the importance of New Orleans. In the minds of most of the thoughtful people of the times it seemed "destined," because of its location, to become the greatest city on the American continent. Even by 1800 its levee wharves were crowded with flatboats from the up-river sections. A direct road was needed between Washington and this future metropolis that would greatly reduce the time of movement of mail and travelers.

Such a road was recommended to the House Committee on Post Offices and Post Roads on December 13, 1803. As New Orleans would unquestionably be the "place of deposit for the products of the Western World," it was declared, its connection with Washington would be incalculably important. The road to and from New Orleans was certain to become the great thoroughfare of the United States, therefore it was certainly an object of prime importance (railroads and steamboats were undreamed of then by practical people) to procure the nearest and most convenient route to the Gulf city. This could be done only by avoiding the road then used through Tennessee, which passed through the Allegheny Mountains (Great

* *Mississippi Valley Historical Review,* VII, 26, 381; *Tennessee Historical Magazine,* VII, 27-35.

Valley), and establishing a route through Virginia, the back parts
of North and South Carolina and Georgia, to (or near) a place
called Jackson's Court House, and thence by a road (to be in part
purchased from the Indians) along a line, as direct as the nature
of the ground would permit, to New Orleans. This route, it was
estimated, would be nearly five hundred miles shorter than the route
through Tennessee. This may be called the Inner Piedmont route.

By 1806 a road or roads had been completed along the route outlined as far as Athens, Georgia. From there on to New Orleans only
a trail was followed. On March 21, 1806, Granger furnished the House
of Representatives estimates for surveying the road southwestward
from Athens, the building of fifteen miles of causeways, and the
throwing of logs across four rivers and twenty-one creeks. All that
was suggested at this time was the improvement of the trail.*

THE FALL LINE ROAD

The road map of 1820 (Fig. 49) shows that roads did develop
along the Washington-New Orleans route, in general as suggested;
but this never became a great thoroughfare. Although this route was
probably the shortest that could be laid out, encountered no exces-
sively steep grades, avoided many rivers and crossed the ones that
lay transverse to it near their headwaters, it never proved as popular
as a highway farther east, which we may well call the Fall Line
Road because it followed, roughly, the outer edge of the Piedmont,
that is, the Fall Line. The latter might also well be designated as
the "Southern Capitals" road for it connected the capitals of the
South Atlantic States, Richmond, Raleigh, Columbia, and Milledgeville, Georgia (once the capital), eventually running westward to St.
Stephens on the Tombigbee (a temporary seat of government in 1817),
and thence to New Orleans.

It seems probable that this Fall Line Road "grew up" as necessity
demanded a communication and traffic route between the cities. Per-
mission to construct the road from Augusta, Georgia, westward to
the river settlements of Alabama was obtained from the Indians in
1805. The Federal Government built small forts and put guards
here and there along the route to protect mails and travelers. Topo-
graphically, the route of this road was well selected. It ran over a high
and dry terrain and forded the rivers at the rapids. In the beginning
some parts of this road were merely a path through the forests,
traversed by horsemen and pack animals, moving in caravans for self-
protection.

---

* *America State Papers,* Class VII, Post Office Dept., **39.**

By 1812 the road westward from Augusta had become a well-traveled thoroughfare, and after the removal of the Indians it was traversed by thousands of pioneers from the South Atlantic seaboard states seeking rich alluvial land in Alabama, Mississippi, Louisiana, and even Texas. The steamboats on the Savannah and Alabama rivers increased its importance for it became the stage route for travelers to and from Savannah and Montgomery. The Florida Peninsula was a barrier to alongshore movements between the Gulf Coast and the South Atlantic and the base of the peninsula in north Florida and south Georgia offered no easy land routes. Travelers from Savannah to Mobile or New Orleans ascended the Savannah River to Augusta, a two or three days' journey; there they took a stage to Milledgeville, on to Macon, Columbia, and Montgomery, and from here again a river steamer down the Alabama River to Mobile.

EARLY TRAILS AND ROADS IN THE TRANSMISSISSIPPI REGION

West of the Mississippi River there were famous trails and roads across Louisiana from both New Orleans and Natchez, the latter center of population being the usual point of departure from the Mississippi. Roads also led from Alexandria and Natchitoches to Nacogdoches in eastern Texas and thence to far-off San Antonio. Both Nacogdoches and San Antonio were founded in the early part of the eighteenth century when Philadelphia was still young and Louisiana was still controlled by the French, and between these two settlements St. Denis, a Frenchman, blazed the San Antonio Road. Along it, as previously seen, passed the usual caravans of traders with their pack animals, immigrants, immigrant wagons, and commercial wagons carrying the products from and supplies to the frontier settlements, when Texas was being overrun by American settlers.

ROADS IN THE ANTEBELLUM PERIOD

The roads of the South continued to multiply in numbers but there was not much improvement in quality until the automobile era. Following 1800 to 1830, toll roads, owned by private companies, were to be found in some states, a response to the thinly-settled conditions of the country, to low valuation of land, and, possibly, mostly to a lack of leadership in the education of the people to the need of good roads. Traffic was so slight, however, that toll roads would hardly pay for their construction. The denser settlements, until the coming of railroads in large numbers, could hardly be divorced from riverside locations. Roads, for the most part, were constructed to serve as feeders to the rivers. Those that traversed the back country, where the population was scarce, hardly deserved the name of highways. In those portions of the South that were fairly well settled, toll roads and toll bridges paid handsomely, as in parts of Kentucky, Tennessee, Maryland, and Virginia; but in the South Atlantic and Gulf States the planters refused to patronize them and many were abandoned. Since the South was opposed to Federal aid in internal improvements little Federal money was spent south of the Mason and Dixon's line.

Most of the highways, even including toll roads, had seasons of almost impassability. Tyrone Power, a European who traveled in America in 1833, 1834, and 1835, described the conditions of the Augusta-Montgomery Road in late fall as follows: "Between Milledgeville and Macon the route became all but impassable, at each mile we anticipated a standstill; the rain was incessant; the creeks were flooded; and the bridges in an indescribable condition. We were frequently compelled to alight and walk, being in momentary expectation of an overturn. . . .*

Lyell in 1843 describes the roads in a similar vein. "We traveled in a carriage with two horses," he writes, "and could advance but a few miles a day, so execrable and often dangerous was the state of the roads. Occasionally we had to get out and call at a farm house to ask the proprietor's leave to take down his snake fence to avoid a deep mud hole in the road."†

Since the beginning of the nineteenth century the "MacAdam" type of road, first devised in England, was rapidly adopted in America, the first in our country having been constructed in eastern Pennsylvania.‡ In the literature of the day it is difficult to distinguish between the terms MacAdam, stone, and turnpike, as applied to roads, for obvious reasons. By 1834 Maryland had many turnpikes. The Baltimore-Cumberland Pike was 135 miles long; at Cumberland it connected with the National Pike which at that time was a free road. There was also a pike from Baltimore to the Susquehanna by way of York, an attempt to divert the commerce of the Susquehanna from Philadelphia to Baltimore. The Havre de Grace Pike, nearly completed, was the Maryland part of the road from Baltimore to Philadelphia.§ Shortly after this a macadam road was constructed from Winchester to Staunton, Virginia.¶ These are only a few of the

---

* Tyrone Power, *Impression of America*, II, 82.

† Sir Charles Lyell, *A Second Visit to the United States*, II, 70.

‡ A. E. Parkins, "The Development of Transportation in Pennsylvania," *Bulletin of the Geographical Society of Philadelphia*, XVI, 105.

§ John Hinton, *The History and Topography of United States*, II, 420.

¶ R. S. Tanner, *Canals and Railroads 1840*, 166.

many hard-surfaced roads constructed in the South in the first half of the nineteenth century.

The state of Virginia had an internal improvement fund for the encouragement of road and canal building. By 1830 it had assisted eleven projects, the state contributing about 46 per cent of the cost.*

Olmsted, in his *A Journey in the Seaboard Slave States*, gives an interesting description of the modes of travel in vogue in the South Atlantic States in the 1840's and 1850's. Near Fayetteville, North

From J. S. Buckingham, loc. cit., I, 1842, 164.

Fig. 50.—A Freighter's Wagon on the Court House Square, Augusta, Georgia, about 1840.

It was reported that as early as 1770, 3000 wagons reached Charleston yearly from the "back country." Fayetteville, North Carolina, was likewise a "wagon" center for more than a half century. The buildings between this court house and the church are those of a medical college.

Carolina (near the head of navigation on Cape Fear), he saw at one encampment thirty to forty wagons for the distant highland districts, laden with cornmeal, flour, or cotton. The wagons were heavily built and drawn by two to four horses, "the rear wheeler always having a large Spanish saddle on his back for the driver. Most of the wagons had come 100 to 200 miles or more. In this tedious way, until lately," the author writes, "nearly all the commerce between the back country and the river towns and seaports of Virginia and North Carolina has been carried on, strong teams of horses toiling on, less than a score of miles a day, with the lumbering wagons, the roads running through a sparsely settled district of clay soil and much

* Jos. Martin, *A New and Comprehensive Gazetteer of Virginia*, 1835, 95, 96.

worse even than those of the sandy lands I have described."* (Fig. 50.)

Fayetteville was the point of transfer from wagon to boat. The destination of such parts of the cargoes of the wagons as were not consumed in Fayetteville was Wilmington; and from there a part moved on to the East, or even to England.

From Edward King, The Great South, 1874, 634.

FIG. 51.—Rolling Hogsheads of Tobacco to Market in Virginia and North Carolina.
This method was first used in Virginia as far back as the seventeenth century.

Olmsted writes that "until within a recent period much tobacco has been brought to market from the remote districts of North Carolina and Virginia by a very crude method called 'rolling.'" (Fig. 51.) Large casks filled with tobacco were fitted with crudely-hewn fellies (forming enlarged hoops, as it were) held in place by pins driven into holes bored in the staves of the casks. A long rod was driven through the casks piercing the heads at their centers, thus forming the axle. To the axle were attached shafts. Motive power was supplied by a horse or two. If two, they were driven tandem. Small farmers often brought their own tobacco to market this way; "but

* Frederick Olmsted, *A Journey in the Seaboard Slave States*, 358, 359.

there were also a set of men who made it their principal occupation, and whose calling was that of 'tobacco-rollers.' " They usually traveled in caravans and kept the country through which they passed in a high state of alarm, for they were a "hard set." They were treated with "respect and consideration . . . by all discrete people for a quarrel of one was made that of the whole body."*

As travel increased in volume, stage lines were introduced, and in all the moderately settled areas stage lines radiated out from every sizable city and town and connected all the larger cities. Stage lines competed with river boats (in those sections where rivers were used) as automobile bus lines now compete with railroads. As an example, the *Tennessee Gazetteer*, issued in 1834, lists twenty-five stage lines out of Nashville, to Louisville, Lexington, Memphis, Natchez, New Orleans, and Knoxville, and most of the county seats of middle Tennessee.†

We generally associate the "pony express," devised to speed up the movement of the mail, with the West. The English traveler Buckingham who visited the South in 1839 describes an attempt to establish a pony express in the South, but predicted that it would be abandoned soon because the expenses were greater than the returns. The route followed is not stated. About five hundred horses were used on a route between the East and New Orleans and were kept "in motion or in constant readiness for mounting." Boys were employed as riders, "each boy rides [riding] only twenty-four miles, twelve onward and twelve back." The speed maintained was about fourteen miles an hour, including stops.‡

Like other sections of the United States, the South was interested in plank roads. The movement began in the 1830's. Many writers extolled their advantages even as late as the 1850's, twenty years after the first railroad in South Carolina and Maryland.§

DECLINE AND REVIVAL OF INTEREST IN ROADS

The increasing number of steamboats on the inland waters up to the 1860's and the expansion of the railroad mileage drove many of the stage coaches and freight wagons off the roads. Certainly all long hauls and long journeys were by water or rail. To the effect of these improved means of transportation there must be added the demorali-

---

* *Ibid.*, 357-360.

† Morris, *Tennessee Gazetteer*, 123. One hundred or more years later one finds a network of autobuses traversing the same routes.

‡ J. S. Buckingham, *The Slave States of America*, I, 259.

§ *DeBow's Review*, XI, O. S., July, 1851, 63.

zation of industry, trade, and commerce, and poverty occasioned by the Civil War. The interest in highways declined, therefore, to be revived only in the late decades, and mainly only after the coming of the automobile.

In the nineties there was a revival of interest in roads, following a general revival in the North. Virginia held a good roads convention in 1894. In 1895 a roads convention was held at Houston, Texas, and in the same year a national roads parliament at Atlanta. This activity was probably stimulated by the establishment of the Federal Office of Public Roads in the Department of Agriculture at Washington in 1893. In the nineties several states organized state highway departments. Maryland, Virginia, West Virginia, North Carolina, and Georgia took the lead in the South.* All this occurred before the automobile was a practical vehicle for travel. Its development to its present efficiency and its widespread use is the one factor in the tremendous road-building program into which this country has entered in the last two or three decades. In 1904 state funds expended by or under state highway departments on rural roads in the United States amounted to $2,550,000. By 1916 the expenditures had reached $40,000,000; and in 1930, $1,140,000,000 was expended by the state highway departments, including Federal aid.† The Southern States in 1932 spent $283,000,000 of the total of $955,000,000 of the country.‡ The registered cars in our country advanced in number from 55,000 to 26,500,000 in the twenty-four-year period from 1904 to 1928.§ The South in 1935 had 6,133,000 registered motor vehicles out of a total of 26,221,000 for the country.¶

Road building was greatly stimulated by the adoption of the policy of building state highways rather than leaving road construction to the respective counties, and again by Federal participation.

The South, for a decade or two, did not keep pace with the other sections of the United States in the building of modern hard-surfaced roads, chiefly because it had fewer people, fewer automobiles, less wealth, and hence less need for roads than the more populous, wealthy, industrial sections in the North. Sections predominantly agricultural lack capital for public improvements. The South, with a total taxable

---

* Article on highways and improved roads in the South, 1865-1910, *Economic History*, VI, 1865-1909, 320, in The South in the Building of the Nation Series.

† *Statistical Abstract*, 1917, 282; 1934, 336.

‡ *Ibid.*, 1934, 336.

§ *Ibid.*, 385; 1934, 341.

¶ *Statistical Abstract*, 1936, 365. In 1937 the auto registrations numbered about 30,000,000.

wealth (in 1922, latest data) equivalent to 58.4 billion dollars, cannot be expected to make the contribution to public enterprises that
the North can with its 203.8 billion dollars of wealth; yet the states
of the agricultural South are keeping pace with, if not surpassing,
the agricultural states of the Middle West in road building. The West
North Central States (between the Mississippi River and the Rocky
Mountains) had in 1930 (latest data) 96,200 miles of rural "surfaced
roads," as compared with more than 96,500 miles in the South Atlantic
States and 73,400 in the East South Central. North Carolina has about
the same mileage as Illinois.*

Today one can travel from Cincinnati or Washington to the tip of
Florida by several routes without leaving asphalt or cement pave-
ment. And a journey on such roads may be made from Washington
to El Paso, or Brownsville, Texas.

---

* *Statistical Abstract,* 1930, 376, 377; 1932, 353; 1936, 358.

CHAPTER VI

THE WATERWAYS OF THE SOUTH

Under the term waterways will be considered bays, sounds, intra-coastal channels, riverways, and canals. In all new countries "the (natural) waterways are the intermediaries between the sea" and the interior. Such they were in America. The first landings of Europeans and first settlements were made on the shores of the indentations of the coast, and the rate of penetration of the interior was in direct relation to the navigability of the rivers. The St. Lawrence and the Mississippi led explorers hundreds of miles into the interior long before the headwaters of the Atlantic rivers were reached, largely because of the numerous shallows and rapids in the Piedmont sections of the latter and also the short courses of these rivers.

Of the three major sections into which we commonly divide our country, the North, the South, and the West (see Fig. 52), the South has by far the greatest mileage of waterways, whether we consider natural or improved waters. It has 1,158 miles of the Atlantic's 1,888 miles of "general coastline" and 1,686 miles on the Gulf, making 2,844 miles out of the 4,940 miles of coastline in our country. Federal Government improvements have provided channels of 30 feet or more at fourteen harbors and 25 feet at two additional ones along the Atlantic and Gulf coasts. Along both the Atlantic and Gulf coasts for most of the total length of 2,844 miles the Federal Government is now constructing an Intracoastal Waterway (most of which is in the South), lying for the most part just behind the barrier beaches and islands of the Atlantic and Gulf coasts. The same map shows the existing riverway project, i.e., sections of rivers that are being improved. The larger rivers of the Atlantic coast and East Gulf are being improved in general to the Fall Line. The Potomac and James are being made deep enough for coastwise or small ocean vessels as far inland as the Fall Line. The other rivers provide navigable channels only for river craft. The waterway of the East Gulf most used today is the Warrior-Tombigbee-Mobile that leads out from the Warrior coal field and by short lines of railroads to Birmingham connects that industrial city with deep water at Mobile.

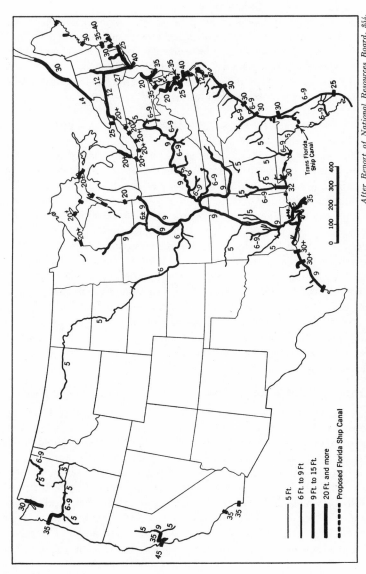

After Report of National Resources Board, 354.

FIG. 52.—Existing Waterways Projects in the United States, 1937.

The Trinity of Texas is the only Gulf river that has been used as a traffic route. Regular schedules on these rivers have never been maintained far from the Gulf waters.

The natural waterways, that have at one time or another been utilized for transportation, have a far greater mileage than that of the "existing projects;" for before railroads and roads were provided stern necessity drove man to utilize shallow bays and sounds and rivers, the latter often during the flood season, that today would be considered valueless as traffic ways.

1. THE RIVERWAYS—THE MISSISSIPPI AS A TYPE

The Mississippi and its tributaries form the greatest of all the river systems of North America and one of the great systems of the world. The Missouri-Mississippi from the Rocky Mountains to the Gulf is 4,200 miles long; and the Mississippi from Lake Itasca to the Gulf is 2,475 miles. There are some 15,000 miles of "natural navigable" (i.e., actually navigated by boats or rafts at some time) riverways within the Mississippi Basin, the main stream of the Mississippi in the South furnishing more than 1,000 miles of riverway, and the Ohio from Pittsburgh to Cairo, 979 miles. These projects have been completed. It may also be seen from Fig. 52 that there is projected a 9-foot waterway on the Tennessee to Knoxville. This is a part of the TVA project. Navigable riverways of lesser depths are being provided in Kentucky, Louisiana, and Arkansas, all a part of the great Mississippi System. We are interested here only in Southern rivers.

SEQUENT UTILIZATION OF THE MISSISSIPPI SYSTEM FOR COMMERCE

The story of the development, decline, and possible revival of commerce on the Mississippi River is in many ways not unlike that of many of the rivers of the United States. On this great inland water system, river commerce surpassed that in any other country of the globe. A certain glamour is associated with the Mississippi, particularly with its history in the middle of last century when it had reached its highest development, that has brought pride to all Americans who know its details (Figs. 53 and 54). The brilliancy of its accomplishment some eighty years ago, when we measured efficiency in transportation in terms of dirt road and horsedrawn vehicles, has blurred our vision to such an extent that we fail to see that new units of measurement have developed by which we should judge its present-day effectiveness.

White man's utilization of the Mississippi dates from the days of the fur trader, who carried into the Indian country a few dollars' worth of civilization's trinkets and returned with a canoe load of valuable furs, so much in demand in Europe. The fur traders' canoes were used on the Ohio before 1700.

The various types of river craft employed, roughly in chronological order of use, were the birch bark canoe and dugout, the raft and flatboat, the keelboat and barge, and lastly the power-driven boat. Many power boats are still used, but the latest models are quite unlike the craft that made transportation history between 1811, the date of the first steamboat, and the opening decades of the twentieth century. Most of the power boats of today are equipped with oil-burning steam engines or internal-combustion power units.

The canoe and dugout were not cargo carriers on a large scale. Of the other man-propelled craft, the only one that was much used for upstream traffic was the keelboat, the largest being 40 to 50 feet long and 7 to 10 feet wide. With much labor it was forced upstream by poling, "bushwhacking," or cordelling. It usually required from seventy to ninety days for the journey from New Orleans to Louisville.

It was the flatboat, cheaply built yet capacious, that carried the bulk of the downriver commerce until well into the middle of the nineteenth century. The flatboat utilized the cheapest of all forms of propulsion—the current of the river. And since many of the products could be marketed during the off-season on the farm (there was little danger of ice in the Ohio until late December, and none whatsoever on the Mississippi below Memphis), labor that was not otherwise occupied could be utilized.

In 1809 Nicholas Roosevelt made a trip down the Ohio and the Mississippi to investigate conditions for steamboat navigation as it was known on the Hudson. He took soundings, estimated the strength of current, secured data of changes of depth, and inquired into the fuel problem. It was his favorable recommendation that resulted in the building of the *New Orleans*, at Pittsburgh, and its trip in 1811, the first steamboat on the Mississippi. The *New Orleans* never returned to its launching place. Its boiler and engine were not able to cope with the strong currents of the Ohio and middle Mississippi. For many years it operated between New Orleans and Natchez where the low gradient of the Mississippi gave more favorable current conditions. But many more boats were built—the *Comet, Vesu-*

vius, Aetna, and others that "belched" fire.* Improvements in the river
boats were made gradually as experience was gained, and the competition became severe. The hull was broadened and the draft lessened,
until it was facetiously declared that an American river steamer
could "navigate in a heavy dew," or "sail wherever it was damp."†
With a hull of this shape the boats navigated *on* the water, not *in* it;
even the largest drew less than 30 inches of water. Along with these

From J. S. Buckingham, The Slave States of America. Vol. I, 1842, 475.

FIG. 53.—Loading an Alabama River Steamer at Night.

Not all landings were at high bluffs.

improvements came for several decades an ever-increasing number
of vessels (Figs. 53 and 54).

The rapid increase in the number of steamboats on the Mississippi
was coincident with the rapid increase in population of the Basin.
For the first time the Basin farmers had comparatively easy and
rapid contacts with markets.

The more *rapid* contacts were due to the increased efficiency of
the engines. In *The Log,* a publication of the Mississippi and Ohio
Rivers Pilots' Association, Percival S. Drown presents some interesting data on the "sailing time" between New Orleans and Louisville.

---

* *The Log,* a publication of the Mississippi and Ohio Rivers Pilots' Association,
113.

† Sir Charles Lyell, *A Second Visit to the United States,* II, 45.

In 1815 the steamer *Enterprise* made the upstream trip in 25 days and 2 hours.

In 1817 the *Shelby*		made the trip in 20 days,				5 hours			
" 1818 the *Paragon*	"	"	"	"	18	"	10	"		
" 1828 the *Tecumseh*	"	"	"	"	8	"	4	"		
" 1834 the *Tuscarora*	"	"	"	"	7	"	8	"		
" 1840 the *Edward Shippe*	"	"	"	"	5	"	18	"		
" 1852 the *Eclipse*	"	"	"	"	4	"	18	"		

The fastest time ever made up to the present for the regular packets was by the *Robert E. Lee* in the summer of 1870 on a trip from New Orleans to St. Louis. The distance, 1,200 miles, was covered in 3 days,

From Edward King, The Great South, 1874, 257.

FIG. 54.—One of the Larger and Faster Steamers on the Mississippi in the 1860's and 1870's.

This type of carrying agent has within the last decade or more been displaced by modern freight carriers. The passenger business is at a very low ebb.

18 hours, and 14 minutes.* The downstream journey of the steamboats was usually made in half the time consumed in steaming upstream.†

There were but 14 registered steamboats on the Mississippi and its tributaries in 1815. In 1820 the number was 72, and by 1826, about

---

* *The Log,* publication of the Mississippi and Ohio Rivers Pilots' Association, 114.

† Frederick Von Rammer, *America and the American People,* 1846, 171; Lyell, *loc. cit.*

95. About this time boat building was given a great impetus by the decision of the United States Supreme Court that the rivers of America were the people's heritage, and that no state or company could hold a monopoly on transportation on them. Fulton and Livingston had secured the exclusive right from several states to use steamboats on their rivers. The Supreme Court decision opened the natural waterways of our country to free competition.*

By 1842 the number of steamers had increased to 450, and there were in competition with those "modern" carriers 4,000 flatboats. It was estimated that some six or seven million people were dependent on the rivers for transportation and 20,000 men found employment on the river carriers.†

The high tide in steamboat traffic on the Mississippi was from about 1847 to about 1860. There were 1,200 steamers registered in 1847, with a total vessel tonnage of 3,250,000 and valued at $16,000,000. Some 40,000 men were employed in river transportation.‡

Some data on steamboat arrivals at New Orleans and receipt of tons of freight for the few selected dates will give an idea of the rapid increase in commerce.

TABLE I

RIVER TRADE AT NEW ORLEANS, 1815–1860[1]

Year	Arrivals	Freight in Tons
1813–1814	21	67,560
1833–1834	1081	327,800
1852–1853	3052	1,328,800
1859–1860	3566	2,187,560

[1] G. S. Callender, *Economic History of United States*, 315; see also J. S. Buckingham, *The Slave States of America*, I, 461, for list of products shipped on the Mississippi; and *Census Report* for 1860, "Agriculture," p. clv, for discussion of grain trade. Also see *Debow's Review*, XVII, O.S., November 1854, 531.

The economic benefits of steam navigation to the country as a whole were enormous. They reduced the cost of transportation and accelerated the rate of movement. Every commodity entering into the regular channels of commerce was affected, and every citizen who purchased or sold commercial commodities was benefited. A reduction of even 1, 2, or 5 per cent in the price of staple articles, like flour, corn, sugar, clothing, and what not, because of cheaper transportation, is a material saving to both the producer and the consumer. As for merchants, their returns were greater, for their "turn

* *Report of Tenth Census, 1880*, "Agencies of Transportation," IV, 671.

† *The American Almanac*, 1849, 220; McMaster, *op. cit.*, VIII, 228; *Hunt's Merchants Magazine*, V (1841), 470; *Ibid.*, IX, 156.

‡ Appleton's *Traveler's Guide*, Part II, 35, 36.

over" was more rapid because of the more rapid movement of commodities and the greater purchasing power and greater buying ability of the customers. Moreover, they were not obliged to carry so large a stock as formerly and thus had less capital involved. The steamboat brought a large part of the commercial products of the Mississippi Basin into national and, to some degree, even into world commercial channels. There was a rapid increase in wealth because of the tremendous increase in the variety, the amount, and value of products offered for sale. Products that formerly were looked upon as worthless or considered "free goods" became of value and contributed their share to the wealth of the producer.

The stimulus given to westward migration increased the demand for land, raised its value (in some sections to a speculative figure), hastened the removal of the East Gulf Indians, and quickened Transmississippi migration. The Oregon Country and California were settled and annexed to the Union about the time of the "golden era" of the Mississippi River steamboat. But there came a time when it was eclipsed and finally practically eliminated.

THE DECLINE OF RIVER TRANSPORTATION

The mechanical genius of man created another steam carrying agent, the railroad, which did for land transportation what the steamboat had done for water transportation—and even more, for the steamboat was restricted in its realm to certain narrow channels, to reach which man had often to make long land journeys over unimproved roads. The railroad finds its realm everywhere on land, lowland plains, plateaus, and even in mountain areas; causeways, trestles, and bridges carry it across rivers, bays, shallow lakes, and even over the borders of the sea. It was the railroad that was by far the chief factor in the decline of the river steamboat. In the struggle between the railroad and the steamboat, victory was not always the result of honest legitimate competition. Yet the dominance of the railroad was, on the whole, due to its superiority. When and where the tonnage of commodities for transport was large enough for only one type of transporting agent the railroad took precedence.

The causes of the decline on the Mississippi, which is used as a type, were many. Most of these same causes persist today to check the revival of inland waterway traffic on the rivers. We list a few in brief.

1. The connected waterways of the Mississippi Basin were not unified as to depth. Only shallow-draught boats could be used on the

smaller streams, and those could not operate economically on the large streams in competition with the larger boats. To transship commodities *en route* from small streams to large proved too expensive.

2. The channel was (and is) ever-changing, changing in depth, in location even, in location of bars and snags, in location of landing points. All these have elements of danger that increase insurance rates.

3. The Mississippi, after the coming of the railroad, which directed traffic in northern United States along an east-west line, cut across the country's major continental traffic routes that came to be developed. See a fuller discussion in Chapter XVII.

4. The area served by riverways was limited to about twenty-five to fifty miles on either side of the channel.

5. The supply of freight along the Mississippi was seasonal, for the river traversed an agricultural country whose products sought markets for the most part only in the fall and early winter.

6. The river steamer was a generalized type. It reached its perfection early. Complete adjustment was attained, and further improvement of the generalized types was apparently not possible; certainly improvements were not made.

7. The steamboat was slow and unreliable. Losses of steamers and cargoes were frequent. The loss on the Mississippi alone in 1855 was 111; and the loss of life, 107.*

8. The terminal facilities were inadequate; all freight was handled by hand or by man-pushed trucks. Warehouses were few. Commodities left in the open were subject to damage from the weather, or to theft, and sometimes to destruction by floods.

The railroads, which can be built almost anywhere and can send branch lines to forests in mountain coves, to mines, and to factory doors without greatly interfering with the free movement of other means of transportation as canals do, were better able to meet the demands of a country advancing rapidly in population, production, consumption, and wealth. Steamboats belong to the slow-going life of the early and middle nineteenth century.

The decline of transportation on most of the other rivers of the South was due to many of the causes ascribed to the decline on the Mississippi. The decline set in earlier on some of the eastern rivers than on the Mississippi, for it was on the Atlantic Seaboard, North and South, that the earliest railroads were constructed. All enterprising Atlantic coast cities, seeing the tremendous economic potentialities of

---

* Quoted from the *Louisville Courier* in *Hunt's Merchants Magazine*, XXXIV, 1856, 369.

the great Mississippi Basin in striking contrast to the limited possibilities of the narrow strip of land that lies between the Appalachian
Highlands and the sea, hastened to establish commercial relations
with it. Boston, New York, Philadelphia, Baltimore, Richmond,
Charleston, and Savannah dreamed first of canals, then later of railroads to tap the great Transappalachian area and draw off its products
eastward—away from the New Orleans markets. Only one of the
cities, New York, was successful in diverting traffic by canal; all were
successful with the railroad, but not to the same degree.

A Recent Revival of Interest in Riverways

In the last two or three decades there has arisen a new interest in
the riverways of our country, stimulated in the beginning as one phase
of the conservation movement for which President Theodore Roosevelt did so much. No doubt the glorious part played by our riverways in the nineteenth century, their inglorious decline, and the
feeling that this decline was the result of unfair competition with the
railroad and a general lack of appreciation of the shortcomings of
waterways and steamboats induced President Roosevelt to appoint the
Inland Waterways Commission on March 14, 1907. A memorable trip
down the Mississippi was made by the Commission in May, 1907
(ninety-eight years after Nicholas Roosevelt had investigated the
possibilities of steamboats navigating this river), and out of this trip
grew the White House Conference (of governors, publicists, and business men, jurists, congressmen, and scientists) which convened May
23, 1908. At this conference there were presented many notable papers
on all phases of conservations. Some emphasized the necessity of Federal support for improvement of the waterways. For the first time
in many decades the people all over the country had their attention
drawn to waterways problems.

Public interest in riverways, as in other phases of conservation, however, waned in the two decades or more following the White House
Conference. Only here and there has there been an organization interested in reviving "the glorious days" of the past. It was the Federal
Government during the World War that made the initial move in what
to some is a new era in inland navigation.

In 1916 Congress authorized the President of the United States to
take over the operation of the railroads of the country as a war
measure. W. G. McAdoo was appointed Director General. With a view
to utilizing all transportation facilities of the country, a committee
was appointed to study the possibilities of reviving or increasing

commerce on its inland rivers, canals, and coastwise waterways. The report of this committee resulted in Congress providing for a fleet of modern river carriers on the Lower Mississippi, the initial cost being about $8,200,000, and a fleet on the Warrior River, which runs southward from the coal fields and some twenty miles from the steel mills of the Birmingham district, at a cost of $3,000,000. The fleet was known as the Mississippi-Warrior River Barge Line (also the Federal Barge Line). It is operated by the Inland Waterways Corporation.

A. E. P.

FIG. 55.—The Inland Waterways Corporation's Terminal at St. Louis, 1935.

Railroad and river barge are coordinated closely and every improvement needed for handling the sorts of freight that pass over the docks (or wharves) are provided. The barges are of steel. Freight is handled through openings in the "roof."

From time to time other appropriations were made by Congress for equipment. The total investment of the IWC in real property and equipment as of December 31, 1934, was $23,461,000.* Government assistance is being furnished with the idea of stimulating private participation in a revival of shipping by private companies.

A few private corporations (mainly large steel companies and oil companies) have become interested. Improved types of barges and tugboats have been devised. Up-to-date terminals at the large cities and at scores of landing places along the routes traversed have been provided (Fig. 55). In 1929 the Interstate Commerce Commission ordered the railroads with connection at river ports touched by the

---

* *Report of Inland Waterways Corporation*, 1934, 22.

Federal barge line "to establish barge-rail and rail-barge rates and routes." In general the rates are arbitrarily set at 20 per cent less than the all-rail rates between the points affected. In fixing the barge rate no attempt was made to determine the actual cost of riverway versus railway transportation *to the people*. The Federal Government provides the carrying agents, no interest is charged on the money invested, and no taxes are paid on the property. But little success has come from all these efforts. The task is not an easy one. Whereas in the early nineteenth century the efficiency of the old-type steamboat was measured in terms of horse-drawn wagons and the flatboat, the modern water carrier has to compete with the American railroad, the most efficient in the world, whose high attainment is the result of some six or seven decades of engineering endeavor; and in addition, in the last decade, there is the automobile truck, which has reduced, by an appreciable percentage, the traffic that the railroad and river boats might otherwise have got.

The revival of interest in waterways, just sketched, is both the result and the cause of a new movement so to improve the channels of our riverways as to fit them better to meet the demands of larger carrying agents. The existing projects designed to fit the waterways for modern transportation, as shown in Fig. 52, have already been referred to.

The Feasibility of Riverway Improvements

How are we to judge of the feasibility of improvements on riverways? Should we be satisfied with a comparison of the posted rates of boat lines and the rates charged by the railroads? Should we accept the statements of secretaries of chambers of commerce, leaders in waterways associations, or even army engineers, all of whom fail to include in their reckoning the actual cost of river transportation to the public? Or should we, in determining relative cost of transportation, put riverways and railways on a truly comparative financial basis?

The public, it should be understood, *pays the entire transportation bill whether by water or by rail, by automobile truck or by air*. When it pays the railroad bill it pays interest on capital investment (watered stock included) in the right-of-way, roadbed, depots, repair shops, and rolling stock. It pays salaries of the officials, attorneys' fees, the cost of operation, taxes on railroad property, and maintenance. Provision is usually made in business enterprises for replacement or amortization of capital investment. All these charges are reflected, over a course of years, in the freight rates charged the public.

When a shipper by water pays his freight bill he, as a shipper, pays or helps to pay, the interest on the capital investment in the boat or boats, the cost of operating the boat (which includes taxes), plus a profit to the boat line. Often the wharves, where there are such, are provided by municipalities. The taxpayers of the United States, in general, provide the improved waterway and provide its maintenance, and, as we have seen in the discussion of the IWC, provide the boats, on which no taxes are paid. Posted boat-line rates are generally lower than posted railroad rates. The shippers by boat, therefore, are bene-fited. So are the boat lines that operate over a right-of-way provided by the public. But what of the public? In determining the actual cost *to the public* of transportation by waterways, to the moneys paid the boat lines there must be added the interest on the cost of river improvements, a certain percentage of their cost for amortization of the capital investment, and also the annual maintenance costs. Let us consider first the Ohio. Up to June 30, 1934, the Federal Government had spent $149,400,000 (including maintenance) for the 979.3 miles of waterway between Pittsburgh and the river's mouth near Cairo. The annual cost of maintenance is more than $2,000,000.*

The public's contribution, annually is as follows:

Maintenance.............................	$ 2,000,000
Interest on investment at 4 per cent..........	5,976,000
Annual amortization (50-year serial bonds)....	2,988,000
Taxes (rate paid by railroads)..............	2,988,000
Total.................................	$13,952,000

This is equivalent to 0.88 of a cent for each ton-mile of freight moved (1,700,000,000 in 1933). The ton-mile rate charged by the common carriers on some sections of the river is 0.8 of a cent. The real freight costs, by water, therefore, are 1.68 cents for a ton-mile. The railroad rate in the Eastern District of the United States is 1.08 cents and, for the Southern, only 0.89 cent. Which is cheaper *to the public*, the Ohio waterway or a parallel railway?

The Ohio is the best located of America's long rivers, to attract water traffic. It heads in the greatest iron and steel center in America, one of the greatest in the world, and also the greatest coal-mining section of the world. On its banks are numerous cities engaged in producing heavy manufactures—Pittsburgh, Cincinnati, Covington,

---

* Data compiled from *Report of Chief of Engineers*, U. S. Army, 1934, 923-925.

and Louisville, each with its satellite industrial towns, and also Wheeling, Huntington, and Evansville. It leads westward to such distribution centers as St. Louis, and westward and southward to Memphis and New Orleans. Yet the Ohio River improvements, so far, cannot be considered feasible. In fact, *freight moved on the Ohio River during the year closing June 30, 1934, actually cost the public $7,500,000 to $10,500,000 more than if the railroads had handled it and the public had paid the railroad freight bill.* If the flow of commerce were in the future to be trebled, the cost per ton-mile to the public would approach that by rail. Will it ever come to carry three times the present tonnage in the face of increasing railroad and truck traffic and especially the latter?

If the admirably located Ohio makes such a poor showing when compared with the railroad what should one expect of the Tennessee? Will the huge sums proposed, $75,000,000 for navigation alone, as given in the *Report of Chief of Engineers,* 1934,* for river improvement on this waterway prove a paying investment *to the country as a whole?* The Tennessee Valley has a much smaller population than the Ohio, far fewer cities, no large cities like Pittsburgh, Cincinnati, and Louisville, very few heavy industries, the kind that do utilize to some degree the riverways; in fact very few factories of any sort in comparison with the Ohio. (See Fig. 7 for map of the Tennessee Valley.) The Tennessee River will never function as does (and has) the Ohio as a transporter of coal. In visualizing the commerce that may flow along any route one must remember that there must be something more than "the way"; there must exist economic-geographic conditions that lead to the exchange of products.

So far in this brief discussion of the future of the Tennessee we have considered only the intravalley commerce. How will the river function in commerce moving in and out of the valley? First of all, its course is indirect, as crooked as a fishhook; that of the Ohio is fairly direct. And still another condition—the Valley of East Tennessee, which is the real heart of the Tennessee Valley, already has its traffic lines established across the valley boundaries. And these are by land, and far shorter than by water. From Knoxville to New Orleans by river is about 1,800 miles, by land 730; to Cincinnati by river, 1,160 miles, by land 300. Freight by water travels 4 miles an hour upstream on the average and 8 downstream and these rates cannot be increased greatly except at tremendous cost in power. By automobile truck or railroad, the rate of movement is 30 to 40 or more miles an

---

* See also *House Document,* 71st Congress, 2nd Session, Part 1, 1930, 325.

hour and can be speeded up. Roads cost less than half as much per mile as the Tennessee waterway and are open to the much-used private and common carrier, the automobile truck. Waterways are no longer the "democratic type" of transportation. Money spent on them is a subsidy to a few boat lines and great industrial corporations owning fleets to move their own products. The savings, if any, are not passed on to the consumer. One must be a blind TVA "patriot," indeed, to see any future for the Tennessee as an important artery for commerce. And yet the navigation of the Tennessee is the corner stone of the river development—hydroelectric power, navigation, and flood control—of the TVA! The building of dams for navigation is the excuse (as presented before the Supreme Court) for the Federal Government developing and distributing hydroelectric power.

Data similar to those used in judging the feasibility of river transportation on the Ohio are not available for the Mississippi. We do not know how much of the total cost for navigation and flood control on the section between Cairo and New Orleans should be assigned to navigation; nor are data available on the ton-mile of freight moved between these two. The busiest section of the Mississippi is that between Vicksburg and New Orleans, the combined upbound and downbound traffic being 8,583,000 tons in 1932. About one-half of this tonnage is petroleum and its products. Between Cairo and Memphis the commerce is less than half that of this most actively used section. The present-day Mississippi from Cairo to New Orleans is a very lonesome river when compared with the activity of the 1840's and 1850's. In fact, none of the riverways of the South is much used. The more the appropriations for river improvement the less the commerce, not because of the improvements but because river transportation on most of our riverways does not form a part of the modern transportation pattern.

A Riverways Policy Needed

And what is the conclusion to the whole matter? We need a riverways commission composed of experienced, trained men, not politicians and office seekers who promise to peddle Federal money for votes, not business men whose interests would be enhanced by river improvements, not local boosters whose horizons are bounded by their own city and its trade territory; but men who will study the problem from every angle and form unbiased, non-traditional judgments. The present and possible future commerce of a stream should take precedence in shaping judgments over its activity in the "glorious" past. Each stream must be considered on its own merits, its location, its

coordination with others. Because the one and three-quarters billion
dollars spent on harbors and rivers have saved us annually $600,000,-
000 in freight costs, a return 230 per cent (as has been claimed)
offers no excuse for squandering money on a Trinity, a Cumberland,
a Tennessee, or a Cape Fear project. Such a commission should try
to establish the practicable and non-practicable relationships of expenditure for improvement and commerce handled, on the one hand,
and the possible saving in freight on the other. The cost of maintenance should always be considered. We need the truth about our
waterways, truth determined by unbiased, honest, experienced investigators. Then we need Congressmen who will accept the truth and
act accordingly, instead of listening to some waterways development
organization which has votes to offer for Federal money. And lastly
we want an informed militant public which will think enough about
the money it spends for transportation to see that it is spent on the
form that will give it the largest returns.

2. CANALS AND THE INTRACOASTAL WATERWAY IN THE SOUTH*

a. CANALS

The oldest canal in the South is the Dismal Swamp Canal (begun
in 1787). It was excavated to connect Chesapeake Bay with Albemarle
Sound and thus give water outlet for the settlements on the sounds
and connecting rivers in eastern North Carolina. This route has now
become a Federal waterway from Norfolk, Virginia, to the sounds of
North Carolina, the purchase having been approved by Congress
March 3, 1899.†

Since 1913 there has been a decline in the amount of traffic along
the Dismal Swamp Canal. The hard-surfaced roads of North Carolina
and Virginia and the decline in timber supply are no doubt the chief
factors in the lower tonnage. The canal serves only a small area and
even without competition could not be expected to carry much tonnage; besides it has a rival, the Chesapeake-Albemarle Canal, a link
in the Intracoastal Waterway.

---

* The *American Almanac* for 1830 lists 22 canals, "finished, in progress, or in
immediate contemplation in the United States." Only two were in the South, the
Chesapeake and Delaware and the Chesapeake and Ohio. The Dismal Swamp
Canal was omitted from the list. Data taken from *Yeoman's Gazette,* quoted in
the *American Almanac,* 1833, 223-224.

† *House Document* 317, 54th Congress, 1st Session; *House Document* 131, 55th
Congress, 3rd Session; Joseph Martin, *A New and Comprehensive Gazetteer of
Virginia,* 1835, 91; *Report of Tenth Census,* 1880, "Agencies of Transportation,"
749.

The Chesapeake and Ohio Canal, which was designed to connect Chesapeake Bay with the Ohio River, but which never succeeded in getting any farther than Cumberland, Maryland, at the foot of the Allegheny Front, was Baltimore's attempt to draw to her marts the rich commerce of the Transappalachian Region. Boston, New York, Philadelphia, Baltimore, Richmond, Charleston, and other cities on the Atlantic Seaboard, as well as New Orleans on the Gulf, were

From J. S. Buckingham, Vol. II, 412.

Fɪɢ. 56.—The James River and Canal near Richmond, Virginia, about 1840.

The Piedmont section of the James River was not navigable in its natural state. Richmond profited much from contacts with a large productive hinterland made possible by the James River Canal, whose western terminus was near Buchannan in the Great Valley.

in active competition for this western commerce. Before the Chesapeake and Ohio Canal was completed to Cumberland, the Baltimore and Ohio Railroad was receiving the attention of Baltimore people and interest waned in the canal.* Finally the railroad purchased the canal property and later abandoned the canal.

The James River and Kanawha Canal and Railroad were Richmond's attempt to reach the Ohio. (See Fig. 56.) As originally planned the James and Kanawha rivers were to be utilized as much as possible, canalized here and there where necessary, and the gap between the

---

* *Report of Tenth Census,* 1880, "Agencies of Transportation," **745**; A. E. Parkins, "Development of Transportation in Pennsylvania," *Bulletin Geographical Society of Philadelphia,* XV, 4.

navigable portions bridged by a canal or railroad, or both. But the actual canal was completed no farther than Buchannan in the Great Valley, a topographic location almost identical with that of Cumberland, Maryland.* This canal, like all others that attempted to scale the Appalachian barrier, is little more than an item in the history of man's attempt to solve the great problem of overcoming the unequal distribution of nature's resources and the products of human industry. It was an experiment that failed. It was a failure almost before it was completed, for a new and more efficient device, the railroad, was developed. The Richmond and Allegheny Railroad acquired all the property of the canal company April 4, 1880, and some time after abandoned the waterway.†

Farther south there was a short canal in South Carolina, the Cooper River-Santee Canal, that connected the harbor of Charleston with the Santee River. The Cooper and Ashley rivers that debouch into Charleston's harbor are only short streams. The Santee Canal was a link in the waterways that connected Charleston with Columbia. Improvements were also made on the Catawbee-Wateree to give barge navigation to the outer borders of the Piedmont. All these artificial waterways were soon abandoned and so also was the Brunswick Canal in southeastern Georgia. In 1850 the South had 1,116 miles of canals; the entire country 4,162.‡

b. THE INTRACOASTAL WATERWAY

The Atlantic section from Massachusetts Bay to the tip of Florida, largely completed in 1937, utilizes the numerous bays, sounds, estuaries, lagoons, and rivers of the Atlantic Coast. The utilization of this series of waters, more or less connected, has long been a dream of man. In the early days when capes Cod, Hatteras, Fear, and other coastal barriers were more of a nightmare to the coastwise navigators than today, the idea was born. The report of the Secretary of the

---

* H. S. Tanner, *Canals and Railroads of the United States,* 1840, 160, 161; Joseph Martin, *A New and Comprehensive Gazetteer of Virginia,* 1833, 90; Jedediah Morse, *American Gazetteer,* 1797, 144; Worcester's *Gazetteer of the United States,* under topic Richmond; Hugh Murry, *Encyclopedia of Geography,* III, 521; *Historical Register,* III, 1814, 255.

† *Report of Tenth Census,* 1880, "Transportation," 31.

‡ *Compendium of Seventh Census,* 1854, 189; J. S. Buckingham, *The Slave States of America,* I, 44; Hugh Murry, *Encyclopedia of Geography,* III, 533; *Report of Seventh Census,* 1880, "Transportation," 31; H. S. Tanner, *Canals and Railroads of the United States,* 1840, 171.

Treasury on Roads and Canals in 1807* describes a "tidewater inland" waterway from Maine to Florida. In 1807 the following canals were completed or under construction: Weymouth to Taunton 26 miles, Brunswick to Trenton 28 miles, Delaware River to Chesapeake Bay, 22 miles (work at standstill because of lack of funds), and finally from Chesapeake Bay to Albemarle Sound (Dismal Swamp Canal) 22 miles. Monroe in his message to Congress suggested the further development of the route. We are interested here in the sections south of Delaware Bay.

A. E. P.

Fig. 57.—The Chesapeake and Delaware Canal in Maryland, 1936.

This is one of the links in the Intracoastal Waterway. The government has recently made improvements to fit it to carry a heavier traffic.

The Chesapeake and Delaware Canal was completed in 1829 at a cost of $2,750,000.† The engineers laid out the route so as to take advantage of drowned creeks, ravines, and marshes. Thus excavation was necessary in only 13.63 miles of the route and this in unconsolidated rock of the Coastal Plain. Two lift and two tide locks were provided.‡ Until the purchase of this canal by the United States Government in 1919 for $2,514,000, the navigable depth was 10 feet. Since then it has been enlarged to a sea-level canal, 10 feet deep

---

* *Historical Register*, III, 1814, 240.

† *Report of Chief of Engineers*, U. S. Army, 1928, 408 gives $2,250,000. Gallatin's proposal may be found in his report of 1807 in *American State Papers Miscellaneous*, I, 914, 915; *Historical Register*, III, 1814, 244.

‡ H. S. Tanner, *Canals and Railroads of the United States*, 1840, 148.

(controlling depth) and 90 feet wide at the narrowest points (Fig. 57).*

That the canal is of value to Baltimore, Wilmington, Philadelphia, and the smaller cities of the section has been well proved by the large amount of traffic it carries. New vessels are being constructed to operate between these cities through the canal, and freight rates have been reduced. Since the new enlarged waterway is on the border of a great

A. E. P.

FIG. 58.—The Intracoastal Waterway at Delray, Florida.

Behind the beach ridge along almost the entire eastern coast of Florida there is a lagoon which with very little dredging is made suitable for small shallow draught crafts.

The Intracoastal Waterway serves its greatest purpose as a route for the small pleasure craft that migrate between the large cities of the East and the winter resorts of Florida. It has no value as a through-traffic route.

industrial region whose factories call for the movement of vast quantities of heavy bulky materials, it will certainly become one of the better used waterways of our country. It materially shortens the distance between Baltimore and Philadelphia. The value of commerce in this canal in 1931 was $51,000,000.†

Chesapeake Bay, with its numerous tributary estuaries, is an extensive waterway that carries an immense overseas as well as a large domestic commerce. Excavation has been necessary in a few sections to accommodate ocean-going vessels. The bay is a link in the Intracoastal Waterway.

From Chesapeake Bay southward to Miami, the Intracoastal Canal

---

* Report of Chief of Engineers, U. S. Army, 1934, 245.

† Report of Chief of Engineers, U. S. Army, 1932, Part 2, 309.

follows, for the most part, the sounds and lagoons that lie behind the barrier beaches and islands (Fig. 58).

As a route for the movement of freight, ships on the Intracoastal Waterway cannot compete with coastwise vessels. The movement of freight is largely local. The waterway is of some recreational value for fishermen and for pleasure craft migration between Northeastern cities and the resorts of the subtropical South.

The Southern Louisiana and Texas Coastal Waterway is intended to furnish shippers a protected route from New Orleans to Corpus Christi.

The Louisiana section of the Gulf Coastal Waterway is proving beneficial to that portion of the state accessible to it. It has been estimated that a fourth of the food consumed by the 400,000 people of New Orleans is brought to the city by some 2,000 motorboats operating nearly every day of the year on the various waterways of Louisiana, the Coastal Waterway and the bayous, whose total length, including the Sabine and the Mississippi on the state borders, measures about 4,800 miles.

The Proposed Florida Canal

One cannot yet predict the future of the Transflorida 200-mile ship canal which was begun in September, 1936, as a PWA project. The army engineers late in 1936 pronounced the project feasible from an engineering standpoint, which, as we have seen in our appraisal of riverway improvements, does not always mean that it is certain to be a paying venture from the taxpayers' standpoint. The state of Florida is "split wide open," to use the expression of one newspaper, over the project. Jacksonville is actively supporting it; Tampa and Miami and the farmers in the section to be traversed are working against the plan. Army engineers have set the construction costs at $162,-000,000; others say that they will be more than twice this amount. Certainly the saving in time will not be great, for vessels in the canal will be forced to cut their speed to at least half that in the open ocean. Moreover, insurance rates on ships and cargoes will be higher than on the high seas, and pilot charges will add to the cost of freight movement; freedom of movement on the land will be reduced unless a bridge is provided on every road crossing the canal. Property boundary lines will need much adjusting. The water table of the land will be lowered naturally along a large part of the route for a considerable distance back from the canal. Along some sections of the route, market gardening and fruit growing must, as a consequence, be abandoned.

3. IMPROVEMENTS TO HARBORS

The entire coastline of the South has been drowned, making estuaries at the mouths of rivers, some of which are large enough to be called bays and sounds. All these coastal waters are shallow. (See Chapter II as to origin of the harbors of the South.) A few of these will be discussed.

Baltimore is on the Patapsco River at the Fall Line, the head of navigation. The portion of the river that carries commerce leads southeastward from the city. Here the width of the Patapsco estuary is from one-half to three miles.

In its original condition a depth of 17 feet at low tide and 18 at high was available for navigation. The larger vessels with cargoes for Baltimore were obliged to lighten a portion of their cargo some 14 miles from city wharves. Since 1836, at long intervals, improvement work has been carried on. The existing project calls for a main channel 35-37 feet deep, from the 35-foot channel (natural) in Chesapeake Bay to most of the wharves in the capacious harbor, the developed water front measuring about 23 miles.

The Federal Government is not called upon to furnish all the improvements desired. In the past Baltimore and the state of Maryland expended $350,000 on the Patapsco River, and the city is now expending $12,000,000 in improving the inner harbor, of which $9,200,-000 is for municipal docks, wharves, bulk heads, and marginal streets, and $2,800,000 for dredging. The city has been authorized to bond itself for $50,000,000 more for port development. The improvements even now are extensive; the addition will give Baltimore a modern harbor. Baltimore harbor handles from $750,000,000 to nearly $1,000,-000,000 worth of commerce each year. Certainly city, state, and Federal expenditures are justifiable.*

Another extensive project in Chesapeake Bay is being carried out to provide a 25-foot channel from Hampton Roads, where there is a depth of 40 feet, to the mouth of the South Branch of the Elizabeth River, about 15.5 miles. There is to be a 40-foot channel 750 feet wide for a part of the distance. This gives ocean vessels access to the wharves of Norfolk and Portsmouth. The Lower Chesapeake ports, Norfolk, Portsmouth, and Newport News, are certain to develop into very important shipping centers, since they are the termini of several

---

* *Report of Chief of Engineers*, U. S. Army, 1928, 4, 39, 446; 1929, 434, 441; 1934, 274-277; Part 2, 8; *The Port of Baltimore, Maryland*, Port Series 16, Part 1, 1933, U. S. Shipping Board; Personal observation.

railroads leading out of the Appalachian coal fields. Hampton Roads is the home anchorage for many of the largest dreadnaughts and other craft of the North Atlantic fleet.* Norfolk handled more than $500,000,000 worth of commodities in 1933, and the value of the total commerce of Hampton Roads that year was $591,000,000.

Space will permit the discussion of only two other ports of the South, New Orleans and Houston. In tonnage of waterbound commerce, both Port Arthur and Beaumont exceed New Orleans but they handle little more than petroleum and its products.

New Orleans is more than a hundred miles up the Mississippi from the Gulf or some 95 miles above the Head of the Passes. The passes are the distributaries at the mouth, five in number, through which the immense volume of water of the Mississippi discharges into the Gulf. The South and Southwest passes only have been improved by the Federal Government for ocean traffic.

Engineering work at the mouth of the Mississippi to maintain navigable depths for deep-draft, ocean-going vessels is the most exacting of any to be found in the world. The first attempt to provide a deep-water channel in Southwest Pass was undertaken in 1833. Other improvements were made about 1837, 1856, and 1873.

Improvements in South Pass were first undertaken by James B. Eads and associates, under authorization of the River and Harbor Act of 1875, subsequently modified in 1878 and 1879. The principles of deposition control worked out by him and put into practice here have been consistently followed since, not only in this pass but in Southwest Pass, and at the entrance to many other harbors where conditions are similar.

By means of jetties of concrete and rip rap on a substructure of brush mattresses, the lower two miles of the pass were constricted in cross section. The water is thereby increased in velocity (as in the nozzle of a hose) and, instead of depositing sediment at the mouth of the distributary, carries it farther on into the Gulf. Eads' work cost the government $8,000,000 and, since the completion of the original project, $150,000 a year has been spent on maintenance.† The perfect control of the sands in the channels leading from the main stream into both the South Pass and the Southwest Pass, and the distribution of the waters to provide proper depths for navigation, are still un-

---

* *Ibid.*, 1934, 314; Part 2, 9. *The Ports of Norfolk, Portsmouth, and Newport News, Virginia,* Port Series 15, 1927, U. S. Shipping Board, 1-67; Personal observation.

† *Ibid.*, 1929, 880, 885.

solved problems and were being investigated, as the author observed, at the Waterways Laboratory at Vicksburg in April, 1934.

South Pass, being the more direct channel for vessels to and from the Atlantic, carries 70 per cent (4,679 vessels annually or about 14 each day) of the traffic. The total expenditures on Southwest Pass (up to the close of 1928) were more than $20,000,000. The value of foreign imports and exports passing through the passes in 1933 was $210,000,000.*

The depth of water and width of channel in the 95 miles of river between the city and the Head of the Passes are far greater than in the passes. Dredging is not necessary. Berthing space within the city limits is large—14 miles on the east bank, 12 on the west. The wharfage has been lengthened greatly by the construction of the Inner Harbor Navigation Canal, about 6 miles long, from the river to Lake Pontchartrain. A lock at the river end of the canal permits the movement of vessels at any stage of water in the river and controls the flow of water through the canal. Port facilities which rank well with the best ports in the world are under the auspices and control of both the city and the state. The value of the foreign and domestic commerce handled at New Orleans in 1933 was $519,000,000. The city is the meeting point of navigable waterways for shallow-draft boats and of course the great Mississippi itself.†

In recent years the port of Houston has gradually drawn to its wharves the exports and imports that formerly were credited to Galveston. Its tonnage of water-borne commerce in 1935 was nearly eight times that of Galveston. Houston is fifteen to twenty miles west of the northern end of Galveston Bay. The project to provide a waterway for ocean vessels from the Gulf called for a canal 50 miles long and 30 feet deep at mean low water, 250 feet wide across Galveston Bay, and 150 feet wide in the section between the Bay and the turning basin near the eastern city limits. The turning basin is about 1,000 feet wide. There is also a light-draft channel 7 miles long from the turning basin to Main Street. A dike more than 5 miles long in upper Galveston Bay will offer protection to passing vessels that might be affected by strong winds across the broad open bay.‡ The value of the commerce of the port of Houston for 1933 was $400,900,000 a

* *Ibid.*, 1929, 874, 888; 1934, 593-602, Part 2, 11.

† *The Port of New Orleans*, Louisiana, Port Series 5 (revised 1932), U. S. Shipping Board, 1, 221; *Report of Chief of Engineers*, U. S. Army, 1934, Part 2, 11; Personal observation.

‡ *Report of Army Engineers*, U. S. Army, 1934, 678-679; *The Ports of Texas City*, Port Series 6, War Department (1924); Personal observation.

year.* Space does not permit a detailed discussion of the port facilities of the other deep water ports of the South.—Richmond, Wilmington, Charleston, Savannah, Jacksonville, Tampa, Miami, Pensacola,
Mobile, Port Arthur, Beaumont, and Corpus Christi (Fig. 59)—each
of which is in close contact, by railroad and highway, with a large
hinterland. The wide spacing of these ports and their large number

A. E. P.

FIG. 59.—The Port of Corpus Christi, a part of Corpus Christi Bay, the estuary of
the Nueces River (1937).

This is one of the newer ocean ports of the South and is busy especially during the cotton-
exporting season. Corpus Christi and Brownsville, also, but recently improved, serve southern and
southwestern Texas.

insure all parts of the South a short land-haul to an overseas shipping
or receiving point.

The Feasibility of Harbor versus Riverway Improvements

Certainly no one would question the feasibility of the expenditures
on the harbors just discussed, when the value of commerce moved
through them is taken into consideration. For the United States the
total expenditures to date on seacoast harbors and channels—some of
the improvements represented by some of this money no doubt are no
longer functioning—to June 30, 1934, was $474,000,000. This sum is
providing channels that, except for maintenance, function for scores
of years. It does not include maintenance. The annual value of the

---

* *Commercial Statistics, Water-borne Commerce of the United States,* 1933,
603.

commerce using these harbors is about $11,000,000,000. Certainly money spent on ocean harbors is money well spent. Indeed such expenditures are absolutely essential for no other traffic ways are available. The justification for harbors *in general* does not, of course, mean that improvements at all harbors are paying ventures. The records for the shallow-draft riverways and waterways show far less returns. Up to June 30, 1934, the Federal Government had donated for navigation improvements ("new work") on the Mississippi and its tributaries $455,000,000, and it will take nearly $200,000,000 more to complete the authorized projects. There is very little likelihood that the riverways will carry much more freight in the future than now, for the reasons already stated. The total value of the commodities (package freight and miscellaneous) carried in 1933 was $679,000,000. The Great Lakes on which $166,000,000 has been spent for improvements have an annual commerce valued at more than $2,000,000,000. The 12-foot channel of the Intracoastal Waterway from Norfolk to Beaufort cost $10,400,000, up to June 30, 1934; the value of the commodities in 1933 was only $25,700,000. This is one of the most-used sections of this waterway. Most other sections make a much poorer showing. The Jacksonville-Miami section, for example, cost $6,200,-000; the value of freight carried in a year is $2,460,000.*

The taxpayers are entitled to know the vast differences in the returns from the money spent on seacoast harbors and channels and the Great Lakes versus the riverways and intracoastal waterways. This is shown, *though only roughly*, in the table that follows, using the type of data presented above:

Class of Improvement	Total Federal Expenditure up to 1934 versus Value of Commerce in 1933
Ocean harbors and channels................	1 vs. 23
Great Lakes, harbors and channels..........	1 vs. 12
Mississippi River and tributaries............	1 vs. 1.5
Intracoastal waterway, Norfolk to Beaufort (12-foot channel)..............	1 vs. 2.4
Jacksonville to Miami.................	1 vs. .4

Data from *Report of Chief of Engineers*, U. S. Army, 1934, 13 and 14.

Surely money spent on our ocean and lake harbors and channels is bringing returns to the taxpayers, and the wide scope of the movement of the commodities that pass through these waterways distributes the benefits; but one has a right to question the advisability of the expenditures on riverways and barge canals.

---

* *Report of Chief of Engineers*, U. S. Army, 1934, Part 1, 13, 339, 469; Part 2. 1, 3, 16, 29, 30.

CHAPTER VII

THE RAILWAYS OF THE SOUTH*

INTRODUCTION

The steamboat even by the late 1820's had about solved the problem of low-cost, efficient transportation for the sections of the South that lay within a score or more miles of navigable waterways. These were the areas of profitable production of farm and forest products. These areas will be called, for short, the "riverine" sections. But beyond these 40- to 50-mile strips of "privileged" lands lay vast areas, in size several times the riverine sections, that awaited only some modern means of transportation to bring them into economic production on a large scale. Life in most respects in the interriverine sections was as isolated and circumscribed as in pioneer days. A few hard-surfaced roads had been built, as previously described, but most of the land commerce was carried over dirt roads at a cost of 25 to 50 cents a ton-mile.

The observations of Michaux and Olmsted on land transportation have been discussed in a previous chapter. It was Olmsted who traversed the South in the period when railroads were just beginning to compete with the waterways for primacy, and who clearly discerned the shortcomings of dirt road transportation—and their retarding influence on economic advancement. A Texas writer in the late 1850's—Texas, having been only recently settled and still having a large debtor class, was fully two decades behind the South Atlantic States in railroad building—presented an interesting view of conditions in his state before the coming of the railroad. "Merchants," he writes, "bought goods in the spring for the fall trade and only received them (in the interior of the State) after a six weeks' or a two months' exposure to the vicissitudes of a voyage on a so-called prairie schooner." Farmers who shipped cotton to market in September or early October never expected returns until Christmas. The prairie schooners were as a rule drawn by slow-moving oxen which rarely made more than ten miles a day and less than that when the roads were muddy. "In the height of the season," to continue the quotation, "our market towns, es-

---

* The writer uses both terms, railway and railroad.

pecially Houston, were one large cattle pen and the streets exhibited from morning till night, only a sea of horns, intermixed with the white covers of the wagons. Long trains of cattle fourteen, sixteen, and sometimes twenty oxen to each wagon—were constantly arriving and departing with a snail-like pace, wearily dragging their loads through the mud."*

THE EVOLUTION OF THE RAILROAD IN THE SOUTH

The increasing success of the steamboat made the contrast of inter-riverine and riverine production exceedingly galling to the people of isolated areas. Even with the high prices of the 1820's, cotton culture was unprofitable on the Piedmont, distant a score or more miles from the head of navigation. The people in the back country of the South Atlantic States, where navigable rivers were fewest or absent, were vigilant of developments in other lands. No more anxious were they to secure some vehicle of commerce for the interriverine land that would be what the steamboat was for the riverine section, than were the commercial interests of the ocean ports like Baltimore, Richmond, Wilmington, Charleston, and Savannah. All these cities had been interested in canals, later in improved roads, but both had failed to solve their problem of transportation. The people on lands near the rivers were living in a modern world. How could the interriverine areas, too, be brought in touch with world markets?

The English had been experimenting with steam railroads since before 1810. But many leading Americans saw little for us in these attempts. Benjamin H. Latrobe in his report to Gallatin in 1808, for example, stated that in view of the efficiency of canals and of the numerous canal companies being organized, the construction of "artificial roads" (railroads) was inadvisable. This in spite of the wonderful tales that were reaching America of the great loads being carried on the railroads of England. Horse-drawn cars on rails had long been used. "The sort of produce which is carried to our markets," Latrobe wrote, "is collected from such scattered points, and comes by such a diversity of routes, that railroads are out of the question as to the carriage of common articles."†

Latrobe's idea dominated, no doubt, in America at that time, but his report probably had little effect in deterring investors. The first railroads in America, as in England, were used to transport stone

---

* Quoted in *Hunt's Merchants Magazine*, XLIII, 1860, 633.

† Latrobe's report in *American State Papers, Miscellaneous*, I, 917; also discussed in L. H. Haney, *A Congressional History of Railways of the United States to 1850*, 183.

and coal (as, for example, the Quincy in Massachusetts, the Mauch Chunk in Pennsylvania, and the Chesterfield in Virginia.)* About 1827 came the welcome news that the locomotive was a success in England. Shortly thereafter two railroad companies, both in the South, the Baltimore and Ohio and the Charleston and Hamburg, were incorporated, and began work. The Baltimore and Ohio was the first to break ground, but the Charleston and Hamburg was more diligent in extending its line. By 1833 the latter had 136 miles constructed, the longest railroad, for a short time, in the world. In 1832 the railroad mileage of the United States was 100, of which 80 miles were in the South. New York had 12 miles, Pennsylvania 6, and Massachusetts 2.†

Many state governments in the South entered into railroad building. State participation was often the result of the initiative of the commercial and merchant interests of the ocean ports, but these interests were willingly supported by the farmers of the interior. Baltimore and Maryland pushed the Baltimore and Ohio westward toward the Ohio; a Washington branch was soon built. Virginia, although it had an improvement fund which in 1833 amounted to more than $2,400,000, about a million of which was "disposable," was slow in entering into railroad building, according to one writer: first, because of "her habitual caution and prudence . . . requiring demonstration" before she embarked "her capital in any new enterprise"; and, second, because of "the sectional jealousies of different portions of the state, the interests of several often conflicting with regard to any specific improvement proposed"; and, third, because "the [mis]management of her first enterprises in this field has contributed to dampen her ardour ever since."‡ North Carolina embarked in state participation in internal improvements in 1833. Three north and south railroads were proposed. The Wilmington and Weldon was begun in 1836.§ The South Carolina Canal and Railroad Company, which built the Charleston and Hamburg road, was financed by the people of Charleston, but a full report of the proposed construction was laid before Congress and the assistance of government surveyors secured.¶ The state of Georgia constructed the Western and Atlantic, as one of the links in a railroad built to prevent Charleston from drawing the commerce of the Georgia Piedmont away from Savannah markets. The governments of both

* Haney, op. cit., 192.

† Data from Hunt's Merchants Magazine, IX, 1843, 95.

‡ Jos. Martin, A New and Comprehensive Gazetteer of Virginia, 1835, 87.

§ James Sprunt, Chronicles of the Cape Fear River, 148.

¶ Haney, op. cit., 192.

Alabama and Mississippi also participated in railroad building, though somewhat later than the South Atlantic States, for they had fewer people and, being much younger, had less capital and less financial backing.

Railroad building became active in the late 1830's and in the 1840's, in the South. Most of the improvements made in American railroads before 1840 were devised by Southern enthusiasts, although often actual construction of the devices took place in Northern factories. The Charleston and Hamburg Railroad was the first to be constructed in the United States with the idea of using steam locomotives. The first engine was built by a West Point, New York, foundry.

When locomotives began to be used it was the general opinion among railroad people that the railroads could be built only over a flat terrain, i.e., "a dead line was thought necessary."* Slopes were to be ascended by stationary engines hauling the cars up and down inclined planes. The Baltimore and Ohio had such devices, and an inclined plane was also planned on the Charleston and Hamburg, where the road had to descend from the uplands of the inner part of the Coastal Plain to Hamburg on the Savannah River.† But the Baltimore and Ohio Railroad after some experimenting succeeded in having a locomotive built that climbed one of its inclines 2,000 feet long, with gradient of 201 feet to the mile, and it "went up with great ease." Later a gradient of 264 feet to the mile was negotiated. This was hailed in Europe (we are informed in American papers), as well as in America, as a great accomplishment. On July 19, 1836, a locomotive on the Columbia road ascended a gradient of 369 feet to the mile. This feat was "witnessed by many scientific men."‡ Most of the locomotives built before 1834 were of the "solid truck" type, that is, they had to travel straight ahead or on curves of large radius. The first four-wheel "swivelled bogie truck" type which supported the front part of the locomotive was tried out, and proved successful, on the South Carolina railroad in 1834. This has remained a characteristic feature of American locomotives ever since.§ Railroads now were equipped to traverse successfully the rough terrain of the Southern Piedmont and the Southern Appalachian Highlands. Man now felt that he could go anywhere and at last the problem of efficient

---

* *Hunt's Merchants Magazine,* IX, 1843, 96; *Niles' Weekly Register,* XLI, Nov. 19, 1831, 259.

† Hugh Miller, *Encyclopedia of Geography,* III, 533; J. S. Buckingham, *The Slave States of America,* 548.

‡ *Niles' Weekly Register,* L, March 26, 1836, 50; July 30, 1836, 362.

§ *Encyclopœdia Britannica,* XXII, Eleventh Edition, 821.

land transportation was solved, and "distance was annihilated." A few of the daring suggested that locomotives could be built to travel 60 miles an hour, but the calmer thinkers seemed to be quite satisfied with 10 or 15, and why not, since 10 to 15 miles a day was the speed (?) of an ox team. In 1835 it was reported that the Charleston and Hamburg Railroad sent "an express daily from one commercial city to another, distant 136 miles, in 12 hours, and that in the day-time."*

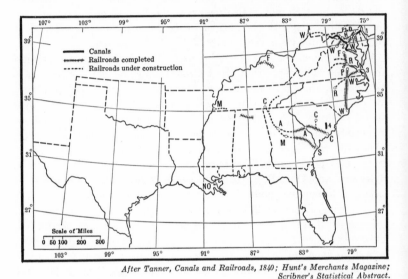

After Tanner, Canals and Railroads, 1840; Hunt's Merchants Magazine; Scribner's Statistical Abstract.

FIG. 60.—Railroads and Canals, 1840. (State boundaries as of 1930.)

The New Castle and Frenchtown Railroad in 1832 worked out what is probably the first railroad signal system, in the United States, at least. At each station on the line, about three miles apart, a tall pole had been erected. As the train passed a station the station master hauled a white ball to the top of the pole. This could be seen through a telescope at the next station. We are informed that the signal the conductor waves to the engineer to go ahead is still known as the "high ball" on most lines.†

But if people's minds appear to us to be cramped as to speed they were certainly not cramped in laying out, in imagination largely, railroad lines which even to us today would be considered far flung.

---

*Quoted in *American Almanac*, 1835, 229.
† Robert S. Henry, *Trains*, 1934, 19.

It was proposed, for example, to extend the Charleston-Hamburg road northwestward to Cincinnati. A convention was held at Knoxville in 1836 to stimulate interest in the venture. The cost, it was estimated, would be about $19,000,000.* In 1835 there also appeared in the *New Orleans Globe* a news item to the effect that "the magnificent undertaking, the New Orleans and Nashville Railroad, is to be commenced immediately, the first fifty miles being advertised for contract." This road was to be 566 miles long and to cost $10,000,000. Nashville and New Orleans would have a 36-hour service going each way. But imagination carried the road much farther. We read, "Should the Virginians determine to connect their contemplated James River improvement with this work, we may expect to travel from Washington to New Orleans in four days, with an ease and comfort never before contemplated."†

In 1836 one could travel between New York and New Orleans in about 13 days, utilizing railroad, steamboat, and stage coach. The Richmond, Fredericksburg, and Potomac Company in connection with other railroads and with certain steamboat companies offered a 54-hour service between Blakely, North Carolina, and New York.‡

By 1840 (Fig. 60) the Southern States had 58 railroads, with a total mileage of 1,462, in operation (with more than 2,000 miles, in addition, building), equipped with 161 locomotives.§ These railroads were distributed as follows:¶

	MILES
In Maryland:	
Baltimore and Ohio to Harpers Ferry (by 1835)	86
Baltimore and Port Deposit	34½
Baltimore and Washington	40
Baltimore and Susquehanna	59½
In Virginia:	
Chesterfield (coal fields) to Richmond	13
Petersburg and Roanoke (to Weldon)	59
Winchester and Potomac (Harpers Ferry to B. and O. R.R.)	30
Portsmouth and Roanoke (to Weldon)	77½
Richmond to Fredericksburg and the Potomac	58
Manchester to Richmond	13

* *Niles' Weekly Register,* L, July 30, 1836, 362.

† *Niles' Weekly Register,* XLIX, Sept. 19, 1835, 41.

‡ Robert S. Henry, *Trains,* 1934, 18.

§ Calculated from data in *Hunt's Merchants Magazine,* IV, 1841, 481, from information furnished by Chavalier Von Gerstner.

¶ Data from *Hunt's Merchants Magazine,* September, 1840, 289; James Sprunt, *Chronicles of the Cape Fear River,* 150; H. S. Tanner, *Canals and Railroads of the United States,* 1840, map.

MILES

In North Carolina:
    Wilmington and Weldon (begun 1836; last spike in 1840) . . 161½
In South Carolina:
    Charleston to Hamburg.............................. 136
In Georgia:*
    Altamaha and Brunswick............................ 12
In Alabama: ·
    Tuscumbia and Decatur (around Muscle Shoals)......... 46
In Louisiana:
    Pontchartrain (New Orleans to Lake Pontchartrain)....... 5
    Carrollton (New Orleans to Carrollton)................. 6
In Kentucky:
    Lexington and Ohio (Lexington to Frankfort)............ 29
    Frankfort and Louisville............................ 50

Tennessee was exceedingly slow in entering upon railroad building. In 1836 the Hiawassee Road was begun, to extend southwestward 100 miles from Knoxville to Ross's Landing (site of Chattanooga) to connect with the Western and Atlantic. About 70 miles were graded at a cost of about a million dollars, but the company was "compelled by financial difficulties to suspend the work" though there were strong efforts to resume it.†

It will be noted that these roads for the most part lay to the east or south of the mountains and extended at right angles to the coast. It was the commerce of the interior that the coastal sections wanted. Even as late as 1840, the idea was generally held that the railroad was the handmaid of the waterway. This was the point of view of some of the projectors of the early Southern railroads, but not of all. The Baltimore and Ohio was to connect Baltimore with the navigable Ohio and thus draw to Baltimore the traffic of the rich Ohio Valley. The Petersburg and Roanoke connected navigable water at the former city with the Roanoke River just below the falls at Weldon. The purpose here was to draw the commerce of eastern North Carolina and particularly of the Sound Country to Petersburg. The Richmond and Petersburg Railroad enabled Richmond to supplant Petersburg as an *entrepôt* for the east Carolina commerce. But to save the Sound

----

* Other sources show that Georgia had in addition to the one short line listed in *Hunt's Merchants Magazine*, the Central of Georgia, 80 miles in operation and 138 miles in addition under construction; the Monroe Railroad from Macon to Forsyth, 28 miles, completed; the Georgia Railroad, westward from Augusta, 80 miles; and work was in progress on the Western and Atlantic which extended from the site of Atlanta—then a point in the "wilderness"—to the Tennessee River at the site of Chattanooga (*American Almanac*, 1840, 250).

† *American Almanac*, 1849, 290.

commerce to herself Norfolk with the assistance of Portsmouth built
the Portsmouth and Roanoke to Weldon, North Carolina, and about
the same time Wilmington started the Wilmington and Weldon. Weldon seemed destined to be a great railroad center. The Charleston
and Hamburg was built to capture the commerce of the outer
Piedmont near the Savannah River in both South Carolina and
Georgia and draw this commerce away from the Savannah River and
the city of Savannah. The Santee Canal and other short canals
brought Charleston in contact with the South Carolina Piedmont to

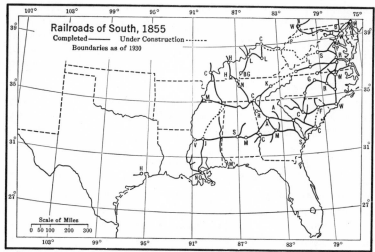

Data for Geo. W. Coulton. *Atlas of World*, Vol. I (1865), checked with Appleton's Guide.

FIG. 61

the east of the Savannah basin and thus Charleston had aspirations
to control the commerce of most of the Southern Piedmont. But later
the navigable Ohio at Cincinnati became the goal. The Georgia railroads from Savannah were extended through central Georgia to secure
the Piedmont commerce and connect with the Tennessee River at
Ross's Landing (now Chattanooga).

In time most of these roads pushing inland from coastal cities developed branches, and sooner or later railroads paralleling the coast
were constructed. In fact, the Wilmington and Weldon and the other
lines that were built northward to Washington, Baltimore, and finally
to New York were of this class.

By 1860 (see Fig. 61 for railroads in 1855) the South had the main
lines of the railroad mesh that covers its surface so completely to-

day. Consolidation of many short lines and the building up of great systems, such as the Southern, the Atlantic Coast Line, the Louisville and Nashville, the Illinois Central, Santa Fe, Southern Pacific, and others, did not come until after the Civil War, and was the work of men who, in addition to the imagination of the railroad projectors of the 1830's, had capital and practical experience to put their systems into the front rank of American railroads. A railroad as long as 300 miles was exceedingly rare in the South in 1860. For example, in 1858 and for many years thereafter, the Washington-New Orleans mail, to cover the 1,249 miles between the two cities, had to travel over ten different, yet connected, lines, as follows: from Washington to Alexandria over the Washington and Alexandria Railroad for 6 miles; then over the Orange and Alexandria road 169 miles to Lynchburg, Virginia; 204 miles over the Virginia and Tennessee road to Bristol on the Virginia-Tennessee boundary in the Great Valley; 130 miles from Bristol to Knoxville over the East Tennessee and Virginia Railroad; over the East Tennessee and Georgia for 83 miles to Cleveland, Tennessee; 29 miles from there to Chattanooga over the Chattanooga and Cleveland Railroad; then 38 miles over the Nashville and Chattanooga Railroad to Stevenson, Alabama; 219 miles over the Memphis and Charleston to Grand Junction in western Tennessee; 165 miles southward to Canton, Mississippi, over the Mississippi Central; and from there 206 miles to New Orleans over the New Orleans and Jackson and Great Northern Railroad. This was the southern portion of a great through-mail route (a "through route," so advertised) between Bangor, Maine, and New Orleans, the longest route in America, 1,996 miles, and was composed of eighteen separate railroads.*

By 1860 the South had about 8,000 miles of railroads in operation and more than 8,000 miles, in addition, under construction.† The older seaboard states, as a group, continued to lead, but Tennessee surpassed North Carolina and South Carolina. Texas had but 230 miles finished, "centering in Houston," and 35 miles in other parts of the state.‡

During the Civil War many of the railroads of the South were effective agencies in offense and defense for the contending armies (Fig. 62). Those of the Upper South to the west of the Appalachians were commanded by the Union forces; those of the Atlantic Coast and Gulf

---

* *Hunt's Merchants Magazine*, XLIII, 1860, 114.

† *DeBow's Review*, XXVIII, O. S., May, 1860, 593; *Statistical Abstract*, 1930, 394, gives 10,048.

‡ *Hunt's Merchants Magazine*, XLIII, 1860, 633.

Coast states were utilized by the Confederacy until captured by the
invading Union army. The Richmond and Petersburg, and Petersburg
and Roanoke, and the Wilmington and Weldon, which formed a north-
south line to Richmond, were, combined, called the Bread Line of the
Confederacy. The major arsenals, as those at Richmond and Selma,
Alabama, sent their supplies to the Confederate front by rail. The
defense, capture, or destruction of railroads formed the major operation of many movements of troops and resulted in many battles. Thus
Southern railroads suffered greatly during the War; and during the
Reconstruction Period the Southern leaders had little money and even
less "heart" to rehabilitate them. Hundreds of miles were crippled if

Fig. 62.—A Reproduction of a Page from Leslie's, January 18, 1862.

Beneath the engraving is the following: "The campaign in Kentucky—The National troops under
General Johnston advancing on the Louisville and Nashville Turnpike, overtaken by the equipage
and baggage train of the Louisville and Nashville Railroad.—From a sketch by our special artist
with General Buell's command."

not destroyed and required entirely new equipment from cross ties to
locomotives. Some main lines were revived readily under Southern
initiative. Many of the weaker ones were incorporated into the larger
systems in process of integration in the 1870's and 1880's. Space permits the discussion of but one example—the Atlantic Coast Line.
In 1869 several Baltimore capitalists acquired an interest in the
Wilmington and Weldon and spent large sums to rehabilitate
it. Subsequently, controlling interests were secured in connecting roads,
north and south, including the Petersburg and Raleigh, the Richmond
and Petersburg, the Wilmington, Columbia, and Augusta, the Northeastern Railroad of South Carolina, and the Cheraw and Darlington.
Although there was unity in operation in these early stages of consolidation of ownership the roads maintained their "corporate identity."
It was not until 1900 that consolidation was complete and the At-

lantic Coast Line Railroad evolved. Absorption of the other lines has taken place since then and will probably continue.*

THE RAILROADS OF THE SOUTH TODAY

The South has about one-third the railroad mileage of United States (82,000 out of the 249,000 miles for the country at large);† one-third the population; and one-third the area. It is, therefore, as well supplied with railroads as the country at large. It has not as many miles to the 1,000 square miles of area or 1,000 people as the North, for there are fewer people. With a lower density of population, and less manufacturing in the Southern States, fewer are needed. The railroad mileage is fairly evenly distributed. The "mesh" is "coarsest" in the Southern Appalachian Mountains, the Appalachian Plateaus, Southern Florida, and western Texas and Oklahoma where the population density is lowest and where there are fewer products to ship. Except in these areas nearly every farm is within 10 or 20 miles, at the most, of a railroad and few are more than 25 miles from a railroad shipping point.‡

Of the three divisions of the South (census classification) the South Atlantic States, which fathered all the early railroads, led until about 1900. In 1910 the West South Central led; the East South Central held second rank until about 1885, then took third place. It has been only during the last three or four decades that the western part of the West South Central Section has become completely won to white civilization. No other section of the South has advanced so rapidly. The growth of railroad mileage is really a "barometer" of this section's economic development. In 1860 the mileage was 680; in 1870, 1,417; in 1880, 5,044. By 1900 the mileage was 18,220 and by 1920, 32,970.§ The opening of Oklahoma, the evolution of west Texas ranches, by the introduction of dry-farming methods, into productive agricultural lands, the development of a few irrigation projects, and

---

* Information from *The Story of the Atlantic Coast Line,* a booklet issued by the A. C. L. Railroad.

† *Statistical Abstract,* 1930, 394, data for 1927.

‡ In 1860 the South had 10,048 miles as compared to 30,626 for the United States. The figures for 1870 were 13,422 out of 52,922; for 1880, 25,977 out of 93,267; for 1900, 54,926 as compared with 193,346 for the country. In 1860 the South had 32.8 per cent of the mileage of the United States; in 1870, 25.4 per cent; in 1900, only 23.2 per cent; and in 1910, 32.4 per cent. It was only about 1910 that the Southern States regained the rank held in 1860. Since 1900 railroad building has been active in the South. (See Chapter I.) Data from *Statistical Abstract,* 1930, 394.

§ *Idem.*

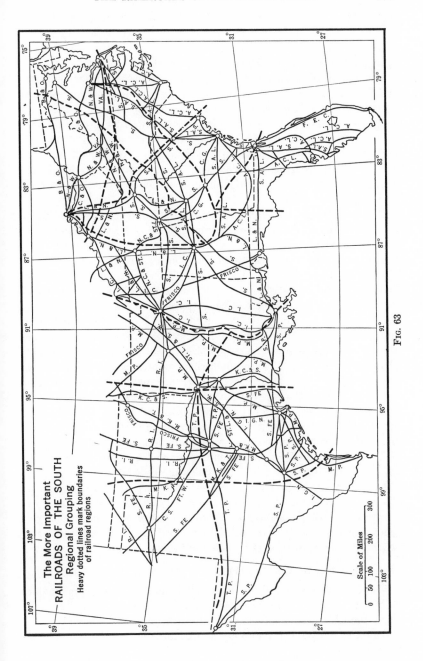

The More Important
RAILROADS OF THE SOUTH
Regional Grouping
Heavy dotted lines mark boundaries
of railroad regions

Scale of Miles

FIG. 63

the rapid rise of this section as the foremost petroleum-producing region of our country, the rise of beautiful, progressive cities, and even developments farther on, in the Southwest, are the major conditions to which railroad builders have adjusted themselves.

The recent industrial advances in the South Atlantic States; the ever-increasing tourist trade, in spite of the tremendous increase of automobiles; and the rise, in recent decades, of an active trade in early vegetables, early deciduous fruit and citrus fruit growing, have kept that section from passing into a "mature" stage in its transportation. The East South Central Section has to a much lesser degree benefited from new developments in agriculture and manufacturing. The advance in manufacturing has been greater than that in agriculture.

Railroad transportation in the South is almost completely dominated by about twelve or fifteen large companies. Most of these companies may be considered Southern, not that their capital is Southern, but they have developed in a Southern environment; i.e., they have "grown up" with the South and are the product of Southern enterprise. They have suffered periods of despondency when the future looked dark and the end of Southern civilization appeared at hand, when panics, droughts, crop failures, and epidemics brought Southern economic life to a low ebb; and they have prospered when it prospered, when the gods of weather favored the agriculturist, when money crops brought abundant returns, and when lumbering, mining, and manufacturing were at a high point of activity. A few, like the Illinois Central, the Southern Pacific, the Missouri, Kansas, and Texas, the Rock Island, and the Frisco, are invaders from the North and West, although their systems in Southern territory have quite generally been built up by the consolidation, both physically and administratively, of short roads built in most cases by Southern enterprise, and, perhaps, by Southern capital in the days when little capital was needed.

Let us now turn to a consideration of the regional distribution of the railroad systems of the South. (See Fig. 63.) For convenience of study we are dividing the South into six railroad transportation regions, areas, or belts. These will be discussed in order from northeast southward and westward as they are on the accompanying map.

REGIONAL DISTRIBUTION OF RAILROAD SYSTEMS

The Chesapeake Bay-Ohio River belt is dominated by three major railroads: in order from north to south they are the Baltimore and Ohio, the Chesapeake and Ohio, and the Norfolk and Western.

The first named, the Baltimore and Ohio, holds a monopoly of the traffic of Maryland west of the Bay and northern West Virginia, north of the Kanawha River. A few other railroad systems have branches in this district, but no other has main, through lines. It connects Baltimore with Philadelphia and New York and with Washington. Westward from Baltimore it serves the Maryland coal fields about Cumberland. It has one main line through Pittsburgh, and on through several Middle West cities. A southern branch crosses West Virginia and Ohio to Cincinnati and on to St. Louis. While its eastern terminus is Baltimore in the South, its western branches form a broad network over the North Central States.

The Chesapeake and Ohio supplies transportation facilities to farms and mines in an east-and-west belt (roughly) to the south of the Baltimore and Ohio territory. It has a main line to Washington, from which city its trains run to New York over the Pennsylvania lines. Its territory in Virginia is mainly to the north of the James River, which it follows from the Great Valley to Richmond. It traverses the James and York River peninsula to its Lower Chesapeake terminus at Newport News. It is in West Virginia that its lines, forming a complete network, follow the valleys to hundreds of coal mines, farms, and mountain forests. Low gradients for its trans-West Virginia lines are found along the Kanawha River. It crosses northern Kentucky to reach its two western termini at Cincinnati and Louisville.

The Norfolk and Western extends westward from Norfolk through Petersburg, Lynchburg, and Roanoke, with a branch line southward into North Carolina to Durham and to Winston-Salem. Its lines traverse the Great Valley from Bristol to Hagerstown. It dominates in the coal, forest, grazing, and farming sections of southwestern Virginia and southern West Virginia. It reaches the Ohio along the Big Sandy, and crosses into Ohio with lines to Cincinnati and Columbus, Ohio.

These three, and particularly the latter two, offer a short cut from the southern Middle West to Chesapeake Bay, which is growing rapidly in importance as an export region for coal. These three run, roughly, at right angles to the Atlantic Coast of the Upper South to the Transappalachian region, the goal of Atlantic Coast transportation enthusiasts since the days of Washington. Roads, canals, and improved rivers have been projected, and partially or wholly developed, but have not met with the success that the railroads have.

South of the Chesapeake Bay-Ohio River traffic belt is an area that may be called the South Atlantic Coast region, the major part of it being on the Coastal Plain from Chesapeake Bay to the tip of Florida and the Florida coast of the Gulf. This railroad traffic region is dominated by the closely formed "meshes" of the Atlantic Coast Line and the Seaboard Air Line in the Carolinas, Georgia, and Florida, and by the Florida East Coast. The latter, as its name signifies, extends for several hundred miles within a few rods to a few miles of the east Florida coast from Jacksonville beyond Miami and out upon the Florida Keys* and then over the shallow waters between to Key West. Other railroads compete actively with the former two for traffic in the Carolinas and Georgia, as the Southern and the Central of Georgia; but nevertheless the major portion of the freight that moves parallel to the South Atlantic Coast on the Coastal Plain is on the Atlantic Coast Line and the Seaboard Air Line. Their northern termini are on Chesapeake Bay and at Richmond, but both run trains over leased tracks northward into Washington, Baltimore, Philadelphia, and New York. They have lines into all the Atlantic and Florida Gulf Coast ports, the more important being Wilmington, Charleston, Savannah, Brunswick, Jacksonville, and Tampa. These two systems are competitors of the coastwise steamship lines. Their main lines lie well back from the coast on the middle belt of the Coastal Plain where they obtain low grades. While they must cross numerous Coastal Plain rivers, they thus avoid the building of long structures that would be needed in the estuarian region.

Both the Atlantic Coast Line and the Seaboard Air Line have also responded to the tendency of freight to move to and from ocean ports. They have lines leading from Wilmington, Charleston, and Savannah across the Coastal Plain to the Piedmont textile region and also westward across Georgia. Both have rails to Atlanta and Montgomery, and the Seaboard has a line into Birmingham.

The Piedmont traffic region is, for the most part, dominated by the great Southern Railway system, the main line of which extends from Washington southward through Charlottesville, Virginia; Danville, Greensboro, and Charlotte, in North Carolina; Spartanburg and Greenville, South Carolina; and Atlanta, all on the Piedmont. But the Southern System has many branches and main lines extending beyond the Piedmont. From Atlanta a line extends westward to Birmingham in the western edge of the Great Valley, and from here one of the main lines gives direct connections with New Orleans. From both Atlanta and Birmingham are lines to Chattanooga, and from here a line extends to Memphis. One may travel from New Orleans, the Crescent City, to Cincinnati, the Queen City, over a Southern Railway-owned road, popularly known as the Queen and Crescent. Its rails also enter

---

* The "Key" section of this road was about destroyed by the 1935 hurricane. Probably will not be rebuilt, it is reported.

Mobile, Jacksonville, Brunswick, Savannah, Charleston, and Norfolk and thus into the territory dominated by other roads, but these may be considered branches of the main stem line. The ports are not connected one with another but to each a separate branch extends from the main stem of the Southern on the Piedmont.

A Southeastern traffic region, in South Carolina, Georgia, and eastern Alabama, forming a sector from the mountains to the Atlantic and Gulf (not including Florida), may be blocked out. It cuts across the Coastal Plain and the Piedmont and hence across both the South Atlantic Coastal Plain and the Piedmont railroad belts. It is dominated by no one railroad system. Its major railroad lines form themselves into two systems that cross each other and thus present a rectangular mesh; but by far the larger number of the lines run back into the interior, almost directly away from the coast. The historic railroads of this belt are the Charleston and Hamburg (see discussion regarding), and the Georgia roads that were built to connect Savannah with the Tennessee River. This is a region of conflict involving the Central of Georgia, which has one main line from the coast to Chattanooga and a "mesh" in eastern Alabama and western Georgia, and the Atlantic Coast Line, the Seaboard, the Southern, and the Nashville, Chattanooga, and St. Louis. The last mentioned leases the Western and Atlantic from Chattanooga to Atlanta and runs trains over the Central of Georgia to the seacoast. No single road seems to dominate in the region.

The East Gulf and Ohio River belt is served by the Louisville and Nashville and the Illinois Central. But these are not competing lines for territory even though they compete for traffic at their termini. Both have freight termini in St. Louis, Louisville, Memphis, and New Orleans. The Louisville and Nashville runs trains to Chicago which is the most important terminus of the Illinois Central. Both have contacts at their northern ends with the great east and west transcontinental traffic route that exends westward from Middle Atlantic ports. At their southern terminus they connect with the numerous steamship lines that use New Orleans as a terminal. The Louisville and Nashville is strictly a Southern railroad, an extension of one of the oldest railroads of the Middle West. Both (L. and N. and the I. C.) connect the subtropical Gulf Coast and the Cotton Belt with the intermediate temperature belt (Hot Summer and Cold Winter). Thus over their lines move cotton, early vegetables, tropical fruit from the Caribbean, subtropical and early temperate zone fruit from the South, lumber, and many other types of commodities originating both within and without the South. Wheat, flour, meal, agricultural machinery, and other manufactures move southward. The Louisville and Nashville has Cincinnati as its easternmost terminus, and thus is nearer the great markets of the Northeast than the Illinois Central. From Cincinnati southward it has a competing line with the Southern Railway's Queen and Crescent to Atlanta.

The dominant trend of the major railroads in the East Gulf and Ohio River Belt is north and south. Running at right angles to these are the Southern Railway (a branch road) from Memphis to Chattanooga and the Nashville, Chattanooga, and St. Louis, also from Memphis to Chattanooga and on to Atlanta. The Paducah-Louisville branch of the Illinois Central also has an east-west trend.

The West Gulf and Interior railroad traffic belt, covering Louisiana, Texas, Arkansas, and Oklahoma, has two main systems of lines (based on direction), a north-south system and an east-west system.

In the Louisiana-Arkansas sub-belt, the north-south railroads (major lines) are the Missouri Pacific, the Iron Mountain, the St. Louis Southwestern, and the Kansas City Southern. The last has practically no branch lines and follows almost a direct route from Kansas City to Port Arthur. The other three cover these two states with many branches.

From the Houston-Galveston ocean termini, several lines radiate northward: a branch of the Southern Pacific to Shreveport and another to Dallas and Fort Worth; a line of the Atcheson, Topeka, and Santa Fe (the Santa Fe) northeastward from Bolivar on Galveston Bay to Longview, Texas; the Missouri, Kansas, and Texas, through Dallas and Fort Worth across Oklahoma to Kansas City; the Colorado Southern northwestward to Denver; and a second line of the Santa Fe northwestward into the Panhandle of Texas called the Galveston, Colorado, and Santa Fe. These connect cotton, petroleum, and wheat regions with the West Gulf Coast ports. Besides the ocean contacts at Galveston and Houston, and Port Arthur, railroads have termini at Corpus Christi and Freeport. The Missouri Pacific has many lines in southern Texas that reach Gulf ports.

Running transverse to these roads that radiate from the Gulf Coast of Louisiana and Texas are the east-west lines, the most southerly of which is the Southern Pacific which extends just inland from the heads of the coastal indentations, from New Orleans westward to Houston and from here westward to San Antonio and El Paso. The Southern Pacific has developed a "mesh" in southeastern Texas; but westward from Houston it has few branches. To the north of the Southern Pacific lies the Texas and Pacific which extends from El Paso eastward through Fort Worth, Dallas, and Shreveport to New

Orleans. It thus competes with the Southern Pacific for through freight between El Paso and New Orleans but it does not serve the same country. The St. Louis Southwestern is an east-west line in Texas as far as Texarkana and Shreveport. It has freight depots in Fort Worth and Dallas, and, like the Texas and Pacific, serves central and northeastern Texas. Its northern terminus is St. Louis.

Farther north in Oklahoma and Arkansas are the Rock Island, the Missouri Pacific, and the Frisco with their eastern termini at Memphis. The Frisco, however, has lines east of the Mississippi.

PART IV

AGRICULTURE IN THE SOUTH

CHAPTER VIII

THE DEVELOPMENT OF AGRICULTURE
IN THE SOUTH

1. AGRICULTURE IN THE FRONTIER REGIONS*

The Chesapeake Bay Frontier

Within two weeks after the landing of the colonists at Jamestown on the James River a small field of wheat was sown. This was the beginning of agriculture in the South and in English America. The French had planted a colony at Port Royal, South Carolina, in 1562, and later one on the St. Johns River, Florida, but these were abortive attempts. The Spanish at St. Augustine had made a beginning in utilizing the agricultural resources of the near-by region, but Spanish agriculture was quite forgotten by the time the frontier of the English-speaking people migrated into Florida. French agriculture in Louisiana began long after the initial attempts in Virginia.

Farming in Virginia was a new experience to most of the colonial pioneers. Many were unaccustomed to hard work, certainly the hard work and privations incident to frontier life in a country quite different in climate and soil from that which had supplied them their meager agricultural experiences. The Virginia pioneers had come from a deforested area and hence had to learn how to "clear" the virgin lands for their crops. The necessity of removing the forests before planting, felling giant pines and oaks, with axe and saw was a herculean task for these gentlemen and must have delayed greatly the expansion of the agricultural area during the first few years. It seems probable that the first wheat was sown on the area cleared off about the fort. This area probably did not exceed four acres. The

---

* The westward movement of the population frontier and of the agricultural frontier were concomitant, related phenomena. Over-crowding, depleted soils, and a need for new lands, coupled with a *wanderlust*, were the dominant dynamic factors in the westward movement. Each frontier in its time made its contribution in people, methods of agriculture, implements, livestock, seed, money, and what not to the newly forming frontier, ever moving westward. It should be clear, therefore, that pioneer agriculture as discussed in the various major regions of the South is not contemporaneous.

first crop was not a success, but, undaunted, the settlers cleared larger spaces of trees and underbrush and the "civilized" area about the fort expanded. What a pitiably small area this was in comparison to the three hundreds of millions of acres in farms in the South today! In 1609, under the wise but exacting rule of Smith, forty acres of land were cleared and planted to corn, two Indian prisoners directing the work. The crop acreage was increased year by year so that by 1631 there was a surplus of wheat for export. Corn soon came to be the chief cereal. Success in growing it was due to its being an acclimated crop, to its high yield, and to the fact that it is well adapted to new lands. It can be eaten in a variety of ways—green, boiled or roasted, ripe, crushed, or ground—which helped in overcoming the monotony of the diet.*

In an old book, entitled *Virginia Richly Valued*, it is written, "The native corne of the country, maiz, is so grateful to the planter that it returneth him his entrusted seed with the increase of 2 or 3 hundred interest, so facilely planted that one man in 48 hours may prepare as much ground and set such a quantity of corn that he may be secure from want of Bread all the year following, though he should have ever so large an appetite to consume it and have nothing else to live upon."† Tobacco growing was also learned from the Indians, but until the production of the sustenance area exceeded the demands of the ever-increasing population, the major energies of the colonists had to be expended in the raising of food crops and at times much trading with the Indians was necessary to secure the requisite amount of food. A law was passed requiring that each farmer should plant two acres of corn. The chief agricultural implements used were of wood, which, though primitive, were of great aid in the cultivation of the land. Corn and beans (usually planted together), pumpkins, squash, and sunflower were the chief food crops of the Indians.‡ These were supplemented by

---

* *Yearbook of Agriculture,* 1921, 174.

† Quoted in Philip A. Bruce, *Economic History of Virginia in the Seventeenth Century,* I, 252, footnote.

‡ Carrier lists the crops grown by the Indians in the Americas as follows: maize, potato (both sweet and Irish), tobacco, peanuts, some varieties of cotton, all edible beans except horse beans and soybeans, all varieties of squash (Hubbard, crook-necked, etc.), field pumpkins, sunflowers, the Jerusalem artichoke, tomatoes, garden peppers, pineapples, watermelons, cassava and bananas. They collected fruits which subsequently have become partially or wholly domesticated as American grapes, strawberries, raspberries, blackberries, gooseberries, and such nuts as pecan, butternut and hickorynut, chestnut, walnut, piñon, and chinquapins. (Lyman Carrier, *The Beginnings of Agriculture in America,* 41.) Not all of these were grown in the South.

nuts, berries, and wild fruit.* All those were readily adopted as essential to white occupancy of the land.

The settlers introduced many field crops and vegetables as well as all the orchard fruits from England. Until 1612 food crops took precedence over others such as tobacco, flax, and cotton.

The Company early decided that subtropical products should, if possible, be grown in the colony. The leaders probably thought Virginia, being in the latitude of northern Africa, should have similar temperatures. All western Europe has a plus temperature anomaly for January of 10° to 40°, while Virginia has a negative 5° to 10°.† Having lived in an oceanic climate, the settlers were unacquainted with the extremes of a continental climate, and it is easy to understand that it might have taken several years for them to get a true conception of the normal temperature conditions. Besides, the science of crop adaptation to climate and soil was little developed in the early seventeenth century. At any rate, it is a matter of history that the Virginia colonists experimented in the growing of rice, indigo, cotton, oranges, olives, the silkworm, and the vine. Men experienced in the cultivation and production of these products were sent over.‡ It was especially desirable that the colonies should produce these and thus keep English gold within the borders of the Empire rather than give it to French, Spanish, or Italian producers. An active trade in some of these subtropical luxuries had long been carried on between England and the Mediterranean. Some of these desired products as rice, indigo, cotton, and wine were grown in Virginia but with little success.

Experimentation in the growing of silkworms continued for many years. The first attempts were made during the time of John Smith, but, during the sickness of the master workman who had charge of the experiment, rats ate the developing worms. Silkworm eggs were later secured from Italy, Spain, and France and a well-trained expert was sent over. George, the Armenian, is spoken of in the reports of the laws passed to encourage silk culture. In 1619 the House of Burgesses decreed that every planter must set out six mulberry trees. A treatise on silk culture was published in England, and many copies were sent to the colony. Bounties were offered for many years for the production of raw silk. In 1657 the Assembly voted that "what person soever shall first make one hundred pounds of wound silke in one

---

* L. H. Bailey, *Cyclopedia of American Agriculture,* IV, 25-29; A. R. Mann, *Beginnings in Agriculture,* 12.

† W. I. Milham, *Meteorology,* 98.

‡ *The Records of the Virginia Company of London,* the Court Book, from the manuscript in the Library of Congress, II, 348-351.

yeare within this colloney shall for his so-doing be paid five thousand pounds of tobacco out of the publique levie."*

One of the most successful phases of agriculture was the livestock industry. In spite of the thieving of cattle and hogs by marauding Indians and the occasional large winter losses—cattle were not housed in the winter as a rule—they increased rapidly in numbers. Cows were brought from England in 1609. In 1611 about 160 were imported. Horses, goats, sheep, and hogs were introduced during the early years. The mortality of these in the first few years was high. The 1623 (April 12) report to the king stated that there were "about one Thousand of beaste Besides Goates and of Swine an infinite number."† Within two or three decades cattle were exported to New England and the West Indies, but even then the total numbers increased rapidly. All these animals were allowed to roam the woods.

How well the Virginia Colony prospered in its agricultural attempts is well shown in the census returns of 1649. In that year there were 15,000 people in Virginia, and in addition 300 negro slaves. There were between 20,000 and 30,000 cows, bulls, calves, and oxen, 200 horses (some pure-bred stock), 3,000 sheep (wolves were constantly decimating their numbers in spite of the bounty offered for killing the predators and the heavy slaughter), 5,000 goats, and more than 5,000 hogs. Many hundreds of acres of land were growing wheat, corn, oats, barley, rice, besides great quantities of potatoes, asparagus, carrots, turnips, parsnips, onions, artichokes, peas, and beans. Indigo was also raised, wine produced, and there was great hope that the raw silk industry would prove a profitable venture.† The success of these early ventures in the production of crops is remarkable when it is known that most of the breaking up of the soil and its cultivation was done with spades, hoes, and mattocks. In 1649 there were only about 150 plows in the colony, i.e., one to 100 people or one to about 20 families. Plows under the system of migratory agriculture were of little use. It was the custom to crop the higher grounds on the average of three years, eight years on the lower lands, and then move on to newly cleared areas. In that brief time the roots of the numerous stumps had not yet rotted sufficiently to permit the use of plows.§

The natural environment of eastern Virginia favored the develop-

---

* Quoted by Lyman Carrier, *op. cit.*, 133; Bruce, *op. cit.*, I, 240-241, 328, 397, and 404.

† Bruce, *op. cit.*, I, 222; data for 1623 in *Records of the Virginia Company, op. cit.*, II, 348.

‡ Bruce, *op. cit.*, I, 336.

§ Bruce, *op. cit.*, I, 338.

ment of isolated plantation units, each of which could be economically self-sufficing. The numerous estuaries of Chesapeake Bay provided a long coastline with water offshore deep enough to float the small ocean-going boats of the time. Each plantation fronting on the water, as most plantations did, had its own private wharf from which export commodities were shipped, and the household and plantation necessities purchased abroad were received. It was the shore lands that were cleared and farmed, the interior of the peninsulas being left in forest and pasture lands. There was little need of roads so long as riparian acreage was available. Thus early Virginia had an estuarian civilization. There was little need of a commercial center for collecting and distributing commercial commodities. It was not until the back country was settled that Norfolk and Baltimore developed as shipping points.

The Virginia Plantation of Early Colonial Days

One gets the impression from the numerous historical and literary writings that large plantations predominated in Tidewater Virginia. It is probable, however, that eastern Virginia was no exception to the general conditions of the South, in which plantations of 500 or even 1,000 acres or more were the exception rather than the rule, except in certain sections. There were many people who, because of ill luck, lack of foresight, low development of acquisitiveness, poor management, and other causes did not accumulate property, and they and their descendants remained on small farms interspersed between extensive plantations. It is the description of the larger plantations that one finds in historical records because they were the exception. William Fitzhugh, a planter in Virginia writing to his brother in England, tells that he had in his possession four plantations of various sizes: a 1,000-acre, a 21,996-acre, a 500-acre, and a second 1,000-acre plantation.* A share in the Virginia Company gave the owner 100 acres of land, but of course a planter could own as many shares as he had money to purchase. Land was cheap, varying in price from 55 cents to $2.57 for the acre (currency of that time).

On the larger plantations the typical dwelling was a two-story rectangular frame building probably 20 by 40 feet, with a brick chimney at either end. The planks and boards after 1630 were supplied for some homes by the sawmill at Jamestown. Sawmills became numerous after 1650. A few homes were of brick, the brick being made in the

* Letters of Fitzhugh, April 22, 1686, quoted by Bruce, *op. cit.*, II, 243.

Colony. Some brick were imported. A layer of clay was found within a few feet of the surface at or near Jamestown, and this was worked into brick. Oyster shells were burned for lime. The walls of the better homes were plastered. Many sorts of paint, including white lead, are found among the records of the imports of the colony. Glass windows were common in the typical home; some of the poorer dwellings had sliding windows. Until after the close of the seventeenth century it is probable that few planters had money enough to construct the pretentious homes to be found on even moderate-sized farms in Virginia today. The characteristic Virginia Colonial type is of later development. Many of the early colonial homes had broad, open halls that were swept by the breezes in the summer. The "dog run" of many log houses found widely scattered throughout some parts of the South today is an architectural adjustment that secures the same results. The columns of the Virginia Colonial house are an adaptation of the Greek stone column. With only slender pines available for columns—no stone was within reach on the Coastal Plain—the sturdy massiveness of the Greek column became the graceful slender column of Virginia.

The heavy yields of crops on the virgin soil and the rapid increase in livestock enabled the enterprising and prudent to accumulate wealth, particularly if they had brought with them sufficient money to purchase large acreages. The standards of living on these early plantations were, apparently, as high as found in the Northern country for similar social levels. Hugh Jones, in 1724, wrote, "The Gentlemen's Seats are of late built for the most part of good Brick, and many of Timber very handsome and capacious and likewise the common Planters live in pretty Timber Houses neater than the Farm Houses are generally in England."* These high standards have ever been maintained in the South among the well-to-do agriculturists.

The homes of the wealthier planters were well furnished with imported furniture of all sorts. Fitzhugh, quoted previously, writes his brother that one of his homes had thirteen rooms, "furnished with all things necessary and convenient . . . for a comfortable and gentle living." Imported rugs, Russian leather chairs, Turkey couches, trunks of leather and brass, and brass-bound chests were found in many homes before the close of the seventeenth century. Porcelain dishes, steel and pewter cutlery, tin, and even silver plates, were common. Musical instruments, like the virginal, lyre, flute, cornet, and violin, were in use.

---

* Quoted by Lyman Carrier, *op. cit.*, 136.

The outbuildings on most plantations included a cellar or two, a dairy, dovecote, stable, barn, henhouse, a kitchen, cabins for slaves, and small homes for white servants. There was also a garden near by and an orchard containing apple, pear, peach, plum, quince, fig, and cherry trees. Water was obtained from a spring, if near, or from a dug well. The plantations were well-stocked with horses (some pure-bred stock), cattle, sheep, goats, pigs, and poultry, as we have seen. The saddle horse was in common use, but a few imported carriages were owned. The pillion and side saddle were provided for the ladies for travel during muddy seasons. One writer says that by 1725 "most females (of the wealthier class) had a coach, chariot, Berlin, or chaise."*

Many travelers commented on the hospitality of the planters, a characteristic of the gentry of the South today. One English traveler, late in the eighteenth century, was told by Jefferson that on his father's plantation a servant was often stationed at the cross roads to beseech any likely-looking travelers to tarry a while, and eat and drink. Isolation, desire for social contacts, infrequency of social calls, lack of newspapers and magazines, and, in some homes, lack of books, and the desire to share with others home comforts and to exhibit the home, have for three centuries been factors in establishing hospitality as one of the cardinal characteristics of the wealthier Southerners. Home-making has become a fixed habit. A beautiful home is one method of displaying wealth and refinement. The beautiful country homes about most of the more enterprising cities of the South today, even where there is no great amount of accumulated wealth, are a modern expression of ideals and habits developed in the days when the plantation home was the symbol of refinement and elegance and comfort. In an industrial and commercial age such wealth would go into factories, banks, and mercantile establishments. Perhaps it were better that the South had more factories and less elegant homes, but who can assert that in the long run the quality of manhood and womanhood would be better?

The interest in agriculture manifested in the Colonial period in Virginia persisted into the early part of the last century and to a certain degree even to our day. The large planters have always been the most persistent experimenters and lent encouragement to improvement in agricultural methods and practices. Washington was considered a "progressive" farmer in his day. He was both a "book farmer" and a "dirt farmer." He experimented with various rotation

---

* Data selected from Bruce, *op. cit.*, II, 133-162.

schemes, and the use of lime, gypsum, and salt as fertilizers. He was interested in improving machinery; grew and grafted fruit trees and ornamental shrubs. Like Jefferson, he was active in American societies for the promotion of agriculture. Jefferson organized the Albemarle Agricultural Society in 1817. Its proceedings were published in the *Richmond Enquirer*. The society gave prizes for improvement and invention of agricultural implements, for livestock and articles of domestic manufacture. Jefferson, backed by many wealthy, prominent Virginia farmers, most of them members of the Society of Virginia for the Promotion of Agriculture, succeeded in getting a chair of agriculture at the University of Virginia which was largely the "child" of Jefferson.*

ON THE FRONTIER OF THE SOUTH ATLANTIC COLONIES

In the Lower South, agricultural prosperity was based in Colonial days on rice and indigo. But tobacco, wheat, rye, oats, and peas yielded in greater abundance than in England.† English cattle, horses, and pigs multiplied rapidly on the pine forest ranges. They were free from disease, and losses were few from the cold winter. There were a few sheep, but these required the attention of a shepherd and hence were not in favor as domestic animals.‡

There were few fruit trees in the coastal sections, figs being about the only edible fruit. Orange trees stood the winter at Charleston, but rarely fruited; at ten miles' distance from the sea the trees were likely to freeze most winters unless well protected. The oranges consumed came from Florida.§ As in Virginia, as wealth accumulated, more thought was given to farming. Agricultural societies were formed; one dating from this time is still active. The shifting from rice and indigo to cotton growing, the constant improvement in the quality of rice, the preparation of indigo for the market, the numerous cotton gins constructed and tried out, all indicate that there was much experimenting on the plantations.

An, agricultural society was formed in South Carolina in 1740 by a group of indigo planters whose meetings at first were for the most part convivial but "talking shop" was permitted. This society—the

---

* Alfred C. True, *A History of Agricultural Education in United States*, 14, 16, 57, 65.

† Edward McCrady, *South Carolina Under Proprietary Government, 1617-1719*, 187.

‡ *Ibid.*, 188.

§ F. A. Michaux, *Travels to the West of the Alleghany Mountains*, 288-292.

Winyaw (or Winyah) Indigo Society—formed a charity agricultural school in 1755. The South Carolina Society for the Promotion and Improvement of Agriculture and Other Rural Concerns was organized August 24, 1785, at Charleston. Many of the leading men of the state, some holding Federal offices in Washington, were included in the membership.*

The success of the South Carolina planters was largely the result of a careful selection of crops. In the cultivation of the subtropical crops, rice, indigo, and cotton, and the warm temperate crop, tobacco, they brought little from England that could prove helpful; but the settlers from the Barbadoes made some contributions, for they had had experiences in exploiting tropical lands. In the formation of the Ashley River settlement, West, who had charge of the expedition, was instructed to visit Barbadoes and bring with him cotton seed, indigo seed, ginger roots, sugar cane, olive sets, and some pigs.† About 1800, cotton began to replace rice, because "it afford[ed] greater returns to the planters." A good cotton crop was considered worth twice as much an acre as rice.

The Georgia colony had every reason for possessing many experimenters in agriculture. The great majority of the people were agriculturists, accustomed to work. Oglethorpe was a practical philanthropist imbued with the idea of advancing the material as well as the spiritual well-being of his charges. The colony drew people from many countries of northwestern Europe, and thus the types of agricultural experiences were many. Oglethorpe purchased livestock in Charleston, and supervised the planting of a few gardens near the Savannah settlement in which were soon growing thyme, potherbs, sage, leeks, celery, and other vegetables. Von Rich, who arrived at Savannah with a body of Saltzburgers, a religious sect from Germany, reported, within a few months, that already they had laid out "a garden for making experiments for Improving Botany and Agriculture. . . . It contains," he writes, "ten Acres and lies upon the River; it is cleared and brought into such Order that there is already a fine nursery of Oranges, Olives, White Mulberries, Figs, Peaches, and many curious Herbs; besides which there is Cabbage, Peas, and other European Pulse and plants, which all thrive."‡ The far southern location of this littoral settlement permitted the introduction of and experimentation with tropical plants such as coffee,

---

* True, *op. cit.*, 8.

† Lyman Carrier, *Beginnings of Agriculture in America*, 200.

‡ Peter Force, *Tracts and other Papers*, Washington 1836, quoted by Lyman Carrier, *op. cit.*, 209.

cocoanuts, cotton, bamboo cane, and tea, as well as those of north-west Europe. After many failures and after the enthusiasm had worn off, the colony settled down to the commercial production of rice and indigo, and, in a few decades, to cotton. The sea islands were found admirably suited to the production of a long-staple (sea island) cotton. Corn became the most important cereal. These were the crops best adapted to the soil, climate, market opportunities, and slavery. Few fruit trees throve in this part of Georgia other than the fig. The European grape proved a failure. The silk industry, as in Virginia, also failed, although for a time there was much interest and some success. Even a public filature was established. Cattle raising was a success from the start.

At first slavery was prohibited. Habits of work were being taught even the young boys and girls. But the rich returns from the virgin soils brought surplus capital, and the great material prosperity of the near-by South Carolina colony, where slaves were numerous, induced the Georgians to abandon, by degrees, their idealism regarding the benefits of free labor and adopt slavery (about 1750). But the slave population was never so large, relatively, as in South Carolina.

AGRICULTURE IN THE GREAT VALLEY—PIONEER PERIOD

Isolation seems to have been more important than climate and soil in agricultural adjustment in the Great Valley in eastern Tennessee. The marketing of cornmeal and meats was difficult, for the mountains and plateaus formed east and west barriers and beyond these were "considerable tracts of country that produce[d] the same provisions and which are [were] more fertile or nearer to the borders of the sea."* Cattle were the chief export, being driven 400 to 500 miles to the Atlantic seaports. Although they were half wild and had to cross numerous rivers, and travel unfenced ways, few were lost.† The driving of horses and cattle to the coast cities continued as a regular method of marketing until the coming of the railroad. One traveler reported that 10,000 horses a year (about 1839) reached the Atlantic Coast cities, and in one day 500 cattle of excellent quality passed through Greenville, South Carolina.‡

Just what contributions to methods of tillage, harvesting, storage, and marketing of crops the settlers from the north and from Europe made in the Great Valley and farther west is not readily discernible

---

* F. A. Michaux, *Travels to the West of the Alleghany Mountains*, 247.
† *Idem.*
‡ J. S. Buckingham, *Slave States of America*, II, 203.

in the literature of the region. It would seem that wherever colonies of foreigners became segregated the prevailing farm practices would be unlike those of the Americans, even though the variety of crops was restricted to that of American communities. Home industries dominated everywhere except in those parts in direct touch with ocean ports. Jefferson reported that home industries dominated in Virginia about 1782, the year he wrote his *Notes on the State of Virginia.** In all the back country, clothing, agricultural implements, crude though they were, and furniture, in most homes, were made on the farm. There was less opportunity for the importation of luxuries than there was in eastern Virginia. Besides, the intermontane and Transappalachian settlers had not yet (in 1800-1820) accumulated a surplus that enabled them to live on the plane of their contemporaries in Virginia. It was many decades later that a gentleman-class arose in Kentucky and middle Tennessee. In frontier regions, whether of high or moderate potential fertility, standards of living are much alike. It requires decades for differentiation to become noticeable.

Farm life in the Blue Grass Region and on the cherty, dolomite lands of eastern Tennessee was much alike when both sections were in the pioneer stage. In the region of "lasting" fertility, as the Blue Grass, beautiful homes, in time, arose with trees, shrubs, orchards, well-built barns and out-buildings, all surrounded by well-tilled fields. The community became wealthy enough to support a good school and a church or two. Sons and daughters went to college. The wealthy planters became state if not national leaders. In the region of moderate or low fertility, as in eastern Tennessee and Kentucky, the soil was depleted in the course of a few years, log houses persisted, schooling facilities were inadequate, tillage was indifferent, and the yields were sufficient only to permit bare existence. It is a rare genius that arises from such an agricultural environment. (See discussion in Chapter IV.)

FARMING ON THE KENTUCKY AND MIDDLE TENNESSEE FRONTIER

The settlers who poured into Kentucky and Tennessee just before 1800 and the decades thereafter carried with them the experiences of the Cisappalachian farmers, whose methods, practices, crops, and livestock had in turn come from the mother countries or had been evolved or modified in America to fit American conditions.

Literature on agriculture is very meager. The attention of the

---

* Thomas Jefferson, *Notes on the State of Virginia,* 323.

farmers on the frontiers was too much taken with matters much more important for their existence than attempts at improving or writing about agriculture, for with virgin soils and farming land in abundance the task of providing food was largely a matter of application of labor. There was little time for experimentation. The records of the frontier settlements are concerned largely with Indian troubles, politics, and elections; agriculture was commonplace. Imlay, who visited Kentucky in 1798, summarizes the agriculture and agricultural conditions as follows:

> Here is found all the variety of soil and climate necessary to the culture of every kind of grain, fibrous plant, cotton, fruits, vegetables, and all sorts of provisions. . . . The superfluous provisions are sold to the emigrants who are continually passing through those settlements in their route to the different districts of the country. . . . Some considerable quantities of spirits distilled from rye, and likewise cider, are sent down the river to a market, in those infant settlements where the inhabitants have not had time to bring orchards to any perfection, or have not a superfluity of grain to distill into spirits. The beef, pork, and flour are disposed of in the same way. The flax and hemp are packed on horses and sent across the mountains to the inland towns of Pennsylvania and Maryland, and . . . in a few years when grazing forms the principal object of those settlers they will always find a market for their cattle in Philadelphia, Baltimore, and Alexandria.*

Michaux, who a few years later, in 1802, traveled through the Blue Grass section of Kentucky, and on southward to the Nashville Basin, also gave interesting details regarding agriculture in the areas visited.

The crops of Kentucky, he observed, were corn, tobacco, hemp, flax, rye, oats, and wheat. The frosts "which began early," he writes, "are unfavorable to cotton." Western Kentucky was unsettled then. On the flatter lands corn grew 10 to 12 feet high and yielded 60 to 70 bushels (English) to the acre. Some areas a second or third year after clearing produced 100 bushels. In the local markets it sold for one-fourth of a dollar as a maximum, but generally was 15 to 18 cents. In the fall, leaves were collected as they became brown and were reserved as a winter sustenance for horses which preferred that kind of forage to the best hay. The corn was ground locally and sent downstream to New Orleans in "slight barrels made of oak."†

Tobacco and corn were the principal articles of export, but there

---

* Gilbert Imlay, *A Topographical Description of the Western Territory of North America*, 60-61.

† F. A. Michaux, *Travels to the West of the Alleghany Mountains*, 178-180.

was some shipment of hemp. In 1802, 42,048 pounds of raw hemp and 2,402 hundredweight in cables and other forms of cordage were shipped. Flax was grown for local use. Linen was made in the homes for home or local use. Only the poorer people used this locally woven linen; the wealthy imported Irish linens.

Horned cattle were numerous on every farm. In herds of 200 to 300 they were driven eastward to Virginia along the Potomac where they were fattened (probably in the Shenandoah Valley and western Piedmont) for the Philadelphia and Baltimore markets. Butter was put in barrels and exported to the Caribbean. Hogs ranged the woods and when turned out did "not make their appearance again for months," he writes. Some farmers had from 150 to 200 hogs. Pork was salted, and, like salt, most of which was brought into Kentucky, was an important article of commerce. Few sheep were bred, but horses were numerous. The better saddle horses brought $130 to $150 locally and, if driven to the seaboard cotton and rice areas, a much higher price. All people, he writes, were interested in "training and meliorating" horses. The saddle and racing horses were descendants of Virginia horses brought by the first settlers.* Some of the Virginia sires of the Kentucky horses were the offspring of imported Arab and Turkish stallions.† Most of the horses raised were for use on the farms. Of these he says, "No attention with respect to improving the breed was paid." Some of these no doubt were interbred with the small Mexican horses which returning boatmen purchased in Natchez. Both saddle and work animals were sold in the numerous sales stables in Kentucky and driven in herds of 15 to 30 to the Lower South, the journey being undertaken always in winter for fear of yellow fever, which was often of epidemic virulency in Savannah, Charleston, and Wilmington. It usually required from 18 to 20 days for the 700-mile journey from Lexington to Charleston.

There were a few peach trees about most homes, and some farmers had small orchards. A part of each crop was turned into brandy (stills were numerous, some commercial where the peaches were exchanged for brandy), of which there was "great consumption." Some whiskey was exported. The price received was about a dollar a gallon. The surplus peach crop was fed to the hogs. Apples grew to great perfection, but the trees were less numerous than the peach. Both were grown in a hit-or-miss way. Peach trees were propagated from

---

* Michaux, op. cit., 187-193.

† Philip A. Bruce, Economic History of Virginia in the Seventeenth Century, I, 472.

peach kernels and grew up on open fields "without being pruned or grafted."*

In the Tennessee Basin most of the crops grown in Kentucky were produced, but in addition the farmers raised cotton. Nashville was the market for the Middle Tennessee-grown cotton, from which city it was shipped by river to New Orleans and from there to Philadelphia, New York, and Europe. Attempts were made to send it east by way of Pittsburgh. Michaux saw barges laden with cotton ascending the Ohio, making about 20 miles a day. Cotton was also sent into Kentucky for domestic use.†

AGRICULTURE ON THE GULF STATES FRONTIERS

By the time Alabama and the Gulf States to the west were invaded by American farmers and planters, cotton had become the major crop of the Lower South, all else being forgotten or shoved to a minor place in agriculture, in the mad scramble to accumulate the wealth that cotton culture assured them. Cotton culture and its accompanying social life were superimposed on an older agricultural regime in Louisiana, the creation of old-world French migrants and Acadian French. The coastal sections of Alabama and Mississippi likewise had an early French culture.

Louisiana's agricultural settlements until late in the nineteenth century were confined largely to the natural levees of the Mississippi and the Red, and their south-flowing distributaries. The draining of the interstream marshes has proved difficult, in fact, impossible, in some sections even at the present day. Livestock, cereals, and the fruits of old France were introduced; but the French early found that cotton, sugar cane, tobacco, rice, and maize were the crops best adjusted to the climate. Perique tobacco, now raised near Baton Rouge on the natural levees of the Mississippi, has come down from French Colonial days. Two varieties of tobacco appear to have been grown.

One of Bienville's reports, quoted by Gayarré, gives a brief review of agricultural conditions in Louisiana in 1736. The planters were disgusted with the cultivation of tobacco "on account of the uncertainty of the crop which is," he writes, "alternately affected either by the incessant rain or by the long droughts so peculiar to this country. We may produce from thirty to thirty-five thousand pounds of indigo if there be no accident in the way. The inhabitants

* Michaux, *op. cit.*, 178, 191.
† Michaux, *op. cit.*, 279, 280.

are turning their attention to this branch of industry. As to silk, very little is made, through ignorance. With regard to cotton, the production is very limited, on account of the difficulty of separating it from its seed, or rather because the cultivation of indigo is more profitable."*

The French introduced a white Siam species of cotton which produced better and was whiter than the American varieties of that day.

Brackenridge, who visited the region in 1810-1811, reported that in the Opelousas Country, though cotton was the principal crop, sugar cane had been found to succeed as well as, if not better than, on the Mississippi. A number of planters had already turned their attention to it. Several sugar mills had been erected to handle the cane. Most of Louisiana sugar was grown on the levee land of the Mississippi. On the levee lands of the bayous west of the Mississippi, he writes, the inhabitants were "generally wealthy and live[d] as luxuriantly as the planters on the Mississippi." In the scantily wooded Opelousas country and on the Attakapas prairies he saw almost "incredible" numbers of cattle. They were marketed in New Orleans, to which they were driven on foot, and brought 15 to 20 dollars a head. The "best cotton in the United States" was grown on the levees of the Red River along with tobacco and indigo.† Southern Louisiana, therefore, in the same temperature regions and with about the same rainfall as southern South Carolina and Georgia had similar crops—cotton, rice, indigo, tobacco, corn, but in addition sugar cane. In both, cattle raising was active.

The Last Agricultural Frontier of the Old South

The first invasion, peaceful, of Texas by Americans was to utilize the grazing lands.‡ For more than two centuries Spanish and Mexican cattle and horses had roamed the vast Texas domain. Spanish agriculture was limited to a small area of irrigated land near El Paso, where a low lateral dam directed water from the Rio Grande into a canal which carried it down valley to the low bottoms.

Moses Austin was the first American to seek agricultural lands in Texas. He offered to plant agricultural colonies in the vast domain that lay so near the American frontier. (See discussion in Chapter IV.) From about 1821 onward, there was active migration of Americans into the region, though the movement was checked materially by the adverse attitude of Mexico when its leaders came to realize

---

* Quoted in Chas. Gayarré, *History of Louisiana*, I, 497, 498.

† H. M. Brackenridge, *Views of Louisiana*, 169, 174.

‡ Henry S. Foote, *Texas and the Texans*, I, 204.

that the peaceful penetration of Americans ultimately meant the loss
of Texas. It was virgin cotton land that attracted American planters,
particularly after Alabama, Mississippi, and Louisiana had largely been
occupied. The invading cotton planters carried with them the farm
practices, wasteful and superficial, learned and practiced in the Gulf
States to the east. Agricultural Texas became a transplanted Georgia,
Alabama, or Mississippi. At first the farmers settled the forested
tracts and avoided the prairies which were, until the 1850's or 1860's,
a vast open range for cattle. But when the advance on the prairie
lands began it was 'rapid. An English traveler reported that in the
preparation of the prairie land "a strong plow and a strong team
[were] required the first year to break up the tough sward and
turn over the sod." The sod once turned rotted down in a single season, and thereafter the soil was mellow and thus easy to cultivate.
In contrast to the agricultural conditions in the forests and prairies,
this traveler discovered that "It would be sounder economy for a
person to settle in the midst of a prairie and draw his fuel and fence
wood five miles, than to undertake the clearing of a farm in the
forest . . . supposing the soil of both to be of equal quality." The
prairie soil was potentially much the more fertile, and was so considered at that time.* See discussion in Chapter II, Soils.

2. THE AGRICULTURAL SOUTH IN THE ANTEBELLUM PERIOD
INTRODUCTION

By the middle of the nineteenth century most of the South, occupied by the whites, had reached agricultural maturity. The older
sections on the Atlantic Slope had become quite thoroughly adjusted
to the physical and market conditions and to the regime of slave
labor; and though a few canals had been excavated and a few hard
surfaced roads had been built, transportation facilities had not yet
been improved sufficiently to disturb the agricultural order that had
dominated for many decades. Here and there a railroad had given
isolated, interior sections an outlet to world markets, but owing to
poor roads the benefits of a railroad were realized only a few score
miles from these harbingers of a new order in transportation.

The decade between 1850 and 1860 is a transition period in the
agricultural geography of the South, largely because of the rapid increase of railroad mileage. From 1851 to 1860, inclusive, more than
7,000 miles were constructed in the Southern States, which was nearly

---

* Kennedy, *Texas*, quoted in Wm. B. Bizzell, *Rural Texas*, **120.**

double the miles in operation in 1851.* The close of the Antebellum
Period brought to an end an economic order that had flourished for
more than two centuries. The Civil War was an economic "revolution" for the South, a change from a regime of slavery to one of free
labor—of free colored labor so debased by the newly given freedom
and corrupted by carpetbaggers in the Reconstruction Period as to
be next to worthless on the plantation. It is for these reasons that
the data for the decade between 1850 and 1860 are selected to present
to the reader a cross section of the agricultural Antebellum South.

THE AGRICULTURAL SOUTH ABOUT 1850 AND 1860

The Southern States in 1850, with 39 per cent of the population of
the country, were producing about 14 per cent of the manufactures.†
In 1860 the factories turned out about the same percentage of the
country's fabricated products.‡ Its economic activities thus were
largely associated with agriculture. An agricultural regime calls for
little mining, though the production of commercial agricultural products involves much transportation. Transportation on the rivers and
railroads and the handling of imports and exports at the ports gave
employment to many men. Table II shows the number of persons
employed in commerce, trade, manufacturing, and mining in comparison with the number in agriculture in 1850. The dominance of agriculture in most of the Southern States is evident.

The slaveholding South had not kept pace with the North and
West in population growth. The presence of the institution of slavery
left little place in the economic order for free labor, hence few
European immigrants had settled in the South.§ Many conditions
and movements were responsible for the slower growth of the South,
no doubt, but slavery was certainly a major one. It also largely
accounts for the slow growth of manufacturing, as will be demonstrated in a later chapter, which explains the slow urban growth.
Virginia, which had held first rank in population among the states
in the Union from 1790 to 1810, inclusive, had dropped to fifth place
in 1860. North Carolina, which was third in population in 1790 and
fourth from 1810 to 1820, held twelfth place in 1860. South Carolina

---

* *Compendium of Seventh Census,* 1850, 189; *Preliminary Report of the Eighth
Census,* 1860, 236.

† Calculated from data, *Compendium of Tenth Census,* 1880, Part 2, 931.

‡ *Ibid.,* 930.

§ Calculated from data, *Report of Eighth Census,* 1860, "Population," p. xxix;
Statistical Abstract, 1928, 91, 93.

TABLE II

EMPLOYMENT OF FREE MALE POPULATION OVER
FIFTEEN YEARS OF AGE, IN 1850[1]

	Commerce, Trade, Manufacturing, Mining	Agriculture
Maryland	47,600	28,600
Virginia	52,700	108,400
North Carolina	20,600	82,000
South Carolina	13,200	41,300
Georgia	20,700	83,400
Florida	2,400	6,000
Alabama	16,600	68,600
Mississippi	12,000	50,300
Louisiana	32,900	18,600
Texas	7,300	28,300
Arkansas	4,300	28,900
Tennessee	23,400	119,000
Kentucky	36,600	115,000

[1] Compiled from *Compendium of Seventh Census*, 1850, 128; There were 132 persons out of every thousand for the whole South engaged in agriculture, 32.5 in commerce, manufacturing and mining, and 3.3 in the learned professions. *Idem*, 129.

had dropped from sixth place in 1800 and 1810 to eighteenth in 1860. Maryland held sixth place in 1790 but nineteenth in 1860. The other Southern States showed similar declines. Texas was too young to be included in our generalizing. Its population in 1860 was 604,000.* Although each of the older Southern States had shown an increase, they had lost a large percentage of their natural population increase by migration to the West. Some of the migrants moved into the North and Northeast. Superficial tillage, a concomitant of one-crop cotton farming, active soil erosion and depletion, and slavery, and the natural increase in the slave population forced the cotton planters to adopt an expansion program. The small farmers in the sections where large plantations were numerous were always glad to sell out at good prices and migrate to frontiers where land was cheap. It was much easier for them to migrate than for the large landowners, for they had less to move. Their hold on the land was weak. They were willing to sell at reasonable prices, and the planters were generally willing to pay all they asked. This constant loss of people was a concomitant, or one of the causes, of the agricultural stagnation of the older South in the 1840's and 1850's. An increasing population in time would have forced the adoption of more intensive tillage practices.

* *Report of Eighth Census*, 1860, "Mortality and Miscellaneous Statistics," p. xx; *Statistical Abstract*, 1929, 8.

The South in 1840 had 6,900,000 people; in 1850, 9,000,000; and in 1860, 11,100,000.* In 1860 it had about 35 per cent of the population of the United States.† Its improved acreage in 1860 was about 41 per cent of that for the country; the value of the livestock about 45 per cent; and of farm implements and machinery, 40 per cent.‡ It was producing less than a third of the wheat, 100 per cent of the cotton, about three-fourths of the tobacco, and 100 per cent of the rice of the United States. Two states, South Carolina and Georgia, produced 93 per cent of the rice of the country. The total production then as now was small, only 215,000,000 pounds. Corn was another important crop, more than half the corn of the country being grown in the Southern States. Tennessee in 1840 ranked as first state in the Union in corn production (total bushels). Ohio took first rank in 1850 and Illinois in 1860. Kentucky held second rank in 1840 and 1850. Virginia stood third in 1840, and sixth in 1850. North Carolina held sixth place in 1840.§

There were fewer swine and horses per capita in the South than in the country at large, and less wool and less butter and cheese were produced.¶ This, of course, is what would be expected, for this section had crops, like cotton, tobacco, and rice, for which it was especially adapted and to which it devoted most of its attention. It had, however, about half the cattle of the country and nearly two-thirds the number of swine.

Although the steamboats on the rivers of the South in the decade after 1850 were numerous and were functioning as they never functioned before or have since, the back-country farmers were about as isolated as ever. Most of the overseas commerce and transportation in agricultural products were in the hands of Northern or European merchants and vessel owners, who had commission houses and banks in many of the Southern seaports.

The Upper and Lower South differed materially in their agriculture. Cotton, rice, sugar cane, corn, and sweet potatoes dominated in the Lower South; corn, wheat, tobacco, oats, hemp, and livestock products, in the Upper South. Virginia led all Southern states in the production of butter, but it produced only one-eighth that of New York. Kentucky led in the number of horses. It surpassed all other

---

* Calculated from data, *Report of Eighth Census*, 1860, "Agriculture," p. xlviii.
† *Statistical Abstract*, 1929, 8.
‡ Calculated from data, *Preliminary Report of the Eighth Census*, 1860, 196-199.
§ *Ibid.*, 200-209.
¶ *Ibid.*, pp. lxxxv, cxxiv.

states in the Union except Ohio, Pennsylvania, and New York. Virginia led the Southern States in the number of sheep, but it had only about 6 per cent of the total for the United States. Kentucky and Tennessee had about 21 per cent of the swine (in number) of the country. Virginia led the Southern States in wheat. It produced more than any one of the North Central States except Ohio. Apple culture on a commercial basis had not yet begun in the South, and the crop of peaches was so small as not to command attention. Interestingly, Kentucky led in the production of market-garden products. The development of the southern part of the Atlantic and Gulf Coastal Plain as an "early" trucking region had to await refrigeration, which came in the late 1870's, and fast railroad transportation. In the Lower South, where climate favored the growth of cotton, rice, and sugar cane (both of the last two very small in value in comparison to cotton), and where overseas and coastwise transportation were close at hand, commercial agriculture dominated. The Upper South was quite self-sufficing, producing supply crops largely. Tobacco, meats, hemp, and livestock on the hoof were the money products.

Because of these differences in type of agriculture there were striking differences in the number of slaves by states and the proportion of slaves to whites. In this connection Table III brings out some interesting facts. Also see Figure 64 for distribution of slaves in 1860.

Within the states of the Upper South, there were strong contrasts in the proportion of slaves to whites in the different physiographic

TABLE III

THE RELATIVE NUMBER OF NEGRO SLAVES AND
WHITES IN THE SOUTH IN 1850[1]

	Slaves	White Population	Slaves to 100 Whites
Upper South			
Maryland..............	90,000	418,000	21
Virginia and West Virginia	473,000	895,000	50
North Carolina.........	289,000	553,000	52
Kentucky.............	211,000	761,000	28
Tennessee.............	239,000	757,000	31
Arkansas..............	47,000	162,000	23
Lower South			
South Carolina.........	385,000	275,000	140
Georgia................	382,000	522,000	75
Alabama...............	343,000	427,000	80
Mississippi............	310,000	296,000	105
Louisiana.............	245,000	255,000	96
Texas.................	58,000	154,000	38

[1] Calculated from data, *Report of Seventh Census*, 1850, p. xxiii.

provinces. These differences in distribution are to be correlated with
the type of agriculture, the wealth of the farmers, size of farm, and
social conditions. The *geo* conditions and forces were more dominant
than the *anthropo*. There were differences in politics and religion in
the physiographic provinces, but these had long since ceased to influence sentiment on the slavery question. They, too, were adaptations, for the most part, to the economic-geographic conditions in the
respective regions. Table IV shows the actual number of thousands of
slaves and whites in selected counties in each of the major physiographic regions in the states of the Upper South, in 1850.

TABLE IV

THOUSANDS OF SLAVES TO WHITES IN SELECTED COUNTIES, 1850[1]

State and County	Location: Physiographic Province, City, etc.	Population Slaves to Whites in Thousands	Page Reference
Virginia			
Surrey County	Middle, Coastal Plain	2.5 to 2.2	(257)
Appomattox	Middle Piedmont	4.8 to 4.2	(256)
Rockbridge	Great Valley	4.2 to 11.5	(257)
Kanawha	Charleston, Allegheny Plateau	3.1 to 12	(256)
North Carolina			
Cravens Co.	Newburn, Coastal Plain	6 to 7.2	(307)
Cumberland	Fayetteville, Edge Piedmont.	7.2 to 12.4	(307)
Burke	Morganton, West Edge, Pied-		
	mont	2.1 to 5.5	(307)
Buncombe	Asheville, Mountains	1.7 to 11.6	(307)
Cherokee	Murphy, Mountains	0.3 to 2.9	(307)
Tennessee			
Monroe County	Great Valley	1.2 to 10.6	(574)
Fentress	Plateau	.15 to 4.3	(573)
Warren	McMinnville	1.7 to 8.4	(574)
Davidson	Nashville	14.2 to 23.9	(573)
Gibson	Middle, West Tennessee,		
	Coastal Plain	4.2 to 15.3	(573)
Kentucky			
Breathitt Co.	Plateau	.17 to 3.6	(611)
Fayette	Lexington, Blue Grass	10.9 to 11.2	(611)
Warren	Bowling Green	4.3 to 10.6	(612)
Graves	Coastal Plain, W. Ky.	1.4 to 10	(611)

[1] Data from *Report of Seventh Census*, 1850. Pages shown on right.

There is much misunderstanding regarding the number of slaveholders of the South in the Antebellum Period, the size of the plantations, and the number of slaves to the plantation. Many picture the

South as being one grand succession of 5,000- to 10,000-acre plantations each manned by 1,000 to 5,000 slaves.*

In 1860 there were in the thirteen Southern States 663,000 farms;
only 4,576 had 1,000 acres or more;* the total number of slaveholders
was 346,000;† and the total number of slaves was about 4,000,000 (Fig.
64 shows their distribution in 1860). The total white population
numbered about 8,000,000. The census data show that only 1 slave
owner in the entire South had 1,000 or more slaves; 13 owned from
500 to 1,000; only 298 held from 200 to 500; 1,980 held 100 to 200.
On the other hand, 77,000 held 1 slave only, 110,000 held 2 to 5, 189,-
000 held 5 to 50. Only about 50 per cent of the owners of farms or
plantations held slaves; and, considering both rural and urban population, probably not much more than one-third of the population
was slaveholding. Plantations of 50 or more slaves, if evenly distributed over the South, would number about 7 or 8 to the county.‡ But
these large plantations were far from being evenly distributed. Hilly,
mountainous regions and regions of poor soil had none. In the Black
Belt of Alabama along most large rivers having broad flood plains,
large plantations dominated. The percentage of farmers that were
slaveholders varied greatly in the states. In South Carolina 81 per
cent of the farmers held slaves; in Alabama about 60 per cent; in Tennessee about 45 per cent; in Kentucky about 42 per cent; and in Virginia about 56 per cent.§ Thus the percentage of slaveholders of total
owners was largest in the Lower South, in the Cotton Belt, and in the
older states of the Upper South.

---

* The term plantation as used by the United States Census Board in recent
decades for census-taking purposes is "any large farm several hundreds or thousands of acres" in extent. Before the Civil War, such would have been operated
as a single unit by slave labor. During the Reconstruction Period the owners
attempted to work their plantations by hired labor, but not finding this feasible,
divided their plantations into small tracts of 20 to 40 acres or more (each called
a farm), and adopted the tenant system that now dominates in many parts of the
South.

The Division of Social Research of the Works Progress Administration has
recently completed a very comprehensive study of the present-day plantation
(see Fig. 83). The study covers only the seven cotton states east of the Mississippi
River. To avoid the tremendous cost of a regular census, a method of wide
sampling was used, 646 plantations being studied in detail. Some of the major
facts discovered are given in the descriptive material on the map. (*Landlord and
Tenant on the Cotton Plantation,* W. P. A. Division of Social Research, Research
Monograph V., Washington, 1936. The investigation was made under the direction of T. J. Woofter, Jr., Coordinator of Rural Research.)

† Calculated from data, *Report of Eighth Census,* 1860, "Agriculture," 221.

‡ This included city and rural owners.

§ *Idem.*

¶ *Ibid.,* 247.

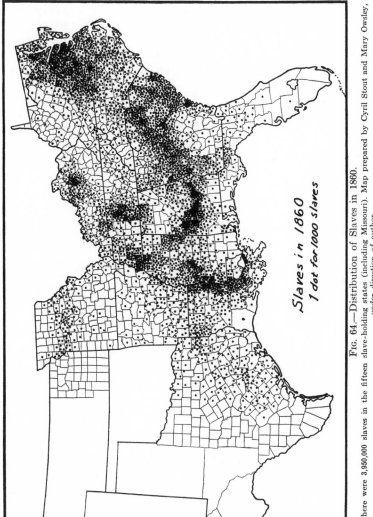

Slaves in 1860
1 dot for 1000 slaves

FIG. 64.—Distribution of Slaves in 1860. Map prepared by Cyril Stout and Mary Owsley, under direction of author.

There were 3,950,000 slaves in the fifteen slave-holding states (including Missouri).

The Population of the Antebellum South Classified*

On the basis of size of farms and ownership of slaves the population of the South in the late Antebellum Period may be divided into
four groups, nearly all being directly associated with agriculture:

First, the large landowners and their families—well-born, well-
educated, well-read, as a rule. They were wealthiest and most numerous in the rice and cotton districts of the Lower South.

A second group was composed of smaller landowners who held
tracts of 100 to 500 acres or more. The vast majority of the landed
Southerners belonged to this group; and though they figure little in
the writings of visitors to the South in Antebellum days they formed
the bulk of the population, and were the most stable of the four
groups. Most of these earned their living by their own labor as did
the farmers of the North; others were assisted by a few slaves. Such
farmers were comfortably well-off, made no pretense at grand living,
were not given to ancestor worship, and participated, but not actively,
in political affairs, unless in a section where their kind dominated in
intellect and experience. The more successful of this group, as wealth
and slaves increased, would qualify for membership in the first
group, unless perchance they were conscientious objectors to slavery,
and there were many such.

A third social stratum, the professional group, composed of lawyers,
doctors, and ministers, was largely drawn from the first and the
second group. Many as their wealth increased became landowners,
large or small. To this third group may be added the large number
of merchants, commission men, bankers, and others. There were a
few men interested in manufacturing and transportation, but men so
engaged did not hold rank in numbers with the large plantation
owners, lawyers, ministers, and doctors.

A fourth group was known as the "poor whites." Some of these
owned land, some not. Some were mere squatters.

The Dominant Influence of the Large Landowners

It was the large plantation owners in the several states, few as
they were in number, whose wealth, experience, culture, training, and

---

* Parts of this section are taken from the author's Presidential address before
the Association of American Geographers at the Worcester meeting, December
29-31, 1930, and later published in the *Annals of the Association of American
Geographers*, XXI, 1-33.

superior intelligence made them leaders. From this group and from the lawyers of the professional group were drawn the politicians and statesmen.

Because of the dominance of agriculture few opportunities were open to young men other than on the land and in the old-line professions of law, medicine, theology, and education. As among the English gentry, the land offered the greatest attraction. But those too poor to live without work, or to procure the land and equipment sufficient to set up even an average establishment, drifted into the professions. Law was above all the profession most respected because it generally led eventually into politics. In these fields, law and politics, Southerners ranked high among representatives from all other sections of our country. "Government," says one writer, "was a passion with Southerners." Politics gave an opportunity for the display of their forensic ability. Even a cursory reading of American history will convince one that the Southern political leaders exercised an influence in national affairs in Antebellum times far in excess of their proportionate representation. Alexander H. Stevens in a speech in the early 1860's asserted that up to 1860 Southerners had occupied the presidential chair 60 years, the Northerners but 24. The South had had 18 judges of the Supreme Court and the North only 11, although four-fifths of the business was Northern. The South had had 24 presiding officers (pro tem) of the Senate to the North's 11. The South had 23 speakers of the House *versus* 12 for the North. The former had 14 attorney generals *versus* 5 from the latter section. The number of foreign ministers stood 86 to 54. The South also had had the vast majority of ranking officers in the army and navy and two-thirds of the comptrollers, clerks, and auditors in the executive offices at Washington.

From a consideration of these facts concerning the dominance of Southerners in national politics and their prominence in state affairs it is not hard for one to understand how it was that, though composing but a very small percentage of the population of the South, the large slaveholders and pro-slavery professional men practically dominated the political and economic philosophy of the Southern population. Among this group of large landowners and slaveholders were many socially inclined. Most of the group lived comfortably. This select group lived elegantly. They were proverbially gracious, open-hearted, honest-minded, and hospitable. To visitors of note they displayed a "violent" hospitality, as one English traveler described it; but, he wrote, an ordinary stranger must be content if a letter of introduction procures for him "a courteous reception and a dinner."* Another British traveler describes the Southern gentleman, the frequenter of fashionable resorts, as he saw him in the North about 1841. "The old men from the South and from Carolina and Virginia especially," he writes, "are what would be called perfect gentlemen of the old school with us: precise, yet elegant in their dress; courteous and affable in their manners; high-toned in their politics and taste; lax in their morality while fashion sanctions their conduct; warm in their attachments, fierce in their resentments, and punctilious in all points of honor and etiquette."†

Lost Opportunities for the Southern Leaders

Yet this privileged group of large slaveholders, powerful as it was, made surprisingly few contributions to the National or even Southern life outside the field of politics. There were probably as many, possibly more, cultured men in the Lower South in the late Antebellum Period than in most other sections of our country. Wealth and leisure gave them opportunity for self-enlightenment and reflection. Valuable contributions to civilization should be expected from such men, and much was expected by many Southerners. But their "light was hidden under a bushel." No outstanding literature and few or no worthy scientific discoveries came from the South. The intellectuals seemed to lack the persistence essential to laborious production. Their efforts were dissipated in politics and oratory, and society. Numerous scientific discoveries could hardly be expected in an agricultural environment and in an atmosphere of classical learning. There was little specialization in any field, an essential for success in most fields of human endeavor. One cause at least for the lack of literary production was the general lack of a reading public in the agricultural sections, as true of the North as of the South. Thomas Nelson Page ascribes the lack of literary production to:

1. The dominance of agriculturists in the social and economic South. Population was dispersed. The people lacked the stimulus of mental contacts.
2. The absence of cities.
3. The absorption of intellectual efforts in the solution of the everyday problems of the plantation.

---

* Frances Hall, *Travels in Canada and the United States, 1816 and 1817,* in Allan Nevins, *American Social History, as Recorded by British Travellers,* 106.

† James Buckingham, *America, Historical, Statistic, and Descriptive,* 1841, I and II, in Nevins, *op. cit.,* 325, 326.

4. Ambition for political distinction.
5. The absence of a reading public.

EDUCATION IN THE ANTEBELLUM SOUTH

The facts that the South was largely agricultural, that the population was scattered, and that the leaders of the people, the wealthier planters, had private schools for their children account for the lack of attention devoted to *public* elementary education. Comparative data for the respective census divisions of the United States in 1860 are presented in Table V.

TABLE V

PUPILS AND EXPENDITURES, BY SECTIONS, 1860[1]

Section	Pupils	Income	Money Spent per Pupil
New England.................	647,000	$2,972,000	$ 4.59
Middle Atlantic States..........	1,365,000	6,441,000	4.71
Western States (North Central)..	2,250,000	8,702,000	3.86
South.......................	586,500	3,461,000	5.90
Pacific......................	33,000	402,000	12.14

[1] *Report of Eighth Census*, 1860, "Mortality and Miscellaneous Statistics," 504.

Before forming conclusions, the fact that the South was about equal in area to the New England, Middle Atlantic, and Western States combined should be taken into consideration; but it also should be remembered that the population of the North was 19,600,000. Reduced to a common population base, there were about three times as many pupils to 1,000 population in school in the North as in the South and the income about twice that of the South.

In academies, however, the South made a much more favorable showing. Reducing the data to a common population base, the pupils to 1,000 population are about equal in number; but in income the ratio of North to South stood as 1 to 1.7.

As for colleges, the South had 194 in 1860 attended by nearly 19,-000 students, the income of the colleges being $1,100,000. The entire North had 235 colleges, 33,400 students, and a total income of less than $1,860,000. If these data were reduced to a common population base, the South surpassed the North in colleges, number of students, and income. The census report states that "next to Michigan, South Carolina and Virginia (each) received the largest appropriations from public funds for public purposes."* It should also be remembered

* *Ibid.*, 503.

that hundreds of young men and women of the South attended Northern colleges and universities.

The South has some of the oldest colleges and universities in our country. William and Mary at Williamsburg, Virginia, was chartered in 1693. One of its initial gifts was from William and Mary of England. It was the second college in America to introduce an elective system. The phantom Henrico College had 9,000 acres of land on the James River set aside for its establishment in 1619. The Indian

From Graham's Magazine, XXV, 1844, 67.

FIG. 65.—The Georgia Female College at Macon, 1838.
The first in the South to grant degrees.

Massacre in 1622 prevented its being the oldest college in English America. Washington and Lee (really Augusta Academy from which it descended) dates from before the Revolution—1749. Tusculum in eastern Tennessee was chartered in 1794; Transylvania, in 1783. The University of North Carolina was chartered in 1787 and opened in 1795. The University of Virginia was founded by Thomas Jefferson in 1817 (see Fig. 65). At many of these there were excellent law schools.

THE POOR WHITES

At the other end of the social scale from the wealthy, educated class were the poor whites, improvident, ignorant, unschooled, degraded morally, and weakened physically by drink and disease. Governor

Hammond of South Carolina, about 1850, gave their number in that state as 50,000 out of a total white population of 300,000. "Some," he reported, "can not be said to work at all. They obtain a precarious subsistence by occasional jobs, by hunting and fishing, sometimes by plundering fields or folds, and, too often, by what is in effect far worse—trading with slaves and seducing them to plunder for their benefit."* The poor whites were largely "outcasts" in the Lower South where slaves were most numerous. Slaveowners rarely if ever employed them. Even the slaves considered themselves superior to the poor whites. In possession of only the poorest land, they labored merely to provide themselves and their families with the simplest necessities. A large percentage were illiterate. They were incompetent to improve their minds or their social and economic status. In few other parts of America could one find such poverty among rural inhabitants.

The life of most of the white mechanics and factory workers, relatively there were few of these, was little better than that of the poor rural whites, for all construction work, repair work, and fabrication by hand or machine on the plantation was done by slaves; and in the cities of the Lower South, at least, planters generally hired out their artisan slaves by the day, week, or month to building contractors and even factory operators. White mechanics were scarce in all parts, and few had experience and ideals to be classed as skilled workers. There were only 32,000 workers employed in manufacturing establishments in the seven Cotton Belt States in 1850; and only 57,000 workers not agricultural.† At times when the demand for negroes on the plantations was active it was difficult for non-slaveholders to secure labor for odd jobs, repairs, and small construction work. The more prosperous contractors had, therefore, to purchase slaves. About the only field open to white labor, and free from slave labor competition, was in transportation. In a slavery regime there was thus little place for a poor man, no matter how ambitious to attain success The few white mechanics who drifted into the South from Europe or from the North were of the poorest sort. Only the thoughtless and incompetent would migrate to sections whose economic life was dominated by slavery. At the close of the Civil War, it is estimated that, out of the 120,000 mechanics in the South, 100,000 were negroes.‡

---

* Quoted by Frederick L. Olmsted, *A Journey in the Seaboard Slave States,* 514.

† Calculated from data, *Compendium Seventh Census,* 1850, 128, 129.

‡ W. T. Couch, "The Negro in the South," in *Culture in the South,* 1934, 453.

ANTEBELLUM PLANTATIONS—SELECTED

A North Carolina Plantation*

A typical plantation would have been as difficult to find in the
Old South as a typical farm or a typical American home today, for
each had an individuality about it, due to its physical environment
and the tastes and whims of its owner. The plantation of this brief
sketch, though it may not be considered typical, was similar in many
respects to others in many parts of the Middle South, particularly
on the Coastal Plain. It was located on the navigable part of the
Roanoke River in eastern North Carolina. The year is about 1860.

The "great house" of the plantation stood on a large bluff overlooking the Roanoke River, in a large grove of elms and oaks, and
commanded a view of the river for several miles. The white owner's
home is described as being "a comfortable old rambling structure in
a green yard and a flower garden, not ugly, but quite innocent of any
pretensions at comeliness."

Scattered about on the higher lands were the overseer's house, a
smoke house, loom house, carpenter's shop, blacksmith's shop, the
cotton-gin house, barns and stables, and others. The negro dwellings,
quite distant from the great house, were arranged, as on most plantations, in two rows with a street between. Each cabin had a front and
back piazza or porch, and behind each was a vegetable garden,
which was cultivated or "allowed to run wild according to the thrift
of the residents." There were apple and peach trees on each slave
allotment, and most allotments had a henhouse and a pigpen. Near
the slaves' quarters was the plantation church, sufficiently large to
accommodate a few hundred negroes, and comfortably furnished with
seats and decorated with colored texts on the walls. A chaplain employed by the owner of the plantation officiated twice a month. On
the other two Sundays of the month the plantation carpenter, an
intelligent old negro, with some oratorical ability, taught in his
homely fashion excellent lessons of honesty and fidelity. The slaves
of the plantation were divided into two groups: the servants and
the field hands. The former were small in number, the latter large.

---

* Some of the data here presented are taken from a small book by Margaret
Devereux, entitled *Plantation Sketches*, published privately in 1906, Riverside
Press. The book is an admirable study and seems singularly free of the sentiment and romance so common in books of this sort. Many other sources were
also used.

In the servant group were a cook and a helper or two, a nurse, a dairy maid, a weaver, also a carpenter and a blacksmith each with assistants, a coachman, a stable boy, and others. The servants were selected from the field hands who had demonstrated their aptitude for particular types of work, and generally were people past maturity. Their assistants were the younger boys and girls or others who were incapacitated for the harder work of the fields.*

On the plantation were made most of the clothing and implements used. Flax, wool, and cotton were woven, raw wool and cotton being produced on the plantation. Most of the slave cloth—coarse wool and cotton—was handicraft goods. The cooperage articles, the wagons, harnesses, and, on some plantations, the plows, harrows, hoes, and other tools were products of handy slaves. Most carpenter work and masonry were performed by the negroes. Negro engineers and firemen ran the steam engine of the gin house, as on most plantations.

The agricultural work of the plantation was carried on by the large group of men and women. Frail women and mothers with several small children were given tasks in and about the great house. Much of their time was given to their household duties, and their regular tasks were spinning, weaving, mending, and similar occupations. Mothers strong enough to do field work left their children in the nursery in the care of an elderly colored woman, known as Mom Diana. Although it was an honor to be selected for work in and about the great house, the barns, and plantation "factories," field work was preferred by many because the hands worked in groups, in which there was an opportunity for the expression of the social tendencies so characteristic of the Negro race.

Field work was done under the supervision of the owner or overseer. To direct the hands and to prevent loss of time and quarrels, "foremen" were selected from among the negro field workers on the basis of maturity, intelligence, spirit of cooperation, and reliability. These negro foremen were generally respected and readily accepted as leaders by their fellows. The foreman took the lead in all pieces of work. He set the pace for his group.

Each season had its round of work as well as pleasure. In late winter and early spring began the preparation of the soil for the staple crops. The summer's work was largely "chopping" cotton and

---

* This specialization in farm and housework prevails today among the colored people. One rarely hires a housekeeper who does general work, but instead a cook, a maid, a washwoman, a window cleaner, etc.

corn. At the close of the summer season in late August, on this plantation, there was a three-days' holiday, preceded by the slaughter of
pigs and poultry in preparation for the big feast. Following this
period of rest came the meanest work of the year, "pulling" the
fodder (leaves of corn). As a rule, during most of the crop season,
field work began at 6 A.M. There was a pause about 9 for breakfast,
then work proceeded until 3 or 4 in the afternoon. But in fodder-
pulling time the hands waited until the dew was off the corn and
weeds. Cotton picking went on during most of the fall. In late November and December when the days were cool and clear there was
hog killing, followed by salting, packing, and smoking of the meat.
In the late fall there also followed the preparation of the cotton,
corn, and other products for market. These were stored in the river
warehouse awaiting the coming of the steamboat which carried the
money crops down the Roanoke to Albemarle Sound. They finally
reached the markets at Norfolk by way of the Dismal Swamp Canal.

Plantation life was often lonesome, being isolated. The monotony
was broken by an occasional visitor, relatives paying a visit, and by
the occasional arrival of the river steamer as it plied between the
many plantation wharves along the navigable part of the Roanoke
and the port at the river mouth on Albemarle Sound. The chief trade
center was Norfolk, where standing orders with one or two reliable
firms were left for a few articles the plantation family considered
useful and desirable on the plantation, and special orders for less
standard things. These commodities reached the plantation usually
by boat.

Life was quiet and peaceful on this, as on most well-administered
plantations. Disorder was generally prevented by using the elderly
negroes to give tone to the whole group. Punishment was rare. Between the slave and his master, many travelers observed, there was
frequently a bond of friendship that resulted often in indulgences
on the part of the owner and strong fealty on the part of the slave.
The bonds of friendship were stronger as a rule on the smaller plantations and wherever the white owner came in direct contact with the
plantation hands. The mistreatment of negroes that existed on some
plantations must generally be laid to the overseer who often was
overanxious to increase the crop returns, as his salary bore a direct
relation to the profits returned by the plantation. He had less of a
financial interest in the welfare of the slave than the owner had.

It seems to have been a general practice on this plantation, as on
many others in most parts of the South, to give the negroes a half
holiday on Saturday, this in addition to the spare time they had

every afternoon, to hunt, trap, work in their gardens, visit, or make trips to the near-by country store for purchases. Many negro families had a few chickens, a pig or two, and hives of bees. Some skilled with tools made crude furniture, wooden kitchenware, and river skiffs which they sold. All but the most improvident had many other items, such as pelts, poultry, and honey, to sell to keep them in ready cash. Often these were sold to the planter or marketed through the planter. The Christmas week was the time for settling the accounts between master and hands for the year. Some slaves in the course of time amassed much money from the sale of such commodities, enough at the end of twenty to forty years to be able to buy their freedom. This became quite a common object in the life of the slave in the latter years of the Antebellum Period. Virginia in 1850 had 54,333 free negroes. There were 27,463 in North Carolina and nearly 9,000 in South Carolina.* (See later discussion on manumission.)

The regular needs of the slaves were supplied by the plantation owner. The regular rations (on the plantation of this sketch) were corn meal, bacon, salt fish, fresh beef in the fall and winter, molasses, and dried peas. If there were children in the negro family a cow was provided.

The conditions varied greatly on the different plantations, as they do on farms today. Some were run efficiently, many very poorly. Some were paying enterprises, others not. On some the slave labor was well managed and responded in work and conduct accordingly; on others the hands were sulky, indolent—certainly as indolent as conditions would permit. Some planters were very indulgent in their treatment of their slaves; others were very exacting and even tyrannical.

A Rice Plantation in Georgia

Sir Charles Lyell on his second visit to America† was entertained for a fortnight on a large rice plantation at Hopeton, fifteen miles above Darien, Georgia, on the Altamaha River. It is his report of his observations at the Hopeton plantation that supplies the material for this study.‡

---

* *Compendium of Seventh Census*, 1850, 63.

† Sir Charles Lyell, *A Second Visit to the United States of North America*, I, 262, 273.

‡ The present writer considers this picture presented by Lyell as free from bias and sentiment as any that has come down to us. He wrote that he had been told that the plantation he visited "was a favorable specimen of a well-managed

Travel to and from Darien was by road or by river. A large dug-out, "rowed" by six negroes "who were singing loudly and keeping time to the stroke of their oars," carried the visitor to the Couper plantation at Hopeton. The landed proprietors along the Altamaha lived much in the style of English gentlemen. The plantation house on the Couper estate stood on a slope overlooking the rice fields on

From Edward King, The Great South, 1874, 431.

Fig. 66.—A Scene Typical on both Rice and Cotton Plantations.

the flood plains of the river. The huts of the negroes were quite apart from the big house, even the servants preferring to remain in their own small huts. The negro homes (Fig. 66) were, Lyell found, "as neat as the greater part of the cottages in Scotland (no flattering compliment it must be confessed)." They were furnished with a table; chairs, a few shelves, a chest, and a bed or beds. A yard was attached to most houses in which there were chickens and "usually a yelping

estate." It was by chance that he visited this particular plantation. He was interested in "scientific objects wholly unconnected with the domestic institutions of the South" or the character of the owner in relation to his slaves. He tried to see clearly and report accurately, as all true scientists endeavor to do, and "relate," he writes, "what passed under my own eyes or what I learnt from good authority, concealing nothing."

cur" kept for amusement. There were 500 negroes on the Hopeton plantation, "a great many of whom [were] children, and [others] old and superannuated."

Rice was cultivated by irrigation on the flood plains of the Altamaha. It took an immense amount of labor to clear and drain these lands, but on the moist virgin soils the returns were heavy. The work was done by simple tools. The seed was sown from late March to early May in trenches made by a hoe, frequent hoeing was necessary in the growing season to keep down the weeds, and the crop was

From Edward King, The Great South, 1874, 429.

FIG. 67.—A Rice Field on the Outer Coastal Plain.

Both South Carolina and Georgia were active producers of rice before the Civil War. South Carolina rice commanded a high price in English markets. The industry was about destroyed during the war. Between 1870 and 1880 there was a slight revival but in the 1880's rice culture got a good start in Louisiana. It had long been grown in Louisiana on a small scale.

harvested by hand in August and September (Fig. 67). Each good negro hand would make about 4.5 barrels of rice a season, 500 pounds to the barrel.

No observations are recorded by Lyell as to the method of conducting the field work or of its nature on the Hopeton plantation. "Old Tom," the head driver, next under the white overseer, had charge of a large part of the work. He was a man of superior intelligence and high "cast of features, a son of a prince of the African Foulah tribe. His memory of the geography of the Sudan, its plants, animals, and people was keen. He was a 'Mahometan,' but his wife and children [were] Christians."

The laborers' rations were meal, rice, and milk, and occasionally pork and soup material. They were usually given more than they could eat and could either return a part of it to the overseer, who made an allowance in money for it at the end of the week, or keep it (such as could be so used) for feed for the fowls. Most negro families had chickens. They sold the fowls and their eggs to purchase tobacco and other luxuries. Some fished and sold the catch to the plantation owners or the white overseer. A few employed their spare

Courtesy Harper's Magazine.

FIG. 68.—Gathering Sugar Cane, Louisiana.
From *Harper's Magazine*, VII, 1853, 760.

time in making canoes out of large cypress trees and sold them for about four dollars, for their own profit. At Christmas they had a week's holiday. Although drinking was uncommon the master always rejoiced when the holiday season was well over, "without mischief." Lyell was told that the "most severe punishment required in the last forty years for a body of 500 negroes at Hopeton, was for the theft of one negro from another."

When negroes were engaged in digging ditches on the rice planta- tion their task for the day was a given number of feet in length, breadth, and depth, with deduction when they encountered a stump or large root. By working leisurely this task could be completed in eight hours, but most laborers could readily do it in five. These gangs were superintended by a black "driver" who held a whip in his hand.

On the estate were many negro mechanics. Lyell watched negro carpenters putting up sluices and constructing "a lock in a canal of a kind unknown in this part of the world." The black foreman was carrying into execution a plan, prepared by the plantation owner, of a lock

Courtesy Harper's Magazine.

FIG. 69.—A Louisiana Planter's "Mansion."

The natural levees of the Mississippi, the Red, and the larger bayous were the sites of the largest and most luxurious homes of the French planters. From *Harper's Magazine*, XIX, 1859, 732.

he had observed in Ireland several years previous, indicating a great deal of mechanical skill. On the plantation a steam engine of fifteen horsepower, of English make, used to run the rice mill, had been operated by a negro for more than twelve years without an accident.

The Hopeton plantation had a hospital of three separate wards all perfectly clean and well-ventilated, one for men, another for women, and a third for lying-in women. There was also a day nursery in which children of women working in the field were looked after by a Mom Diana.*

* *Ibid.*, 263-269.

Fanny Kemble, an English actress who played at many opera houses and theatres in the North, and who married a Georgia rice planter near Darien, Georgia, some years before the Civil War, gives us a far different picture of the treatment of slaves on the rice plantation. She writes (after being divorced from her husband) that on her husband's rice plantation (he owned two) the huts were poorly constructed and dirty. The slaves were worked hard, fed poorly, and mistreated in time of sickness. On the sea-island estate (the second plantation) the huts were miserable, even lacking the comforts of a stable.* Her picture undoubtedly could be as true as was Lyell's of the Hopeton estate, for there were all sorts.

Figure 68 is a scene on a Louisiana plantation in the 1850's; Figure 69 an Antebellum home.

A Plantation in Middle Tennessee

Middle Tennessee in the 1850's had some of the most enterprising farmers of the South. They read widely and were well acquainted with the advances being made in the United States and western Europe. In 1854 some of the farm leaders succeeded in getting the state legislature to incorporate a state agricultural bureau and support financially a state fair, as a means of stimulating farmers in all parts of the state to a higher conception of their calling, to the necessity of preserving soil fertility, of introducing the better breeds of farm animals, and of using greater care in selecting seeds, and also of adjusting crops to climate and soil. By 1855 bureaus also were organized and fairs held in the three natural divisions of the state and in seventeen counties. The farmers of middle Tennessee took the lead. As one method of encouraging better farming, prizes were offered annually to the best farm in a given section as judged by a committee selected by the bureau.

The following description of a plantation in middle Tennessee—owned in 1854 by Mark R. Cockrill, Esq.—is taken from a report made by an examining committee appointed by the State Agricultural Bureau. The plantation was one of several entered in the contest. The report is descriptive of the plantation and its operation; nothing is said about the technique of handling the "hands" and of the plantation life of the slaves. In fact, the word slave is not mentioned.

The Cockrill plantation, 5,000 acres in extent, lay 5 miles north-

---

* Fanny Kemble, *Journal of a Residence on a Georgia Plantation in 1838-39.*

west of Nashville on the Charlotte Road. Much of it is now within the
corporation limits of the city. The plantation included both sloping and
flat valley lands. The low ground the committee considered very productive, but a considerable portion of the upland, some rocky, very
unproductive. The farm economy was based on livestock, some 3,000
animals in all—2,300 sheep, the balance consisted of horses, mules,
and cattle. Mr. Cockrill believed in pure-bred animals—Saxon sheep
and Durham cattle were his preference. The committee was "gratified
to bear testimony to the superior quality of Mr. Cockrill's stock and
especially to his world renowned herd of Saxon sheep and his excellent
Durham cattle." No farmers of the state, it declared, "can boast of
so many superior animals; and we doubt not they will favorably compare with the best herds in other states." The high quality of the wool
clipped from the Saxon sheep was evidenced from the fact that in 1851
he received first prize for his exhibit at the London (England) Exhibi-
tion. This prize also won him a gold medal, suitably inscribed, ten-
dered by the State Agricultural Bureau.

The committee also thought Mr. Cockrill's system of farming the
correct one for middle Tennessee. In the expressive words of the report, "He feeds the soil by sowing oats, clover, and blue grass and
pasturing his cattle on them." Besides these three fodder crops, 120
acres of the land that year were in corn and 100 in wheat. He was
also careful, the investigators pointed out, to remove as little as possible from the land that could otherwise be used to maintain its productiveness.

As for the returns—there was at the time on the plantation not
yet sold 18,000 pounds of Saxon wool. He had sold that year mules
to the value of $7,000, one jack at $1,000, and 12 head of pure-bred
Durham cattle. He had several other animals ready for market that
he estimated should bring $3,000. The beautiful home and its sur-
roundings, the committee admired. The slave-built fence that enclosed
the land, except along the Cumberland River, they considered equal
to or "perhaps superior to any in the state."

A "family" of 40 persons was supported on the plantation. This
probably included whites and the colored slaves.

But Mr. Cockrill did not get the prize that year in spite of the
excellence of his farm and equipment. The committee criticized Mr.
Cockrill for not employing "a much stronger force, sufficient at least
to take the amount of wood to market which [was] rotting on his land
and [to] remove the bushes, briars, and noxious weeds which so seri-
ously retard[ed] the growth of his grasses."*

* *Report and Circulars of the State Agricultural Bureau,* Part I, 1854-55, 20-44.

The first award that year went to an owner of a 500-acre farm—
a Mr. Harlan, who lived six miles east of Gallatin. The notes prepared
by the committee in its report are as follows:

> Amount of land, 500 acres,—one hundred thirty in corn, fifty in
> wheat, fifteen in rye, eight in barley, sixty in oats, one hundred and
> forty in blue grass, and the balance in lots of convenience but every
> portion of the land is actively employed, except a lot about the
> stables and barns. . . . Keeps an average of thirty horses and mules;
> fifty head of cattle, one hundred head of sheep, one hundred fifty
> swine, raises a large amount of poultry, of the improved varieties.
> Sells beef, mutton, pork, horses, and mules, from twenty-five hun-
> dred to three thousand dollars' worth per annum, and supports a
> family of forty persons. Most of his clothing is made on the place.
> Employs but four efficient hands on the farm.
> Mr. Harlem . . . is scrupulous to feed the land whilst he feeds
> his stock and supports his family. . . . He has taken great pains to
> stop washes, trim out undergrowth and fence rows, and to destroy
> all the briars, and what ever he considers injurious to the land, its
> products or his stock.*

Space will not permit further sampling, even though the illustra-
tions presented have by no means exhausted the many phases of life
on the plantations, and are very inadequate as regards the farms of
which there were far more in number than plantations. Generalizing
is always dangerous and particularly so when types of economy in a
region as great as the South with its many strongly contrasted subregions are under consideration.

We are safe undoubtedly in saying that the rural economy on the
smaller farms of the Antebellum Period was in many respects quite
like that of the small farms of today. Emancipation little affected
communities where slaves were few or non-existent; but where the
plantation and slavery dominated, emancipation and the impoverish-
ment of the planters as a result of the war forced the tenant system
in its worst form upon a large part of the South.

Before advancing to the third phase of the theme of Part IV, The
Development of Agriculture in the South, the writer wishes to devote
a few pages to the discussion of the effect of slavery on the economic
development of the South, in the Antebellum Period, in particular.

3. SLAVERY AND ITS EFFECT ON AGRICULTURAL ADVANCEMENT

THE DISTRIBUTION OF SLAVES

Slaves were unequally distributed over the South, as stated in previous pages; but in all the Southern States, although the number of

---

* *Idem,* 47.

slaveholders formed less than a third of the population,* most of the leaders of each state were drawn from the slaveholding classes. It may be asserted, therefore, with much data to substantiate the contention, that the institution of slavery dominated the economic, political, and social life of the entire South, though not to the same degree in the various states and not to the same degree in all parts of any one state.

SLAVERY, AN INHERITANCE IN THE SOUTH†

Slavery was as natural to the South as free labor was to the North. It was natural to both the environmental conditions of the South and the social order inherited from the Mother Country. It was not New England's conscience that drove it into the camp of the Abolitionists in the 1830's and 1840's of the last century, but the economic-geographic unfitness for slavery of the New England environment. In 1807 a bill was introduced in Congress postponing the operation of the provision in the Constitution which forbade the importation of slaves after 1808. The representatives of Massachusetts, New Hampshire, Rhode Island (which had 150 ships engaged in the slave trade in 1777), and Connecticut, dominated by the maritime interests engaged in the slave trade, joined with the slaveholders of Georgia and South Carolina in support of the bill. Virginia's representatives strongly opposed the bill. Virginia was not a producer of rice and indigo, the crops that made slavery profitable in Colonial days. It was Southern leaders in Congress that advocated and supported the original clause in the Constitution prohibiting the importation of slaves after 1808. Jefferson, though a slaveholder, was opposed to slavery, and wrote in his *Notes on Virginia*, "The whole commerce between master and slave is a perpetual exercise of the most boisterous passions, the most

---

* The Census Bureau gives us estimated data, for 1850 on the percentage of the total white population that held slaves, as follows:

	Per Cent
Southern States	32.1
Maryland and District of Columbia	22.
Virginia (West Va. included)	35.
North Carolina	29.
South Carolina	53.
Georgia	42.
Kentucky	29.
Tennessee	25.5

A Century of Population Growth, 1790-1900, Bureau of Census, 1909, 138.

† Parts of this section are likewise taken from the author's Presidential address. (See footnote, p. 208.)

unremitting despotism on the one part and degrading submission on the other. Our children see this and learn to imitate it." He is reported to have once said, "I tremble for my country when I reflect that God is just." Washington in his will made provision for the freeing of his slaves. For several decades before 1800 there was a feeling in Virginia against the "traffic in souls." Twenty-three times the Virginia Colonial Legislature petitioned the Crown, or the proprietors, to abolish the slave trade. In 1772 the House of Burgesses again prepared a petition to the Crown, in which one may find these words, "The importation of slaves into the colonies from the coast of Africa hath long been considered as a trade of great inhumanity . . . [which if continued] we have every reason to fear will endanger the very existence of your Majesty's American Colonies."

Thus the nineteenth-century South inherited slavery. The institution was introduced when the people of all civilized nations of the world held slaves.* It was found ill-adapted to industrial countries and those where diversified agriculture dominated and where there was a long "off season" for labor. In the United States the slavery frontier gradually shifted southward out of New England, later out of the Middle Atlantic States, and in the 1840's and 1850's was rapidly on the decline in Virginia, North Carolina, and Kentucky.† It would have declined relatively in the Lower South had its subtropical agriculture remained associated with rice and indigo, the natural environment of which was the low, flat lands near the coast. But the invention of the cotton gin and the rapid expansion in cotton culture fastened slavery upon the South. Both whites and negroes in general came to look upon it as a necessary institution, as natural as hunger and work.‡ Ministers of the gospel preached sermons and wrote books

---

* Although the first slaves were introduced into Virginia in 1619, the trade in negro slaves before 1753 was too small to warrant attention. In 1753, 511 were imported into Charleston, largely for the plantations in South Carolina. In 1765 and 1766 more than 1,400 were brought into Georgia from Africa and the West Indies. From 1783 to 1787 the British West Indies exported about 300 per annum. From 1715 to 1808, 333,000 slaves were imported into English America; probably the total number imported was between 375,000 and 400,000. (*Compendium of Seventh Census,* 1850, Sen. Doc., 83.)

† G. W. Featherstonhaugh, *Excursions through the Slave States,* 1849, I, 191. Confirmed by numerous other contemporary documents.

‡ In 1760 there were 195 free colored families holding slaves in South Carolina; in Charleston alone there were 132 slaveholding negroes. Negro slaveholders were to be found all through the South. The Indians also held slaves. One Choctaw owned 227 and ten of the largest owners held on the average 64. (*Preliminary Report on the Eighth Census,* 1860, 10, 11.)

upholding slavery, finding numerous passages in Holy Writ showing it a God-ordained institution; just as the ministers of the coastal cities of New England were accustomed to offer up prayers for the safe return of slave ships bound on the most barbarous and unchristian enterprises in which man has ever been engaged. One church at or near Farmville, Virginia, owned a few slaves and rented them out to people of the community, the money thus obtained went to the support of the church. The demand for slaves in the cotton fields of the Gulf States prolonged its life in the Upper South, for slaveowners in these states bred negroes for the Lower South.* It was retained in the Lower South because it, apparently, was adjusted to one-crop, large-scale agriculture. Here, the long growing season, and still longer season favorable for outside work, made it possible to keep the hands employed most of the 300 working days of the year, either by tillage of the soil or clearing lands for future crops of cotton. The production of tobacco, rice, and indigo made slavery profitable in the eighteenth century. The tropical-bred negro, immune to the diseases of wet, hot climates, was a godsend to Southern rice growers on the low, swampy, outer margins of the Coastal Plain. The climate was so "deadly" there that all the whites who could get away sought the mountains or the sea islands during the summer months.

Commercial agriculture, for which the South was fitted because of its subtropical climate and location with respect to ocean transportation, demanded a stable labor supply. Owing to the ease of obtaining land there was a constant tendency for the more energetic and ambitious whites to become landowners. The indentured whites, who were numerous in the early days of some of the colonies, were continually leaving their plantations and taking up lands for their own profit. Negro slavery was, therefore, the logical labor system for such conditions and times.†

When cotton culture discovered the more healthful, interior uplands, the negro for a time was not so essential to the agriculturist. But with the removal of the Indians from the Gulf Plains, westward expansion continued and the demand was resumed. Even in the Lower South, the institution was profitable only when cotton prices were high, where land could be purchased cheaply, and virgin soils utilized.

---

* One slave trader stated that 100,000 slaves were purchased annually in Virginia, North Carolina, and Tennessee for use in the cotton fields of the Lower South. (Quoted in Emerson I. Fite, *The Presidential Campaign of 1860*, 82.)

† Also see F. V. Emerson, "American Slavery," *Bulletin of the American Geographical Society*, XLIII, No. 1, 14-16.

THE SOUTH WOULD OUTGROW SLAVERY IN TIME

In the course of time, slavery would have demonstrated its unprofitableness. Moreover, the public sentiment of the world would have shamed the Southern planter into emancipation. The United States was the only large Western nation in 1860 that had slavery within its territorial boundaries. In 1792 Denmark abolished slavery in all her possessions; and one after another of the European nations did likewise. England outlawed the slave trade in her realm in 1808. Mexico abolished it about 1820-1825. Other Latin American nations freed their Indian slaves when they passed from under the Spanish yoke.

The strong defense of slavery by Southerners for two decades before the Civil War was to a certain degree a reaction to the agitation of the Northern Abolitionists. Their onslaught, their vilification of Southern institutions, and everything Southern, put the Southerners on the defensive. An English traveler wrote in 1842 that the Southerners were "in the position of a froward child who takes delight in doing just the contrary of what he is desired to do in order to show his independence." "They believe," he writes, "slavery an evil, know that they would be better off under a system of free labor, but will not abolish it because other persons have told them they ought."*

A perusal of the works of the numerous English travelers who visited the South in the 1820's to the 1850's will soon convince one that emancipation sentiment was strong. Manumission was active everywhere, but particularly in the Upper South. Virginia had 54,000 and North Carolina 27,500 free negroes in 1850. South Carolina, even, had 9,000, as earlier stated. The first active leaders of emancipation, the first societies, and the first emancipation journals were Southern. In 1826 there were 143 emancipation societies in the United States, 103 of which were in the South. North Carolina and east Tennessee Abolitionists took the lead. But the proportion of antislavery advocates declined during the decades as cotton culture expanded.

Antislavery sentiment was strongest in the Upper South for two reasons. First, a large part of this section was unsuited for the type of crops in the production of which slave labor was profitable. Diversified agriculture dominated. Farms were small in regions of plateau and mountain topography. A regime of local economy (now classed by the census as self-sustenance farming) for the most part prevailed in agriculture as in manufacture. Second, the planter-farmers near the

---

* J. S. Buckingham, *The Slave States of America,* II, 403-410.

northern borders of the Upper South in Virginia, Maryland, and Kentucky looked with amazement, and perhaps envy, at the rapid progress and general prosperity of such states as Pennsylvania, Ohio, and Illinois, and could not suppress the feeling that did a free labor regime prevail in their states they would show similar advancement.*

Most of the urban dwellers in the South were opposed to slavery, particularly the merchants who suffered materially because the plantation owners traded directly with out-of-the-South markets or insisted on reduced prices because they bought in large quantities.†

To offset this growing feeling for emancipation or manumission the pro-slavery leaders in the Lower South endeavored in many ways to convince the slaveowners in the Upper South that, after all, if they would only recognize the fact, quite as much money could be made in raising slaves for the cotton plantations of the Gulf States as in the production of commercial agricultural export products.

Slavery had got to be such an unwieldy institution that the Southerners in general feared to disturb its *status quo*. The possibilities of slave insurrection greatly disturbed the slumbers of a large portion of the population. Lyell remarks that on careful observation of the problem of slavery one is caused to "moderate his enthusiasm for emancipation. He is forced continually to think of the responsibility which would be incurred, if several millions of human beings were hastily set aside, like so many machines, by withdrawing from them suddenly the protection afforded by their present monopoly of labor. In the opening of the market freely to white competitors before the race is more improved, consists their danger."‡

Gradual emancipation or manumission was the only feasible way out of slavery. But this would need be *very* gradual, for most of the poorer sorts of negroes were likely to become public charges. Although the Abolitionists of the North shouted for emancipation the free negroes who wandered into the free North were treated with "scorn and neglect," more so than in their home section, for the prejudice of Northern people was strong against the colored race.§ To turn four million slaves free would have been calamitous, as forced emancipation and Reconstruction in 1862 and 1865 proved, and no sane person would have suggested such a movement. Randolph of Virginia said that the South was in the position of a man holding a wolf by the ear.

---

* Lyell, *op. cit.*, I, 206; II, 83.
† J. W. Burgess, *The Civil War and the Constitution*, I, 31.
‡ Lyell, *op. cit.*, II, 79.
§ J. S. Buckingham, *op. cit.*, I, 403.

It was equally dangerous to hold on or to let go.* But all that could be done was to "abide their own time and act independently of all fear or intimidation."†

The Uneconomical Economics of Slavery

In these days of improved agricultural and industrial accountings it takes but little reflecting to realize the uneconomical economics of slavery.

1. There were far too many workers doing servant duties, duties that in another type of regime would be performed by the proprietors. About the households of the more wealthy planters there were, as a rule, a chief cook and a scullion or two as helpers, probably also a second cook; a nursemaid, if there were small children; often a servant for each member of the family; a dairymaid and an assistant or two; a laundrymaid; a coachman or two; a miller; a gardener and helper; a weaver and a seamstress and tailor; a carpenter; a cooper; a mason; often an engineer; and old negroes in charge of the negro children while the mothers were at work in the fields. (See lists in the section on the North Carolina plantation.) The number varied according to the wealth of the family and varied from time to time in a given family. The average large plantation, judged on the basis of the retinue of servants, would have put to shame the average contemporary Englishman's country estate. Thus a large percentage of the slaves were too young or too old to be effective economic producers. In terms of the modern agriculturists they were "boarders."

An analysis of the statistics of slave population for 1850 shows that in South Carolina only 40 per cent of the slaves were between the ages of 21 and 59 inclusive, and thus capable of doing hard field work. About 47 per cent of the total number were under 15 or over 69 years of age, and thus were incapable of work save that of the most trivial sort.‡ It was generally the young and the old slaves that were detailed for servant duties, largely unproductive, even though quite essential.

2. An immense amount of money was tied up in labor which in a free regime would be invested in more land or machinery. In the eighteenth century mature negroes cost the planters $200 to $400. After

---

* Page, *op. cit.*, 36.

† Buckingham, *op. cit.*, II, 403.

‡ Calculated from *Report of Seventh Census*, 1850, xliv; also in George W. Colton, *Atlas of the World*, I, Statistical Section III.

the suppression of the slave trade (1808), and after cotton became the dominant crop in the Lower South, the price steadily mounted to $1,000, and later to $1,500 for a mature, healthy field hand, and even $2,000 for a good mechanic. This meant that, for labor on a plantation of fifty slaves, the unit considered economically essential to offset the unproductive work of servants and the unproductive periods of the slaves' lives and other items, there was an investment for labor of $25,000 to $50,000. In nearly all the states of the Lower South the value of personal property far exceeded the real estate because of the heavy investment in slaves. In 1860, the first year in which such data were presented, the real estate of South Carolina was valued at $130,000,000, the personal property at $360,000,000. In Georgia the figures were $180,000,000 and $438,000,000; in Alabama $155,-000,000 and $277,000,000.* By 1860 the South, no doubt, had more than $2,000,000,000 tied up in slaves. Although this property was increasing in quantity at the rate of 24 to 33 per cent every decade,† it was open to danger of decimation from contagious diseases and from desertion. The overhead was tremendous. Each plantation thus virtually carried capital, old age pensions, and sickness and unemployment insurance for each of its employees.

Society in general supported and educated the wage earner in the North and equipped him as a mature, efficient laborer with no expense to his employer beyond the regular taxes the employer paid as a member of the community. In youth and old age and during sickness, off-seasons, cold days, and holidays the employer was at no expense for labor. Even the workday was longer in the North—ten to twelve or more hours in factories and from sunrise to sunset on farms. What a striking contrast in the South! The slave was clothed, fed, sheltered, and given medical attention from the cradle to the grave— and the owner supplied all!

3. Although it is quite impossible to get at all the facts, most non-Southern writers who visited the Antebellum South agree that on the majority of the plantations neither the workday nor the work week was long. Lyell reports that the work of the slaves, in general, was not so strenuous as that of English workers of that day.‡ There were indulgent planters and "nigger driving" planters, as one would expect.

---

* *Report of Eighth Census*, 1860, "Mortality and Miscellaneous Statistics," 294.
† *A Century of Population Growth*, 80.
‡ Capt. Basil Hall reports that tasks were completed by 2, 4, or 5 o'clock. (Capt. Basil Hall, *Travels in North America in the Years 1827 and 1828*, I, II, III, quoted in Nevins, *American Social History as Recorded by British Travellers*, 154); also see J. S. Buckingham, *Slave States of America*, II, 428.

It is quite certain that on but few plantations was the work as strenuous as the Abolitionists preached.

There were periods even on the plantations of indulgent operators when the days of labor were long. But so were the hours from sunrise to sunset on many if not most of the farms in the free North; and a ten- to twelve-hour day in a mill or factory in Europe and America was common until recent decades.

A bit of reflecting ought to convince one that with slaves—high-class field hands—costing the planters $1,000 to $1,500 or even more, it would be a foolish owner indeed who would mistreat his labor by excessive work. While he, by necessity, would be forced to get as large a return as possible, he had to think of these returns in terms of the lifetime of the slave. Employers of free labor had no such restrictions. A crippled, maimed, rheumatic laborer, even were the employers responsible, placed no financial obligations on them. Most owners of slaves gave much attention to the health and physical perfection of their charges. Olmsted, for example, found one Virginia planter employing Irish workers for ditching on his plantation. The reason given was that the work was unhealthful and "a negro's life is too valuable to be risked at it. If a negro dies it is a considerable loss, you know."*

In the literature dealing with the Antebellum South one finds repeated instances of this solicitude of the planter for his charges, his property.†

4. At best the negro slave was a slow, unwilling, indifferent worker, born with a superabundance of hereditary, tropical inertia; and there was little incentive in the institution of slavery to develop diligence, enterprise, and a desire for work. This applies specifically to field hands. There was no pleasure in work, for work was slavery and slavery meant work. Because of these conditions the cost of supervision was enormous. One writer-observer says, "They seem to go through the motions of labor without putting strength into them."‡ Lyell quotes a Northern observer as saying, "Half the population of the South is employed in overseeing that the other half do their work, and they who work accomplish half what they might under a better system."§ Few negroes liked to work alone. Even for the most trivial tasks two were assigned, so there would be one "to help the other do nothing."¶

---

* Olmsted, *A Journey in the Seaboard Slave States*, 91.

† For example see "Terms of the Overseer's Contract" as printed in John Spencer Bassett, *The Plantation Overseer as Revealed in His Letters*, 27-28.

‡ Olmsted, *op. cit.*, 91.

§ Lyell, *op. cit.*, II, 72.

¶ Olmsted, *op. cit.*, 46.

Specialization, particularly in services about the barn, yard, house, and shop, was carried to the extreme, probably more so than is demanded by our modern labor unions—this in an economic regime not demanding specialized labor was expensive.

Thus slavery from an economic standpoint was really a curse to the planter, for as one Kentucky farmer assured Buckingham, an English traveler in the 1840's in the South, "It absorbed their capital, ate up their profits, and proved a perpetual obstacle to their progressive prosperity." "It took," the Kentuckian calculated, "$2,000 to purchase a good male slave." Considering interest (10 per cent) on the capital invested, insurance ($100 a year), wages of white overseers "to see that they do their duty," and the cost of sustenance, "a slave cost not less than $500 a year"; and "After all," he concludes, "he would not do more than half the work of a white man who could be hired at that same sum, without the outlay of any capital or the encumbrance of maintenance while sick."[*]

Olmsted found that in Virginia planters hired out able-bodied negro field hands to neighbors at the rate of $100 a year. The contracting party clothed, housed, and fed the laborer thus secured. On his own farm in New York, he paid $105 and boarded and housed the men but they clothed themselves, the cost of which he estimated was about $20 per year. The white laborer on the New York farm required no overseer. Olmsted would not venture an estimate of the relative efficiency of the two classes of workers, but declared that owing to the clumsy hand tools used by the slaves, the whites, who could safely be trusted with light, efficient implements, had an advantage of at least 10 per cent.[†]

SLAVERY DOOMED

The institution of slavery was deeply rooted only in the Cotton Belt, and here it was a financial success on most plantations only because of the high price of cotton (which was the condition up to about 1840 and again in the late 1850's) and the abundance of cheap land. Low prices and the lack of cheap virgin land would have meant its demise. Long before 1790 the slavery frontier was retreating southward, as previously stated. New England held 3,760 slaves in 1790; the Middle Atlantic States, 45,000; and the South, 649,000. Only 23 remained in New England in 1840 and 3,347 in the Middle

[*] Buckingham, *op. cit.*, II, 404.
[†] Olmsted, *op. cit.*, 46.

Atlantic, more than two-thirds of these being in Delaware.* In 1860
New Jersey had only 18, Delaware, 1,798, and Maryland showed
a decrease in numbers. For some of the older slave states the increase
in the latter decades was less than 5 per cent.† The slave population
in these states was, therefore, experiencing a declining decennial increase. In other words, the curve of negro population which for two
centuries had shown an upward trend was tending toward the horizontal. This is what would be expected, for the acreage curve of
agricultural land was tending toward the horizontal and the demand
for slaves was declining.

The most active demand for slaves in Virginia, northern North
Carolina, Kentucky, northern Tennessee, and Missouri was in tobacco
growing, but the acreage of this money crop increased but slowly.‡
Owing to the rapid natural increase of slaves in the older, agricul-
turally stationary sections and where soil fertility was declining year
by year, planters found themselves oversupplied. The slaveowners of
Virginia, Kentucky, Tennessee, and the Carolinas were forced either
to free a portion of their slaves, sell them to the newer states, or sell
their farms at a sacrifice and move their slaves to new territory.
Manumission was common. But to free all the increase meant economic
ruin, for those that were given their freedom had to be supported
until they were self-supporting. For most this meant the remainder
of their lives, for they often refused to leave their masters when
freed. Many of the younger and more enterprising planters migrated
to newer states. Evidently the institution of slavery was becoming
a "white elephant" in the older states, for when the expansion of the
cotton acreage should end because of lack of virgin land (by 1850
the cotton planters had about reached the western edge of the humid
Cotton Belt), the slaves would become a drug on the market. The
Southern planters were destined "to be eaten out of house and home,"
or free their slaves.

How long it would have taken to have the natural turn of events
to do the job cannot be told. The Civil War came on and rudely, yes
convulsively, disturbed the order that had so long dominated the
South, displaced it, and introduced a regime of free labor. But there
are after-effects of the slavery regime that have lingered on—habits,
attitudes, ideas, and destruction wrought on some of the resources. It is
to these that the writer now wishes to direct the reader's attention.

* In this volume we have classed Delaware as a Southern state.
† *A Century of Population Growth*, 134, Tables 60, 61.
‡ *Yearbook of Agriculture*, 1922, 401-402, article on Tobacco.

SOME AFTER-EFFECTS OF THE SLAVERY REGIME

1. Slavery tended to stigmatize manual work in general. Manual labor and slavery became synonymous, to be shunned by white men and women. Not all the proverbial "intolerance of physical fatigue" of the Southerner is the result of this false conception of man's relation to his maladjustment in nature. The easier life with some Southerners was and is a physiological adjustment to a hot, humid climate and an activity adjustment to an agricultural regime in an environment that is not exacting as to time of planting and time of harvesting—such, for example, as exists for much of the year in the Cotton Belt. Among the poorer classes the easier life is partly the result of a feeling of helplessness in the face of adversity, of isolation from markets, of ignorance and lack of leadership, of poverty, and of diseases that sap human energy.

2. The South learned extravagant habits and ways of living. The standard of living in the South today is undoubtedly higher than in any other section of our country for people of comparable incomes. In Antebellum days there was much grand living on a few plantations. In the rice region society was the gayest in America. Yet there were few men of opulence. Many with moderate means followed the leadership of a few wealthy, in display. As a result there was much bankruptcy and many forced sales of estates and negro slaves. The court receivers generally had slaves for hire or for sale.

3. As to the effect on the poor victim of this institution, the negro, the writer believes that one must conclude, in the end, that hard as was his lot on some plantations—and yet it was no harder than for many poor whites of that time in the South and even in the North and European countries, and his thraldom on most plantations was certainly no more galling than jungle life in Africa—he was benefited more than the whites. He was taught habits of work and order; civilized living, as regards home, clothing, and sanitation; lessons of sobriety, honesty, and faithfulness; and, to some extent, a respect for marriage vows. The "old time" religion, adapted from that of the whites, has always had a sobering and civilizing effect.

This burden of dealing with an ignorant, unskilled, undeveloped, most foreign of foreigners was a severe drag on the energy of the dominant race. Whether the period of tutelage was long enough no one can say. Perhaps it was. For most of the negroes it certainly was not too long. When the desired results had been attained and the rudiments of civilization had been planted, to prolong an institution that restricted individual freedom and limited one's vision of a broader life and the prospects of improving one's lot would be unchristian and inhuman. "Every man has a right," says Channing, "to exercise and invigorate his intellect and whoever obstructs or quenches the intellectual life of another, inflicts a grievous and irreparable wrong." The sacredness of individual man no matter what his color should never "be forgotten in the feverish pursuit of property. It is more important that the individual should respect himself and be respected by others than that national wealth, which is not the end of society, should be accumulated."*

Slavery had its evil effects on the negro. For his labor he was assured a home, clothing, food, service in time of sickness and old age, and these are as many blessings as come to the lot of many unskilled free, white workers even in our day; but these "blessings of slavery," as they were designated by Southerners, probably did him harm. They made him dependent, they deadened his initiative and did not correct his tropical improvidence. A large percentage of the negroes today must be treated as children, a condition that permits their exploitation by the unscrupulous. But are we certain that slavery is responsible for their failures, or are they vestiges of primitive jungle life that the slavery regime did not correct? The civilizing of the negro was more successful, all observers assert, on the smaller plantations where contact between the whites and blacks was greater, and it was also more successful with house servants than with field hands.

4. On the other hand, the whites who were thrown with the negroes in everyday dealings in slavery days must have absorbed some of the traits and ideals of this undeveloped race, even though they were the negro's masters and considered themselves superior. Many whites to some degree, no doubt, sacrificed ideals of workmanship, moral standards, tolerance, sympathy for suffering humanity, and the spirit of true democracy; for wherever there are masters and slaves, be they chattel slaves or wage slaves, there is no true democracy.

5. In this relationship of master to slave may lie the cause of the uncompromising attitude of so many Southern political leaders in the decade or so before the Civil War and that still crops out on various occasions in the descendants of these slaveowners. The autocracy displayed on the plantation would naturally be carried over into the political world. The slave rulers were not accustomed to being dictated to as they were by the Abolitionists, and resented outside interference in what they considered purely state matters. Yet, on the other hand,

* Quoted by Lyell, *op. cit.*, I, 242.

but for this feeling of superiority on the part of the whites—a spirit of mastery in their own section—during those tragic days of the Civil War and Reconstruction, white civilization in the South would have been submerged by a black and mulatto one, as it was in the island of Haiti a half century earlier. Southern autocracy combined with buoyant optimism after all saved a white South for the American Union.

6. Another effect of slavery, certainly a contributory factor, is to be seen today in the worn-out, worked-out, badly eroded soils in so many parts of the South. In a young country where land is abundant and people few, agriculture is in the exploitive stage of adjustment. Soil conservation is not natural to such an environment— certainly not in the minds of most tillers of the soil. This was notoriously true in the sections of the South where slaves were numerous. One observant traveler comments, "Every planter considers himself only a temporary occupant of the plantation on which he is settled, he thus goes on from year to year 'racking it out,' and making it yield as much cotton or corn as he can without considering the future. Always ready to sell out and travel farther west."* Migratory agriculture stripped the land of the protecting forests and exposed the surface to erosive forces.† There is abundant evidence in the journals and newspapers of the times, however, to show that soil deterioration was troubling a few at least in the South in the Antebellum Period.

An agricultural observer, writing in 1858, said that nature had surely not "arranged things so badly as to make it necessary . . . to wear out our lands in order to make a living from them." That some improved system of tillage was necessary especially in the old Cotton States was admitted by all "for the purpose of retaining what little soil is still left us, as well as in order to renovate our old worn out soil." He recommends winter plowing, returning to the soil all the vegetable matter available—decaying vegetables from the plantation should be piled up to rot or preserved in pits—diversification of crops, and allowing one-fourth of the usable land each year to rest.‡

7. The plantation system, because of the type of crop and the ignorance of the field workers, made little use of agricultural machinery even after machines had become common in the Northern States. The value of farm machinery in use in selected states, North and South, is shown in Table VI. The Southern planters and farmers failed there-

---

* J. S. Buckingham, *op. cit.*, I, 258.

† This topic is treated at greater length elsewhere.

‡ *De Bow's Review*, I, N.S., Oct. 1858, 395; see also J. S. Buckingham, *Slave States of America*, I, 173.

fore to get the benefit that comes from multiplying man power and
animal power through machines and implements.

TABLE VI

VALUE OF FARM IMPLEMENTS IN 1860[1]

(Five leading states in North and South)

New York	$29,167,000	Louisiana	$20,392,000
Pennsylvania	22,443,000	Virginia	9,380,000
Ohio	16,790,000	Mississippi	8,860,000
Illinois	18,276,000	Tennessee	8,371,000
Indiana	10,420,000	Kentucky	7,475,000

[1] *Preliminary Report on the Eighth Census*, 1860, 197.
The figure for Louisiana is not in harmony with that for other Southern States. The schedule covering implements in this state was undoubtedly not interpreted as it was in the other states. It probably included the machinery of sugar mills, which is very expensive.

CHAPTER IX

THE AGRICULTURAL SOUTH TODAY—THE AGRICULTURAL REGIONS

INTRODUCTION

The estimated gross income from crops in the South in 1933 was $1,409,000,000; for the entire United States $2,876,000,000. Thus the South produces, measured by value, nearly 49 per cent of the crops of the United States.* The income from livestock in the Southern States was only about 22 per cent of that for the country. The remarkable showing in the production of crops for a section having less than 30 per cent of the land area and a little more than 30 per cent (for 1929 and 1930) of the crop land of the country is due largely to the high money returns of a few of its crops, as cotton, tobacco, early vegetables, early peaches, and citrus fruits. No section of our country, probably, exceeds the South in the variety of products grown, chiefly because of the large latitude range and the long growing season. The long season makes possible the practice in some sections of growing both cold-weather and hot-weather crops. The South grows nearly every crop that is produced in the North and in addition has many peculiar to its latitude that cannot be grown in the North. Having a continental climate with hot summers, it can grow a few crops that are not produced profitably in the Pacific Coast States, with their mild oceanic summer temperatures. Florida could be and is to a large degree a veritable "herbarium" of crops of nearly every latitude. On the "keys" and on the southern tip of the mainland the vegetables of Canada's latitude are produced beneath tropical palms, in January and February. In the summer, the Gulf Coast lands grow crops natural to the *rainy* lands of the subtropics, while the High Plains of Texas are producing wild grasses, cultivated fodders and grains of semiarid and even arid temperate lands. Most of the crops grown were originally European in origin, as stated in previous pages, but there have been in recent decades importations,

---

* *Statistical Abstract,* 1934, 572. Data in Chapter I are on a slightly different basis from these estimated figures and for a different year.

some for trial, from Australia, Asia, Africa, South America, and the West Indies.

Although the variety grown is large the bulk of the acreage of Southern farms, gardens, and orchards is devoted to only a few products, as Table VII indicates.

TABLE VII

LEADING CROPS OF THE SOUTH IN ACREAGE COMPARED WITH
ACREAGE FOR THE UNITED STATES[1]

Crops	Acreage of the Crops in the South	Acreage of the Crops in the United States
Cotton	40,000,000 (Av. 1928–1932)	40,554,000
Corn	32,429,000 (1928–1932)	102,768,000
Wheat	9,835,000 (1928–1932)	59,885,000
Sorghums (Kafir, milo, feterita, dura)	5,026,000 (1928–1932)	6,855,000
Oats	4,357,000 (1928–1932)	39,887,000
Tame hay (all forage plants cured)	8,442,000 (1927–1931)	54,420,000
Tobacco	1,694,000 (1928–1932)	1,874,000
Peanuts	2,000,000 (1928–1932)	2,000,000
Rice	830,000 (1927–1931)	954,000
Sugar (cane)	234,000 tons	(cane and beet) 3,811,000 tons
Apples	35,510,000 bushels (1927–1931)	161,333,000 bushels
Peaches	19,073,000 bushels (1927–1931)	56,282,000 bushels
Oranges: Florida	18,100,000 boxes (1933); California	28,439,000
Grapefruit: Florida	10,700,000 boxes (1933); California	1,713,000
Texas	1,130,000 boxes (1933); Arizona	700,000

[1] Data from *Yearbook of Agriculture*, 1935; and *Agricultural Statistics*, 1936, U.S.D.A.

The data just presented show that the South has most of the acreage of our country in cotton, tobacco, peanuts, and rice. These are distinctly Southern crops, though some are raised to a limited degree elsewhere. Tobacco is grown as far north as Wisconsin and Connecticut, rice is raised in the Sacramento Valley and some cotton in the West. The South produces only a small part of the acreage in wheat, oats, and hay, and about its quota, based on acreage of farm land in crops, of corn. Most of these are Northern crops. Florida and Texas (each) lead California in grapefruit but are behind in oranges; Georgia is far behind California in the production of peaches; and in the output of raw sugar the South trails far behind the North. In this latter comparison it is cane sugar *versus* beet sugar. There is a far larger acreage of sugar cane in the South than the figures for raw sugar indicate, for thousands of farmers in the southern portion of the Gulf States raise cane for syrup. Cane for sugar has a very limited acreage, being grown in only a very small portion of Louisiana; while the sugar beet belt extends from Ohio to California, inclusive. Sugar cane is really a wet tropical product.

In several specialty crops like tomatoes, watermelons, cantaloupes, cabbage, celery, onions, and others, the Southern States produce a goodly share of the country's total. For many of these specialties the returns to Southern producers are large because these products get on Northern markets as "early vegetables and fruits." It is estimated that the commercial truck crop of the South for 1935 had a value of $65,000,000; that marketed was valued at $55,000,000.

That each product of the field, orchard, and garden has an environmental complex—temperature, moisture, sunlight, growing season, soil minerals, soil biology, and other conditions—in which it does its best is a fact well recognized. The optimum environmental demands of plants are inheritances that have been stamped upon their structures and in the life habits of their ancestors through hundreds perhaps thousands of years of occupancy of specific habitats. Man has created new varieties of crops by hybridization, but most of his work in the breeding of plants and animals has been confined to a modification or improvement of the wild species. Even in the new there are certain inheritances from the old.

For about three centuries the farmers of the South have been experimenting, chiefly by trial and rejection, often aimlessly, yet at times and particularly in late decades assisted by scientific workers in our experimental stations, to find the environment complex best suited for each of the crops grown and animals raised. The farmers have been in possession of these lands long enough to have discovered, to a fair degree, the various crops and methods of tillage best suited to the various environmental complexes with which they have to deal. These types of land utilization and crops grown, therefore, have become fairly well stabilized, so that there has been but little change in the distribution of crops from several decades. This generalization applies for the most part only to the major crops. It is very probable that a century hence corn will be growing where it now grows, and the same may be said of tobacco, cotton, winter wheat, citrus fruits, and rice. But there will be great changes, certainly, in the acreage distribution and the number of acres of the minor crops, particularly special crops, such as early vegetables, small fruit, peanuts, and others, which now are grown in most of the Southern States but only in small and isolated areas in these states. While to be grown successfully they must have optimum or nearly optimum physical environmental conditions, their distribution today is due largely to adaptations to markets and marketing facilities, to initiative of successful producers, and to stimuli given production by railroads and state or Federal agricultural field agents. These motivating influences are less stable than the natural environmental conditions. Each of these minor crops is capa-

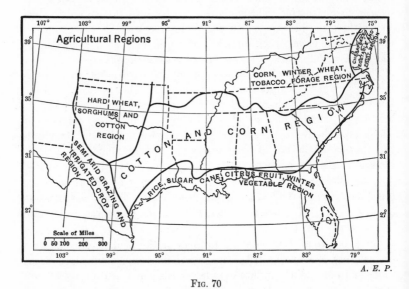

FIG. 70

ble of immense expansion, for the area in which each may be grown is immense.

We now turn our attention to the distribution of the various crops raised in the Southern States, grouped into crop regions, and to the major environmental conditions and the social and economic conditions of man in these crop regions. For convenience, the sections in which they are grown are grouped into regions and subregions or areas (Fig. 70).

THE MAJOR AGRICULTURAL REGIONS AND SUBREGIONS

The Agricultural Regions map of the South, Fig. 70, is based on the actual acreage distribution of the dominant crops and groups of crops. A large area in which a crop or a group of crops dominates is here called a *region*; the land covered by the minor crops is called an *area.**

Six major crop regions may be recognized in the South, namely:

1. The Corn, Winter Wheat, Tobacco, and Forage Region.
2. The Cotton and Corn Region.
3. The Rice, Sugar Cane, Citrus Fruits, and Winter Vegetable Region.

A. E. P.

FIG. 71.—A Blue Grass Pasture in the Nashville Basin.

Blue grass is not so adapted to the climatic conditions of the Nashville Basin as to those of the Kentucky Blue Grass Region. This is near the southern edge of the Graybrownerth Region.

4. The Chesapeake Vegetable and Fruit Region.
5. The Hard Wheat, Sorghum, and Cotton Region.
6. The Semiarid Grazing and Irrigated Crop Region.

The remainder of the South, not included in the above, is largely non-agricultural, at present.

1. THE CORN, WINTER WHEAT, TOBACCO, AND FORAGE REGION

The Corn, Winter Wheat, Tobacco, and Forage Region covers almost the entire Upper South from the Mississippi flood plains to the Fall Line of Maryland and Virginia. Most of the Ozarks should also be included. This crop region is to a certain degree the southern extension of two crop regions that reach their greatest development in the

---

* The plan in general follows that used by O. E. Baker in the publications of the Bureau of Agricultural Economics, United States Department of Agriculture. The data used are those presented in the *Yearbooks of Agriculture*, and are checked up in detail with the reports of the 1930 Census.

A. E. P.

FIG. 72.—A Cultural Landscape South of Maryville, East Tennessee, in the
Great Valley.

Shales and limestones tend to weather into flat lands, which are highly productive.

FIG. 73.—The Upper Cumberland River Valley in the Allegheny Plateau, near
Harlan.

This is largely a limestone valley, one of the best in the South. Only the lower slopes of the
hills and ridges and the lowlands are cultivated. The rise in mining has given local markets to
supply and the building of hardsurfaced roads has partially reduced isolation. There is some
part-time farming, the mines supplying the off-farm work.

states to the north. It is south of the Corn Belt (of the North Central States), and is the southern portion of the Hay and Forage Belt. To the crops dominant in these two northern regions are added winter wheat and tobacco, both grown to the north. Most of the tobacco acreage of the South is in this region. See Fig. 75.

FIG. 74.—A Small Mountain Farm in Western North Carolina.
The valley flats are cultivated. The slope behind the house once grew corn but now is too stony for any use except for pasturing during the wet season.

Environment and Limits

Rainfall and temperature are two environmental conditions that are fairly uniform over the Corn, Winter Wheat, Tobacco, and Forage Region. The region lies almost wholly in the Hot Summer and Cool Winter Temperature Region (Fig. 19) and has an annual rainfall of 40 or more inches (Fig. 20). Droughts are infrequent (Fig. 21). This region is almost entirely within the Graybrownerth Region (Fig. 27), whose soils, as we have seen, evolved under a deciduous forest cover. There is, however, within this agricultural region great diversity in topography and productiveness of soil. The best farming sections with flat topography and deep, rich soil are the Nashville Basin (Fig. 71), the Blue Grass, parts of the Pennyroyal of Kentucky, the Great Valley (Fig. 72), especially the Shenandoah Valley, and some of the wider limestone valleys of the Ozarks and the Allegheny Plateau (Fig. 73). Contrasted with these in fertility are the stony slopes of the dissected plateaus, the ridges of the Great Valley, the surface of the flat Cumberland Plateau, and the eastern part of the Piedmont. The natural and agricultural landscape, likewise exhibit much variety and as great contrasts. There are homes of wealth, comfort, and culture in the limestone basins and valleys where the soil is deep and soil depletion at the minimum. From these come the leaders in enterprises of all sorts. In striking contrast are the small farms on the eroded slopes of plateau and mountain (Fig. 74) where isolation, poverty, and mean living are associated with illiteracy, conservatism, and limited horizons for advancement. Independence, self-assurance, self-respect, and potential human greatness are certainly not wanting, however, in these less-favored localities. Rural rehabilitation, hard-surfaced roads, closer markets, education, and currents of modern life are necessary to stimulate the many dormant superior qualities of these people to fuller fruition.

Our whole country, the United States, should be interested in the rehabilitation of these so-called backward sections, for they are the most active breeding grounds for the next generation of Americans. The excess of births over deaths (see Fig. 148, data for 1933) per 1,000 population in 1932 among the whites of Kentucky was 13; that of Ohio, Indiana, and Illinois just across the Ohio 3.8, and 3.7, and 4.4, respectively. The rate for West Virginia was 11.8, for Virginia, 11.3, for North Carolina 15, and for Arkansas 11.4. The rate for all industrial states with numerous large cities is low. For Massachusetts it is 4.4, for Maryland 4.7, Connecticut 4.1, New York 3.9, New Jersey 3.9.* The rate for the undeveloped sections of these Southern States is much larger than that for the states as a whole. Many investigations and Census reports reveal the fact that the industrial states like Massachusetts, Rhode Island, Connecticut, New York, and New Jersey are not raising enough children to maintain their population and most of the great agricultural states from Ohio westward to the Great Plains are barely producing their quota. It is from the mountain and plateau sections of the South and the Rocky Mountains, therefore, that the future population must come to maintain the present population numbers of these states. Is it not, therefore, to the interest of the whole country that these undeveloped regions send healthy, strong, intelligent, educated, law-abiding citizens to replenish the depleting ranks?†

---

* *Statistical Abstract*, 1934, 85.

† Ellsworth Huntington, "The Conservation of Man," in *Our Natural Resources and Their Conservation*, a symposium, edited by A. E. Parkins and J. R. Whitaker, 1936, 559-574; O. E. Baker, "The Agricultural Prospect," *op. cit.*, 214-236.

Corn and Hay

Corn is the most widespread of the crops of this agricultural region and has by far the largest acreage.* Except in the forested areas corn is a feature of nearly every landscape. Corn, as previously pointed out, was first cultivated by English Americans in eastern Virginia in 1609. The corn frontier moved westward with the westward-moving pioneers, for it soon became the staple food of the Southern farmers and certain of the farm animals and has remained so to this day. Little of the corn of this agricultural region leaves the farms on which it is grown. The largest acreage today is in Tennessee, Kentucky, and North Carolina.

Tame hay† ranks second in acreage of the farm crops. The largest acreages are in Tennessee, Kentucky, and Virginia, the limestone sections of these states being the largest producers.

The variety of hays is large—timothy, legumes, most of the clovers, and blue grass. The acreage of hay in proportion to the total area is far less than in the states of the North. The acreage in hay, however, is no measure of the forage-producing power of this agricultural region because for every acre in hay crops there are seventeen in pasture—plowable pasture, woodland pasture, and others. The most productive and most actively grazed lowland pastures are in the Blue Grass, the Nashville Basin, the Shenandoah Valley, and the eastern foot-hill region of the Piedmont. There is much summer grazing in the higher portions of the Allegheny and Cumberland plateaus and on some of the ridges of the Great Appalachian Valley, the cattle being finished for market in the lower limestone valleys. The percentage of land used for pasturage is far from being uniform over the regions just listed. As a whole we may say that far more acres are available than are used. The total acreage and number of cattle involved, however, is small indeed when compared with the same type of livestock culture in the Rocky Mountains and the Corn Belt. In 1934 (on January 1) the total number of cattle in the six states of this agricultural region was about that in Iowa.

Livestock

English cattle were brought to Virginia on some of the first ships, as earlier mentioned. By 1631 there were more than 5,000 cattle in the colony, and soon after this date exportation to Barbados was begun. By 1654 many farmers owned herds of 80 or more. The

---

* *Yearbook of Agriculture*, 1935, 380.
† *Yearbook of Agriculture*, 1935, 534-536.

number soon outgrew the fenced spaces and the cattle were allowed to roam the woods at will. Branding and annual "round-ups" were Virginian cattlemen's inventions and institutions. Many cattle escaped, to be preyed upon by Indians and hunters, licenses being granted the colonists for cattle hunting. Saddle horses were trained for this form of sport. It is estimated that 50,000 cattle perished of cold and lack of feed during the winter of 1673.* The mortality apparently was always high. Flint, a Virginian, writing of pre-Revolutionary days, informs us that "in those days they [the cattle] were utterly neglected," that it was quite common for such "multitudes" to starve to death every winter as to supply hides enough for shoeing the negroes on every farm. He writes that "this was a matter so generally and constantly anticipated that my own grandfather, as I have heard from unquestionable authority, was once near turning off a good overseer because cattle enough had not died on the farm . . . to furnish leather for the above purpose."† In spite of the heavy mortality, the number increased rapidly, and Virginia and Maryland cattle from the Tidewater furnished the basis of the herds to be found on the Piedmont, in the Great Valley, and the transmontane country; by 1800 the cattle of these regions totaled hundreds of thousands.

Many a pioneer family took with them a cow or two, as they rode horseback, trudged on foot, or drove the slow-moving oxen the hundreds of weary miles through dense forests and mountain passes across streams, to new homes in the West, in the fertile Blue Grass, the Nashville Basin, and later even to the arid plains. It was not man alone that conquered the wilderness, but man, the ox, and the cow.

A few cattle raisers in states like Virginia, Kentucky, and Tennessee began the purchase of English pure breds in the early part of the nineteenth century. It is reported that Matthew Patton drove a herd of cattle from Virginia to Kentucky in 1794. These were descendants of pure-bred cattle imported from England into Maryland just before 1783. It is reported that they were a fine quality of beef cattle, of large size, and that the cows were good milkers.‡ In 1817 Durham or "shorthorn" pure-bred bulls were imported into Kentucky direct from Europe. It was not until about 1832, however, that much interest was developed in Kentucky in improving the breeds of cattle. County fairs are reported as aiding to some degree the de-

---

* Philip A. Bruce, *Economic History of Virginia in the Seventeenth Century*, I, 372; L. H. Bailey, *Cyclopedia of Agriculture*, IV, 43.
† Quoted in The South in the Building of the Nation Series, *Economic History*, V, 217.
‡ *Report of Eighth Census*, 1860, p. cxxxii.

velopment of better herds. Importations from Europe continued until
after the Civil War. During this time the state was a breeding and
dispersal center for blooded stock that was sent into parts of Ohio,
Illinois, Missouri, and even Texas.*

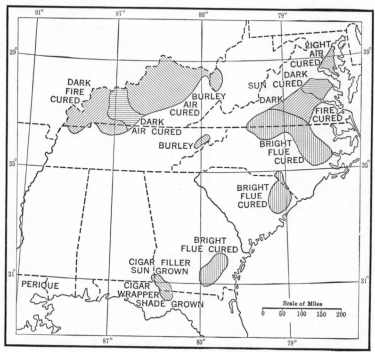

Fig. 75.—Distribution of Types of Tobacco.
Data from Yearbook, Department of Agriculture 1922, p. 410; *Ibid.*, 1931, 701.

Wheat

Winter wheat†—soft winter wheat is the variety raised—is a declining crop in this agricultural region, largely on account of competition from the more important winter-wheat-producing states to the
north and west. The open winters with frequent alternate freezing and
thawing destroy a large percentage of the young plants. In Antebellum days, before the railroad mesh was much developed in these
states, the relative acreage was much larger than now, enough being

---

* L. H. Bailey, *Cyclopedia of American Agriculture*, III, 37.
† *Yearbook of Agriculture*, 1935, 355.

produced to meet home demands. Wheat has always been largely a home supply crop, rarely leaving the farm except to be taken to a grist mill. These states are at present classed as "wheat deficiency" areas. Moreover, the demand for soft winter wheat is declining because of the increasing use of hard wheat, yeast bread (light bread) both by bakers and in the home. Light bread is invading the "hot-biscuit country." Electric toasters and rural electrification play no small part in this shift in food habits. The shift, of course, is more active in the urbanized sections.

Tobacco

Tobacco* has the smallest acreage of the major crops yet the money returns are far greater to the acre than from other crops—from $75 to $150. The six states in this agricultural region produce about 80 per cent of the tobacco crop of our country. Figure 75 shows the location of tobacco areas of the South, classified, largely, as to type of tobacco produced and method of curing.

Tobacco is the most labor-consuming crop of this agricultural region. Studies show that it takes 262 hours of man labor and 89 hours of horse labor to produce an acre of Kentucky dark fire-cured tobacco; for the bright tobacco of the Atlantic slope the demands are about 400 for man labor and 90 for horse labor. Much of the work must be done by hand or with very simple machines. In the spring comes the sterilization of the seedbed by steam or wood fires to kill disease germs, spores, insect pests, and weed seeds. The seedbed, the size depending upon the acreage to be planted, is covered by cheese-cloth and must be watched carefully. Transplanting in the fields is done by hand or machine, after the ground is thoroughly worked. Cut-worms may attack the plant the first night or two and destroy most of the crop. Other enemies are wireworms, budworms, grasshoppers, tobacco budworms, tobacco horn worms, besides rust, spotted leaf, root-worm, wilt, hollow stalk, wildfire, and mosaic disease. Spraying or dusting for many sorts of enemies and diseases must be frequent. At an appropriate time in its growth the plant must be topped and suckered that its strength may go into the production of prime leaves. A few plants in each tobacco field are permitted to go to seed for next year's planting. Frequent cultivation is necessary to check the growth of the weeds and keep the soil porous.

Cutting takes place before the frosts of fall. The entire plant above

* *Yearbook of Agriculture*, 1935, 452, 453.

ground is cut and suspended, top down, on sticks, about three feet long, pushed through the main stalk. The plants are left on these sticks during the movement of the crop from the field and also during curing. The practices vary somewhat in the different regions.

After cutting and sticking, the plants, if the weather permits, are often left in the field for a few hours or a day or two before being taken to the curing barns. The barns are provided with racks or poles

A. E. P.

FIG. 76.—A "Barn" in the Bright Flue-Cured Tobacco Area of North Carolina, near Kingston.

Heated air, not heat and smoke as in the dark fire-cured tobacco district in Kentucky and Tennessee, does the curing of the tobacco. Long stove pipes with many elbows, thus giving much radiating surface, carry the heat from the brick furnace (or furnaces) to all parts of the barn. The furnace is fired from the outside beneath the porch. The barn is built "tight" to check the loss of heat.

arranged in stories; on these the tobacco is hung loosely to permit freedom of movement of air.

The type of curing varies in the several districts. In the dark fire-cured region (Fig. 75 for location), curing is done by a wood fire and smoke, the fire being made on the dirt floor of the barn. Usually the burning wood is covered with sawdust to subdue the blaze and create the maximum of smoke. In the dark air-cured and light air-cured tobacco regions of Kentucky, the barns are built with numerous narrow doors extending from the ground floor to the roof. In the bright flue-cured tobacco region the tobacco barns (Fig. 76) are built "tight," as in the dark fire-cured tobacco region, but the heat is a clean heat from flues—really stove pipes—that carry the fire and smoke from small furnaces (often two to a barn) that are fired from outside the barn.

A type, a class, or brand (the last refers more to manufactured tobacco) of tobacco is distinguished by the color of the leaf, its thickness, firmness, elasticity, smoothness, degree of prominence of veins and midribs, its aroma, its absorptive power, and its content of nicotine, lime, phosphate, and other compounds. The methods of curing and manufacturing also affect the quality of the finished product. It is known that climate and soil have a dominating influence in giving the tobacco its characteristics and its qualities. Some close students of tobacco culture go so far as to declare that if a type from one tobacco region is carried to another, within a few years, the plant migrant will come to have the dominant characteristics of the tobacco long grown in the region to which it is carried. Says one authority "climate imparts flavor; soil determines texture." Southern tobacco is characterized by sweetness and delicacy of flavor. The leaf is smaller than that of Northern-grown tobacco, but it is thicker. "The long period of growth in the Southern States gives tobacco ample time for the elaboration in its vesicular (and vascular) system of the oils and gums that contribute to its sweetness and fragrance. Even saccharine juices have been found stored up in large quantities in some of the yellow tobaccoes of North Carolina and Virginia."[*]

Soil and subsoil affect "the development of those properties of the leaf which determine its usefulness in the trade." Leaves light in color and body, with a fine texture but weak aroma, used for cigarettes and granulated pipe tobacco, are generally found growing in light top soil and porous subsoil. The flue-cured tobacco of the Carolinas and Georgia grows on light sandy and sandy loam soil. On heavy soils the leaf tends to be small, dark in color, heavy in body, and strong in aroma. The dark fire-cured and air-cured tobacco of Virginia, Kentucky, and Tennessee grows on heavy soils. Burley grows best on soil rich in phosphate.[†]

Indirectly, soil and climate affect the method of curing. Light, thin, fine-textured leaves do not need to be fired so long or so intensively as heavy leaf tobacco to attain the desired color and dryness. Much heat is needed for the Carolina bright tobacco, rich in gums, oils, and waxes. The clean heat of flue-curing destroys little of the aroma. The farmer gives much attention to the weather—moisture and temperature—in his curing operations.

---

[*] Joseph B. Killebrew and Herbert Myrick, *Tobacco Leaf*, 30.

[†] Garner and others, "History and Status of Tobacco Culture," *Yearbook of Agriculture*, 1922, 416.

Since the beginning of white colonization of America the Corn,
Winter Wheat, Tobacco, and Forage Region has grown the bulk of
our tobacco. It was in Virginia that many of the practices of tobacco
growing were worked out. Cultivation began in 1612, and by 1616
tobacco was the staple crop; even the streets of Jamestown were
planted to it, and as the cultivated area expanded so did the acreage
of tobacco. Laws had to be passed to force the settlers to grow food
crops to keep them from starving and also to prevent the glut-
ting of the English market.* Not only did export tobacco enrich the
growers, it also yielded a handsome revenue to the Crown. An official
known as the Cape Merchant handled all exports and imports of
commodities from and to the colony. Tobacco warehouses were erected
in 1619 to aid in inspecting the export tobacco in order to insure a
high quality. Stringent laws were passed governing its cultivation,
cutting, stripping, and packing for market. Each hogshead of tobacco
presented for export had to have stamped on it the name of the cooper,
the owner, the weight, and the serial number among the planter's
exports.

The large casks or hogsheads, which weigh 1,000 pounds, were difficult to handle. They were rolled from the plantations (Fig. 57) to
the water's edge and from there transported by flatboat or bay sloops
to the overseas ships. The first river improvements undertaken in
Virginia (and probably in America) were to aid the movement of
tobacco to the overseas ships. In 1664 the export crop from Maryland and Virginia amounted to 50,000 hogsheads. A ship could carry
from 200 to 600 hogsheads. In 1666 the export crop required 100
ships.

The methods of cultivation first used were learned from the Indians.
These methods were modified as the acreage of the crop increased.
Tobacco barns were first erected about 1619. Bruce writes that it is
probable that the Indians grew several "natural" varieties of tobacco.†

Shortly after the Revolutionary War tobacco culture was carried
by Virginians to Kentucky and Tennessee, and as early as 1784 con-
tracts were made with the Spanish at New Orleans for several boat-
loads. Warehouses were erected along the Ohio, Cumberland, and

---

* *The Court Book,* records of the Virginia Colony of London, I, 325, 315.
(Manuscript in Library of Congress; date of record, March 26, 1619.)

† Philip A. Bruce, *Economic History of Virginia in the Seventeenth Century,*
I, 210, 222, 253, 254, 303, 308, 318, 361, 383, 385, 391, 394, 436, 440, 442, 444, 447,
449, and others.

other rivers in which the tobacco was stored awaiting shipment by flatboat.*

The production of bright fire-cured tobacco on the Piedmont in Virginia began about 1852 by the Slade brothers. It soon came to command a high price because of the excellent quality. Cultivation was checked by the Civil War, but there was a revival in its production between 1870 and 1880.†

Many minor crops are grown within the Corn, Winter Wheat, Tobacco, and Forage Region, like apples, small fruits, and vegetables grown for home use or for distant markets.

Special Crops—Apples and Peaches

Among the special crops apples are the most important. Commercial apple growing is centered in the Shenandoah-Cumberland valleys of Virginia, Maryland, and West Virginia, on the eastern slope of the Blue Ridge in Virginia, North Carolina, and Georgia; in northeastern West Virginia; in the Southern Appalachians; in northwestern Arkansas; and in a few other areas. The South has about 35 per cent of the apple trees of the United States and produces about 23 per cent of the bushels of apples. There are tens of thousands of acres in the South suitable for apple growing.

Apple experts in advising prospective growers say that for profitable cultivation the soil must be well drained, never waterlogged, yet retentive of moisture. Hilltops and upper slopes of hills and ridges, if the soil is deep, are recommended for two reasons: the drainage of underground water is sufficient, and fruit buds or blossoms are likely to be saved from late frosts in the spring because air drainage (colder air moving down the slope to the lower lands) is possible.

Apples have been grown in the Upper South since Colonial times. The first seeds or stock were brought from England, but because seeds rarely produced trees like the mother tree, owing to cross pollination, most varieties grown in America originated here. Hundreds of varieties are known, but only a few have commercial importance.

Frederick County, Virginia, today has the largest number of apple trees in the South, more than 900,000. Winchester, its county seat, the "apple capital of the South," has an apple blossom festival each year that is known internationally. Berkeley County, West Virginia, near by, has about 795,000 trees; and Albemarle County on the eastern

---

* Killebrew and Myrick, *op. cit.*, 7; Russel Whitaker, "The Development of the Tobacco Industry in Kentucky," *Bulletin of the Geographical Society of Philadelphia*, January, 1929.

† Killebrew and Myrick, *op. cit.*, 10.

slope of the Blue Ridge about 650,000. Several other counties have from 300,000 to 500,000 each. In Habersham County, Georgia, on the eastern slopes of the Blue Ridge are about 267,000 trees. Another large commercial region is on the rugged hill lands of the Ozark Plateau in Arkansas, in Benton and Washington counties. Here there are about 1,800,000 trees.

The Arkansas area finds markets in the Middle West for its apples. The Virginia, West Virginia, Maryland, and North Carolina areas send apples to Britain and cities of the Northeast, and of course supply Southern markets.

Peaches are grown not only in the apple regions of the Corn, Winter Wheat, Tobacco, and Forage Region but also in the humid parts of the Cotton and Corn Region, where the largest plantings are found.

The largest commercial peach area in the South is in central Georgia. The state of Georgia, however, is second to California in both number of trees and production. In 1929 Georgia had 9,200,000 trees to 11,855,000 in California. California, from 1927 to 1931, averaged 23,300,000 bushels to Georgia's 6,400,000.* Commercial peach growing is also practiced in northeastern Texas, northwestern Arkansas, in Tennessee, North Carolina, and in Maryland.

The edaphic and water demands of peaches and apples are quite similar, but temperature demands are very different. Fruiting of apples is weak or absent in latitudes where there is not a distinct season of cold that forces upon the plant a period of rest. The peach tree is not so affected by warm or mild winters, in fact, the Peen-to, a Chinese variety grown in the South, is subtropical. Peach trees are quicker to respond to warm spring temperatures than apples. The opening of the fruit buds comes before the formation of the leaf, a characteristic which often results in the destruction, wholly or partially, of the fruit crop, by late spring frosts.

Maryland and Virginia at one time were the largest peach producers in the South. One man, Thomas Robinson, had 20,000 trees in Anne Arundel County about 1800. Many other large orchards were in existence by 1830 and 1840. There is a record of an orchard of 63,000 in Accomac County in Virginia in 1814. It is reported that by 1865 the water front of the three northern counties of Maryland "presented the appearance of a continuous peach forest" and the orchards extended inland many miles. Peach orchards are still numerous on both the west and east shores of Chesapeake Bay and also in the apple regions of the Blue Ridge and the Great Valley.

* Data from *Yearbook of Agriculture,* 1934, 497.

Although this section is devoted to the crops and products of the Upper South, it seems best to continue here the brief discussion regarding peach growing even though the story carries the reader into the two agricultural regions to the south of the Corn, Winter Wheat, Tobacco, and Forage Region.

Even though peaches have long been grown in the Upper South, in the Lower South their culture is of greater age. The Spanish brought the "Spanish blood" peach, or the "Tinsley," thought to be its descendant, to Florida in the sixteenth century. The Tinsley is still considered "one of the chosen fruits on the earth."[*]

The peach industry in central Georgia dates from the 1870's, about the time the early-maturing Hale and Rivers varieties were evolved and about the time of the first successful shipment to New York. It usually took three or four days for the journey, and because the fruit reached market during an off season it sold for very high prices, some years as much as $12 to $20 a bushel. But not all shipments were successful. Refrigeration had not then been developed, and the shipments frequently if not usually spoiled en route. The first refrigerator car load of Georgia peaches reached New York in 1889. That year the Elberta variety got into bearing. It became "famous in a day." The planting of peach trees became active. In 1890 Georgia had 3,800,000 trees; in 1899, 11,140,000; in 1919, 12,000,000, and in 1925, nearly 15,000,000. But a decline set in. In 1929 there were only 9,200,000.[†]

The Georgia Fruit Exchange and the Georgia Experimental Station in the peach region are working to improve the crop and put better peaches on the markets. Georgia has a standardizing law providing for compulsory grading and standardization. There is a tendency for the peach region to shift to the slopes of the outer Piedmont. Many old orchards on the hilly lands of the Coastal Plain are being uprooted as a result of negligence in controlling insect pests and diseases, old age of trees, poor varieties, and low prices, particularly for the later-maturing varieties. Peach growing on most farms is secondary to cotton and corn production.[‡] Peach tree planting is active now on the Piedmont between Greenville and Spartanburg in South Carolina.

Types of Farming

Most people when the South is mentioned think of cotton, negroes, and a high degree of tenancy. This is the Lower South. There is an

---

[*] L. H. Bailey, *Standard Cyclopedia of Horticulture*, V, 2, 500; H. H. Gould, *Peach Growing*, 384, 406.

[†] Data from Census reports.

[‡] Georgia Experimental Station, *Bulletin* 155, 1929.

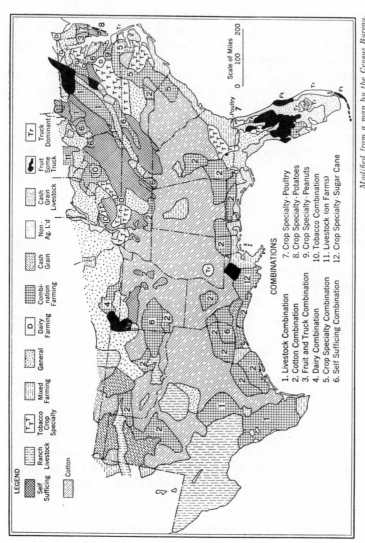

FIG. 77.—Types of Farming in the South.

Modified from a map by the Census Bureau.

LEGEND

Self Sufficing

Ranch Livestock

Tobacco Crop Specialty

Mixed Farming

General

D Dairy Farming

Combination Farming

Cash Grain

Non- Ag. L'd

Cash Grain Livestock

Fruit Some Truck

Tr Truck Dominant

Cotton

COMBINATIONS

1. Livestock Combination
2. Cotton Combination
3. Fruit and Truck Combination
4. Dairy Combination
5. Crop Specialty Combination
6. Self Sufficing Combination
7. Crop Specialty - Poultry
8. Crop Specialty - Potatoes
9. Crop Specialty - Peanuts
10. Tobacco Combination
11. Livestock (on Farms)
12. Crop Specialty - Sugar Cane

Scale of Miles
0   100   200

Upper South in which the agricultural economy is far different from that in the land of cotton. The Upper South, largely in the Corn, Winter Wheat, Tobacco, and Forage Region, has as great a diversity in types of agriculture as any other section of our country of similar area.

Proof of this is to be seen in Fig. 77, a slightly simplified form of a map prepared by the Census Bureau. In pioneer days most of the Upper South practiced a self-sufficiency economy (sometimes described as local economy), but as the steamboat, the railroad, and later, the hard-surfaced road, each in its turn came to serve the region, combined with the introduction of mining, industrialization, and recreational activities, there has appeared a tendency in some sections to produce money-crop products and even specialties. Self-sufficing agriculture, however, is still practiced in the plateau regions, in parts of the Highland Rim Plain, in West Virginia, Kentucky, and Tennessee, and in the Southern Appalachians, as Fig. 77 shows. The Boston Mountain section of the Ozark Plateau also has self-sufficing farming. In the Southern Appalachians the visitor will see pasture land with beef cattle, dairy cattle, horses, and sheep; fields of corn, wheat, oats, buckwheat, and hay; patches of potatoes and vegetables; orchards with a few apple and peach trees; and besides this variety of crops there are likely to be hogs, chickens, and turkeys. The good roads of the Southern Appalachians are gradually changing the type of farming, where contacts are readily made with resort and recreational centers; and there is a tendency to specialize in such products as are in local demand. The rise of mining centers of the Plateaus in West Virginia, Kentucky, and Tennessee is also having a limited effect in bringing about a change.

General farming (Fig. 77), which, as interpreted by the Census Bureau, is several types of farming on the individual farms, dominates in the Nashville Basin and the plains sections of the Great Appalachian Valley. It is the type of farming, also, in the better portions of the Ozarks and the North Carolina Piedmont. Variety of crops dominates, as in the self-sufficing areas, but there is an advantage in this for a variety of products reaches market to be used to purchase the many essentials associated with the higher standard of living that is found in these general farming areas.

Even where the income of the farm is based on specialties, such as fruit, vegetables, tobacco, or dairy products, or on combination farming (as 4, 6, and 10 on the map), the variety is large; but the old staples, such as corn, wheat, oats, and hay—"leftovers" from the self-sufficing days—cover most of the cultivated farm acreage. A similar regime prevails in the fruit regions of Maryland, West Virginia, and

Virginia. In the dark fire-cured tobacco region (T, Fig. 77) of south-western Kentucky and near-by portions of Tennessee, tobacco is the money crop, but it is grown only on a small part of the cultivated land, the remainder of the acreage being devoted to staple crops. Various combinations are to be encountered in the tobacco region (T) of southern Virginia and North Carolina, but tobacco makes up more than half the farm income.

This diversity of types of farming in the Upper South accounts for the greater stability, as compared with the Cotton and Corn Region, in agriculture. Tenancy is far less prevalent in the Corn, Winter Wheat, Tobacco, and Forage Region than in the Cotton and Corn Region. Less than 19 per cent of the farms in West Virginia in 1930 were run by tenants. In Maryland the figure was 26.5, in Virginia 25.1, in Kentucky 32, and in Tennessee 32, while in South Carolina and Alabama it was 65, in Louisiana 67, and in Mississippi 72. These northern states are saved to a certain degree the evils inherent in tenancy that fall upon their sister states to the south.*

There is far less soil erosion and soil depletion in the Upper South than in the Lower. The dominance of forage crops in this northern region is of major importance in checking erosion, and the livestock raised supply the best of fertilizers, far better than commercial brands so much used in the Lower South. The farmers, moreover, are nearer the great domestic markets of our country and have more marketing, buying, and financing cooperative associations than the agriculturists in the agricultural region to the south.†

2. The Cotton and Corn Region

Environment and Limits

The Cotton and Corn Region, the largest of the agricultural regions of the South, extends from west central Texas, the eastern edge of the subhumid lands, eastward almost to the Atlantic. (See Figs. 70 and 77.) Its northern border is the northern limit of the cotton acreage, and coincides rather closely with the line of 200 days of frost-free weather, i.e., the 200-day growing season. The eastern and southern border of the Cotton and Corn Region is fixed definitely by the northern border of the forests and marshes of the Flatwoods. The southern limit of the corn acreage coincides almost exactly with the southern limit of the cotton acreage. The 11-inch isohyet for the autumn has

---

* *Statistical Abstract*, 1934, 553.

† Data for statement in *Statistical Abstract*, 1934, 568, 569.

been assigned as the southern limit of cotton culture; but both isohyets and contours, which may be used to mark the limits of the Flatwoods, coincide with the southern limits of this Cotton and Corn Region.

There is greater uniformity of environmental conditions and types of land utilization in this agricultural region than in the region just discussed, in the Upper South. Everywhere, almost, the land is of low relief, the exceptions being the ridges of the Great Appalachian Valley in Georgia and Alabama, the Ouachita-Arbuckle highland and mountain area, and the southern end of the Cumberland Plateau. The last, in Alabama, is not high but rough. Its soils are poor and its temperatures much lower than the lowlands northeast, south, and west. Here mixed farming, as Fig. 77 shows, is the dominant type of land utilization. In the ridge and valley sections, just mentioned, cotton is a valley crop.

For 1,200 miles from the Virginia boundary line to central Texas, and for 400 miles north and south, the observant traveler sees almost a continuous succession of cotton or corn fields. The cotton acreage in the South in 1934 was about 27,000,000 acres (the normal average is about 40,000,000); the corn acreage, in the cotton states, about 25,000,000 acres.*

There is also great similarity in length of growing season, in temperatures, in rainfall, and in soils. The length of growing season, as previously stated, is 200 days and more. The Cotton Belt covers parts of the Hot Summer and Cool Winter Temperature Region; has 30 or more inches of rain; and the soils, from east central Texas eastward, belong to the rederth-yellowerth group. The Black Prairie Region of Texas is included in the Cotton and Corn Region as delimited in this chapter.

While the Cotton and Corn Region is in general of low relief, most of the land is in slope (mature topography); and the loose porous topsoils offer excellent conditions to the natural forces for rapid and disastrous soil wash and erosion. Most of the hopelessly eroded agricultural lands in our country are found in the Cotton Belt. The valley slopes of the edge of the Piedmont and the hilly lands of the inner edge of the Coastal Plain have almost everywhere been eroded beyond repair, certainly beyond redemption for agriculture in the next few generations. The dominance of red in the outer Piedmont agricultural landscapes and of yellow in the Coastal Plain is evidence of the destruction of the topsoil (A horizon), due to sheet wash. Nature offers

---

* Calculated from data, *Yearbook of Agriculture*, 1935, 380, 427. Note that corn acreage is for all portions of the states that produce cotton.

the conditions, as just stated, for the destruction of these lands, but
ignorance, neglect, laziness, and even lawlessness, on the part of man
have aided and abetted nature. If steps had been taken in time man
could have checkmated the natural tendencies. Little else would have
been necessary than to maintain a plant cover. Rainfall, temperature,
and length of growing season are all highly favorable for plant life.

The tendency to erode is not the only unfavorable condition of the
soils of this region. The parent soil material of the Coastal Plain is
of marine origin, largely siliceous sands and silts and thus low in
soluble minerals. The soils of the Piedmont have a more favorable
inheritance.

Both Coastal Plain and outer Piedmont soils developed under a
coniferous forest, largely, and thus when first attacked by man were
low in humus and unfavorable for soil biota and humus colloids. The
parent soil is low in clay and hence in mineral colloids. The rainfall
is heavy, as previously stated, over most of the Rederth and Yellowerth
Region, and thus leaching has been favored, aided by high temperatures. These soils, weak in the beginning of their occupancy by white
man, have little regenerative power, and have for three centuries
been miserably treated by one-crop farming during a commercial-
agricultural regime.

The topsoil, the A horizon, where left, is gray in color, porous, and
easily tilled; the B horizon is compact and red or yellow in color.
Climatic conditions and acidity of the soils have never favored grasses.
The almost continuous cultivation of tilled crops, with a minimum of
cover crop particularly during the winter, and winter neglect, have
resulted in soil depletion and the destruction of the A horizon. A rotation scheme involving the turning under of green crops or the application of barnyard manures coupled with the free application of essential soluble minerals would have sufficed to keep these soils in as
productive a condition as when the forests were removed. Redemption
is still possible over a large area.

The most depleted cotton lands (the result of erosion and leaching,
and loss of soluble minerals, humus, and colloids) are in the east. By
"drugging" the soil with commercial fertilizer a fairly large yield is
obtained. The three states, North Carolina, South Carolina, and
Georgia, spent more than $84,000,000 for fertilizers (amount for cot-
ton lands not differentiated) in 1929.* The percentage of farms using
fertilizer in the South Atlantic states ranges from 84 to 88, the largest
percentage of any states of the Union. Most of the farms using fer-

* *Statistical Abstract,* 1934, 562.

tilizer are on the Coastal Plain and in the Cotton Belt. The total cash income from crops in 1930 for these three states was only $385,000,000. Thus 22 per cent of the cash income from crops went to buy commercial fertilizer, which is soon leached out and in the long run leaves the soil poorer than when its application was begun. In a large part of Alabama (which spent nearly $22,000,000 in 1929 for fertilizer) much the same procedure is followed.

A. E. P.

FIG. 78.—A Cultural Landscape in the Black Prairie Region of Texas, ten miles southwest of Austin.

The land here is gently rolling. The soil is deep and mellow and as dark, when wet, as coal dust. Some freshly turned soil is in the immediate foreground in the low terrace.

Some sections of the Cotton and Corn Region, however, are inherently fertile, such as the flat lands of the Tennessee Valley, the alluvial lands of the Mississippi Valley, the Arkansas valley, the Red River valley, and the Black Prairie lands of Texas (Fig. 78).

The Black Belt of Alabama is no longer one of the important cotton regions of the South. The black moist lowlands with a calcareous subsoil or bedrock are now producing grasses which feed increasing herds of excellent beef and dairy cattle. The boll weevil brought about the change. On the moist lowlands cotton matured slowly and is ravaged more by the weevil than early maturing cotton. On farms having both highland and lowland, cotton is grown on the higher, drier, though less fertile, uplands. Large-scale production dominates in southwestern Oklahoma and in the brown soil lands of the Coastal

Plains and Low and High Plains regions of southern and western Texas (Fig. 79).

West of the Cotton and Corn Region is a large area of subhumid land in which cotton is the leading crop but is in combination with other crops, and hence not included in the Cotton and Corn Region.

The Variety of Crops

There is a tendency in some parts of the Cotton and Corn Region to introduce special crops. In the Carolinas are grown tobacco, pea-

A. E. P.

Fig. 79.—Cotton Picking near Corpus Christi.

The large trucks carry the cotton from the fields to the gins. Most of the pickers are itinerant Mexicans who generally travel about the country in trucks. On large plantations they may be engaged for a duration of several weeks, living at such times in barns, sheds, tents, or even in the trucks. Cheap labor, high yields, and large-scale farming enable the Texas farmers to produce cotton far cheaper than the East Gulf planter.

nuts, truck, strawberries, pecans, sweet potatoes, early Irish potatoes, watermelons, and legumes. Near the cities are found dairies. These specialties tend to be segregated, as a rule, one specialty to a community. In many hilly regions cotton culture is associated with self-sufficing agriculture, as in parts of the Great Valley, the hilly lands on both sides of the Fall Line; and with combination agriculture in the piny woods of Texas and Louisiana (Fig. 77). Scrubby livestock are allowed to roam the piny woods and grow up as they may, while the attention of the farmer, the little that he spares to agriculture, is given to cotton raising. In Louisiana some sugar and rice are produced within the borders of the Cotton and Corn Region, but the larger acreage of these crops is in the subtropical crop region.*

In the Cotton and Corn Region, in general, the attempt at diversification is far too meager. On many farms not even corn is grown, cotton being the exclusive crop. Some detailed figures based on census data for 1929 and 1930 for Butts and Henry counties, on the Piedmont of Georgia, give us a fairly concise picture of the agricultural practices in that part of the South. In these two counties in 1929

A. E. P.

Fig. 80.—A Cabin in a Cotton Field, near Camden, South Carolina, the House of a Tenant or a Small Farmer.

there were 2,554 farms; 1,484 (60 per cent) did not grow vegetables for home use, 2,025 (80-90 per cent) did not grow Irish potatoes, 2,477 (97 per cent) did not grow sorghum for syrup, 2,273 (89 per cent) did not have swine, 1,233 (48 per cent) did not have milk cows, and 526 (20 per cent) did not have chickens.† All these products require but little additional work.

The farm land of Butts and Henry counties is of medium to poor fertility, yet a detailed examination of a county (Sunflower County in the Yazoo Delta) in one of the most fertile sections of the South reveals similar conditions. There are 14,700 farms in this county, 11,600 being operated by colored farmers, mostly croppers. The average size of the farm is 26 acres. The horses and mules numbered 16,279 or a little more than one to a farm. Cattle numbered 11,000, swine 22,000, chickens 162,000. Only two farms raised winter wheat, 6 sugar cane for syrup, 44 sorghum, 422 Irish potatoes, 1,700 sweet potatoes,

---

* Data from map, Type-of-Farming Areas in the United States, 1930, *United States Census,* Foster F. Elliott, editor.

† *Report of Fifteenth Census,* 1930, II, Part 2, 564-640.

A. E. P.

FIG. 81.—The Home of a Middle Class Farmer, Choccolocco Valley, East of
Anniston, Alabama.

This valley lies between the quartzitic Choccolocco Mountain and the Piedmont.

A. E. P.

FIG. 82.—A Black Belt Planter's Home, near Uniontown, Alabama.

There are many such large plantation homes scattered over the Black Belt. Many, however, are
not so well kept as this one.

6 tomatoes, 9 watermelons, and 3 mixed vegetables.* The soil here is deep, fine-textured, friable, excellent for any sort of crop.

Farming for such farmers consists of a few weeks of concentrated work then long periods during which few duties call. There is no discipline under such a regime. Without discipline any people are likely to slip backward in civilization toward the indolence of savagery. It is the women that are the burden bearers in such regimes.

Figures 80, 81, 82 show three grades of farm homes in the eastern Cotton Belt.

Tenancy

Of all the deleterious features of agriculture in the Cotton and Corn Region none is quite so disastrous as the system of tenancy. In fact, most of the evils that befall this agricultural region are rooted in tenancy. Widespread tenancy, as we now have it in the Cotton and Corn Region, was evolved in those dark days following the close of the Civil War, when the majority of the freed slaves, demoralized by the wild promises of Northern politicians of "a mule and forty acres of land for everybody," roamed the country without knowing where they were going and why, or assembled at army posts or camps to receive sustenance. As roamers they were a menace to the safety of life and property. Few could be depended upon as agricultural laborers. White labor was scarce, even scarcer than before the war, owing to heavy losses of Southern man power. Fortunately a few of the more dependable freedmen remained on the plantations and tilled the greatly reduced acreage of crops. Some cotton was produced and sold. Little money, however, was available. Much of the small cotton crop of 1865 was seized by Federal agents, and what was left was taxed three cents a pound by the Federal Government. Besides, tools, animal power, wagons, gins, and even the necessary houses to shelter workers had been destroyed over large areas by raiding parties during the war. The planters had an abundance of land, in fact were land poor, not being able to utilize it. Many a plantation worth, say, $100,000 before the war was sold for $5,000 to satisfy creditors. The large plantation owners were worse off than the small owners and infinitely worse than the farmers who had only a few or no slaves.

Negro laborers after a time came to the realization that as freedmen they had to work as hard as or harder than in pre-emancipation days and that now there was no one to "paternalize" them. If the planters were poor the negro laborers were even worse off, and when

---

* *Ibid.*, 1061-1096.

Federal care lessened they found themselves "on their own." The planters generally found it impossible to pay monthly wages, but they could get a certain amount of credit from bankers and merchants for themselves and their tenants. Large plantations were divided into "farms" having the acreage that a tenant could, or would, readily cultivate with the animal power and the "hands" (including women and children) available.* The negro supplied the labor; the planter the land, the seed, the tools and work animals, and the fertilizer, if any were used. The planter also went security for sustenance for the cropper and his family until the cotton crop was matured, picked, ginned, and sold. And thus the cropper-tenant system developed and has continued to our day. Fig. 83 is a map of a typical plantation of today.

Croppers are not always destined to remain croppers. Frequently, the more enterprising provide themselves with work animals and "step up" a notch in the scale of tenancy. They become share tenants, later cash renters, and, finally, occasionally, landowners. There has been and is a constant movement up the scale or down the scale as dame fortune smiles or frowns.

There are all sorts of landowners, some kind, some "nigger drivers" or cheaters; and likewise all sorts of tenants. The virtues and vices are as widely distributed in the social levels in the Cotton Belt as in other sections. Each planter or tenant, to succeed, must work hard and use good judgment. A planter "soft" with his tenants is headed toward bankruptcy; one who robs his charges at every turn succeeds as well as a business man who follows the same practices; but he dies with his virtues unsung—so far as tenants and neighbors are concerned.

There were about 2,700,000 farms, out of a total of 6,300,000, operated by tenants in the United States in 1930; 1,800,000 of these tenant-operated farms, or 66 per cent, were in the South. Of the 1,800,000 tenants in the South, 800,000 were croppers; 238,000 were cash tenants or renters; and 776,000 "other tenants." The white tenants in the South number about 1,000,000, the colored about 800,000.† In the United States, in 1930, 42.4 per cent of all farms were operated by tenants. The percentage in the South ranged in the three sections from 48.1 to 62.3. In New England only 6.3 per cent of the farms are tenant operated; 15 per cent in the Middle Atlantic States; and 27.3 per cent in the East North Central section. In 1880 only 25 per cent of the farms of our country were operated by tenants. Tenancy continues to increase.

---

* *Economic History 1863-1909*, VI, The South in the Building of the Nation Series, 87-93.

† *Statistical Abstract*, 1934, 649, 551, 553.

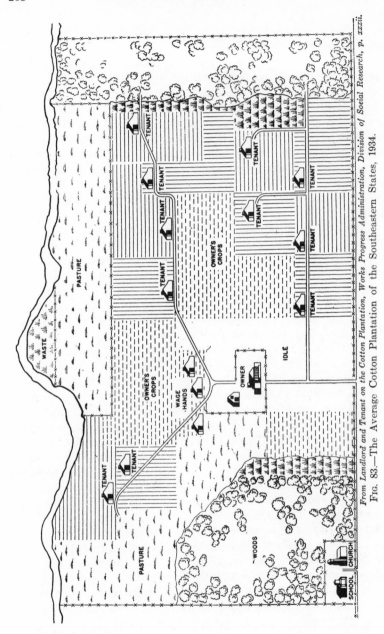

From *Landlord and Tenant on the Cotton Plantation, Works Progress Administration, Division of Social Research, p. xxxii.*

FIG. 83.—The Average Cotton Plantation of the Southeastern States, 1934.

Tenancy is unequally distributed in the South. It is larger in the Cotton and Corn Belt than in other regions, about two-thirds of the farms being so operated. In the Yazoo Delta, 92 per cent of all the farms are operated by tenants, 64 per cent of the tenants are croppers, and most of the tenants are colored. Texas, of the states largely in the Cotton and Corn Region, has a smaller percentage of tenant farmers than other cotton states—about 60 per cent.

The Dominance of Cotton

Cotton, since the early part of the nineteenth century, has been the dominant money crop of the Lower South. Figures 84 and 85 show the distribution of production in 1791, 1801, 1811, 1821, and 1859.

For more than a century the degree of prosperity or financial distress of the Cotton Belt has been determined by the price of cotton. When the export price stood at 15 or more cents, as it did during the early part of the nineteenth century up to 1824, and even at 33.9 cents as it did in 1817, the highest in peace time in America, there was prosperity. Plantation owners had money in plenty, improvements were made, new houses were built, the slaves were better fed and worked fewer hours, the planters' families spent more weeks at the summer resorts, more of the young men and women were sent to Northern or European schools, more purchases were made, and thus the mercantile business of the entire United States and sections of Europe was benefited. But when the price stood at 10 cents or lower (export price), as it did during most of the twenty-eight years between 1828 and 1856, even going down to 5.6 cents in 1844, largely because of overproduction, there was great financial distress, planters became bankrupt, migrations to new territory became more active, banks handled less money, merchants sold fewer goods, there was much talk about the economic unfitness of slavery and an increase in sentiment in the South for emancipation, certainly for manumission. Since the Civil War a part of the distress occasioned by low prices has been shifted to the tenant.

The rank of the cotton crop in comparison with others in our country is readily seen by comparing the relative crop values listed in Table VIII.

Between 1916 and 1920 the average annual returns to the South for cotton (lint and seed) was about $1,720,000,000. The cotton crop outside the South (California, Arizona, Missouri) amounted to some $28,000,000. In 1919 a "high-water" mark was reached: $2,034,650,000.

TABLE VIII

VALUE OF SELECTED CROPS, UNITED STATES, 1929[1]

Corn (harvested for grain)	$2,048,000,000
Cotton (including cottonseed and products)	1,483,000,000
Hay (excluding corn forage)	1,244,000,000
Wheat	841,000,000
Oats (grain)	538,000,000
Potatoes (Irish or white)	470,000,000
Tobacco	286,000,000

[1] *Statistical Abstract*, 1930, 682–686; 1934, 624.

From 1921 to 1930 the average farm value was about $1,400,000,000.[*] In 1932 the farm value was only $465,000,000.

Since 1800 (to 1930 inclusive) the cotton crop, if the average price be taken as fifteen cents, has brought to the South, roughly, $70,000,000,000.[†]

The dominance of United States in cotton production among the nations of the world is readily seen by a glance at the data of Table

TABLE IX

AVERAGE ANNUAL COTTON PRODUCTION OF WORLD, 1926–1930[1]

	Bales
World	26,720,000
United States	15,268,000
India	4,724,000
China	2,000,000
Egypt	1,600,000
Russia (U.S.S.R.)	1,012,000
Brazil	547,000[2]

[1] *Yearbook of Agriculture*, 1935, 427, 428.
[2] In 1937–38 Brazil produced about 2,000,000 bales; the United States, 18,750,000.

IX. From these data it will be seen that the United States produced between these dates about 60 per cent of the cotton of the world. The percentage has declined greatly since about 1930; in 1934 it was only 36 and in 1935, 44 per cent. Our exports of cotton have also declined.

American monopoly of world production began about 1800. Before the invention of the cotton gin, Britain, the greatest user of raw cotton in manufacturing, particularly after her epochal inventions of spinning and weaving machines (devised chiefly during the latter half of the eighteenth century), secured most of her cotton from Asia,

[*] *Ibid.*, 1928, 660; 1934, 606; *Yearbook of Agriculture*, 1922, 714. In the last few years the production of California has been greatly increased.

[†] Calculated from data in *Statistical Abstract*, 1922, 689; 1928, 632; *Yearbook of Agriculture*, 1931, 672, 673.

Africa, and the Americas other than the United States. Soon, however, after the perfecting of the cotton gin, about 1793, America became the chief source of supply.

In 1790 the United States produced 3,135 bales of cotton (see Figs. 84 and 85); in 1800, 73,145; in 1861, 4,485,893; in 1926-1927, nearly 18,000,000 bales. Yet we are far from the limit of our produc-

From U. S. Department of Agriculture, Bureau of Agricultural Economics.

Fig. 84

tion. The total area of the Cotton Belt is about 300,000,000 acres. Between 60 and 70 per cent is in farms. Some 30 per cent of the total area is improved land.* The average acreage in cotton in the United States in late years has been about 30,000,000.† Why does America hold so dominant a position in cotton production?

---

* *Yearbook of Agriculture*, 1935, 427.

† *Yearbook of Agriculture*, 1931, 674, 675. The cotton-acreage-reduction schemes instituted in 1933 and 1934, and the Bankhead Bill, which put a tax on cotton offered for sale above the previous five-year average at any market, were only

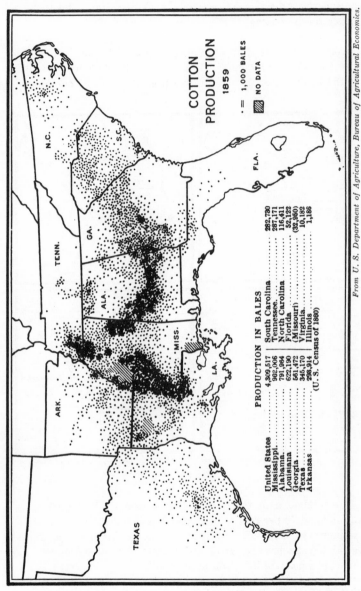

COTTON
PRODUCTION
1859

· = 1,000 BALES

▨ NO DATA

PRODUCTION IN BALES

United States	4,309,517	South Carolina	282,730
Mississippi	902,006	Tennessee	287,171
Alabama	791,064	North Carolina	116,411
Louisiana	622,190	Florida	52,122
Georgia	561,472	(Missouri)	(32,960)
Texas	345,170	Virginia	10,182
Arkansas	298,914	Illinois	1,186

(U. S. Census of 1860)

From U. S. Department of Agriculture, Bureau of Agricultural Economics.

Fig. 85

The chief reason is that America has the largest area of cultivable land of any country that has the temperature and rainfall optimum for the growth of the cotton plant. Through long study it has been found that the best conditions are a cold winter with much freezing to destroy insect pupae; and wet weather to store up moisture in the soil; "a mild spring with light but frequent showers," and this gradually merging into "a moderately moist summer, warm both day and night, followed by a dry, cool and prolonged autumn." Cool, wet weather causes the seeds to rot. Surface roots develop rather than deep roots, and the plant later in dry weather is stunted in its growth. Rainy weather also interferes with cultivation and thus the destruction of weeds. An abundant supply of ground water stimulates the growth of stalk and leaf at the expense of seed and fiber. Dry, cool autumn weather is favorable, as it forces the plant into the production of seed and the attached fiber, just as though nature "feared" that there might be a break in the line of succession of generations of cotton plants. Each plant produces seed that that plant species may be perpetuated. Cotton fiber is nature's device to help perpetuate the cotton "race," not to clothe man. If the dry, cool, autumn weather comes too soon, however, the plant is stunted and the lower bolls on the plant develop earlier than top bolls. Early frosts, though affecting the lower bolls but little, often reduce growth of the top bolls. There is thus a long period during which weather conditions must be favorable for the maximum production of bolls. The plant demands as to climate and weather are, therefore, very exacting for the maximum production of seed and fiber. The soil demands are far less so.

Cotton is grown on practically all well-drained types of soils in the Cotton Belt. In wet seasons the higher and better-drained lands give the best yields; in dry seasons, the clay and alluvial lands. "The most productive lands in normal seasons are the dark-colored clay lands, particularly those rich in lime, such as the black prairies, and the reddish brown, and black, well-drained river bottom land and second bottoms." The sandy lands of the Coastal Plain and the red clay of the Piedmont give satisfactory yields if well fertilized.*

There is a constant shifting of cotton production, small as a rule, from year to year, very pronounced over a long period. During the one and a quarter centuries of cotton culture in America there has

temporary measures, attempts to maintain a reasonable profitable price for cotton. The crop-control programs are attempting to hold the production between 10,000,000 and 12,000,000 bales.
* *Atlas of American Agriculture*, "Cotton," 8.

been a gradual shifting inland and later westward as new lands were opened, traffic lands established, and old lands worked out.

The hold that cotton culture has on the farmer of the Cotton Belt is due

1. To the almost certain sale of the crop at a fair price. In late years the Government has stepped in to maintain prices when over-production threatened to lower the price—a very dangerous act, from an economic standpoint, in the long run.

2. To the fact that cotton is a dependable cash crop. It is not a perishable crop in comparison with many others; stocks can be carried over from year to year or for several years, and it is a fairly certain crop. Money can be borrowed on crop prospects, and, when picked and baled, the cotton may be stored and deposited as collateral on borrowed money.

3. To its being a traditional crop. The Southern farmer is by tradition thoroughly acquainted with its cultivation, although there is much chance for improvement on most farms.

Though other crops have been introduced it is certain to remain the major crop of the present-day Cotton Belt. Cotton growing has become a habit in the Cotton Belt.

The essential practices and conditions that made cotton a profitable crop in a slavery regime—simple tasks, comparatively light work, the long growing season, little machinery, long harvesting season, high money yield to the acre—are favorable to its cultivation under the present-day plantation system with small farms. With one mule, a man can readily plow and cultivate from twenty to thirty acres, and this is as much as an ordinary family can pick. With two mules and a large family, or extra help during picking season, he may care for thirty or even forty acres.

The greatest demand for labor comes during the harvesting season. Picking represents about one-fifth the cost of producing cotton. In many parts of the Cotton Belt the school vacation is arranged so as to come during cotton-picking time. The wages paid cotton pickers are often such that many hands are enticed from households and factories.

In spite of the many attempts at the invention of cotton pickers, and many heralded successes, nearly all the cotton is still picked by hand. The would-be inventor of a successful cotton picker has a far greater task than had the inventor of the grain harvester, for with cotton the picker must in reality be able to select ripe from green bolls, harvest bolls at many levels, and, besides, must not mutilate either the leaf or the stalk. If there could be bred a cotton in which the bolls would be bunched as are the heads of wheat and all at or near the same level, or a cotton in which all the bolls will mature at the same time so that the entire fiber crop could be harvested at the same time, the making of a harvesting machine would be much easier. Cotton-picking machines to be successful must call for far lower labor cost than the hand method requires to offset the high cost of the machine.

A spindle type of picker with friction fingers is now being experimented with. The Rust picker was introduced to the public in 1936. The fingers are moistened steel spindles, 1,344 in number, carried on a revolving drum. The ripe cotton adheres to the wet spindles as they pass through the plant, "the bolls and leaves of which are left uninjured." It takes four men to operate it, but it picks an acre an hour, the work of a hundred hand pickers. Several improvements are yet to be made before the Rust machine can be considered as nearly perfect as a grain harvester.* A much improved Rust picker was announced in 1937.

In 1926 the cotton sled or stripper came into use in the subhumid semiarid sections of Oklahoma and Texas. This device enables one man to do the work of eight or ten picking by hand. The cost of ginning is higher than for hand-picked cotton for the lint is much dirtier. "In all probability this mode of harvesting cotton in the newer cotton areas has come to stay." This method, however, is applicable only to frost-bitten cotton, from which the leaves have fallen as a result of the frost and on which the stems of the bolls are brittle. In the High Plains region where the sled is most used, the bolls open late, and the leaves of the plants are caught by early fall frosts before the bolls mature. To let cotton remain in the fields in most parts of the South until the fall frosts would ruin much of the crop because of fall rains. Much cotton is lost when the sled is used, but labor is scarce and the extensive type of farming dominates. Sled-picked or snapped cotton also calls for special types of cleaners at the gins. These are being provided at most of the western Texas gins.†

"Snapping" cotton, by hand, is practiced in some parts of the South, especially for the late crop.

3. THE SUBTROPICAL AGRICULTURAL REGION

General Characteristics

In the Rice, Sugar Cane, Citrus Fruit, and Winter Vegetable Region (or the Subtropical), the distribution of the acreages of the major

---

* Data from the *New York Times*, Sept. 6, 1936, Rotogravure Section.

† *Yearbook of Agriculture*, 1927, 223; Dan Scoates, "Cotton Picker Progress," *Country Gentleman*, June, 1931, 6, 65.

crops is wholly unlike that in the other regions. (See Figs. 70 and 77 for the location of this region and the types of farming dominant.) In the Cotton and Corn Region, fields of corn mingle with fields of cotton; moreover, a corn field one year may be a cotton patch the next; and in the Corn, Winter Wheat, Tobacco, and Forage Region fields of corn, patches of tobacco, and areas of forage may be found on the same farm. But in the Rice, Sugar Cane, Citrus Fruit, and Winter Vegetable Region, the crop areas, for the most part, are mutually exclusive, although there may be general or mixed agriculture with a variety of crops in each subregion. In Florida vegetables and citrus fruits may be found on the same farm or even same acreage. This region, therefore, is really an assembly of several lesser crop regions or areas and each of these subregions is isolated for the most part by forests or swamps.

In so far as climate dominates, this is the optimum agricultural region for crops in the South. It has heavy rains that are well distributed throughout the year and an abundance of moisture during the summer. There is plenty of sunlight. The growing season is long because of the region's low-latitude location and also because of the protection from untimely frosts given by the ocean waters. Killing frosts do reach the northern three-fourths of the region, as previously observed, but severe freezes are infrequent. The ocean also tempers the summer heat. This area has lower summer maxima than lands two or three hundred miles farther north. The soil is low in soluble minerals, a condition due to both inheritance and excessive leaching in spite of the flatness of the land. The soils of a large part of Florida are similar to lateritic tropical soils. They have an abundance of iron oxides and alumina and are thoroughly leached. The flatwood soils are largely immature. The soils, whether on lowlands or uplands, because they are light, friable, porous, and fine-grained, lend themselves to the intensive cultivation practiced in many sections.

There are strong contrasts in the degree of agricultural development. In the piny woods a modified self-sufficing regime, begun a century or more ago by immigrants from Carolina and Georgia, prevails. This is dominant in the region of general farming shown on the map, Fig. 77. Cotton, corn, livestock, garden truck, and fruit are raised. Most of these are sustenance crops. Cotton and tobacco are the money crops. A few farms practicing general farming (several distinct sources of income on the same farm) also sell truck, especially early Irish potatoes. Some farms should be classed as part-time, some members of families working in the lumber woods and mills, in turpentine "orchards," or at the resort hotels, and elsewhere.

In the region indicated as mixed farming (several distinct types of farming in the same region) in Georgia, some farms are self-sufficing, some part-time. On some, forest products supply the needed cash; on others are grown truck, tobacco, and cotton.

Capitalistic agriculture is dominant in the "Sugar Bowl" of Louisiana, region 12 on the map, Fig. 77. Labor is paid wages. The sugar mills and railroad tracks to connect field and mill call for much money. The money investment in agriculture per farm is very high. In the rice area, largely to the west and north of the sugar cane area,

A. E. P.

FIG. 86.—The Mississippi Levee below New Orleans.

This landscape is about fifty miles below New Orleans, near Pointe à la Hache. The river on the left is bordered by timbered groins to protect the levee from washing; on the right are the road, homesteads, garden plots, and orange groves. The large iron pipe in the middleground is a siphon to carry water from the river to the truck gardens.

most of the farms are of moderate size though the farm equipment is expensive, rice culture calling for dikes, ditches, and pumps, besides threshers and other agricultural implements.

The farmers in the mixed farming region on the natural levees bordering the Mississippi River (Fig. 86) and along the Gulf Coast to the east of the Florida line raise truck and fruit for local and Northern markets, and dairy products for New Orleans, Mobile, Pensacola, and the smaller resort towns. Truck crops dominate on the Mississippi natural levees, irrigation water being secured by siphons from the Mississippi, the surface of which at normal stages is higher than the lands. The cultivated strip is narrow and is well protected from sudden changes in temperature by the abundance of ocean or marsh water on either side. Satsuma orchards cover a large acreage to the west of Mobile Bay and a smaller acreage to the east of the bay.

Citrus Fruit

The largest citrus-fruit area of Florida covers the central hilly upland, Karst topography (Fig. 87). "Round" orange and grapefruit trees have the largest acreage. But cabbage, beans, lettuce (Fig. 88),

A. E. P.

FIG. 87.—An Orange Grove in Central Florida.

The hilly lake country (Karst) of Central Florida offers admirable conditions for the growing of citrus fruits. Water and air drainage are excellent.

strawberries, and poultry, all largely money products, lend diversity to the farming and assure a more certain income. On the Florida Keys the citrus fruit trees are largely limes, an almost tropical climate being necessary for a tree that cannot stand "the least bit" of frost. Some truck, as in other citrus fruit regions, is raised. Marsh lands, with cultivated areas only here and there made possible by expensive drainage, cover most of the southern half of Florida (Fig. 89).

The citrus fruits of the South* include "round" oranges, satsumas,

---

* Material for this section was obtained by personal observations in all the citrus-fruit sections of Florida and at a few points on the Gulf Coast and also from *Farmers' Bulletin* 1343, by E. D. Vesbury and T. Ralph Robinson, Department of Agriculture. This publication supplied the historical data for the Florida region and was of great value in checking up the writer's observations. *The Standard Cyclopedia of Horticulture* was also consulted, II, 782, 783, 2229; also the reports of the census. This section was critically read by J. B. Smith, Orange County Citrus Subexchange, Orlando, Florida.

tangerines, grapefruit, limes, lemons, and kumquats, besides citrons, shaddocks, and a number of others grown for ornamental shrubs or trees or for local use. "Round" oranges, or just plain oranges, are

A. E. P.

FIG. 88.—A Lettuce Field near Gainesville, Florida, in March.
Central Florida truck gardeners try to have a vegetable or vegetables for shipment to Northern markets every month in the year.

A. E. P.

FIG. 89.—A Sugar Cane Plantation near the Eastern Shore of Lake Okeechobee.
This is south of the normal frost line. In both Florida and Louisiana there has recently been tried out very effective sugar-cane harvesters—the Muench and the Falkiner. The latter was being used on the above plantations in March, 1931. Sugar-cane planters have also been devised.

produced in all the citrus fruit sections in Florida and also in the Lower Rio Grande Valley. The bulk of the citrus fruit trees of the South are round oranges. Polk County, Florida, had more than

2,600,000 trees, bearing and non-bearing, in 1929; Orange County, about 1,500,000; and Lake, 1,200,000. These are the three leading orange-producing counties in Florida.*

Grapefruit ranks second to oranges in number of trees. It is slightly less hardy than oranges and hence must be grown where protection from unseasonable frosts is more certain. In Florida, Polk led all counties, with 1,309,000 trees in 1929. Pinellas had 423,000, Lake 257,000, St. Lucie 211,000, and Highland, the third in rank, 261,000. Polk, Lake, Orange, and Highland are inland counties, hilly, and dotted with numerous limestone sinks and basin lakes. Most of the oranges and grapefruit groves cover the hill slopes and hilltops. Pinellas has a long coastline—the Gulf and Tampa Bay. Texas has about 2,900,000 grapefruit trees to Florida's 4,500,000.†

Satsumas rank next to grapefruit in acreage. Being much hardier than either round oranges or grapefruit, they are found widely distributed over the Gulf Coastal sections—in northwestern Florida, and the southern parts of Alabama, Mississippi, and Louisiana. Mobile and Baldwin counties on the shores of Mobile Bay are the commercial producing areas of Satsumas. The Satsuma orange was introduced into United States by American Ambassador Valkenberg in 1869.

The citrus fruit industry on a commercial scale in Florida dates from about 1870. Oranges, however, have been grown in Florida and here and there along the Gulf Coast since the time of the early Spanish and French settlements. A few groves along the St. Johns River were producing fruit for out-of-state markets long before 1870. Charleston and Savannah and the plantations about were regular markets for Florida oranges early in the nineteenth century. Commercial production on a large scale in Florida, however, had to await direct and rapid railroad connections with the Northern markets. The value of all orchard products in 1850 (Census Report) was only $1,280. Such contacts with large markets were provided in the 1860's; and soon after, the planting of orange groves began in earnest. Hundreds of Northern investors held sole or part interest in Florida orange groves. The losses to investors were heavy as a result of the 1886 and the 1894-1895 freezes. The 1899 freeze also was severe but, undaunted, planting was continued. The last severe freeze, up to 1932, was in the winter of 1916 and 1917. Each freeze spurs the planters on to exercise more care in the selection of sites for groves. Man had to learn by trial and success or failure. A complete failure once in four

---

* *Report of Fifteenth Census*, 1930, "Agriculture," II, Part 2, 713-724.
† *Idem.*

or five years may not deter a farmer, providing he can get adequate financial returns during the favorable years, but the complete destruction of a citrus grove means that for four or five years there will be no returns. Not all *frozen* orchards are a total loss, however, for if the roots and the lower parts of the trunks are unharmed, and they usually are unharmed, new trees may be started profitably by budding or grafting on the old.

Because of the constant danger of frosts that may bring ruin to the citrus groves, many of the most successful citrus horticulturists make provision for frost protection. In some groves trees are kept banked or mounded for several years after planting. If frozen, the upper parts only are likely to be harmed and new sprouts will come up and the tree will be back to bearing within a very few years. A certain amount of protection may be secured from light "killing" frosts by wood fires or oil and coke. Wise orchardists keep a stock of wood in their orchards all the time, or particularly during the winter.

Besides seeking frost protection, as from bodies of water, and windbreaks from cold northern winds, the grower, or would-be grower, must look for areas where there will be favorable soils, soil drainage, and air drainage. Hills, knolls, and hummocks or hammocks are preferred to flats and hollows, for both air drainage and soil drainage are better. Small hollows or depressions—limestone sinks—in regions of Karst topography, as in many parts of central Florida, may have water drainage but not air drainage. On the west and east coast of Florida flat lands are utilized, for a certain amount of natural frost protection is furnished by the moderating effects of breezes off the ocean; and such flat lands, even if elevated only a score of feet above mean water level, may be drained readily. In the interior of the state the ideal locations are the slopes and crests of the hills in areas interspersed with lakes, in moderately steep-sided basins. The lakes vary in size from a few acres to a few square miles.

Florida has much to learn from California in citrus fruit culture, in the selection of sites, selection of standardized varieties, the care of the groves, and marketing. Until the organization of the Florida Citrus Exchange there was little or no concerted action in the growing and marketing of fruit. In California the growers' organizations take full charge of the crop from the sorting and grading, through the packing, loading in refrigerator cars, and marketing. Advertising, purchasing of supplies, lobbying in the state legislature, and even in Congress, for favorable laws, and dickering with the Interstate Commerce Commission for favorable rates are not beyond their activities. The Florida

Exchange which handles about 30 to 40 per cent of the state's crop has greatly aided the growers in late years in securing favorable legislation and in setting high standards for the products marketed. All citrus fruit offered for sale or shipment must be inspected. Railroads and express companies are forbidden to accept immature fruit.* The Florida legislature has also passed a law permitting counties to establish public cold-storage warehouses, but little or no attempt has yet been made to provide means to hold the fruit over to avoid market gluts. California oranges may be purchased in our markets almost any time of the year. This spread of market season is secured by selecting varieties whose crops mature at different periods, but it is also the result of storage, a large part of each crop being held in storage for later deliveries. Florida oranges hold the market for much shorter periods.

Grapefruit has come to be a much-called-for fruit only in recent decades, mainly since 1890. People had to learn to like its acid, bitter tang, but its consumption is increasing rapidly and would be further increased by careful standardization and by low prices. Its propagation is similar to that of the orange. As with oranges many varieties are marketed.

The most important problem before Florida citrus-fruit growers is the putting of their products on the markets of the states to the north at a price that will give the grower a fair profit yet will be so low as to stimulate consumption. For large consumption—and large consumption is necessary if the Southern citrus fruit producers are to prosper, or even live—citrus fruit must be removed from the list of luxuries for several months in the year.

The Trucking Areas

The trucking areas (Tr on the map, Fig. 77) of Florida, in which truck takes precedence over all other crops, are widely distributed in the northern part of the state, along the eastern coast, in the west central part, and around Lake Okeechobee.

The low-latitude location of Florida giving it a long growing season —twelve months in the southern third—and an early spring, its sandy

---

* There is, however, much "orange running" by trucks which all too often deal in inferior oranges. In late years there has also been marketed by rail much immature fruit bearing the title "color added." By this means much immature fruit gets by the inspectors. Florida growers are certain to pay for such deception. In many markets California fruit is preferred. Consumers are becoming wary of "color added" fruit. Florida can produce oranges as excellent as those grown in any other section. The growers should see that the consuming public get only superior fruit.

soil which warms up quickly, its peninsularity, and railroad refrigeration and rapid transit to great Northern markets are the basis for the Florida slogan, "A product for market every month in the year." Florida begins to ship lettuce (Fig. 88) to the north about Thanksgiving, green beans late in November, tomatoes (Fig. 90) and cucumbers about December 1, celery and cabbage in January, Irish potatoes by March 20, green corn in May, and sweet potatoes by July. With little competition from other sections at these periods Florida truck growing brings handsome returns. As the season moves northward, and a truck-

A. E. P.

Fig. 90.—A Tomato Field on Key Largo, near Tavernier, Florida.

This is near the edge of the tropics. Limestone, the bed rock, is partly covered with a scanty layer of silt and humus. The tomato plants grow in the small earth-filled pockets in the rough surface of the bed rock.

ing area nearer market comes into competition, vegetables become more plentiful and Florida loses its monopoly.

There is a tendency toward regional specialization in truck growing in Florida as in other sections of the South, probably not due to an attempt to adapt crop to soil and climate, but to marketing demands. Crops may be shipped in carload lots at lower freight rates, and are marketed better in carload lots in large consuming centers.

Florida has the lowest percentage of farms operated by tenants of the states of the Lower South. Of the 57,000 farms in the state in 1930, more than 39,000 were operated by owners and only 17,000 by tenants. Most of the vegetable and fruit farms are owner operated.

4. The Chesapeake Vegetable and Fruit Region

This agricultural region is limited almost entirely to the Coastal Plain of Virginia, Maryland, and Delaware; but not all the Coastal

Plain of Virginia is in this region. It is a region of peninsulas between swamp-bordered estuaries. The large peninsula between Chesapeake Bay and the ocean and Delaware Bay is known in chamber of commerce circles as *Delmarva*.

The marketable products are sweet potatoes, white potatoes, sweet corn, tomatoes, cabbage, green peas, onions, watermelons, cantaloupes and muskmelons, cucumbers, strawberries, and some apples and peaches. The West Shore of Maryland also produces tobacco. Not all these products compete for the same land, but as a rule several of the above crops may be grown on the same farm.

A. E. P.

FIG. 91.—A Well-kept Dairy at Laurel, Delaware.

This dairy region has near-by markets in Baltimore, Wilmington, and Philadelphia.

The crops raised in this agricultural region and the type of farming are adaptations to the deep, porous, sandy, moderately fertile soils (the Sassafras in the graybrownerth group), the humid, littoral climate, and the excellent marketing facilities. The Pennsylvania Railroad traverses Delmarva, lengthwise, and gives fast service into Wilmington, Philadelphia, and New York. West of the bay there are several railroads near or west of the Fall Line. Most of the peninsulas west of the bay in Virginia are without railroads, but hard-surfaced roads now serve these farming sections. There are excellent roads also on the large peninsula.

Agriculture is traditional and has been the dominant occupation for about three hundred years. The cities have long been absorbing the surplus agricultural population but not so rapidly as to deplete the farms of available workers. Fishing in the estuaries of the Chesapeake and off the Atlantic coast is also an old industry, but it is largely the farmers at the off-season that man the boats and own many of the luggers and schooners. These bay vessels, some supplied with auxiliary gas engines, often serve a dual purpose. They are used for fishing during the fishing seasons and at other times transport the farm products, watermelons, tomatoes, and others, to the markets of Baltimore and Philadelphia, Wilmington, Norfolk, and smaller cities.

There is also some lumbering in this region, so that part-time work is open to the farmers in the woods, the sawmills, and the crate, basket, and box factories.

Many types of agriculture are to be found in this small agricultural region, as the map, Fig. 77, indicates: mixed, general, part-time, and

A. E. P.

FIG. 92.—A Truck Garden, near Norfolk, Virginia.

Truck growing in the South for Northern markets had its beginning at and near Norfolk.

specialty. The specialty products are truck, deciduous fruits, tobacco, peanuts, and milk and cream (Fig. 91). Some farms produce live-stock and grain. Intensive agriculture dominates. The tendency is to shift from general and self-sufficing farming, with their variety of crops, to specialty production. The people of this region are about as prosperous as in any of the better farming sections of our country. Many of the houses are modern in equipment with running water, electricity, and telephones. Stationary gas engines, tractors, and autos are found on a large fraction of the farms.

The Norfolk trucking area (Fig. 92) was about the first Southern region to ship vegetables and strawberries to Northern marketing centers, the first attempts being made by two or three New Jersey farmers who began truck gardening in the Norfolk section about 1844.

In an old journal it is written that 600 bushels of green peas and 500 quarts of strawberries were shipped to Baltimore and 400 bushels of peas to Boston in May, 1850. By 1854 the steamer *Roanoke* was carrying truck products to New York nearly every trip during the marketing season. It required 36 hours to land the shipment on New York wharves. This was before artificial ice and refrigeration. Often the shipments reached their destination unfit for sale.

Commercial vegetable growing, or truck gardening, is not confined to the Chesapeake Vegetable and Fruit Region and the subtropical regions, in fact it is widely scattered, in isolated areas, over the Coastal Plain from Delaware Bay to the Rio Grande. Among the more important producing regions are Crystal Springs, Mississippi, western Tennessee, northeastern Texas, Crystal City in the Nueces Valley; and the Lower Rio Grande Valley, called "the Valley."

The earliest truck comes from the far South, the Rio Grande Valley vying with Florida in supplying late fall and winter markets. As the spring season advances northward, region after region comes into production, each in turn supplanting its competitor to the south.

There are still large areas in the Coastal Plain for the expansion of truck growing, but of course the whole vast region cannot become a succession of gardens for market demands are not now and will not be in the future.

5. The Hard Wheat, Sorghums, and Cotton Region

This subhumid and semiarid region (Fig. 70) covers more than half of Oklahoma, the Panhandle of Texas, and the land between the Break of the Plains and the Prairies of central Texas. It covers two major physiographic provinces (see Fig. 9): the High Plains and the Central Lowlands. The surface, as a whole, is flat, but there are several belts of dissected lands, too dissected for agriculture but usable for grazing. The lands bordering the Canadian River in northwestern Texas and the Break of the Plains (the eastern border of the High Plains) present the steepest slopes and the highest relief. In the Central Lowlands are several rocky valley borders and rock scarps. Everywhere agricultural operations are limited by the low rainfall and the long periods of drought, for this agricultural region is on the border of and partly within the "danger" region for agriculture. The northwestern part of this region is in the southern part of the "Dust Bowl" which was so devastated by wind erosion in the summer of 1935. The normal annual rainfall at Plainsview, Hale County, near the middle of the High Plains is 21 inches. See Figures 20 and 21 for the normal rainfall and the average frequency of droughts. At Fort Worth on the eastern border, the precipitation is 33 inches. The evaporation rate is high and so also is transpiration, hence more rainfall is needed for crops than in the northern Great Plains. It has been stated that two times as much water is needed to grow a bushel of corn in Texas as in North Dakota. The subhumid, climatic conditions, with a tendency toward the semiarid some years, affect the character of the soil, the crops, and the types of farming.

Blackerths (chernozems) and dark brownerths, both Pedocals, cover the area, where erosion has not removed them (Fig. 27).

The sorghums like Kafir corn, milo, feterita, and durra, grown for seed or forage, are to be found in most counties and compete both with wheat, which is produced mainly in the northwestern part of this region in Texas and Oklahoma, and with cotton, in the southern part, for acreage.

In the cash grain region as shown on the map, Fig. 77, wheat dominates. North of the Canadian River some range livestock is raised along with the wheat, both being found on some farms. South of the Canadian River, cotton and sorghums are companion crops of wheat but the acreage of wheat decreases southward. In Oklahoma general farming with some dairying and poultry raising are associated with grain production. In the region of combination farming (2) there are similar mixtures. Even in the regions where cotton dominates, most farmers may raise sorghums and livestock. The differentiation into the various subregions is a matter of dominance of some crop or crops. In fact, a wide variety of products is raised. Besides these just mentioned there are sheep, some oats, alfalfa, barley, rye, some corn, and orchard fruits—the last on the low plains in the eastern part of this agricultural region.

This vast agricultural area was for several centuries, during Spanish and Mexican occupancy and until just before the beginning of the present century, a great grazing domain. During this long period all these tens of thousands of square miles were open range country to be used by anyone strong enough to hold possession. (See discussion in next section.) American ranchmen began to secure government claims for ranches on the High Plains in the early 1880's. In 1887 the Fort Worth and Denver City Railroad was built across the High Plains to the coast and thus easy contacts with markets were opened up. No longer were the long "drives" to the "cow towns" on railroads to the north necessary. But the railroads also made it easy for agricultural products to reach markets, and soon farmers came and the agricultural frontier swept westward. Ranchmen broke up their large holdings and sold them to the newcomers. Public lands not yet alienated were "homesteaded" by farmers (Fig. 93). The first farming was largely supplementary to the cattle industry. Milo maze, Kafir corn, and grain sorghums were grown for fodder to be fed during dry spells and periods of heavy snow and cold.

Progress has been rapid. Cities, villages, and well-kept farm homes have replaced the lonely, widely spaced ranches. In the larger centers one finds the best that modern life offers in the way of comfort, pleasure, contentment, and culture. Schools, churches, improved roads, and

A. E. P.

FIG. 93.—A Homestead of a High Plains Farmer, near Lubbock, Texas.

A house of the cottage type, neat in appearance, a wind mill, a poultry house, garage, and stable are the usual equipment of a ranch. Most houses have shrubs and flowers and an attached garden.

the telephone system are everywhere to serve the people. Several colleges supply facilities for higher education.

The future of the western, drier portion of this region is problematic. Dust storms are of frequent occurrence. Though the storms in the summer of 1935 were apparently not so devastating in Texas as farther north, the constant removal of dirt must in time result in disastrous soil depletion. The burning of wheat stubble, clean tillage of corn, cotton, and sorghum, and the removal of the original grass cover are all dangerous procedures. Chambers of commerce of Panhandle towns may not agree with climatologists, geographers, ecologists, and soil scientists that the High Plains is a semiarid region and its agriculture should be a semiarid type, but nature may put on a demonstration some day, as it did farther north, that will be very convincing. Surely steps should now be taken to forestall what *might* happen, by a more

widespread use of the land for livestock and the maintenance of the
humus content in the topsoil.

6. THE SEMIARID GRAZING AND IRRIGATED CROP REGION

This large region in southern and southwestern Texas includes the
dry, stony Edwards Plateau; the Pecos Valley and the dry Trans-
Pecos Plains; the Guadalupe, Davis, and Santiago mountains; and
the valley plains of the Rio Grande (see Figs. 9, 70, and 77). Grazing lands dominate in acreage. The largest irrigated area is in the
southern part of Texas, in the lower Rio Grande Valley. Other small
and widely scattered areas are found along the Rio Grande, the Pecos,
the Colorado, and a few other rivers. Well-irrigation is practiced in
a few sections.

This large area, about a third of Texas, is arid and semiarid (Figs.
15 and 20), and except where water is available for irrigation, and
topographic conditions permit, grazing is the only productive use to
which the surface land may be put. In the mountain areas there is
woodland and grassland pasturage somewhat better than on the lower
dry plains covered largely with bunch grass. Texas leads all states in
the number of sheep and goats. San Angelo is known as the goat center
of America, and nearly all these animals and most of the sheep are
raised on the Edwards Plateau. Cattle dominate over the remainder
of the grazing area.

Cattle

Cattle went with the first American colonists into what is now
Texas and soon found their way to the vast grasslands of that state
as large as several European countries.* Even before American colonization, French and Spanish herders from Louisiana grazed cattle
on the Coastal Prairies of Southeastern Texas. Stephen Austin who
began the planting of American colonies in Mexican territory in the
early 1820's took cattle from Missouri with him. But already there
were hundreds of thousands of longhorn cattle on the Texas humid
and subhumid grasslands, descendants of Spanish Andalusian longhorns, the earliest of which reached the Mexican Plateau before the
middle of the sixteenth century. In the tall grass and short grass
plains of central Texas and, to a lesser degree, in the subhumid pastures, these Spanish cattle found a natural cattle habitat, the like

---

* The cattle region in the early days included all of Texas west of the eastern
forests.

of which they and their ancestors probably never had experienced; for Old Spain with its summer droughts, winter rains, and high summer temperatures is anything but a natural grass region. With all-year grazing in Texas and all-year breeding, and with the buffalo about the only competitors for forage, the herds multiplied rapidly. In 1830 the cattle in the American's herds numbered 100,000 or more. This does not include the wild cattle. The cattle in possession of the Spanish missions in Texas in 1833 numbered 424,000, it is estimated.

By 1837-1838 droves of wild, unbranded cattle, numbering 300 to 1,000 each, were being collected by cattlemen in Texas, from both wild and tame herds, and driven to the cities of the Northern interior. In 1842 Texas cattle were driven to New Orleans to market, a movement that continued well into the Civil War days. That same year (1842) 1,500 were driven to Missouri, and in 1846, 1,000 Texas cattle reached Ohio.*

From these dates on, Texas has been a great "dispersal center" for cattle. In 1850 came the first drive to California to feed the gold seekers and to restock the California ranges which had become depleted of their Mexican-Spanish cattle, owing to the great demand for meat after the gold rush.† This continued for two decades or more, until Oregon began active competition with Texas in supplying beef cattle. In 1856 Texas cattle were driven on foot to Chicago. Figure 94 shows the number of cattle (enumerated) on farms and ranges in the United States in 1860. There were large numbers in western Texas though not so shown on this census map.

After the Civil War the drives to the north became more numerous. Railroads were being built westward into the Great Plains section, and Texas cattle were driven north to the "cattle towns" on these railroads, like Abilene, Junction City, Ellsworth, and others, on the

---

* *Report of Tenth Census*, 1880, "Agriculture," 965.

† The extremely high prices paid for feed in California, an economic phenomenon incident to the heavy returns from great activity in gold digging, made a cattle and sheep drive to California profitable. According to Olmsted, one Texas driver made $100,000 by buying Mexican sheep at $1 per head and selling them in California at $20. Cattle that cost $14 in Texas were selling, as a rule, in the late 1850's for $100 in California. The driving of cattle to California was hazardous in many ways, owing to the poor pasturage en route; but when once in California there was little chance of loss since the cattle usually could be put on the California ranges for a time and fattened if the market was found overstocked. Olmsted writes that the usual herd numbered 600 and was under the charge of experienced drivers, about four men to each 100 cattle. (Frederick Law Olmsted, *A Journey Through Texas*, 274.)

Kansas Pacific.* During the Civil War, Texans while at the front, necessarily paid little attention to farming and cattle raising and on their return found the ranges stocked with hundreds of thousands of unmarked cattle, "mavericks," which could be claimed by the first energetic cattle man that got his branding iron on them. Emerson Hough writes: cattle "in Texas were hardly looked upon as wealth. The people could not eat a tithe of the beef, they could not use a hundredth of the leather. Over hundreds and hundreds of miles of ownerless grasslands, by the rapid waters of the mountains, by the slow streams of the plains, or the long dark lagoons of the low coast country, the herds of tens grew into droves of hundreds and thousands and hundreds of thousands."† The abundance in Texas meant low prices there. Mature cattle were worth no more than $5 a head, but if driven to the Northern States (the Middle West) would bring $50. The assembling of a herd for a drive just after the Civil War was not called a "round-up" but a "cattle hunt," and every man on the hunt could be a cattle owner if he so wished.‡

In 1866, when the movement northward really got under way, 260,000 cattle crossed the Red River. From 1865 to 1881 more than 4,000,000 cattle moved northward out of Texas, the average annual drive being about 282,000. It is estimated that 70,000 to 100,000 were driven to California in this period, and 100,000 to 150,000 to New Mexico and Arizona. These figures do not include the entire number leaving Texas, for tens of thousands no doubt were driven off by raiders. See Figure 95 for the distribution and number of cattle in 1880. The largest drive took place in 1884, when more than 1,000,000 cattle left Texas under charge of 4,000 men. The Kansas Pacific Railroad was the more accessible to Texas drivers, but when the "cow towns" along this road were overstocked, the drives were continued northward 300 miles farther to the Union Pacific.§

Thus Texas for about four decades was the cattle center of the western half of the United States. Texas cattle stocked the ranges of the Great Plains from the Rio Grande to the Canadian border; formed the nuclei of many herds in New Mexico, Colorado, Arizona, Oregon, and Washington; fed hungry gold seekers in California and gold prospectors in many parts of the West; supplied meat to New Orleans

---

* *Report of Tenth Census,* 1880, "Agriculture," 966.

† Emerson Hough, *The Story of the Cow Boy,* 4.

‡ Ernest S. Osgood, *The Day of the Cattle Men,* 29.

§ *Second Annual Report of the Bureau of Animal Industry,* 1885, 300; *Report of Tenth Census,* 1880, "Agriculture," 966, 972; *Report of Eighth Census,* 1860, pp. cxxiii-cxxix.

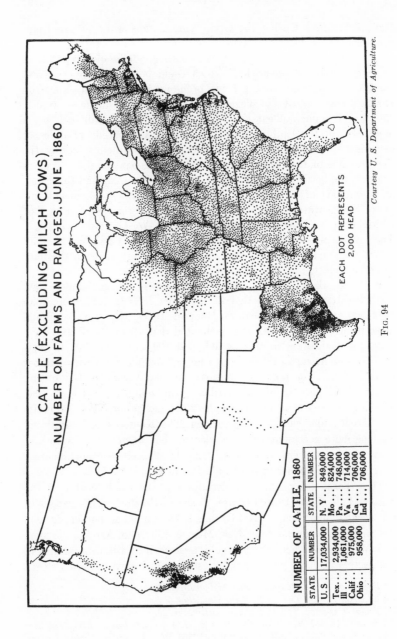

CATTLE (EXCLUDING MILCH COWS)
NUMBER ON FARMS AND RANGES, JUNE 1, 1860

EACH DOT REPRESENTS
2,000 HEAD

Courtesy U. S. Department of Agriculture.

NUMBER OF CATTLE, 1860

STATE	NUMBER	STATE	NUMBER
U.S.	17,034,000	N.Y.	849,000
Tex.	2,934,000	Mo.	824,000
Ill.	1,061,000	Pa.	748,000
Calif.	975,000	Va.	714,000
Ohio	958,000	Ga.	706,000
		Ind.	706,000

FIG. 94

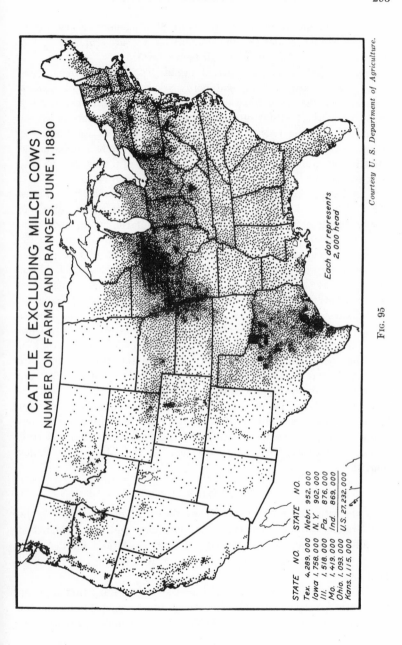

CATTLE (EXCLUDING MILCH COWS)
NUMBER ON FARMS AND RANGES, JUNE 1, 1880

Each dot represents
2,000 head

STATE	NO.	STATE	NO.
Tex.	4,289,000	Nebr.	952,000
Iowa	1,758,000	N.Y.	902,000
Ill.	1,518,000	Pa.	876,000
Mo.	1,419,000	Ind.	869,000
Ohio.	1,093,000	U.S.	27,232,000
Kans.	1,115,000		

Courtesy U. S. Department of Agriculture.

Fig. 95

and the Confederate armies in the Gulf States before the closing of the Mississippi; besides sending millions to the farms and slaughtering houses of the Middle West, all before 1885.

Long before the pre-war drives began, Texas steers—long, lean, lanky, agile, hard of hoof, and hardy—drew "argosies" of traders' wagons from the Great Bend of the Missouri to the Mexican town of Santa Fe in the foothills of the southern end of the Sangre de Cristo Mountains. In the twenty odd years that the Santa Fe trade was active, many millions of dollars' worth of goods were hauled across what is now Kansas, Oklahoma, the Panhandle of Texas, and on into New Mexico to this half-savage, half-civilized frontier town.

Since 1880 a great change has come in the cattle industry of Texas. The longhorns, descendants of Spanish Andalusian cattle, inured to scanty pastures for hundreds of years in semiarid Spain, and again for a few hundred years in Mexico, were admirably adjusted to the semiarid or subhumid plains of western Texas; but they were poor beef animals and still less valuable as milk animals. The Herefords (Fig. 96) have been found admirably fitted to west Texas conditions and, moreover, are among the better beef animals. Many ranchers raise fodder to feed their cattle in the off-season.* In past decades Texas cattle raisers were content to produce feeders for the Corn Belt farmers who made great profits in finishing the cattle; but of late the west Texas farmers (particularly in the High Plains) are more and more "finishing" their beef cattle. More cattle today are being raised to the square mile than formerly, and the mortality is being reduced to that of the more densely settled cattle areas. Yet Texas continues to supply feeders for the Corn Belt, from the grama-grass pastures of the Osage Hills of Oklahoma, and the Flint Hills region of Kansas. They later are sent to the Mississippi Valley markets.

The Irrigated Areas

In the irrigated area in the far western part of Texas, along the Rio Grande, the dominant crops are vegetables and fruit, which find a ready market in the growing city of El Paso. Alfalfa for the dairy cattle, needed to supply milk and butter for the city, is the chief field crop.

The Lower Rio Grande irrigated area stretches along that river on the south for some 60 miles and along the Laguna Madre on the east for 40 miles. More than 385,000 acres were under cultivation in

---

* George Scott, *Farmers' Bulletin* 724, June, 1916.

1930; the enterprises already developed were capable of irrigating a maximum of 490,000 acres. The Bureau of Reclamation has reported that "it may be possible to reclaim as much as 1,000,000 acres by constructing storage reservoirs on the middle Rio Grande and its tributaries lower down," and use all the normal flow of the stream. How much of this water can rightfully be utilized by American citizens will need to be determined by negotiations with Mexico. The Mexicans are building dams on rivers that now supply a large amount of water to the Lower Rio Grande. Irrigation along these rivers will reduce greatly the amount of water available in American territory.

A. E. P.

Fig. 96.—White-faced Cattle (Herefords) on Natural Pasture, near Ballinger, Texas. This breed has been found well adapted to the semihumid conditions of western Central Texas.

Oranges have been grown under irrigation in the lower Rio Grande valley since 1750; but it has been only since about 1920, following the completion of extensive tests as to the best root stalks to use for grafting in this region, that heavy planting has taken place. Between 1920 and 1923, 477,000 trees were set out. By April 1, 1930, the number had reached more than 6,000,000, of which 4,200,000 were grapefruit.* The Census Report (Fifteenth) gives 2,765,000 grapefruit trees for 1929 for Cameron and Hidalgo counties. The orange trees numbered 973,000.

The irrigated land is all in the valley of the Rio Grande with the land on three levels: the first bottoms, the second bottoms, and the third bottoms. These, locally, are called "lifts," for the water used

* Data issued by the Plant Quarantine and Control Administration, Harlington, Texas, of the U. S. Department of Agriculture, July 1, 1930.

in irrigating the land is lifted by pumps from the Rio Grande (Fig. 97), three sets of pumps being necessary to get the water to the third bottoms or bench. Although the general level is flat, each of these benches dips slightly away from the river so that when once the outer edge of the bench is reached by the water it is easy to distribute the life-sustaining fluid to the land (Fig. 98).

A. E. P.

FIG. 97.—The Intake Pipes at the Pumping Station for the Lower Rio Grande Irrigation District (or Division) No. 6, above Brownsville.

The active pumps are electrically driven; the supplementary have Diesel engines. The silt-laden water taken from the Rio Grande is carried in huge ditches some 25 feet wide and 8 to 10 feet deep about 25 miles or more northward from the river. The major ditches are on elevated ridges, the tops of some being 15 or more feet above the level of the land.

Drainage and floods, besides the lifting of the water to the lands to be irrigated, are problems confronting the irrigators. Floods of the Rio Grande from upstream and floods due to the backing-up of the water during Gulf storms occasionally cover the lower bottoms or benches. Drainage is difficult because of the lay of the land. The higher lands, being of coarse material, drain well; but the two lower benches, composed of heavier soil, silty clays, and clays, require tile draining or ditching. "Over" irrigation has resulted in elevating the water table, and alkali, unless the practice is stopped, is sure to give the farmers trouble; and already has in some sections. Since the rainfall is but slightly more than 20 inches (24.15 inches at Brownsville), on the average, the rains make but little contribution to the water needs of the crops.

Irrigation works by several development companies were begun about 1905-1906, after the completion of the St. Louis, Brownsville, and Mexico Railroad into the Valley. Tracts of 2,000 to 100,000 acres were purchased at $3 to $10 an acre. Each company worked independently, "the prime object (of the companies) being to get water upon the land at the lowest first cost and dispose of their holdings at

A. E. P.

Fig. 98.—An Agricultural Landscape, South of Mercedes in the Lower Rio Grande Valley.

In the right foreground is a lateral (to main supply canals) ditch. The cement wall is a part of a siphon that carries the water under the road. The level of the water in the ditch is here some 6 or more feet above the road level. Palms and citrus fruit trees are in the background.

a profit as quickly as possible."* At the close of 1929, sixteen major irrigation districts were operating in the Valley and eleven additional major districts were under process of organization. The works of many of these districts have been purchased by farmers' organizations from the original irrigation companies. Besides these major systems there are thirty small systems operated also by private capital.

Success has been far from universal. The water supply in some systems has been both inadequate and unreliable. Many farmers

* Mimeographed sheet issued by Bureau of Reclamation, Department of the Interior; Personal Study.

bought land—some never saw the land before making the purchases —at fictitious prices; many under the pressure of high-powered salesmanship bought so heavily as to impair their working capital and have not been able to survive in periods of adversity. But on the whole the growth of the area in population, wealth, and productive power has been phenomenal. Cameron County has increased in population from 1,600 in 1900 to 55,000 in 1930, and Hidalgo County from 6,800 to 68,000 during the same period; Willacy County, from 1,000 in 1920 to 6,400 in 1930.*

There was a little irrigation before the coming of the railroad in 1904. A sugar plantation about seven miles east of Brownsville was irrigated by water lifted from the river as early as 1870. Another sugar plantation on this river near Hidalgo dates from 1884.

The far-southern location of the Lower Rio Grande Valley and the proximity of the Gulf, with a dominance of Gulf winds, give it a climate as favorable for the production of fruits and vegetables as that of Southern California or Florida.† In this subtropical climate the 32° temperature is reached only about three or four times a year, on the average, and a killing frost comes only occasionally. The principal summer crops are cotton, corn, broom corn, sorghum, Rhodes grass, sugar cane, vegetables, and citrus fruits. On the same ground winter vegetables may be grown, such as cabbage, carrots, beets, and potatoes, besides watermelons, peas, beans, eggplant, onions, anise, broccoli, and escarole. Swine raising, poultry raising, and dairying are associated activities.

The rapid development of the valley is due more to citrus fruit than to vegetables. Texas grapefruit is "conceded to be by Federal agricultural experts, the best in the world." Anyone who has had the opportunity to make fair comparisons will without doubt subscribe to this bold statement.

Rio Grande citrus fruit raisers had little competition from Florida-grown fruit in 1928 and 1929 because of the embargo occasioned by the Mediterranean fruit fly. The citrus-fruit industry in the Lower

* General Phil Sheridan who led an army across the Rio Grande near its mouth in the Mexican War is said to have declared that if he "owned Texas and hell, [he] would rent Texas and live in hell." (*National Geographic Magazine*, LIII, 637, quoted by Frances Potts, *Some International Problems of the Rio Grande*, master's thesis, Peabody College, 1931.) This low estimate by one of America's brilliant generals is in striking contrast to what visitors now make of this highly productive region.

† Data from report of Weather Bureau for Southern Texas, U. S. Department of Agriculture; *Circular* 34, July, 1924, Texas Agricultural Experiment Station, Agricultural and Mechanical College of Texas.

Rio Grande therefore started off under very favorable market conditions. It is estimated that, when the present acreage gets into full bearing, the potential movement of citrus fruit from the Lower Rio Grande will range from 25,000 to 30,000 cars a year.* The effect of this large crop, in addition to the potential crop of Florida, on market prices will certainly prove disastrous to the growers in one or both areas. How can the markets absorb the product of new acreages?

---

* Data on shipments from *New Reclamation Era*, May, 1929, 77.

PART V

MANUFACTURING IN THE SOUTH

CHAPTER X

THE DEVELOPMENT OF MANUFACTURING IN THE SOUTH

INTRODUCTION

Manufacturing, in its broadest sense, the fabrication of raw materials for human use, is an activity as widespread, almost, as the distribution of man and as ancient as the human family. In its crudest form it may be as simple as the shaping of a stone weapon; in its highest it requires the erection of vast plants, equipped with expensive and intricate machinery, and manned by thousands of workers. It is only in its crudest phases that it is widespread; in its highest, its localization demands are exceedingly exacting. Hence modern manufacturing regions are few in number. The highest phases of manufactures have evolved from the simpler, an evolution that has required long periods of time. Power-machine-factory manufacture is scarcely one and a half centuries old. In America, for many types, it is scarcely a century old. Here the development of manufactures, as in other phases of evolving civilization, has been rapid. The stream of American civilization, a distributary of the European, branched off from the mother stream at a time when tremendous changes in manufacturing, the introduction of machines, the resultant of many centuries of development, were about to occur.

The epoch-making inventions of Kay (about 1733), Hargreaves (1764), Compton (1779), Arkwright (1771), Cartwright (1784), Watt, Stevenson, Bessemer, and other Englishmen, laid the foundations of modern manufactures in Europe. Nearly all our early attempts were for the most part but echoes from across the Atlantic. Yet these attempts, aided by governmental encouragement in the form of tariffs, were the foundation stones of America's leadership of today. In America, as in other parts of the world, manufacturing, as intimated above, is localized in but few sections, because but few sections possess the requisite natural environmental conditions that encourage development from the crudest stages to the advanced. Again, some regions possessing the physical requirements of power, raw materials, and natural transportation facilities lack the human factor, as essential as the physical-environmental. Such was the situation in the South for more than a half century, as will be shown in a later discussion.

We are to look upon the environmental-natural or physical conditions for manufacturing as static. The dynamic urge is supplied by an increasing population which calls for consumers' goods in ever-increasing amounts, produces raw materials in greater volume, and supplies the necessary factory labor. But the evolution of more adequate, abundant, and efficient transportation facilities is of great, if not of paramount, importance. It is the degree of adequacy of transportation facilities that determines the range of movement of commercial commodities.

Three stages or eras, based on the range of movement of commodities, are recognized in this study of the evolution of manufacturing in the South.

1. Manufacturing in a regime of local economy, in which producer and consumer were within the same household or within the same neighborhood. Transportation facilities were for the most part not essential. Household manufacturing dominated. Few or no machines were used, and if used were perhaps of household manufacture.

2. Manufacturing in a regime of regional economy. Producer and consumer were joined by such types of transportation facilities as are to be found in newly settled regions, such as rivers or dirt roads. Centers of manufacturing had developed. The term region, as here used, is the area that may be reached by the meager transportation facilities of an economically young region and thus is necessarily limited in extent. Where wagons on dirt roads were the only carrying agents the area of the region was small indeed, 25, 50, possibly 100 miles in radius at the most. Where there were broad sweeps of navigable waterways the manufactured goods could be transported economically hundreds of miles downstream, even with the crudest form of water carriers. River manufacturing centers, before the coming of the steamboat, lay near the headwaters of the regions they served because the downstream movement of commodities was easier than upstream. It is in this second stage of economic development that commercial production started. Factories equipped with machinery developed here and there.

3. Manufacturing in a regime of national or world economy. It was the railroad which for almost a century now has dominated in land transportation and the ocean steamer that made this regime possible. The steamboat in its day on the inland waterways made its contribution, serving as a feeder to the major ocean traffic lines. The South is only in the beginning of this era of modern manufactures.

These three stages were in the main chronologically fairly distinct in any one section of the South; but in the whole area of the Southern States there has been until the last half century, or even quarter century, much overlapping. It was along the inland waterways and the coasts that people advanced most quickly to the second and third stages. The interior parts have been regions of retarded economic development. Even as late as four decades or so ago homespuns, the product of the hand spinning wheel and hand loom, were being produced in the mountain sections, not just at mountain schools or centers of mountain industries for sale to tourists, but for widespread use in the communities. But the civilizing influence of the steel rails has penetrated plateau surface and mountain valley; and in the humblest home, along with Brazilian coffee, Ceylon tea, Hawaiian or Cuban sugar, advanced agents of world commercial commodities, are to be found Grand Rapids furniture, Illinois agateware, Rhode Island worsted, New England or North Carolina cotton goods, "ready to wear" clothing made in New York shops, Syracuse chinaware, and New Jersey victrolas and radios. The implement house may shelter a Chattanooga plow and harrow, an Indiana wagon, an Illinois binder and tractor, as well as a certain celebrated, Detroit-made automobile. Within the last few decades the "back country" of the South has evolved from a condition of local self-sufficiency and provincialism to one of dependence on and activity in the commercial maelstrom that circles the world.

MANUFACTURES IN THE COLONIAL AND THE EARLY NATIONAL PERIOD

No reliable official data are available on manufacturing in the United States until the 1830 census year. The 1790 census was taken only to serve as a basis for the apportionment of representatives. For the first thirty or more years of our national existence, and earlier in Colonial days, therefore, we must depend on estimates by various writers and annalists.

As for Virginia, Jefferson gives a few brief statements about its manufactures in 1781 and 1782. He reports that "the most necessary articles of clothing" were manufactured within the families and that the cotton cloth would bear comparison with that of Europe, but cloth from flax and hemp was both "unsightly and unpleasant."* What was true of Virginia, there is reason to suspect, was true of Maryland and North Carolina. Blacksmiths, shoemakers, cabinetmakers, and others

---

* Thomas Jefferson, *Notes on the State of Virginia,* 323.

were found in every community. But there was little necessity for manufacturing in those sections that had contact with the ocean ports, such as Baltimore, Wilmington, Charleston, and Savannah. Except in the distant parts of the Piedmont and in the Great Valley the Southern colonists depended largely upon European manufactures.

There were a few iron furnaces in eastern Maryland and Virginia all during the eighteenth century. Jefferson reports that in 1781-1782 there were three on the south side of the James River, one on the north side in Albemarle County, three in Frederick County, and two in a valley between the Blue Ridge and North Mountains. One of these made 1,600 tons of pig iron a year, another 1,000 tons, and three others about 600 tons each. Four of the furnaces carried the manufacturing process to the bar-iron stage. Besides these, a forge at Fredericksburg made 300 tons of bar iron a year from pig imported from Maryland; and a forge on the "Potowmac" also used Maryland pig iron. He writes that the toughness of the cast iron at Ross's and Zane's furnaces was very remarkable, that the pots cast from iron produced at these furnaces were "thinner than usual" and could be "safely thrown in and out of a wagon." Saltpans, he says, "cannot be broken up in order to be melted again unless previously drilled in many parts."[*]

These were not the first ironworks erected in Virginia. Skilled workers in iron were sent over to the Jamestown colony from England in 1619 to "set up three iron works" as well as sawing mills and salt plants. Not a few of the prominent men in Virginia in the eighteenth century were interested in the making of iron furnaces. Colonel William Byrd wrote a treatise entitled "A Progress of the Mines," in 1732, in which he lists Augustine Washington, father of George Washington, Colonel Spotswood, and others, as interested in iron making.

There were many furnaces in Maryland by 1715; and in 1719 the Maryland legislative assembly offered a bounty of 100 acres of good land to any "who would set up a forge or a furnace in the province." In 1718 Maryland and Virginia exported "3 tons 7 cwt. of bar iron to England." By 1776 there were some eight to ten furnaces in Maryland, located mainly on the Coastal Plain. Bog iron was dug from surface deposits near Fort Henry. Charcoal was the fuel. In 1778 Baltimore had a slitting mill and two nail factories.

There were several furnaces in North Carolina before the Revolutionary War, on the Cape Fear, Yadkin, and Dan rivers.[†] These iron industries were developed to meet a pressing local need for iron, a commodity cheap and yet bulky, and producible even with crude devices. Until the era of cheap transportation and strong competition, all the furnaces were small and crude. The quality of iron could bear no comparison in purity and uniformity with that made today, with chemists watching and testing every step in its production. Modern blast furnaces have a capacity of 100,000 to 150,000 tons a year. The largest listed by Jefferson in 1781 produced but 1,600 tons. The forges used in the making of wrought iron were still more crude, similar in principle to the forge, which, in its main features, had apparently been devised by people independently in many parts of the world. Its use had been generally abandoned in Europe in the fourteenth century. The forge was not unlike the blacksmith's forge of our day. There was a wood and leather bellows operated by a hand lever that forced cold air into a small cavity made in powdered or crushed charcoal. This cavity contained the charge of crushed limestone and iron ore. After a long period of heating the red-hot mass was removed from the forge and pounded to break off the hard coating of slag, steel, and cast iron that formed on the outside, a result of excessive carbonizing and unequal heating within the mass. A bloom of rather poor wrought iron was formed as the core of the mass. The forges thus used produced crude wrought iron by the direct process, the most primitive of methods. The early furnaces in America, known in Europe as the Osmund, were also small, rarely more than twelve feet high. The iron produced was called an osmund or a bloom. There were all sizes of furnaces, one may well imagine, some little larger than the forge. The process of making steel was also slow, and one could never be certain of its quality, for the carbonizing process was so crude that the carbon was very unevenly distributed. Hollow ware, made by casting at the finishing works, was generally of poor quality.

Most of the iron-making establishments in the Great Valley were forges. Several were built before the Revolutionary War, one as early as 1725. Some of these forges were replaced by furnaces as the market expanded and more experienced iron making resulted.*

Industries on the frontier are always of a generalized type. The mechanic can do many things well enough, but few things or nothing perfectly. Perfection comes with specialization. Iron making on the frontier was characteristic, for the most part, of a regime of local economy. Although the exportation of refined iron was not unknown, it was apparently of rare occurrence. Owing to the lack of competition, very

---

* Swank, *loc. cit.*

low-grade ore—the only sort available—could be used. The plants at any one locality were short lived, as a rule, owing to the exhaustion of ore deposits and wood for making charcoal, and the lack of land transportation to bring ore and fuel to the furnace.

The early attempts at manufacturing represented the work of only a small part of the total population. The great bulk of the people were agriculturists who saw a greater future in the acquisition and tillage of land than in manufacturing. In frontier regions, where land is abundant, and therefore cheap, and people are few to the square mile, agriculture, not manufacturing, is the normal economic activity. Hewett, an eighteenth-century chronicler of the Carolinas, wrote of conditions in South Carolina about 1770 as follows: "Nor is there the smallest reason to expect that manufactures will be encouraged in Carolina while landed property can be obtained on such easy terms. The cooper, the carpenter, the brick-layer, the ship-builder, and every other artificer and tradesman, after having labored for a few years at their respective employment and purchased a few negroes, commonly retreat to the country and settle tracts of uncultivated land . . . Even the merchant becomes weary of attending the store and risking his stock on the stormy sea or in the hands of men when it is often exposed to equal hazards, and therefore collects it as soon as possible and settles a plantation."*

The progressive, well-read, freedom-loving Jefferson lent little or no support to the encouragement of manufacturing, because he feared that the growth of urban centers and a large factory population would undermine the moral foundation of the rising republic. He also felt, probably, that advances in such economic activities were bound to result in failure because the social and economic environments were not favorable. He writes in his *Notes on the State of Virginia* that political economists in Europe had established the principle that every state should manufacture for itself. In America such a principle was held by not a few, but conditions in these two continents were wholly unlike. "In Europe all lands," he says, "are either cultivated or locked up against the cultivator," therefore manufacturing must be resorted to for relief. "But," he writes, "in America we have [had in his day] an immensity of land courting only the industry of the husbandman." The farmer, to him, was the hope of the nation, as stated in a previous chapter. He wished to see the majority of the people on the land and independent, for, he says, "Dependence [as among factory workers]

---

* Hewett, an early chronicler of the Carolinas (S. C.), quoted by M. Trescott in an address before the Historical Society of South Carolina, printed in *Charleston Mercury* and *De Bow's Review*, XXVII, O. S., December, 1859, 678.

begets subservience and venality, suffocates the germ of virtue and prepares fit tools for the designs of ambition. . . .

"While we have land to labour then, let us never wish to see our citizens occupied at a work bench or twirling a distaff. . . . A degeneracy in these [in an industrial population] is a canker which soon eats to the heart of its laws and constitution."*

During the Revolutionary War the people of the struggling colonies were forced to provide themselves with manufactured goods. Just after the war they felt the necessity of a protective tariff (the first of its kind in America and the second act to be passed under the constitution), "for the support of the government, for the discharge of the debts of the United States, and the encouragement and protection of manufactures." It was passed on July 4, 1789. Baltimore merchants, among many in the Northeastern States, sent a petition to Congress, favoring such an act, on April 11, 1789. The state legislature of Maryland, for which the petition was first prepared, realizing that but one "sovereign legislature" should exercise this right of laying duties, sent it on to Congress.† This tariff apparently stimulated the growth of manufactures in all the older parts of the country for a decade or two, but more particularly in the North. Among the Southern States, Maryland and Virginia, the oldest and most densely settled and having by far the best contacts with the ocean, took the lead. In other words, the tariff benefited those states in establishing manufacturing that were about ready to become manufacturing states. Hamilton saw little benefit to be derived from a protective tariff. He wrote in 1791 that it was his belief that "To leave industry to itself . . . [was], in almost every case, the soundest as well as the simplest policy," for he believed that manufacturing was "the offspring of a redundant, or at least of a full population."‡ To this philosophy the economic geographer has long subscribed.

MANUFACTURING IN 1810

Gallatin, in his report on manufactures for 1810, classified the manufacturing industries of the United States into three groups:

1. Those manufactures "carried on to an extent which may be considered adequate to the consumption of the United States" were (only important listed):

---

* Jefferson, *op. cit.,* 323, 325. Bracketed enclosures are the present author's.

† *American State Papers,* "Finance," I, 5.

‡ Alexander Hamilton, Report of Secretary of Treasury, *American State Papers,* "Finance," I, 123.

Manufactures of wood or of which wood is a part.
Leather and manufactures of leather.
Soap and tallow candles, spermaceti oil and candles.
Flaxseed oil.
Refined sugar.
Coarse earthenware.

2. Manufactures firmly established:

Iron and manufactures of iron.
Manufactures of cotton, wool, flax, and hemp.
Hats, paper, printing types, and printed books.
Gunpowder.
Glass.
Jewelry and clocks, etc.

3. Those in which some progress has been made in providing the needs of the country:

Paints and colors.
Chemical preparations and drugs.
Salt.
Manufactures of copper, brass, japanned and plated ware, calico, and some type of glassware.*

As for details of manufactures in the several states, it is possible to get only the sketchy reports of annalists and chroniclers of the time. In a large, two-volume geography compiled by Morse† it is stated that Maryland about 1810 had 80 grist mills, 2 glass factories, 2 iron furnaces, 2 paper mills, a few tanneries, and 400 distilling plants. The total value of manufactured products was $11,500,000.

In *A Geographical Dictionary* by Scott, it is found that forges and furnaces were in operation in six Maryland counties, making pig iron and bar iron, hollow ware, cannon, stoves, and other useful articles. The manufactured products of Baltimore were flour, sugar, rum, tobacco, snuff, cordage, paper, woolen goods, cotton cords, saddles, boots and shoes. There were 54 mills within 18 miles of the city, one of which had 4 pairs of stones that ground 150 barrels of flour a day.‡ The flour industry was therefore of long standing. Baily, who visited Baltimore about 1796, wrote that "on a little run of water which empties

---

* *American State Papers*, "Finance," II, 425-426.
† Jedidiah Morse, *American Universal Geography*, I, 458.
‡ Joseph Scott, *A Geographical Dictionary*, topics, Maryland, Baltimore.

itself into the harbour" there were several mills making flour and that a great quantity was exported.*

Scott reports that the water power at Richmond, Virginia, was much used. There were several mills at the west end of the city, "one of which is not inferior to any in the United States," being built in such a way as to have the water pass through the mill so as to run a machine for grinding corn and another for making paper. He reports that lately "the inhabitants of Virginia were beginning to pay more attention to the manufacture of clothing."†

Iron manufacturing plants were active in "different parts of the state." Northwest of the Blue Ridge there were "numerous manufactories of cast and wrought iron and also lead." At Richmond small arms were made on "an extensive scale," iron and coal (brought to the city by water) and water power were at the very door of the factory. But we are told that the people as a whole were "much attached to agriculture, and preferred foreign manufacture."‡

The Moravians in North Carolina had a paper mill at Salem, and there were iron works in three counties on the Yadkin River. Whiskey and brandy were made for home consumption. Tar, pitch, and turpentine were the chief exports.§

Swank wrote that there were four forges, two bloomeries, and two furnaces in operation in Lincoln County (now Catawba, Lincoln, and Gaston counties and a part of Cleveland) that had been in operation before 1800. One was built in 1780 and continued to produce iron until 1873.¶

Charleston, apparently, had little interest in manufacturing in the early decades of the eighteenth century, for no mention is ever made in the many descriptions of the city, read by the writer. It was active in commerce and at times ranked only below New York, the leader. Its fabricated wares could be obtained readily from New England or Europe.

In 1810 Tench Coxe reports nine bloomeries, besides a small nailery (nail factory) and a steel furnace in the upper Piedmont in South Carolina.‖ As for manufactures in general, Morse writes that "Domes-

---

* Francis Baily, *Journal of a Tour in Unsettled Parts of North America,* 1796 and 1797, 105.

† Scott, *op. cit.,* topics, Richmond, Virginia.

‡ Jedidiah Morse, *American Universal Geography,* I, 481.

§ Morse, *op. cit.,* 499.

¶ Swank, *op. cit.,* 832; changes in counties from *A Century of Population Growth in United States,* 68.

‖ Swank, *op. cit.,* 833.

tic manufactureries in the upper districts [were] carried on to an extent which [went] far to supply the wants of the families, but none [were] made for exportation, articles of iron excepted."* One at least of the mills, erected in 1790, was rather extensive. A correspondent of the American Museum told of a man who "had completed and had in operation in the High Hills of the South, near Statesburg, ginning, carding, and other machines driven by water, and also spinning machines with eighty-four spindles each, with every necessary article for manufacturing cotton."† Much water power was available, according to Morse, and this resource offered opportunities for an expansion of manufacturing. In some towns hats were made of palmetto; tanneries, and shoemaking shops were common; but little advance had been made, for "the genius of the people leads them," he writes, "to agriculture."‡ The total value of manufactured products in South Carolina was $3,624,000.

Georgia in 1810 produced in the homes, factories, and mills cotton, woolen, and linen cloth, cotton bagging,§ lumber, tanned hides, whiskey and beer, and sugar. Swank reports that in 1810 a bloomery, a forge, and a nailery were in operation near the coast in Georgia. This probably used bog iron ore.¶ The total value of Georgia's manufactured products was slightly more than that of South Carolina. For both Alabama and Mississippi there were no returns. Louisiana exported 10,834,000 pounds "of sugar of domestic growth" and production

---

* Morse, *op. cit.*, 517.

† Quoted in "Factory System of United States," *Report of Eighth Census, 1860,* 539.

‡ Morse, *loc. cit.*

§ "The application of machinery to the manufacture of textile products began very early in the South. Before Slater erected the first Arkwright mill in Rhode Island, power and automatic machinery were applied to cotton spinning in South Carolina. In 1790, a small band of English weavers and spinners established in the tidewater region of the state an eighty-four-spindle mill for the manufacture of fine cloths. Before 1800, spinning jennies and water-driven spinning frames were to be found in two South Carolina towns, and carding and spinning machinery were in use in eastern Tennessee. Early in the century three Rhode Island manufacturers erected in South Carolina a mill of 700 spindles—the first to be built in the Piedmont region,—hauling their machinery 250 miles over rough roads into the interior.

"In 1810 the value of textiles produced was greater in North Carolina than in Massachusetts, and the census for that year records more homespun cotton manufactured in Virginia, South Carolina, and Georgia than in the other thirteen states and territories combined, also more flax was spun in Virginia than in any other state." (Mary Anderson, *Women's Place in Industry in Ten Southern States,* Women's Bureau, U. S. Department of Labor, 1931-1932.)

¶ Morse, *op. cit.*, 541; Swank, *op. cit.*, 833.

from New Orleans in 1816. Markets for these products were found in Baltimore, Philadelphia, and New York, as well as in the Mississippi Valley towns.*

The lack of markets was undoubtedly one cause for the undeveloped condition of manufacturing in Louisiana. New Orleans was not even active in up-river commerce. Before the coming of the steamboat, Morse writes, "The difficulty of ascending the Mississippi [had] cut off New Orleans from supplying the western states [North Central] with foreign merchandise." It was found cheaper to purchase articles in New York and Philadelphia, carry them *by land* to Pittsburgh at the forks of the Ohio, and thence down that river to the various towns on its banks, than to transport them up the Mississippi and the Ohio.†

By 1810 Tennessee and Kentucky seemed to have made, as did the Cisappalachian states, some advance in manufacturing. Isolation from the older manufacturing sections to the east of the Appalachian barrier, the abundance of local raw materials, and the facilities offered to some of the then rapidly growing towns for the distribution of manufactured goods favored the development of manufacturing. They were under a regime of both local and regional economy.

Michaux, who visited the Transappalachian country in 1804 (quoted in chapter on agriculture), wrote that Knoxville did "not yet possess any kind of establishment or manufactory, except two or three tan yards"; and Nashville had "no kind of manufactory, although built upward of fifteen years." But Lexington, the most important trading center in the Blue Grass Region, had two extensive hemp rope-walks constantly in operation supplying the ships (some ocean) that were built on the Ohio. There were also several tanyards, several common potteries, and one or two powder mills which used sulphur brought across the mountains from Philadelphia, saltpeter from the numerous caves of Kentucky, and charcoal from the near-by forests. He considered the articles manufactured "very passable." The "want of hands," he writes, "excited the industry of the inhabitants of this country" to invent machines to speed up manufacturing. A Lexington man "had just obtained a patent for a nail machine." But manufacturing was developing slowly for, he writes, "There are few of them [families] who put their children to any trade, wanting their services in the field."‡

In 1810 Kentucky had 267 tanneries, 2,000 distilleries, 24,450 looms (probably in the homes), 53 powder mills, 33 fulling mills, 36 salt

---

* Morse, *Geography,* I, 511.

† Morse, *op. cit.,* 665.

‡ Michaux, *Travels to the West of the Alleghany Mountains,* 124.

works, 6 paper mills, 38 rope walks, 13 cotton-bagging manufacturies, 15 spinning machines, 3 forges, and 4 furnaces. Its manufactured products were valued at $5,099,000.*

Swank reports that there were probably four furnaces and three forges in Kentucky in 1810. The government built the Slate furnace in 1790 on the Licking River and operated it until 1838.† There were several iron works in eastern Tennessee in 1810. He remarks that the mountaineers were apparently "born with an instinct for making iron." Charcoal, limestone, and beds of iron ore were in close proximity, offering excellent opportunities to the iron workers. The difficulties of transporting iron goods over the mountains or across the Blue Ridge and along the poor roads of this time made it necessary to have local iron manufacturing plants to meet local needs. Their wide distribution was a response to poor transportation and wide distribution of the essential raw products used for manufacturing.

Iron making was a frontier industry and could be carried on wherever beds of iron ore were found. The products were those that found a ready sale in the near-by farming territory, such as nails, horseshoes, straps for plows, plow points, wagon tires, harrow teeth, and hollow ware. Some iron was floated down the Tennessee River from the iron works on the Holston and other rivers.‡

After perusing the previous paragraphs on the state of manufactures in the South in 1810, one would be inclined to conclude that for this early date a great advance had been made, yet the data available show that this generalization is far from the actual facts.

Seybert, basing his estimates on several reliable (he so considered them) sets of data, gives the total value of manufactures for the United States (17 states) at about $128,000,000, and apportions the values to the various states as shown in Table X.§

The value of the products of the three leading Northeastern States at this time (1810) was more than 2.8 times that of the three leading Southern States. At this early date then there had begun a differentiation of economic activities, the greatest advance in manufacturing having been made in the North.

This differentiation in economic-geographic interests in three sections is also voiced in Gallatin's report: "Not only do the middle and

---

* Jedidiah Morse, *American Universal Geography*, I, 594.

† Swank, *op. cit.*, 834.

‡ Swank, *op. cit.*, 835.

§ Tench Coxe estimates the value to have been $173,000,000. Gallatin places the value at $120,000,000. These estimates are unlike the estimates given by Morse in the previous pages. Each writer, apparently, had his own estimates.

TABLE X

VALUE OF MANUFACTURES, 1810[1]

	Million Dollars		Million Dollars
Pennsylvania.......	32.1	Kentucky..........	4.1
Massachusetts......	19.7	New Hampshire.....	3.1
New York..........	14.6	Rhode Island.......	3.1
Virginia............	11.4	Georgia...........	2.7
Maryland..........	6.6	Tennessee..........	2.7
Connecticut........	5.9	South Carolina......	2.2
North Carolina.....	5.3	Ohio..............	2.0
New Jersey........	4.7	Delaware..........	1.0
Vermont...........	4.3		

[1] Adam Seybert, *Statistical Annals of United States*, 11.

northern sections of the United States manufacture all their own raw materials, but they have so fully entered into the domestic and mill manufactory of our southern and western cotton, that almost every retail store in the ten middle and northern or eastern states effects, in every year, more sales of cotton than of wool, flax, and hemp, and the state and vicinity of Rhode Island exhibits a water spinning cotton mill in or for every township. The presence then of this only redundant American [population] and raw material has produced these pleasing and successful exertions in this interesting manufacture, amounting already to one-third of the whole value of the foreign manufactures imported into the U. S., in the first year of the present constitution."*

What are the reasons for the difference in degree of development of manufacturing? Political and economic philosophers, particularly of the Northern school later on in the century, have ascribed the retarded state of manufacturing in the South as due to slavery. In 1810 slavery existed in both North and South, but there were more slaves by far in the South. The New England States had 418, the Middle Atlantic 31,000, and the Southern 1,090,850.† Both sections bordered the ocean and thus could import and export readily to the same degree. In the 1790's Virginia and South Carolina frequently stood second or third in rank in commerce and manufacturing. Much of North Carolina's exports generally went to Virginia or South Carolina ports.‡ Neither section had the advantage of the other in inland transportation. Both sections had stores of iron ore, water power, forest resources, and agricultural products.

Among the other natural conditioning factors that may possibly

---

* Quoted by James Mease, *Archives of Useful Knowledge*, I, 251.
† *A Century of Population Growth in the United States, 1790-1900*, 133.
‡ Seybert, *op. cit.*, 142.

explain the differentiation in economic activity in the two sections was a difference in population density.

In the Western countries, where social, religious, and political factors permit economic developments to follow the normal trends, conditioned by soil, climate, minerals, power, forests, and transportation facilities, there is a close relationship between density of population and type of economic activity. Manufacturing tends to be more active in the more densely settled sections. The population density of the North Atlantic States in 1810 was about 22; and of the South Atlantic, only 10. In 1800 New England density was 19.9; that of the Middle Atlantic States 14; and of the South Atlantic, 8.6.* Although the density in the Northeast was greater, the densities in both is far from that of the manufacturing type. Other considerations must be noted.

Differences in social ideals and traits of the leaders in both sections, brought with them from across the Atlantic, no doubt were powerful factors in this differentiation. The gentleman cavalier of Virginia and the wealthy colonist of South Carolina from the first had as their ideal the acquisition of large estates. Though relatively small in numbers, they fashioned the social and economic milieu for their contemporaries and successors who had acquired, or might through economy and enterprise acquire, sufficient wealth to possess landed estates manned by negro slave workers. It may be pointed out, however, that while this was a social, a human factor, its functioning in the South was conditioned by the abundance of cheap land and a low population density. Great trends in the historical development of regions or sections, it must be remembered, are not set in motion by the whims or ideals of any one social group, though the trend may be warped at times. The major trends or lines of development are deeply rooted in the natural condition of the environment. In the *long run* the social and political institutions of a country tend to adapt themselves to the natural environmental tendencies, or the country or region will lose out in the struggle that will arise with the people who accept nature and adapt their lives to its laws and opportunities. The South, because of its humid, warm temperate and subtropical climate and vast areas of agricultural land, was "destined" (not to be interpreted in the same sense ascribed by the political schools of expansionists in America in the fourth and fifth decades of the nineteenth century) to be a great agricultural section so long as its population was not great enough to exploit, to an advanced degree, its manufacturing resources.

---

* Data from *Statistical Abstract*, 1928, 9.

MANUFACTURING IN THE SOUTH IN 1850 AND 1860

Owing to the dearth of statistics on manufacturing for the decades between 1810 and 1850, it is next to impossible to trace in detail the changes in the ranking of the states in total manufactures and the changes in the individual industries. We must be content therefore to contrast manufacturing in 1810 and 1850.

Even though the South made some remarkable advances in manufacturing between 1810 and 1850, these advances were small in comparison with the progress in the North. The South, relatively, suffered a remarkable decline.

In 1810, according to Seybert, the value of the manufactured products of the South was $36,068,000; that of the North, $88,632,000.* The South was producing 28 to 30 per cent of the commodity value of the country, and its population was about 46 per cent of that for the United States—not a bad showing in manufacturing.†

By 1850 the South was manufacturing slightly less than 14 per cent of the products of the United States.‡ Its population was 39 per cent of that for the country.§

Before the causes of the decline between 1810 and 1850 and the attempts made by Southern leaders to build up manufactures are discussed, a brief study of the conditions of manufactures in 1850 will be presented. J. B. D. De Bow, a Southern journalist and superintendent of the Census for 1850, groups the states and the value of their manufactures as shown in Table XI.

Cotton manufacturing in 1850 was fairly widespread in the South. A beginning had been made, however, in the localization of mills on the outer edge of the Piedmont where there was abundant water power. Georgia had the largest number of factories and turned out the greatest value of products among the Southern States in both 1850 and 1860. In 1860 Virginia, North Carolina, and Alabama each had an output of more than $1,000,000.¶ Here and there were large and active manufacturing plants developed through the enterprise and hard work of some one man or firm. William Gregg, who may be called the father of modern cotton manufacturing in the South, had erected a "complete" textile plant at Graniteville, South Carolina, modeled after

---

* This includes products of mines and mechanical arts.

† Data from Adam Seybert, *Statistical Annals of United States*, 11. Totals and percentages, calculated.

‡ *Compendium of Seventh Census*, 1850, 179; *Report of Twelfth Census*, 1900, VII, Part I.

§ *Statistical Abstract*, 1928, 6.

¶ *Report of Eighth Census*, 1860, "Manufactures," pp. xii, xiii.

TABLE XI

VALUE OF PRODUCTS OF MANUFACTURES, MINES, AND
MECHANICAL ARTS, 1850[1]

New England	$ 274,700,000
Middle Atlantic	472,000,000
Southern States	
(So. Atlantic)	53,600,000
Southwestern States	
(Ala., Miss., La., Tenn., Ark., Texas)	26,300,000
Northwestern States	
(All remainder including Pacific States)	186,700,000
Non-slaveholding	845,400,000
Slaveholding	167,900,000
Total for the United States	$1,013,300,000

[1] *Compendium of Seventh Census,* 1850, 179.

those of the Lowell Company near Boston and at Lowell. He worked hard, and with some success, to interest Southern capital in cotton milling.* Greenville, South Carolina, in the foothills of the Southern Appalachian Mountains, had several large cotton mills, run by water power, in its vicinity. Here also was located a coach factory, the largest in the South, that employed a hundred skilled mechanics and turned out $80,000 worth of coaches a year, which found a ready sale all over the Lower South. One writer states that the factory was well equipped with machines for sawing, planing, boring hubs, turning spokes, smoothing wood, and cutting tenons.†

In a factory at Prattsville, Alabama, were produced 600 cotton gins annually that "acquired a celebrity throughout all the South."‡

The iron industry, for the most part still in its primitive state, was widely distributed; but by far the larger number of plants were in the southern part of the Appalachian Highlands—Piedmont, Mountains, Great Valley, and Cumberland Plateau—and along the lower Cumberland and Tennessee rivers. Maryland and Virginia (Fig. 99) still had a few iron works. Lesley reports that North Carolina in 1856 had 40 bloomeries and 6 furnaces, and a few forges, "mostly in operation," besides 2 or 3 rolling mills. South Carolina the same year had 8 furnaces (6 in Spartanburg County), 3 small rolling mills, and 2 bloomeries. North Georgia had a small iron works near the Chattahoochee River on the western edge of the Piedmont. "This whole country possesses an incalculable, inexhaustible abundance of

* Victor S. Clark, *History of Manufactures in the United States,* I, 459.
† *De Bow's Review,* XXVII, O. S., December, 1859, 694, 695.
‡ *Ibid.,* XI, O. S., July, 1851, 102.

the richest ore, while its production of iron still remains at a minimum." Such statements clearly illustrate that the "theory of relativity"
needs to be applied to the interpretation of all statements, even those
of the *Census Reports*. At Atlanta a rolling mill was constructed in
1858, employing 150 skilled mechanics. The writer comments that no
longer would it be necessary to transport old rails to the North, to be
reworked.* Tennessee had 75 forges and bloomeries, 71 furnaces, and
4 rolling mills. Not all were in continuous operation, indicative in
general of a decline either in supply of ore or in market demands.

Courtesy Harper's Magazine.

FIG. 99.—Mount Savage Iron Works, Western Maryland, about 1856.

The Great Valley from the Hudson to Central Alabama has been the site of scores of iron
works, for the most part small and ephemeral in their span of life. The iron works above were
near Cumberland on Jenning's Creek. From *Harper's Magazine*, XIV, 1858, 603.

There were about this time 41 forges and furnaces in operation on
the Cumberland River in Tennessee and Kentucky, using lean brown
ores of the Highland Rim. Blooms from these plants were floated down
to the rolling mills of the Ohio Valley.†

By 1860 many of these ceased operation, or else the census enumera-
tions are somewhat awry. The *Census Report* for 1860 lists 6 iron
bloomeries for the South out of 97 for the whole country; 39 pig-iron
furnaces out of 286; 84 bar, sheet, and railroad iron plants for the
South out of 256 for the country; 96 foundries out of 1,412; 4 locomotive works out of 19; and 6 nail and spike factories out of 99.‡

---

* *Ibid.*, I, N. S., October, 1858, 475.

† *Report of Eighth Census*, 1860, "Manufactures," pp. clxxv, clxxvi; *Report of
Tenth Census*, 1880, Swank, "The Iron and Steel Industry," 832, 835.

‡ *Report of Eighth Census*, 1860, "Manufactures," pp. clvii-cxcv.

CAUSES OF DECLINE IN MANUFACTURES, FROM 1810 TO 1850 AND 1860

The relative decline of manufactures in the South during the first half of the nineteenth century was due certainly to the expansion of cotton culture. The invention of the cotton gin in 1793, following the invention and perfection of cotton spinning and weaving machines in England during 1733-1785 (see page 303), greatly reduced the work necessary for the separation of seed and fiber and gave a demand for American cotton. Nowhere in the world has man found vast areas better fitted by climate, surface features, and natural transportation facilities for the growing of this staple. It has been shown that the rapid expansion of cotton culture was due to the high prices received. During the first decade of the eighteenth century the lowest export price was 15.6 cents, the highest 24.6. In the second decade prices ranged from 10.7 to 33.9 cents. Would any people be so stupid as not to feel the stimulus of great wealth with abundant prospects of still greater wealth? It speaks for the enterprise and business acumen of the Southern planters of the times that their money went into new lands and increasing numbers of slaves, instead of into the untried (by them) fields of manufacturing. Some no doubt realized that the economic ship of the South was drifting into dangerous shoals. Most, however, were no doubt as satisfied in the rôle the South was playing as the author of the following lines, written from Virginia in 1854: By not developing manufactures "we have lost nothing, the world has gained a great deal, and we have fulfilled a mighty destiny in the moral and political field, greater than the achievements of trade and arts in the physics of other States. We have no cities, but we have a meliorated country populace, civilized in the solitude, gracious in the amenities of life, and refined and conservative in social habits. We have little associated but more individual wealth than any equal number of white population in the South."*

It was in the late 1830's and the 1840's that the supply of cotton began to exceed the demand and prices fell. Great distress followed. The immense sums of money tied up in land and slaves lay dormant or were as rapidly being dissipated. Neither form of property could be sold. In the meantime commerce and manufacturing, economic activities absolutely essential to every civilized land, had by degrees fallen into the hands of vessel owners and factory operators of the

---

* *De Bow's Review,* XXIII, O. S., July, 1857, 61.

Northeastern States. Even the farmers of the Middle West found in the South excellent markets for their grains, meats, horses, and mules.

The desperate economic situation in which the South found itself in the 1850's and 1860's is well described in the following extended quotations which breathe both a defense of the economic order of the South of that date and a recognition of the direful position in which that section had drifted. The writer asks:

> Why is it that the North has so far outstripped the South in commerce, the growth of its cities, internal development, and the arts of living? A false philosophy and a false philanthropy at once point to our slave institution, and say, "Behold the barrier to your advancement in the curse of African bondage!" The bigot who utters this can't be blind to the fact which historical experience has graven upon the tablets of time. Slavery, so far from being the cause of our retardation, is the nursing mother of the prosperity of the North. It is the production of slave labor that furnishes the pabulum of its commerce—it is sugar, cotton, and rice that freight its ships, and supply the capital and credit on which its vast foreign commerce is built. Slavery is the back-bone of the Northern commercial as it is of the British manufacturing system; and it is a question of doubt today, whether immediate emancipation would entail more of devastation and ruin on the States of the South, than on those of Old and New England. With two thousand miles of seacoast, we own hardly a ship, and are destitute of a commercial marine. Yet we have all the aptitude of genius and geographical position for commerce that the North has. Deprive us of our system of labor— the best organized, the most humane and efficient, that the world has ever seen—and what is to prevent us from launching our energies in the new direction of the ocean?

Then he asks:

> What is to prevent us from competing with them in the manufacturing arts? We have waterfalls tumbling from a thousand hills in exhaustless motive power—our fuel for steam is superabundant. Why, then, do we depend upon our Northern brethren for every article of industrial manufacture? Why do they spin the very clothes that we wear, out of the produce of our fields? Why do we look to them for every hat, shoe, saddle, blanket, carriage, and even down to the humble horn combs, buttons, and lucifer matches, that we require? The answer is ready and simple, and is itself an eloquent vindication of the splendid success of our system of slave labor, and an eulogium on the glorious soil and climate on which a bountiful Providence has cast our happy lot. It is that our labor, almost without diversity of application, and devoted to agriculture alone, has enabled us, not only to accomplish the great civilization which we enjoy, but has enabled us, with the surplus, to bear a heavy proportion of the burdens of our common government, and yet make New England rich by the millions we annually pay for her indus-

try, her arts, her luxuries, the use of her ships, her railroads, her hotels, and her bracing summer climate. Why, does any one suppose we could have done all this and be solvent, without slavery? How prodigious the resources, how efficient and telling the labor, that could bear this splendid annual tribute! . . .

The defiant writer then tells how the octopus of the North has enmeshed the economy of the South. He writes:

With his ships, protected by beneficial navigation laws, he engrosses all of our carrying trade, at highly remunerative charges. He manages all our business for us, fiscal as well as industrious. He not only carries, but he ships our cotton, negotiates for its sale, and reaps the reward of that profitable transaction. What he cannot make himself, and we want, he imports for us from Europe, and from Asia, and from the uttermost parts of the earth, and after the article has gone through the mill of commercial manipulation, and paid all possible profits in a northern port of entry, it is sent out to us, and slavery planks down the money for it. Nay, more than this—not content with attending to so vast an amount of business for us at home and abroad, the Northern man brings his skill and his thrift, and his usefulness in our very midst, and obligingly occupies and fills the most profitable places and functions for the interchanges of our trade. Who is it that buys the bulk of your cotton, and sugar, and rice, in the Southern markets? The Northern man with Northern facilities. Do you want a civil engineer to project a road or canal? You send to the North for him. Do you want a locomotive and trains to equip your road? They come from the North. Nay, we import our very schoolmasters to teach our children—the primers and Bibles out of which they read—our divines, our editors, lawyers, and doctors, and a vast deal, too, of our politics.*

Then the expediency philosophers of the South got to work. Convention after convention was held in an attempt to work out some solution to extricate the South from the economic doldrums into which it had drifted. A perusal of some of the orations delivered at these conventions and of scores of magazine articles shows that the political philosophers had but a meager understanding of the fundamental principles underlying the operation of economic-geographic laws. Their suggestions for shifting the economic order in the South from an agricultural regime to one in which manufacturing, commerce, and transportation integrate with the industries producing raw materials are naïve indeed. They little realized that great movements require decades and decades of time to get into operation and are "tuned" to the economic-physical environment in which they operate.

---

* *De Bow's Review,* XVII, O. S., October, 1854, 365-367.

There were saner and more practical men in the South who understood the drift of things and saw also the way out, but they were all too few in number.

Another sums up the solution in a very few words. "We must," he writes, "do something else besides growing cotton; [we must] educate our children to other employments than planting, physic, divinity, and law."*

Among the many suggestions offered were:

1. That the Southern people boycott the goods of Northern manufacture by patronizing local factories. Writes a Judge of the Supreme Court of Alabama in 1860, (1) Buy nothing which is made or grown north of the Mason and Dixon's line if you can obtain a substitute for it that is made or grown anywhere else. (2) Buy nothing imported into a Northern port if you can obtain a substitute which was imported into a Southern port. "Such patriotism for Southern institutions," he writes, "may cost privation or money for a year or two but trade will soon adjust itself."†

2. Direct trade from Europe should be encouraged to free the Southern people from the New York, Boston, and Philadelphia ship owners. This might be done, one writer says, by levying an excise tax on all goods imported that reached the South by way of Northern ports. South Carolina in 1833 passed an act relieving vessel owners of the state from paying taxes on their shipping.‡

3. Many believed that slave labor should be used in the factories, to offset the lack of factory hands. In a factory at Saluda near Columbia, South Carolina, in 1851 there were 128 workers in all, including children—"All slaves and the large proportion of them [were] owned by the company." The mill operated 5,000 spindles and 120 looms. The average cost of labor per annum at this mill was $75 per employee in comparison with $116 for white operatives at other mills. The mills, it was claimed, would give work to slaves "not strong enough for the cotton fields."§

4. Others advocated the opening of the slave trade in order that more workers would be had for the fields and thus release negro hands for the factories. An editorial in *De Bow's Review* in January, 1859,

---

* John Forsyth in *De Bow's Review*, XVII, O. S., October, 1854, 376.

† *De Bow's Review*, XXVIII, O. S., May, 1860, 589; XXIX, O. S., July, 1860, 81.

‡ John Forsyth, paper before the Franklin Society of Mobile, *De Bow's Review*, XVII, O. S., October, 1854, 375.

§ From report by a *New York Herald* reporter, quoted by E. Steadman of Tennessee, in *De Bow's Review*, XI, O. S., September, 1851, 319. The cost of the slave was probably not included.

pointed out that the pages of the past year or two of the *Review* had
contained many arguments advanced pro and con upon the slave trade.
"Certainly," the editor states, "no cause has ever grown with greater
rapidity than has that of the advocates of the slave trade, if we may
judge from the attitude it is assuming in most of our Southern legislatures."*

5. Still others thought that the South should encourage the immigration of white mechanics or mill workers. Says one "The Republic
owes its existence to original immigration. There should be a continued influx of this element." There could be "no danger to slavery.
The non-slaveholder knows he is not responsible for slavery, hence
will not feel obligated to abolish it."†

It has been shown in previous pages that, on the basis of percentages,
there was apparently no increase in Southern manufacturers in the
decade between 1850 and 1860. Yet on the basis of value of manufactures there had been a large increase—from $142,000,000 to $251,-
000,000. But the increase was far less than in the other sections of
the United States. That some of this increase was the result of the
propaganda carried in the newspapers and magazines of the South
and delivered orally from public platforms, there is no doubt; but
something more than talk is necessary to change the economic order
of a section of 11,000,000 people, scattered widely over thirteen or
fourteen states, long accustomed to the tillage of the land. The vast
stores of minerals and forest resources and water power, the physical
basis for the rapid progress now being made in manufactures, were
then even more untouched than today, for the people lacked experience and capital for their exploitation.

The South was not yet in an economic-geographic condition and
position to develop manufacturing activities. Even had there been no
Civil War, and had slavery continued, there would have been no
marked turn toward manufacturing.

MANUFACTURING DURING AND AFTER THE WAR

During the Civil War manufactures—home and factory—flourished
as never before. The Union blockade was exceedingly effective within
a few months after the war began. In 1861 the cotton exported was
valued at $42,000,000; in 1862 at only $4,000,000. For imports of manufactured goods the blockade was just as effective. Old spinning wheels
long since relegated to the attics were brought out. Looms in the
homes were repaired. Forges, furnaces, and bloomeries that had been

* *De Bow's Review,* XXVI, O. S., January, 1859, 51.
† Boswell in *De Bow's Review,* XVII, O. S., August, 1858, 184.

practically if not actually out of commission in the face of severe competition from Northern-made iron introduced by the expanding railroad lines were rehabilitated and new ones constructed for the manufacture of cannon, guns, railroad iron, and iron articles of every sort used by the Confederate armies. Rails when worn out were replaced only when the need was greatest. The country was combed for every bit of scrap iron or brass available. The few tanneries, even by working overtime, could supply only a small part of the leather needed to equip the soldiers. Civilians had to go without. Men followed the armies to collect the hides of horses that fell in battle. The riding saddles were stripped of their excess leather. No people in modern times ever went into a great war so ill-equipped in manufacturing as the Southerners, and no people fought more valiantly against such odds. But before the end came all the industrial plants in the vicinity of the invading Union armies were destroyed, many not to be rebuilt, certainly not by the people of the impoverished South, for many a year.

Up from the ashes and out of crumbling walls of the Antebellum factories there has arisen within the last half century or so a new creation, a new economic order, dedicated to the task of making (if given time) the New South as self-sufficient and as powerful in a regime of world economy as the natural resources and the toil of free-born laborers will permit. In 1860, the South, it has been shown, was producing 13.3 per cent of the manufactured goods of the United States. In 1870, five years after the War, but five years of Reconstruction that to many Southern leaders was worse than war, the Southern States produced 6.6 per cent and by 1880 6.2 per cent of the manufactures of the country. Although there had been some actual growth in manufacturing as Table XII shows, there had been a de-

TABLE XII

VALUE OF SOUTHERN MANUFACTURES AT
SPECIFIC DATES[1]

1860	$193,500,000
1870	277,700,000
1880	388,800,000

[1] Data from census reports of these dates.

cline relative to the whole country. Since 1880 the Southern States have been making steady but significant advances in manufacturing, as Table XIII indicates.

Since both the area and population of the South are about 30 per cent of the total for the United States, it is evident that this section

TABLE XIII[1]

Year	Value of Manufactures	Percentage of Total of U. S.
1880	$ 338,800,000	6.2
1890	706,800,000	7.5
1900 (1899)	1,184,400,000	9.1
1910 (1909)	2,637,100,000	12.1
1920 (1919)	8,375,400,000	13.4
1930 (1929)	9,993,600,000	14.3

[1] *Idem; Statistical Abstract*, 1932, 845.

is still far from doing its share in manufacturing. But the gains it has made in recent decades, when considered in terms of its vicissitudes in the past, is very reassuring for the future. Growth is certain to gain momentum as time passes.

SUMMARY

In the preceding pages there have been discussed many social, economic, and political conditions of the South that have been operative in retarding the development of manufacturing. Among the more important are:

1. The dominance of agriculture. Vast areas of cheap agricultural land, a mild humid climate, and a long growing season made the acquisition of the necessities of life an easy problem. Like that of the landed aristocracy of England, the Southern planter's ambition in life was to acquire land and still more land. Men in the professions—doctors, lawyers, preachers, or teachers—had as their goal in life a landed estate, of thousands of acres and hundreds of negro slaves, field hands, and servants. Accordingly, contemporary Southern planters and professional men were constantly "inveighing against the vices of manufactures, the mercenary speculation of commerce." "Perhaps," one writer comments, "they adopted too readily the industrial theories of Hobbes, Sir Thomas More, and the pastoral poets generally." They certainly "lauded the superior nature of those engaged exclusively in agriculture."*

2. Slavery. The negro tended to keep out the free, white, skilled mechanics, foreign born and native born, that have meant so much to the development of manufacturing in the North. The movement of population in the United States from the older industrial sections of the Northeast has been for a century or more a westward movement. There were no economic prizes to offer in the South of that day at all comparable to those of the West. Moreover, migrants have

---

* Mr. Burwell in *De Bow's Review*, XVII, N. S., October, 1858, 178.

always preferred to move along isotherms rather than across them. Likewise the white landless laborers were constantly being pushed out of the South for want of work and forced to seek a livelihood in the North and West. In 1860 there were living outside the South 960,000 Southern-born whites. Since the Civil War there has been little check in the emigration movement. It is estimated that 5,000,000 people left the South between 1865 and 1900. Free labor before the Civil War felt that it could not adjust itself to a slavery regime; and since the War it has not cared to compete with low-class negro labor. Until the last decade or so the South has lacked that surplus of factory workers, skilled mechanics, essential for manufacturing.

3. Little capital was available in the South. When "Cotton was King" in the Southern economic world all surplus money went into the purchase of lands and slaves.

During the period of low cotton prices, just before the War, the salvaging of the immense amount of capital invested in land and slaves was impossible. Then came the tragic eras, the Civil War and Reconstruction, when the property of most of the Antebellum leaders, the wealthy, was entirely swept away, leaving only bare, depleted, washed cotton fields, half grown to weeds and bushes with no dependable labor to restore them to their former state of production.

4. Northern bankers, manufacturers, and traders dominated Southern business. While the South, largely because its leaders found it easier and more satisfying, remained the producer of great staples of commerce, the North was developing commerce and manufacturing. Northern* ships carried Southern cotton, hemp, rice, sugar, and other staples from the numerous ports on the Gulf and South Atlantic to Northern industrial centers and Europe, and brought in return the necessities and luxuries, the products of their own and European factories. When the South came to realize the poor economy of exporting raw material and bringing back these same materials fabricated into necessities, usable commodities, at greatly enhanced prices, when they had at home every condition necessary for carrying on commerce and manufacturing, it was too late—they had become enmeshed in the tentacles of "the Northern octopus." Denunciations against the Northeast were of no avail, and there was little sense in them. Criticism of the South because of its peculiar institutions and its retarded economic development was likewise senseless. People in both sections had developed in perfectly normal ways, true to the peculiari-

---

* Although the Southerners inveighed against the North, it was the Northeast or the East that they were critical of.

ties of their environments. The Northeast, because of limited agricultural opportunities, advanced into the manufacturing-mining-commercial stage early. The South, with "soil, climate, habits, and a peculiar labor," was destined to be "staple states," to use the phrase of Calhoun, as long as such habits and slavery persisted. Its commercial forests and its minerals remained unexploited, its waterfalls and rapids undeveloped, and its harbors unused by ships of its own construction.

It seems probable that the South, had it been isolated physically and politically, and had it never experienced "accidents," would have continued to hold the rank it had attained in manufacturing in 1810; and gradually would have developed a manufacturing and commercial population along with the agricultural in such a ratio as to make itself largely self-sufficient. But the invention of textile machines in England and the cotton gin in America, the expansion of cotton culture in the Lower South, and the perpetuation of the institution of slavery, all created an abnormal, predominating interest in agriculture to such an extent that manufacturing languished. While manufacturing in the South was in a state of coma, Northern industrial and commercial men were awake and doing, and gradually threw out their lines of control, until the South came to be, apparently, inexorably bound to the industrial North, to be a producer of foods and raw materials and a market for manufactured goods. Now that population is somewhat catching up with agricultural expansion, modern transportation facilities are conditioning the development of diverse types of agriculture and the exploitation of forest and mineral resources; inventions are making it possible to harness the energy of waterfalls and rapids and distribute this energy over hundreds of square miles of territory; and America in general is coming to be an investor nation instead of a borrower, the South is beginning an advance that ultimately will carry it to the position it would have attained two or three decades ago had it not met with accidents in the otherwise normal economic-geographic line of development, normal to regions so richly endowed.

THE NEW SOUTH

The New South dates from about 1880. It is both new and old. It still retains its interest in the land, but it is slowly but surely building a manufacturing structure on the broad foundation of a wide variety of agricultural products, mineral deposits of many sorts, large areas of virgin forest land, which by careful husbanding may be made to furnish a perpetual supply of raw materials. The industrial structure it builds (and is building) will be much more secure than that of New England, for all the essentials of an advanced industrial order are in greater abundance and also in regional proximity.

In this chapter the environmental conditions for manufactural development have been stressed repeatedly, but superficially for the most part. In the chapters that follow the more important physical environmental conditions essential for and utilized in the establishment, maintenance, and growth of specific types of industries will receive more careful and systematic consideration.

CHAPTER XI

THE POWER RESOURCES

INTRODUCTION

Coal, petroleum, natural gas, and water power are the four sources of power of which the Southern States have a large share. For a few decades wood was the fuel most used for generating steam in the boilers of mills, factories, steamboats, and locomotives. The mineral fuels, coal, petroleum, and gas, have largely supplanted wood as fuel in industries; and the larger number of textile factories by far are powered by electricity. Data as to the relative importance of these sources of power in the South are not available. In the United States in 1930, 61.5 per cent of the annual supply of energy came from coal, 21.9 per cent from domestic oil, 6.8 from natural gas, 1.9 from imported oil, and 7.9 per cent from water power. In the last 20 years coal has declined from about 88 per cent to about 61 per cent of the total power used, while oil (petroleum) has increased from 6 per cent to nearly 24 per cent and water power from 2 per cent to about 8.* Coal, of which the South has large reserves, is by far the most important and will continue to hold high rank as a fuel for a long time to come.

1. THE COAL SUPPLY AND PRODUCTION

Three of the larger bituminous coal fields of the United States lie wholly or partly within the borders of the Southern States (Fig. 100). Their area and estimated original supply are as follows:

1. Appalachian Field, in the South—42,500 square miles, 350 billion tons—in West Virginia, Virginia, eastern Kentucky, Tennessee, Georgia, and Alabama. The South has about 60 per cent of the total area and coal supply of this field.

2. The Eastern Interior Field in western Kentucky—6,400 square miles, 55.5 billion tons of coal.

3. The Western Interior and Southwestern, in Texas, Oklahoma,

---

* *Statistical Abstract,* 1930, 367.

and Arkansas—86,100 square miles (includes brown coal in Texas), 88 billion tons.*

In addition to these are two small Atlantic Slope fields in Virginia and North Carolina. There is little or no mining in these today.

How much the original supply has been depleted is rather difficult to determine from the statistics available, but suffice it to say that the depletion is less than 1 per cent of the original supply of the South. Table XIV gives the area, original supply, and the 1929 pro-

TABLE XIV

DATA ON COAL IN THE SOUTH[1]

State	Area, square miles	Original Supply, tons	Production 1929, tons
North Carolina	60	200,000,000	
Maryland	455	8,000,000,000	2,700,000
Virginia	1,900	22,500,000,000	12,700,000
West Virginia	1,700	152,000,000,000	138,500,000
Kentucky	16,670	123,000,000,000	60,500,000
Tennessee	4,400	25,700,000,000	5,400,000
Georgia	167	900,000,000	....
Alabama	8,500	68,600,000,000	17,900,000
Oklahoma	10,000	55,000,000,000	3,500,000
Arkansas	7,600	1,900,000,000	1,800,000
Texas	68,500	31,000,000,000	1,000,000

[1] *Idem;* Production in 1929 from *Commercial Yearbook*, I, 1931, 288.

duction in the Southern States having coal supplies. The total production of coal in the South in 1929 was about 40 per cent of the total coal mined that year in the United States, or 46 per cent of the bituminous coal mined. Not only does the South produce much more coal than its share, on the basis of area and population, but it has more than half of the reserves of the United States.†

THE MORE IMPORTANT FIELDS

The Appalachian bituminous field.‡ This field has a longitudinal extent in the South of about 650 miles. Its width in northern West Virginia is approximately 175 miles. Near the Alabama-Tennessee border it is less than 30 miles wide but again expands to several times this width in northeastern Alabama. About 60 per cent of its reserves, as

* Data on area and original supply from *Statistical Abstract*, 1917, 22, 23.
† *Statistical Abstract*, 1930, 770.
‡ *Birmingham Folio* 175 U.S.G.S., 110, 152; State Geology reports of Alabama, Mississippi, Louisiana, Arkansas, Kentucky, Virginia, West Virginia; W. M. Emmons, *General Economic Geology;* Heinrich Reis, *Economic Geology.*

has been stated, is in the South. Stream dissecton has been very active, particularly in West Virginia, Virginia, and Kentucky (Fig. 100), and immense quantities of coal have been carried away to the sea; but dissection aids the miner greatly in his operations. Nowhere else in the world is mining easier. The coal seams lie, for the most part, essentially horizontal. Many, if not most, of the seams outcrop on the valley sides. Coal seams occur at several horizons. Any one seam may extend over many hundred square miles; but probably no single seam extends over the entire Appalachian field. The Pittsburgh

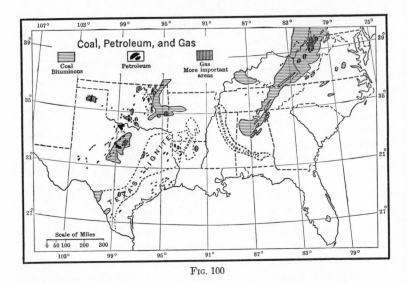

Fig. 100

seam, from which more coal has been lifted than from any other in our country, is probably the largest. It extends southward from southwestern Pennsylvania into western Maryland and eastern Ohio, and lies beneath a large part of West Virginia, and beneath about a million acres in western Virginia. The coal of this seam is one of the best to be found in the whole Appalachian field. It came into prominence when it was found that it made a high-grade metallurgical coke. Connellsville coke from the coal of the Pittsburgh seam has played an important rôle in the development of the iron and steel industry of western Pennsylvania. In Maryland and West Virginia coal from this seam is used mostly for fuel. For a long time it supplied most of the coal carried to Tidewater along the Potomac by canal and rail. In Maryland it is mined near Cumberland, but is approaching exhaustion in this state. Above and below the Pittsburgh seam are several others, though none assume the importance of the Pittsburgh, and nowhere are the seams so thick.

Another famous coal is the Pocahontas in western Virginia and near-by portions of West Virginia. This formation lies nearly horizontal in the dissected Allegheny Plateau just to the west of the folded and faulted strata of the Great Valley. In the Valley it has been entirely removed by the deep erosion which has changed the ancient Great Valley mountain system into the series of ridges and valleys. At Pocahontas, West Virginia, where the vein was first opened by a drift mine the seam is about 12 to 13 feet thick. It is an excellent steaming coal, high in caloric energy and low in ash (rarely over 5 per cent). It is a semibituminous variety.

The New River seam, which occurs in a horizon above the Pocahontas, is also of high grade. Many seams above the geologic horizon of the New River coal are mined in West Virginia.

Coal is taken from many different horizons in eastern Kentucky but all are high-grade, low in sulphur, phosphorus, and ash. The coal-bearing strata of Kentucky extend to the western edge of the Great Valley like those of the Pocahontas formation in southwestern Virginia. But the coal measures in southeastern Kentucky have been interrupted by the Pineville fault and the monoclinal fold of Pine Mountain. The area of coal lands in western Kentucky is much less than in eastern Kentucky. Most of the coal used in smelters, blast furnaces, factories, for transportation agencies, coke, and gas making in the entire Northeastern States and a large part of the North Central States (even as far west as Montana, and also much of Canada), comes from the Pennsylvania, Maryland, Ohio, West Virginia, and Kentucky (Fig. 101), coal mines.

The Wartburg and Sewanee coal basins are associated with the Cumberland Plateau in Tennessee. The seams have been but little disturbed by the tremendous earth movements that occurred in the Great Valley. Their many seams are mined by shafts dug from the top of the Plateau and by drift mines on the slopes of the sides of the Plateau, or the sides of the very few valleys that are carved in the Plateau. Near Chattanooga, coal taken from the Cumberland Plateau and Walden Ridge is (or was) used for iron smelting; but most that is mined is for household use or steaming purposes. Furnaces, now closed at Rockwood, Dayton, and elsewhere on the border of the Great Valley, were localized at their respective sites because of the coal measures and near-by iron ore.

The Appalachian field covers only a small area in northwestern

Georgia, but, as has been stated, it has a large area in Alabama. The coal-bearing strata of the Birmingham area are of the same geologic horizon as in Pennsylvania. In the Birmingham district coal seams are found in gentle synclines in the Warrior River and Plateau fields, but in comparatively steep synclines in the Cahaba and Coosa fields. The Warrior and Plateau fields are on the Cumberland Plateau; the Cahaba and Coosa, in the Great Valley. It seems probable that

A. E. P.

FIG. 101.—A Part of the Coal-mining Town of Lynch, in Southeastern Kentucky. The town and the openings to the mines are in the deep valleys of the Allegheny Plateau. Most of the homes in Lynch are far superior to the general run in coal-mining towns.

farther to the northeast, in northeastern Alabama and eastern Tennessee, coal seams once extended over the site of the Great Valley; but they have been eroded away because they lay above the base level of the streams that covered the valley. The Allegheny Plateau in Kentucky has lost much coal.

The coal of the Birmingham region is ranked second only to that of the Pocahontas and New River coal of West Virginia. It is used (as coke) in blast furnaces, in steel mills, in steam-electric plants, in factories and homes; and much is shipped to near-by cities and the Gulf Coast.

The Arkansas-Oklahoma coal areas cover about 13,000 square miles. There are seven seams of 2 to 5 feet in thickness in Oklahoma and several others that yield coal for local consumption, when not in competition with better-quality coals. Only two seams, 3 to 6 feet thick, are exploited in Arkansas. The coal measures have been slightly folded, as a result of the Ozark uplift. Thus the coal is in the advanced stages of evolution, nearly semibituminous. It is high in fixed carbon. Little of the coal of these two states is shipped far, for it is in competition with coal from other fields north, east, southwest, and west.

The central Texas field (the Southwestern) has several seams but not of coking grade. It is high in ash and sulphur, and is practically useless for metallurgical purposes and for gas making. However, Texas has little need for metallurgical coke for now it is an exploiter of petroleum and natural gas. Texas cities and the railroads consume most of the coal output.

There are two main fields of lignite in the South (Fig. 100), both near the inner edge of the Coastal Plain. The Mississippi field, crescent shaped, in the Cretaceous formations, is mined to a very limited extent locally, but has poor heating qualities. Experiments have shown that some lignitic fuels are valuable for making producer gas. Some of the beds of lignite in Mississippi are 7.5 to 8 feet thick.

The south Arkansas, Louisiana, and Texas lignite deposits are similar to the deposits in Mississippi, but they are utilized more extensively, locally, probably because better-quality fuels are more distant than in Mississippi.

On the Rio Grande border of the lignite region of Texas are deposits of commercial cannel coal of good quality. Cannel coal yields both gas and oil when distilled. It is a very young coal, younger even than the lignites of the Gulf Embayment. Some day when the oil and gas deposits of Texas are depleted, these valuable cannel coals will be exploited.

The small field in eastern Virginia, in the Chesterfield coal basin some 15 to 20 miles west of Richmond, is interesting because it was here that coal mining in America had its birth. The deposits were known as early as 1770 and were worked by 1775, and for a long time were the only source of supply of domestic coal. In 1789 Chesterfield coal (also called Richmond coal) was sold in Philadelphia for 1s. 6d. a bushel. In 1836 it was delivered to consumers in Richmond for 15 to 16 cents a bushel, and later for 10 to 12 cents, i.e., $2.80 to $3.50 per ton. At times some was exported to Boston. In 1822, 48,000 tons were mined in Virginia; in 1833, 142,000 tons; and by 1843, 65,770 tons. Mines were opened in the 1840's in the western part of Virginia (now West Virginia) and shipments made. It was about this time that Pennsylvania got its start in coal mining and soon surpassed agricultural Virginia.*

By 1860 coal was mined in Alabama, Georgia, Kentucky, Maryland, Tennessee, and Virginia (including West Virginia), the aggregate output being about 1,700,000 tons a year on the average, between 1856 and 1860. There was no abatement in mining during the Civil War, for coal was needed. The annual output was about 1,900,000 tons. Since 1865 there has been a rapid increase; the output in decennial years is shown in Table XV.

TABLE XV

COAL MINED IN SOUTH BY DECADES[1]

	Tons
In 1870	3,437,000
1880	7,002,000
1890	24,925,000
1900	54,510,000
1910	120,856,000
1920	178,061,000
1930	202,092,000

[1] Calculated from various Government documents.

No better barometer of the status of industry is needed than the amount of coal mined—if all is used within the coal-producing area. No statistics are available to show the total consumption, but in the period since the Civil War it is known that there has been an ever-increasing demand for fuel and power, due to the growth of urban centers, and the increasing number of coke ovens, iron and steel plants, cement and brick plants, steam-electric plants, artificial gas plants, and also a great increase in railroad mileage. Much coal is being exported from the Chesapeake Bay (Fig. 102) and the Gulf Coast ports and much also is shipped by rail and water to Northern industrial sections. Although it would be better to have the coal consumed at home, in the South, not all the benefits at present accrue to the North. In time the excellence of these Southern coals when better known should attract industry.

In Pennsylvania, Britain, Belgium, and Germany people have found it economically advantageous to locate industries near coal deposits. Particularly is this true of some industries requiring large amounts of fuel or power. It is only in the Birmingham districts, to be discussed later, the small Chattanooga district, and the Ohio River-Kanawa Re-

* Report of Eighth Census, 1860, p. clxviii.

gion in West Virginia and Kentucky that the cheap fuel and power have been taken advantage of. Wheeling, back in the first half of the last century, had an important glass industry, and the evaporating of brine, near Charleston, used large quantities of coal and natural gas. At Ashland, Kentucky, and Huntington and Charleston, West Virginia, there are today numerous coal-using industries.

Coal has been a factor in the localization of the several types of industries now found in the valley of East Tennessee. Under the

A. E. P.

FIG. 102.—The Great Coal Dock of the C. & O. Railroad at Newport News, Virginia.

The coal originates in western Virginia and West Virginia. Much coal is exported from the Lower Chesapeake ports.

supervision of the Tennessee Valley Authority, industrialization should move on apace. At present the trend is toward the development of water power. Politics has dictated thus. Some day, possibly, the opinion of engineering science will be heeded and steam-electric plants, fueled by the excellent coal of the Cumberland Plateau, will supply much of the needed power.

Without coal and iron ore, the site of Birmingham would still be occupied by a small country town. Only a beginning has been made in the Birmingham district in industrialization.

2. PETROLEUM AND NATURAL GAS

The petroleum era had its beginning in 1859 when Drake at Titusville, Pennsylvania, discovered the dark green liquid at a depth of only 69.5 feet.* This accidental digging at a particular spot where the oil existed so near the surface was indeed fortunate, for the technique of sinking deep wells was in its infancy. Except for the experience gained in northwestern Pennsylvania and elsewhere in the Appalachian oil fields, the deep pools now being discovered at 3,000 to 10,000 or more feet below the surface would be unworked.†

All the early oil developments were in the northern Appalachian field which covers much the same area as the northern part of the Appalachian coal field. The close association of coal and oil, and the fact that oil is sometimes distilled from some coals, led people to the use of the term "coal-oil" in some sections as the name for kerosene, which at one time was the most valuable derivative of petroleum. But most of the petroleum-bearing strata of the Appalachian field lie below the coal measures.

The surface indications of oil and gas, that led to the discovery in Pennsylvania, also exist in southwestern New York, West Virginia, Ohio, and the states to the southwest in the Appalachian Plateau. These areas were soon invaded by the exploiters of petroleum "pools." From the original center at Titusville, Pennsylvania, therefore, the industry spread out, to the westward and southwestward. Ohio in 1880 produced 39,000 barrels, West Virginia 179,000. In 1880 Pennsylvania's output was more than 26,000,000 barrels. By this time oil had also been discovered in California, the output in that year being 41,000 barrels.‡

Kentucky and Tennessee, in the same field (Appalachian) as West Virginia and Pennsylvania, came in in 1883 as producers—only 5,000

* The *Louisville Courier Journal*, in an article published in 1929, claimed that the first oil well in United States was dug near Burkesville, Kentucky, and that the oil was used for medicinal purposes. To quote, "On Renox Creek, three miles above Burkesville, in Cumberland County, stands a marker on the site of the famous American well drilled in 1828. Salt-well drillers hit a gusher at 175 feet, which spouted fifty feet in the air for several days. Flowing into the Cumberland river, the oil one night caught fire. For a week residents of the surrounding territory traveled for miles to see a river on fire. This has been related many times, and also that of Dr. White's supposed discovery that this oil was a remedy for various ills. 'American Oil,' as it was called, was sold for many years as a cure-all, and many a rural family probably has one of the original vials, with the name blown in the glass, standing on a cupboard shelf."

† In the Oklahoma City field (the first well brought in December 4, 1928) the oil comes from a depth of 6,500 feet. Texas has one of the deepest wells in the world, in the Big Lake field, Reagan County, the oil coming from a depth of about 8,500 feet. (*Daily Oklahoman*, Sept. 21, 1930.) California has a well about 10,000 feet deep. In the summer of 1937 oil was struck in a well near Howna at 11,630 feet (*New Orleans Times-Picayune*).

‡ *Statistical Abstract*, 1917, 240.

barrels. Neither has ever made very large contributions. Kentucky up to 1927 had produced only 0.9 per cent of the total of the country. And Tennessee's total production is less than 1/400 of Kentucky's. In these two states the anticlinal folds, beneath which the oil of the Appalachian field in West Virginia and Pensylvania is found, play out and only small domes exist. These are soon exhausted by the exploiters.

Texas came in as a producer in 1896, its output that year being 1,000 barrels. Two years later its yield was 546,000 barrels; in 1901, 4,400,000. Oklahoma produced its first 1,000 barrels in 1897. By 1904

A. E. P.

FIG. 103.—In the Oklahoma City Oil Field.

One of the city's numerous skyscrapers may be seen in the middle background. This central Oklahoma field extends 75 miles east and west.

its output was 1,400,000; and by 1907, 43,500,000 barrels. Louisiana wells in 1902 produced 549,000 barrels and in 1904 nearly 3,000,000. By 1910 the respective outputs of these three Southern states were: Oklahoma 52,000,000 barrels; Texas 8,899,000; and Louisiana 6,841,-000. The chief competitor of any one of these states for first rank in the United States was California.

In 1915 Oklahoma's output (Fig. 103) was 98,000,000 barrels, and California's, 87,000,000. Since that date, now one, now the other, has held first rank. Texas in late years has surpassed both combined.

From 1931 to 1935 the South produced, annual average, 66 per cent of the petroleum of the United States or 40 per cent of the total of the world.*

---

* *Statistical Abstract*, 1936, 724, calculated. Data on page 12 was for 1932.

In the rapid rise as a petroleum producer the South owes much to the contributions the other older producing regions have made in the technique of petroleum exploration, drilling, control of the liquid, transportation to market, refining, and salvaging of equipment used in exploitation. But by far the most important of all factors or conditions is the rapid increase in number of motor vehicles that has taken place since about 1895-1900. In 1900 only 8,000 automobiles were registered in the United States; in 1913, 1,258,000; in 1930, more than 26,545,000;* and in 1937, about 30,000,000.

There must be an end to petroleum production, sometime. We cannot expect to continue to draw a billion barrels a year (and the amount increasing about 50,000,000 or more each year) forever. The next development will be to recover what has been left in the ground, which according to good authority is three, four, or more times what has been removed. How this may be done is receiving† the attention of the best oil experts of the country. The South will certainly be as much benefited by any methods devised in oil recovery as any other section. All fields, as the history of oil production shows, have their periods of prosperity, and then comes on a slow decline. The productive life of a field depends, of course, upon the amount of oil originally in the ground and the rate of exploitation. An oil geologist can form a fair estimate of the volume of possible oil-bearing rock in a given field if he knows its area and the dip of the limbs of the anticline,‡ but the extent of the oil in the rock is difficult to determine. An estimate of the oil reserves of the South, as of January 1, 1922, in barrels of 42 gallons, is as follows:

Gulf Coast (Texas and Louisiana)	2,100,000,000
Oklahoma	1,540,000,000
Northern Louisiana and Arkansas	525,000,000
Texas, except Gulf Coast	670,000,000
West Virginia	200,000,000
Kentucky, Tennessee, etc.	175,000,000
Total	5,030,000,000

* *Statistical Abstract*, 1932, 358; Associated Press notice.

† Henry L. Doherty in a statement before the Federal Oil Conservation Board, on Feb. 10, 1926, said, "In my opinion we leave more than four barrels of oil in the ground for every barrel we now recover by flowing or pumping. . . . There is no certainty of recovering a substantial amount of oil from our abandoned fields or recovering it except at very slow rate of production."

‡ Geo-physical exploration by a portable seismograph is now being used with success.

The total given for United States is some 9,150,000,000,* thus the South has, according to estimates, more than 50 per cent of the total for our country. Since then many new fields have been discovered, many of them in the South, and reserves have correspondingly increased. New estimates made by experts in 1935 give the reserves of the United States as about 12,000,000,000 barrels.†

A. E. P.

FIG. 104.—A Gas-compression Station in West Virginia.

THE PETROLEUM FIELDS OF THE SOUTH

West Virginia, as previously stated, is in the Appalachian oil and gas fields (Fig. 104). The oil and gas occur in long, narrow anticlines that have a northeast-southwest trend parallel to the trend of the main axis of the folded Appalachians. The area actually underlain by oil- and gas-bearing strata is probably but little more than 3,500 square miles. The pools occur largely in sandstone, overlain by shale, which forms impervious layers. There are several layers of oil-bearing sandstones. The same oil-bearing strata may be 500 feet from the surface in one part of the field but 2,500 or more in another, owing to warping or folding of the oil strata and to surface erosion. The wells vary in depth from 100 to 4,000 feet. In recent years deep test

* These data were prepared by the United States Geological Survey and the American Association of Petroleum Geologists, working independently, at first, later in conjunction in subcommittees.

† *Bulletin of the American Association of Petroleum Geologists,* Tulsa, Oklahoma, January, 1936.

wells have been sunk to discover if possible the presence of oil in very deep strata that were known to bear oil in other parts of the field. The oil-bearing strata are in the Devonian, Mississippian, and Pennsylvanian formations. Appalachian oil has a paraffin base, is easily refined, and is a very high grade.

The oil and gas fields of Oklahoma, Arkansas, northern and central Texas, and northern Louisiana are all included in the Mid-Continental Fields. The oil and gas of Oklahoma are found in sands, largely (about six strata in number), but some in porous limestone. Most of the oil-bearing layers are in the Pennsylvanian rocks. The bearing strata are as a rule on a low dome or anticline, but some are on terraces. Some of the individual fields are isolated. Among the better-known minor fields are the Cushing, the Garber, the Glenn, and the Oklahoma City.

The gas in western Arkansas near Fort Smith is in Pennsylvanian sandstones that form low anticlines.

The oil and gas fields of northern Texas and Oklahoma near the Red River belong to the same geologic formation. The best-known minor fields in Texas are the Burkburnett and Petrolea in minor domes and anticlines in the larger synclinal fold that formed south of the Arbuckle Mountains when they were folded. Oil in the Electra field was first discovered by a driller seeking a domestic water supply, at a depth of 147 feet. This discovery started a boom and a rapid exploration of the whole region. The Burkburnett was one of the most productive of the Mid-Continental Fields. The eastern Texas fields are now more productive.

West of Fort Worth is a large field, forming a part of the north central Texas field, with many inner areas or fields as the Duke, Caddo, Ranger, Breckenridge, Brownwood, and others. Oil occurs here in "wrinkles" or small anticlines in about eight horizons. Owing to the small size of the anticlines and the ready escape of the gas, this North Central Texas oil and gas region declined rapidly.

From Hunt County, northeast of Dallas, southward to Bexar County, in which San Antonio is located, is a great fault zone known as the Balcones Fault belt. In this region are many small folds in which both oil and gas are found. The better-known fields are the Corsicanna, Mexia, Grosbeake South Bosque, Thrall, and Elgin and San Antonio.

In northwest Louisiana and northeastern Texas is a broad dome (it underlies several counties) called by geologists (Veatch, Harris, and others) the Sabine uplift. In this broad zone are several anticlines that have a northeast-southwest trend. Each has one or more oil and gas fields, as the Caddo, Shreveport, Homer, Monroe, and others. The opening of the Caddo field was an important event in the history of northern Louisiana. The gas of Monroe has for a decade or more been the raw material for a large carbon black industry. Recently gas is being used as fuel in the generating of electricity, which is carried by transmission lines to large areas in Louisiana.

The Coastal Plain of these two states, as previously described, is characterized by numerous domes or islands that contain oil, gas, salt, and gypsum deposits. Oil and gas do not occur in some of the domes nor are these minerals confined in paying quantities to domes that come to or above the surface. Spindletop, Sour Lake, Damon Mound, Goose Creek, Evangeline, and New Iberia are the most celebrated of the oil fields here.

In the Panhandle of Texas, near the Canadian River, about 40 to 50 miles from Amarillo, is a new field, opened in 1926. Within a few weeks a ranch region was turned into an active oil-producing center with a population of 25,000.

In northeastern Texas in Van Zandt County a new field was opened in 1929. On Sunday, October 13, 1929, Van was, according to a press notice, "a community of seven houses, two general merchandise stores, one church, a school, and a population of approximately twenty. By Wednesday the number of inhabitants had increased to 1,200 and then to 1,500. Land in all directions two miles from the well was leased for $300 to $2,000 per acre.*

In the transportation of crude oil by pipe line and in refining, the Southwestern oil men have practices and methods well established. Pipe lines connect all the large producing fields of Oklahoma, Texas, Louisiana, and Arkansas with the refineries in the North and East or the Gulf Coast (Fig. 105). Movement to the Gulf is greatly assisted by gravity, but pumping or boosting stations are scattered all along the lines. The Gulf Company has 4,481 miles in operation; the Humble Pipe Line, a Southern company, 6,300 in 1930; the Magnolia, 5,700; the Prairie, that operates lines from Texas to Indiana, 13,300 miles; and the Texas Pipe Line Company, in Texas and Oklahoma, 6,300.†

More than 150 refineries are located in the South. There are 4 in Baltimore, the largest being the Standard. The larger refineries in Louisiana are on the Mississippi between or at New Orleans and Baton Rouge, many of the old plantations of "The Coast" (page 108) are now

---

* *Dallas Morning News,* Oct. 18, 1929.
† *Statistical Abstract,* 1932, 724.

owned by oil refining or exporting companies. The larger in Texas have a coastal location, on navigable channels. Arkansas had 10, Louisiana 13, Oklahoma 45, and Texas 83 at the last census year, 1929.*

Crude and refined oil are shipped from many Gulf ports to the Eastern States and overseas.

The gas fields of the South are numerous and widely scattered. Most of the cities of the Southwest are supplied with natural gas, and

A. E. P.

FIG. 105.—An Oil-pumping Station near Cisco, Texas.

Many of the pipe lines of Texas run seaward, down hill, to Houston and other Gulf ports. The spacing of the pumping stations along the line is adjusted to the topography of the land traversed.

a large percentage of the homes are heated with gas. In 1931 a pipe line more than a thousand miles long was completed from the Panhandle of Texas to Chicago and other cities in the North Central States. Pipe lines are now being constructed from the western gas regions of the South to some of the cities east of the Mississippi River, even to Middle Tennessee and into Kentucky.

3. THE WATER POWER OF THE SOUTH, POTENTIAL AND DEVELOPED

INTRODUCTION

The distribution of the potential and developed water power of the several sections of the United States, measured in horsepower, is shown in Table XVI.

From this table it is readily seen (by calculation) that the South

---

* *Report of Fifteenth Census*, "Manufactures," 1929, II, 7711.

TABLE XVI

DEVELOPED AND POTENTIAL WATER POWER OF THE UNITED STATES,
BY SECTIONS (JAN. 1, 1934)[1]

Section	Potential		Developed, i.e., Installed Capacity of Wheels Jan. 1, 1934
	90 % of Time	50 % of Time	
	Horsepower	Horsepower	Horsepower
New England.............	998,000	1,978,000	2,004,000
Middle Atlantic............	4,373,000	6,050,000	2,421,000
E. North Central..........	742,000	1,426,000	1,186,000
W. North Central.........	929,000	1,937,000	762,000
South Atlantic.............	2,924,000	5,048,000	3,036,000
E. South Central..........	1,328,000	2,272,000	1,298,000
W. South Central..........	559,000	1,110,000	150,000
Mountain.................	10,844,000	15,552,000	1,209,000
Pacific..................	15,413,000	23,793,000	3,848,000

[1] *Statistical Abstract*, 1934, 332. The unit of rating for water turbines is horsepower (hp.); for the dynamo kilowatt (kw.) or kilowatt-hours (kw-hr.). This last is equivalent to about 1.34 horsepower-hours. KVA is kilowatt-volt-amperes. This is a better unit for rating a dynamo, for it includes three units of measurement.

has only 13 per cent of the potential water power of the United States (based on data for 90 per cent of the time, and 14 per cent, 50 per cent of the time) but has 34.5 per cent of the power of the installed water wheels.*

Development has progressed farther in the Southern States east of the Mississippi than in any other section with the exceptions of New England and the East North Central States, both of which have very little power. In New England the capacity of the installed wheels is nearly twice as great as the potential for 90 per cent of the time. In the Middle Atlantic States only a little more than half of the potential has been developed; in the South Atlantic and the East South Central the installed exceeds the potential for 90 per cent of the time; in the Pacific Section only about a fifth of the potential is being utilized.

---

* The data given of the power of the installed wheels is only roughly a measure of the actual developed power, for in some sections steam power supplements or supplants water power during the dry seasons. At the Wilson Dam power plant the installed capacity is about 260,000 hp. but before the Norris and other dams were constructed there was water sufficient to generate only about 60,000 hp. the year round.

There has been a very rapid development in the Southern States in recent years. The South had 34.5 per cent (as stated above) of the developed power of United States on January 1, 1934, whereas in 1921 it had but 17 per cent. The installed capacity of the water wheels on November 1, 1921, was 1,339,000 horsepower, but on January 1, 1934, 5,484,000 horsepower.

Water power is widely though unevenly distributed in the Southern States as Table XVII indicates.

TABLE XVII

POTENTIAL AND DEVELOPED WATER POWER OF THE SOUTH, BY STATES[1]

States	Potential Water Power Available		Developed Water Power, Jan. 1, 1936, Installed Capacity Data from U.S.G.S.
	90% of Time	50% of Time	
	Horsepower	Horsepower	Horsepower
South Atlantic States.......	2,924,000	5,048,000	3,215,000
Maryland and District of Columbia.............	106,000	238,000	410,000
Virginia................	459,000	812,000	156,000
West Virginia...........	355,000	980,000	269,000
North Carolina..........	852,000	1,160,000	980,000
South Carolina..........	555,000	860,000	811,000
Georgia................	572,000	958,000	569,000
Florida.................	20,000	30,000	20,000
East South Central.........	13,280,000	2,272,000	1,363,000
Kentucky................	172,000	280,000	145,000
Tennessee...............	654,000	882,000	291,000
Alabama................	472,000	1,050,000	867,000
Mississippi..............	30,000	60,000	
West South Central.........	559,000	1,110,000	144,000
Arkansas................	200,000	300,000	95,000
Louisiana...............	1,000	2,000	
Oklahoma..............	70,000	194,000	2,000
Texas..................	288,000	614,000	48,000

[1] Idem; special bulletin of U.S.G.S.

The leading states in developed power in order, as the table shows, were North Carolina, Alabama, South Carolina, Georgia, and Maryland. All the power plants of these states are on rivers that flow out of the Southern Appalachian Highlands, and most of them by far are on rivers that have their headwaters in the Southern Appalachian

Mountains. A few important power streams take their rise in the Great Valley (Holston, Clinch, and Powell), the Appalachian Plateau, and in the Ozark Plateau and Ouachita Mountains.

THE POWER REGIONS OF THE SOUTH

The power streams and power developments of the South may be grouped into seven power regions, namely:

(a) The Maryland-Virginia region, including sites and developments on the Potomac, the James, and the Roanoke.

(b) The Carolina-Georgia Piedmont region, i.e., the rivers of North Carolina, South Carolina, and northeastern Georgia. This is the major power region of the South.

(c) The Southwestern Piedmont region, in which are grouped the sites, undeveloped and developed, on the Chattahoochee and its tributaries, the Tallapoosa, and the Coosa.

(d) The Appalachian Mountain power region, in western Carolina and near-by portions of Tennessee.

(e) The Great Appalachian Valley region, in Virginia and Tennessee.

(f) The Appalachian Plateau region, in Kentucky, Tennessee, and northern Alabama.

(g) The Ozark-Ouachita region.

The discussion of these regions will largely center around the developments that had been made up to 1934.

The Maryland-Virginia Power Region

Maryland has several small power plants on the Patapsco River, on Antietam Creek, and on Deep Creek. One of the largest plants in the South is the Conowingo (Fig. 106), on the Susquehanna, near the Pennsylvania boundary. The eleven power units are housed in a power house 950 feet long. The ultimate capacity of the turbines when installation is complete will be 360,000 horsepower. The maximum head is 89 feet. The large variation in the flow of the Susquehanna is partly regulated by a 14-mile pool created by the dam; but at times the water is so low that a steam plant in Philadelphia is called upon to supply the required load. During the dry season the hydroelectric plant runs only part of the day, thus permitting the water to be stored for the "peak" demand.*

---

* Data from booklet of Philadelphia Electric Company; Personal observation and interview.

Virginia has some 60 power plants but all small. The total capacity
is only 156,000 horsepower. Several are on or near the Potomac. Several large developments are contemplated, a 25,000-horsepower plant
on the James River, between Richmond and Lynchburg, and four on
the New River. The Potomac has some 225,000 horsepower available
for development for both Maryland and Virginia.

A. E. P.

Fig. 106.—The Power Plant and Dam of the Great Conowingo Power Project on
the Susquehanna River in Maryland, near the Maryland-Pennsylvania boundary.
The electricity generated here is used at present in Philadelphia. The total installed capacity of
the seven units is 378,000 hp. The operating "head" is 89 feet. The dam is 4648 feet long.

Virginia, in comparison with the other South Atlantic states, is poor
in potential power resources and very backward in development. Its
developed power is less than one-third that of Georgia, one-fourth
that of South Carolina, and one-fifth that of North Carolina.

The Carolina-Georgia Piedmont Region

The most important power region in area and installed capacity is
in the Piedmont of North Carolina, South Carolina, and northeastern
Georgia (Fig. 107). Here is developed 70 per cent of the total for the
entire Piedmont. This region, about 170 miles long and 100 miles
wide, may well be called the major power region of the South.

The rivers of this major power region have most of their headwaters in the Blue Ridge, the divide of the Southern Appalachian
Mountains. The more important of these rivers are the Yadkin-Pedee,
the Catawba-Wateree, the Broad, the Saluda, and the Tallulah-

Tugaloo. There are several reasons for the abundance of water power in this area:

(a) The fall of the rivers is great. Most of the tributaries of the rivers rise in the Blue Ridge.

(b) There are numerous shoals and falls along the streams, the former offering sites for power plants.

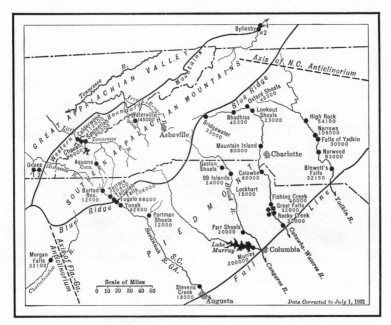

Fig. 107.—The Piedmont and Mountain Water Power Developments.
The location of only one lake, Lake Murray, is shown.

(c) The third condition is the heavy rainfall. In the mountain area of northeastern Georgia and northwestern South Carolina it is more than 80 inches. Over all this area it is more than 50 inches.

The rainfall is well distributed seasonally. See Figure 22 for rainfall types. Even in the driest seasons the power plants are fairly well supplied. Although the streams must be classed as "variable flow" rivers, yet the variability is not any greater than in most parts of eastern United States.

(d) Topographic conditions tend to hasten the runoff, for the land is all in slope, and the slopes are steepest near the mountains; but there are large forests about the mountain headwaters, covering from 80 to 90 per cent of the watershed, and farm woodlots are numerous on the flatter lands. Under provisions of the Week's Bill, and through numerous Congressional appropriations, a large acreage of forest, mainly virgin, has been purchased. The Pisgah, Nantahala, Cherokee, and Unaka National forests have a total area of more than 1,000,000 acres. The new Great Smoky Mountains National Park will add a large acreage to these protective forests.

The largest power developments in this major power region are on the Catawba-Wateree River, under the control of the Duke Power

A. E. P.

FIG. 108.—A Part of the Murray Power Dam on the Saluda River near Columbia, South Carolina.

This is a dirt dam 7825 feet long and about 95 feet high, the material having been obtained near by. A core of clay makes the dam impervious to water. The spillway is of cement. The power plant is below the dam and to the right, the intake for which may be seen in the center background (white tower). A cement tunnel runs through the dam from the intake to the turbines. A highway crosses the dam, shown on the right, bordered on the left by cement rail—very conspicuous in the photograph.

Company; the huge Murray Dam on the Saluda River (Fig. 108); and the six dams and plants belonging to the Georgia Power Company on the Tallulah-Tugaloo River in northeastern Georgia.

The present developments on the Catawba-Wateree River are the most outstanding for several reasons. The entire stream is under the control of one utility corporation, the Duke Power Company (Fig. 109). From the beginning it was planned, ultimately, to utilize the absolute (economic) maximum foot-pounds of power, and the dams, completed to date, have been located with that in view. The developments extend along the river for about 220 miles and, with the exception of the two or three gaps at which power plants will probably be constructed in the near future, most of the potential power is uti-

lized. The total fall of the water from the surface of the Catawba
Dam above the Bridgewater Station to the tailrace of the Wateree
Plant on the edge of the Piedmont is 1,056 feet, of which 752 feet to
date have been utilized. The total installed capacity of the plants is
about 600,000 horsepower. The turbines operate under heads of from
60 to 90 feet at the various stations.

The river is so controlled today that in normal conditions 550
pounds of water—nearly 9 cubic feet—in the Catawba Dam at the
headwaters will have produced about 700 horsepower by the time it
flows down the tailrace of the Wateree Dam. The Duke Company

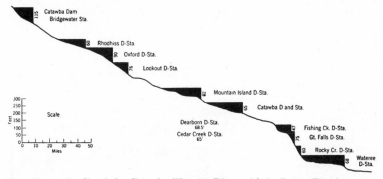

FIG. 109.—A Profile of the Catawba-Wateree River with its Power Developments.
D is for dam; Sta is for Power Station or Plant. The power developments of the entire river
are operated as a unit.

owns or controls not only the plants on the Catawba-Wateree River,
but also a large number of other hydro plants on the Broad, the
Yadkin, the Saluda, and the Seneca rivers, besides eight steam plants.
The total installed capacity of the power units, all interconnected, of
this company is 1,154,000 horsepower.*

The great Murray Dam (Fig. 108) and plant on the Saluda River,
some 15 miles from Columbia, South Carolina, will eventually have
a turbine capacity of 222,600 horsepower. The supply of water comes
from the huge lake 41 miles in length that is impounded behind an
earthen dam 7,825 feet long and 208 feet high.†

---

* Map issued by State of North Carolina Department of Conservation and
Development; a letter July 1, 1930; booklet, Industrial Department of the Duke
Power Company; letter, Carolina Power and Light Company; Personal obser-
vations and interviews.

† Booklet from Lexington Water Power Company, Associated Gas and Electric
System.

The six plants in northeastern Georgia on the Tallulah-Tugaloo River (Fig. 107) have a total installed capacity of 260,000 horsepower. The large power development on such small streams is due to the high heads. The Terrora power plant operates under a head of 190 feet, and the Tallulah Falls plant under a maximum head of 608

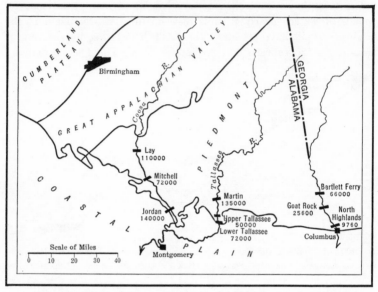

FIG. 110.—Power Developments in the Southwest Piedmont Region.

feet. The latter has a water-wheel capacity of 108,000 horsepower and a generating (electricity) capacity of 72,000 kilovolt-amperes.*

The Southwestern Piedmont Power Region

The power sites on the Coosa, Tallapoosa, and Chattahoochee are all on the Piedmont (Fig. 110). Dams have been constructed at three sites on the Coosa: the Lay Dam (at Island No. 12), Mitchell Dam, and Jordan Dam. The total installed capacity at these dams is 316,000 horsepower.

Three developments along an 11-mile stretch of the Tallapoosa as it plunges over the edge of the Piedmont into the inner lowland of the Coastal Plain, when completed, will have a total installed capacity of 257,000 horsepower.

* Data from booklet supplied by the Georgia Power Company

The Appalachian Mountain Power Region

The plants of this region utilize the waters of the mountain tributaries of the Tennessee that flow out of the natural forests and transverse to the northeast-southwest trend of the ridges and rocks, thus giving numerous rapids and pools and narrow' water gaps. These are all high-head plants. The Aluminum Company of America has three plants: the Santeetlah, Cheoah, and Calderwood (Fig. 107).

The Carolina Power Company has a plant on the Pigeon River at Waterville. The reservoir of this latter covers but 400 acres, but the turbine capacity of the plant is 145,000 horsepower. This large power from such a small reservoir and stream is due to the 861-foot head, to secure which the water is conducted from the reservoir by means of a large pipe 6 miles—most of the way in a tunnel beneath a mountain —to the turbines in the gorge far below the reservoir.* Under such a high head the water requirement to the horsepower is small. In a 100 per cent efficiency turbine it would require only about 0.7 pound (less than one pint) a second. Owing to the perfection reached in turbine design and installation, the actual water requirement probably does not exceed one pound a second for a horsepower.†

Power Development in the Great Appalachian Valley and Appalachian Plateaus Region (Steam and Water Power)

Hydroelectric developments in the Valley of East Tennessee and on the borders of the Appalachian Plateaus are few in number and mostly small. (See later discussion for Norris Dam.) Southwestern Virginia has only a few small developments. A plant is being constructed at the junction of the Gauley and New rivers that will have a capacity of 120,000 horsepower. The other plants now in operation on the borders of or well in the Cumberland Plateau are the Dix River plant in Kentucky (40,000 horsepower), Rock Island plant on the Caney Fork in Tennessee (33,000 horsepower), and the Hale's Bar hydro and steam plant in the gorge of the Tennessee River. There are also two small plants on the Ocoee River in southeastern Tennessee and a third in northern Georgia. The latter three are just outside the Valley. In the Valley the gradients of the streams are low and sites where economical

---

* Data from Carolina Power Company; *Electrical World,* Aug. 30, 1930, 384–389.
† Correspondence with Carolina Power Company; *Tenth Annual Report of Federal Power Commission,* 1930, 4.

dams may be constructed are few; besides, coal is near, outcropping in many places on the face of the Cumberland and Allegheny escarpments. Cheap coal of excellent quality is an important competitor of hydro power in the development of electricity. The many improvements that have been made in engines and boilers in recent years have greatly reduced the cost of generating power by steam. In the steam plants of North Carolina, for example, it is officially stated, that the coal consumption to the kilowatt-hour was reduced from 4.64 pounds, the amount required in 1920, to 1.94 pounds in 1925.* Other competent authorities have stated that more recent improvements have reduced the consumption to about one pound to the kilowatt-hour, and further improvements are expected. Says Leighton, "If improvements [in steam engines] continue water power developments will be installed only under special circumstances and in really favorable places." Many undeveloped water-power sites considered of great value twenty years ago are now not economically worth developing.†

When water plants were small, the cost of developing hydroelectric power was as low as $70 to $100 a kilowatt. By 1900 the average cost had arisen to $150, and by 1920, $200 to $250, a kilowatt. Power interests have searched the country for possible dam sites and have already secured most of the more easily developed ones. As far back as 1908, the United States Commission of Corporations called the attention of conservationists of our country to the activity of several large power corporations in the acquisition of rights to power sites.‡ Because most of the sites permitting low-cost installation have been taken up, it is claimed by the best authorities that the cost for further development will range from $300 to $600 a kilowatt-hour.§ With such high costs for new developments it is certain that "cheap power" from now on will be supplied by steam-electric plants placed near sources of good steaming coal rather than from hydroelectric plants.

That these conclusions are shared by many competent engineers is shown by the numerous large steam-electric plants constructed

---

* *The Power Situation in North Carolina,* Department of Conservation and Development, Cir. 16.

† Marshall O. Leighton, "Water Power Obsolescent," *Manufacturers Record,* p. xcvi, Part 1, July 4, 1929, 66.

‡ Charles R. Van Hise, *The Conservation of Natural Resources in the United States,* 135.

§ Frank Williams, "Water Power and its Conservation" in *Our Natural Resources and their Conservation,* Parkins and Whitaker, Editors, 329.

during the last decade or so in the coal regions of the South. The largest steam-electric plant in the Plateau is the Gorgas plant No. 1, constructed by the Federal Government during the war but now controlled and owned by the Alabama Power Company. It is in the Warrior River Coal Field west of Birmingham. The present engine installment generates 100,000 horsepower. Other units will be constructed that eventually will generate 320,000 horsepower. The Hale's Bar steam plant generates 53,000 horsepower, and several in Kentucky and West Virginia, mostly in the coal fields, can each generate 50,000 to 80,000 horsepower.

The water-power resources of the entire Tennessee River (which crosses three of the physiographic provinces of the Southern Appalachian Highland) are estimated at 4,000,000 horsepower, with the aid of auxiliary steam plants or if sufficient reservoirs are constructed.* The development of most of the water-power resources in the mountain sections of the Tennessee River and its tributaries, even in the face of the tremendous improvements made in boilers and steam engines, is economically possible; but it is doubtful if any power site on the rivers of the Great Appalachian Valley and the Appalachian Plateaus can in the future be utilized economically, in competition with the near-by deposits of excellent coal.

The Muscle Shoals project is by far the most talked-of hydroelectric plant in America, yet after all it is one of the least known. Our newspapers and politicians have so magnified its actual dimensions and potential power output that most people have come to believe that the future industrial development of the United States depends upon its being utilized. It was a tremendous asset to politicians in the 1920's in securing the vote of agriculturists; it opened up the question of Federal versus state rights in the disposal of water-power sites on navigable rivers and tributaries of navigable rivers; and it caused much debate over Federal versus private control of hydroelectric plants. The controversies were not ended as was supposed in May, 1933, when Congress provided for the Tennessee Valley development, and created the Tennessee Valley Authority.

The shoals section of the Tennessee River (Fig. 111) in northern Alabama extends downstream from Brown's Island, above the mouth of Elk River, to Florence, Alabama, a distance of about 37 miles, and has a drop, measured vertically, of 134 feet. The army engineers have selected three sites for dams in this section. The lower site,

---

* *Tennessee River and Tributaries, Part 1,* 71st Congress, 2nd Session, House Document 328, 14. Without reservoirs the potential, it is estimated, is 3,000,000 hp.

near Florence, is known as Muscle Shoals No. 1; just above Florence
is Muscle Shoals No. 2; and the third, just below the mouth of Elk
River, is Muscle Shoals No. 3. There are other sites for dams in
northern Alabama. These shoals are on the edge of the old land to
the east of the eastern edge of the Coastal Plain. In reality they
constitute a fall zone similar in origin to the Fall Line, except that
the rocks of this old land in northern Alabama are not so old as those
of the Piedmont. The Wilson Dam, constructed by the Federal Government during the World War to supply energy for the manufacture
of nitrates for munitions, has been built across the river at the lower

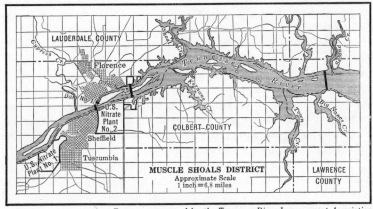

From map prepared by the Tennessee River Improvement Association.

FIG. 111.—Water Power and Navigation Dams on Tennessee River in Alabama.

end of Muscle Shoals No. 2, near the eastern edge of the little city
of Florence.

The dam, 4,600 feet long, stores water for both power and navigation. The north end of the Wilson dam is pierced by a canal with
two locks, the total lift of which is 91 feet. The power house built
into the downstream side of the dam provides space for 18 water
wheels and dynamos. The dam provides a "maximum available head
of water on the wheels of 96 feet, and a minimum head" of 68 feet.
Wilson Lake formed above the dam, in normal water (501 feet above
sea level) extends upstream 14.7 miles to the site of Dam No. 3,
the General Joe Wheeler Dam. This, like the Norris Dam, is an ad-
junct of Wilson Dam. Both will have turbines and dynamos for power
development, however.

The Norris Dam was completed in 1936. Its site, long known as the Cove Creek dam site, is at or near the junction of the Clinch and Powell rivers. The Norris Dam and plant is to cost about $35,000,000. A transmission line to cost $6,000,000 will be built to connect the Norris plant and the Joe Wheeler power plant with the Wilson Dam plant.*

The total rated capacity of the Wilson Dam plant at Muscle Shoals when installation is complete will be about 624,000 horsepower. Only four units of 30,000 horsepower and four of 36,000 horsepower are now installed, making a present rated capacity of 264,000 horsepower; but because of the small storage possible before the Norris and Wheeler Dams were completed, not more than about 60,000 continuous horsepower (the year round) is available. The storage of flood-season waters at these dams will somewhat augment the low-season flow. It is estimated that the continuous or firm horsepower will be 120,000.†

Under Federal control, through the TVA, the Wilson Dam plant and the Norris and Joe Wheeler plants will be run as a unit just as are the Duke plants in North Carolina. Electricity will be distributed to cities and towns both within and without (if near by) the Valley. The steam plant near the Wilson Dam will be held by the TVA "in a stand-by condition." Norris Dam and plant and transmission line, Joe Wheeler Dam and plant, Wilson Dam and plant, and the steam-electric plant, all, will represent an investment of more than $100,000,000. Many other dams will be necessary before the Wilson Dam hydroelectric plant can be run the year round at its present installed capacity.

The Ozark-Ouachita Power Region

This region has little potential power (200,000-300,000 horsepower) in comparison with the Southern Appalachian Highlands region, and so far very little has been developed. As of Jan. 1, 1936, 95,000 horsepower had been developed—installed capacity. The largest power rivers are the White and the Ouachita.‡

---

* At the close of 1937 three other dams were being constructed by the Federal Government above Wilson Dam—Guntersville, Chickamauga, and Hiwassee, on Fowlers Bend. The total Federal expenditures, if Congress appropriates in 1938 what the President recommends in his message of January, 1938, will be $250,-000,000 for hydroelectric power, flood control, and navigation. Other dams are in prospect calling for additional funds.

† Letter from *TVA*, June 15, 1934. The additional dams will increase this.

‡ The Arkansas Geological Survey (letter from director, April, 1930) gives 296,000 horsepower for 100 per cent of the time. On Jan. 1, 1930, the four plants

Texas, Louisiana, and Oklahoma also are poor in potential power, largely because of the low relief and the scanty, unreliable rainfall. Oil and coal in Texas and Oklahoma in particular compete with water power. In Texas in 1929 only 19 million kilowatt-hours of electricity were generated by water power but 2,782 million by fuel power. Louisiana had no water-power plants in 1930, and Oklahoma only four.*

THE SUPER POWER SYSTEM IN THE SOUTH

All or nearly all the larger power plants of the Southeastern States are interconnected by high-voltage transmission lines forming the Southeastern Super Power System, that spreads over the Piedmont of North Carolina, South Carolina, Georgia, and Alabama, and the Great Valley of Tennessee and extends for some distance into bordering regions. The lines are most numerous where the power plants (the hydroelectric and steam-electric) are most numerous, where the population is densest, and where there are the largest number of industries. There is a tendency toward a grouping of the lines within state boundaries and for the plants and lines within a given state to be dominated by one or at most a few large power companies. In fact, the super power system is for the most part the outcome of agreements between large companies.

The advantages of such an interconnected system are many. Connecting hydroelectric and steam-electric plants over a large area assures consumers a reliable, non-variable supply of power. Low water in any one section or the washing out of one dam, or even several, means no cessation and even little variation in the delivery of power. The linking of steam plants with hydroelectric takes care of the natural decline in output occasioned by the normal low-water season of late summer. Such interconnecting permits a much more complete utilization of the potential power resources of the streams. Economy (at present) demands that the hydroelectric plants be utilized as long as they are capable of meeting the power demands; then and only then are the steam plants called into action.

---

of the state in operation had an output of 15,530 hp. *Developed Water Power in United States,* Geological Survey, Jan. 1, 1930, # 40062; data for 1936 from U.S.G.S.

* *Statistical Abstract,* 1930, 368; *Developed Water Power in United States, loc. cit.*

HISTORY OF POWER DEVELOPMENT IN THE SOUTH

The evolution in the utilization of water-power resources of the South has followed the developments in other parts of the country. The first steam-electric plant in the United States—the Central Station in New York—was constructed by Edison in 1882 for lighting. The first hydroelectric plant was built at Appleton, Wisconsin, in 1882. Alternating current for lighting purposes was first generated on a large scale in a plant at Great Barrington, Massachusetts, in 1885; and the first electric street cars in United States ran in Binghamton, New York, and Richmond, Virginia, in 1887. These were the initial developments in the generating and consuming of commercial electric currents. But transmission of the current to areas away from the plant had to await the perfecting of the transformer, and other developments, by Tesla and others. By 1888 power development and transmission, much as we have them now, were possible.

Up to this date, then, large hydroelectric developments were unknown in America. Mills powered by falling water date, in the South, from the early seventeenth century. In 1620 the Virginia colonists petitioned the proprietors to send over skilled millwrights to build water mills. It is known that by 1634 two such mills were in operation, and by 1649 five were grinding grain. This was a beginning of a type of water utilization that has persisted for three centuries, but of decreasing importance after about 1820. Grist mills, powered by overshot wheels, may still be found here and there in the South in the Appalachian Highland areas and in the Ozarks.

In the early part of the nineteenth century, and before, there were large merchant grist mills (as shown in the discussion of the development of manufacturing) at Baltimore and Richmond, run by water power at the Fall Line. Other cities in the Upper and Middle South had large water-driven merchant mills before the Revolutionary War, some on the Cape Fear River at Fayetteville, on Pine Creek, near Camden, at Greenville, South Carolina, and elsewhere in the South. By 1790 spinning, carding, and weaving mills were run by water power in many parts of the cotton-growing states. Mention has been made in Chapter X of the numerous factories being run by water power at or near Baltimore, Richmond, and elsewhere in the Upper South. One of the large power plants (about 1845) was the Augusta Canal and dam at Augusta, Georgia, where a head of 50 feet was developed, giving a potential of 20,000 horsepower. A canal 7 miles long brought water above the dam to several factories below.

In 1849 the city took over the ownership and leased some of the power. Other large dams and canals were on the Chattahoochee, the Catawba, and the Tallapoosa. In 1849, in Georgia, water power was used by 36 cotton factories, 19 wool carders, 1,129 flour mills, and 744 sawmills.*

In 1880, the steam engine, the old types of water wheels, and the hydraulic turbines were in use in the South, as shown by the very comprehensive survey of power and water power by the Census Bureau. From 1870 to 1880 the report shows that the steam engine as a source of power for factories was increasing at the expense of the water wheels.

The degree and character of water-power developments in 1880 may best be shown, briefly perhaps, by data on the tributaries of the Altamaha, in Georgia, which without doubt may be considered typical of streams of this size throughout the eastern South. Water power was used in 73 flour mills, 37 sawmills, 7 cotton factories, 13 cotton gins, 6 furniture factories, 3 paper mills, 2 agricultural implement plants, 2 leather plants, 6 woolen mills, and 1 wheelwright's shop. Most of these plants were on the Piedmont and the inner portion of the Coastal Plain. The report says that the number of water-power developments on the tributaries of the Altamaha on the Coastal Plain were "not worth mentioning."†

The total development in the South in 1870 was 185,188 horsepower; and in 1880, 195,509. From 1880 to 1890 many water-power plants were enlarged and modernized. Beginning with 1890 there was a notable increase in developments, but the greatest activity dates from 1923.‡

---

* The South in the Building of the Nation Series, *Economic History,* V, 580, 584; *Report of Tenth Census,* 1880, "Water Power," 820, etc.

† *Report of Tenth Census,* 1880, "Water Power," 820-822.

‡ *Water Supply Paper,* 206, 579.

CHAPTER XII

THE EXPLOITATION OF THE MINERAL RESOURCES

In 1930 the Southern States produced in value more than one-third (35 per cent) of the mineral output of the United States—$1,809,-000,000 out of $5,165,000,000. In two of the most useful minerals, coal and petroleum, it leads the other sections, the North and the West.

As yet, a large part of the coal mined in the South goes to the North to mills and factories, and a large part of the petroleum is refined in Northern refineries; but industries and refineries are increasing in number, and the benefits to the South of the complete manufacture of its raw materials are increasing year by year.

Mining is, as a rule, allied to manufacturing. The rapid growth in mining in the South is, therefore, remarkable, when it is remembered that this section is predominantly agricultural, 12,900,000 people in 1930 being classed as urban and 24,950,000 as rural. That is, only 36 per cent of the people of the South Atlantic were urban; 28.7 per cent in the East South Central section; and 36.4 per cent in the West South Central.*

Non-metallic minerals—coal, petroleum, natural gas, clay, gypsum, salt, phosphate, and others—take precedence over the metallic in quantity of reserves and in extent of distribution. This is largely due to the fact that sedimentary rocks are more widely distributed than igneous or meta-igneous.

Table XVIII gives the value of the total mineral output of the South in 1932 by groups of states and individual states.

From this table it is seen that Texas in 1932 took first rank in the South as a producer of minerals; indeed, it stood second only to Pennsylvania among all the states. It was petroleum, largely, that gave Texas its high rank, and it was petroleum that made Oklahoma the second of the Southern States in mineral production. West Virginia held third place, largely because it was one of the leading coal-producing states of our country. Coal also brought more than $150,000,000 in 1929 to Kentucky.

The distribution of the minerals of the South in relation to the

---

* *Report of Fifteenth Census*, "Population," 1930, I, 15.

TABLE XVIII

MINERAL OUTPUT OF THE SOUTH, 1932[1]

South Atlantic	$ 199,741,000
Delaware	300,000
Maryland	7,234,000
Virginia	16,927,000
West Virginia	156,643,000
North Carolina	2,466,000
South Carolina	951,000
Georgia	6,293,000
Florida	7,108,000
East South Central	95,527,000
Kentucky	59,076,000
Tennessee	14,562,000
Alabama	19,170,000
Mississippi	2,719,000
West South Central	651,545,000
Arkansas	15,540,000
Louisiana	60,921,000
Oklahoma	185,121,000
Texas	389,963,000
Total for the United States	$2,284,600,000 for 1932;
	$5,164,963,000 for 1929.

[1] *Statistical Abstract*, 1935, 678.

bedrock of the physiographic provinces has been sketched in a previous chapter (see Figs. 16, 17, 18 and 100). The principal minerals of each state, in order of value or production in 1929, are as follows:[*]

Delaware	clay products, stone, and sand and gravel
Maryland	coal, clay products, cement, and sand and gravel
Virginia	coal, stone, clay products, cement
West Virginia	coal, natural gas, clay products, and petroleum
North Carolina	stone, clay products, copper, and sand and gravel
South Carolina	stone, clay products, sand and gravel, and barite
Georgia	stone, clay products, cement, and fuller's earth
Florida	phosphate rock, stone, fuller's earth, and cement
Kentucky	coal, petroleum, clay products, and natural gas
Tennessee	coal, stone, cement, and clay products
Alabama	coal, iron, cement, and clay products
Mississippi	sand and gravel, clay products, stone, and natural gas
Arkansas	petroleum, coal, natural gas, and natural gasoline
Louisiana	petroleum, natural gas, natural gasoline, and salt
Oklahoma	petroleum, natural gas, natural gasoline, zinc
Texas	petroleum, natural gas, sulphur, natural gasoline

The variety of minerals of the Southern States is far greater than shown in the above list but it is largely those listed above that have

[*] *Statistical Abstract*, 1931, 776.

the natural environmental conditions—quality, topographic location, quantity, and nearness to traffic lines and markets—that permit their exploitation in competition with numerous other sections. The long formidable lists of minerals of a region or a state so often displayed in publications of development bureaus have little or no economic significance. To be of value the deposits must be workable deposits— workable in a competitive world.

Coal, natural gas, and petroleum have been discussed in Chapter XI. Each of these is also a raw product in manufacturing. Coal is a raw product for the production of coke, asphalt, tar, coal gas, and a wide variety of by-products. Petroleum must undergo a manufacturing process before it is available for use; and natural gas in northern Louisiana is the basis for a large lampblack industry.

1. PHOSPHATE ROCK

The phosphate rock of the South is found in Florida, Tennessee, and South Carolina. The output in 1930 was about 3,926,000 tons, valued at $13,997,000—a small yet important industry. About four-fifths of the output now comes from Florida, which not only supplies rock to our country but also has large exports.

South Carolina was the first to exploit phosphate deposits, but the production now is very low. Florida became a producer in 1888, and since about 1903 has led all other states.

In Florida the workable deposits are in a belt 100 miles long and of varying widths, to the north of Tampa. The rock occurs as hard rock, land pebble rock, river pebble, soft phosphate, and phosphate marl. The hard rock and land pebble furnish most of the shipments; and the land pebble is most important, making about 90 per cent of the output in recent years.

In Tennessee the classes of phosphate rock are white, blue, and brown. The brown is the one most mined. Open-pit mining is used. The overburden is about three or four feet.

The reserves in our country, as worked out by the United States Geologic Survey, are as follows:[*]

	Tons
Florida	294,000,000
Tennessee	84,000,000
Idaho	5,068,000,000
Montana	391,000,000
Utah	327,000,000

[*] W. H. Voskuil, "Phosphate Industry and Resources of the United States," *International Bergwertschaft,* June, 1928; C. A. Whittle, "The Fertilizer Industry," in *Manufacturers Record,* LXXXVI, Part 1, Dec., 1924, 202.

2. SULPHUR

All the natural sulphur and most of the salt of the South are derived from the domes or islands in Louisiana and Texas, as previously stated. In the production of sulphur the Southern States hold the world monopoly, but in salt they hold low rank, the output of the salt plants being only 683,000 tons out of the 7,569,000 of the United States. Louisiana is the chief producer of salt in the South—606,000 tons, which is slightly more than one-fourth the output of Michigan, one-third that of New York, and one-half that of Ohio.

When sulphur production began on a large scale in the Gulf Coast section in 1902 as the result of the invention of the Frasch process, we were importing most of what we consumed. Some was obtained from pyrites, but at a heavy cost. Some sulphur is still obtained from pyrites in California and Virginia. From 1904 to 1916 our production of sulphur was 365,000 tons a year. But in 1935 it was 1,635,000 tons.* We now meet all our domestic needs, which have increased materially because of the growth of the chemical industries, and export about 700,000 tons. The value at the mines is only $18 to $22 a ton.† Sulphur was first discovered in Louisiana in the 1860's, by a prospector for oil, at a depth of about 1,000 feet. The 100-foot bed, however, could not be exploited, for quicksand prevented the sinking of shafts. Herman Frasch, of Cleveland, Ohio, devised the method that has since been used for the recovery of this useful product. The first well using this process was put down in 1894, but the process was not really a success until 1903. Water under pressure, at a temperature of 300° F., is forced down a large pipe, about 10 inches in diameter, to the sulphur beds, 300 to 1,200 feet below the surface. Sulphur melts at 237-346° F. The melted sulphur is forced upward, assisted by compressed air, through vertical pipes encased within the large 10-inch pipe and therefore surrounded by the superheated descending water. At the surface the sulphur is carried by hot pipes to huge bins, some 40 to 150 feet on a side, where it cools into a solid mass and is later "mined" when shipment is desired. The sulphur thus obtained is 99.8 per cent pure. Galveston and Freeport are the leading exporting ports. Railroads carry the sulphur to interior consuming centers.

Sulphur plants are expensive. The largest cost $2,000,000 or more. Large heavy boilers using fuel-oil heat the water under pressure.

---

* *Statistical Abstract*, 1934, 673; 1936, 699.

† Louisiana and Texas were our chief sources of sulphur from 1903 to 1924; but in the latter year the Union Sulphur Company of Louisiana, which operated the only mine of the state, suspended operations, having exhausted its resources, it is reported. Texas in 1928 produced 99.88 per cent of the total of the country.

Louisiana once had a producing sulphur mine (or well) about ten miles from Lake Charles, in Calcasieu Parish, but operations have ceased, due, it is claimed, to exhaustion of the supply.

Sicily was the chief source of sulphur used in the United States before the invention of the Frasch process. In fact, Sicily had furnished about 90 per cent of the world's supply of 400,000 tons. The sulphur was quarried out of pits as deep as 350 feet by crude devices.*

3. SALT

The widely distributed salt licks, found in marine sedimentary rock, were the sources of the first salt produced in the South. Some were worked several decades before 1800. "Boiling down" brine was the work of the individual farmer for his family during the off-season from work, though he sometimes produced enough to barter with the neighbors. Commercial salt making began where concentration of population furnished a market and where waterways offered transportation facilities. One of the celebrated salt-making sites was near Charleston, West Virginia (then Virginia), on the Kanawha River (Fig. 112). There were works here in 1797, 150 pounds a day being produced and sold for 8 to 10 cents a pound. Surface brines were first used. By 1817 the establishments in this vicinity numbered 30, the output being 600,000 bushels a year. After about 1817 coal was the fuel used for evaporation. By 1880 West Virginia had 15 establishments with a total output of 2,700,000 barrels a year. The Kanawha Valley today is the seat of an important chemical industry, using salt as one of the raw products.

Salt licks were a source for brine in Louisiana during the War of 1812-1814. During the Civil War, Judge Avery began salt making on a large scale, using surface brine. But the surface resources were soon exhausted, and a shaft 16 feet deep was sunk to a bed of solid rock salt and the salt quarried like stone. After the Civil War deeper shafts were sunk here and there, one 350 feet deep; but salt mining met with intermittent success. New York capital became interested in 1880. Jefferson Island now has an active salt mine, the salt being quarried, hoisted to the surface up shafts, and ground in surface workings.†

---

* Robert H. Ridgeway, "Sulphur and Pyrites in 1928," *Report of Bureau of Mines,* Department of Commerce; W. H. Emerson, *General Economic Geology,* 362; Many newspaper clippings.

† *Report of Tenth Census,* 1880, "Manufactures," 1014-1026; Personal observation and interview.

4. CEMENT MATERIALS

Cement-making materials are found in all the limestone sections, as the Great Valley, the deep valleys of the Cumberland Plateau, the Highland Rim, and the Blue Grass and Nashville basins, and in parts of Arkansas, Oklahoma, and Texas (Fig. 18).

Alabama, Tennessee, and Texas are the chief producers of cement in the South, but only about 7 per cent of the output of the country

From Edward King, The Great South, 1874, 690.

FIG. 112.—A Large Salt Works in the Kanawha River Valley, about 1870.

Salt was made in this region soon after the settlement of the valley. Large chemical plants now utilize the salt deposits.

comes from the Southern States. The low production is due to the relatively low demand in the South for cement. In 1900 there were three plants, one each in Virginia, Tennessee, and Texas. Indeed, the United States was slow in entering the industry. The process was devised in England in 1824, but it was not until 1872 that the first plants were built in America. Natural cement, a natural mixture of clay and lime carbonate, an argillaceous limestone, has long been used in many parts of the South, but nature's product is not uniform in its composition. For the immense bridges and buildings, for which

Portland cement is now used, it is essential that the chemical composition and crushing strength be uniform.

Texas was probably the first to have a Portland cement plant in the South, at San Antonio in 1880. The story goes that an Englishman who was familiar with the making of Portland cement in his native land, and who knew the characteristics of the rock used, discovered what he thought was cement-making rock near San Antonio. A test was made and the rock proved suitable. The old quarry and the first plant are now (or were until lately) interesting features in Brackenridge Park in San Antonio.

A plant was constructed in Arkansas in 1897, and in Maryland in 1898. The industry in the South really got its start about 1900. The rotary kiln has been a wonderful factor in stimulating the industry. Road building and the growth of urban centers give excellent local markets for the product of the cement plants.

The raw materials entering into the manufacture of Portland cement are limestone and clay. These two ingredients are ground to extreme fineness, so fine that they may pass through a 200-mesh screen (200 wires to the inch). Fuel—finely powdered coal, gas, or oil—is the other essential. But since the weight of limestone and clay is so much greater and the cost of shipping is so much more than for the coal necessary for the fusing of these two ingredients, the cement plants must be located where limestone and clay are available.

Because of the low value of the cement per hundredweight and the high freight charges, relatively, there is a tendency, as stated above, for cement plants to be widely distributed, to be wherever market demands are sufficient to warrant construction of the expensive plants, and the two minerals and fuels may be assembled. The other factor, of course, is enterprise and capital.

There are plants in Alabama, Tennessee, Georgia, Virginia, Kentucky, and Oklahoma. The Department of Commerce, however, does not list the number of plants or the output. The South in 1929 consumed (apparent consumption) about 20 per cent of the total of the United States.*

5. BUILDING STONES AND GRAVEL

Building stones are available in surface exposures almost anywhere in the South except on the Coastal Plain and the valley flats of the larger rivers. (See Figure 18.) The great activity in road building in the last decade or so has called for vast quantities of sand,

---

* *Commerce Yearbook,* I, 1931, 361.

gravel, and crushed limestone. In the limestone regions, limestone quarries may be opened up almost anywhere. As a rule the sides of valleys or slopes of hills are generally selected, since here the soil covering is thin, the rocks less weathered, and transportation from the quarry does not require the elevating of the rock. Where possible, the stone crusher is located below the level of the quarry and above the road on which the trucks may carry away the crushed rock. Macadam roads were common even in Antebellum days in the Great Valley and the Kentucky and Nashville basins. Many new asphalted roads have been built on the old limestone road base.

Sand and gravel roads predominate in mileage on the Coastal Plain, for these materials are available there and crushed rock is not. In parts of southern Louisiana where clays and silts predominate, clay at one time was burned to hard lumps as a substitute for gravel.

Stone, brick, and cement or stucco are the most-used materials for the walls of homes and public buildings and business blocks in most parts of the South, away from the sections where lumbering and saw milling are active. Limestone, sandstone, and granite are the leading building stones.

Granite is quarried in the Piedmont and in a small area in Texas west of San Antonio, where a granite mass projects through the surrounding sedimentary rock. Granite quarries, like limestone quarries, are for the most part located on slopes. Solution is a dominant process in the weathering of the feldspar in the granite; and where the bed rock surface is flat, weathering may progress to a depth of 50 feet. Quarrying here would mean the removal of 50 feet of overburden. The sides of mountains, of monadnocks, and valleys are thus selected for the "workings." Typical examples are the great quarries on the lower slopes of Stone Mountain, near Atlanta. The faces of the monadnock are absolutely free of weathered rock, soil, and vegetation. Most of the granite quarries in North Carolina, which produce both paving block and building stone, are at the bases or on the lower slopes of monadnocks. Southern granite is as good as any found on our continent. Grays predominate. As it is generally free from joints and cracks, large blocks may be quarried for special uses.

Marble quarries at or near Tate, Georgia, and Knoxville, Tennessee, the two leading quarrying centers, supply stone of beautiful shades and grades that find markets all over the South and even in the North. Excellent marble outcrops at many places in the Great Valley (Fig. 113).

6. BAUXITE

The entire American supply of bauxite, from which aluminum may be extracted, comes from Arkansas, Georgia, Alabama, and Tennessee; but Arkansas is the largest producer. The Arkansas deposits which produce 95 per cent of the total have long been known, having been described by Branner in 1891. They have been concentrated by weathering and solution from syenite (closely related to granite), the syenite containing 27 per cent of aluminum silicate and the bauxite

A. E. P.

FIG. 113.—A Small Marble Quarry at Gantt's Quarry, Alabama, near the Line of Contact of the Great Valley and the Piedmont.

The stone is uniform in color, rich in tone—a velvety white with a very faint tinge of pink —and perfectly flawless, even in large blocks. It is an excellent grade of statuary marble, although not so used.

37 to 57 per cent. Arkansas bauxite has to meet strong competition with ore imported from South America. The north Georgia deposits were the first to be worked in the United States, operations beginning in 1889. Alabama's mining began in 1891. Shipments began from Arkansas in 1896, but they were insignificant until 1900. Tennessee began as a shipper of the ore in 1907. In 1929 only 331,000 tons were mined in the United States, valued at $1,928,000. This is less than half the consumption of the aluminum industry. Our imports come chiefly from British Guiana. In 1929 we imported 410,000 tons. Imports are increasing relative to domestic production.*

---

* *Commerce Yearbook*, 1937, I, 404; *Statistical Abstract*, 1931, 772.

A. E. P.

FIG. 114.—A Feldspar Mill near Micaville, North Carolina.

Mica and feldspar occur in such large masses in some parts of the mountains as to make mining of individual minerals profitable. It is on the basis of the larger masses of the individual constituents of granite that the geologist bases his belief that this mountain area has long been nature's "quarry" that has supplied material for sedimentary rock both west and east. Large crystals form deep in the crust of the earth where cooling is slow.

A. E. P.

FIG. 115.—A Gypsum Plant near Sweetwater, Texas.

The high quality of the gypsum, its abundance, and the low price of the land were the localizing factors.

Bauxite is consumed chiefly east of the Mississippi in the making of aluminum, certain chemicals, and abrasives. The largest reduction plant producing aluminum oxide is at East St. Louis.* Metallic aluminum from this oxide is produced at Maryville, Tennessee. Nearly all the deposits and reduction plants in the United States are owned or controlled by the Aluminum Company of America.

Most of the Arkansas bauxite mines are near Bauxite (Saline County) and Little Rock. The mines are easily reached by spur tracks from the main tracks of trunk-line railroads. In general, open-pit mining is practiced. The overburden is stripped off and the deposit handled by steam shovels. The ore is dried near the mines but is shipped out of the state for refining.

Bauxite has uses other than in the manufacture of aluminum. It is used in the manufacture of abrasives, in the preparation of aluminum salts as alum, aluminum sulphate, and aluminum chloride. It is one of the ingredients of refractory brick and is used in aluminous cement, in petroleum refining, and in the preparation of calcium aluminate for quick-setting plaster compounds.

Figure 114 shows a feldspar crushing mill in North Carolina and Figure 115 a gypsum plant near Sweetwater, Texas.

* In late December, 1937, the Aluminum Company of America was constructing a large plant at Mobile, to reduce British Guiana bauxite to a more concentrated form before shipment inland.

CHAPTER XIII

THE IRON AND STEEL INDUSTRY

THE RISE OF THE INDUSTRY

Although iron ores are widely distributed in the South in every form used in blast furnaces (Fig. 16), there is today little mining other than in the Birmingham district. The Birmingham area, however, produces only about 10 per cent of the total ore mined in the United States.

It is believed that the South in 1810 was producing nearly one-fifth of the pig iron of the country. By 1840 the percentage had reached nearly 26, but a relative decline set in soon after. In 1850 the production was 23.4 per cent, and in 1860, 12.8 per cent. At the close of the Civil War nearly every forge and plant was destroyed, as earlier stated, and by 1870 a revival had been experienced in only a few sections. The relative output in 1870 was about 8 per cent. By 1880 the output had returned nearly to the Antebellum figure, 11.7 per cent; in 1900, 14.2 per cent; and 1930, 11 per cent.[*]

Although there has been a percentage decline during the last century

TABLE XIX

PIG-IRON OUTPUT OF THE SOUTH, BY DECADES

Year	Output in Tons	Percentage of U. S.
1810	No data	18.1
1840	No data	25.9
1850	131,541	23.4
1860	No data	12.8
1870	No data	8
1880	448,878	11.7
1890	1,833,937	
1900	1,965,000 (in Md., Va., and Ala.)	14.2
1910	2,710,000	10
1920	3,346,000	9
1930	4,480,000	14

[*] Edwin C. Eckel, "Iron and Steel Possibilities of the South," The South: The Nation's Greatest Asset, Part II, *Manufacturer's Record*, 1912, 37; *Statistical Abstract*, 1936, 700.

or more, in actual tons of pig iron produced, there has been a great
increase in total tons, as Table XIX indicates.

The bog iron and other small ore pockets in the Coastal Plain and
parts of the Piedmont, worked in Colonial days and well into the
nineteenth century, are not considered of economic value today.
Neither are the magnetite areas of North Carolina. Up and down
the Great Valley from central Alabama to near Staunton, Virginia,

From Edward King, The Great South, 1874, 533.

FIG. 116.—The Rockwood Iron Furnaces, Rockwood, Tennessee, about 1870.

Federal officers who were stationed in this portion of the Great Valley during the Civil War
recognized the admirable opportunities offered for the making of pig iron. Soon after the war
this plant was constructed and was in almost continuous operation until 1929. Under the merciless
competition from the larger furnaces at Birmingham and Pittsburgh this small furnace has
drawn its fires.

are old blast furnaces—about forty in number—that in recent decades
have been "in blast"; but at present the active furnaces are confined
almost exclusively to the Birmingham districts. The Rockwood furnace (Fig. 116) closed in 1929, never to be in blast again, it is reported. These furnaces are on or near ore deposits. Red hematite and
brown limonite outcrop or come near the surface here and there in
the entire length of the Great Valley in the South. The brown ores
are too low in iron to be used, except in the Birmingham district,
at present prices for pig iron.

The red ore of the South is mixed with lime carbonate and silica.
It is fossiliferous and is known to geologists as Clinton or fossiliferous

ore. The red ore is uniform in quality. Where leaching has been active and much lime carbonate removed, the ore is soft and produces as much as 50 to 55 per cent of metallic iron, when smelted. The hard ore is rich in lime carbonate, some containing from 15 to 19 per cent, but it has a smaller percentage of metallic iron than the leached, some deposits as low as 37 per cent. The hard ore contains so much lime carbonate that a very small amount of limestone, or none at all, is needed in the blast furnaces (see Table XX). If more limestone is present than is needed, brown ore of the region is added to offset the excess carbonate. From one to four iron-bearing horizons are mined in the Birmingham districts.

TABLE XX

ANALYSES OF HARD AND SOFT ORES,

BIRMINGHAM DISTRICT[1]

	Hard %	Soft %
Iron	37	51–55
Silica	13.4	18.5
Alumina	3.2	3.65
Lime	16.2	1.2
Sulphur	Traces	Traces
Phosphorus	6.37	0.5

[1] Walter B. Jones, *Bulletin* 28, Alabama Geologic Survey, 120, 127, 157.

Some of the red ore, particularly in the early years of mining in the Birmingham district, was mined by open pits (Fig. 117); later by underground workings, combined with the open pit. Now most of the mining is underground. The strata dip from 15 to 45 degrees; the shafts or slopes follow the dip. The vertical shaft is also used in some parts of the central Alabama fields. The output of the Birmingham district in late years has been about 2,000,000-5,000,000 tons. The Lake Superior districts in 1930 mined 49,383,000 tons* and the Birmingham 5,552,000 tons.

The same class of ore was worked near Chattanooga and at Rockwood. Red hematite forms one of the underlying strata (Rockwood formation) of the Cumberland Plateau. The iron-ore output of Tennessee was only 102,000 tons in 1929.†

The brown iron ore of the Highland Rim between the Nashville Basin and the Tennessee River (Fig. 16) was worked in the earlier half of the nineteenth century to supply ore to the numerous furnaces on the Cumberland and Tennessee rivers. A small furnace at

* *Statistical Abstract*, 1931, 774; 1934, 664; 1936, 700.
† *Idem.*

A. E. P.

FIG. 117.—A Cross Section of Red Mountain, in the southern part of Birmingham.
Much of the rock in the left is a hematite seam.

A. E. P.

FIG. 118.—The Ferro-phosphate Blast Furnace at Rockdale, in the Nashville Basin.
Iron ore and phosphate rock are near at hand. A Nashville Iron worker, J. J. Gray, Jr., after
much experimentation, devised a method of making ferro-phosphate in a small blast furnace.

Rockdale, Tennessee (Fig. 118), makes ferrophosphorus from local ores and near-by rich phosphate rock. About a dozen furnaces in the brown ore region have been in operation off and on in late decades (Fig. 119), but competition from Birmingham is almost too severe for them to be run on a paying basis. Little ore, therefore, is mined.

A. E. P.

FIG. 119.—Charcoal Kilns at the Old Shelby Furnace, South of Columbiana, Alabama.

The use of the more efficient coke as fuel in large-scale plants at Birmingham forced the Shelby furnace, and ten others along the Mineral Belt (L. and N.), to close about a decade or more ago. Even a large-scale chemical plant to utilize the by-products of the charcoal kilns and forty thousand acres of forested land, assuring an abundant supply of wood, could not save the Shelby furnace.

It was only when iron prices were high that they could run at a profit. During and for a few years after the World War many were in blast, and they could again be rebuilt and brought into production were the price of pig iron increased.

TABLE XXI

BLAST FURNACES IN THE SOUTH, BY STATES,
IN 1917, 1925, AND 1930[1]

	1917	1925	1930
Alabama	47	35	24
Virginia	19	3	0
Tennessee	16	5	6[2]
Kentucky	7	?	0
Georgia	4	?	0
Texas	2	?	0

[1] *Statistical Abstract,* 1917, 234; *Biennial Census of Manufactures,* 1925, 423; *Report of Fifteenth Census,* 1929, Industry Series, Table 12, 10.
[2] In 1936 only two blast furnaces—at Rockdale and Wrigley—were operating.

Brown ore occurs in the Ozarks in northern Arkansas and in northeastern Texas, but in neither section are the deposits worked at present.

THE IRON AND STEEL INDUSTRY IN THE BIRMINGHAM DISTRICT

The South in general, until recently, had gone but little farther in iron manufacturing than the pig-iron or wrought-iron stage. Its crude iron has been shipped elsewhere for further fabrication. In this arrangement the profit that comes to the manufacturer and the wages to the laborer are lost to the South. For example, a ton of pig iron worth $18 to $21, if manufactured into rails, sells for $43 a ton, and if cast into furnaces or stoves, from $150 to $250. Nearly all this advance in the value of the iron as the result of manufacturing goes to the manufacturer and to labor, for both of which if they are Southern the profits remain in the South to be spent for other goods. It is chiefly in the Birmingham district (some in Chattanooga) that one finds a beginning in the more advanced stage in iron and steel manufacturing. Here are fabricated such products as sheet and bar iron, water and sewer pipe, cast-iron and lap-weld pipe (black and galvanized), rails, structural steel, bolts and rivets, steel cars, wire, stoves, furnaces and radiators, sugar mill machinery, cotton gins, and a wide variety of other products. But these types of industry are after all only early stages in the evolution of iron manufactures. The highest stages are represented by plants that turn out high-class machinery, engines, firearms, auto accessories, cutlery, and tools. When larger and more active markets are available and more experience is gained in manufacturing, the higher types of iron and steel goods will be turned out. In time the Birmingham district should supply the needs of the entire South for the many sorts of machinery, implements, tools, and small metal products as well as the heavy iron manufactures now produced.

Nowhere else in America—in fact in the world—are the three essential raw materials—iron ore, fuel, and fluxes—so easily assembled.* Nature has done her part in offering to man wonderful opportunities for iron manufacturing in the Birmingham district. The failure to exploit these opportunities to their fullest rests with man. A beginning has been made, but only a beginning. Alabama in 1927 was mining only about 10 per cent of the iron of the country, as compared with 80 per cent for the Lake Superior district, and was turning

---

* Iron ore from Red Mountain moves over a high line railroad, down grade, to the Fairfield plant of the United States Steel Corporation in less than 30 minutes. The proximity of the plant to coal is equally advantageous.

out less than 8 per cent of the pig iron and ferro-alloys. The distant "future" in iron ore production rests, however, with Alabama. Burchard in 1927 stated that the Lake Superior resources of iron ore would be exhausted in about 33 years, at the present rate of production, but Alabama's stock would last 333 years (at the present rate of consumption).* The total iron ore reserves in the Southern States amount to about 10 billion tons, as estimated by Eckel in 1906, but

A. E. P.

FIG. 120.—Part of the Ensley Pig Iron and Steel Plant at Ensley, in the Birmingham District.
At Fairfield is a more up-to-date plant.

most of this is low grade. The estimates of the better grade ran from 5 billion to 7.5 billion tons for the United States, one-third of which is in the South.

The Birmingham district lies near the western edge of the Great Appalachian Valley and spreads over the eastern edge of the Cumberland Plateau, in north central Alabama. The northeast-southwest extent of the district, from Irondale to Bessemer, is about 15 miles; the northwest-southeast extent is less than 8 miles. Within this area are Birmingham, North Birmingham, East Birmingham, Ensley (Fig. 120), Bessemer, Irondale, Oxmoor, West Bessemer, Woodward, Brynton, Fairfield, Edgewater, Bayview, Shafton, Ridge-

---

* E. F. Burchard, "The Iron Ore Situation in the South," *Circular* 13512, U. S. G. S., March, 1927, 8; Burchard, "Alabama Ores Equal Lake Supply," *Iron Age*, p. cxix, No. 12, 847-850 (March, 1927); E. C. Eckel, *Mineral Resources of the United States*, 1906, 7.

field, Laketon, Tipton, and Thompson, and a score or more of smaller population groups, all interested directly in mining coal and iron ore or quarrying fluxes and manufacturing pig iron and iron and steel goods.

The iron mines are distributed for some fifteen miles along the slopes of Red Mountain (Fig. 117), a long narrow ridge which skirts the eastern edge of both Birmingham and Bessemer. Many of the cities listed above lie west of a line from Birmingham to Bessemer, and thus on the Cumberland Plateau, beneath which are the coal measures of the Warrior-Plateau fields, that have an area of about 12,000 square miles. To the east of Red Mountain is the Cahaba Coal field and still farther east is the Coosa Field. Flux is available, both limestone and dolomite, near by. These latter are accessible in the longitudinal outcrops in the valleys, with a northeast and southwest trend, that lie between the coal basins and the iron ore mountain.

Some five large companies dominate the iron and steel and associated industries. The largest of all is the Tennessee Coal, Iron, and Railroad Company, a subsidiary of the United States Steel Corporation. Its blast furnaces have ten stacks in all as follows:*

At Ensley......................... 6 stacks
Bessemer...................... 2 stacks
Fairfield..................... 2 stacks

The company operates several open-hearth furnaces for producing steel, several blooming mills, a billet mill, a rail mill, a guide mill, two plate mills, a combination bar and structural mill, a basic slag plant, several coal mines, a by-product coke plant, a benzol plant, and several iron mines and dolomite and limestone quarries and has its own railroads that bring furnaces, steel mills, and coal and iron ore mines and quarries into close proximity. The Woodward Iron Company has furnaces at Woodward and Vanderbilt—five stacks in all—coal and ore mines and by-product coal and benzol plants.

The Sloss Sheffield Steel and Iron Company has furnaces at Birmingham and North Birmingham, four in all, and the necessary coal and iron ore mines and coke ovens. The Republic Iron and Steel Company has three stacks at Thomas, with coal, ore, and fluxing material deposits. The Chickasaw Shipbuilding and Car Company has a car-building shop, a forge, a car-repair shop, a machine shop, and a

---

* The Alice, Oxmoor, and Little Bell once owned by the Company were all dismantled by 1927. The two stacks at Bessemer may not be put in blast again. Fairfield is the newest and most modern of all the plants.

380 THE IRON AND STEEL INDUSTRY

bolt, nut, and rivet plant. Smaller companies produce stoves, ranges, and ornamental iron ware. The American Steel and Wire Company turns out galvanized wire, nails, barbed wire fencing, woven wire fencing, and staples. Steel billets are supplied to this wire company by the Ensley plant.

The iron ores used in the blast furnaces of Alabama have been previously described. The total length of exposures of the red hematite (or Clinton, known also as the Red Mountain ore) in Alabama is about 150 miles. Nearly 95 per cent of the ore of Alabama comes from the Red Mountain formation, but only about 5 per cent of the area of the iron-bearing rocks has so far been mined, showing the tremendous iron resources of the state. Although most of the ore used in and about Birmingham comes from Red Mountain, there are other outcrops near, in fact, in all the anticlinal valleys separating the coal basins, except where faulting has pushed the iron-bearing layer too far beneath the surface to be reached readily. Borings have struck ore 800 feet below the surface and measured along the dip 5,000 feet or more from the outcrop. The outcrops have a north-east-southwest distribution.*

The iron and steel industry of the Birmingham district is for the most part a post-Civil War development. One of the best known pre-war furnaces, at Tannehill, was built in 1836 on the site of an old forge, on Roupe's Creek in Tuscaloosa County, some sixteen to eighteen miles southwest of the city of Bessemer. Bar iron, kettles, ovens, and skillets were poured and sold to the farmers in the region about. In 1855 Moses Stroup bought the old furnace and erected a much larger one, which was one of the chief sources of cannon ball, gun barrels, cannon, pots, skillets, and other iron articles for the Confederate army. This old furnace, affectionately known as "Old Tannehill," (Fig. 121) was wrecked in 1865 by Union forces and has never been rebuilt. Its vine-covered stack is still to be seen in an excellent state of preservation, a tribute to the careful work of its builders.

During the Civil War about sixteen plants were in operation in central Alabama, smelting iron and casting necessary utensils, implements, and tools. This includes only the larger works. There were many smaller forges and blacksmith shops that often were called iron works.

It was in 1863 that the Oxmoor furnace, five or six miles south of Birmingham in Shades Valley, at the foot of the western slope of

---

* Walter B. Jones, *loc. cit.;* Henry McCalley, *Miscellaneous Paper* 6, Alabama Geological Survey.

Shades Mountain, was erected by the same Moses Stroup who built
Old Tannehill. This furnace was probably the largest up to that date.

Most of the furnaces of Civil War days used brown ore, but the
Oxmoor used red ore from near-by deposits that was hauled to the
furnace by wagons. The output was 10 tons a day. A furnace at
Irondale was also built about this time in an attempt to meet the

A. E. P.

FIG. 121.—The Remains of One of the Stacks of Old Tannehill, southwest of
Bessemer, Alabama.

This, a pre-Civil War furnace, was destroyed by Union forces in the war.

demands of the Confederacy for this "precious" metal. Red Mountain
ore was used. The fuel for these forges and furnaces was charcoal.
All were destroyed in 1865 when the Union army overran this section
of Alabama. Associated with these were six rolling mills with a daily
capacity of 85 tons. Pig iron was also shipped to other parts of the
state, particularly during the Civil War to Selma, which was the
seat of the Confederacy's great manufacturing arsenal. Of the sixteen
furnaces in operation during the War only six were restored, most of

the owners having lost everything in that tragic era. These were Oxmoor, Irondale, Shelby, Brierfield, Salt Creek, and Rock Run. The
Irondale furnace was the first to be rebuilt, the owner having secured
capital from Ohio sources. It went into blast in 1866. It finally ceased
operations during the panic of 1873. Oxmoor went into blast in 1872,
with two 25-ton stacks, but the management was so poor that the
output of each was only about 10 tons a day. Oxmoor was closed for a
time in 1873 and during the cholera plague. Birmingham, founded in
1871 by a land company that was promoted by railway officials, was
still a tiny city and suffered greatly; but both city and furnace weathered the storms. After these calamities a new organization which took
over Oxmoor made many improvements.

Between 1880 and 1886 there were rapid developments in the iron
industry in the Birmingham district. The Alice, Sloss, Williamson,
Woodward, and Mary Pratt iron companies were organized and began the construction of iron works. The Alice furnace, the first within
the city of Birmingham, went into blast November 30, 1880, with
an output of 53 tons a day. Near by was the Williamson furnace. The
Sloss Company put two 70-ton furnaces in blast in 1881. This company was backed by Louisville and Cincinnati capital. By 1881
Birmingham was beginning the development that has continued down
to this day.

In 1882 and 1883 Birmingham was jubilant over the purchase of
Alice furnace and large tracts of coal and iron land by Colonel Ensley—a million-dollar deal. Ensley and the capitalists that backed him
were Tennesseans. This company became the Platt Coal and Coke
Company. It was later taken over by the Tennessee Coal, Iron, and
Railroad Company. But this deal was nothing in comparison with the
$50,000,000 purchase consummated by the United States Steel Cor-
poration in 1907. This giant in the iron world took over the holdings
of the Tennessee Coal, Iron, and Railroad Company (the name was
retained), which was sailing in financial straits and was likely to be
wrecked on the rocks of low prices and poor markets.

The Tennessee company had holdings in coal lands on the Cumberland Plateau north of Sewanee. Its success was tied up with the
Nashville, Chattanooga, and St. Louis Railroad which transported its
coal to Chattanooga and Nashville. It entered the Birmingham field
in 1886, "perhaps the most significant event in Southern coal and
iron records of (that) interesting year." Much capital was borrowed
from New York houses to finance the Birmingham deal, and by 1888
the majority of stock was held by bankers and steel men of New
York. The entrance of the Steel Trust into the Birmingham field was

sanctioned by President Roosevelt, even though he was at that time
wielding his "big stick" against the great American trust, because he
considered that the taking over of the Tennessee Company's interests
was the only preventive of a financial panic in the iron industry of the
South which might indeed affect the financial stability of the whole
country. The year 1907 is considered the greatest of all years, to date,
in the history of the iron and steel industry of Birmingham. The
dominance of this subsidiary of the United States Steel Corporation
has been indicated in previous paragraphs.*

Until the "Pittsburgh plus" plan was abolished by the Steel Trust
upon the recommendation of the Federal Trade Commission, the
Birmingham district was not able to profit from its admirable geographic situation as regards the distribution of the three essential raw
products: ore, fuel, and flux—a situation that, in so far as natural
conditions control, makes possible the production of iron and steel
more cheaply than anywhere else in the world. The cheapest place
until the Birmingham resources were opened up was in the Cleveland
coal and iron district of northeastern England (Yorkshire), where
the average haul to assemble the essential ingredients is about twenty
miles.

The Pittsburgh plus plan, in the words of a member of the Federal
Trade Commission, operated in this way: "The United States Steel
Corporation's price at Chicago, which is a Pittsburgh plus price, is
made up by taking the price at which the particular products are
sold at Pittsburgh, say $30 a ton, and to this is added that amount
which is equivalent to what the freight charge on the product from
Pittsburgh to Chicago would be, as if the products were actually
shipped from Pittsburgh, or $7.60 per ton, making a total of $37.60.
The Chicago steel user, therefore, who buys steel from the Corporation's mill in the city of Chicago, must pay $7.60 a ton more than
his Pittsburgh competitor pays. In like fashion, the Duluth steel user
must pay $43.20 per ton for the steel he buys from the Corporation's
mills at Duluth, while his Pittsburgh competitor pays only $30 per
ton, because the Duluth man must pay the imaginary freight charge
on the goods which never were shipped from Pittsburgh to Duluth, or
$13.20 per ton."

Though Birmingham is not mentioned in the above lucid description
of the operation of the plan, this city could be substituted for either

---

* Ethel Armes, *The Story of Coal and Iron in Alabama*, 157, 420; Walter B.
Jones, *The Mineral Resources of Alabama*, Bulletin 28, Geological Survey of
Alabama, 153, 154.

Chicago or Duluth. In all three cities the United States Steel Corporation has iron plants.

The Tennessee Coal, Iron, and Railroad Company, a part of the Steel Trust, was benefited by any profit accruing from such monopolistic control, but all industries and the public in general in the Birmingham district were harmed. The plan stifled all attempts at competition and prevented the lowering of iron and steel prices that often results from free competition. Nearness to Birmingham and the natural advantages of cheap production there meant nothing to Southern consumers. Their iron and steel cost them as much as if they purchased them in Pittsburgh, which has to transport its iron more than a thousand miles and its coke some fifty to sixty miles.

At present, as we have seen, the Birmingham region (which may be thought to include Gadsden) dominates the iron and steel industry of the South. When, however, the high-grade ores of Alabama are exhausted and low-grade ores come to play a part in the industry, there are a score or more localities that will see an active iron industry. On the sites of many old furnaces long since rusted to nothing and forgotten there will arise new creations in steel and stone to serve mankind.

CHAPTER XIV

FOREST RESOURCES AND FOREST INDUSTRIES

INTRODUCTION

Before the farmer and the lumberman began their labors in the South, forests, as shown in a previous chapter, covered the entire area from approximately the 30-inch isohyet eastward to the Atlantic. Two great commercial types of forests are recognized, namely, Southern pine (longleaf, shortleaf, and loblolly) and hardwood. See Figure 23 for the distribution of the forests of the South and leading species in each region. About 150 species of commercial timber grow in the South. Though some species are very scarce, every one is being put to some use; and with the developments that are going on in the industrial world there will come greater demands for special woods for particular uses.

THE SOFTWOODS AND SOFTWOOD INDUSTRIES OF THE SOUTH

The commercial exploitation of the hardwood forests is an activity of our day. Throughout the history of the South, Colonial and after, however, the Southern pine forests have been yielding a revenue to the people. There are several reasons for this. Pine is much preferred to hardwoods in general construction. Until the invention of the admirable woodworking machinery of our day, hand saws, planes, adzes, and broad axes made the finishing of wood for building construction, furniture, implements, bridges, vessels, and what not, even with soft wood like pine, very laborious. The conifers, pines, have in this country furnished fully 80 per cent of the lumber for commercial use. Then, too, the coastal rivers that crossed the pine belt furnished the cheapest form of transportation known to man, particularly where there was a current. From the Southern pine was obtained crude turpentine, from which by a simple distillation process, spirits of turpentine, pitch, and rosin could be extracted. A much cruder process was used for the manufacture of tar. These several products, because of their high commercial value in comparison to weight, could, commercially speaking, stand a transatlantic journey to the shipyards and paint shops of Europe, even in those days when ships were small and an overseas voyage was a matter of many weeks. The deep water of the estuaries made it possible for ocean vessels to load overseas cargoes almost in the heart of the forests.

Sequent Exploitation of the Softwood Forests

Forest exploitation began in Virginia very early. The pine was not a conspicuous species in Virginia's forests, being confined to the Chesapeake Bay region, and even there it was (and is) mixed with hardwoods. The naval-stores industry, therefore, never thrived as in North Carolina. There are, however, many records of naval stores exportation.*

From the works of John Smith it is learned that the English Commercial Company, under whose enterprise Virginia was settled, very early arranged to establish sawmills in the colony. Captain Newport who brought over the Second Supply had with him Polish and Dutch millwrights whose work was to construct sawmills to prepare timber for home construction and ship building. Trained workmen from Hamburg were brought in 1619.

Very little can be found regarding lumbering and the manufacture of lumber and forest products in the South for the first century or two. The lists of exports reveal a few facts; and from these, inferences may be drawn. Jefferson in his *Notes on the State of Virginia*, in listing the exports of the state for 1782, mentions masts, planks, scantling, shingles (valued at $67,000), and tar, pitch, and turpentine ($40,000).†

We know that the exportation of naval stores began from North Carolina very soon after settlers pushed from Virginia to the borders of the Sound. But the active center of the industry remained near the coastal rivers and east of the Cape Fear River until far into the first half of the nineteenth century.‡

As for South Carolina, Governor Johnson in his report to the Royal Government, September 17, 1708, writes, "We are sufficiently provided with timber for masts and yards of several sizes, both pine and cypress, which may be exported very reasonably and supplied at all

---

* Philip Bruce, *Economic History of Virginia in the Seventeenth Century*, II, 431.

† Thomas Jefferson, *Notes on the State of Virginia* (First "Hot-Pressed" Edition), 1801, 328.

‡ C. S. Sargent, "Report on Forests of North America," *Report of Tenth Census*, 1880, 516.

times of the year."* In 1724, 52,000 barrels of pitch, tar, and turpentine were exported from South Carolina.†

In Georgia the early settlers cleared land only in the southeast and eastern part of the state, as the population maps show, until after the removal of the Indians. By 1830 the frontier had been pushed to the western border of the state on the Piedmont, covered largely by hardwood forests, but the pine lands of the Coastal Plain had hardly been invaded. Even in 1840 the southern third of Georgia was thinly settled.

Commercial lumbering had not yet begun in Alabama, Mississippi, and Louisiana, by 1830, and Arkansas was just being settled. Kentucky and Tennessee had nearly 700,000 people each and hence had made great slaughter of their forests; but little timber had been cut for sale, except locally.‡

The census report of 1840 gives us the first official data on the forest industry in the South (Table XXII).

TABLE XXII

SAWMILLS, FOREST PRODUCTS, AND FURNITURE MANUFACTURES, 1840[1]

	Number of Mills	Value of Lumber	Barrels of Tar, Pitch, and Turpentine	Value of Furniture
Maryland................	430	$226,977	...	$305,360
Virginia.................	1,987	538,092	5,809	289,391
North Carolina...........	1,056	506,766	593,451	35,002
South Carolina...........	746	537,684	735	28,115
Georgia.................	677	114,050	153	49,780
Alabama................	524	169,008	197	41,671
Mississippi..............	309	192,794	2,248	34,450
Louisiana...............	139	66,106	2,233	2,300
Tennessee...............	977	217,606	3,336	279,580
Kentucky...............	718	130,329	700	273,350
Florida (Terr.)...........	65	20,346		
Arkansas................	88	176,617	36	20,293

[1] *Report of Sixth Census*, 1840, 227, 239, 247, 251, 257, 261, 265, 269, 275, 281, 399, 408, 409; also in *Hunt's Merchant Magazine*, IX, 1843, 137, 239, Summary.
    Softwoods not differentiated from hardwoods in this table.

The data show that Virginia, South Carolina, and North Carolina

---

* Edward McCrady, *South Carolina under the Proprietary Government, 1620-1719*, 478.

† Edward McCrady, *South Carolina under the Royal Government, 1719-1776*, 60.

‡ Statistical Atlas, 1914, Census Bureau, 7; *Statistical Abstract*, 1928, 6.

were the most active states in the manufacture of lumber, on the basis of value of product. The total value of lumber for the South was $2,967,000 and for the United States about $13,000,000. The seat of the naval stores industry in 1840 was still in North Carolina, more than 95 per cent of the products coming from that one state. Maryland, Virginia, Tennessee, and Kentucky, each with large acreage of hardwoods, were the leaders in furniture manufacturing.

By 1849 the total value of lumber had reached $12,442,202; and by 1859, $24,817,736. In 1850 it is reported that the South was producing 13.6 per cent of the forest products of the country.*

The relative cut of the Southern States and the number of sawmills in 1880 are shown in Table XXIII.

TABLE XXIII

THE LUMBER INDUSTRY IN 1880 IN THE SOUTH[1]

	Establish-ments	Lumber Cut Bd. Ft. M.
Georgia	655	451,788
Texas	324	328,968
Virginia	907	315,939
Kentucky	670	305,684
Tennessee	755	302,673
Alabama	354	251,851
Florida	135	247,627
North Carolina	776	421,822
South Carolina	420	185,772
West Virginia	472	180,112
Arkansas	319	172,503
Mississippi	295	168,747
Louisiana	175	133,472
Maryland	369	123,336

[1] *Compendium of Tenth Census*, 1880, Part 2, 1,162. Both hardwoods and softwoods included.

The lumber industry in 1880 was widely distributed in the South, but the total cut was only 13.8 per cent of the total for the country.† Some of the older states, like Virginia and North Carolina, ranked well with the newly settled Gulf States.

It is not so easy to trace the migration of the lumber industry in the Southern States as it is in the North. In the North, migration in general was northward in New England and westward across New

* R. C. Bryant in H. T. Warshow, *Representative Industries of the United States*, 477; R. A. Johnson, in *Manufacturers Record*, LXXXVI, Part 2, South's Development, 314.

† R. C. Bryant, *op. cit.*, 477.

York and Pennsylvania and on to the Lakes States. Lumbering operation began in southern Michigan long before the middle of the nineteenth century and spread northward and on into Wisconsin and Minnesota. Between 1879 and 1889 most of the lumber of the country
was cut in the Lakes States, 34.7 per cent of the total of the United
States.* The movement was fairly orderly and rapid, for the rapidly
increasing population in the Northeastern States and especially in
Ohio, Indiana, and Illinois (these three in the hardwood forests)
made a rapidly increasing demand for pine lumber. In no given region
did forests replant themselves and reach maturity before the advancing agricultural frontier swept on and the region passed from a lumbering to an agricultural régime.

Rate of Reproduction of Southern Forests

In the South the agricultural frontiers in the pine belt moved more
slowly, and because of the lower population density and larger farms,
or plantations, the agriculturist did not make such a clean sweep as
he did in the North. Many woodlots were left. Moreover, the forests
reproduced themselves more rapidly than in the Northern States. The
migratory type of agriculture meant a constant abandoning of farm
land and its reversion to the forest state. It takes but thirty to forty
years in the South for pine seedlings to reach maturity, suitable for
commercial lumbering. It is because of this rapid growth that the
lumber industry has been active so long. In Georgia, the youngest
of the South Atlantic colonies, for example, sufficient time has elapsed
since its first settlement for forests to have reproduced themselves
five or six times. Some of the early advocates of forest conservation
did not realize the rapidity with which forests reproduce themselves.
An early conservationist, who wrote of the Georgia forests in 1859,
asserted that the forest crop was not like cotton and rice for it takes
"centuries for the crop to mature and when the forest is once culled
over the crop is forever gathered, for we are altogether too fast a
people to think of waiting a hundred years for another crop." He was
of the opinion that it would take 300 to 400 years to grow a tree large
enough for a mast.

This constant renewal of the pine is the most astonishing fact about
Southern forests. In some forest regions the existing stand if removed
is not followed by trees of the same species. In the hardwood areas,

---

* *Idem.*

for example, if the beech and maple are removed completely and fires sweep over the region so as to burn the humus of the soil, many stages will need to be passed through in plant succession before conditions are again suitable for a natural growth of beech and maple. But the Southern pine is a primitive type. As its evolutionary history (paleobotany) shows, it is a much earlier and more generalized type of plant than the broad-leaved trees. It has not been weakened in its ability to cope with adverse conditions by becoming specialized, i.e., adapted to some particular habitat. It can and does occupy young subnormal soils, and thus is a "rough and ready" type wholly unlike most hardwoods which require mature or nearly mature soils (see Chapter II) for active reforestation. If seed trees are present and the soil does not wash too rapidly for the sprouting plant to get a root hold, longleaf pines will be followed by longleaf pines, or at least by some one of the Southern pines, as one may readily observe almost anywhere in the pine belt.

Fires and ranging pinewoods hogs are the worst enemies of the young pines in their first year of growth. These conclusions are based on the reported results of studies carried on in Louisiana. Two lots were allowed to be reseeded by nature. One was carefully protected from fires and grazing animals. The other was treated as pine forests are usually treated in the South, that is, grazed and fired each year.

Harper, who has made studies of forests and forest conditions in all the East Gulf States, is of the opinion, however, that forest fires do not harm the pines two or three years old or older, because the bark is thick and non-combustible and therefore is not burned much by the blazing grass and herbage on the forest floor, and that if during two or three years there should be no fires reproduction would take place.* Whether the pines are harmed or not depends, probably, on the quantity of litter on the forest floor and thus the intensity of the flames.

Hu Maxwell, writing in "The South; The Nation's Greatest Asset," in 1910, says, "The long leaf pine (*Pinus palustrus*) is in more real danger of extermination than any other important tree of the United States. It is a noble specimen of the vegetable kingdom; but like the Indian who is a noble specimen of the animal kingdom, it seems unable to thrive among civilized surroundings. Few seedlings are coming on and the primeval stands are disappearing. Short-leaf, loblolly, and

---

* Roland M. Harper, "The Natural Resources of Georgia," *Bulletin of University of Georgia*, XXX, No. 3, 1930, 82, 83.

Cuban pine (*Pinus heterophylla*) hold their ground and if given half a chance are perfect missionaries to push into new lands."*

THE SOUTHERN PINE INDUSTRY TODAY

It is only in the last decades that the lumber industry in the South has been stimulated by the active demands of outside markets. Hewn lumber, masts, and naval stores, as has been stated previously, have long been exported to the Northern States and Europe. Until about 1880 to 1890 the chief market for Southern forest products was the South or overseas; but with the decline of the forest resources of the Lakes States, the Southern forests came to be the chief source of lumber for the rapidly growing North. The decline of the forests in the Lakes States brought Northern lumbermen to the Gulf Coast forests and rapid commercial exploitation of Southern forests was begun. After a time, when cheap railroad rates with the Pacific Northwest were maintained, Pacific coast lumber came to compete with that from the South, and thus to a certain degree relieve the intensive demand on Southern forests.

The rise of the lumber industry in the South is shown in Table XXIV.

TABLE XXIV

PERCENTAGE OF LUMBER CUT OF THE UNITED STATES
PRODUCED IN THE SOUTH[1]

	Per Cent for the Country
1850	13.6
1870	9.4
1880	13.8
1890	20.3
1899	31.7
1909	44.9
1919	46.6
1926	46.2
1929	47

[1] R. C. Bryant, "The Lumber Industry," in H. T. Warshow, *Representative Industries of the United States*, 476, 477. Data from R. V. Reynolds and Arthur Pierson, *Professional Paper*, 1,119, United States Department of Agriculture, 1923, 62 pages; *Statistical Abstract*, 1935, 662.

LUMBER CUT OF UNITED STATES, IN LAST DECADE

The lumber production in the South for the last decade or more has been in excess of 40 per cent of the total of the country. More

___
* Published by the *Manufacturers' Record*.

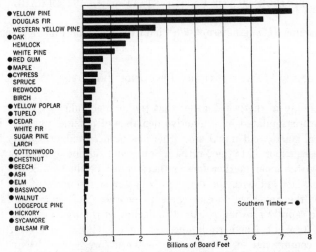

Fɪɢ. 122.—Lumber Cut of the United States, by Species, 1929.

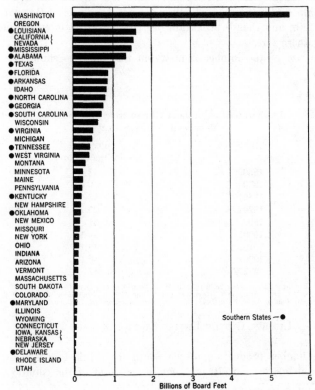

Fɪɢ. 123.—Lumber Cut of the United States, by States, 1929.

than 31 per cent of the total lumber cut of the United States in 1929
was the yellow pine of the South. Douglas fir, next in importance,
furnished 24 per cent of the total, and western yellow pine about 8
per cent (Fig. 122).*

Washington and Oregon are the leading two states (Fig. 123), but
Mississippi and Louisiana stand third and fourth. Table XXV, Column
I, indicates clearly the most active lumbering centers of the South
today; and Column II, the timber resources in 1926.

TABLE XXV

PRODUCTION OF LUMBER IN SOUTHERN STATES, 1929[1],
AND RESOURCES IN 1926

	I Production, 1929 Millions of Feet	II Resources in 1926 Millions of Feet
Mississippi.........	2,670	81,200
Louisiana..........	2,232	30,000
Alabama...........	2,059	50,000
Texas..............	1,452	38,000
Arkansas...........	1,348	76,200
Georgia............	1,386	42,000
North Carolina.....	1,202	30,000
South Carolina......	1,068	28,300
Florida............	1,137	48,400
Tennessee..........	714	65,000
Virginia............	709	?
West Virginia.......	633	47,600
Kentucky..........	339	37,400
Oklahoma..........	200	12,000
Maryland..........	55	8,800

[1] *Statistical Abstract*, 1932, 676; B. A. Johnson, "Forestry and Lumbering in the South," *Manufacturers' Record*, LXXXVI, Pt. 2, South's Development, 318. Both softwood and hardwood included, mostly softwood for states of Lower South.

The states producing more than a thousand million feet a year each
are the Gulf Coastal Plain states, and with the exception of Arkansas
the lumbering is almost entirely in the pine forests of the Coastal
Plain. It is the interstream forested areas reached by log railroads
that run to sawmills or to railroads doing general traffic business that
are being cut. The good roads constructed in these states in recent
years have made the use of the motor truck possible in the transportation of logs to the sawmill, or lumber from the small portable sawmill
placed in the forest.

Some of the largest mills in the world are to be found in the pine
belt of the South today. These large, well-equipped, substantially built

* *Statistical Abstract*, 1932, 675.

mills require immense forest areas to feed their greedy saws. It is
largely the railroad that connects the sawmill with the forest areas.
Many of the larger companies have adopted a forestry policy that
insures for their mills a perpetual supply of timber. The South today
then has reached the last and final stage in lumbering and is advancing from the exploitive stage to a forest-crop stage. Only a beginning is being made in this latter.

THE FUTURE OF LUMBERING IN THE SOUTH

How long will the lumbering industry last in the South? That depends on our present resources, the rate of exploitation, the rate of
growth, and the rate of adoption of the forest-crop system. With so
many factors involved no one can predict. Prophets have arisen now
and then during the last few decades warning people in general, and
the lumbermen in particular, of the impending danger of timber exhaustion. A few figures may aid us somewhat in formulating a rough
answer to the above question.

TABLE XXVI
AREA OF FORESTS IN THE SOUTH
THOUSANDS OF ACRES[1]

	Original Area	Present Total	Saw Timber Virgin	Area Growing
Central Forest Belt[2] only partly in the South............................	170,560	31,901	7,600	24,301
South Atlantic and East Gulf.......	170,240	46,200	18,300	27,900
Lower Mississippi (Includes Texas)..	128,400	41,035	20,835	20,200

[1] *Statistical Abstract*, 1931, 749, data from "Forest Service."
[2] Ohio, Indiana, Illinois, Iowa, Missouri, Eastern Kansas, Eastern Nebraska, Kentucky, Tennessee, and West Virginia.

A more detailed statement, though probably not to be considered
as official, is presented in Table XXVII.

These data on the present forested area include virgin, cut-over,
and idle lands, capable of growing timber but needing replanting.*

From statistical tables furnished by the Forestry Bureau it appears
that the stand of saw timber in the South Atlantic and East Gulf
States and the Lower Mississippi (this does not include Kentucky,
West Virginia, and Tennessee) is 501,485 million board feet, and that,
in 1926, 15,572 million board feet were cut. Leaving out of account our

---

* J. H. Platt, "The Lumber and Forest Products Industry of the South,"
Annals of the American Academy of Social and Political Science, CLIII-CLV,
63-75.

TABLE XXVII

TOTAL ORIGINAL AND PRESENT FORESTED AREAS, IN ACRES

State	Original Forested Acres	Present Forested Acres
Alabama	32,000,000	20,000,000
Arkansas	32,000,000	21,500,000
Florida	28,800,000	19,000,000
Georgia	36,500,000	20,000,000
Kentucky	24,300,000	9,400,000
Louisiana	25,600,000	17,400,000
Maryland	5,800,000	2,200,000
Mississippi	28,800,000	17,000,000
North Carolina	30,100,000	18,000,000
Oklahoma	12,000,000	8,000,000
South Carolina	18,000,000	10,000,000
Tennessee	25,600,000	12,000,000
Texas	30,000,000	15,000,000
Virginia	25,000,000	12,000,000
West Virginia	15,400,000	8,500,000

annual growth, our forest resources would last about 32 years, provided the annual cut remains the same. It takes about 30 years in the pine region of the South to grow a tree to commercial timber maturity. The total annual growth of saw timber is placed at 4,180 million. At the end of 32 years, the accrued annual growth, based on the figures for 1926, would keep the saw mills running more than 8 years. We are cutting each year, however, about 4 times as much as we are growing, according to figures presented by the Forest Service about 1921.* Thus the growth increment is being made on a constantly decreasing total stand. With no widespread attempts on the part of the states and lumber companies to provide for a permanent supply of timber, our forests, if the present rate of cutting continues, can hardly last longer than 35 or 40 years. But the present rate will hardly continue, for prices are constantly mounting and standards of construction, increasing wealth, and desire for fireproof construction material is forcing a relatively increasing use of brick, stone, and cement. Steel and cement are now the chief materials in bridge construction. Steel is being used in office furniture. Moreover, the forest conservation movement is gaining ground. Many states have forestry departments and have laws encouraging the planting of trees; and since about 1932 the Federal Government has begun the reforestation of marginal lands that it has acquired from the states or by purchase. Forest economists assert, however, that such forests cannot compete with those naturally

---

* This figure is disputed by lumbermen.

planted and grown so long as the latter are numerous enough to dominate the lumber market.

Fully 70 per cent of the lumber sawed is not reworked by further manufacturing in the South. The South must therefore continue to supply lumber, but it should not be content with supplying it in the rough form. The manufacture of rough lumber adds but little, comparatively, to the cost of raw material, labor, and capital involved. Northern factories return the lumber in the form of furniture, agricultural implements, musical instruments, etc., at prices enhanced several times. The profits of this complete or secondary manufacture are far greater than from primary fabrication. This advanced manufacture should all be done in the South.

The degree of development of an industry is always, or nearly always, a reflection of the general economic conditions. We can hardly expect manufacturing to be in the advanced stages, in which beauty and careful and painstaking workmanship characterize the output of the factories, in a region in the first stages of industrial development. Primary, rough manufacturing tends to dominate in regions in the primitive stages of industrial development; but it is perfectly possible for man to modify this tendency if he has the will. The natural ingenuity of the American, and the daring and enterprise, combined with the piecework system and the wide use of machines in American factories, enables any factory owner to develop in a short time a body of skilled workers. It will be some time before Southern workmen will turn out the beautifully finished furniture, for example, of the Grand Rapids craftsmen, but there is a wide market for low and medium-grade furniture which Southern factories can and do produce. High-grade furniture is being produced in the South in increasing amounts. Hardwood industries will be discussed in the next section.

THE HARDWOODS AND THE HARDWOOD INDUSTRIES
OF THE SOUTH

The original hardwood forests of the South had, by far, a larger acreage than the Southern pine. The Forest Service recognizes four types of hardwood forests:

1. *The oak-hickory,* largely oak in the South, that covers about half of eastern Texas and Oklahoma and a small area in northwestern Arkansas.

2. *The oak-pine,* which has a large acreage in eastern Texas and western Louisiana and which covers about a third of Arkansas and the higher lands of the East Gulf and South Atlantic states. The

oak predominates on the lower lands, the pines on the higher and drier. In Virginia it covers both Coastal Plain and Piedmont.

3. *The oak-chestnut-yellow poplar* forest of Tennessee, Kentucky, West Virginia, the Great Appalachian Valley, the Southern Appalachian Mountains, and the Blue Ridge. Within this forest area on the highest portion of the numerous peaks there are spruce like those of Canada.

4. *River bottom hardwoods and cypress.* In most of these areas there are a vast number of species. The oak-hickory area of Texas is largely oak, but at the other extreme is the great mixture to be found in the oak-chestnut-yellow poplar forest.

Among the hardwoods, in general, are:

1. The *ash*, of which there are seven species of commercial importance. About two-thirds of the supply of eastern United States is second growth. Its chief use is for handles, spokes, and cooperage. The supply is decreasing rapidly, and the annual cut is declining.

2. The *chestnut*, valuable for the tannin in its wood, telephone and telegraph and electric wire poles, and, to a small degree, for its nuts. The trees were most numerous in the Southern Appalachian Highlands, and it is here that one found the most beautiful stands. Mature trees ran from 3 to 5 feet in diameter—some to 7—and had a height of 60 to 90 and even 120 feet. In the Southern Appalachian Highlands chestnut once formed about 25 per cent of the total hardwood stand. The total stand was estimated as 15 billion board feet. In 1909 production reached its maximum for the chestnut—664 million board feet— from which time the cut has been declining year by year. The chestnut blight which has swept southward from the Middle Atlantic States is destroying the bulk of the remaining trees. Within a few years the lumberman and the blight will have about exterminated the species.*

A few tanneries and a few tannin extract plants in or near the forests utilize much of the cut. The extract plants take bark or wood, green or dead, and, by "hogging" (cutting into chips) and boiling it in water under pressure, extract the tannin. The liquor drawn off from the boilers is concentrated to a thick liquid or dried to a powder. In some plants the chips coming from the boiling after the liquor is drawn off are used to make coarse paper, building paper, coarse kraft, and corrugated cardboard.

3. *Hickory* has long been a symbol for toughness, elasticity, great strength, and, where properly used, durability. Its chief use is for the spokes and rims of vehicle wheels, for golf sticks, and handles,

---

* Saplings are now springing up from the roots of some of the old trees but these will never be the beautiful specimens that the mother trees were.

worked up in small woodworking plants throughout the hardwood area in Mississippi and Ohio basins. It rarely grows in dense stands but is scattered widely through the forests. It is both a Northern and a Southern tree. Most of the stands of hickory today are in the South. It was estimated, as of 1920, that the stand in the Lower Mississippi forests was about 5.20 billion board feet; in the South Atlantic and East Gulf States 3.2; and in the Central States (largely in the South) 6.8.

4. *Red Gum* is predominantly a Southern hardwood. The total stand is estimated to be in the

Lower Mississippi	26.9	billion board feet
South Atlantic and East Gulf	13.4	billion board feet
Central Forest	3.7	billion board feet
Middle Atlantic	.17	billion board feet

It is being much used in late years in furniture, solid and veneer, and for boxes and slack cooperage. It serves as a substitute for both mahogany and walnut, for the core of veneered pieces, and for veneer itself. If stained brown it is sold in the less expensive furniture as "walnut"; if red or brown, "mahogany"; by special treatment it becomes satin walnut or Circassian walnut, and some pieces having peculiar coloring and grain are sold to the public as "figured red gum." All in all, red gum is a versatile wood, particularly in the hands of some furniture makers and dealers. It has honest merits, however, that the honest furniture dealers are not ashamed to advertise.

The trees grow to 2 or 3 feet in diameter and a mature height of 80 to 120 feet. It is a slow grower like most hardwoods. It takes 50 to 60 years to produce a tree 12 to 16 inches in diameter.

When hardwood is plentiful, red gum was frowned upon as a timber tree because of the tendency to warp in seasoning. But this difficulty has been overcome by specially devised methods, and, in number of cubic feet, more red gum is used in furniture today than any other wood.

5. *Maples*. Several species of maples have commercial value. The most important is sugar or hard maple, but silver maple and red maple are also used. Tennessee, Kentucky, West Virginia, and the mountains and the Piedmont of Virginia and North Carolina are the leading source regions. The chief use is for flooring and furniture, shoe lasts, and musical instruments. Bird's-eye and curly maple growths, the result of accidents in the life of a tree, are much valued in furniture.

The habitat range of these trees is largely in New England and the

Middle Atlantic States where the largest stands are today. The South has less than 20 per cent of the stand of our country.

6. *Oak* has been for a long time the most important hardwood in our country, largely because of its abundance, its strength, and its beauty. Quarter-sawed oak, in which the medullary rays of the wood are displayed on the surface in a wide variety of patterns, is the most expensive and the most sought for in furniture and interior "trim." There are about 50 species of oak, botanically; but commercially these are thrown into two great groups, white oak and red oak. The Upper South is in the center of the white oak region. Memphis and Nashville are the leading hardwood centers of the country.

The total stand of oak timber in our country in 1920 was estimated at 157 billion board feet, distributed as follows:

Central Forest Area	65	billion board feet
Lower Mississippi	49.5	billion board feet
South Atlantic	28	billion board feet
Northern States	14.5	billion board feet

7. *Yellow poplar*, or *tulip tree*, is one of the less important trees, in quantity of stand, of the Southern hardwood forests. It is a *soft* wood, but is not classed as a commercial soft wood. It grows to great size, 6 to 8 feet in diameter and from 100 to 160 feet high; and because its boll is generally free from defects it produces boards and planks of great width and length. Because it is durable, takes paint and varnish readily, and is light in weight and tough, it has a wide variety of uses—for sash, doors, siding, boxes and crates, etc.

Similar in character of wood and size of tree is the cottonwood or Carolina poplar.

Among the other hardwoods of the Southern States, of commercial value, are the cherry, elm, tupelo gums (black, water, and sour gums are included in the trade), and black walnut.

The hardwood forests serve man in many other ways. They supply interior trim for his houses, and to some extent the exterior, his furniture, the wood of his implements and tools, vehicles, baseball bats, golf sticks, and innumerable other objects. They are the chief element of beauty and attractiveness in his recreation grounds; and in the South where lakes on the uplands are wanting, they serve as regulators of the flow of streams. These latter considerations have prompted Federal and State governments to establish forest reserves and parks here and there in the South.

The creating of national forests in the South has been a much more difficult task than in the West, where all that was needed was for

Congress to set aside a given tract, exempt it from entry, and provide for its supervision. This cost little or nothing, for grazing permits and the sale of forest products more than meet the expenses of road building and supervision. In the Southern States nearly all the public lands had been preempted by the time that the establishment of national forests was thought necessary.

Sawmills, planing mills, flooring mills, furniture factories, tanneries, tannin extract plants, spoke, handle, and golf-stick plants, and cooperage plants are found here and there in cities, towns, and mere villages throughout the hardwood area.

A. E. P.

Fig. 124.—A Street of Furniture Factories in High Point, North Carolina.
Factories are found on several streets. The numerous automobiles of the factory workers—this is distant from the trading center—is evidence enough that the workers are well paid.

The sawmills, planing mills, and flooring mills are mostly in the larger cities, because, being large-scale enterprises, they draw their raw products and seek markets from and in large areas. Furniture-making on a large scale is limited in its localization to only a few sites. High Point, North Carolina, and Chattanooga, Nashville, and Memphis, in Tennessee, are the more important centers. High Point, called "the Grand Rapids of the South," is the leading furniture-manufacturing center (Fig. 124). Its furniture is sold largely in the Grand Rapids market. The total output for the South, however, is only a half to a third that of the Northern States.

There are excellent opportunities in the South for the growth of the furniture industry.

There is also an opportunity for the further development of hard-wood distilling plants, yielding acetic acid, wood alcohol, wood tar from which a variety of products may be further separated, and charcoal, although synthetic products as substitutes for some of these may come to be produced more cheaply than the natural.

The South for many years has been an important source for railroad cross ties, oak (about 50 per cent), and Southern pine being the chief timbers for this purpose. Cypress, chestnut, beech, and maple are used in small quantities. The oak-tie regions of the South are the Highland Rim, the Cumberland Plateau, the Ozark Plateau, and eastern Texas.

NAVAL STORES

For more than three centuries tar, pitch, turpentine, and rosin, called naval stores because in the days of wooden sailing vessels the chief use for these commodities was in the navies and merchant marines, have been produced in the South in greater quantities than in any other forest region in the world. Only tar and pitch really should be called naval stores, but the term later on came to include turpentine and rosin. In recent decades the uses of these forest products in industry have greatly multiplied. Most of the distilled turpentine now finds its way into paints and varnishes, to thin these liquids and "cut" the solid matter. In varnishes it dissolves the resins (amber, copal, and others). The thinned liquid penetrates the wood, if it be wood that is being coated, and the turpentine evaporates readily, thus aiding in the drying.

The extensive use of lacquers is reducing the demand on turpentine. But this is offset by other demands such as a solvent for rubber or caoutchouc. Turpentine has long been utilized in the manufacture of cotton and woolen print goods, to prevent the running of colors.

Rosin, one of the resins made from crude turpentine by distillation, finds its chief application in the making of soap, paper, oilcloth, linoleum, printing inks, roofing material, and other products. Japan drier for paints is a metallic salt of resin acids. Rosin oil with lamp-black is a very excellent black paint. Ceramic enamels include various resins among their ingredients; some, rosin. One of the important applications of rosin is to size paper, that it may take ink without too much spreading. The distillation of rosin yields many very useful products.

What is needed greatly in the naval-stores industry—really an out-grown name, as just shown—is chemical research comparable to that which has been going on in the petroleum industry for many years. Crude turpentine being an organic compound undoubtedly has a host of by-product derivatives that may be isolated. New uses may be found for these derivatives. The production of turpentine and rosin is not a permanent industry, but certainly its life is as long as that of the petroleum industry. Chemical research might even extend its life through the discovery of synthetic products as substitutes.

Tar and pitch in the earlier days, as previously shown, were much-used products on ships. The term "Jack Tar" comes down from the wooden-ship days, and the title "the Tarheel State," the nickname for North Carolina, from the great activity of its people in the production of tar. The making of tar and pitch was a forest industry, a crude form of manufacture. Tar is an extract from pine wood, obtained by "baking" in pits. Thus tar-making means the destruction of the forest trees. Pine logs in former days were sawed and split into pieces convenient to handle and the pieces stood on end, close packed in a pit, forming a conical heat, and covered with turf. The wood was fired, the combustion being checked by lack of air, and the pitch in the wood is "fried out." It was black in color because of the carbon in it. All gases, the more volatile products of the pine, were lost. The pit has been quite generally replaced by steel ovens in which all vapors are saved and all products are clean.

Probably no other industry in America remained unchanged for so long in its methods as that of the naval stores. It is only in recent decades that the box method of tapping the trees has been replaced by the gutter and cup method, patented in 1868. It has taken a long time to induce turpentine orchardists to adopt the improved and more economical method. Although no figures are available, it is probable that at present the number of cups in use exceed the number of boxes, and that cups have been hung on 75 per cent of the trees tapped.*

The longleaf pine is the most copious producer of the resin known as crude turpentine, the base for all the naval-stores products. But other pines produce resin in fair quantities. The slash pine of the South is a heavy producer, but not so heavy as the loblolly. Northern pines in both United States and northern Europe produce naval stores. One of the reasons assigned for the planting of the English colony in Virginia was that here naval stores could be obtained and thus free the mother country from the monopoly held by "Northern Crowns" in Europe.

* A. W. Schorger and H. S. Betts, *The Naval Stores Industry*, Bulletin **229**, contributions from Forest Service, United States Department of Agriculture.

In the Public Record office in London, England, there is preserved "Instructions for such things as are to be sent from Virginia" that makes mention of "hard pitche," "tarre," "turpentine," and "rosen." Instructions are given the leaders in the colony as to the methods of tapping the trees. "Pyne trees, or Firre trees," it states, "are to be wounded within a yard of the ground, or boare a hoal with an agar the third pte into the tree, and lett yt runne into anye thing that may receye the same, and that wch yessues owte wilbe Turpentine

A. E. P.

FIG. 125.—The Improved Method of Tapping the Longleaf Pine.
The galvanized iron or burnt clay container has replaced the "box" cut into the dead heartwood of the tree.

worthe 18 £ Tonne. When the tree begenneth to runne softely yet is to be stopped up agayne for preserveinge the tree."

Captain Newport carried the first shipment of naval stores, so far as records show, to England. Until the Revolutionary War encouragement was given the industry. Bounties were granted at times, prices set, and standards established. In 1720, for example, encouragement was given "such persons as will [would] take up and improve such piney and remote lands for the increase of his Majesty's Quit Rents and for rendering the Colony yet more useful and advantageous to Great Britain by supplying the aforementioned commodity, so necessary for his Majesty's navy and the increase of shipping and navigation." In Colonial days, and later even, when specie was scarce, pitch and tar were legalized media of exchange.

Whether the instructions given the early colonist of Virginia regarding the tapping of the pines were ever tried is unknown, but it is known that in very early days the box method was worked out.

The new method, the gutter and cup (Fig. 125), or simply the cup method, does not require so large a wound or blaze as the box method; and if the cups are properly hung little "scrape" forms, nearly all the resin that exudes reaches the cup, and thus much turpentine, which with the box system was evaporated, is saved.

The end sought in forest conservation in turpentining is "pure gum and minimum damage to the timber." It has been proved that better and more turpentine and resin are secured by the cup system than the box, and the tree is damaged much less. Moreover, the fire hazard is not so great (Fig. 125). Care is always taken in all well-run orchards to clear away grass and rubbish for several feet around the trees to prevent fire, if it starts, from reaching the exposed resinous-coated surface of the trees and the cups. From experiments carried on in Georgia in 1902 it was shown that the excess of dip and scrape in percentage of gallons from cupped trees *versus* boxed trees was:*

> First year............ 23.43 per cent
> Second year.......... 5.51 per cent
> Third year........... 58.58 per cent
> Fourth year.......... 66.29 per cent

Turpentining is a migratory industry and a dying one. In 1849 North Carolina produced 86.7 per cent of the total crop of the United States, and continued to lead for thirty years. Until about 1840 the industry was centered chiefly to the east and north of the Cape Fear River, for it was thought that only the longleaf pine on the lower lands would yield resin in paying quantities; but about that time operations began farther west and far up along the western branches, often several miles from streams. Cape Fear was the chief outlet for naval stores in the crude or finished form for a large area in southeastern North Carolina, and Wilmington was the chief exporting port. Crude turpentine from forests distant from navigable streams was barreled and rolled, just as was tobacco before roads and railroads were provided, sometimes many miles, to streams navigable by rafts. Much crude turpentine was shipped during freshets, the rafts carried to the headwater of tidewater by the river currents. In the tidewater section progress toward Wilmington was made only when the tide was going out and there was a down current—only about six hours a day. At other times the rafts lay moored to the banks. The

---

* *Bulletin* 229, *op. cit.*, **22**.

white owner often left the transportation operations to his slaves, he going by horse and carriage to Wilmington, to be present when the shipment arrived and was inspected, and also to make the sale.

During the Civil War the industry was at a low ebb; nearly two-thirds of the establishments ceased operation. By 1870 there was a revival, and South Carolina superseded North Carolina (in 1879) as the leading producer; from 1889 to 1899 Georgia led. Then Florida assumed leadership. In 1924 and 1925 Georgia surpassed Florida in the production of both turpentine and rosin. Savannah, in 1890, became the export port and has so remained since; but Jacksonville, Pensacola, and New Orleans are active exporters.*

In a few sections of the South, large companies have secured extensive tracts of land and are preparing for permanent operations by reforestation, scientific tapping and caring for the trees, and balancing production of naval stores and growth. One company in the South, which has distilling plants in many states, immense tracts of pine, numerous marketing agencies, and its own ocean carriers, has decided to adopt a plan of perpetual operation. Could the example of this company lead to the organization of others, the life of the turpentine industry might be greatly lengthened.

The naval-stores industry involves two major operations: the securing of the resin or crude turpentine, described above in detail, and the distilling of this crude to make spirits of turpentine, or simply turpentine, and rosin. An average still of 30- to 40-barrel capacity a day will handle the yield of about 80,000 to 100,000 trees or of 4,000 to 5,000 acres.

The still consists of an air-tight copper container in which the crude turpentine—"run" and "chip" and "scrape"—is heated; a gooseneck pipe carries the volatile distillate to a worm immersed in cold water; and the distillate is cooled to a liquid form. Rosin with much trash is left in the container. This may be run out through a pipe that leads away from the bottom of the container to a vat sunk in the ground; or the bottom part of the container may be separated at a joint and rolled from its bed, and the contents poured into barrels. Rosin is barreled while still in the plastic or liquid state.

The latest development in the naval-stores industry, and one which will tend to prolong the life of the naval-stores resources, is the distilling of turpentine from refuse wood. Pine stumps, old logs, and mill refuse of pine are heated in an oven. This in reality is displacing

---

* Bulletin 229, op. cit., 2, 3; pamphlet issued by the Gillican-Chipley Co., 8; article in Raleigh News and Observer, Raleigh, North Carolina, April 20, 1924, 4; Report of Fourteenth Census, 1920, X, 679.

the old tar kiln and pit. The process is known as wood distillation. When pine is used the products are spirits of turpentine, pine oil, tar, and charcoal. The pine oil and tar may be further separated into paint oil, insecticides, disinfectants, and medicinal products. The turpentine does not have the same quality as that obtained by distilling the crude turpentine, but improvements are likely to be made. In 1929, 31,321,000 gallons of turpentine were made from gum and 4,619,000 gallons from wood.* Thus it is seen that, though of recent introduction, wood distillation is being rapidly developed. The first government reports of data on softwood distillation date from 1904.

The introduction of steam distillation and extraction of resins from pine woods may prove to be better conservation practice than to bake the wood to the charcoal stage, for it may be found that paper can be made from the by-product. In this process wood is "hogged" as in the making of paper. The wood is thoroughly chipped to small pieces and treated with live steam in low-pressure boilers. Turpentine and pine oils are largely removed. A solvent such as naphtha, most of which may be recovered, is also used in the process. The de-resined wood may be used for fuel or perhaps for paper. The turpentine by this process is nearly as high in quality as that obtained from crude turpentine, but the resin is a low grade.†

The widespread practice of turpentining trees before cutting them for lumber will tend to prolong the life of the naval-stores industry also. Until 1900 there was a prejudice against lumber cut from turpentined trees. Such lumber commanded a relatively low price; and where transportation facilities were not available for the lumber, the turpentined trees were abandoned and left to nature to destroy. This old practice has meant a great waste of forest. The cup method now used in turpentining does not harm the tree for lumber as the old box method did. Turpentining in some forest tracts is practiced for two to three years on mature trees before cutting. The United States Forest Service has furthered the practice but condemns the activity of some companies in their tapping of young trees. Many large lumber companies, however, do not favor turpentine operations on trees that are to be cut for lumber.‡

THE PAPER INDUSTRY

Paper mills have long been in operation in the South, but the paper industry has never been important. In 1820 the Southern States had

* *Statistical Abstract,* 1931, 760.
† N. C. Brown, *Forest Products,* 231.
‡ *Bulletin* 229, *op. cit.,* 40.

only 12 mills—3 in Delaware, 3 in Maryland, 3 in Tennessee, 2 in
Kentucky, and 1 in North Carolina—out of 108 in the United States.*
The Moravians long before this date, in fact in 1766, had a small
mill at Salem, North Carolina. During the Revolutionary War "local
bounties and other means" were provided to encourage paper making,
and after the Revolutionary War North Carolina granted mill owners
loans. But paper making is always most active near the markets for
paper. About 1860 there were 63 paper mills in English America, 48
of which were in Pennsylvania alone. In these early days cotton and
linen rags were the only material thought to be available.†

The paper was made entirely by hand, sheet by sheet. Shortly after
the beginning of the nineteenth century a Frenchman invented an
endless web upon which the pulp was spread evenly and from which
it could be taken to be pressed into paper, but this idea was not
practical until further developed by the Fourdriniers in England. The
Fourdrinier device is the basis of all the great paper-making machines
today that turn out sheets of paper 3 to 6, even 20, feet wide and
miles in length. The Fourdrinier machine was imported into the
United States from England in 1825. In 1830 two citizens of Mead-
ville, Pennsylvania, secured a patent for making paper from wood,
basswood being used. In 1840 Keller in Germany patented a wood-
grinding machine, which was introduced into United States in 1866.
It was used mostly in the North.‡

The census of 1840 lists 17 paper establishments in Maryland, 12
in Virginia, 2 in North Carolina, 1 in South Carolina, 5 in Tennessee,
and 7 in Kentucky, or 44 in all. The number for the United States
was 426. The plants in the South were apparently about as large as
those of other sections, if we may judge from the relative value of the
product and the number of mills. The Southern States produced paper
to the value of $530,000. The total for the country was $5,640,000.§

In 1860 there were 204 paper mills in New England, 273 in the
Middle Atlantic States, 53 in the West (Middle West), and 24 in
the South. Of the last, Virginia had 9, North Carolina 6, South Carolina 3, and Tennessee 2.¶

The making of chemical pulp dates from 1867. Tilghman had discovered that salts of sulphuric acid would dissolve wood when chipped

---

* *Report of Eighth Census,* 1860, "Manufactures," p. cxxvi.

† *Ibid.,* p. cxxiv.

‡ N. C. Brown, *Forest Products,* 21; *Report of Eighth Census,* 1860, "Manufactures," p. cxxxix.

§ *Report of the Sixth Census,* 1840, 408.

¶ *Report of Eighth Census,* 1860, "Manufactures," pp. cxxi, cxxii, cxxxi.

or splintered. The first chemical pulp process used was the sulphite. Next to the mechanical process, using wood-grinding machines, it is the most used in the United States today. In 1932, 1,200,000 tons of pulp were made by the mechanical process; 1,167,000 tons by the sulphite; 291,000 tons by the soda (caustic soda) process; 1,032,000 tons by the sulphate process. The sulphate process is the latest developed and the one used where coniferous wood is the raw material.*

Until the last two decades or so, the paper industry in the South, never large in number of establishments and in output, as previously stated, used rags, spruce from the higher lands of the Southern Appalachian Mountains, and hardwoods.

In 1906 the Forest Service began its investigation of pulpwood possibilities in our country; and since 1930 the Forest Products Laboratory at Madison, Wisconsin, has, in its paper and pulp section, devoted the major part of its time to the utilization of Southern woods. Some 94 species of trees have been tested by the soda, sulphite, and sulphate processes. Out of these experiments has grown the application of the sulphate process to Southern pine. The resinous nature of conifers, and of the Southern pine in particular, was the chief hindrance in the use of these woods earlier in paper making. The longleaf pine was found to have several commendable qualities: long thick-walled fiber, high specific gravity and thus heavy yield in weight to the cord, and, most important of all, large acreage of timber, the largest of any wood. Besides, the longleaf pine is quick growing.

A press notice in February, 1932, stated that the Chemical Foundation and the state of Georgia had completed an experimental paper plant at Savannah (the Savannah Paper and Pulp Laboratory), and that it would be under the direction of Dr. Charles Herty, a former professor at the universities of Georgia and North Carolina, who was convinced, through experiments, that slash pine was a suitable pulpwood for the production of newsprint paper. Herty believed that he could make a paper stronger and lighter than that from Canadian spruce and just as clear if only young pines, which are almost entirely sapwood, are used.

By June, 1934, after about two years of experimenting, Herty had overcome the minor difficulties that first bothered him. He found that the blue stain in the pine, resulting from a fungus growth (one of the difficulties) could be neutralized. Slash pine 7 to 9 years old was used. He found later that the alpha cellulose content of Southern pine is

* *Statistical Abstract,* 1935, 665. Some years sulphate-process pulp exceeds mechanical pulp, in tons.

higher even than that of spruce, and hence this Southern wood can be used in the manufacture of rayon, lacquer, and other cellulose products.* He later demonstrated also that even old trees could be treated to produce excellent ground pulp. He used in these later trials the wood of trees 40 to 45 years old. This means that any pine forest in the Lower South is potentially a pulpwood forest for newsprint paper.† It is believed by many, however, that it will be best to cut the trees for pulpwood in their seventh to ninth year. Later in 1937 Herty announced that black gum which grows on an immense acreage of wet lands in the South is a pulp wood.

A careful survey shows that there are available for the making of paper, in the United States:

977.8 million cords of Southern yellow pine...... (South)
521.4 million cords of Western yellow pine....... (West)
414 million cords of spruce and fir............ (North)
381 million cords of birch, beech, and maple.... (Central)
311 million cords of hemlock................ (North and South)
209 million cords of white and sugar pine...... (North and West)
168 million cords of red gum................. (South)
141 million cords of lodge pole pine........... (West)
132 million cords of black and tupelo gum..... (South)

Other woods suitable are basswood, yellow poplar, tamarack, and larch and jack pine.

With the rapid decline of available pulpwood in the North, one can see readily from these data that the paper industry must shift southward if the chief reliance in the future is to be domestic woods. The West and Alaska have great stores of wood available, but the South is nearer the great consuming centers and has excellent transportation facilities to these centers. Moreover, it can grow pulpwood more rapidly than any other section of the country. It takes 60 to 80 years to grow pulpwood in Canada, but only 15 to 20 years in the South and only 7 to 9 years if the original Herty process is used. A 100,000-acre tract of forest will grow as much pulpwood in a year as 300,000 to 400,000 acres in northern United States or southern Canada. Northern mills now import much pulpwood: about 30 per cent of the spruce wood, nearly 50 per cent of the poplar, and 13 per cent of the balsam fir used in 1926, and in addition 1,496,222 tons of wood pulp—about 34 per cent of the domestic production. The Canadians now and then threaten to raise the price of pulpwood and wood pulp. It is in the South that the Northern mills can find an answer to the threat if the

* Associated Press, *Nashville Banner,* June 1, 1934.
† Associated Press, *Nashville Banner,* June 22, 1934; also, Jan. 29, 1937.

prices become much higher. Unfortunately the majority of the Northern mills have been localized to utilize Northern domestic and Canadian supplies of pulpwood and are too far inland to take advantage of water transportation offered by the Atlantic. In readjusting to a Southern supply it will be more economical to move the mills to the pine forests of the South.

So far most of the Southern pine used in the industry has been made into "kraft" paper, a tough, light-weight, brown wrapping paper

A. E. P.

FIG. 126.—Cut-over Lands on the Coastal Plain in North Carolina.

If fires were prevented, this area could be reforested readily by nature. Many if not most landowners see greater returns, certainly more apparent ones, in the use of the land for grazing. In the far South fires are necessary to improve the grasses, particularly to keep the non-edible growths in check. With the rise of a pulp and paper industry such lands will be used to grow timber crops.

devised in Germany. Wrapping paper stands about third among the variety of paper products, hence there is little danger of Southern-made paper not finding a market. Besides, Southern pine sulphate pulp may be bleached to fit it for newspaper, magazine, and similar high-grade products at reasonable manufacturing cost.

The sulphate process has been used in America since about 1900. Dahl used it with straw as a raw material in 1833 and soon after it was used on wood.* Its adoption for paper making in the South was shortly before 1909. In that year less than 91,000 cords of yellow pine

* N. C. Brown, *Forest Products*, 47.

were consumed in the pulp mills of our country. In 1919 there were more than 234,000 cords; and in 1926, 685,000 cords, only a little more than 10 per cent of the total consumption of United States. Excellent authority asserts that the South can practically dominate the American kraft paper industry.

The industry is growing so rapidly that statistics would be out of date before published. Mr. Earl Tinker of the Forest Service in a speech before the Southern Agricultural Workers' convention at Nashville in February, 1937, said that $70,000,000 had come to the South during the previous year to be invested in the wood pulp industry and "other millions would be invested as the industry developed." Later reports estimated that there were, in 1937, 15 mills or more under construction representing an investment of more than $100,000,000.

A few of the large lumber companies have erected kraft paper mills near their sawmills and use waste bark, edgings, and slabs, instead of burning them in giant incinerators as has been done for decades.

The South has an abundant supply of pulpwood which, with proper measures, may be made perpetual by the utilization of the millions of acres of cutover land (Fig. 126) now supporting only a few scrubby cattle to the square mile. It has cheap labor, cheap power, and clear water. There is, therefore, a great future for the pulp and paper industry in the South if "sustained-yield" forestry is practiced.*

Paper has been made in Louisiana for a decade or more from rice straw. Cotton linters have been used successfully for a very high-grade bond paper, and writing paper from saw grass.

Closely related to the pulp and paper industry are those producing celotex, masonite, and other building materials. Celotex is made from the waste of the cane sugar mills of Louisiana, the bagasse being treated and pressed into thick sheets that, because of their loose texture, are excellent insulators. Masonite from wood fiber is a product of a plant in Laurel, Mississippi. It is dark reddish brown in color, more compact than celotex, and much finer in texture. Early in 1937 came announcements from a Northern laboratory of revolutionary methods in the separation of cellulose from lignin, applicable not only to forest products but to plants raised on farms as well.

The Southern States are in the beginning of a new era in the utilization of its forest and crop resources. It will continue for a few

---

*It is estimated that there are 200,000,000 acres of pine land that may be kept in pulpwood production. Late in March, 1937, the first shipment of 3,000 tons of pine sulphate pulp went from the wharves of Savannah to Hudson Falls, New York.

decades, at least, to export rough lumber; but science and capital are working together to devise and develop new ways of utilizing its resources more completely (yet with due regard to the best principles of conservation) and in such a way as to bring far greater returns to the South for units of raw materials consumed, capital invested, and wages received.

CHAPTER XV

THE TEXTILE INDUSTRIES OF THE SOUTH

COTTON MANUFACTURES

THE SOUTHERN MOVEMENT

It is only in cotton manufacturing that the South can claim leader-ship over other sections of the United States in the fabrication of raw products. Agriculture, lumbering, and mining, yielding raw materials for manufacturing, still engage the larger bulk of the workers of the South. In 1929 the entire North (fairly comparable in area to the South) had more than 75 per cent of the wage earners of our country engaged in manufacturing, as compared with 18 per cent in the South; or, on the basis of population, about 9 per cent of the entire population of the North were engaged in manufacturing and only 4 per cent of the South.*

The growth of cotton manufactures in the South has indeed been remarkable. At last after many decades of retardation in the fabrication of raw cotton, even though fiber and seed were right at hand, this section is only now taking advantage of the opportunities that have long existed.

This growth is well brought out in Table XXVIII, which shows the number of active spindles in the South and in the New England

TABLE XXVIII

GROWTH IN ACTIVE SPINDLES IN THE SOUTH AND THE NORTHEAST[1]

	South	Northeast
1840	181,000	1,597,000
1860	324,000	3,859,000
1880	561,000	8,632,000
1900	4,369,000	13,171,000
1930 (July 31)	18,586,000	11,351,000
1936 (November)	17,463,000	5,608,000
1937 (June)	18,881,000	7,131,372

[1] *Statistical Abstract*, 1931, 866, also 521; *Report of Tenth Census*, 1880, "The Factory System of the United States," 442; *Census of Manufacturing*, 1927, U. S. Department of Commerce; *Preliminary Report*, Department of Commerce, Dec. 1936, post card; news item for June 30, 1937. There are slight differences in data from the different sources.

* *Statistical Abstract*, 1932, 8, 9, calculated.

States in 1840, 1860, 1880, 1900, and 1930. It was in 1923 that the South came to surpass the New England States in number of spindles.

Although the growth in cotton weaving has not been so spectacular as that in cotton spinning, much progress has been made in establishing this most valuable phase of cotton manufacturing in the South. See Table XXIX for the growth of weaving.

TABLE XXIX

NUMBER OF LOOMS AT SELECTED DATES[1]

	South	Northeast
1831	91	33,000
1860	7,000	118,000
1880	12,000	212,000
1929	344,966	268,404

[1] Idem; Report of Fifteenth Census, "Manufactures," 1929, "Cotton Goods," 16.

By 1925 the active spindles in the South came to exceed those of New England. In 1927 the value of the products of the cotton-goods industry of a Southern state for the first time exceeded the leading Northern state. North Carolina in 1927 produced about 20 per cent of the cotton goods of the whole country (Massachusetts 18.7 per cent), South Carolina nearly 15, and Georgia nearly 12.*

A large part of this development is the result of Southern enterprise and capital, but many New England firms in their expansion programs have constructed new mills in the Southern States. Said one New England operator, about 1923, "There isn't a cotton mill under construction in the New England States today. There isn't an addition of any consequence being made to any cotton mill in New England today. But at this very minute millions of dollars are being expended in the South in new cotton manufacturing establishments." The conditions in the two sections in the cotton industry in 1923 have been little changed since then, but the shift southward is gaining in momentum if anything. About a hundred new textile mills were constructed or were under construction in 1928. Some of these were knitting mills. A few were built to produce rayon. About 20 per cent of the new plants were cotton mills. Some of the new mills weave fabrics in which cotton or wool is combined with silk or rayon.

That this industry in the South is in a "healthy" condition is shown by the activity of the spindles in place, the percentage being, on the average, between 95 and 98 per cent. In New England scarcely more than 60 to 65 per cent of those in place were active (1935).

What are the possible causes for the shifting of the major amount

* Commerce Year Book, 1930, I, 461.

of cotton manufacturing of the country from New England to the
South?*

ASCRIBED CAUSES FOR THE SOUTHWARD MOVEMENT EXAMINED

One factor generally cited favoring the industry in the South is
nearness to the supply of cotton. The importance of this factor rests
on the location of the competitive markets and the relative freight
rate on raw and manufactured cottons. New England has a large
market at or near home and is as near the markets of the Middle
West as the South. Besides, it is near the more important export ports
of our country.

Of particular advantage to the Southern manufacturer is the attitude of the railroads toward the cotton industry. The Southern railroads, for example, are now providing special cotton-goods trains that
assemble the goods daily direct from the doors of the mills. The cars
are run to transfer points in the cotton-manufacturing region where
there is a reassembling, and through-cars from there carry the goods
to Cincinnati, Louisville, St. Louis, Chicago, Kansas City, and other
points to the northwest. Connections are made at Knoxville and Chattanooga for Memphis and New Orleans and beyond. Goods reach the
East by all-rail conveyance or are sent to Charleston and other South
Atlantic and Gulf ports where connections are made with the coastwise and even with overseas lines of steamers. Moreover, a commodity
rate lower than the rate on raw cotton is given the manufactured
goods by some railroads. This is done, as the railroad managements
frankly state, to stimulate Southern cotton manufactures. What is
greatly needed is a lower rate for the freight moving from the South
to the North.

As to the quality of the raw cotton purchased, the New England
manufacturer has the advantage, for he has a large market from
which to buy and is able to select "more even-running goods." It
seems possible that the widespread adoption of the system of grading
advocated by the Bureau of Markets will offset the seeming advantage
New England has in procuring uniform quality. But if variety in
staple is desired, the Southern manufacturer, in order to adapt quality
of fiber to specific use, is at a disadvantage, for the New England
mills do select cotton from a larger producing area than the Southern

---

* Many of the points brought out in the discussion which follows are taken
from letters, papers, and speeches of New Englanders interested in cotton
manufacturing.

mills, being near the commercial nodal points, like New York and Boston, and world traffic routes.

The Southern mill, of course, is not confined to the immediate region for its raw cotton; but to secure an advantage in the cost of production over the New England manufacturers, the Southern mill is limited in its raw-material area. Anywhere east of the Mississippi freight charges from cotton markets to Southern cotton mills are lower than to New England, and it is from this region that most of the cotton comes. In 1929-1930 the four leading cotton-manufacturing states of the South consumed 4,219,000 bales of American cotton and produced in 1929 4,260,000.* Thus these states in most years produce about as much raw cotton as they consume. If consumption should advance beyond production then near-by cotton areas, as Mississippi and Louisiana, may be called upon. But these four states are far from having reached their maximum in cotton production.

In the purchase of cotton grown in Texas, New England mills are on a footing with the Southern mills, but not for cotton from Oklahoma and Arkansas. The rail-water rate from Oklahoma City to Lowell, or Providence, is $1.54 and $1.52; the all-rail rate from Oklahoma City to Gastonia, North Carolina, is $1.34. But for some time now the number of spindles in Texas has doubled every decade, therefore more cotton is being worked up in Texas mills every year, and consequently, for Texas cotton, New England mills will be losing their advantage as time goes on. A new cotton-mill center of no mean proportions may develop in central Texas. In 1928 there were 24 active cotton mills in the state, having 246,000 spindles. The scarcity of labor due largely to the oil boom and other developments prevented rapid growth, but these conditions are likely soon to pass. Some mills were employing Mexicans. Texas mills may find markets for their goods in their own state and the Middle West and Southwest.† Nearness to the raw cotton is undoubtedly a factor of considerable importance favoring the Southern manufacturers now and in the future.

The South with 31 per cent (in 1930) of the population of our country is a large market in itself, and in all this vast area Southern mills have the advantage. On the other hand, New England has the advantage of a well-earned reputation for good goods in both domestic and foreign markets, and this is undoubtedly of particular advantage in overseas trade. In some branches of the cotton trade the South does not have goods that can compete with those of New England,

---

* *Statistical Abstract*, 1931, 867; *Yearbook of Department of Agriculture*, 1930, 683.

† *Manufacturers' Record*, XCIV, Pt. I, July 5, 1930, 84.

particularly the finer qualities.* This is probably a factor of small importance, as one New England manufacturer points out, for only about one-tenth of the volume, measured in dollars, of the cotton trade is in the finer goods. In the future this will be even less of a factor favorable to New England, for the Southern mills are turning out annually an increasing proportion of the better cottons, and a reputation for goods is being more firmly established each year.

In the cost of constructing and equipping factories the South probably has no advantage, for, although building materials and labor are cheaper in the South, the cost of machinery is greater, for New England dominates the cotton-machinery industry. Many cotton manufacturers of the South are asking that machinery plants be constructed near Southern cotton mills. At a recent international textile show at Boston, a committee from the South presented the advantages for this industry in the South: cheap fuel, a near-by growing market, and iron and steel as cheap as, if not cheaper than, in New England. In 1930 the Cotton Manufacturers Association of North Carolina prepared and sent to New England a resolution urging the building of Southern plants. With about 75 per cent of the active spindles of the country, and therefore 75 per cent of the wear and tear of the cotton machinery of the whole country, in the South, there ought to be a profitable market here for locally constructed machines.†

There is apparently no economic-geographic reason for cotton machinery not being produced in the cotton-manufacturing states of the South. Heavy machine manufactures tend, generally, to be located near where the machines are used, thereby reducing freight charges; but, also, of greater importance, the manufacturers should be near so that the performance of their machines may be watched and improvements made to keep up with competitors. Machinery plants if once established in the South would give this section cheaper machines than those now obtainable, and cheaper machinery would mean lower-cost cotton manufacturing. The freight charges and express charges on tex-

---

* That New England does make the better quality of goods is shown by a comparison of value of product and value added by manufacture—this latter is really the basis for judging extent of development and quality of manufactures. Take for example Massachusetts and North Carolina for comparison:

	Total Value of Products	Value added by Manufacture
Massachusetts	$285,000,000	$139,000,000
North Carolina	$310,000,000	$126,000,000

† *Manufacturers' Record*, XCVII, Pt. 8, Feb. 6, 1930, 60.

tile machinery and repairs amount to a very large sum each year. Large stocks of parts must be kept by each of the Southern mills.

Evidently, if Southern cotton manufacturers are ever to have textile machine plants close by, such plants will need be built by Southern enterprise. Southern machine producers, however, would encounter great difficulty in securing manufacturing rights on patents that have not run their allotted time for expiration. Here and there all through the cotton-manufacturing districts in the South are small repair plants; and though the mechanical ingenuity of Southerners has never received much encouragement because of the extensive dependence on

A. E. P.

FIG. 127.—A Finishing Mill at East Spencer, North Carolina.

Many of the textile plants in the South are "complete" mills handling cotton (or cotton mixed with other fibres) from bale to cloth in the bolt. The South, however, supplies much cotton yarn to the New England mills. Finishing and dyeing call for labor more skilled than that in the cotton spinning mills.

hand labor and the dominance of one of the simplest of man's industries, agriculture, an occasional genius has come forward with a labor-saving device. It seems probable that with the gradual shifting of man's activities in the South from an environment of nature to one of machines more inventors will arise. So far the patent office at Washington has been and is a Northern institution. Southern industry, and cotton manufacturing in particular, will be handicapped in its development so long as Northern machine manufacturers hold patent rights. We must develop inventors.

The equipment of most of the Southern mills is the best and the most modern to be had (Fig. 127). There was a time when Southern mills "were to all intents and purposes graveyards of antiquated and worn-out machinery from Northern mills," but today most of the mills are "equipped with the latest improved machinery planned and engineered by the best of Northern millwrights."* For example, in the four cotton-manufacturing states of the South, 71 per cent of the looms used in plain goods are automatic in comparison with 38 per cent in the four leading New England states.†

Although the South has at present no advantage in the actual construction and equipment of factories, it does offer cheap land and low taxes. In recent decades, and in fact to a limited extent since 1870, nearly all the factories have been located on sites outside cities. Land is cheap; and since each company constructs the cotton mill town in its entirety and owns it, there are no taxes except those of the county and state. The expenses of running the town are borne by the mill owners, and these are reduced to the minimum. The majority of the mills in New England are in large urban centers where taxes are high and where land, if new mills are to be erected or old ones enlarged, is expensive.

Another important consideration favoring the South is power. Most of the Southern cotton mills in the four low-cost, cotton-manufacturing states are 400 or more miles nearer coal deposits than the New England mills are. Coal is as easily and cheaply mined in the South as in western Pennsylvania. Railroads carry coal from the Appalachian coal region, celebrated for its excellent coal, through the Southern Appalachian Mountains to western North Carolina and northern South Carolina, where other Piedmont railroads distribute it widely. Georgia and Alabama mills may draw coal from the Cumberland Plateau. Water, however, is the chief source of power in the South. Since 1895 nearly every factory erected has been equipped to use hydroelectric power. In fact, the localization of cotton factories on the Piedmont is due to the abundance of power in the streams. (See section on water power.) There are numerous sites for power plants. The first electrically equipped mill in the South began operations at Columbia, South Carolina, in 1894; and in 1896 a mill at Anderson, South Carolina, installed "direct-connected spinning frame motors." The census report on manufactures for 1929 indicates that in the factories in the South Atlantic States more than half (52 per cent) of the total power used was hydroelectric power (mostly purchased from utility companies), and that next in rank was power from "steam engines and turbines"— about 40 per cent.‡

---

* President Loving of the Arkwright Club, New England.
† Calculated from census data for 1929.
‡ *Statistical Abstract*, 1932, 732.

Although water power is not abundant in the Southern Appalachians it is sufficient to supply more than the present minimum potential power demands of the region east of the Mississippi River, as stated in a previous section. With the "hook-up" of steam and water power in a super power system in the Southeastern States, it is possible to use, to much advantage, power "available for 50 per cent of the time." On this basis the South Atlantic States in 1934 were using, in actual installation, about 57 per cent of the potential power, and the East South Central about 60 per cent. In the New England States, as a whole, the "installed capacity" of water wheels even exceeds the potential "90 per cent of the time," and in Massachusetts and Connecticut exceeds the potential available for 50 per cent of the time. Most power plants in the New England States use coal as a source of power for many months during the year.* Such development of potential water power is possible in the South. In fact, it may be carried still farther than in New England, for coal for the supplementary steam plants is cheaper than in New England and probably will continue to be so.

Whether the relative climatic conditions favor the New England or the Southern producer is problematic. The colder and longer winters of New England are a handicap, for much more fuel is needed to provide optimum working temperatures. The summer temperatures of New England outside the factories, however, are more stimulating and permit greater physical exertion; but is it not possible that in the winter the closed, highly heated, poorly ventilated factories (for many New England factories were built long before modern sanitary science had developed) are as enervating as Southern summers? And is it not possible that people who for generations have become acclimatized to the conditions of the Piedmont, far different from those of the Coastal Plain, can turn out as much work as South and Central European mill workers in New England? No conclusive data have yet been collected, that the writer is aware of, to show that the cotton factory hand of the Piedmont is any more inefficient as a producer, by reason of adverse climatic conditions, than the worker in New England. The tempo of his operations is undoubtedly slower. The working conditions in the factory are probably more important than the climatic conditions external to the factory. The factories of the South are newer than those of New England and are the product of the best millwrights of both New England and the South; no reasonable

---

* Data from *Statistical Abstract*, 1935, 332.

expense is spared to provide the most comfortable working conditions possible.

Closely associated with the question of climatic conditions is the length of day. Throughout the year there are more daylight hours in the working days in the South than in New England. But this advantage, if any, is partially overcome by the fact that the normal work week in New England is about 48.5 to 53.6 hours and that of the South 55 to 57.

That the work week should be longer and the pay of the workers lower in the newly developed industry in the South is not surprising. Labor has always had to take the initiative in securing reasonable returns for its contributions. Southern labor union leaders are not so aggressive as those of the North.

The work week in the newly risen industry in the South is far shorter than it was in New England when its industry was only a score or more years old. For example, in 1849 the average week for male doffers in the mills of Massachusetts was 75 hours. In 1852 it was cut to 72, and in 1861, through labor agitation, further reduced to 60. By 1875 the average week for all workers was 70 hours. In 1880 doffers in New York factories worked 66 hours; in Pennsylvania 60; in Virginia and Georgia 68. In 1928 the work hours a week were 55 in Alabama, 56 in Georgia, 54 in Maine, 50 in Massachusetts, 54 in New Hampshire, 56 in North Carolina, 53 in Rhode Island, and 55 in South Carolina.*

The relative merits of the cotton-mill worker of New England and the South have received much attention by men both North and South who have discussed the causes for the rapid shifting of cotton manufactures. The statements made as to response to leadership, pride in work, respect for authority, loyalty to employer, and other characteristics are largely the expressions of opinion. In a few sentences that follow, the writer is expressing his own opinion, formed as a result of personal observation and the study of the opinion of others.

Nearly all labor in the South is from the Southern Appalachian Highlands—mountains, valleys, and plateau—and from the farms of the Piedmont. It is predominantly Anglo-Saxon and English-speaking (Fig. 128). There were only 8,788 foreign-born whites in North Carolina in 1930, or 0.4 per cent of the total white population. In South Carolina the percentage was 0.6; in Georgia 0.8; and in Alabama 0.9. The negro population ranges from 29 per cent in North Carolina

---

* *Bulletin* 499, U. S. Bureau of Labor Statistics, 363-366.

to 46 per cent in South Carolina; but the negro is a small factor in the textile industry in the South, being employed only in a menial capacity in the mills.*

On both the mountain and Piedmont farms these workers before coming to the mills lived in small, unattractive, unsanitary houses. Their yearly incomes had never been large—for many not more than $100.00 a year, cash. They had never been persistent, constant work-

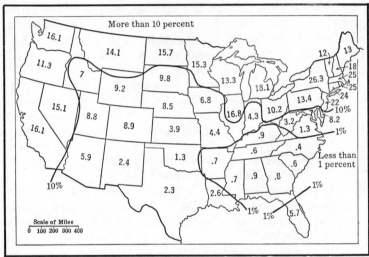

Data from *Statistical Abstract, 1935, 18.*

Fig. 128.—Percentage of White Population That Is Foreign Born in the United States, 1930, by States.

In most of the South the percentage is less than 1 per cent.

ers. They may have at times exerted themselves physically, but rarely in a gainful occupation. Conditions had never developed a high degree of foresight, nor had the acquisitive instinct developed many wealthy farmers. These mountain people are not a uniform type, of course, for there are wealthy, educated mountain people, just as there are unschooled; yet they are uniform enough for a thoroughly democratic society. They are loyal to each other; they consider people outside their horizon as foreigners. They are as intelligent (this is apart from school education) as the average run of farmer folks, and their moral standards are undoubtedly as high. They are law abiding. A few are moonshiners, but only a few in any community, and these are the men too lazy and too shiftless to earn a living

* *Statistical Abstract,* 1931, 14, 19.

otherwise. Southern teachers who have taught city-bred children and children of the mountain sections of western North Carolina and South Carolina in the cotton-mill towns see little difference in their intellectual ability. This last generalization is not a mere matter of opinion but is based on official school data, the results of standardized tests (the writer has many such on file). Mountain children are as keen, as adaptable, as amenable to regulations, and as resourceful as city children. Newcomers at the mill-town schools often exhibit the effects of poor and scanty food and isolated environment, but within a few months the stimulating effect of good food, sanitary living, and contacts with large population groups is quite discernible.

Young boys and girls, often whole families, from farms of both the Piedmont and the mountains move to the mill towns because the opportunities, economic and social, are better than in their old homes. It is but one phase of the cityward drift of population. How long the movement to the factory centers will continue is difficult to predict. In North Carolina there are on the average 14.4 farm people on 100 acres of tilled and pasture lands; in South Carolina the figure is about the same. In Georgia it is 10; so, also, for Alabama. In striking contrast to this are the figures for selected states in the Middle West. In Ohio, for example, there are only 4.5 persons (farm population) to 100 acres of used land; in Wisconsin, about the same number; in Iowa, 3; and in Kansas only 1.7. There is no evidence, therefore, that the South will have its industrial expansion curbed by a lack of local hands. The population increase is higher in the South than in the North as shown in Fig. 148.

The rate of cityward movement depends on the wage differential between city and country and the relative availability of jobs. The wages offered in the South are several times the money returns on the farms, and as long as this condition persists there is conceivably no reason for a cessation of factoryward migration. Increased use of farm machinery will tend to reduce rural demands for labor as it has in the North and create a surplus for the factories. Because of the much higher wages offered in the cotton factory, the workers are willing to work long hours, but rarely 12 hours, as was the rule until recently, in the steel mills of Pennsylvania and Ohio. Hours of labor is a matter of agitation of labor unions, of legislation, public sentiment, attitude of factory managers, and the degree of poverty or prosperity of the workers.* There is probably not so much poverty among the farming class in the Piedmont and Southern Appalachians,

* And possibly Federal legislation.

the class that supplies most of the cotton-factory labor, as among the foreign born in New England cities. In the scores of cotton-mill towns in the South, visited by the writer, he has never yet seen such evidences of poverty and squalor and mean living as he has seen in the slums of New York and Chicago, or in many of the coal-mining towns of Pennsylvania. It cannot be denied that improvement in labor conditions in the South are needed, but not more so than in the North.

That the cotton mills of the South are run chiefly by women and children, driven there by poverty, seems to be a prevalent idea in some parts of our country.* *The Monthly Labor Review* (Vol. 42, No. 6, June, 1936) states, "In 1930, at the time of the latest census of occupations, female operators were relatively more numerous in Northern than Southern mills." The percentage of workers that were women in cotton-textile manufacture in the two sections was, for the Northern states, 42 and for the seven Southern states 36 (p. 1479).† In the same year the percentage of total number of children working in non-agricultural occupations was 2.6 for Alabama, 5.8 for Georgia, 3.9 for North Carolina, and 6.4 for South Carolina. In Rhode Island the percentage was 5.7; in Massachusetts, 3.9; Connecticut, 5.5; New Hampshire, 2.3.‡ Evidently the story of the large number of children in Southern cotton mills is largely a matter of fiction. These are unbiased Federal Government figures.

The wages offered in the South are far larger than the returns the workers ever received on farms, as previously stated. This condition

---

* When the cotton industry was young in the South the percentage of women and children was large. John Trotwood Moore, in his novel, *The Bishop of Cotton Town,* gives us a picture of the sordid conditions following the Civil War in one mill town in Alabama, owned by New England capital. Possibly other mill towns controlled by Southerners were equally bad. If we may judge from a few samples we have in literature and history, the cotton industry North and South in its early stages (and for that matter most industries in a comparatively new country) exploit women and children. In New England, according to Adams, the cotton-mill operators declared for several decades after 1800 that tending the machines did not require men but was *better* done by girls from six to twelve years of age. Whole families often hired out to factory owners, mostly poor families, for generally they had the greatest number of children. There is a record of a man signing a contract for $5 a week for himself, $2 for his sixteen-year-old son, $1.50 for a thirteen-year-old boy, $1.25 for a daughter of twelve, 83 cents for a boy of ten, $2.33 for the man's sister, $1.50 for her son of thirteen, and 75 cents for her daughter of eight. (Data from James Truslow Adams, *The Epic of America,* 131.)

† Bulletin of the Women's Bureau, No. 111, U. S. Dept. of Labor, 44, gives 32.5 per cent for South Carolina, 47 per cent for Maine, and 39.1 per cent for Texas.

‡ *Fifteenth Census,* 1930, "Population," V, 388.

tends to make the worker contented. According to census data, the monthly variation in number of laborers throughout the year is about the same North and South.

Inasmuch as the Southern mill hand speaks English, it is easier for the mill managers to instruct the raw recruits than in New England where 21 to 29 per cent of the total population and 60 to 80 per cent of the mill hands are foreign. Another favorable characteristic of the Southern mill worker is that he is more loyal to his employer than are the foreign mill hands in New England. The reason assigned is that most of the mills were started by local men with local capital secured from stocks sold to local people. Employers and employees are Southern, and, as one writer puts it, "they speak the same language, they cherish to a large extent the same traditions and are moved by the same sectional pride." This argument may be classed as a sentimental one, yet some people are moved by sentiment as much as by economic consideration. The fact is that there are few or no strong, radical unions in cotton mill towns in the South. Southern cotton-mill workers are not advocates of strikes as a means of settling differences between capital and labor; and several strikes in recent years have been failures, not especially because of the antagonism of the owners of the mills but because of lack of support by the mill workers.* So strongly do Southern mill hands believe in the justice of American institutions that foreign labor agitators find hard going among them. Conservatively led labor unions in the South will in the long run prove as beneficial to the employees as to the employers, for

---

* The "labor war" in North Carolina in late 1929 was due to the activities of labor radicals, according to a statement by T. N. Wilson of the North Carolina State Federation of Labor. Opposition to the "foreign" agitators, leaders of the National Textile Workers Union, came entirely from American-born mill hands, many of whom belonged to the United Textile Workers Association. The Associated Press reported President Wilson of the North Carolina office of the Association as saying, "The United Textile Workers Association (affiliated with the American Federation of Labor) favors scientific management of industries and the elimination of waste and stands ready to co-operate with friendly employers and is doing so in New England. . . . [It] recognizes that our government. is a success but not perfect and is attempting through evolution to better working conditions." As for the local organizations in the South, he says, "The officers have arisen from the ranks of the workers in the trade and even though they may not have as much book learning as some others, they look at their work from the standpoint of the practical needs of the workers and economic welfare of the mass of the employees and the industry as a whole. They are just as much interested in seeing the textile industry on a prosperous basis as the employers are." This organization has at present many thousand members in the Southern textile region.

both labor and capital suffer in strikes and labor wars. Such unions are needed to assure proper working conditions and fair wages for labor.

Pennsylvania has had its Homestead strike, and New Jersey, Rhode Island, New York, Massachusetts, and Michigan their strikes and labor riots by the score. Whether or not the South in its industrial development will repeat the turmoil of the North on so many occasions will rest largely on the treatment the mill operators of the South give their workers, and the sanity of the labor leaders. The American-

A. E. P.

Fig. 129.—Cottages for Cotton Mill Workers, Greensboro, North Carolina.

At most of the cotton mills in the South small neat frame cottages are provided for the workers at very low rentals. In many villages prizes are offered for neat premises.

born worker of the South, even though reared in poverty, has not that natural tendency toward radicalism that characterizes so many workers from the congested industrial districts of western Europe. The procuring of a living is not so strenuous a task in the South as in Europe or even New England, and consequently the Southern workers are not as likely to be driven to desperate action. Southern labor has not evolved in an environment of hate, suspicion, and wrath.

Possibly the evident content, so far, of the cotton factory worker of the South is due to the excellent living conditions that surround him, the improvement in living conditions that has come to him, and the low cost of living. The genial winters do not call for the well-built homes and high fuel bills that the New England workers must finance. Most of the cotton mills of the South are outside the cities on tracts of land purchased at a low price, and large enough to permit the carrying out of "social betterment" schemes. Even though some mill villages leave much to be desired in comforts and decency, most of them are models of sanitation, attractiveness, and comfort. Alabama, about 1929, passed a law which gave cotton-mill communities until 1931 to provide a complete "water carried" system of sewerage for every home. The homes erected in some of the mill towns stand favorably in comparison with those of mill workers in any city in

A. E. P.

Fig. 130.—A Home of a Cotton Mill Foreman, Judson Mills, Greenville, South Carolina.

Some of the mill workers take great pride in the appearance of their houses, even though they are renters.

the country. The houses (Figs. 129 and 130) are neat, comfortable, though small, and modernly equipped, and they are rented to employees at very reasonable rates—a common charge being 25 cents a week a room, or $6 to $8 a month, with water and light free. New England workers would pay $20 to $30 a month for a similar habitation. Prizes are offered by the Southern mill owners for well-kept yards and well-cultivated, productive gardens. Many of the streets are paved, and all are well lighted. Parks, schools, churches, and amusement halls and theaters are provided. The company stores (or stores which have an agreement with the mill operators to handle checks and accounts) supply goods at prices as low as those found at other places of business. The equipment of the schools and the teachers are even better than those of the public schools of the same states.

In many mill towns trained nurses and medical clinics are provided along with the excellent schools, gymnasiums, day nurseries, parks, baseball fields, and church buildings. Some companies supply wood at cost and have power saws to cut it to the proper length. Model dairies are maintained by some companies, which furnish the workers with pure milk at low prices. A community director supervises boy and girl scout activities and women's clubs in some towns. Some communities have golf clubs for the mill workers. All these factors—houses, free water and light, free schools, recreation parks, church buildings, and other conveniences at low cost—should be taken into consideration when one is comparing the wage returns to the laborers in the South and New England.*

The "poor, down-trodden" cotton-mill workers, that one unacquainted with actual conditions in the typical Southern mill villages pictures after reading "labor literature," are after all relatively well paid and well taken care of.† The excellent schools offer opportunities, too, for almost any boy or girl to get at least a high-school education. An employee in a cotton mill, or the child of an employee, is not in a "blind alley." Many rise to better positions in the mills, go into business pursuits, banks, the law, or the schools. The vast majority of parents have high ideals for their children, and a high-school education at least is their aspiration. There are, of course, all grades of workers, based largely on wages. The homes of the better-paid employees have pianos, radios, and electric refrigerators, as those in other industrial towns.

The relative skill of New England and Southern workers has always been a question of debate. We usually associate fineness of goods with skill of workers. Some writers, some of the New Eng-

---

* Wages are lower in the South than in the North but so are living expenses —rents, fuel, clothing, food, education, and recreation. The United States Department of Labor gives the average hourly wage in the cotton textile industry for August, 1934, as ranging from 33.5 cents to 68.6 cents in Northern mills and from 30.4 cents to 60.7 cents in Southern mills, making a differential ranging from 3.1 cents to 7.9 cents per hour. This was the "basic code rate" under the N.R.A. These rates have been maintained fairly well since the demise of the N.R.A. The differential was greater, however, before the establishment of the basic code rate. (*Monthly Labor Review,* U. S. Department of Labor, March, 1935, 614.)

† For a time during the depression the majority of the teachers in the public schools of North Carolina received a lower salary than the wages paid mill workers.

landers, acquainted with Southern conditions, contend that Southern
mills *can* produce as fine cloth as New England mills. The fact is,
however, that most of the finer goods are made in New England;
yet the number of orders secured for the finer goods by Southern
mills is increasing. Southern workers are gaining in experience and
skill. Undoubtedly, New England mills are at an advantage in comparison with Southern mills in having a large body of skilled workmen, yet this advantage is not an important one and will be overcome in time. It is partly offset by the wide use of the new modern
automatic machinery in Southern mills.

We have no definite data to show that Southern workers are either
more or less efficient than New England workers, but we do know
that Southern mills are turning out good fabrics and are producing
them 14 to 18 per cent more cheaply than New England mills. This
lower cost of production in the South, whatever the causes, the aggressiveness of the labor unions in New England; and the adverse
legislation in New England are forcing many New England companies
in their expansion program, and new textile companies seeking sites
for new mills, to move southward.

SUMMARY

The great growth in cotton manufactures, in the South in the last
few decades seems to be due to natural environmental and economic
forces. It has developed under free competition and is, therefore, undoubtedly a sound growth. This growth in the South does not mean
the passing of New England as a cotton-manufacturing section but
that New England will need to develop a more intensive type of
manufacturing. This will demand larger markets for New England-
made finer goods and an intensification of the competition with Old
England. As a Rhode Island cotton manufacturer has recently said,
success for the New England operator depends on getting his mill
"running on goods that [will] not compete with the South," or better
that the South cannot compete with. New England's chief contribution to the industry in recent years has been new weaves and new
designs of ever-increasing attractiveness. Long-time leadership in this
field and well-developed textile schools are her chief assets, combined
with the excellent reputation of her goods and her business methods.
Southern States will probably never be as dominant in America in
the production of manufactured cotton as in the production of raw
cotton. But the growth in cotton manufactures is sure to continue,
possibly until most of Southern-grown cotton will be consumed in
Southern mills. The average annual consumption in all Southern mills

from 1926 to 1933 was 4,720,000 bales. In 1890 is was only 539,000 bales; by 1900, 1,523,000; and by 1915, 3,027,000.*

There are interesting limitations to the cotton-manufacturing industry of the world which in turn affect the South to a large degree. One is the cost of producing raw cotton; another is the ability of consumers to purchase cotton goods. Cotton has for decades been slowly pushing wool and linen into a lower and lower rank as raw materials for fabrics. Many new devices and methods for making cotton cloth more attractive and serviceable have greatly increased its consumption. Rayon is its newest competitor. The power of consumption, world wide, depends on world prosperity and the price of American raw cotton. War, with accompanying high prices, greatly reduces consumption; so, also, do high prices for raw cotton in times of peace. Prosperity for the American cotton planter, that comes with 15- to 35-cent cotton, is always at the expense of cotton manufactures and the machinery of the whole cotton exchange system, because of the curtailment of cotton-goods consumption the world over.

The extent of development in the future of cotton growing and cotton manufacturing in the South depends on the ability of the world to absorb American cotton. Environmental and economic, natural and human, factors, as previously stated, are favorable in the South, for a doubling of the cotton crop and cotton manufactures, but when can the world absorb such volumes?

There is great need of research laboratories in Southern cotton mills, manned by chemists and other experts, that cotton manufacturing may keep pace with the rayon industry.

The Federal Government is performing a most useful service in the creation of the "New Uses Section" of the Textile Division of the Department of Commerce. It has planned, and investigations are progressing in accordance with these plans, first, to make a study of all present-day uses of cotton; and, second, to work in cooperation with all industrial plants, research organizations, and technical schools and laboratories in a study of the technical problems related to the manufacture of cotton and the discovery of new uses. Experiments have begun on the development of new synthetic, artificial fabrics using cotton as a base or in combination with other cellulose products. Experiments have been conducted to produce yarns or cloth less susceptible to wrinkling, which is the present objection to cotton dress goods. These are only a few of the investigations planned or

* *Statistical Abstract*, 1934, 746.

completed. The Cotton Textile Institute and the Farm Chemurgic Council are studying and advancing the industrial uses of cotton.

In the South, as cities multiply and increase in population, as new industries arise, and more intensive tillage calls for more rural residents, as wealth multiplies and standards of living rise, will the Southern mills now manned by the boys and girls from the farms be replaced by foreign labor as were the "blooming and energetic, naturally intelligent" girls and boys of New England replaced by French Canadians and later by South and Central Europeans? Will Southern-born mill operators exercise the paternalism they now do toward their employees? The South is destined to suffer great changes in the future as its industrial development progresses. Old Southern traditions are already fading from memory and practice in many parts as a new economic order comes in. The business man is gradually rising into prominence above the traditional country gentleman or planter. The rise of cotton manufactures is largely responsible for this.

THE RAYON INDUSTRY

The newest textile material in America and elsewhere is rayon, the commercial name for artificial silk. Its rapid growth in use in the United States is an indication of the favor it has won, chiefly among the women purchasers. In 1911 only 300,000 pounds were produced in the United States. In 1921 the output was 15,000,000 pounds; in 1931 132,632,000 pounds (approximate); and about 295,000,000 pounds in 1936. The imports had shrunk from 13,000,000 pounds in 1926 to 1,804,000 pounds in 1931. There were 29 rayon establishments (rayon yarn and allied products) in the United States in 1929.* Of these 14 were in the South. The Southern plants were located in Virginia (5), Tennessee (4), Georgia (1), Maryland (1), Delaware (1), West Virginia (1), and North Carolina (1). Any data given regarding the industry are out of date almost before the ink is dry. Rayon produced in 1925 was valued at $88,061,000; in 1929, $149,546,000, and the output was increasing rapidly.† The depression, of course, reduced production. Tennessee has the Du Pont Rayon plant, near Nashville, and the Glanzstoff and Bemburg plants (companies now united) near Elizabethton and Johnson City, in Happy Valley, eastern

---

* *Commerce Yearbook,* 1932, I, 427; *Statistical Abstract,* 1932, 745; 1934, 712. The plants numbered 34 by 1933. In 1936 the consumption of rayon was 7.6 per cent of the consumption of all fibers in our country. It was only 0.3 per cent in 1920 (*The American Silk and Rayon Journal,* March, 1937, 28).

† *Report of Fifteenth Census,* 1929, Industries Series, "Rayon and Allied Products," 13.

Tennessee. The Virginia plants are at Roanoke (the oldest), Covington, Waynesboro, Hopewell, and Richmond. At Rome, Georgia, the
American Chatillon Corporation has built two plants, and in 1930
the American Euka Corporation constructed one near Asheville. Bur-
lington, North Carolina, also has a new plant. Others have recently
been constructed or are being constructed in the Shenandoah Valley
where freestone water and cheap labor are available.

Several reasons may be given for the active growth of the industry
in the South. This section is now the leading cotton-manufacturing
region of our country. Allied industries tend to locate in close proximity. Much rayon is mixed with cotton (as well as with wool, linen,
and real silk) in the weaving of fabrics. Rayon manufacturers come
to the South for the same reasons that Northern cotton manufacturers
do: cheap labor, cheap and abundant power, soft water, cheap land,
favorable tax rates and legislation, and general freedom from labor
troubles. One writer reported in 1936 that the tendency has been to
increase the capacity and number of mills in the South more rapidly
than in the Northern States during the last ten years.*

Capital also stands ready to enter a rapidly growing pioneer enterprise because of the large profits that are assured before active competition sets in. In 1929 the value of manufactured rayon (and allied
products) was $149,546,000 and the value added by manufacture
$116,211,000.† Although the rayon plants are very expensive to build,
ranging in price from $4,000,000 to $15,000,000 or more, and although
the labor costs are high because of the large number of workers,
there is evidently much left of the "value added" that may be classed
as profits. All the companies in the South have ambitious plans for
expansion.

The rapid growth in consumption of rayon is due largely to the
low price as compared to natural silk, in general, about 50 per cent
less. While rayon is inferior to real silk, and in the end is not so
economical as the difference in price would indicate, this lower price
makes its appeal to certain classes of shoppers. But the chemists,
some of the best in the country, are active in rayon laboratories.
Wonderful improvements have been made, and still more wonderful
may be expected. Eventually it may be made as serviceable as natural
silk in all particulars.

Data supplied by the Du Pont corporation indicate the type of
trade that absorbs the rayon skeins it produces. Some 21 per cent

---

* *Rayon.* September, 1936, 30.
† *Statistical Abstract,* 1932, 745.

goes into hosiery, 19 per cent is mixed with cotton, 18 with silk, 34 per cent goes into underwear, and the remainder into braids, art goods, and others.

Several different processes are used in this country in the production of rayon, but all duplicate, as far as possible, the work of the silkworm in changing cellulose plant fiber into a liquid. With rayon, the liquid, forced through small holes in a plate or through tubes, forms into small thread. The wood pulp used so far, imported from Canada, is from northern spruce. Herty has already demonstrated that rayon can be made from Southern pine.

Artificial silk was first produced in France in 1884 by Count Hilaire de Chardonnet. It was exhibited at the Paris exposition in 1889; and soon after, a small plant for its manufacture was erected in northeastern France. In 1903 Stearn, an Englishman, discovered the viscose process, and it is this that is most used in the United States. The French, English, and Germans have formulas and processes that have been patented in all the manufacturing countries of the world. American plants use these patented formulas. Japan, which has recently surpassed the United States in the production of rayon, uses European processes.

Four formulas are in use in America: the viscose, which accounts for 89 per cent of the total production; the nitrocellulose (Chardonnet's process), 6 per cent; cellulose acetate, 4 per cent; and the cuprammonium, 1 per cent. The total production from 1921 to 1930 by these processes was as follows:

	Pounds
Viscose	562,000,000
Nitro	40,000,000
Acetate	23,000,000
Cuprammonium	6,000,000

The use of the nitro process is declining, the fiber produced lacking tensile strength. The acetate process produces the strongest fiber, but production costs are high.

The rayon industry in America dates from about 1911, the first plant having been constructed at Marcus Hook, Pennsylvania, in 1909. Production began in 1911. The greatest development has come since 1925.*

---

* *Rayon*, XII, July, 1931, 19, 20.

CHAPTER XVI

THE CHEMICAL INDUSTRIES OF THE SOUTH

Chemistry is entering more and more into the industrial life of the United States. There are two reasons at least for this increasing participation. First, chemistry, particularly the industrial phase, is developing rapidly in its usefulness; and, second, our industries are advancing into more intensive phases. Chemistry is finding new uses for old things and uses for new things, and is using by-products that once were waste. It is the handmaid of conservation and economy. It is because of this increasing activity in industry, as industry intensifies, that the degree of development and use of chemistry becomes a criterion for judging a nation's or a region's economic development. The great chemical plants and chemical laboratories in industrial plants are largely in the Northeastern States. One could hardly expect the South, because of its youth in the manufacturing world, to have made much of a start in the chemical industries, yet an actual southward movement is on its way.

One of the largest chemical concerns in the South is the Davidson Chemical Company, with manufacturing plants and raw products in many of the Southern States. Its main plant near Baltimore, at Curtis Bay, produces sulphuric acid from pyrite, once considered worthless. Pyrite is brought from Cuba by ships to the wharves of the Curtis Bay plant, and so also are other raw materials. A silica gel and a copper leaching plant are associated with the sulphuric acid plant. A variety of products are turned out, such as magnesium fluosilicate and hydrofluosilicate. Sulphuric acid is used in the production of soluble phosphates. The company owns 1,400 acres of phosphate lands in Florida, and several chemical fertilizer plants, the Southern plants being at Baltimore, New Orleans, Norfolk, Suffolk (Virginia), Tennessee, and North Carolina.

The Eastman Kodak Company at Kingsport, Tennessee, makes pyrogallic acid and other organic products used in photography. At Copper Hill (Fig. 131) and Ducktown, where once the sulphur fumes

---

* *Manufacturers' Record*, XCIV, Pt 1, July 12, 1927.

from the copper smelters destroyed all plant life for a radius of five to ten miles from the plants, there are now great chemical works that utilize the sulphur dioxide in the manufacture of sulphuric acid, bringing returns of more than a million dollars each year. The normal output of sulphuric acid is from 1,000 to 1,200 tons a day. Chemical laboratories all over the South are associated with brick plants, ce-

A. E. P.

FIG. 131.—The Acid Plant at Copper Hill, Tennessee.

About 1890 the copper mining and smelting company was forced by court action to install a sulphur gas-recovery plant. Copper mining and smelting were begun before the Civil War. The drain on the forests for fuel and the fumes from the smelting operations destroyed the vegetation over 100 square miles of territory. The farmers of Georgia—the state boundary is a few hundred feet to the south of the plant—instituted the suit.

The Copper Hill plant has an advantage in marketing its products over the one at Anaconda, Montana, since it is nearer the great Eastern markets.

ment plants, paper mills, iron furnaces and steel mills, sugar refineries, softwood distillation and naval stores plants, oil refineries, tanneries, tannic acid extract plants, fertilizer plants, and cottonseed oil mills.

In a few products involving chemistry in their manufacture, or products that will be used in chemical industries, the South leads or stands high in their preparation, as shown below.* It has produced, in late years:

---

* Lauren B. Hitchcock, "Chemical Research and Industries of the South," *Annals of the American Society of Political and Social Science,* CLIII-CLV, 81, 82.

PRODUCT	PERCENTAGE PRODUCED BY SOUTH
Refined petroleum products....	40
Cottonseed oil................	97
Fertilizers....................	70
Rayon.......................	62
Naval stores.................	100
Sulphur......................	100
Carbon black.................	75
Tanning material.............	27
Clay products................	16
Coke........................	15

At the Standard Oil refinery at Baton Rouge there has been erected an experimental plant for testing out the hydrogenation of petroleum in an attempt to produce a gallon of gasoline from a gallon of oil. The process of hydrogenation originated with the I. G. Farben Industries of Germany in the liquefaction of coal. The American rights to the process were secured by the Standard Oil Company and since there has been no call for liquefaction of coal in America yet, the company's chemists began experimenting on crude petroleum. The Baton Rouge plant is one of three in the United States selected as centers for experimentation. A second is being erected at Baytown, Texas, on the Houston Ship Canal. Already millions of dollars have been spent in construction work, an indication of the faith this great company has in the science of chemistry.*

Oil refineries are numerous in the Southern States. No data are reliable very long, as the number is constantly changing. Only a few of the larger companies will be noted. The Standard Oil Company owns a 10,000,000-barrel (a year) plant at Baltimore, another large plant at Charleston, South Carolina, one at Baton Rouge, just described, and another at Baytown, Texas. The Humble Oil Company, a subsidiary of the Standard, controls the Baytown plant, with a capacity of 135,000 barrels a day. Thousands of miles of pipe lines connect these plants with the oil fields of Louisiana, Texas, Arkansas, and Oklahoma.

The Gulf Petroleum Company has a huge plant at Port Arthur, Texas, with a daily capacity of more than 55,000 barrels. Here also is the parent plant of the Texaco Company, which can refine 60,000 barrels a day. Texaco owns smaller plants at Port Neches, West Dallas, Amarillo, Houston, San Antonio, and El Paso in Texas; West

* *Manufacturers' Record*, XCVII, Feb. 13, 1930, 56.

Tulsa, Oklahoma; and Pryce, Kentucky. (Those of the North and West are not listed.)

Sulphur production, as carried on in Texas and formerly in Louisiana, is classed among the chemical industries, although few or no chemical processes are involved in the mining. That a great industry could be built up about the plants, and will be in the future, there is little doubt. Yet the raw product sulphur is more easily shipped than any of the acids, and therefore sulphuric or sulphurous acid plants, or allied industries producing such acids, would tend to be located near the markets for these products. At present the Texas plant is interested only in the production of crude sulphur. Salt beds, gypsum deposits, and limestone, all in close proximity, offer admirable opportunities for the development of a great soda ash and alkali industry, with its many products and by-products. Soda ash is consumed in the making of glass, caustic soda, soap, cleaning compounds, pulp and paper, and textiles, and in oil refining.

Sulphuric acid and salt are the chief raw products in the production of muriatic or hydrochloric acid, used in the preparation of glucose, glass, and scores of other products. Sulphuric acid is used in making alum consumed in paper mills and in water purification. Sulphuric and sulphurous acids are employed in the preparation of paints, glue, textiles, explosives, galvanized ware, chemicals and drugs, besides fertilizers, soda, and other products listed above.

The development of great hydroelectric plants in the Southeast and in and about the Southern Appalachian Mountains makes available electric power and heat for a nitrogen-fixation industry. So far, however, Americans have had little success in the production of artificial nitrates. The Duke Power Company operated a small plant at Great Falls, South Carolina, for a time, using the Pauling process that combines nitrogen and oxygen by an electric arc. The cyanamid process tried out at Muscle Shoals in the United States Nitrate Plant No. 2 (Fig. 111), that cost $75,000,000, was considered a failure; some chemists said nitrate could not be made in the plant to compete with the imported product. There is some reason for believing that the Haber process, known also as the synthetic process of nitrogen fixation, ammonium nitrate being the end product, is highly feasible. The first plant in America was the United States Nitrate Plant No. 1 near Sheffield, Alabama, to the west of Nitrate Plant No. 2. This process requires but little electricity.

For several years cellulose and its derivatives have held a prominent place in synthetic chemistry. Nitrocellulose, the product of the action of nitric acid (formed from sulphuric acid acting on sodium nitrate) on cellulose (as cotton linters), is the base for smokeless gunpowder, celluloid, photographic films, lacquers, artificial leather, viscose rayon, cellophane, and plastics. The South has all the essential raw materials for the manufacture of all types of nitrocellulose.

The Forest Products Laboratory of Madison in 1937 announced feasible methods of extracting lignin from wood. Heretofore only cellulose was obtained. Lignin in woody plants is closely associated with cellulose, which forms the cell walls while lignin cements the cells together and constitutes the woody part of the plant. By boiling under pressure with a weak acid, sawdust or woody material in any other minute form may be made to give up its lignin. While hot and moist, lignin, as taken from the cookers, is plastic and can be molded or pressed into any form desired. When hard it can be turned on a lathe, planed, bored, or sawed just like hard rubber. It is a non-conductor of heat and electricity. It is one of the cheaper new plastics. It can be made for about 2 or 3 cents a pound, in the bulk. Now sawdust and other refuse of mills can be put to the service of mankind.

It was Thomas L. Willson and associates who discovered a commercial method of making calcium carbide, the source of acetylene gas, at Spray, North Carolina, in 1892, while experimenting in the production of aluminum in an electric furnace. The commercial process is simple, merely the fusing of carbon and lime by an electric arc. Acetylene gas had been discovered by Davy in 1837, and calcium carbide was made by Wohler in 1862 but not in commercial quantities and by a method commercially workable. The carbide industry has never developed in the South. The products that may be derived from calcium carbide are valuable and the gas is used in the oxyacetylene flame for welding and cutting iron and steel. The flame is 1,000° C. hotter than the oxyhydrogen flame.

Coal, coal tar, coke, petroleum, natural gas, salt, limestone, phosphate rock, gypsum, sulphur, naval stores, hardwoods, softwoods, rare earths, corn, soy beans, cotton, cottonseed and cotton linters, steel alloy materials, the refuse of industrial plants, and a host of other raw materials exist in the South in great abundance and merely await the coming of chemical laboratories and chemical plants to turn them into valuable products. Dr. Herty, frequently mentioned in this volume, has done much toward the advanced utilization of forest products. Certainly no one chemist in the South has done more toward the industrial utilization of farm products than the negro Dr. George Washington Carver of Tuskegee Institute. He has made 300 useful products from peanuts, and more than 100 from sweet potatoes. These are only two of the many products of field, forest, and ground with which he has worked.

Since the World War the production of helium has become important in Texas, not because of the great amount of the product nor its great value measured in dollars, but because in few or no other sections of the world does it occur in such large quantities in natural gas. Helium was discovered in the sun in 1868, by spectroscopic methods, long before its existence on earth was known. Sir William Ramsay was the first to isolate it in a chemical laboratory, in 1894. It was not until the last war that the United States began its production. A large plant, designed and operated by the Luide Air Products Company, was constructed at Fort Worth. This company held the patents for its isolation. Recently the Federal Government has developed a large plant about seven miles from Amarillo and has secured control of a virgin gas field of 50,000 acres. New methods developed in 1930 or 1931 have cut the cost of production to half. The natural gas after being purified is cooled to 300° below zero and liquefied. The helium evaporates from this liquefied gas; in short, the helium is frozen out of the natural gas. It is shipped in specially designed triple-sheeted cylinders filled and sealed under a 2,000-pound pressure. It has several uses other than for the inflation of dirigibles, but its non-inflammable nature makes this, so far, its most valuable use.* Little use has been made of it in America, but in 1937 it was decided that the gas could be sold to foreign powers or firms for peace-time uses. Recently it has been discovered that helium has great medicinal value in the treatment of pulmonary afflictions. Some medical experimenters are very enthusiastic regarding its future in medicine. Large scale production is planned by the Government.

---

* *Scientific American,* CXLIV, February, 1931, 132; *Mechanical Engineer,* LI, 1929, 941; Henry Wigglesworth, "Chemical Industries," in H. T. Warshow, *Representative Industries of the United States,* 130-182; Reports of the Farm Chemurgic Council, office at Dearborn Inn, Dearborn, Michigan.

PART VI

URBANIZATION OF THE SOUTH

THE RISE OF SOUTHERN CITIES

CHAPTER XVII

THE RISE OF SOUTHERN CITIES

INTRODUCTION

First the village, then the town, eventually the city,* are the well-recognized stages through which a close settlement passes if its site possesses natural environmental advantages sufficient to attract large numbers of people. Many sites for settlements are selected, but few chosen ever attain size and importance. The environmental conditions which attract men of enterprise and capital, professionals and laborers engaged in occupations of many sorts to a site are many and complex. What some of these attractions are will be revealed in detail in subsequent paragraphs in this chapter.

The rate of growth of urban groups depends largely on the variety and superiority of the attractions. Man must always play a part in urban growth, but his activities will be of little avail unless supported by favorable environmental conditions.

Transportation and urban growth are indissolubly associated. The urban dweller, not being a producer of food sufficient for complete sustenance, must be connected by means of transportation to pastures, fields, gardens, and orchards, for existence.

The size of the city is limited by the extent of its sustenance area. In the thousands of years that the horse-drawn vehicle was the sole carrier of food to the urban dwellers, the sustenance area was rarely

---

* These terms are loosely used in America as they undoubtedly are in other countries. At what point in its growth a "close settlement" passes from the village stage into the town stage has not been established. The Census Bureau since 1910 has classified all incorporated places having a population of 2,500 or more as urban. Before the 1910 Census only incorporated places of 8,000 or more were called urban. In the 1930 Census the term urban has been extended to include townships and other political subdivisions (not incorporated as municipalities) which have a population of 10,000 or more and a population density of 1,000 or more to the square mile. (*Report of Fifteenth Census,* 1930, I, "Population," 9.) In this chapter the writer is more or less arbitrarily selecting 8,000 as the minimum population for a city, recognizing fully that owing to the "gerrymandering" of municipal boundaries census data mean only approximations as to a city's population.

more than 30 to 40 miles in radius (3,000 to 5,000 square miles), and the size of the city was limited accordingly to a few hundred thousand people. Seaports had a much larger sustenance area. Few cities, probably, in ancient or medieval times ever reached the sustenance limitation, for, owing to the insanitary conditions, the death rate at times nearly equaled and sometimes surpassed the cityward migration of ruralists. The railroad and the steamship, particularly since they have reached such a high degree of perfection, along with the other modern means of transportation, have made it possible to bring the whole habitable world within the sustenance sphere of great seaports, and also of interior cities. For these urban centers there are few physical limits to size. Competition, however, makes any city share its possible sustenance area with others, and hence there are many dominating cities, but no all-dominant one, and there certainly never will be. Here reference is made to geographic cities, not civic. Scarcely a village or town today in America, no matter how isolated, is as circumscribed in its possibilities of growth as were the inland cities of the eighteenth century.

The industrialization of America, as of other countries, with its concomitants—improved transportation, the advances in division of labor, and growing complexities of social and economic institutions—has been the chief factor in the growth of cities. A redundant rural population would naturally result from an increasing use of agricultural machinery, and of course from natural population increase. The increasing number of factories has made it possible for the cities to absorb this superfluous rural population as well as a large proportion of the immigrants, and the normal urban increase.

The major activities which make possible the existence and growth of cities are commercial, transportational, manufactural, governmental, and recreational, and for some, educational. In most cities such as Baltimore, Charleston, and New Orleans, the commercial and transportational activities dominated in the earlier days of their evolution. The manufactural activity has been, for most parts of the South, a factor in city growth only for the last half century or so. Recreational centers are of more recent origin.

The dominant activity of a city tends to be related to the environment of its site and its sustenance area or situation. New Orleans, Houston, and Baltimore are great commercial centers largely because their location on the border of the world ocean makes commerce the most profitable activity into which capital and enterprise may flow. San Antonio, Dallas, Atlanta, and others are predominantly jobbing centers, for they are in the midst of great agricultural and grazing regions. In both of these groups of cities manufacturing is secondary. Population centers near great stores of power and fuel, regardless of their early activities, drift toward manufacturing. Baltimore, Birmingham, and Chattanooga are examples. Among the elements that make recreational centers attractive are landscapes, or "seascapes," pure bracing air, moderate temperatures, clear skies, natural wonders, general freedom from diseases and obnoxious insects, and historic relationships. Most cities combine two or more activities. Moreover, growth in one type affects growth in others. As the industrial city grows, its commercial activities become greater. And on the prosperity and age of both depends the number of patrons of recreational centers. So far the South has made fewer contributions to the population and wealth of the recreational centers than the North.

Common sense leads one to the conclusion that the city possessing the environmental conditions that are attractive for the largest number of these activities is the city that is likely to grow the most rapidly. But the type of the combination is essential, for some activities have more attractive power than others. The city that specializes in one or a few actively is the one that attracts the most attention but not always the largest number of people; nor does such a city possess the maximum stability and continuity of growth.

City growth is thus a normal phenomenon in a region or country having a normal population increase and an evolving economic order. In 1790 only 3.3 per cent of the people of the United States were in cities of 8,000 or more; but by 1930 the percentage had advanced to 49.1. The number of cities of 8,000 or more population during these 140 years increased from 6 to 1,208. In 1930 there were 5 cities in the United States having a million or more people (New York alone had nearly 7,000,000) ; 13 of 500,000 or more; and 93 of 100,000 or more. In the agricultural South in 1930 there was no "million city," the largest being Baltimore with 805,000; and only 23 (including Washington) out of the 93 cities of the 100,000-or-more size were in the Southern States. The industrial-agricultural North had 59, and the West only 11.*

The pages that follow in this chapter are an attempt to trace the evolution of many of the cities of the South in size and function. There are presented also certain possible outstanding causes for their growth or lack of growth. The first consideration is the localization of population centers.

---

* *Report of Fifteenth Census,* 1930, I, "Population," 9; *A Century of Population Growth,* Census Bureau, 11.

SELECTING VILLAGE SITES

Many of the villages in America, particularly those of the isolated frontiers of the seventeenth and eighteenth centuries, were palisaded, defense being the dominant reason for the segregation of the people. About the palisaded villages lay the farm lands on which the farmers lived most of the time, seeking protection in the fort only during impending dangers. The rapid changes that came to the frontier by the ceaseless migration of land seekers and the early subjugation of the Indians soon reduced the necessity for palisades, and many "forts" soon became trading centers, with a store or two, a blacksmith shop, a school, and a church, as the localizing factors of social, commercial, and religious life.

Villages, other than those for defense—and these were on the frontiers as stated above—often developed at cross roads, at a ferry or ford, near mountain passes, at small falls about a gristmill or sawmill, at a mine or a blast furnace, at the head of navigation of rivers, at the confluence of rivers, at river bends, or about a county courthouse. Nearly every county in the South has a village, town, or city (some have two or more) that started as the county seat. In eastern Virginia, however, many county seats were nothing more than a courthouse in the forests that everywhere covered the centers of the peninsulas, the plantation homes and cleared lands being on tidal waters. Trading centers often developed and were fairly evenly spaced along well-traveled roads, rivers, or, later, along the railroads.

In sketching the rise of Southern cities the writer divides the 140 years since the first census, when for the first time official data were available, into two periods: a 90-year period, from 1790 to 1880, during which the South was overwhelmingly agricultural; and a 50-year period, from 1880 to 1930, during which increasing attention was paid to manufacturing. The year 1880 may be considered to mark the beginning of this New South.

NINETY YEARS OF URBAN DEVELOPMENT (1790-1880)

The first census (1790) revealed the fact that there were but five cities in the United States with a population of 8,000 or more. Two of the five cities (Fig. 132) were in the South—Baltimore with a population of 13,503, and Charleston with 16,359 people. For future comparisons, New Orleans, which became a part of the United States in 1803, must be added to the list. It had a population of about 10,000. The total urban population in the South (using 8,000 as the urban-

population basis and including New Orleans) was about 39,800; that
of the North, 93,613 (in Philadelphia, New York, and Boston).* The
South at this time had about 30 per cent of the total urban population of the country (not including New Orleans). Thus city growth
was more rapid in the North than in the South, largely because of the
leadership of the former section in manufacturing, a fact brought out in
previous chapters.

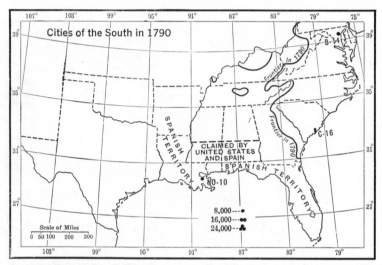

Fig. 132.—Data from Adam Seybert, *Statistical Annals; a Century of Population
Growth*, U. S. Census Bureau. (Boundaries of States as of 1930.)

Baltimore at this date was the most active of the Southern cities
in manufacturing, had "a considerable trade," and was growing rapidly. Although in 1790 its population was less than that of Charleston,
it soon surpassed the latter.†

Charleston's economic interest lay largely in commerce, it being the
only large port of South Carolina which was at that time, as it was
for many decades, an active producer of rice and indigo.

---

* Data from *A Century of Population Growth*, Census Bureau, 11. New Orleans is not included in the report. *Report of Fifteenth Census*, 1930, "Population," I, 18, 19.

† Joseph E. Worcester, *Gazetteer of United States*, 1818, topic, Baltimore;
A. E. Parkins, "The Development of Transportation in Pennsylvania," *Bulletin
of the Geographical Society of Philadelphia*, XIV, 25, 28.

Besides these two larger cities in the South there were numerous other population centers—villages and towns—scattered over this section, that within a few years reached city status (Fig. 219).

By 1810 (Fig. 133) the South had only four cities of 8,000 or more people, New Orleans and Richmond being added to the limited list for the year 1790. Washington, the nation's city, a political not a geographic creation, though south of the Mason and Dixon's Line,

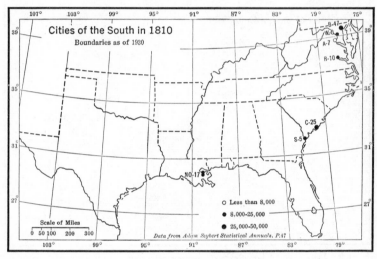

FIG. 133

is not included in this study. Baltimore had become a city of 35,600, and Charleston nearly 25,000. Richmond had 9,735 people.*

Baltimore, near the head of ocean navigation (for vessels of that time) on the Chesapeake, the logical site for a port, had expanded its trade territory. It had commercial traffic lines that reached to all parts of Maryland, down the Great Valley even to the Valley of eastern Tennessee, across the Appalachian Plateau to the Ohio country; and it competed with Philadelphia for the commerce that floated down the Susquehanna. Livestock was driven from Kentucky to its markets. It was also active in manufacturing, as described in previous chapters. With all this activity, the rapid increase in the population of the city "even surpassed" the expectation of its friends. It contained more men of "wealth and probity in commercial transactions in proportion

---

* Adam Seybert, *Statistical Annals,* 47.

to its population than many of the seaport towns in the Union."* Its exports were much larger in proportion to its population than those of either Philadelphia or New York. It was the third city in size in the country. Its merchant fleet numbered 102 vessels. It had so established itself by 1810 in its commercial sphere, its sustenance area, that there was little possibility of Philadelphia, its nearest competitor, ever winning much of its trade territory. From the beginning even to the present its growth has been steady and comparatively rapid. It was greatly benefited by the construction of the National Road which was completed to the Ohio in 1817; and by the Chesapeake and Ohio Canal and the Baltimore and Ohio Railroad, the latter dating from about 1828-1830. It was the steamboat on the Mississippi, which drew the traffic of the Ohio Valley southward to New Orleans, that forced a group of some twenty-five of the leading citizens of Baltimore, at a meeting held February 12, 1827, to propose the construction of a Baltimore and Ohio railroad "as the best means of restoring to the city of Baltimore that portion of the western trade which [had] lately been directed from it by steam navigation and other causes."† (See Chapters VI and VII.) In both the Revolutionary War and the War of 1812, Baltimore was benefited by "privateering" on British commerce; and in the clipper-ship days, in the early decades of the nineteenth century, the Baltimore clipper was the pride of American merchant shipping and, of course, of Baltimore. When the power demands of its factories surpassed the potential power of the Patapsco rapids it had access by canal and railroads to the coal deposits that outcropped on the eastern edge of the Allegheny Front near Cumberland. Thus its commercial and industrial activities experienced no abatement and it grew in numbers of people accordingly.

The economic life of Charleston was not so varied as that of Baltimore. Commerce with the back country which, as previously stated, was carried on by wagon, some commodities coming even from the Valley of eastern Tennessee, and an extensive overseas trade with Europe and the West Indies, brought much wealth to its people.‡ Though channels across the bar which had formed at the entrance of the harbor had but 16.5 to 18 feet of water, this provided ample depth for the small ships of that day. There are several reasons, apparently, why it did not grow so rapidly as Baltimore. It had a

---

* Joseph Scott, *A Geographical Dictionary of the United States of North America*, topic, Baltimore.

† John Moody, *The Railroad Builders*, 97, 98.

‡ Joseph Scott, *op. cit.*, topic, Charleston.

much larger negro population, more than 46 per cent of its population in 1790 being negro; its contacts with the back country were
not so well developed as Baltimore's; and its hinterland was not so
productive. It was not so active in shipping. It was more of a recreational and rest center than Baltimore.

New Orleans, the third city in size in the South, was just at the
beginning of its commercial career in 1810. Flatboat traffic on the
Mississippi was assuming great importance and was certain to increase as the great Mississippi basin was won to civilization.

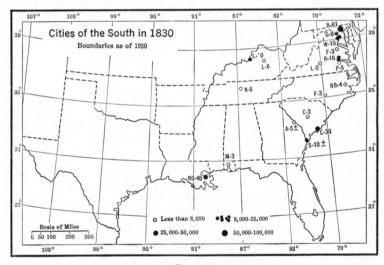

FIG. 134

The cities (8,000 or more population) of 1810, it is to be noted, were
seaports, and all were *grown-up, original settlements*. Richmond may
be considered a continuation of the original James River settlement,
the commercial activity merely shifting from the lower James to the
head of ocean and bay navigation at the Fall Line. The practical
geographer, John Smith, recognized the value of this site, and it was
through his influence that a settlement was made there in 1609, but the
hostility of the Indians caused its abandonment. Fort Charles was
erected at the falls in 1645. Permanent settlement dates from about
1737. The new settlement was named Richmond from Richmond on
the Thames, to which its site bore some resemblance.

The Census of 1830 lists Baltimore (80,620), Richmond (16,060),
Charleston (30,289), New Orleans (46,300), and Louisville (10,352),

five in number, as the cities of the South (see Fig. 134). The population of Savannah is not given, apparently on account of the inefficiency of the census takers or recorders. Since four of the cities, and the largest at that, were seaports, it is evident that a seacoast site continued to be the most favorable for urban growth. Louisville was the only exception and it was on a navigable river. Among the larger towns (less than 8,000 in population) were Petersburg at the Fall Line in Virginia on the navigable Appomattox; Lexington, Kentucky, with 6,104 people; and Nashville, Tennessee, with 5,566.* The growth of Nashville, like that of Louisville, was associated with river navigation. The steamboat on the Mississippi had now reached a high degree of efficiency and was competing successfully with the flatboats. The steamboat was also the chief factor in the rapid growth of Louisville, for this city was at the Falls of the Ohio which, though not forming a barrier to navigation in high-water periods, did cause a break in transportation in the dry season. Nor did its site prove less advantageous by the construction of the Louisville and Portland Canal, some two and one-half miles long, in 1830. Louisville for a time was second to Lexington in population, which was larger because it was near the centers of the original settlements in Kentucky. A writer stated in 1815 that next to Lexington Louisville was "the most considerable town in the state" and that an extensive commerce was carried on with Natchez, New Orleans, and St. Louis.† The superiority of its site and situation over those of Lexington, and the westward movement of the farming frontier, soon began to tell to its advantage.

Between 1830 and 1850 there was an appreciable growth both in population of individual cities and in the number of cities. Wilmington, Delaware, in 1850 had a population of nearly 14,000. (See Fig. 135.)

Baltimore continued to be the only city of Maryland. Its population was 169,000; and, owing to the conservative policy of Philadelphia in not extending its municipal boundaries as the geographic city grew, Baltimore was the second city in the United States in population. In 1854 when Philadelphia's boundaries were extended to the borders of the county, thus taking in its suburbs and increasing its population to 500,000 or more, Baltimore took third rank. Its transportation facilities were extended and multiplied over those of 1830. The railroad that spread out north and south of the city brought a large and productive hinterland with a wide variety of products into

---

* *Report of Fifth Census,* 1830, 81, 85, 91, 95, 97, 101, 111, 115.
† Joseph E. Worcester, *A Gazetteer of the United States,* topic, Louisville.

close touch with its markets; and the river, bay, and ocean, along
with harbor improvements which were begun about 1836, contributed
to its commercial prosperity. The excellent transportation facilities,
cheap coal, water power, and varied raw materials continued to stimulate its manufactures.

Alexandria, Richmond, Petersburg, Norfolk, and Portsmouth, all
on Chesapeake Bay or the navigable tidal tributaries of the bay, had
attained city status. Richmond now had a population of 27,600. The
only interior city of Virginia was Lynchburg. This had water trans-

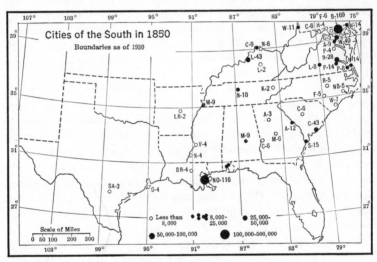

Fig. 135

portation by means of the James River Canal to Richmond and, being
the only city of the Piedmont so favored, was an active collecting
and distributing point for a large area. It had (about 1845) 128 stores,
32 tobacco warehouses (some of which manufactured tobacco), a cotton factory, an iron foundry, 3 large flour mills, and 3 banks. On the
canal there were "handsome packet boats for passengers" and 40
freight boats of 60-ton burden.*

Railroads in Virginia in 1850 had not yet begun to be numerous
enough to affect, appreciably, the growth of cities. The rapid growth
of Richmond during the preceding decade led some to prophesy a

---

* Daniel Haskell and J. Calvin Smith, *A Complete Descriptive and Statistical
Gazetteer of the United States of America,* 1846, 304.

From Edward King, The Great South, 1874, 631.

FIG. 136.—The Gallego Flour Mill, Richmond, Virginia, about 1870.

In its day this was one of the largest flour mills in the United States. It was located here to utilize the water power of the James River at or near the Fall Line. Wheat came from the Piedmont and Great Valley by way of the James River Canal.

From Edward King, The Great South, 1874, 637.

FIG. 137.—The Tredegar Iron Works, at Richmond, Virginia, about 1870.

For many decades Richmond was one of the most important foundry and machine-shop centers in the South.

bright future for its manufactures. Writes Martin,* "There is no
doubt . . . of its final destination as a manufacturing city (Figs.
136 and 137), as there is probably no [other] spot in the Union endowed by nature with finer facilities for that kind of industry." With
the James River canal extending westward to the Great Valley; with
an extension by canal, river, or railroad (then projected) to the Ohio;
with ocean and deep-water navigation within a few miles of the city
limits; with coal mines scarcely more than a dozen miles distant;

Engraved by Fisher, Son, and Company, London.
From J. S. Buckingham, op. cit., Vol. I, 46.

FIG. 138.—Charleston Harbor about 1840.

with "unlimited" water power; and already with numerous factories
turning out flour, cotton yarns and goods, paper, and other products,
there was everything that would stimulate prophets to prophesy. But
nature, the timidity of man (see Chapter VII), and an accident, the
Civil War, prevented the fulfillment of the prophecy.

North Carolina, whose exports for the most part always moved
northward to the Chesapeake Tidewater ports or southward to Charleston, was still without an 8,000-population center. Wilmington, its only
deep-water seaport, had a population of but 7,264. Fayetteville, near
the Fall Line, had less than 5,000.

Charleston (Fig. 138) continued to be the only city in South Carolina, but Columbia was approaching the status of a city. The state
government had already been moved from Charleston to this more

*Joseph Martin, *A Gazetteer of Virginia,* 1835, 75.

central location. Columbia could ship products to the seacoast by the river and the Santee Canal, but it seems unlikely that river navigation contributed to its growth. The railroad which had but recently reached it from Charleston was beginning to increase its importance as a collecting and distributing center. Politics and education were its major interests, however.

In Georgia, Savannah had nearly 16,000 people (Census for 1850 gives 15,312), some two-thirds of whom were "connected with commerce and trade and the greater part of the remaining third with her manufactures and mechanical arts"; yet only 164 whites were classed as laborers. As a market for lumber, cotton, and rice, Savannah ranked among the first cities of the South. The average depth of the seaward channel was 19 feet, and thus the largest of seagoing boats could reach its wharves. It had by this time built up numerous traffic lines to the interior of the state. Besides the Savannah River, on which 20 steamboats of large size and 50 steam towboats operated as far inland as Augusta, there was a "great line of railroad reaching into Tennessee and Alabama." Another railroad was being built to the Flint River, and the Savannah and Ogeechee had been improved for steamboats.*

The only other population center in Georgia that had reached city size was Augusta, on the Fall Line and at the head of navigation of the Savannah. While Augusta had railroad connections with Charleston, the major part of its trade moved to and from the sea by way of the river. A railroad connected it with Milledgeville; and this, with the numerous roads that extended over the Piedmont, served to give it "a very active trade." It contained 12 commission agents engaged in foreign trade. Cotton, tobacco, and grains were the more important farm products handled.†

Like Georgia, Alabama had two cities: Mobile, the larger, an ocean port; and Montgomery, a river city. Montgomery had steamboat connections with Mobile. Mobile (20,515) was larger than Savannah. The admirable situation of the city for commerce—it has the longest system of navigable waterways of any city in the South, with the exception of New Orleans—was partly nullified as a factor in urban growth by the unhealthful conditions of its site. It had devastating epidemics in 1819, 1825, 1829, 1839, and 1843. About the last date a marsh on the northern border of the city was filled, and shortly after a drainage system was provided. In 1850 Mobile was second only to New Orleans as a commercial mart on the Gulf. An 18-foot channel

---

* Richard S. Fisher, *A New and Complete Statistical Gazetteer of the United States of America*, 773, 775.

† Haskell and Smith, *op. cit.*, 43; R. S. Fisher, *op. cit.*, 51.

led across the bar at the mouth of the bay, which, in its original condition, had only 11 feet of water over it.* This for a time greatly
restricted the size of ocean-going crafts that could reach the city.
Improvements to the harbor by the United States Engineers were
authorized in 1826, 1830, and 1832.†

In 1850 three railroads were under construction from Mobile: the
Mobile and Ohio, projected northward; the Gerard and Mobile extended eastward toward the Atlantic Coast; and a small railroad
westward to New Orleans. Contacts by rivers were made with a large
trade territory to the North. Most of the cotton exported from Mobile
—one-sixth of all produced in the Union in 1852—reached its 46
wharves by river. More than half the cotton exported went to England. The port also handled forest products as exports, and imported
manufactured goods.‡ Later New Orleans began to push its trade eastward and northeastward into Alabama and eastern Mississippi. Thus
Mobile was not left sovereign in its natural hinterland. Its growth was
slow for several decades after 1850.

Montgomery owed some of its prestige over the less populous centers of the state to its being the capital city. It was, for a time, an
important shipping point for a large cotton-producing area in eastern
Alabama. For two or more decades before the railroad era it was
one of the important stopping points on the river-and-land route between Savannah and Mobile. The completion of the La Grande Railroad extended Savannah's and Charleston's trade territory into Alabama, and their gains were losses to Mobile and Montgomery. The
Florida Peninsula, a barrier to commerce between the eastern Gulf
Coast and the South Atlantic, favored Savannah and Charleston in this
struggle. The Montgomery and West Point Railroad was already carrying cotton and other farm products to the Chattahoochee River, down
which it moved to Pensacola.

New Orleans, which from the beginning has been the second city
in the South, in 1850 was in the zenith of its monopoly of the trade
of the vast, fertile Mississippi Basin, which by this time was occupied by aggressive farmers as far west as the semi-humid prairies.
(See Fig. 46.) Most of the commerce between the cities and rural
districts of the Mississippi Basin and eastern United States and
Europe passed over the wharves at New Orleans, where river steamers
and flatboats met ocean carriers (Fig. 139). In the far northern part

* Fisher, *op. cit.*, 500, 501.
† *Mobile*, Port Series, 3, Part I, Corps of Engineers, U. S. Army and U. S.
Shipping Board, 1, 5.
‡ Fisher, *loc. cit.*

of the country the Erie Canal (completed in 1825) had tapped the commerce of the Lakes Region and there resulted a large movement of freight between the old Northwest and New York. But this had little effect on New Orleans, for its trade territory hardly touched the Great Lakes Region. It was not until 1854 that all-rail connections were established between Chicago and New York by way of the Michigan Central, the Great Western, and the New York Central,* and soon thereafter railroad lines were projected westward from Chicago into the borders of New Orleans territory. The Pennsylvania Canal, completed to Pittsburgh by 1834, was drawing off some of the traffic of the upper Ohio Basin to Philadelphia; but it was not

Engraved by Capewell and Kimmel, New York.
From "The Home Circle," Vol. II, 1856, 97.

FIG. 139.—The New Orleans Harbor about 1850.

until after 1853, at which date the Baltimore and Ohio Railroad reached Wheeling, and 1854, when Philadelphia was given rail connection with Pittsburgh by way of the Pennsylvania Railroad,† that New Orleans began to lose the monopoly of the trade of the Ohio River region and the upper Mississippi Basin. These regions gradually were annexed to the sustenance areas of Baltimore, Philadelphia, and New York, as their three master railroads extended their feeders westward.

In the Lower South, the railroads that were projected westward and northwestward from the Atlantic Coast cities were slow in getting to the Mississippi, so that this waterway continued to dominate in transportation in the South in a large area tributary to that river.

---

* A. E. Parkins, *The Historical Geography of Detroit*, 266.
† A. E. Parkins, "Development of Transportation in Pennsylvania," *Bulletin of the Geographical Society of Philadelphia*, XIV, 28, 39; XV, 1, 15.

Thus while the railroads of the North destroyed or greatly reduced New Orleans' commerce with the upper Mississippi region, the Southern lines benefited the city.

The chief interests of New Orleans in 1850 were associated with commerce. The most active part of the city was the levee which served both as a protection to the city from floods and as a wharf or quay for river and ocean craft. Writes one author graphically,[*]

> The quay is here all action, and the very water is covered with life. Huge vessels float upon its bosom which acknowledge none of the powers of air and wait no tide. One is weighted down to the guards with cotton, a freight of 3,000 bales. Twenty more lie side by side laden with the same commodity. Huge piles, bale upon bale, story above story, cover the levee. Pork without end, as if the Ohio had emptied its lap at the door of New Orleans, and flour by the thousands of barrels rolled out upon the quay and heaped up—a large area is covered with these two products from the up-country, and still appears seemingly undiminshed, although the seller, the buyer, and drayman are busy in the midst of it. Here is a boat freighted with lead from Galena; and another brings furs and peltry from the headwater of the Missouri 3,000 miles to the northwest. The Illinois, the Ohio, the Missouri, the Arkansas, and the Red River, all are tributaries to this commercial depot and send down annually to its wharves merchantable material to the value of $100,000,000, more or less. Nearly 20,000 miles of inland navigation is tributary to the city. The quay appropriated to the foreign and coastwise shipping presented another and a different scene. Here the cotton bales, tobacco hogshead, pork and flour barrel, and the whiskey cask yield to bales of foreign and domestic manufactures, pipes of wine, and crates of wares. The shipping stretches away as far as the eye can reach, two miles or more in extent three tiers deep with their heads to the current curving with the river—a beautiful crescent. The English, the French, the Spanish, the Dane, the Russian, the Swede, the Hollander, etc., are here commingled and compete for the commerce of the teeming West.

In 1849-1850 there arrived at New Orleans from upriver 951 flatboats, and 2,918 river steamboats.[†]

Manufacturing was of much less importance probably because the rapidly growing stream of commerce absorbed the energy and increasing capital of its business men.[†]

Commerce called for banks (seven in number), commission houses, wholesale houses, and importers and exporters of a wide variety of raw and manufactured products.

The site of New Orleans was unhealthful and continued to be so

[*] Fisher, *op. cit.*, 554.
[†] *Idem.*

for several decades until improved methods of sewage disposal and drainage were provided. Yellow fever epidemics were of frequent occurrence. The city's location at the nodal point of a vast system of land and ocean traffic lines made it cosmopolitan. On its streets, in the hotels, and in the residential section itself mingled Creoles from the West Indies, Central America, South America, or Mexico, with Europeans and Americans, Asiatics, and Africans, in great numbers. No other city in the South had such a variety of races, such a babel of tongues and such a variety of vices. Its population growth was directly and indirectly the result of man's taking advantage of a site on a great inland waterway, near its mouth, and one that had a deep-water contact with the world's oceans. The immediate physical environment was anything but favorable. Man made here a great emporium, a great population center, by overcoming the immediate unfavorable conditions of topography, climate, domestic water supply, lack of stone, and other items, and by building upon the opportunities offered for connecting a great productive hinterland, covering half the Mississippi Basin, with the markets and manufacturing centers of the world at large.

The Mississippi Basin in the South in 1850 had five urban centers above New Orleans that had attained a population of 8,000 or more. (See Figure 135.) They were all on navigable rivers. Louisville had a population of more than 43,000, having more than doubled in number of people every decade since 1830. In its growth it had left Lexington far behind and now dominated completely the commercial and manufacturing activities of the state. But it had rivals. Covington, a satellite of Cincinnati and on the Ohio, and Newport near by had a combined population of 15,000. Being in reality "Cincinnati in Kentucky," these two cities shared with Cincinnati much of the environmental advantages of that city's situation. The river, however, served always to prevent freedom of movement between the parts of the greater urban center, and to a certain degree industrial expansion. Differences in state governments no doubt at times interfered with their geographic unification. "Greater" Cincinnati had a total population of about 170,000, or more than four times that of Louisville.

Wheeling in Virginia on the Ohio where the National Road crosses that river had grown by 1850 to a city of 11,435. A wire suspension bridge, "one of the finest structures in the world," had replaced the ferry. This facilitated travel east and west. The Baltimore and Ohio reached the city early in the 1850's.

Memphis had a population of only 8,841 in 1850, but the superiority of its situation over that of other Tennessee cities was certain to give it the lead when once it secured control of the productive territory naturally tributary to it. Unlike New Orleans, its immediate environment is favorable for city growth, favorable for the extension of traffic lines into the territory. Its location on a bluff 30 or more feet above the highest floods of the Mississippi, and the most favorable site for a city between the mouth of the Ohio and Vicksburg on either side of the river, early attracted enterprising men. It became the mart for a trade area that covered much of three states. Though much of its success was intimately associated with the commerce of the Mississippi, it was early sought as a terminal point of or an important way station for Mississippi Basin railroads. The first railroad to reach it from the east was the Memphis and Charleston, early in the 1850's. It became a bridge city, the high bluff offering conditions for the construction of high-level bridges far beyond the reach of floods. Here were the only bridges across the Mississippi below Cairo until the construction of those at Vicksburg and New Orleans in recent years. The city was admirably situated for manufacturing. Coal could be secured by river barge from the Appalachian fields in Ohio, West Virginia, and Pennsylvania, or from West Kentucky; and all about were hardwood forests and a wide variety of farm products. Its early growth was aided materially by the location here of a Federal navy yard. Among the industries in 1850 were a shipyard (other than the navy yard), a large flour mill (62,000 barrels capacity annually), and a large cotton "manufactory."*

It should be noted that the cities of 8,000 or more people in 1850 were either seaports or river ports with but one exception—Petersburg, Virginia.

Between 1850 and 1870 there was a large increase in the number of cities in the South (see Fig. 140). Many centers which in 1850 were small towns had now become cities. Wilmington (30,842) stood alone in Delaware. Baltimore had grown to more than 267,000. Cumberland and Frederick were now of city size. No new cities had arisen in Virginia. On the other hand, Lynchburg had lost its city status. Richmond had a population of 51,000; the Norfolk-Portsmouth center, 30,000; and Petersburg, about 19,000. The Great Valley centers had made little advance. An ocean harbor site with numerous railroads into the interior seemed to be favorable conditions for urban growth in Virginia in the decades between 1850 and 1870.

Urban growth in North Carolina was slow. The railroads continued to hold the northern counties within the Chesapeake Bay commercial

---

* Fisher, *op. cit.*, 460.

sphere. Wilmington had a population of 9,550 in 1860; its population in 1870 was 13,400. In South Carolina the cities still numbered two: Charleston (49,000) and Columbia (9,300). Georgia now had four active cities, Atlanta and Macon being new (city status).

No other city in the South, up to this time, had had such a rapid growth as Atlanta. In 1843 it was a mere railroad station on a hilltop in central Georgia. It was given railroad connections with the seacoast in 1845. In 1850 it had a population of 2,372; in 1860, 9,554; and in 1870, 21,789. Its rapid growth up to 1870 and since is largely

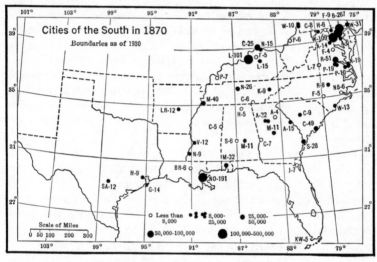

FIG. 140

or partly the result of its geographic location on the broad inter-stream area on the Piedmont, to the south of the rough mountain and gorge lands of the Southern Appalachian Highlands, and opposite low-grade gaps across these highlands. It is central to most of the Southeast. Atlanta could have been a few score miles north, south, east, or west of its present location and still be the active Atlanta that it is; but the placing of the southern terminus of the first railroad in northern Georgia, the Western and Atlantic, fixed its location and it became a crossroads of railroads in the early 1850's when a line was built northwestward from Augusta and another from Atlanta to Montgomery. During the Civil War it was the seat of large manufactures for the Confederate army and a depot for supplies. The effects of these activities on the growth of the city were largely overcome by its being in Sherman's "path of destruction" in 1864. A large part of the city was burned, and thousands of people fled its boundaries. Its remarkable growth between 1860 and 1870, 28 per cent increase, is evidence that its situation has environmental attractions in abundance for urban growth. But it must not be forgotten that Atlanta had enterprising, aggressive, and progressive leaders, who realized its geographic advantages for trade and exploited every opportunity that presented itself.

Florida was still without an 8,000-population city in 1870; and in Alabama, Mobile (32,000) and Montgomery (10,600) were the only cities. In Mississippi, Vicksburg, near the mouth of the Yazoo, down which steamboats brought the cotton of the then-settled parts of the Delta, now had a population of 12,443, and Natchez, 9,000. Natchez is one of the oldest settlements on the lower Mississippi, and at one time was the only receiving port in American territory for the commerce of the upcountry. (See Chapter IV and Fig. 44.) By degrees its river commerce was absorbed by New Orleans, and its trade interests became associated only with the immediate farming region. Its status as a city was short lived, for in 1880 its population numbered less than 8,000.

Tennessee had three cities by 1870, Memphis taking the lead and Nashville ranking second. Both had much better river and rail contact with the outside than Knoxville, the third city.

In Kentucky, Lexington, one of the older population centers of the state, had now become a city of nearly 15,000. Louisville was in the 100,000 class, and Covington and Newport had expanded somewhat in size. Two cities therefore had been added to Kentucky's list.

West of the Mississippi, city growth had been rapid. Little Rock, which in 1850 had 2,167, now had 12,380 people. Its location on the Arkansas probably contributed something to its growth. It was the nearest trading center for Fort Smith at the eastern border of an Indian territory. The Arkansas Valley was the most productive part of the state.

Texas now had three rapidly growing cities: San Antonio (12,256), Houston (9,382), and Galveston (13,818). Galveston, the seaport, was the largest. Though lacking harbor facilities it was the chief port of the state (Fig. 141). San Antonio was the oldest city of the state, having been an important Spanish settlement when Texas was a part of the Spanish Empire. Houston, the third city, located on the coastal prairie far up on Buffalo Bayou, had poor connections with the ocean. In 1856 it was connected with Galveston Bay by the Buffalo Bayou,

Brazos, and Colorado Railroad. Galveston handled that part of its trade which moved to and from the Gulf and continued to do so until recent years. Houston's growth all along until the completion of the Houston Ship Canal was due to its railroad connections with the interior. By 1860 there were 320 miles of railroads in Texas centering in Houston, out of the 711 for the state.* San Antonio remained isolated until railroads reached it in the 1870's.†

From *Edward King, The Great South, 1874, 103.*

FIG. 141.—Before the Days of Federal Harbor Improvements at Galveston, Texas.

In 1880 the South had 39 centers of 8,000 or more population. (See Fig. 142.) There were 35 in 1870. Lynchburg had regained city rank. Key West was Florida's first city. Paducah, Kentucky, Shreveport, Louisiana, and Dallas and Austin in Texas were the new cities. Natchez and three others had fallen below the 8,000 figure.

In 1880 there were only three cities in the South with a population of 100,000 or more: Baltimore with 332,000, New Orleans with 216,000, and Louisville with 124,000. The two larger were ocean ports, the third a river port. Baltimore and Louisville owed some of their growth to Northern trade, Baltimore more than Louisville; for by now the former had spread a mesh of railroad lines far and wide, and had brought a large part of the Transappalachian territory, north of the

---

* Latter figures from *Statistical Abstract*, 1930, 394; former from *Hunt's Merchants Magazine*, XLIII, 633.

† Map, *Mitchell's New General Atlas*, S. Augustus Mitchell, publisher, 1866.

Ohio, within its trade area. Baltimore's factories were producing $78,-
000,000 worth of goods in 1880, and Louisville's, $36,000,000.* The
Louisville and Nashville Railroad lines had by 1880 extended Louisville's trade territory far into the Gulf States, but the Ohio hindered
its development of traffic lines into the North. Louisville was thus
largely a Southern city. There were only two 50,000 cities: Charleston (nearly 50,000) and Richmond (63,600). Both of these were sea-

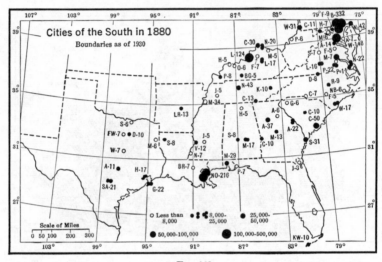

Fig. 142

ports, but only coastwise and smaller ocean-going craft could reach
their wharves.

Of the eight cities of 25,000 to 50,000 (see Fig. 143A) three were
seaports: Wilmington (Delaware), Savannah, and Mobile. Wilmington's contacts with the interior were by rail; Savannah's and Mobile's,
by both water and rail. Savannah's harbor could accommodate the
largest of ocean boats of that time. Wilmington, whose interests were
largely in manufacturing, had only a shallow-water connection with
the deep-channel of the Delaware River. Wheeling, Covington, Nashville, and Memphis were on navigable waterways and also had railroad connections with most of the larger cities of our country. Atlanta depended upon railroads alone to keep it in touch with its trade
territory and the world outside.

* *Compendium of Tenth Census,* 1880, Part 2, 973-977.

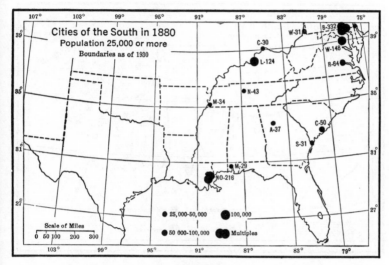

Fig. 143A

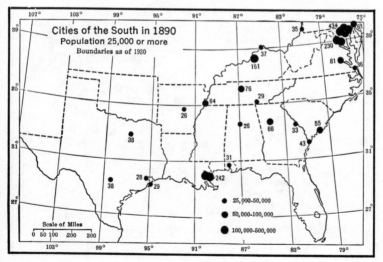

Fig. 143B

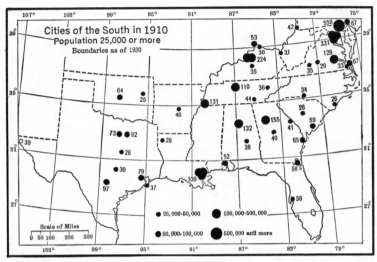

FIG. 143C

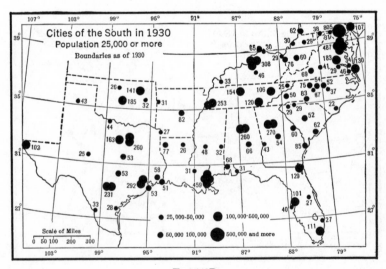

FIG. 143D

A HALF CENTURY OF GROWTH (1880-1930)

The growth of cities in the New South in the last 50 years has been remarkable. (See Table XXX; also Figs. 143A, 143B, 143C, and 143D.) There were 3 cities of 100,000 or more people in 1880 as previously shown; the number had increased to 22 by 1930 (Fig. 143D). The combined population of the "100,000-or-more" class cities in 1930 was more than seven times the population of this class in 1880. There were only 2 cities with populations between 50,000 and 100,000 in 1880; in 1930 there were 24. At the former date there were 8 in the 25,000-50,000 class; in 1930 the number was 36. As would be expected there have been great variations in the rate of growth. Yet urbanization is progressing rapidly. A large number of Southern cities have had growths that are many times the *normal multiple* for our country. By normal multiple is meant the number of times the urban population of our country in 1930 was of the urban population in 1880. The total urban population of the United States in 1880 was 14,000,000, in 1930 more than 69,000,000.* This latter figure is 4.8 times the former. This 4.8 is here called the *normal urban population multiple* for the United States. Using the 4.8 as the normal urban population multiple in a comparison of the urban populations at these two dates, Table XXX shows that the South had 6 cities in 1930 in the "100,000 or more" class that were below the normal multiple in their growth, but 16 that were above. The growth of a few is more than 20 times the normal multiple.

The cities with a low multiple growth, as shown by the table, were Baltimore, New Orleans, Louisville, Wilmington, Richmond, and Nashville. The first three were the largest in the South. The actual numerical increase of these three has been great. Baltimore in this time had actually added more than 470,000 people to the 1880 population, an equivalent of four Miamis of 1930 with some to spare. New Orleans had added 243,000, or the equivalent of two Chattanoogas; and Louisville, 184,000. Thus though their ratios seem small the actual numerical increase was great. The slower growth of Wilmington, Richmond, and Nashville was to some extent associated with the smallness of their trade territory, and to the fact that none possessed superior advantages for manufacturing. The cities that have had the most spectacular rise in the last half century, some in forty or even thirty years, are Tampa and Miami in Florida, Birming-

---

* No adjustments were made for the different bases employed for differentiating urban and rural population at the two dates.

TABLE XXX

THE GROWTH OF THE LARGER CITIES OF THE SOUTH, BETWEEN 1880 AND 1930[1]

Cities	Population in 1930	Population in 1880	Actual Population Multiples
(Old) Baltimore	805,000	332,000	2.4
(Old) New Orleans	459,000	216,000	2.1
(Old) Louisville	308,000	124,000	2.5
Houston	292,000	17,000	17.2
Atlanta	270,000[2]	37,000	7.3
Dallas	260,000	10,000	26.
Birmingham	260,000	3,000	86.6
Memphis	253,000	34,000	7.4
San Antonio	232,000	21,000	11.
Oklahoma City	185,000	(4,000 in 1890)	46.5 (since 1890)
(Old) Richmond	183,000	64,000	3.
Fort Worth	163,000	7,000	23.3
(Old) Nashville	154,000	43,000	3.6
Tulsa	141,000	(1,400 in 1900)	100. (since 1900)
(Old) Norfolk	130,000	22,000	6.
Jacksonville	130,000	8,000	16.2
Chattanooga	120,000	13,000	9.2
Miami	111,000	(1,700 in 1900)	65.4 (since 1900)
Wilmington	107,000	42,000	2.6
Knoxville	106,000	10,000	10.6
El Paso	102,000	700	146.
Tampa	101,000	700	145.7

[1] The writer recognizes that the population figures for the respective cities, and for the different dates for any one city, are capable of rough comparison only, for they represent the population of civil not geographic cities. Yet, since the supreme goal of all American cities is large size, it is generally the practice to push the municipal boundaries as far toward rural sections as they may be stretched; and thus the population of the municipal city quite generally represents the population of the geographic city.
[2] Atlanta City, not "municipality of Atlanta," which has 361,000.

ham in Alabama, Tulsa and Oklahoma City in Oklahoma, and El Paso in Texas.

A city in its evolution, its life, is in many respects like an organism. It has birth, growth, decay, and power of revival. It may suffer accidents and be affected with diseases, yet, like living matter, it has the power of repairing damages and overcoming diseases. Its life is a struggle for space, for the control of trade territory and resources. Large cities demand large sustenance areas; small cities, lesser ones. As a city grows in population, and its industries increase in complexity and in number, it endeavors to enlarge its sustenance space; if this be accomplished, further growth is stimulated. The size it may ultimately attain depends upon the area and extent of resources of the area it controls. If in this expansion of sustenance area it comes into competition with other cities, a combat is on for territory. The physical weapons in this struggle are seaways, canals, interior waterways, railroads, and, to a lesser degree, highways and airways. The more successful cities often are directed by intelligent leaders, civic organizations, and business men of foresight, who advertise honestly, and who are best acquainted with the practical working of geographic laws of human utilization of physical environments.

Eventually in this struggle for space the boundaries of the sustenance area of a city tend to become fairly fixed; but there is never any assurance that they will remain so. The location of a trade boundary, or the boundaries between contending cities, depends upon the relative activity of the civic leaders, past and present, of these cities; so also do the direction and the rate of movement of the trade territory boundary. When the boundaries of the sustenance area of a

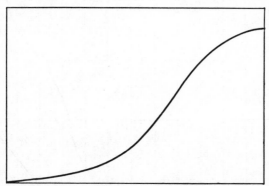

Fig. 144.—A Normal Curve of Population Growth

city become fairly well fixed and the resources of the area have about reached the maximum of development, the city tends to slow up in its population growth. Eventually the population becomes stationary. Very few cities have reached this stage in America. But the discovery of new resources within the city's realm and the discovery of new methods of utilizing hitherto little-used resources are stimuli to renewed growth. In the early periods of a city's growth minor accidents, but momentous to them, such as an epidemic, a fire, the severing, the shifting, or the decline of an artery of commerce, have profound effects upon its development; but as it increases in size such accidents disturb the population growth but little. All these trends and modifications in the growth may be expressed graphically by curves (Figs. 145 and 146).

The curve of normal population growth has a fairly definite form (Fig. 144), though the "size" of the curve for the different cities varies. In the early periods the up-trend of the curve is slight (this may be called the plains). This is followed by a strong up-turn, which may even become nearly vertical, if the city has a rapid growth. In time

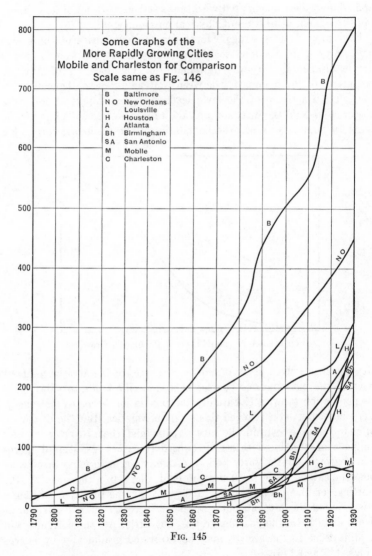

FIG. 145

the curve flattens out and eventually becomes horizontal (the plateau). The size which the city may attain, we have seen, is roughly proportional to the size and richness of its sustenance area. The population curve of a city which dominates a small sustenance area is relatively small; the plateau is but a few units above the plains; but the curve (abscissa) of a city that dominates a large area has its plateau far above its plains.

THE POPULATION GRAPHS OF SELECTED CITIES INTERPRETED
(For Some Cities a Summary)

Baltimore, the oldest of the large cities of the South and the city that has had the largest growth (see Fig. 145), has many environmental conditions that are highly favorable. It has been shown that it was the first of the Southern seaports to push a railroad into the interior. Its zeal in canal construction was less successful than that of Philadelphia, but its Baltimore and Ohio Railroad reached the Ohio about a year earlier than Philadelphia's road. All along, Baltimore has been more active than other Southern cities in expanding the boundaries of its sustenance area. This has been done by sheer enterprise, for it was no mean engineering feat to construct a railroad across the Allegheny Front in the days when railroad engineering was a young profession. Commerce was its major economic activity for a century or more. Distance from industrial regions from which manufactured goods could be obtained, water power and raw materials at hand, and, later, proximity to the coal mines of the Appalachian field, all favored man in developing manufactures. It is a seaport and has always had deep-water navigation to the world's traffic routes. Yet this fact and its value to the city was nearly lost sight of at times. After the passing of the Baltimore clipper the major interests in commerce seemed to swing to the railroad. The Baltimore and Ohio was Baltimore's own line; but the Pennsylvania, when it extended a line to Baltimore, tended to make that city a dependency of Philadelphia and New York. Its leaders eventually came to realize this fact and began the development of their own ocean outlet. Chesapeake Bay and Patapsco River, though deep enough for the smaller boats of the past centuries, came to be considered inadequate and the inadequacy increased with time. In late years the Federal Government and the city have appropriated millions of dollars for turning basins and deeper channels, wharves, warehouses, elevators, wharf machinery, and dry docks,* as discussed in a previous section, Chapter VI. Today Baltimore ranks sixth among the manufacturing cities (on the basis of *value added by manufacture*) of the country, its leading products being steel and other heavy-

---

* *Report of Chief of Engineers*, U. S. Army, 1930, 460-462.

industry products, chemicals, fertilizers, industrial alcohol, and refined petroleum.

An early start, location on an arm of the sea, and a sustenance area rich in power and raw material are the major natural conditions and factors in the growth of Baltimore.

New Orleans, the second city in size and in growth in the South, had its sustenance area in the Mississippi Basin established for it by nature. Its location near the mouth of the trunk stream of a vast river system, and at the same time an ocean port, "destined" it to be an emporium. In the days when the products of farms, forests, and mines of the great Mississippi Basin moved by rivers, New Orleans flourished; and for a few decades its sustenance area (trade territory) extended from the Appalachian to the Rockies and from the Gulf nearly to the borders of Canada. But the ingenuity of man, as we have seen, lessened, and later destroyed, the monopoly that waterways enjoyed in interior commerce; and, as railroads spread westward from the Middle Atlantic Seaboard, the northern boundary of its trade territory receded ominously southward. But for the rapid settlement and exploitation of the Mississippi Basin in the South and the selection of New Orleans as a Gulf terminus by numerous railroad lines in 1870's and later, its growth would have received a noticeable slump with the passing of the river steamer. There is little evidence that the people of New Orleans were ever active in developing great traffic lines, by river or by land. A few short lines of railroads were constructed, eastward, northward, and westward, to near-by productive sections, but these were later absorbed by large developing systems anxious to profit from the superior location of the city for world commerce. Environmental conditions did not demand enterprise of its citizens in expanding its sustenance area. But the apparent lethargy of past decades and centuries is in striking contrast to the enterprise shown in late decades. New Orleans, now that it has strong competition on the Gulf Coast, is fighting for traffic and has succeeded in winning the support of the whole of the state of Louisiana in its attempts to develop one of the most efficient river and ocean terminals in the South.

The Federal Government has, as has been learned in previous pages, adopted a project that will give not only a 9-foot channel to Pittsburgh, Chicago, and St. Paul, with lesser depths on many tributaries, but also a 35-foot channel in the 110 miles of river from the city to the Gulf. It is the opinion of this writer that the value of up-river improvement in attracting trade to New Orleans is yet to be demonstrated. The value of its 35-foot channel to the Gulf has been and is being demonstrated.

With active Houston to the west and Mobile, now being developed through state assistance, New Orleans must from now on struggle to retain its trade territory, for the railroad has reduced the monopoly the Mississippi gave it over the traffic of the Mississippi Basin. Its manufactures are supplementary to commerce and form in a way a symbiotic relationship to the major activity. The opening of a "cheap" (to the shippers) water route, the Warrior River navigation, to the Alabama coal fields gives New Orleans cheaper coal than it hitherto

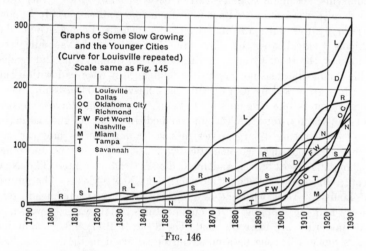

Graphs of Some Slow Growing
and the Younger Cities
(Curve for Louisville repeated)
Scale same as Fig. 145

L Louisville
D Dallas
O C Oklahoma City
R Richmond
F W Fort Worth
N Nashville
M Miami
T Tampa
S Savannah

FIG. 146

had. Although there is little prospect of New Orleans attaining a high rank as a manufacturing center, industrial plants are being established in increasing numbers, utilizing the admirable riverside sites available as far upstream as Baton Rouge.

Since the beginning of the nineteenth century, its population graph has had a consistent upward trend with no evidence that the present rate of growth will receive a serious check in the near future. The extension and expansion of ocean traffic routes to the ports of the South Atlantic and the Pacific, and the rerouting of freight along the logical traffic lines between the Gulf and the North Central States (instead of by way of New York or Philadelphia), would be of great benefit to New Orleans.

Louisville (Figs. 145 and 146), in its attempts to hold its sustenance area, suffers from being surrounded by aggressive cities each endeavoring to make inroads into its commercial realm. In the early part

of the nineteenth century its commercial life depended upon the
river. Some twenty years after the beginning of the railroad era (say
1850-1860) Louisville conceived the idea of expanding its trade territory to the South. It was without competitors and hence, by means
of the Louisville and Nashville Railroad, it drew Nashville and even
Memphis and the territory between, into its trade area. Later, lines
were extended into southern Kentucky, eastern Kentucky, eastern
Tennessee, even Mobile to New Orleans and Pensacola on the Gulf.
In time its railroad, which in the beginning was meant to benefit only
Louisville, became a common carrier between many cities. Other railroads also were built to Louisville from many directions. It is now
served by the Baltimore and Ohio, the Chesapeake and Ohio, the
Illinois Central, the Big Four, the Louisville and Nashville, the
Southern, the Pennsylvania, and the Chicago, Indianapolis and Louisville. Louisville does not enjoy the dominance it once had within the
territory traversed by its railroad, the Louisville and Nashville. Some
larger centers like Cincinnati, St. Louis, and Chicago have absorbed
some of the territory, for certain commodities at least; and, as in all
sustenance areas of large cities, minor trading centers have arisen.
Some exchange their commodities with Louisville; others, for some
commodities, seek larger and more distant trading centers like New
York, Chicago, St. Louis, Cincinnati, and New Orleans. The future
of Louisville rests with the development of its restricted trade territory and the building up of manufactures. Coal, water power, and
raw materials are close at hand. The flood of 1937, though a major
catastrophe, will soon be a minor historical event in the city's industrial and commercial life.

The present-day status of Houston, as the major city of Texas
(Fig. 145), and the constant upturn of its population curve are readily
explicable on the basis of its environmental advantages, although one
must pay tribute to the enterprise and persistence of its people. The
selection of its site for a city meant that so far as nature was involved
it would be only a small coastal prairie population center; but man
has made it a railroad center and an ocean port that is fourth (in
cargo tons, 1935) among the American ocean ports. It is the port of
a large hinterland, only now being exploited, an area rich in timber,
mineral resources, and agricultural and pastoral lands. Ten or more
railroads (some main lines or connections with the main lines of large
railroad systems) and extensive systems of state highways, and petroleum and gas lines put it in close and direct touch with all parts
of its large sustenance area, an area that is certain to continue expanding. It is the ocean port for most of the other enterprising cities

of Texas, such as Fort Worth, Dallas, Waco, Austin, and San Antonio. It handles not only the outgoing ocean shipments from these cities but also the incoming. Corpus Christi (Fig. 59) is developing as a port of southwestern Texas, but its growth can affect Houston but little. In the late 1890's Houston had the same population as Galveston. In 1930 its population was nearly sixteen times Galveston's. Houston profited by Galveston's misfortune of 1900. Its population more than doubled in the last decade.*

As for its environmental conditions for manufacturing, what it lacks in cheap coal is offset by the abundance of petroleum and natural gas. Eastern Texas had in 1936 the most active petroleum-producing fields of our country. It is in the midst, or within easy reach, of large areas of pine forests in eastern Texas. Texas in normal years has about 40 per cent of the cotton acreage of the United States, most of which is within the territory reached by the railroads touching Houston. Petroleum lines and gas lines give it access to most of the oil and gas fields of its hinterland. Salt and sulphur are found in great quantities in the West Gulf Coastal Plain. The types of manufactures in the future will be much as they now are, those closely associated with the fabrication and preparation of the raw materials of its trade territory for distant markets and those in the cities, towns, and farms of its hinterland. It is one of the leading oil-refining centers of the South. A dozen or more refineries have been erected along the Houston Ship Canal to prepare for shipment the ever-increasing flow of oil that runs down hill from Kansas, central and western Texas, Oklahoma, Arkansas, and Louisiana. Its refining industry received its initial impulse from the tremendous production of the nearby Coastal Plain fields. A large part of its outgoing oceanwise commerce, coastwise and foreign, is made up of petroleum and petroleum products. Houston has cotton compresses, oil mills, and a million-bushel grain elevator with ultimate construction planned to handle from four to six million bushels. There are foundries, rice mills, railroad repair shops, and a wide variety of lesser plants.

Atlanta and Dallas (see Figs. 145 and 146 for graphs of growth) are similar in some respects in their location and in the factors conditioning their development. Both are largely the product of railroads; both are great jobbing and distributing centers, the former for the Southeast and the latter for the Southwest (in Texas). Atlanta, as previously stated, has been greatly benefited in its growth by its location to the south of a terrain ill-adapted to the development of

---

* *Report of Fifteenth Census,* 1930, "Population," 18.

traffic routes. Dallas grew up on a broad flat plain in one of the most fertile agricultural sections of the South. Both are in the Cotton Belt, but Atlanta's old cotton lands have long since reached their maximum production under existing methods while those in the Dallas sustenance area are still in their prime, though beginning to show the evil effects of one-crop agriculture. Neither has superior advantages for manufacturing. Both are within ready reach of coal deposits but more distant than some of their rivals. Atlanta is on the border of two important water-power regions. One would expect that both cities will continue to dominate as commercial centers in their respective regions and that each will continue to support some manufactures, but manufacturing will be subordinate to trade. The graph of the population growth of Dallas (Fig. 146) is similar in most respects to that of Atlanta, but Atlanta is twenty years the older and its graph is not quite so steep. The population multiple of Dallas in 1930 was 26; that of Atlanta 7.3.

Fort Worth, the rival of Dallas, only thirty miles distant, possesses all or most of the advantages for growth enjoyed by the latter city. It is nearer the cattle country (now fast being reduced in area by the dry-land farmer) than Dallas, and hence it is a packing center. Dallas is in the wonderfully fertile Black Prairies and is more of a cotton center. Fort Worth is nearer the Ranger and Burkburnette oil fields of central and western Texas and is thus central to most of the developments of the state. It has many central offices of oil companies, is the focus of several pipe lines, and has many refineries. Dallas is scarcely less important in the oil industry. While both are jobbing centers, Dallas has more of the larger companies. Most of the railroads of central Texas, in extending their main lines and developing feeders, have not been partial to either one. They are equally supplied by highways. Here in the center of the great Southwest have developed within the last half century two urban centers, sufficiently near to be considered one, with combined population of 423,000, nearly as large as New Orleans, more than two centuries old and on one of the great rivers of the globe. Is this not strong evidence that the railway has supplanted the waterway as a carrier in interior commerce and as a city builder?

Similar to the growth of Fort Worth and Dallas (and also Atlanta) is that of San Antonio. It came up with the development of a large farming and ranching country in south central Texas. Its reliance for transportation is the railroad. Its historic interests and the mildness of its winters attract winter visitors, and its numerous colleges make it an educational center. It has some manufactures, but most of its economic life is associated with trade and commerce. In 1920 it was the largest city in Texas.

El Paso, the fifth city in Texas having 100,000 or more people in 1930, has had, like most of the "frontier" cities of Texas and Oklahoma, a spectacular growth. In 1880 its population was 700; in 1930, 102,000. Its attractions are many. It is an important railroad center. It is the southern terminus of a branch of the Santa Fe and the Rock Island systems; the western terminus of the Texas and Pacific; the northern terminus of two Mexican railroads (Juarez just across the Rio Grande is actually the Mexican terminus); and is on the main line of the Southern Pacific. These transportation facilities enable it to develop as an important jobbing and distributing center, not only for a large area in Texas and New Mexico and parts of Arizona, but also for northern Mexico. It is a "port" of entry for Mexican goods. The great distance from large manufacturing centers, its central location in a web of traffic lines, and coal within economic distance are favorable for its manufacturing plants, which turn out a variety of products, such as mining machinery, cement, and chemical products, that find ready sale in its sustenance area. Its railroads enable it to draw metallic minerals from near-by mining districts to its smelter, one of the largest of the country. The dry mild winter climate of this region fits it as a resort for patients afflicted with pulmonary diseases. Its proximity to old Mexico, a land of romance and tradition, attracts not a few tourists.* Grazing and irrigation farming are low-rainfall types of land utilization. The region about is not an environment that will support a large city, certainly not a city many times the present size of El Paso.

Birmingham, whose population multiple, as Table XXX shows, is nearly 87, is the only large iron and steel center in the South and can manufacture iron and steel more cheaply than any other center in the United States (and even in the world). Where else in the United States are good coking coal, fairly rich ore, and a suitable flux from twenty to sixty minutes apart? Nature made it possible here to develop the greatest iron and steel center in America. Man has exploited the opportunities remarkably well—and Birmingham has grown thereby—but the region has the physical environmental conditions that permit man to make it far more important than it now is. It should dominate completely the iron trade of three-fourths of the

---

* The new Pan American highway that leads southward from Nuevo Laredo (opposite Laredo) is drawing automobile tourists from the El Paso route into Mexico.

South and supply iron and steel implements and machinery, railroad equipment, pipe, wire, nails, sheet metal, rods, and other goods to the west coast of North and South America and even the Orient.

Memphis is the third of the river cities to maintain a high rank among the growing urban centers of the South. Like most cities east of the Mississippi, its early growth was slow. The Civil War and Reconstruction seem to have had little effect in retarding its growth. In fact, none of the graphs of Southern cities bears evidence of a population decline during the Civil War. Manufacturing and commerce were stimulated to supply the manufactured products that in pre-Civil War days came from the North. Thus the urban population increased. Plantation abandonment was probably another factor, as many whites and colored people moved to the cities. The decline in the population of Memphis between 1870 and 1880 was due to yellow-fever epidemics. Such calamities had more disastrous effects on Memphis than on New Orleans because the population was smaller. Epidemics in 1873, 1878, and 1879 resulted in more than 7,600 deaths, and two-thirds of the population in 1879 fled the city. Since 1880 its rise has been rapid. With nine railroads touching it or passing through it, and with renewed interest in the utilization of the Mississippi, there is every assurance that Memphis will continue to grow. Its civic leaders have courage and enterprise enough, in opposition to real estate developers of suburban property and tax-dodging business men, to push out the city's boundaries as the suburbs grow.

The rapid growth of Oklahoma City (population multiple 46.5 since 1890) was based largely on agriculture and is quite in harmony with the rapid settlement and development of the state of Oklahoma which has been discussed in previous pages. Tulsa's growth (multiple 100 since 1900) is founded mostly on oil, but its interests are also in agriculture. Oil has added to the economic attractions of Oklahoma City in the last few years. Oklahoma City and Tulsa, like Dallas and Fort Worth, are in the prairies of the Great Central Plains, in the Prairyerth and Darkerth (soil) regions. The cities are trading and jobbing centers for large farming, grazing, oil, gas, and coal areas, and both have manufactures for the working up of the local products. Oil pools of Oklahoma some day must decline in output, as the history of production in Pennsylvania shows. Agriculture, trade, and such manufactures as will continue to meet local demands must then form the bases of the economic life of these two cities and hold the people as best they can.

Of the three Florida cities in the 100,000-population class that have had a spectacular rise in the last thirty to fifty years, Jacksonville is the largest; and it is likely to retain the leadership it now has. Its prosperity rests on a much broader and more substantial base than that of either of the other cities. It lies at the southern end of the South Atlantic crescent and is the natural trading and jobbing center and ocean port of an area that covers parts of Georgia, Alabama and Florida. This area it dominates largely by means of railroads and highways, although the St. Johns River is navigable for a long distance and is a link of the Florida section of the Intracoastal Canal. There is little mineral wealth in the area, but there have long been pine forests furnishing lumber and naval stores for manufacture and shipment; and there is an increasing amount of farm products, particularly vegetables, fruits, and tobacco. The deep, broad St. Johns River gives it one of the best of harbors (the bar at the mouth has been dredged) for ocean shipping and serves also as a refuge for fishing fleets. Both Miami and Tampa were carried into the 100,000 class on the crest of the "Florida boom," although Tampa was a sizable city with a large commerce a decade or more previous.

Miami's prosperity rests upon the mildness of its winter climate, its location on the ocean and an excellent bathing beach, and the ability of man to transform mosquito-infested swamps, infertile sand dunes, and lagoons into cultural landscapes as attractive as the imaginary cities in *Arabian Nights*. Its future, so long as the recreational business dominates its life, depends largely upon the size of the "leisure class" that can be induced to come or remain. It is an important center for winter conventions of many sorts. Its location makes it a port of call and terminus for passengers, mail, and freight that move by airways and seaways between eastern United States and the vast lands of Hispanic America. It has few or no environmental advantages for manufacturing. The citrus fruit and garden truck area may be expanded. But can the country absorb even the production of the present, not to mention the potential, acreage of the South?

Tampa's early (1900-1920) economic life rested on the exploitation of pine forest and phosphate beds. Federal harbor improvements have made it a deep-water port. It has an important trade with many ports in the West Indies. It is claimed that more Havana cigars are manufactured in Tampa than in the city that gives them their name and fame. Other manufactured products are ships, boilers, fertilizers, and foundry products. With the decline in the supply of timber and phosphate and the infertility of much of the Tampa area for crops other than citrus fruits and garden truck, its future must rest largely

on its attractiveness as a health and winter resort,* on the returns
from early vegetables and fruits, and on the retention of its trade
with the West Indies. Miami is now a competitor in the passenger
traffic to Cuba.

SLOW GROWTH OF THE "SOUTH ATLANTIC CRESCENT" PORTS

The slow growth of the ports of the South Atlantic crescent, north
of Jacksonville, is seemingly anomalous. If growth of population be
an indication of economic activity—commerce or manufacturing—as
has been assumed all along in this chapter, then these ports have
existed in a comatose economic and commercial state for many decades. The combined population (in 1930) of Wilmington, Charleston,
and Savannah is less than that of Richmond; and the total population of these three and Mobile (a total of 247,691) is less than that
of the city of Atlanta (not the municipality of Atlanta which includes five near-by cities) by 23,000. Yet these were prominent towns,
some cities, from a half century to more than a century and a half
before the site of Atlanta was selected for the terminus of the Western
and Atlantic Railroad. Charleston was once (1790) the fourth city
in the United States, as earlier stated, with a population about half
that of New York City. There are few sites in the South, other than
Baltimore, New Orleans, and Galveston-Houston, seemingly better
located for commerce with the interior than Savannah and Mobile.
Any practical geographer would select Savannah as a winner in a
population race over Jacksonville, and certainly over Tampa. It has
a vastly larger area "behind it" if it would stir itself to make good
its natural claim. Of course cities generally do not build railroads,
certainly small cities do not; but civic leaders, if they are alive,
may succeed in attracting railroads to their city if their "home town"
possesses attractions, and Savannah does. It has been shown that
for a time the Savannah River between Savannah and Augusta was
the most-traveled trans-Coastal Plain route in the South, between
Chesapeake and Mobile bays. Savannah lies near the middle of the
broad concave crescent that indents the coast of southern South Carolina and Georgia, and is the nearest large city in the South Atlantic
States for commodities moving southeastward to the ocean from Tennessee and parts of Kentucky. It was the first of the cities of the
Southeast to build a railroad to the Tennessee River. Why then has
it fallen behind scores of other Southern cities?

---

* St. Petersburg, the largest winter resort on the west coast, only a few miles
distant and within its trade territory has a census population of more than
40,000.

As for Charleston and Wilmington, their back country, their hinterland, is restricted greatly in area, the width of the Atlantic Slope being less here than in Virginia, North Carolina, or Georgia. The mountains behind have served to discourage the development of railroads to the interior beyond. Charleston, it will be recalled, proposed a railroad northwestward to Cincinnati across Georgia and around the mountain barrier, but Savannah surpassed her in these attempts to reach the Tennessee River in Tennessee.

In striking contrast to the slow growth of the urban centers on the South Atlantic crescent is the rise of several cities of 25,000 to 75,000 (largest 83,000), on the Carolina Piedmont, within the last few decades. North Carolina now has seven Piedmont cities larger than Wilmington, the only seaport of the state, with deep-water navigation. Again it may be asked, why have Wilmington, Charleston, Savannah, Mobile, and Pensacola fallen behind in the rise of Southern cities?

Apparently the coast of the South Atlantic States from northern Florida to the northern border of North Carolina is a "blind alley." The Piedmont with its cities in the Carolinas and Georgia (including the Fall Line cities) has become the active section of these three states. Water power as a resource, and the textile industry, have attracted more capital and enterprise than the ocean's marginal lands and the coast cities. The railroad as an artery for commerce has surpassed the coastal waters. How much the barriers to commerce, the Florida Peninsula, the Carolina coastal shoals, Cape Hatteras, and the eastward protrusion of North Carolina have been responsible for the shift is difficult to estimate. The Piedmont, it seems clearly, has been drawn into the trade territory of Atlanta, and to some degree that of Baltimore and other Northern centers, by the railroads. It has been noted in a previous chapter that the main lines of the major railroad systems of the South Atlantic States parallel the coast. The railroads have prevented the coast cities from becoming active terminal points and are drawing some of their commerce to the great northeast-southwest land traffic routes. This apparently is the explanation. These railroads therefore have "beheaded" the traffic routes that in the earlier periods extended from the South Atlantic seaports into the back country, and have given traffic a northeast-southwest trend. The railroads offer to the Piedmont in these states shorter, more direct, and cheaper routes (transshipment not necessary) to the Northeastern States. There is also a large saving in time.

But the Carolinas and Georgia need not let their coast lines and harbors remain a "blind alley" if they but bestir themselves, as

Louisiana is now doing, and "go after" some of the industrial plants that are, in increasing numbers, seeking locations in the South.

OTHER CITIES THAT LOST OUT IN THE STRUGGLE

There were a few cities in the 25,000-50,000 class, in 1930, fairly prominent among their sister cities in the 1830's and 1840's, that have been retarded in their growth for diverse reasons. Lynchburg, whose importance nearly a century ago warranted discussion as to its rapid rise, has taken a century to grow from less than 5,000 to 41,000. Being a city on the only canal and "modern" means of transportation in Piedmont Virginia in the early decades of the nineteenth century, it drew traffic from great distances north and south. The railroads stripped it of its trade territory and annexed much of Virginia directly to Richmond's sustenance area. Much the same conditions checked the growth of Petersburg. It had a population of 11,000 in 1840, 21,000 in 1880, and 29,000 in 1930. It has become in many respects a "suburb" of Richmond.

In the center of one of the richest agricultural regions of the South, Lexington was once the largest city of Kentucky, active in trade and manufactures. But it was great when urban cities on the larger Ohio were not developed. Louisville soon surpassed it, and later Covington-Newport. An inland town before the days of the railroad had little chance in competition with a city on a large river that was one of the great arteries of transportation. The Louisville and Lexington Railroad probably benefited Louisville more than Lexington. It has taken seventy years for Lexington to advance in population from 10,000 to 46,000.

Among the numerous other population centers that warranted mention in the gazetteers and geographies of a century or more ago but that have never reached the 25,000-population level are Frederick and Annapolis in Maryland; Alexandria, Fredericksburg, Winchester, Staunton, and Danville in Virginia; Fayetteville and New Bern in North Carolina; Milledgeville in Georgia, once the capital of the state; Vicksburg and Natchez in Mississippi, which have been discussed in previous pages; and Maysville and Frankfort in Kentucky.

A few like Fayetteville, Alexandria, Natchez, and Vicksburg seemed to have been well located for active commerce and rapid population growth; but fate ruled otherwise. Was it because of the shortcomings of man, the greed or lack of foresight on the part of a few, the shifting or decline of traffic routes due to new methods of transportation, or the capture of trade territory by other and better-located cities? Comprehensive generalizations are not possible. Small cities and cities in the days of their youth may be harmed beyond recovery by seemingly slight causes. The successful cities, large or small, are not necessarily on the best urban sites for growth. A few of the larger in their early years of struggle may have been guided by thoughtful minds, or fortune may have smiled upon them and given them the early start that enabled them to forge ahead of their one-time rivals. As for some of the few that have fallen behind in the "onward and upward movement" that seemingly dominates all life, the "fault" may not have been in their "stars" (environmental conditions) but in themselves that they remained "underlings." Yet this apparently is not true of the majority of cities, for there seems to be a close correlation of rate of growth of cities with the quality and size of the sustenance area that they come to control; and control of the sustenance area is conditioned on adequacy of transportation.

SOME GENERAL CONCLUSIONS

The rise of cities in the South is a phenomenon normal to the geographic-economic evolution of a region richly endowed with natural transportation facilities, with agricultural, forest, and mineral resources, and occupied by a race and a civilization with a capacity for continued progress. It is probable that the South will never catch up with the North in urban growth; but inasmuch as industrialization is only in its beginning in the South, so also is city growth.

Is further city growth desirable? There are many in the South who say *no*, and who deplore the passing of the dominance of agriculture in its political, economic, and social life. Like Goldsmith they might assert,

> Ill fares the land to hastening ills a prey
> Where wealth accumulates and men decay.
>
> .   .   .   .
>
> A time there was ere England's [the South's] griefs began,
> When every rood of ground maintained its man.
>
> .   .   .   .
>
> But times are altered; trade's unfeeling train
> Usurp the land and dispossess the swain.

But city growth is inevitable; and, instead of bringing decay, it brings and will continue to bring material, intellectual, and spiritual progress. The city, if its economic or commercial life be active, offers an escape, for the small farmer and the landless, from continued poverty. For the boy and girl of the overpopulated rural areas, who have ambition and talent, it offers opportunity, a way out of the blind alley into which they might drift. The increasing urban population in the South,

484   THE RISE OF SOUTHERN CITIES

whether in large aggregations or in small, will make farming more
profitable, for no longer will the Southern farmer be forced to compete in Northern markets with Northern farmers for many of his
money crops. Urbanization will stimulate diversification in agriculture.

Not only is the city a center of opportunity, but it possesses the
material wealth for advancement in education, in fact for advancement in civilization in all its phases. Here are to be found the best
in architecture, the best in art, the best in music, the largest number
of workers in science, the most active work in social betterment, the
best of our literary writers, and the most advanced thinkers in religion and philosophy. Since the dawn of life on the earth, progress
has come only where and when life is forced into an intensive struggle
for existence and new creations arise. Progress is the result of new ideas.
The agricultural frontier made men, for here man had to fight to
overcome the savagery of both inanimate and animate nature. There
was ever before the adventurer a hope that victory meant peace and
plenty, a hope which spurred him on to excessive physical and intellectual effort. Action, struggle, progress, are what men crave. The
farm has ceased to attract men of enterprise and ambition, for its
labors no longer challenge their best efforts; and even for him who
has the requisite capital, success is not assured. The city has become
the arena where man competes with man, and out of which come
strong men. It is therefore the center toward which men of energy,
enterprise, and intelligence have been moving for many decades. It is
in the cities that new ideas germinate, flourish, and bear fruit.

The more prominent and more promising states in the South today
are those with the larger number of cities. It is the progressive cities
that are leading the South today out of its traditions in politics, theology, educational methods, and social organization.

The city is the culminating episode of human occupancy of a region.
It is the fruit; its sustenance area is the vine. It is one of the major
resultants of the complex human developments in the exploitation of
the natural resources.*

---

* See discussion on pages 495 and 496 regarding advantages of "garden cities" or
rurban areas, as one author styles them. Such a type of close settlement gives
many of the advantages of the urban center yet permits the economic security,
for a large part of the population, that is possible in rural areas. Suburbanization,
associated with part-time farming, is advancing more rapidly than is generally
appreciated in the South.

PART VII

THE SOUTHERN PROSPECT

CHAPTER XVIII

THE SOUTHERN PROSPECT

SUMMARY AND CONCLUSION

BREAKING DOWN SECTIONALISM

A facetious Southern judge many years ago remarked that there were still a few Southerners who thought that damn Yankee was one word. Although such exhibitions of sectionalism have not always been confined to the South, and "Jonnie Reb," as a term of reproach, has been uttered with as much vehemence as damn Yankee, both expressions happily are passing out of use in serious conversation. It was during the Democratic administration of a Southern-born president and a war in which North and South and East and West fought together against common foes that intolerant sectionalism was largely forgotten and the Stars and Stripes, born in a war against a common enemy, now again waves over a politically united country, revered alike by all sections.

Regional differentiation in English North America began before the Revolution. Madison commented on the sectionalism in the Constitutional Convention. He declared that "the real difference of interest lay not between the large and small but between the Northern and Southern states." The institution of slavery was the basis of the differences of opinion. The feeling of antagonism between North and South increased as one vital question after another was up for discussion, and the differences culminated finally in the Civil War. Except for the ruthlessness of a few Northern leaders during the Reconstruction Period who sought to dispossess Southern landowners and divide their lands among their former slaves and thus destroy Southern civilization, the Civil War would have settled some, at least, of the points of difference. Reconstruction, however, reopened the breach, and hates continued for several decades. Commerce, the tie that tends to bind nations and regions together, was not active and had little influence, until late in the past century. The South had little other than cotton and tobacco to send to the North. Most of its manufactured goods came from the North, but high freight rates and profits made

487

for high prices. Because the Southerners were forced to meet their commercial obligations with the maximum of money there was generally the minimum of good will. Commercial transactions make for friendship when all parties concerned believe that each is benefited.

Today the South has a multitude of products to send northward, and since many Northern articles now must meet Southern competition and the cost of transportation has been greatly reduced, both sections are on a more equitable basis in their commercial transactions.

Besides cotton, tobacco, and timber and its products, from early November, after frosts have blighted the fall gardens of the Northern States, there begins a movement of vegetables and fruits that continues until the local gardens and orchards of the North get into production. For many months a steady stream of refrigerator cars laden with vegetables, peaches, oranges, grapefruit, apples, and a wide variety of other products speeds northward.

In the fall begins the southward migration of winter residents to our subtropical playgrounds—Florida, the "Gulf Riviera" (Mississippi Sound coast), New Orleans, Galveston, Corpus Christi, San Antonio, and El Paso. Even Asheville, Pinehurst, and Southern Pines, too, have winter residents. In addition to these winter residents there are hundreds of thousands of tourists at all seasons who remain but a few days. An estimate for the year 1936 gives 2,000,000 as the number of visitors to Florida, spending approximately $200,000,000.* North Carolina and Virginia have a year-round tourist business. The estimates of annual expenditures of tourists in North Carolina range from $25,000,000 to $50,000,000. The National Park Service reported in 1935 a half million visitors to the Great Smoky Mountains Park. The season of 1937 saw more than 725,000. The Virginia State Chamber of Commerce estimates that in 1935 tourists spent nearly $74,-000,000 in Virginia, and the State Highway Commission estimated that 12,145 automobiles entered Virginia daily in 1935.† These figures are largely estimates, it is true, yet they do give a fair idea of these temporary migrations. No doubt a majority of the tourists recorded in these states were from the North. When the national parks and forests of the South become better known far greater numbers will certainly come. There is at present a far greater migration of Northerners to the

---

* Letter from Harold Colee, president, Florida Chamber of Commerce, Jacksonville, Florida.

† Letter, Paul Kelley, North Carolina Department of Conservation and Development, March 18, 1937; letter, R. F. Nelson, Direction of Publicity, Virginia State Chamber of Commerce, March 19, 1937.

South than Southerners to the North. Yet tens of thousands of Southerners each year visit New York, New England, Niagara Falls, the Great Lakes, and Canada.

Thousands of operators, managers, and agents of commercial houses are coming southward to establish offices and take up permanent residence. A large percentage of the faculties of all the larger educational institutions are from the North or have been educated in the North. The migration northward from Southern farms, and cities as well, of men and women seeking greater opportunities and higher financial returns, has been immense. This movement was most rapid during the prosperous years, from 1917 to 1929, at least 100,000 to 200,000 a year.

Wilson Gee in a recent issue of *Social Forces* from a study of *Who's Who in America* found that 2,229 of the 6,051 Southern-born listed in that volume had migrated to other sections—to the North and West. This loss was partly offset by a migration of 1,416 natives of other sections to the South. The South still suffers a loss of 813 men of talent and training and leadership.

Southerners should not forget the gestures of friendship and good will of Northern philanthropists in the establishments of educational funds in the South for various purposes. Probably the oldest of these gifts to Southern education is the Peabody Education Fund. Other funds are the Carnegie, the Rosenwald, the Slater, and the Jeanes. The greatest contributions have been made by the General Educational Board and the Rockefeller Foundation. These funds and boards, besides many other donors, have largely endowed Peabody College for Teachers, Vanderbilt University, Lincoln Memorial, Berea, Fisk University (Negro), Tuskegee (Negro), and Maharry Medical School (Negro).

Once more Southern political leaders and statesmen are prominent, as before the Civil War, in the Congress of the nation. The man-made barriers between North and South are breaking down. Physiographic barriers there never were.

THE PROSPECT FOR POPULATION

To social scientists who have long associated the rapid changes in American economic life with an increasing population, it comes somewhat as a shock to discover that already the nation's birth rate is on the decline (Fig. 147, inset). The births per 1,000 population in 1915 were 24.7; in 1920, 23.7; in 1930, 18.9; and in 1932, 17.4. In the cities in 1932 the rate was 16.7; in the rural districts, 18.1. The

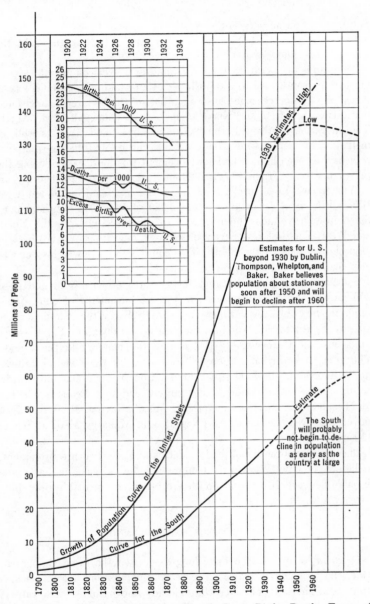

FIG. 147.—Some Graphs of Population Growth. Inset: Births, Deaths, Excess of Births over Deaths, 1920-1933.

rural rate is higher than the urban, but both show a gradual decline over a period of years. This decline is correlated with and is certainly due to the advancing standard of living and urbanization.* Industrialization, urbanization, advancing standards of living, and decline of birth rate are concomitants. Children, to parents on a farm, are an asset from seven or eight years of age on to as long as they remain under the parental roof; but most city children are liabilities. As a rule they make little or no contribution to the family income. The cost of clothing, food, recreation, society, and shelter is far greater than for farm children. Though the gross family income is far greater, comparatively, in the city than in the country, the overhead is also greater. There are far fewer "free goods" in the city. Parents therefore by economic necessity are forced to restrict the size of the family. Often

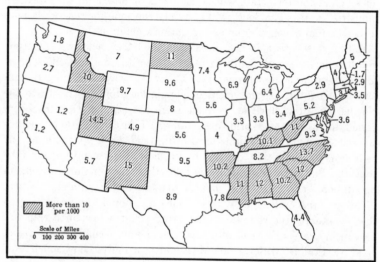

Data from *Statistical Abstract*, 1935, 87.

FIG. 148.—Excess of Births over Deaths per 1000 of Total Population, 1933, by States.

the woman of the family becomes a bread winner and therefore cannot also assume the duties of motherhood.

The declining birth rate of the United States in its effect on the population curve is partly offset by the decline in the death rate (Fig. 147, inset). The average death rate for the "registration states" from 1901 to 1905 was 15.9; in 1915 it was 13.3, and in 1932, 10.9, or a

* Data from *Statistical Abstract*, 1934, 84; 1917, 77.

decline of 5 per 1,000 in about 30 years. Figure 148 shows the excess
of births over deaths for the year 1933, in the states.* It will be noted
that the largest number of states with the highest excesses are in
the South. The difference in the rate of reproduction of the industrial North and the rural South will, as time passes, result in
far greater differences in reproduction rates, for the child-bearing
women of the North and the Pacific states are getting "older" (average age) more rapidly than the child-bearing women of the South.
Fresh stock is being introduced in the South. Industrialization and
urbanization of the South will in time reduce the birth rate as they
have in the North; but it will be several decades before this section
will have attained the rank in manufacturing and urbanization held
by such states as Illinois, Ohio, Pennsylvania, New York, New Jersey,
Connecticut, and Massachusetts; and it will therefore be several decades before the birth rate will be as low as it now is in the Northern
industrial states. The South will certainly continue for several decades
to be the major contributor of the nation's children.

Baker states that in the decades 1920-1929, inclusive, 4,000,000
youths migrated from Southern farms—some to Southern cities, some
to Northern cities and farms (Fig. 149).† One cannot predict the extent in the future of movement of population from the South to the
Northern States, which as we have seen was rapid during the boom
period following the World War. Improved rural conditions and increased amount of manufacturing will tend to keep more of the
Southern youths within the South. In short, the conclusion must be
that the South in time will overtake the other major sections in
population, relatively, as it has in manufacturing, mining, railroad
building, and other activities. But it should be remembered
that eventually the conditions that bring about a low birth rate will
prevail in the South as in other sections. Dame fecundity is a wilful
creature. Stalins, Hitlers, and Mussolinis, no matter how much they
command her, she heeds them not. In poverty and squalor as in India,
China, and uncivilized society, where man is motivated largely by
instinct and little by reason and discretion, the birth rate is high;
but so also is the death rate. Among cultured people the rate is always low. This was as true in ancient Rome and Greece as in the
highly civilized nations of western Europe and America today. Such
trends are normal. Man can do little to change them.

* *Statistical Abstract,* 1917, 88; 1934, 79.

† O. E. Baker, "The Agricultural Prospect," in *Our National Resources and
Their Conservation,* A. E. Parkins and J. R. Whitaker, Editors, 223.

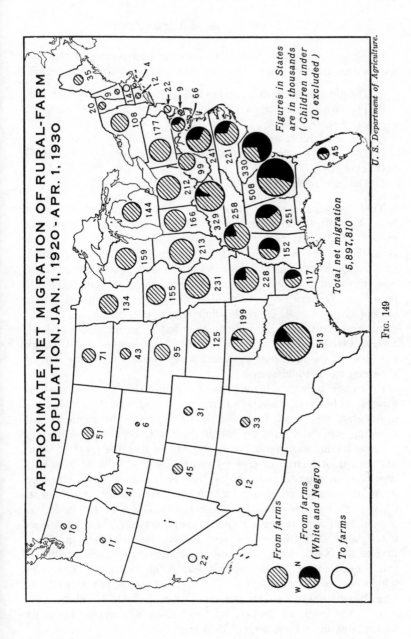

APPROXIMATE NET MIGRATION OF RURAL-FARM POPULATION, JAN. 1, 1920 - APR. 1, 1930

Figures in States are in thousands (Children under 10 excluded)

Total net migration 5,897,810

From farms

From farms (White and Negro)

To farms

U. S. Department of Agriculture.

FIG. 149

The Prospect for Manufacturing

Economic geographers and economists hold as postulates that the localization and rate of growth of manufactures in a region depend on:

1. The abundance, variety, and quantity of workable raw materials.
2. The cost and extent of the fuel and power resources—coal, oil, gas, water power.
3. The availability of capital.
4. The absorbing power and accessibility of markets for the products fabricated.
5. The cost, reliability, experience, and skill of laborers.

That the South is highly favored as regards the first two items has been demonstrated in preceding chapters in this book. The recency of industrialization, now scarcely beyond the initial stages, means that the drain on Southern resources to date has been slight. Of our fundamental resources related to the land, serious inroads have been made only on our soils and forests, and these are renewable resources. We have no measure of the degree of exploitation of our oil and gas resources. Of coal, sulphur, salt, iron ore, bauxite, limestone, and clays there is an abundance; but lesser quantities of lead, zinc, and copper. These all are non-renewable resources. A little more than half of the maximum potential water power (for 50 per cent of the time) has been harnessed.

Up to the present a large part of the financing of our industrial enterprises has been undertaken freely and gladly by Northern capitalists; but under such financing the profits leave the South. It will take time to accumulate capital in the South, as it always does in a region having an agrarian economy; but to reap the greatest benefits from its industrial enterprises and utilize to the fullest extent its superb environmental advantages, the South must have adequate financial resources at home to match those that nature has given it. Cheap, reliable, non-unionized labor has been one of the more important conditions favoring Southern manufactures. There have been a few labor difficulties, a few very serious, but relatively far fewer than in the North. How long these comparatively peaceful conditions will prevail in the South depends largely on the sanity and fairmindedness of labor leaders and of the factory owners as well. As long as agriculture remains dominant there is little likelihood that labor in the South will be permitted to become as unreasonable in its demands as in sections largely industrial.

Labor will always be cheaper in the mild temperate South than in the cold North, for food, clothing, and shelter cost less. At present rents are lower in the small factory villages than in the congested towns and cities of the North. If labor can be induced to avoid forming congested districts but instead develop "garden"—or "small farm" —villages or cities, as has been done in parts of England and Belgium, rents or the cost of homes may be kept low and a greater means of social security attained. The automobile and the modern road are making it possible for workers to live twenty or thirty miles from their work, out in the country, and yet be far nearer their work, measured in time, than most of the industrial workers in large cities. Not only would the factory workers and their families benefit by such a home economy but so would the factory owners, for a home owner is a more stable creature than a mere renter.

So far the South has not developed a large body of experienced skilled workers, for there has not been a demand for them. Automatic, precision machines make skilled workers less a factor in localization of industry than formerly when work was done largely by hand. A few factories established in the South have had to bring some skilled workers from other sections, but the shoe factories, textile mills, paper mills, and machine shops have for the most part trained their men from local supplies of labor. The automobile industry of Detroit, now manned by some of the most skilled workers in America, has developed its workers during the last twenty-five years. The first products of the factories were crude, made by workers of relatively crude workmanship. As the automobile became refined so did the skill of the workers. This is the normal procedure in industrial evolution. Lack of skilled labor in the South will not retard industrialization, for the factories of the North will continue to dominate in production that demands the most skilled workmen and if highly skilled workers are ever needed in the South they can be developed. The major contribution that the South has to offer, and will continue to offer for several decades to attract industries, are low-cost raw materials, low-cost power, and cheap labor. These are associated with industries producing rough or at the most semi-refined products.

Where will the industrial areas of the South be four, five, or more decades hence? The writer believes just about where they are now. The Carolina Piedmont will continue to lead in textile production, but the textile region is likely to expand westward across Georgia and into Alabama; in fact, it already is doing so. Water power and proximity of factory to factory and excellent rail transportation are dominant factors. A small textile section will probably develop in central Texas. The iron and steel and related industries are likely to remain in the Birmingham-Gadsden section of the Great Valley, for here are the major ingredients—iron ore, coal, and carbonates. The pulp and paper plants now beginning to increase in numbers will find their best locations at Atlantic and Gulf river ports to which pulpwood may be floated by river or carried by rail and where clear fresh water may be secured, but near the port that their export, which will mostly be pulp, not paper, may have low-cost transportation to Northern paper mills. A second (to Birmingham) heavy metal industry in which iron and steel products bulk large is now located on the upper Ohio in West Virginia and the near-by portions of Kentucky. This is likely to decline as the Lake Superior iron ore mines decline in production; but the industries depending on coal as fuel and other minerals, as glass sand and salt, surely will continue to expand; so also will the wide variety of industries in the Valley of Eastern Tennessee, utilizing the raw materials of forest and mine and cheap electricity supplied by an indulgent Federal Government, which permits the TVA to sell electricity at less than actual cost. There is little likelihood that the oil refineries, although expansion is going on, will shift far from where they now are, for undoubtedly most of the oil regions in the South have been discovered. Baltimore with its superior advantages, Louisville, Memphis, Atlanta, New Orleans, Houston, and Dallas-Fort Worth and lesser centers are likely to continue to expand their plants and to supply the wide variety of products they now fabricate for their respective trade territories.

The manufacture of woolen blankets, of overalls and men's jackets, caps, and cotton gloves, of hosiery and other knit goods, women's apparel, shoes, automobile tires, certain chemicals, agricultural implements and tools, and many other products, most of which involves simple operations which may be performed by women and children with simple and automatic machinery and which call for only a small variety and quantity of raw material, are now widely distributed in the smaller towns in many parts of the South, mainly east of the Mississippi River. Often a town offers free land, free water, sometimes free power, and no taxes. Often local capital assists in the financing. These bonuses, along with electric power and non-union labor, are often the decisive factors in selecting a location. The local chambers of commerce must be given some credit for their activity. Such developments will probably continue. These factories are a boon to many a small town with a surplus of young people. Each small town can be made the nucleus of a "garden city" industrial center, though few may develop beyond the initial stages. Each supplies work for a goodly number of farmers who live in the surrounding region.

When one looks into the future and tries to visualize the extent of expansion of manufacturing in our country, the sinister downward trend of the nation's birth rate which eventually will flatten the national population curve (Fig. 147, large curves) deadens one's enthusiasm. To what extent will the South be affected? (See predicted curve for South, Fig. 147.) Will the evident Southern tides of industrialization continue? Will the South advance because of its newness irrespective of the trends in the East or North? Will America secure foreign markets to absorb the present surpluses of its factories and still larger surpluses if expansion continues? The answer to these queries must be left to the future. This we know: the South has industrial potentialities as great as or greater than any other section, and the Southern press now carries, frequently, such headlines as "Southern Tide of Industrial Empire Brings Hundreds of New Plants to Dixie."

THE PROSPECT FOR AGRICULTURE

General statements and conclusions on the prospect for agriculture in the South are more difficult to make than for any other major region of the United States because of the diversity of environmental conditions and types of farming.*

Some remarkable advances have been made in some sections of the South in late decades in specialty farming: citrus fruit growing, peach growing, apple production, the production of garden truck, and rice growing in Louisiana; also irrigation crops on a large scale in the Rio Grande. Tobacco culture has been improved somewhat, and a beginning has been made in the dairy industry. These are mostly young enterprises, still in their vigor, and each has space for further expansion. Only in few regions are the specialties as yet fully established, however. Specialty regions are enclaves of intensive agriculture in larger agricultural sections in which extensive methods of tillage dominate. Droughts, untimely frosts, uncontrolled insect pests, poor markets, competition from rival regions, any one or more for a few years, might so discourage the farmers as to cause the abandonment of a specialty's cultivation. There is much experimenting here and there in the South in early season specialties, and this type of farming is certain to continue and increase. Market

---

* For a map showing types of agriculture in the South see Fig. 78.

demands, both North and South, determine the area that may profitably be devoted to special crops; but the markets will be likely to continue to expand for the next few decades, particularly in the South with
its increasing industrialization. Dietary habits are also slowly changing. Advancing standards of living will call for a wider variety of
foods.

In sections of the South where large farms and plantations have
long dominated there seems to be the same decline in agriculture
that is met with in other parts of our country where general and
commercial types of farming prevail. Maturity apparently has been
reached. Emigration is active. In all established agricultural sections
that have about reached the limits of acreage utilization and advancement in farm practices there is little room for an increasing population.
Among the emigrants leaving the farms there are certain to be the more
ambitious, progressive, and aggressive of the sons and daughters. In the
cities they find greater opportunities for advancement and the ac-
cumulation of wealth. Along with them, of course, are many who
leave because they lack the capital essential to start independent
farming. This cityward movement has been active since the beginning of industrialization and urbanization of our country, about 1890.
Thus the farm no longer attracts the leaders that it once did when
the occupations open to young men and women were few. (See Figure
149.) The economic security of the farm is being traded for the un-
certainties, yet possibilities, of the factory, the mart, and the counting house. The depression has forced a return of many of the unsuc-
cessful and unfortunate to the farm. How many of the "adventurers"
remain will depend on the relative attractiveness of farm and factory
in the future. Many students of rural life are of the opinion that if
the agriculturalists of America are not to sink to the level of the peas-
ants of Europe something must be done to assure greater returns for
the money invested and the time and energy expended by the farmers.
Subsidies of some sort seem to many to be essential. There must be
some form of crop control, preferably by co-operatives, for the be-
setting problem of American agriculture is that it is too prolific.

In many ways the agricultural South, in general, falls far below
the norm for the country in attractiveness of countryside, and in the
quality and value of farm homes and home equipment. The farm
"mansions" in the plantation sections of the South are far more
numerous than the "best" houses in any of the other regions of our
country (see Fig. 83), but the dwellings on the average-sized farms
and small farms (Figs. 81 and 82) are quite generally cheap, unattractive, and unhomelike, and the premises are in keeping with the

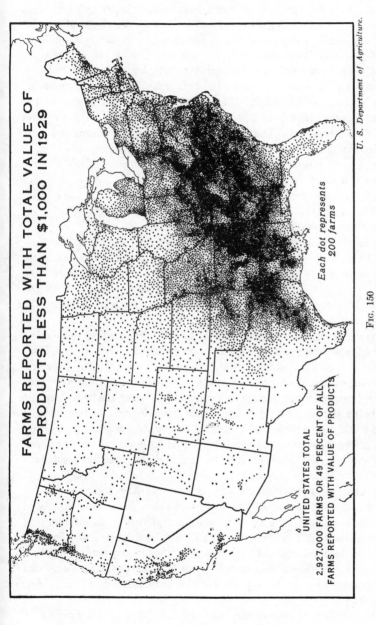

FIG. 150

U. S. Department of Agriculture.

In most of the older states of the South, the percentage of farms having less than $600 of annual gross income (or value of products) is 40 or more. In West Virginia 43 per cent and in Kentucky 44 per cent of the farms have an income of less than $600. The cash returns from crops sold on a large percentage of the tenant farms of the Cotton Belt are less than $300.

houses. Very few farms in the South have running water in the kitchen, bathrooms with running water, and electricity for lighting and power.* In other words, rural standards of living are lower than the national averages; and lower standards are associated with low returns per family or farm. Although the gross return from crops is high, as pointed out in preceding pages, the high density of rural population, in proportion to acreage of tilled land gives low per capita or per farm returns. (See Fig. 150.) We are here dealing with averages based on census data. The raising of farm family standards is a task before us. Farmer, merchant, manufacturer, educator, and health agent are all concerned.

Most of the low-income farms of the South are:

1. In areas of eroded lands.

2. In mountain and dissected plateau areas where topography restricts the cultivable area per farm.

3. In the areas where tenancy dominates, particularly in the Cotton Belt. Here erosion has long been dominant and the originally poor soils greatly depleted; but an additional factor is the small area of land each tenant is permitted to work, or can work, with the power equipment available. The owners of small farms suffer for the same reasons.

Agricultural improvement in areas of the first category must come through soil conservation. This is being undertaken by the Soil Conservation Service and many other separate and affiliated agencies. The soil-conservation program of the United States Department of Agriculture instituted (temporarily probably) after the abandonment of the ponderous AAA, *if honestly and carefully administered,* is the wisest and most economical plan ever devised to subsidize agriculture and at the same time obligate the farmer to build up his soil. Such conservation contributes to the "general welfare," and its result will pass on to future generations.

In many sections of the South erosion has advanced too far for soil reclamation to benefit the farmer of this generation. Millions of acres of such land have already been purchased for reforestation and more millions must be. (See Fig. 154.) Soil conservation and reforestation are the most-talked-of movements today in the South. What to do with the landsmen displaced introduces a new problem. Many can find employment in the rapidly increasing factories or in the forest projects.

The problem of raising the standards of living of the farmers of

---

* Data from *Statistical Abstract,* 1934, 566.

A. E. P.

FIG. 151.—A Cultivated Slope in Southern West Virginia.

The light streak across the middle of the picture is a hard-surfaced highway built by the state.

A. E. P.

FIG. 152.—A Cultural, Mountain Landscape near Junaluska, North Carolina.

In most of the mountain valleys cultivation utilizes all the flat land and often extends up the mountain slopes. On the mountain slopes corn or grass is grown. The growing of grass is the safer type of land utilization on the slopes.

the mountain and dissected plateau sections (Fig. 151) of the Southern Appalachian Highlands concerns neither soil erosion (but little)
nor tenancy for they are largely valley dwellers (Figs. 152 and 153)
and home owners. Coal mining gives whole or part-time employment
to many near coal mines in the Plateaus. Here and there are a few
small industries, largely woodworking. Good roads, consolidated
schools, automobiles, movies, and mail-order catalogues are gradually
bringing these people out of their seclusion. Public nurses, farm agents,

A. E. P.

FIG. 153.—Rough Land in a Mountain Basin near Murphy, North Carolina.

There are numerous broad basins with flat to hilly surfaces in Southern Appalachian Mountains.
The land in this landscape is too rough for safe and profitable tillage. It is used mostly for pasture.
An excellent road system connects most mountain valleys with the near-by cities or shipping points.

and perhaps industrial agents, to introduce them to new industries
that will utilize their resources, are some of the advances necessary
to increase their income and raise their standards of living. Most of the
farm and village people possess vigor, enterprise, and inherent intelligence that merely need stimulating for active participation in the economic life of the South. Lumbering, woodworking, fruit raising, truck
gardening, canning, livestock raising, dairying, weaving, and pottery
making are activities already started in sections most open to inter-
course with outside markets.

How to improve the lot of the tenants of the Cotton Belt, the
victims of an economic system born in the hectic post-Civil-War days
and now numbering four million, more or less, is a problem that is
challenging the most experienced and best thinkers of the South. Some
investigators are prone to blame the planter, but it seems certain that

the real basis of the tenants' poverty is the low price of cotton that has prevailed for several decades and the gradual depletion of the soil. From 1875 to 1914, inclusive, in only eight years did the "producer's" price of cotton reach 10 cents a pound. During and following the World War, the price for most years was about 15 cents, even reaching nearly 36 cents in 1919.* The depression crashed the prices, and but for their "pegging" by the Federal Government they might have sunk to the lowest ever. The reduction of cotton exports due to depressed conditions in consuming countries, the rise of new cotton regions, particularly Brazil, the increasing use of rayon, changes in styles, and the great potential producing power of the South—some four or five times the present crop—means that we are in for a period of low prices unless some control measures are devised and/or active foreign markets opened up. If our foreign exports are cut off then the Cotton Belt will have only American mills and the American public to supply.

Many suggestions are being made to improve conditions. No one plan is applicable to all sections, and certainly no one plan is a complete solution. First of all, many believe that something should be done to take many millions of acres of marginal or near-marginal land out of production (Fig. 154). The acreage yield does not pay for the expenditures for seed, tools, and labor; and all the time the soil is being depleted. The method of withdrawal of lands has not been worked out—whether by condemnation and repurchase, or by starving out the farmers on the marginal lands by refusing to assist in pegging prices. Perhaps the most lasting improvement will come from a slow system of education and the demonstration of new crop regimes in which cotton plays only a minor part. Some advocate a campaign to educate the tenants (and many planters) to diversify their crops so that they will be less dependent on other regions and have farm tasks that will utilize more of their available work-time. The success of Iowa and New England farmers is, to a certain degree at least, due to their year-round activity and the variety of their undertakings. No farmer can succeed whose annual labor does not sum up to more than three or four months a year. There is no plausible explanation, except ignorance and shiftlessness, why each cotton tenant and small farmer should not have a garden, fig and peach trees, a few pigs, poultry, and a cow or two. Some plantation owners insist on such; others are either indifferent or prohibit such profitable undertakings. More livestock must be introduced. Now that the tick is

* *Yearbook of Agriculture* 1931, 672, 673; 1935, 425, 426.

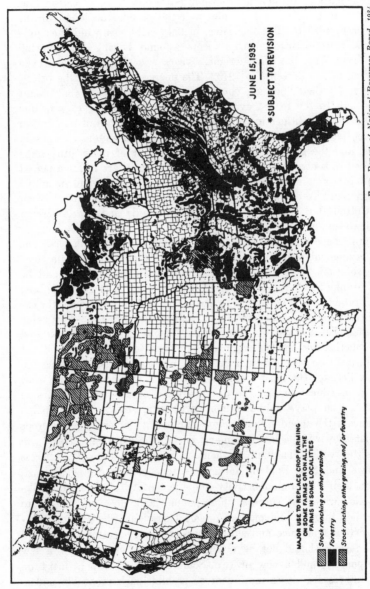

JUNE 15, 1935

* SUBJECT TO REVISION

MAJOR USE TO REPLACE CROP FARMING
ON SOME FARMS OR ON ALL THE
FARMS IN SOME LOCALITIES

▨ Stock ranching or other grazing

■ Forestry

▧ Stock ranching, other grazing, and/or forestry

From Report of National Resources Board, 1934.

FIG. 154.—Areas in Which a Shift in Type of Land Utilization is Recommended. See legend for recommended major uses in the future.

nearly eradicated, the year-long grazing possibilities in the Cotton Belt (by the planting of winter crops and storing of legume hay) should be utilized. No region can maintain soil fertility, except at great expense, that does not have livestock and grass or cover crop in its farm program. The Cotton Belt soil and climate are not optimum for nutritious grasses, but the farmers can and do grow abundantly all forms of leguminous forage crops. The activity of the Georgia farmers in the growing of legumes of all sorts may well be copied by those of other states.

A proposal for tenant betterment that has received wide publicity is the establishment of the surplus tenants on land, the purchase of which is to be financed by the state or the Federal Government, the would-be owners to recompense the government by small annual payments. A bill passed in July, 1937, authorized an immediate appropriation of $10,000,000 to begin the program, $25,000,000 for the fiscal year 1939 and $50,000,000 in 1940.* The expenditures are to be under the supervision of the Resettlement Administration. The aim of the plan is to establish permanent homes. Some hail this proposal as solving the tenant problem; others point to the slow progress that has been made in Ireland, after more than a half century of effort; and to the failure of the Reclamation Bureau operating under the Reclamation Act of 1902 to collect a large percentage (about 63 per cent) of the contracted payments from the farmers who settled on irrigated land, the works for the watering of which were built by the Federal Government.†

Certainly the major objective should be to assist the unfortunates to assist themselves and avoid developing permanent dependents and dole takers. As with the mountain people, leaders must be supplied the tenant and small farmer, such as public school teachers, farm agents, home agents, and public health nurses to start cooperative organizations, boys' and girls' clubs, women's clubs, and better farmers' clubs and to lead the farmers to envisage their work as did the Antebellum farmer—the noblest on earth, the most essential of all occupations.

---

* United Press dispatch in *Nashville Banner*, July 23, 1937, 7.

† Data on irrigation in the United States, in *Statistical Abstract*, 1931, 626; George J. Miller and A. E. Parkins, *Geography of North America*, 400; data on Ireland in *Statesman's Yearbook*, 1910, 64; *Country Gentleman*, March, 1937, 20, article by James Edmonds.

BIBLIOGRAPHY

(Abridged)

I. BOOKS LISTED BY AUTHOR

ALVORD, C. W., and BIDGOOD, LEE. *Trans-Allegheny Explorations,* Cleveland, A. H. Clark, 1912.

ARMES, ETHEL. *The Story of Coal and Iron in Alabama,* published under auspices of the Chamber of Commerce, Birmingham, 1910. (University Press, Cambridge, U. S. A.)

ARMROYD, GEORGE. *A Connected View of the Whole Interior Navigation of the United States,* Philadelphia, Carey & Lea, 1826.

ARNOLD, B. W., JR. *The Tobacco Industry of Virginia, 1860-1894,* Baltimore, Johns Hopkins University, Studies in Historical and Political Science, Series 15, 1 and 2, 1897.

BAILEY, L. H. *Cyclopedia of American Agriculture,* IV, New York, Macmillan Co., 1912.

BAILY, FRANCIS. *Journal of a Tour in Unsettled Parts of North America in 1776 and 1797,* London, Baily Brothers, 1856.

BARTRAM, WILLIAM. *Travels Through North and South Carolina, Georgia, and Florida,* Philadelphia, James & Johnson, 1791.

BASSETT, JOHN SPENCER. *The Southern Plantation Overseer As Revealed in His Letters,* Northampton, Mass., printed for Smith College, 1925.

BAUM, FRANK G. *Atlas of U. S. A. Electric Power Industry,* New York, McGraw-Hill Book Co., 1923.

BENNETT, H. H. *The Soils and Agriculture of the Southern States,* New York, Macmillan Co., 1921.

BIRKBECK, MORRIS. *Notes on a Journey in America,* London, printed by Severn and Co. for James Ridgway, 1818.

BIZZELL, WILLIAM BENNETT. *Rural Texas,* New York, Macmillan Co., 1924.

BLOWE, DANIEL. *A Geographical, Historical, Commercial and Agricultural View of the United States of America, Forming a Complete Emigrant's Directory,* London, Edwards & Knibb, 1820.

BOLTON, HERBERT E. *The Spanish Borderlands,* XXIII, New Haven, Yale University Press, 1921. (The Chronicles of America, edited by ALLEN JOHNSON.)

BOWMAN, ISAIAH. *Forest Physiography,* New York, John Wiley & Sons, 1911.

BRACKENRIDGE, H. M. *Views of Louisiana; together with a Journal of a Voyage up the Missouri River in 1811,* Pittsburgh, Cramer, Spear, Eichbaum, 1814.

BRADBURY, JOHN. *Bradbury's Travels in the Interior of America, 1809 to 1811,* Cleveland, A. H. Clark, 1904; originally printed for the author by Smith and Galway, 1817.

BROOKE'S *Universal Gazetteer or a New Geographical Dictionary,* Darby's Edition (William Darby), 1823.

BROWN, NELSON C. *Timber Products and Industries,* New York, John Wiley & Sons, 1937.

BROWN, W. G. *The Lower South in American History,* New York, The Macmillan Co., 1902.

BRUCE, PHILLIP A. *The Rise of the New South,* Philadelphia, George Barrie & Sons, 1905.

Economic History of Virginia in the Seventeenth Century, two volumes, New York and London, Macmillan, 1895.

Institutional History of Virginia in the Seventeenth Century etc., New York and London, G. P. Putnam's Sons, 1910.

BUCKINGHAM, J. S. *The Slave States of America,* two volumes, London, Fisher, Son & Co., 1842.

BUNKER, PAGE S. *Forestry in the South,* Washington, The American-Tree Association, 1928.

BURGESS, JOHN W. *The Civil War and the Constitution, 1859-1865,* New York, Charles Scribner's Sons, 1901.

CAMPBELL, JOHN C. *The Southern Highlander and His Homeland,* New York, Russell Sage Foundation, 1921.

CARRIER, LYMAN. *The Beginnings of Agriculture in America,* New York, Mc-Graw-Hill Book Co., 1923.

CLARK, VICTOR S. *History of Manufactures in the United States, I, 1607-1860* (1929 Edition), New York, published for the Carnegie Institution of Washington by McGraw-Hill Book Co., 1929.

COLTON, GEORGE W. *Colton's Atlas of the World,* two volumes, New York, J. H. Colton & Co., 1856.

COOK, J. H. *Fifty Years on the Old Frontier, etc.,* New Haven, Yale University Press, 1923.

COUCH, W. T. (Editor). *Culture in the South,* Chapel Hill, University of North Carolina Press, 1934.

DARBY, WILLIAM. *View of the United States Historical, Geographical, and Statistical,* Philadelphia, 1825.

Universal Gazetteer, A New Geographical Dictionary, Second Edition, Philadelphia, 1927.

DEBOW, J. B. D. *Industrial Resources of the Southern and Western States,* three volumes, New Orleans, 1853.

DEVEREUX, MARGARET. *Plantation Sketches,* Cambridge, privately printed at the Riverside Press, 1906.

DODD, WILLIAM E. *The Cotton Kingdom,* New Haven, Yale University Press, 1921.

DUBLIN, L. I. *Population Problems in the United States and Canada,* Boston, Houghton Mifflin Co., 1926.

DUGGAN, J. F. *Southern Field Crops,* New York, Macmillan Co., 1911.

Southern Forage Crops, New York, Macmillan Co., 1925.

DUNBAR, SEYMOUR. *A History of Travel in America,* four volumes, Indianapolis, Bobbs-Merrill, 1915.

EARLE, F. S. *Southern Agriculture,* New York, Macmillan Co., 1908.

ECKEL, EDWIN C. *Iron Ores,* New York, 1907.

EMBREE, E. R., ALEXANDER, W. W., and JOHNSON, C. S. *The Collapse of Cotton Tenancy,* Chapel Hill, University of North Carolina Press, 1935.

EMBREE, EDWIN R. *Every Tenth Pupil, the Story of the Negro Schools in the South,* reprint from *Survey Graphic* by Julius Rosenwald Fund.

EMMONS, W. H. *General Economic Geology*, New York, McGraw-Hill Book Co., 1922.

FEATHERSTONEHAUGH, GEORGE W. *Excursions through the Slave States*, London, J. Murry, 1844.

FISHER, RICHARD S. *A New and Complete Statistical Gazetteer of the United States*, in Vol. 1, *Colton's Atlas of the World*, New York, Colton, 1856.

FLINT, TIMOTHY. *The Last Ten Years in the Valley of the Mississippi*, Boston, Hilliard & Co., 1826.

   History and Geography of the Mississippi Valley, I, Cincinnati, Flint & Lincoln, 1832.

FOOTE, WILLIAM H. *Sketches of Virginia: History and Biography*, Second Series, Philadelphia, 1855.

   Sketches of North Carolina, etc., New York, R. Carter, 1846.

FOSTER, J. W. *The Mississippi Valley: Its Physical Geography*, Chicago, Griggs & Co., 1869.

FRANK, ARTHUR DeWITT. *The Development of the Federal Program of Flood Control on the Mississippi River*, New York, Columbia University Press, 1930.

GAINES, FRANCES P. *The Southern Plantation*, New York, Columbia University Press, 1924.

GAYARRÉ, CHARLES, *History of Louisiana*, New Orleans, James A. Gresham; also Hawkins, 1885 (third edition).

GLINKA, K. D. *The Great Soil Groups of the World, and Their Development*, translated by C. F. MARBUT, Ann Arbor, Edwards Brothers, 1928.

GRAY, L. C., assisted by ESTHER KATHERINE THOMPSON. *History of Agriculture in Southern United States to 1860*, two volumes, Washington, Carnegie Institution of Washington, 1933.

HALE, WILLIAM T. *The Farm Chemurgie*, Boston, Stratford Co., 1934.

HANEY, LEWIS HENRY. *A Congressional History of Railways in the United States to 1850*, Madison, Wisconsin, University of Wisconsin Bulletin 211.

HASKELL, DANIEL, and SMITH, J. C. *A Complete Description and Statistical Gazetteer of the United States of America (1843)*, New York, Sherman & Smith, 1843.

HENDERSON, ARCHIBALD. *The Conquest of the Old South West (Virginia, Carolinas, Tennessee and Kentucky), 1740-1790*, New York, Century Co., 1920.

HODGES, LeROY, Editor. *The South's Physical Recovery*, one hundred addresses by national leaders, Proceedings of the Third Annual Convention, Southern Commercial Congress, Atlanta, Georgia, 1911.

HOSMER, JAMES K. *A Short History of the Mississippi Valley*, Boston, Houghton Mifflin Co., 1901.

IMLAY, GILBERT. *A Topographic Description of the Western Territory of North America, etc.*, New York, Campbell, 1793; London, J. Debrett, 1797.

JEFFERSON, THOMAS. *Notes on the State of Virginia* (First Hot-Pressed Edition). Philadelphia, R. T. Rawle, 1801.

KELLEY, WILLIAM. *The Old South and the New*, New York, Putnam, 1888.

KEMBLE, FANNY. *Journal of a Residence on a Georgia Plantation in 1838-39*, New York, Harper & Brothers, 1863.

KEPHART, HORACE. *Our Southern Highlanders*, New York, Macmillan Co., 1922.

KERR, JOS. G. *Historical Development of the Louisville and Nashville Railroad System*, Louisville, published by L. & N. Railroad, 1925.

KILLEBREW, J. B., and MAYRICK, HUBERT. *Tobacco Leaf, Its Culture, Marketing, and Manufacture, etc.*, New York, Orange Judd Co., 1915.

KING, EDWARD. *The Great South*, Hartford, American Publishing Co., 1875.

LYELL, SIR CHARLES. *A Second Visit to the United States*, two volumes, London, John Murray, 1849.

McCRADY, EDWARD. *The History of South Carolina under the Proprietary Government, 1670-1719*, New York, Macmillan Co., 1901.

The History of South Carolina under the Royal Government, 1719-1776, New York, Macmillan Co., 1901.

McMASTER, JOHN BACH. *A History of the People of the United States*, Vols. I-VIII, D. Appleton & Co., 1895.

MARSHALL, HUMPHREY. *The History of Kentucky*, two volumes, Frankfort, George S. Robinson, printer, 1824.

MARTIN, JOSEPH. *A New and Comprehensive Gazetteer of Virginia*, Charlottesville, published by Joseph Martin; Moseley & Tompkins, printers, 1835.

MELISH, JOHN. *A Geographical Description of the United States*, Philadelphia, 1816.

MICHAUX, FRANÇOIS ANDRÉ. *Travels to the West of the Alleghany Mountains*, London, D. N. Shury, 1805.

MIMS, EDWIN. *The Advancing South*, New York, Doubleday Publishing Co., 1926.

MITCHELL, BROADUS. *The Rise of Cotton Mills in the South*, Baltimore, Johns Hopkins University Press, 1921.

William Gregg, Factory Master of the Old South, Chapel Hill, University of North Carolina Press, 1928.

MITCHELL, SAMUEL A. *Principal Stage, Steamboat, and Canal Routes in the United States*, Philadelphia, Mitchell & Hinman, 1834.

MITCHELL, S. AUGUSTUS, JR. *New General Atlas*, Philadelphia, 1866.

MOODY, JOHN. *The Railroad Builders*, Vol. 38 in Chronicles of America Series, New Haven, Yale University Press, 1921.

MORRIS, EASTIN. *The Tennessee Gazetteer*, Nashville, W. Hasell Hunt & Co., 1834.

MORSE, JEDIDIAH, *The American Gazetteer*, Boston, Thomas & Andrews, 1797.

The American Universal Geography, Vol. 1, Charleston, S. Etheridge, printer. 1819.

NELSON, JOS. P. *A History of the Chesapeake and Ohio Railway Company, Its Antecedents and Subsidiaries*, Richmond, Lewis Printing Co., 1927.

NEVINS, ALLAN. *American Social History as Recorded by British Travelers*, New York, Henry Holt & Co., 1923.

ODUM, H. W. *Southern Regions of the United States*, Chapel Hill, University of North Carolina Press, 1936.

OLMSTED, FREDERICK LAW. *A Journey in the Seaboard Slave States*, New York, Dix & Edwards, 1856.

A Journey through Texas, New York, Dix & Edwards, 1856.

PARKINS, A. E., *The Historical Geography of Detroit*, Michigan Historical Commission, 1918.

PARKINS, A. E., and WHITAKER, W. R., Editors. *Our Natural Resources and Their Conservation*, New York, John Wiley & Sons, 1936.

PECK, JOHN MASON. *A New Guide for Emigrants to the West, etc.*, Boston, Lincoln & Edwards, 1831.

PHELAN, JAMES. *History of Tennessee, The Making of a State*, Boston, Houghton Mifflin Co., 1889.

PHILLIPS, U. B. *A History of Transportation in the Eastern Cotton Belt to 1860*, New York, Macmillan Co., 1908.

Life and Labor in the Old South, Boston, Little, Brown & Co. 1929.

POPE, JOHN. *A Tour Through the Southern and Western Territories of the United States of North America*, Richmond, John Dixon, printer, 1792.

POPE, WILLIAM F. *Early Days in Arkansas*, Little Rock, Frederick W. Allsopp, publisher, 1895.

POWER, TYRONE. *Impressions of America*, two volumes, Philadelphia, Carey, Lea & Blanchard, 1836.

RAMSEY, J. G. M. *The Annals of Tennessee*, Philadelphia, J. B. Lippincott & Co., 1853.

RHYNE, J. J. *Some Cotton Mill Workers and Their Villages*, Chapel Hill, University of North Carolina Press, 1930.

RIES, HEINRICH. *Elementary Economic Geology*, New York, John Wiley & Sons, 1930.

SCHIMPER, A. F. W. *Plant Geography*, Oxford, Clarendon Press, 1903.

SCOTT, JOSEPH. *The United States Gazetteer, etc.*, Philadelphia, F. and R. Bailey, 1795.

A Geographical Dictionary of the United States, Pittsburgh, Cramer, Spear & Eichbaum, 1811.

SEMPLE, ELLEN CHURCHILL. *American History and Its Geographic Conditions*, Boston, Houghton Mifflin Co., 1903.

SEYBERT, ADAM. *Statistical Annals of the United States*, Philadelphia, Thomas Dobson & Son, 1818.

SHELFORD, V. E., Editor. *Naturalist's Guide to the Americas*, Baltimore, Williams & Wilkins Co., 1925.

SPRUNT, JAMES. *Chronicles of the Cape Fear Rivers, 1660-1916*, Raleigh, Edwards & Broughton, 1916.

TANNER, HENRY S. *A Description of the Canals and Railroads, Comprehending Notices of all the Works of Internal Improvement throughout the Several States*, New York, T. R. Tanner & J. Disturnell, 1840.

TANNER, HENRY S. *The American Traveler or Guide through the United States*, Philadelphia, published by the author, 1834.

VANCE, RUPERT B. *Human Geography of the South*, Chapel Hill, University of North Carolina Press, 1932.

VON RAUMER, FREDERICK. *America and the American People*, translated by W. W. TURNER, New York, 1846.

WARD, GEORGE W. *The Early Development of the Chesapeake and Ohio Canal Project*, Baltimore, Johns Hopkins University Press, 1899.

WARD, ROBERT DEC. *The Climates of the United States*, Boston, Ginn & Co., 1925.

WARSHOW, H. T., Editor. *Representative Industries in the United States*, New York, Henry Holt, 1928.

WEBB, W. P. *The Great Plains*, Boston, Ginn & Co., 1931.

WILLIAMS, W. *Appleton's United States Guide Book for Travelers*, Southern and Western States, New York, D. Appleton & Co., 1850.

WILSON, WOODROW. *A History of the American People*, Vols. I-V, New York, Harper & Brothers, 1902.

WINSOR, JUSTIN. *Narrative and Critical History of America,* Vols. I-VIII, Boston, Houghton Mifflin Co., 1894.

WOLFANGER, LOUIS A. *The Major Soil Divisions of the United States,* New York, John Wiley & Sons, 1930.

WORCESTER, J. E. *Gazetteer of the United States,* Andover, Flagg & Gould, 1818.

ZON, RAPHAEL, and SPARHAWK, WILLIAM. *The Forest Resources of the World,* New York, McGraw-Hill Book Co., 1923.

II. PUBLICATIONS OF FEDERAL, STATE, MUNICIPAL GOVERNMENT AND OTHER OFFICIAL BODIES
Also includes series
GENERAL

AGRICULTURAL DEPARTMENT, UNITED STATES. Publication series: *Yearbook,* annual, contains statistical data on crops in the United States and foreign countries, beginning with yearbook for 1936 statistical section in separate volume; Circulars; Farmers' Bulletins, numbers 1-1625; Leaflets; Miscellaneous Publications; Statistical Bulletins; and Technical Bulletins.

AMERICAN STATE PAPERS. Legislative and Executive Documents of the Congress of the United States, 1789—March 1, 1823, selected and edited under authority of Congress, Gales and Seaton—1832-1861, 38 volumes. Documents grouped under ten classes: Indian Affairs, 2 vols.; Finance, 5 vols.; Commerce and Navigation, 2 vols.; Military Affairs, 7 vols.; Postoffice, 1 vol.; Public Lands, 8 vols.; Miscellaneous, 2 vols.

Atlas of American Agriculture, prepared under the supervision of O. E. BAKER, Washington, Bureau of Farm Economics, U. S. Department of Agriculture. *Part II.* Climate, precipitation and humidity, temperature, sunshine, and wind. *Part III.* Soils of the United States (colored maps), 1935. *Part V.* Crops: Section A. Cotton. *Part IX.* Rural Population and Organization. Washington, Government Printing Office.

Census Reports, United States. First census, 1790, population only; second census, 1800, population only; third census, 1810, population only; fourth census, 1820; fifth census, 1830, statistical view of the population of the United States, 1790-1830, a résumé; sixth census, 1840, population and statistical view; seventh census, 1850, population, statistical view, compendium, and abstract; eighth census, 1860, population, preliminary report, statistics in an abstract; ninth census, 1870, population, social statistics, compendium, statistical atlas; tenth census, 1880, most complete and comprehensive to that date, historical treatments of transportation, agriculture, manufactures, descriptive of forests, soils, etc.; eleventh census, 1890, population, compendium, abstract, statistical atlas; twelfth census, 1900, do; thirteenth census, 1910, do; fourteenth census, 1920, very complete; fifteenth census, 1930, very complete.

Commerce Yearbook, Vol. 1 United States; Vol. 2 Foreign Countries. Began publication in 1922. (Since 1933 Vol. 1, covering the United States, has been discontinued.) Washington, U. S. Department of Commerce.

Drainage and irrigation, in late census reports.

Folios of the United States Geological Survey (selected). Alabama—Birmingham No. 175; Arkansas—Eureka Springs—Harrison No. 202; Georgia—Ringgold No. 2; Kentucky—Richmond No. 46, Kenova No. 184; North Carolina—Asheville No. 116, Nantahala No. 143; Oklahoma—Tishomingo No. 99,

Tahlequah No. 122; South Carolina—Pisgah (N. C. of C.) No. 90; Texas—
Van Horn No. 194, Uvalda No. 64, Austin No. 76; Virginia—Pocahontas
Special (Pocahontas No. 26), Tazewell No. 44, Norfolk No. 80, Staunton
No. 14, Fredericksburg No. 13; West Virginia—Buckhannon No. 43.

GEOLOGICAL SURVEY, UNITED STATES (U. S. G. S.). Established in 1879. Surveys
1804-1865 are largely exploratory, made mostly by the War Department.
From 1867 to 1879, the geologic and geographic work was under the Geographical and Geological Surveys. Annual reports, 1880- ——; Bulletins,
1883- ——; Monographs; Professional Papers, 1902- ——; Water Supply
Papers, 1896- ——; Miscellaneous Publications; Topographic maps; and
geologic folios.

Geology, Commercial, World Atlas of U. S. G. S. Miscellaneous Publication, Part
1 Minerals. Part 2 Water power. Washington, Government Printing Office
1921.

MINES, BUREAU OF, UNITED STATES. Publication: Annual report of Director,
1912-——; Bulletins, 1910-——; Economic Papers, 1925-——; Handbook
1916- ——; Miners' Circulars, 1911- ——; Mineral Resources of United
States, 1882- ——; Technical Papers, 1911- ——.

Mississippi River, Charts of. Mississippi River Commission, created in 1879, and
annual reports since 1880.

National Resources Board, Reports of. Part 1 Findings and Plans; Part 2
Land; Part 3 Water; Part 4 Minerals; Part 5 Surveys and Maps, Washington, Dept. of Documents, 1934.

NATIONAL RESOURCES BOARD, *Supplementary Reports of the Land Planning Com-
mittee to the.* Part I General Conditions and Tendencies Influencing the
Nation's Land Requirements; Part III Agricultural Land Requirements
and Available Resources; Part V The Problem of Soil Erosion; Part VI
Maladjustment in Land Use; Part VIII Forest Land Resources; Part IX
Planning for Wild Life; Part XI Recreational Use of Land in the United
States. Washington, Supt. of Documents.

National Resources Committee, Reports of. Inventory of the Water Resources
of the United States, 1935; State Planning in the United States, 1936; Land
Planning in the United States, 1936; Regional Factors in National Planning and Development, 1936; Washington, Supt. of Documents, 1936.

Population Growth in the United States, A Century of, 1790-1900. Heads of
families in 1790, industries, education, newspapers, periodicals, slavery, etc.
Prepared by Rossiter, Chief Clerk of the Bureau of the Census. Washington, Government Printing Office, 1909.

Port Series, Issued by War Department. Publications began in 1921. Series practically complete for ports of the United States. Revisions issued from
time to time.

Power Commission, Reports of Federal, Annual, 1920 to date. Washington, Government Printing Office.

Soil Reports, Bureau of Chemistry and Soils, U. S. D. A. Areas widely scattered
over the United States. County or district or regional basis of areal de-
limitation, mostly county. Each accompanied with map and text, gives brief
summary of history of agricultural development of area, description of
soils, farm practices, etc. Washington, Supt. of Documents. Several published each year.

Statistical Abstract of the United States. Vol. 1, 1878, to date. An annual. Washington, Government Printing Office.

Transportation Series, 1926-29, prepared by Bureau of Operations, United States Shipping Board.

Water Power, Potential and Developed, of the United States in Statistical Abstract, data supplied by U. S. G. S., also mimeographed sheets.

Waterways Corporation, Report of Inland, Annual, 1924 to date. Cooperation with War Department, successor to Inland and Coast Waterways Service which was established in 1920, Washington.

Specific, Arranged by Topics

"Agricultural Outlook for the Southern States, The," *U. S. D. A. Miscellaneous Publications,* No. 102, 1930.

American Agriculture, A Graphic Summary of, based largely on the census, BAKER. Washington, U. S. D. A., May 1931.

Bauxite. ASHLEY, *Resources of Tennessee,* Vol. 1, 211, 1911; HAYES. *U. S. G. S., 21st Annual Report,* 111; VEATCH. *Georgia U. S. G. S., Bulletin* 18.

"Beef Cattle Industry of Virginia, Economic Factors Affecting," BURMEISTER. *U. S. D. A. Bureau of Agric. Econ., Tech. Bulletin* 237.

"Beef Supply, Our," SHEETS and others. *Yearbook of Agriculture,* 1921, 227-322.

"Beef, The Production of, in the South," WARD. *Yearbook of Agriculture, U.S.D.A.,* 1913, 259-282.

"Cattle Ranges of the Southwest—A History of the Exhaustion of the Pasturage, and Suggestions for Its Restoration," *U. S. D. A., Farmers' Bulletin* 72.

"Citrus Fruits in the Gulf States, The Culture of," VASBURY. *U. S. D. A., Farmers' Bulletin* 1343, 1923.

"Coal," CAMPBELL and others, *U. S. G. S., Prof. Paper* 100, 1917.

"Copper in Western North Carolina," LANEY. *North Carolina Geological Survey, Bulletin* 21, 1910.

"Copper Deposits of the Appalachian States," *Bulletin* 455, *U. S. G. S.,* 1911.

"Copper, Ducktown Manufacturing District, etc.," EMMONS, LANEY, and KEITH. *U. S. G. S. Prof. Paper* 139, 1926.

"Cotton, Diseases and Control," *U. S. D. A., Farmers' Bulletin,* 1187, 1921.

"Cotton Plantation, Landlord and Tenant, etc.," WOOFTER and others. *Research Monograph V, Division of Social Research,* Works Progress Administration, Washington, 1936.

"Cotton Production and Distribution in the Gulf Southwest," MOULTON. *U. S. Department of Commerce, Domestic Commerce Series* 49, Part III, 1931.

"Dairy Industry, The," LARSON and others. *Yearbook of Agriculture,* 1922, 251.

"Farm Lands Available for Settlement," *U. S. D. A., Farmers' Bulletin* 1271, 1922.

"Flood Disasters, The Mississippi Valley, of 1927," pamphlet from American Red Cross, 1929.

"Floods in the Lower Mississippi Valley," CLINE. Board of Trade of New Orleans, 1927.

"Florida, Physiography of," SANFORD. *2nd Annual Report, Florida Geologic Survey.*

"Florida, The Geology and Vegetation of Northern," HARPER. *Report of Florida State Geologic Survey,* 1914.

"Forage for the Cotton Belt," TRACY. *U. S. D. A., Farmers' Bulletin* 1125, 1920.

"Forage Situation, Our," PIPER and others. *Yearbook of Agriculture,* 1923.

"Forest Situation in the United States, The," *Publication of U. S. Forest Service, U. S. D. A.,* 1932.

"Geography and Geology of the Black and Grand Prairies," Texas, *21st Annual Report U. S. G. S.,* Part 7, 1900.

"Geology of Portions of the Edwards Plateau and the Rio Grande Plains," HILL and VAUGHAN. *Annal Report. U. S. G. S.* Part 2, 1898.

"Geomorphology of the Southern Appalachians," HAYES and CAMPBELL. *19th Annual Report U. S. G. S.,* Part 2, 1898.

"Georgia, The Natural Resources of," HARPER. *Bulletin of the University of Georgia,* 1930.

"Iron Ore (Hematite), Mining Practices in the Birmingham District, Alabama," CRANE. *Bureau of Mines, Bulletin* 239, 1926.

Iron Ores (Clinton), McCALLEY. *State of Georgia Geologic Survey, Bulletin* 17, 1908; STOSE. *Economic Geology,* XIX, 405, 1924.

"Land Utilization and the Farm Problem," GRAY and BAKER. *U. S. D. A. Bureau Agri. Econ.* 87, November, 1930.

Lead and Zinc, KEITH, *U. S. G. S. Bulletin* 225, 1904; OSGOOD. *Tenn. Geological Survey Bulletin* 2, 1910; PURDUE, *Tenn. Geological Survey Bulletin* 14, 1912.

"Loblolly Pine in Eastern Texas," ZON. *Forest Series, U. S. D. A., Bulletin* 64, 1905.

"Long Leaf Pine for Paper Pulp, Suitability of," SURFACE and COOPER. *U. S. D. A., Bulletin* 72, 1914.

"Marketing Fruits and Vegetables," McKAY. *Yearbook of Agriculture,* 1925, 633-710.

"Maryland, A General Report on Physiography of, Including the Development of the Streams of the Piedmont Plateau," C. ABBE, JR. *Maryland Weather Series,* Vol. 1, part 2.

"Migrations, Interstate, among the Native White Population as Indicated by Differences between State of Birth and State of Residence," GALPIN and MANNY. *U. S. D. A. Bur. of Agr. Econ.,* Washington, 1934.

"Mineral Resources of Alabama, The," JONES. *Geological Survey of Alabama, Bulletin* 28.

Mississippi River, The Physics and Hydraulics of the, HUMPHREYS and ABBOT. United States Army, Washington Government Printing Office, 1867.

"Mobile, Alabama, The Port of," *Port Series* No. 3, Part 1. War Department, Corps of Engineers, United States Army and United States Shipping Board, Washington, United States Government Printing Office, 1930.

"Naval Stores Industry, The," SCHORGER and BETTS. *Forest Service, Dept. Bulletin* 229, July 28, 1915.

"New Orleans, Port of," *Report of Board of Commissioners,* New Orleans, 1928.

"Oil Fields of the Gulf Coastal Plains," HAYES and KENNEDY. *U. S. G. S., Bulletin* 212, 1903.

"Paper Pulp, The Suitability of American Woods for," RUE. *U. S. D. A., Bulletin* 1485, 1927.

Phosphate rock in the South: ROGERS, *U. S. G. S., Bulletin* 580, 1914; SELLARDS, *Florida Geological Survey, 3rd, 5th, and 7th reports;* HOOK. *Resources of Tennessee,* IV, No. 2, 1914; WATSON. *U. S. G. S., Bulletin* 604, 1915.

"Potash in Texas and New Mexico," MANSFIELD and LANG. *American Inst. of Min. Met. Engrs., Tech. Pub.* 212, 1929.

"Power Situation in North Carolina," *Department of Conservation and Development, Circular* 16, Raleigh, N. C.

"Problems, Economic and Social, and Conditions of the Southern Appalachians," GRAY and others. *U. S. D. A., Miscellaneous Publications* 205, Washington, Government Printing Office.

"Ranching Area in the Edwards Plateau of Texas, An Economic Study of a Typical," YOUNGBLOOD. *Texas Agric. Exp. Station Bulletin* 297, 1922.

"Rural Problem Areas, Six: Relief—Resources Rehabilitation," BECK and FOSTER. *Division of Research, Statistics and Finance of Federal Emergency Relief Administration,* Washington, 1935.

"Salt Domes of Texas and Louisiana," BARTON. *Univ. of Texas Mineral Survey, Bulletin* 2801.

"Sheep Industry, The," SPENCER and others. *Yearbook of Agriculture,* 1923, 229.

"Soils of the United States, Their Genesis and Development," MARBUT. *Lectures in the Graduate School of the United States Department of Agriculture,* February to May, 1928. (Unpublished, in mimeograph form.)

"Southern Appalachian Region, Denudation and Erosion in the," GLENN. *U. S. G. S., Prof. Paper* 72, 1918.

"Sugar," BRANDES and others. *Yearbook of Agriculture,* 1923, 1-95.

"Sulphur in the South," *U. S. Bureau of Mines, Bulletin* 184; BARTON. *Univ. of Texas Bulletin* 2801, 1928.

"Tenantry, Farm, in the United States," BIZZELL, WILLIAM BENETT. *Bulletin* 275, *College Station,* Texas.

"Tennessee River and Tributaries in North Carolina, Tennessee, Alabama, and Kentucky." *Report of Chief of Engineers United States Army,* to Secretary of War. *71st Congress, 2nd Session. House Document* No. 328, Pt. 1. Washington, United States Government Printing Office, 1930.

"Timber," *Yearbook of Agriculture,* 1922.

"Types of Farming in the United States," ELLIOTT. Washington, U. S. Census Bureau, 1933.

"Underground Water Resources of Alabama, The," SMITH. *Annual Report of the Geol. Survey of Alabama,* 1907.

"Underground Water Resources of Northern Louisiana, Geology and," VEATCH. *U. S. G. S., Prof. Paper* 46, 1906.

"Virginia Company of London, The Records of the Court Book," manuscript in the Library of Congress, 11.

"Weather and Crops in Arkansas 1819-1879," HICKMAN. *Monthly Weather Review,* XLVIII, August, 1920, 447-451.

"Women's Place in Industry in Ten Southern States," ANDERSON. Pamphlet of *United States Department of Labor, Women's Bureau.* Washington, United States Government Printing Office, 1931.

III. MAGAZINES OUT OF PRINT

American Almanac and Repository of Useful Knowledge. Vols. 1-32, 1830-1861. Boston, Publishers changed from time to time: Charles Bowen in 1834; Charles C. Little and James Brown, 1845, etc.

Annals, The, of America, 1492-1826, two volumes. Edited by ABIEL HOLMES, Cambridge, Hilliard & Brown, 1829-1830.

Archives of Useful Knowledge, three volumes, 2 parts, edited by James Mease. Philadelphia, published by David Hogan, 1810-1813.

DeBow's Review (Agricultural, commercial, industrial progress, and resources).
Edited by J. B. D. DEBOW, New Orleans, Vols. 1-34 (January, 1846-August,
1864); after the war series, 1-8 (January, 1866-October, 1870); N. S. (October, 1879-June, 1880). Suspended at times. Issued under various names:
*Commercial Review of the South and West; DeBow's Review of the
Southern and Western States; DeBow's Commercial Review of the South
and West.*

Historical Register, The, of the United States, three volumes. Edited by J. H.
PALMER, 1812-1814.

Hunt's Merchants Magazine and Commercial Review. Edited and published by
FREEMAN HUNT. 1840-1870. New York, F. Hunt.

Niles' Weekly Register, Baltimore, printed by Niles, Editor. 1811-1849. At one
time known as *National Register.* Suspended at times.

IV. MISCELLANEOUS PUBLICATIONS

Booklets, Pamphlets, Magazine Articles, Research Series, Theses;
Arranged by Topic

"Agricultural Regions of North America," O. E. BAKER. *Econ. Geog.,* II, IX,
1926-1929.

"American Slavery, Geographic Influences in," EMERSON. *Bulletin Amer. Geog.
Soc.,* XLIII, 1911, 13-36.

"Atlantic Coastline, The Story of the," booklet issued by the Atlantic Coastline
Railroad.

"Black Belt of Alabama, Economic Geography of, FRED ARNOLD. Master's thesis,
George Peabody College, 1928.

Calahan Divide, The Geography of the, L. G. KENNAMER. Doctor's dissertation,
George Peabody College, 1932.

"Cattle Industry in Oklahoma, History of the Ranch," E. E. DALE. *Annual Report Amer. Hist. Assoc.,* 1920.

"Chemical Plants in the South," *Manufacturers' Record,* XCIV, July 5, 1928, 71.

"Child Labor in the South," A. J. McKELWEY. *Annals of Amer. Acad. of Pol.
and Soc. Sci.,* XXXV, 1910, 307-156.

"Cincinnati Southern Railway, The: A Study in Municipal Activity," JACOB
HARRY HOLLANDER. *Johns Hopkins University Studies in Historical and
Political Science,* Series 12, 1894, 1-116.

Clays, The Ceramic, of Henry and Weakley Counties, Tenn., H. J. PRIESTLY.
Master's thesis, George Peabody College, 1936.

"Cotton Boll Weevil, Weather and the," *Monthly Weather Review,* LVI, 1928,
301.

"Cotton Crop, Financing the," H. S. REED. *Acad. Pol. and Soc. Sci.* XXXV, Jan.
1910.

"Cotton Goods, Industry, Wages and Hours of Labor in the," *Monthly Labor
Review,* XXIV, February, 1927, 300-305.

"Cotton Mill, The South Carolina—A Manufacturer's View," THOS. F. PARKER.
So. At. Quarterly, IX, 1909, 325.

"Cotton Mill Village, The South Carolina," THOS. F. PARKER. *So. At. Quarterly,*
VIII, 328; 1910, 349.

"Education in Virginia, The Evolution of Public," EDGAR KNIGHT. *Sewanee Review,* XXIV, 1916, 24-41.

"Farm Crops for the South, New," S. M. TRACY. *Ann. Amer. Acad. of Pol. and Soc. Science*, XXXV, No. 1, January, 1910, 52-59.

"Fertilizer Industry, The," C. A. WHITTLE. *Manufacturers' Record*, LXXXVI, Pt. 1, Dec. 11, 1924.

"Fertilizer Problem, Fundamentals of Our," SAMUEL WYER. Booklet, *Fuel-Power-Transportation Educational Foundation*, Columbus, Ohio, December, 1927.

Graphic Summary of the Agricultural South, 1850, The, J. E. GUARDIA, doctor's dissertation. George Peabody College, 1933 (unpublished in 1937).

Great Appalachian Valley, The, in Alabama. J. F. GLAZNER. Doctor's dissertation, George Peabody College, 1934 (abstract).

"Growth of an 'Oil Town'—Van Zandt County, Texas," J. E. FEE. *The Dallas Morning News*, Friday, Oct. 18, 1929.

"Internal Improvement, The North Carolina Fund for," W. K. BOYD. *So. Atlantic Quarterly*, XV, January, 1916, 52-67.

"Iron and Manganese in the South," C. WILLARD HAYES. *Economic History*, VI, The South in the Building of the Nation series, Richmond, 1909.

"Iron and Steel in the South," C. M. STANLEY. *Independent*, CXVII, 1926, 587.

(Iron Ores) "Alabama Ores Equal Lake Supply," BURCHARD. *Iron Age*, CXIX, March, 1927, 847-850.

"Iron Ores, Brown, in Alabama," BURCHARD. *Econ. Geology*, XXIII, No. 4, 1928.

"Iron Ores, Brown, of Alabama, Occurrence and Age of," ADAMS. *Econ. Geology*, XXIII, No. 1, 1928.

"Iron Ores, Clinton Group, in Alabama," ALDRICH. *Amer. Inst. Min. and Met. Engineers, Transactions*, LXXI, 1925.

Joplin Mining Industry, History and Development of, W. A. BROWNE. Master's thesis, George Peabody College, 1927.

"Land Utilization in the United States, Geographic Aspects of the Problem," O. E. BAKER. *Geog. Rev.*, XIII, January, 1923, 1-26.

Llano Estacado, The, A Geographic Interpretation, W. A. BROWNE. Doctor's dissertation, George Peabody College, 1935 (abstract).

Log, The, publication of the Mississippi and Ohio Rivers Pilots' Association.

"Malaria, Report of a Symposium on," *So. Medical Journal*, XXII, April, 1929.

"Maryland, Beginnings of," STEVEN. *Johns Hopkins Univ. Studies in Hist. and Pol. Sci.*, Series 21, Nos. 8, 9, 10.

"Maryland, Internal Improvements in," MARTIN. *Johns Hopkins Univ. Studies in Hist. and Pol. Sci.*, Series 19, No. 10.

"Middle Country, South Carolina, at End of Eighteenth Century, The," BACOT. *So. At. Quarterly*, XXIII, January, 1924.

"Movement of Northern Cotton Mills to the South, etc.," HENRY G. LORD. *Textile World*, LXXVIII, February, 1925, 670.

"Natchez Trace, The," COTTERILL. *Tenn. Hist. Mag.*, VII, April, 1921, 29.

"Natural Regions, The Subdivision of North America into," JOERG. *Ann. Assoc. of Amer. Geographers*, IV, 1914, 55.

Naval Stores Industry, The, ADA MARVIN. Master's Thesis, George Peabody College, 1937.

"Negro and Agricultural Development, The," ALFRED HOLT STONE. *Ann. Amer. Acad. of Pol. and Soc. Sci.*, XXXV.

"Negro Education in the South," FRED S. McCUISTION. Paper read at 1930 Conference on Negro Education, George Peabody College.

"Negro Exodus and Southern Agriculture, The," *Rev. of Revs.*, LXVIII, 1923, 401-407.

"South, The New—The Textile Development," E. T. H. SHAFFER. *Atlantic Monthly*, CXXX, 1922, 562.

"Southern Expansion, Decentralization, Working Demonstration of a New Order of," D. G. WOLFE. *Textile World*, LXXVII, February, 1925, 671.

Tennessee, Geography of Western, FLOY ROBBINS. Doctor's dissertation, George Peabody College, 1930 (unpublished, 1937).

Texas, Black Prairies of, A Regional Study, HARRIET SMITH. Master's thesis, George Peabody College, 1920.

Texas, The Minor Interior Prairies of, ELTON M. SCOTT. Master's thesis, George Peabody College, 1936.

"Tennessee Valley Project, The," A. E. PARKINS. *Journal of the Tennessee Academy of Science*, VIII, 1933, 345.

"Transportation and Traffic on the Ohio and Mississippi before the Steamboat," W. W. CARSON. *Mississippi Valley Historical Review*, VII, No. 1, June, 1920, 26-38.

"Southern Agriculture, Plantation System, and the Negro Problem," GRAY. *Ann. of Amer. Acad. of Pol. and Soc. Sci.*, XL-XLI, March, 1912.

(Vegetables) *Tomato Growing and Marketing in the Crystal Springs Area, Mississippi*, MYRTLE HAMPTON. Master's Thesis, George Peabody College, 1936.

"Water Power of the Southern Appalachians, The," A. E. PARKINS. *Journal of the Tenn. Acad. of Sci.*, VI, 1931, 97.

"Water Power Obsolescent," MARSHALL LEIGHTON. *Manufacturers' Record*, XCVI, Pt. 1, July 4, 1929, 66.

Waterways of the South, The River-Foot, W. W. SPELLINGS. Doctor's dissertation Group, Peabody College, 1936 (abstract).

"Weather Conditions and Thermal Belts in the North Carolina Mountains and Their Relation to Fruit Growing," H. J. COX. *Ann. Assoc. of Amer. Geographers*, V, 1915, 51.

Wild Life, The Conservation of, VERA RALEIGH. Master's Thesis, George Peabody College, 1934.

Yazoo Basin, The, A Study in Geography, FERN DORRIS. Master's thesis, George Peabody College, 1925.

INDEX

526   INDEX

Roads—(*Continued*)
  decline and revival of interest in, 135ff.
  Fall Line, 130
  Nashville-Louisville, 126
  National Pike, 124
  of pioneer, 123
  of Transmississippi region, 131
  the major early, of South, map, 125
  Wilderness, 124

S

Salt, 365
San Antonio, discussion of growth, 476
  in 1870, 114
Sawmills, number of, 1840, table, 387
Sectionalism, breaking down, 487ff.
Settlements in Spanish and French territories, 99ff.
Shift in type of land utilization, map, 504
Signal system, first railroad, 168
Silk-raising in Virginia Colony, 188ff.
Slavery, after effects, 235ff.
  an inheritance in the South, 225ff.
  doomed, 233ff.
  effect of, on agricultural advancement, 224ff.
    on manufacturing, 327
  supported by church, 237
  uneconomical economics of, 230ff.
  "white elephant," becoming in 1860, 234
Slaves, distribution of, by states, 1850, 204
  by regions and counties, 205
  in 1860, map, 207
  importation of, 226
  indifferent workers, 232ff.
Softwoods of South, 385ff.
Soil erosion, 70ff.
  loss in acres, 70
  reason for active erosion, 73ff.
  remedies for, 74ff.
Soil profile, 62
Soils of the South, 57ff.
  map, 59
  Pedalfers, groups of, 60ff.

South, The Advancing, 1
South, The, an epitome of development of, 2
  cities of, classified, 463
    in 1790, map, 447
    in 1810, map, 448
    in 1830, map, 450
    in 1850, map, 452
    in 1870, map, 461
    in 1880, map, 464, 465
    in 1890, map, 465
    in 1910, map, 466
    in 1930, map, 466
  general conditions of agriculture in 1860, 206
  in comparison 1850 and 1860, 203
  location in Westerlies, effects, 42
  physiographic provinces of, map, 27
  railways of, 164ff.
  Upper, economic stability, 259
  useful minerals of, 36
  waterways of, 138
  would outgrow slavery in time, 228ff.
South Atlantic "Crescent" ports, opportunities for growth, 481
  slow growth of, 480ff.
South Carolina, agriculture, 193
  canal and railroad company, 166
  cities in 1850, 454
Southern advancement, contribution of railroads to, 16
Southern Appalachian Mountains, 29ff.
Southern cities, rise of, 443ff.
Southern cotton industry, healthy condition of, 414ff.
Southern leaders, lost opportunities of, 210ff.
Southern ports, activity at, 15
Southern prospect, 487ff.
Southern unity, basis of, 117
Southward movement of cotton manufacturing, ascribed causes examined, 415ff.
Special crops in cotton and corn region, 263
Specialization in work on plantation, 233
Spindles, cotton, growth in number in South *vs.* New England, 414
Stages in manufacturing, 304
State railways, 166ff.